This book is dedicated to all those (almost completely) anonymous 'lit secs'.

Bibliography of the Communist Party of Great Britain

Bibliography of the Communist Party of Great Britain

Dave Cope

Lawrence and Wishart,
London 2016

Lawrence and Wishart Limited
99a Wallis Road
London
E9 5LN

© Lawrence & Wishart 2016

Typesetting: e-type
Cover design: Andrew Corbett

The author has asserted his rights under the Copyright, Design and Patents Act, 1998 to be identified as the author of this work.

All rights reserved. Apart from fair dealing for the purpose of private study, research, criticism or review, no part of this publication may be reproduced, stored in a retrieval system, or transmitted, in any form or by any means, electronic, electrical, chemical, mechanical, optical, photocopying, recording or otherwise, without the prior permission of the copyright owner.

ISBN 9781909831032

British Library Cataloguing in Publication Data.
A catalogue record for this book is available from the British Library.

Contents

Acknowledgements	6
Introduction	7
General introduction	7
The Communist Party in Fiction – Andy Croft	18
The Communist Party on the Stage	26
Communist Party Films – Bert Hogenkamp	26
Artists and the Communist Party	39
Historiography of the CPGB – Kevin Morgan	45
Sources and Locations	53
Bibliographies and reference works	55
Internet sites	59
Associated publishers	61
Discography	73
Factory papers – not traced	74
Some foreign language material	78
Abbreviations	79
1. National Publications	85
2. Local Publications	123
3. National Magazines	156
4. Local Magazines	163
5. *Our History*	175
6. YCL Publications	178
7. YCL Magazines	186
8. Students	189
9. *Daily Worker/Morning Star*	192
10. Modern Books	198
11. About the CP – Books and Pamphlets	204
12. About the CP – Magazine Articles	263
13. Unpublished Memoirs	330
14. Theses	332
Indexes	338
Introduction to Indexes	338
a. Introduction to Names	338
b. Introduction to Topics	339
Names	344
Topics	355
Periods	361
Regions	363
Industries	365

Acknowledgements

Thanks first to Sally Davison, Avis Greenaway and Katharine Harris at L&W for their work and incisive clarity in getting such an untidy monster of different texts and formats into a more than presentable book format.

This book would not have been as comprehensive as it is without the help of dozens of individuals. Among them I must mention: Sid Brown, Barry Buitekant, Ralph Darlington, Audrey Canning, Nina Fishman, Alison Gilchrist, Ron Heisler, Paul Hogarth, Alun Hughes, Monty Johnstone, Francis King, Trish Newland, George Matthews, Bill Moore, Kevin Morgan, Bert Pearce, Andy Simons, Harold Smith, Ray Watkinson, Andy Whitehead and Matthew Worley. It is a pity so many of these cannot see the outcome of their contributions, but that is my fault not theirs, and their names should be remembered.

And without the help over the years of my brother, Robin Cope, it would not have been possible at all.

Updates

The author and publisher will co-operate in providing updates to this Bibliography.

Please send any corrections, omissions and new titles to the author. These will appear on the web sites of both author and publisher. Printed copies will be issued annually, on request, from the author.

Dave Cope,
Left on the Shelf,
Yard 91, 87 Highgate,
Kendal,
LA9 4ED
leftontheshelf@phonecoop.coop
www.leftontheshelfbooks.co.uk

Introduction

(All sections in the introduction are by Dave Cope unless stated otherwise.)

General Introduction

The Communist Party of Great Britain was founded in July 1920 and dissolved itself in November 1991. There are some historians who argue that too much importance is attached to the existence of the CPGB (between 1943 and 1957 it described itself as the British Communist Party). And yet, more and more books and articles are being written about it. Since the demise of the Party there have been four books to complete Lawrence and Wishart's history of the CP; five one-volume histories and three dozen full scale biographies or autobiographies of communists (plus many more on people who passed through briefly); there have been over thirty important academic studies of different aspects of the Party's activities (ranging from different industries to its cultural life and influence); and there have been over 350 articles in journals (excluding book reviews and obituaries). There have been numerous theses, academic conferences and oral history projects; the Socialist History Society continues the work of the Historians' Group with its own excellent journal, as well as occasional talks and conferences. A Communist History Network was set up, but later replaced by a Communism Specialist Group of the Political Studies Association. And there have been exhibitions, such as the one at the People's History Museum in Manchester in 2003-04.

The Communist Party cannot be ignored by those interested in the history of twentieth-century socialism, industrial relations, cultural politics, literary criticism, anti-colonialism and anti-fascism. It was a strange creature – like other communist parties in some ways, like the rest of the British left in others; moving from Stalinist orthodoxy (though even this assertion requires some qualification) early on, to a form of libertarian socialism at the end. It had the common sense to disband before it faded away completely, though some will disagree with me on this. Having a clearly defined start and end date appeals to historians studying organisations and periods: they can summarise them, categorise them and attempt to provide a definitive interpretation – hence this deluge of material since 1991. It needs to be stated that both the New Communist Party, from 1977, and especially the Communist

Party of Britain, from 1988, claim to have taken on the mantle of the CPGB, but for the purposes of this study the Party ended in 1991 when the majority at the 43rd Congress decided to dissolve it and transform it into Democratic Left.

When it was formed, it was a party 'of a new type' that wanted to be completely different to previous socialist parties, and often it was a party that was ostracised and treated as the 'enemy within' and whose members suffered blacklisting at work. Yet it attracted some of the century's most interesting artists and writers; some of the best trade union leaders; some of the leading academics and scientists, and a host of grassroots activists from all social backgrounds, involved in all aspects of civil society. Many passed fleetingly through the organisation, most brought something to it and took something from it. It is a commonplace to say that the influence of the Communist Party far exceeded its small size – but it was due to the collective work of these individuals that this is true. Generally, and despite the occasional demagogue, bully, timeserver and cynic, its members were articulate, thoughtful, active, and selfless in their attempt to work for what they believed would be a better world for all. These characteristics describe many socialist organisations, but while Communists were hardly 'of a different mould', there can be no doubt that the CP attracted a significant number of exceptional people.

The communist project failed, but communism in Britain produced a rich heritage. In the field of the written word, which concerns us here, no other organisation on the left comes near it for quantity, and this includes the Labour Party, which was always many times bigger.

The belief in the written word was boundless; money from Moscow may have helped, but even when none was available pamphlets, papers and journals were churned out. Some of the pamphlets had print runs of 100,000; a network of 'literature secretaries' picked up weekly piles of magazines and pamphlets which were then distributed to members and were sold in factories and communities. There was the huge effort to maintain a daily paper from 1930 onwards. Bookshops were set up all over the country – there were thirty-two in 1945, excluding Collets, which had very close links with the Party. Printing companies, a book distributor and a publishing house were all established and were quite successful (Central Books and Lawrence and Wishart have even survived the demise of the CP and exist to this day). The Party played a large role in the success of the Left Book Club in the 1930s and 1940s – not just in commissioning, writing and distributing but in organising the various LBC groups.

Many of the journals the Party distributed were imported from Eastern Europe and the Soviet Union, but many more were home-grown. *Labour Monthly* was widely read and respected (at least until the late 1960s), and *Marxism Today* in the final years was the most widely known and influential, but there were hundreds published by national committees, specialist groups and branches.

The picture is not entirely rosy – the quality and content of the magazines and pamphlets were variable, and some appear risible or utopian now. And the significance of the immense written legacy of the CPGB, in itself of variable quality and interest, is also open to debate. This bibliography lists many a dull pamphlet (in both content and style) and sometimes an even duller study syllabus about that dull pamphlet, but there is much material still worth reading and still sought by students, historians and collectors. This ranges from the publications of the Historians' Group to first editions of Lenin and Marx (including the *Communist Manifesto* in Welsh). At least many of the texts can now be more easily accessed and assessed through this listing.

If content was not always matched by style, production was not always equalled by distribution and sales – this is a problem anyone who has been active in a political organisation will recognise. There exists a wonderful anonymous report from 1935 titled *Printed Propaganda*, possibly written by a manager of the Communist Bookshop in London, which berates the poor quality of most pamphlets (from a political, grammatical and legal perspective), the production of the same titles by different organisations in or close to the Party, the haphazard commissioning and reprinting and vast overproduction. The report begins 'Complete chaos exists in the production of printed propaganda'. It mentions one pamphlet (*Small Study Course: The State*) that was printed in an edition of 10,000 – then had to be withdrawn and pulped. Another predicted that Hitler could not come to power – two weeks before he did. Articles from journals were reprinted as pamphlets without checking to see if there was a market for them – 10,000 copies of William Rust's *For Indian Independence* were printed and none sold. The Russian contribution was not always well planned either: 'they issued over 104 pamphlets of one sort or another during the first Five Year Plan, some 150,000 of which were shipped here. Without asking anybody here, of course'.

Many autobiographies testify to the importance of books and self-education for CP members; Ruth Frow's biography of her husband (*Edmund Frow: The Making of an Activist*) is a vivid example. Libraries were set up for members in the 1920s and 1930s – Scotland had the P.M. Dott Memorial Library, and the Midlands District had its Workers' Library with a very attractive bookplate. Party bookshops sometimes organised their own lending libraries (the one in Gloucester appears to have been one of the largest), and so did some factory and local branches. The Working Class Movement Library and the Marx Memorial Library are closely associated with the CP; James Klugmann, historian and bibliophile, had an unequalled collection of books on labour movement history. Not only did many ex-CP members end up in the book trade, new and second-hand, but also in publishing, sometimes setting up their own businesses. As well as Lawrence and Wishart (preceded by Martin Lawrence), the Party had other publishing enterprises at different times: these are listed below.

Despite the comment above about dull pamphlets, this is not the whole story: artists contributed to the design and illustration of pamphlets – and for three decades some of the best political cartoons ever produced in this country graced the covers of some Party publications, as we shall see.

The tradition of education and self-education in the Communist movement is found in all other sections of the labour and socialist movement, but the CP produced much more material. There were regular meetings and classes, study sessions, day schools, summer schools and 'Communist Universities'. There are many syllabuses and guides to reading in this bibliography testifying to the importance of the written word in British Communist culture.

The British CP produced some significant literary critics – notably in the 1930s. This theme can be followed in practically all the CP journals from the 1920s to the 1980s, as well as in the lists and catalogues of its publishing houses. The CPGB played a crucial role in the recovery, publication and selling of the full version of *The Ragged Trousered Philanthropists* by Lawrence and Wishart in 1955. This much-loved novel remains part of the fabric of British working-class culture and was taken to heart by CP members. The Liverpool bookshop alone sold some 3000 paperbacks and 500 hardbacks over a decade from the mid-1970s – and much of this was due to individual activists, especially building workers, selling them to workmates. Literature secretaries would regularly take radical and working-class novels and sometimes poetry to meetings.

Some of these critics were also novelists and poets, and another book could be devoted to Communist authors and to writers who passed through the CP. Andy Croft's contribution below, together with other work he has published, could be the basis for such a project.

The lines become blurred with some writers: Graham Greene may have been in the CP for a very brief period (one month?) but wrote often about communism and its relation to Catholicism. Sean O'Casey was on the board of the *Daily Worker*, but not a Party member. Rex Warner sold the *Daily Worker* but he, too, never actually joined. Was Hamish Henderson a member or not? His biographer says not, but Andy Croft states that Henderson told him he had joined at one time. For the purposes of a bibliography, such blurring is a nuisance – membership of the CP is a rigid parameter for entry, but the existence of such ambiguities reflects the influence of the Party and the importance of literature in its culture.

One of the aims of this work is to help recover the work of lesser known writers – such as those 'worker-writers' who addressed a small local audience – as well as to pinpoint the many more famous writers who may have gained experience from their membership of the CP, and indeed, in some cases, owe their start in the literary world to the Party. There are many cases of CP members being involved in local poetry magazines, writers' groups etc – some achieving considerable local success (e.g. Harold Hikins in Liverpool). Local Party organisations occasionally published collections of poems (especially in Scotland) and, though this was more uncommon, works of fiction. These can all be traced in this bibliography.

What has been said about writers applies to the other arts. The list of musicians who were members of the CP is, for example, surprisingly rich and ranges from classical composers and performers to the worlds of avant-garde, jazz, folk and rock. In the field of classical music we find Alan Bush, Bernard Stevens, Michael Tippett, Elizabeth Lutyens, Humphrey Searle, Christian Darnton, Benjamin Frankel, Rutland Boughton, Diana Poulton and in the field of musical administration Tom Russell and Edward Clark.

The influence of the CP in the folk world is widely acknowledged – A.L. Lloyd, Ewan MacColl, Roy Palmer, Hamish Henderson, Ian Campbell, Harry Boardman and Dick Gaughan are the most famous, but there were dozens of others active in setting up local folk clubs and magazines, and in collecting and publishing songs (Lawrence and Wishart published the key texts *Come All Ye Bold Miners* and *Folk Song in England*). There are few songs about Communists, but there is one fine one; this is Leon Rosselson's *Song of the Old Communist*, a long and moving song based on his father, which says more about the ideals and disappointments of the British Communist movement than some of the books listed here.

The rise of pop music coincides with the decline of Communism in Britain, so it is no surprise to find that few rock singers were ever members of the YCL or CP. On top of this, the CP hierarchy – and certainly the CP Musicians' Group – were often openly hostile to pop music, which was portrayed as an unhealthy American influence. Children of Communists are not unknown in successful groups (Kirstie MacColl, Hank Wangford, plus members of The Who, Pink Floyd, Frankie Goes to Hollywood, UB40). There were YCL members in several post-punk groups (e.g. Scritti Politti – named after Gramsci's work, rather than Harry), and in one of the incarnations of The Fall, but perhaps the only well-known musician who was also a longstanding Communist was Robert Wyatt from Soft Machine.

Of course, not all the writings of these writers and musicians and artists will be reflected in this bibliography. If someone wrote a crucial text in their field, such as Francis Klingender's *Art and the Industrial Revolution*, Lloyd's *Folk Song in England*, or Caudwell's *Illusion and Reality*, the importance of the book is irrelevant – inclusion depends on references to the Communist Party, or to an individual's activity in the Party. Thus, none of Caudwell's seminal Marxist literary criticism is included, but there are eleven articles or books, which discuss his membership and are therefore given entries. Each of these will have its own bibliography to help those who wish to explore further.

The listing of individuals has two problems. Firstly, it glosses over the way the CP and its members worked with other individuals and organisations. The CP was instrumental in setting up many organisations; in the cultural arena alone there were the Workers' Music Association, Unity Theatre, the Edinburgh People's Festivals, the folk magazine *Sing*, the Artists' International Association, the magazine *Artery*. But these bodies, often disparagingly referred to as 'front organisations', often owed more to the individuals involved than to the Party as such. In other cases, it was individuals on their own who had a major input into their creation; one example is Claudia Jones and the Notting Hill Carnival. Even in cases where the

Party was more in control of organisations (the NUWM is an example of a major body, the First of May Demonstration Committee a smaller one), these bodies developed a life of their own, and it does them, and the many non-communists active in them, an injustice to regard them solely as adjuncts of the Party. This is why I have not dealt with them in this bibliography. They deserve, and sometimes already have, histories and bibliographies of their own.

The second, related, problem is that it divides CP members from rest of the left; it separates them and can appear to magnify their importance; it makes them appear 'special'. The aim is not to somehow glorify them; it is to show the contribution they made to so many different areas of life. A similar work on other left organisations would also reveal many exceptional individuals – including the actors, film directors and playwrights associated with the WRP, the journalists and comedians with the SWP, the anti-colonialists with the ILP, the community activists with Militant, the intellectuals with the IMG. It might not have the breadth and variety seen here, but of course this is partly due to the length of time we are considering. A bibliography of the Labour Party would not have as many official publications as the CP, though the biographies and autobiographies of its leading figures would obviously be more significant in terms of political importance. However, if one discounts those of MPs, and if one uses the same criterion, i.e. that the book describes their political activity, such books may be fewer in quantity than can be traced here of CP members. The Labour Party produced hundreds of pamphlets, but a comparison reveals that they invariably published fewer than the CP. A quick comparison of publications over three years from the ILP, LP and CP (largely using the bibliography of the ILP by Woolven, for the 1926 figures, and the official LP bibliography, plus the COPAC libraries database and my Left on the Shelf database) shows this:

1926: ILP 25; LP 24; CP 33.
1936: ILP 10; LP 24; CP 51.
1946: ILP 5; LP 45; CP 111

This excludes YCL publications, but does include those by the '*DW*' (although this only applies to 1946 – there were none for the earlier years). The number of local (branch and District) pamphlets by the CP is interesting: 2, 14 and 59 respectively.

The Labour Party never had a cultural journal of any sort, nor did it have a women's paper, a theoretical/discussion journal or even an internal discussion magazine. The only time Labour opened any of its pages to non-members was with *New Socialist* (its first issue was in September 1981) – an excellent publication but one which clearly owed its inspiration to *Marxism Today*.

It is the wealth of Communist Party autobiographies and biographies that surprised me in the course of compiling this work. The reasons for this are varied. Looking at the autobiographies, many are self-published or come from small local publishers; there is undoubtedly an element here of evangelisation, of a desire to convert to the cause. In the case of those published since the CP's demise, there is an element of self-justification, or of soul-searching, of trying to come to terms with 'what went wrong'. While hardly any of the biographies of British CP leaders are as hagiographic as those of some leading Communists in other countries, they can be a bit too timid and official – John Mahon's *Harry Pollitt* is a case in point. The lack of an official biography (or any sort of biography) of John Gollan, the General Secretary who followed Pollitt, or any subsequent General Secretary, is interesting. Obviously this reflects the decreasing size and influence of the CPGB and the fact that none of his successors had the national impact that Pollitt had, but there is an implied recognition that the cult of personality should be avoided.

More common is a written celebration of a lesser-known figure, perhaps published by trade union colleagues, friends or family. By listing these, this bibliography will be a useful tool for family, local and social historians. Many of these subjects are hidden from history, precisely because they never became MPs, because they worked selflessly within their industry, locality or cultural field. What this mass of material reveals is a deep belief in the value of the individual, of the importance of the contribution of individuals to the collective and historical process to change society. There is almost an urgency to communicate: to convert, yes sometimes, but to testify, to explain and to convince. There can be an almost religious aspect involved in this committing to paper. There are, certainly, many comparisons that can be made between religion and communism – the texts, the prophets and saints (and apostates), the schisms, the self-righteousness, the commitment and selflessness, and even the concept of a promised land. The quality of these biographies and autobiographies varies. Some of them are poorly written and poorly produced, some are simply boring, while others are excellent pieces of writing; cumulatively they provide an exceptional body of material for the student of twentieth-century politics, culture and social history.

To historians, autobiographies are not always as significant as one may imagine. Authors often provide self-justification for their actions, are selective with their memories and are not always honest about their motivations. Especially in the context of controversial political activity, authors may consciously or unconsciously play up the importance of their role. But it is even more likely that some will play down their membership of the Communist Party, as their political positions change over the years and this membership perhaps becomes an embarrassment. The best writers will avoid this trap (Denis Healey and John Mortimer are examples who relate their brief membership with humour), but it is a pity that, for instance, Ted Willis, after becoming Lord Willis, did not write in more detail about his time as editor of *Challenge* and Chairman of the YCL, even from a critical perspective. The main danger facing Communist autobiographies is the desire to convince the reader (perhaps even, subconsciously, the authors themselves) that all their decisions were justified, that there was nothing at all wrong with the Communist project and that it was due to the strength of the enemy, or the actions of traitors within, that this project failed. There are depressingly too many autobiographies – usually self-published – that contain little self doubt or self criticism; they are often the same ones that spend much space explaining the politics of the period they are dealing with in a rather simplistic way.

A different trap for Communists writing their autobiography is modesty – for instance, we learn little about Wal Hannington from his books. Perhaps one reason for this modesty and for the lack of hagiographic biographies referred to above, is that members of the CP in Britain had to write for readers outside the CP – just as they had to work in wider organisations if they were to achieve anything. The CP itself was just too small to provide a reading or political audience. Material intended primarily for the CP itself was often timid, uncritical and disappointing – such as Mahon's biography or Klugmann's two volume history.

The literature of those who left the party and who became active anti-Communists (the apostates) can provide a mirror image to Communist autobiographies. These people also have to convince their readers of the correctness of their decisions, they risk magnifying their own role, and they, too, often provide simplistic political analysis. Some had to defend themselves against charges that they were profiting financially from this anti-Communism. Others had a religious conversion and exchanged one certainty for another. This type of autobiography – from both sides – was typical of the Cold War period but they are limited in number in Britain: they are more common in the United States.

It is to be expected that there will be many biographies of trade union leaders and leading union activists. But members, and ex-members, of the CP turn up in surprising areas. The list includes: the Secretary of the Vegan Society; the owner of a big Sheffield bakery; government ministers (including a Foreign Secretary); a leading civil servant in India secretly working with the independence movement; an internationally renowned historian writing pseudonymously as a jazz critic; a pioneer of soap operas; an artist who studied under Diego Rivera in Mexico; a model for, and lover of, the painter Modigliani; a founder of African archaeology; a working-class suffragette married to the son of a freed slave from Guyana; a cab driver who came to head the Thompson Holiday Group; a member of the House of Lords calling for its abolition in his maiden speech; an organiser of political discussion classes in Japanese prisoner of war camps; a Literary Executrix of James Joyce; a librettist for Benjamin Britten; a nanny to Bertrand Russell's family. I hope the discovery of some of these characters will be one of the pleasures of perusing this bibliography.

One only has to read the obituaries in the broadsheet newspapers since the demise of the CP to discover how many people who reached a high level of recognition in their profession had been members at some time or other.

Apart from the trade unions, CP members played a key role in the peace movement, the anti-fascist and anti-racist movements (there were specific organisations and journals for Jewish comrades, there were Advisory Committees for black members, and many Communists featured prominently in local CREs). The CP initiated, or helped maintain, many international campaigns (Movement for Colonial Freedom, Liberation, Anti-Apartheid), solidarity movements with India, Ethiopia, Chile, the Portuguese Colonies, West Africa, Kurdistan, the Caribbean, China, Vietnam, as well as being the moving force behind support for the International Brigades in Spain. The links with the countries of Eastern Europe also took up a lot of effort through participation in the Friendship Societies – but these turned out to be more ambiguous in their significance. Nearer to home, the CP was deeply involved in the Co-operative movement, in progressive educational campaigns (notably for comprehensive education and adult education), in workers' sports organisations, in campaigns for civil liberties, in women's organisations etc.

Some of the parameters involved in this bibliography have already been referred to, and some of the problem areas are looked at more closely in the following section. Material published by the CPGB is comparatively simple: items selected have to be priced for sale, so this excludes leaflets, election addresses and most internal bulletins. It includes all national and local pamphlets, books – but these are few in number – and journals. I have allowed the occasional pamphlet that is unpriced to appear; these have to be important documents of some substance – one example is the eight page *Three Communist Councillors Report to the People*. Of course, there is always the possibility that a pamphlet was actually sold, and that the price was left off in error.

Material about the CPGB presents more problems. Included are all books, pamphlets and articles from journals that contain substantial or important references to the Party or to individual members. It is perhaps inevitable that famous people will be included even where the references to their CP activity are brief. However, many books about well-known individuals who were in the CP, even for a long time, are excluded; an instance is Sean French's *Patrick Hamilton*, which does include a little on his Marxism, but nothing on his membership of the CP – though we are informed that he taught his parrot to repeat 'Pretty Pollitt'!

Inevitably, there are books that are borderline and the decision whether to include or exclude from this bibliography cannot be completely objective. George Lansbury's autobiography has one sentence about the CP – it is about his attitude to the CP and of some historical interest given his importance in British labour history – but inclusion could not really be justified. There are hundreds of books with fleeting references to the CP, its members and activities. These will include autobiographies of little known figures such as Mary Craddock, who describes her attempt, when at grammar school, to convert her father to communism or George Scott, who describes Pollitt speaking at a Second Front meeting in Middlesbrough. These two are not included, but R.L. Wild's description of Charlie Bateman – 'Winchester's only Communist' – is included. The extent of the reference to the CP is obviously crucial but so is the uniqueness of certain specific references, as in Wild's case, which gives a vivid sketch, however brief, of an individual in a specific location. I hope such entries may prove helpful to researchers following up personalities or localities. The even larger category of books that record a writer's opinion of communism in general is clearly irrelevant; if the opinion is of British Communism in particular then inclusion depends on the passage being about activity rather than policy – or how important the author is. Other categories of books and pamphlets that will have many passing references to the CP are those dealing with industrial relations and espionage. Many descriptions of strikes mention individual members and, particularly in the case of those written by anti-communists (e.g. the long series of pamphlets by the Economic League), emphasise their party affiliation – not always correctly: it was in the authors' interests to exaggerate the influence of the CP. In this area, again, entries may be questioned – are too many omitted or too many included? And this only applies to material I have traced – there will be many items that should be included but that I missed. I can only hope there are not too many obvious ones.

While excluding 'front organisations' from the Bibliography, I have listed separately the publications of some bodies and publishers associated with the CPGB. These vary from the Workers' Bookshop (directly controlled) to the Marx Memorial Library – whose publications can be seen, up to the late 1960s, as an integral part of the Party's publishing and educational programme – to Fore Publications, whose directors, while CP members and prominent literary figures, had an ambiguous relationship with the leadership. These are divided into those under CP control and those with loose connections, but this relationship was often fluid, and no simple formula can describe these varied and interesting publishers and their relationship to the Party machine – a relationship which could change considerably over time. The ultimate example of this is of course the relationship of the *Morning Star* and the CPGB.

Other publishing ventures have been omitted: the Labour Research Department had close links with the CP. Future CP members played a key role in its establishment in 1913 as the Fabian Research Bureau (it became the LRD in 1918). Members were on its leading body for many years. Many anonymous pamphlets – and the output of LRD was huge – must have been written by Communists, and most of the credited authors were members; the CP distribution network handled the pamphlets for many years. LRD concentrated on economic and social issues and trade union research and had a very distinct identity and support structure within the labour movement. But in the 1920s and 1930s there were studies of industries and localities that clearly reflected Communist class-war views.

The CP put a lot of effort into friendship and solidarity organisations for the Soviet Union from the 1920s onwards, and they produced hundreds of pamphlets. The first organisation was the People's Russian Information Bureau, followed by Friends of the Soviet Union, Russia Today Society, British Soviet Friendship Society and the parallel Society for Cultural Relations with the USSR. The quantity of publications increased massively during the Second World War – and printing figures were huge after the Nazi attack on the USSR when the CP basked in the reflected popularity of the Red Army. The post-war period saw a decline in these sales with the onset of the Cold War – but also saw the creation of more Friendship Societies with all the Eastern bloc countries and China. Each country would have a main Friendship Society, with Communist and prominent non-communist figures elected to leading positions. Each would have at least one regular journal, and there might be specialist societies – e.g. for education or health – with their own publications. In the 1950s and 1960s these publications were given a high profile by Central Books and branch Literature Secretaries, partly because they were heavily subsidised by the countries concerned and provided a good income source for the party organisations. They also featured prominently in CP bookshops. The Soviet Union took over printing and distribution of most of their pamphlets (through Soviet Booklets and then the Novosti Press Agency), but CP members were employed by the London Novosti office and as regional reps. The Soviet Union had the largest number of journals, but China sent over *China Pictorial, China Reconstructs, Chinese Literature* and *Women of China*. In the 1970s and 1980s, there was some low-key hostility from the Party hierarchy and members to the prominence given to all of these publications from the socialist countries: they did not reflect the politics of the Eurocommunist period. However, they were still imported, distributed and sold by the party, though in much lower quantities. Once again, an enormous collective effort of time and resources was involved. These are all excluded from this Bibliography.

The major publishing body omitted from this book is Martin Lawrence and its successor, Lawrence and Wishart. A fully rounded overview of the CPGB's publications needs a study of the official publishing house and a listing of its books. Such a study will be difficult given the lack of archives, but a bibliography is a lengthy, but quite feasible, proposition.

This is almost exclusively an English language bibliography. I have included non-English language material published by the CP itself in the main body of the bibliography (a couple of Welsh pamphlets and a few French language ones from the Second World War), and I list below a few foreign language items I have come across more or less by chance that are about the CPGB. Russian speakers will find material in collections in the former Soviet Union; the other former 'socialist' countries in Eastern Europe will all have some material (probably predictably similar in perspective); there are also theses in French and German, sometimes very useful ones; and no doubt more besides. Of course there may also be some articles in Welsh. Locating such material is particularly difficult. Some foreign language material is listed in the British Library's Subject indexes and some in the SSLH Bulletins.

Finally, a few words about myself – my hinterland, or 'where I'm coming from' as the current expression has it – and my interests and prejudices that may be reflected in this work. I was in the CP for over twenty years, right up to the end. I worked in the CP bookshop in Liverpool and then in Central Books for sixteen of these years, and subsequently in a post-CPGB Central Books for a further thirteen. For part of this latter period, I ran a second-hand book business which then became a full-time occupation. This business specialises in left-wing publications, and inevitably communist ones feature prominently. My approach to the CP is coloured by an element of emotional attachment (rather than nostalgia), which is not surprising given that my working life was so interwoven with it; and of course, there were the family and friendship links. My work also gave me a certain antiquarian approach to the Party's publications, which has been helpful in compiling this work but which can have its negative side. Having said all this, I have tried to be objective in the Introduction and in annotating some of the entries. Very occasionally I have deliberately allowed myself the luxury of letting my politics show – perhaps in reaction to the worst excesses of a Trotskyist or Maoist tract, or an example of hard-line communist sectarianism. I hope the reader will forgive this lapse.

The Communist Party in Fiction

Andy Croft

No political organisation in Britain ever attracted so many distinguished writers as the Communist Party once did. Kingsley Amis, Robert Bolt, Elizabeth Bowen, Graham Greene, Doris Lessing, Iris Murdoch, John Prebble, Arnold Wesker, Raymond Williams and – for two weeks – Stephen Spender, were all Party members in their youth. Others who wrote their best work while they were Communists include Patrick Hamilton, Hamish Henderson, Cecil Day Lewis, Joan Littlewood, Ewan McColl, Hugh MacDiarmid, Edgell Rickword, Randall Swingler and Sylvia Townsend Warner. Moreover, a number of working-class writers – notably Fred Ball, Len Doherty, Harry Heslop, Lewis Jones, Dave Wallis, Ted Willis and Roger Woddis – may be said to have learned to write while they were in the Party. Among CP leaders, Wal Hannington once wrote an unpublished novel, Willie Gallacher published a book of poetry and Palme Dutt a play about Dimitrov.

Unsurprisingly, then, the Communist Party and individual Communists make a number of notable appearances in twentieth-century fiction. Arthur Seaton votes communist in Alan Sillitoe's *Saturday Night and Sunday Morning* (1958); the Party's principal publishing house, Lawrence and Wishart, turns up as 'Boggis and Stone' in Anthony Powell's *The Acceptance World* (1955); the gamekeeper in the first draft of D.H. Lawrence's *Lady Chatterley's Lover* is secretary of a Party cell in Sheffield.

The distinguished Cambridge crystallographer – and lifelong Communist – J.D. Bernal appears in C.P. Snow's *The Search* (1934). The character of Guy Pringle in Olivia Manning's *Balkan Trilogy* is based on her husband, the legendary 'Red' BBC radio producer Reggie Smith. The 'finely featured' NUWM leader assaulted by the police in Walter Greenwood's bestselling *Love on the Dole* (1934) was the Young

Communist Eddie Frow, later AEU Manchester District Secretary, bibliophile and historian. Arthur Seaton in *Saturday Night and Sunday Morning* (1958) attends a factory-gate meeting addressed by John Peck – later a Communist councillor in Nottingham. CP National Organiser, Dave Cook, is one of the main characters in Alison Fell's *Tricks of the Light* (2003). There is a comic portrait of Palme Dutt in Nigel Williams's *Star Turn* (1985). And in *Goodbye to Berlin* (1939) Christopher Isherwood based Sally Bowles, the most famous character in 1930s English fiction, on the *Daily Worker* film-critic Jean Ross.

For many novelists membership of the Communist Party was once a shorthand for Bohemianism, as in Howard Spring's *Shabby Tiger* (1934) or William McIlvanney's *The Kiln* (1996); the rock-star narrator of Iain Banks's *Espedair Street* (1987) gives away large sums of money to the Party and the ANC. Elsewhere, Communists were frequently represented in British fiction as humourless and uncompanionable zealots, as in George Orwell's *Coming Up for Air* (1939), Cecil Day Lewis's *Child of Misfortune* (1939), J.B. Priestley's *Daylight on Saturday* (1943) and Evelyn Waugh's *Unconditional Surrender* (1961). The figure of the sad and solitary British Communist working for Soviet intelligence is a variation on this – Sawbridge in C.P. Snow's *The New Men* (1954), Halliday in Graham Greene's *The Human Factor* (1978), Stott in Nicholas Blake's *The Sad Variety* (1964) and George Blake himself in Ian McEwan's *The Innocent* (1990). But on the whole, whether they are knaves like Illidge in Aldous Huxley's *Point Counter Point* (1929), fools like Lord Erridge in Anthony Powell's *Casanova's Chinese Restaurant* (1960) or sympathetic characters like those in Storm Jameson's *None Turn Back* (1936), William Golding's *Free Fall* (1959) and William McIlvanney's *Doherty* (1975), British Communists were usually represented in fiction as lonely representatives of an idea rather than members of a real political organisation.

The following list is not therefore a comprehensive record of every reference in fiction to the British Communist Party, but a selection of those in which membership of the Party or the actions of Party shape the narrative, characters or argument of the novel in important ways.

Ruth Adler [Ray Waterman], *Beginning Again* (Hodder and Stoughton, 1983)
Post-war sequel to *A Family of Shopkeepers* (see below) although the names have changed. Good picture of Hampstead CP life.

Jim Allen, *Days of Hope* (Futura, 1975)
Revolutionary unrest in Britain from 1916 to the General Strike, culminating in the resignation of Trotsky's supporters from the Party.

Brian Almond, *Gild the Brass Farthing* (Lawrence and Wishart, 1963)
The Party's attempts to organise in the Lancashire textile industry in the 1930s, including a portrait of *Daily Worker* editor Bill Rust.

James Barke, *Major Operation* (Collins, 1936)
Cinematic novel of Glasgow life, starring a heroic NUWM leader and the Party organiser in Partick.

James Barke, *The Land of the Leal* (Collins, 1939)
Family saga beginning in rural Galloway in the 1820s and ending in Glasgow in the 1930s, includes a portrait of the CP and YCL in Glasgow.

Alexander Baron, *The In-Between Time* (Macmillan, 1971)
Coming of age novel set in North London in 1937, exploring the rival attractions of the Labour League of Youth and the Communist Party. Includes a brief portrait of Harry Pollitt.

Alexander Baron, *Rosie Hogarth* (Jonathan Cape, 1951)
Eponymous character is an undercover Party member, liaising with secret Party members in sensitive government jobs.

Alexander Baron, *Seeing Life* (Collins, 1958)
Set in London in 1956, includes a character allegedly based on John Gollan.

Ralph Bates, *Lean Men* (Peter Davies, 1934)
British Comintern agent arrives in Barcelona in 1931 to organise the PCE.

Anthony Bertram, *Men Adrift* (Chapman and Hall, 1935)
Experimental novel with many plot lines, including the murder of a Party member.

Simon Blumenfeld, *Jew Boy* (Jonathan Cape, 1935)
Whitechapel *Bildungsroman*, which rejects the immigrant culture of the Ghetto and the inaccessible culture of England in favour of the universal and international claims of the Communist Party.

Robert Bonnar, *Stewartie* (Lawrence and Wishart, 1964)
Labour Party corruption in a small town in Fife helps a young railwayman decide to join the Party.

Alec Brown, *Daughters of Albion* (Boriswood, 1935)
Picture of unhappy middle-class society where emotional and sexual honesty is enjoyed only by those who have joined the Communist Party.

Alec Brown, *Breakfast in Bed* (Boriswood, 1937)
The intellectual journey of an English Liberal couple, one towards Fascism, the other to the Party and Spain.

Arthur Calder-Marshall, *Pie in the Sky* (Jonathan Cape, 1937)
Experimental state-of-the-nation novel, which includes several Party members and a character possibly based on Harry Pollitt.

Cecil Day Lewis, *Starting Point* (Jonathan Cape, 1937)
Story of four friends from Oxford in the 1920s, as they make their way in the world, one as a scientist, one as a writer, one as a philanthropist and one as a Communist who fights in Spain.

Len Doherty, *A Miner's Sons* (Lawrence and Wishart, 1955)
Party life in a South Yorkshire pit village.

Len Doherty, *The Man Beneath* (Lawrence and Wishart, 1957)
NUM politics in South Yorkshire coalfield, including CP fraction.

Peter Elstob, *The Armed Rehearsal* (Secker and Warburg, 1964)
Spanish Civil War novel (by ex-member of the International Brigades) containing portraits of Douglas Hyde, Kit Conway, George Nathan, Fred Copeman and Tom Wintringham.

Waguih Ghali, *Beer in the Snooker Club* (André Deutsch, 1964)
A young Egyptian comes to London in the early 1950s. During the Suez crisis he joins the CP, but is deported after hitting a policeman on a demonstration in Trafalgar Square.

Lewis Grassic Gibbon [Leslie Mitchell], *Grey Granite* (Jarrolds, 1934)
The third of Grassic Gibbon's celebrated *A Scots Quair* trilogy, in which Ewan leaves Glasgow with the 1932 Hunger Marchers to work full-time for the Party in London.

Willie Goldman, *Light in the Dust* (Grey Walls Press, 1944)
An ambitious young writer is torn between the attractions of literary London and the intellectual culture of Whitechapel Communism to which he belongs.

Graham Greene, *It's a Battlefield* (Heinemann, 1934)
The events surrounding the trial of a Communist bus driver charged with manslaughter after the death of a policeman on a demonstration.

Frank Griffin, *October Day* (Secker and Warburg, 1939)
The battle of Cable Street.

Bruce Hamilton, *The Brighton Murder Trial: Rex v Rhodes* (Boriswood, 1937)
Supposed verbatim record of the trial, set in the near future, of a Brighton Party

member framed with the murder of a local Fascist. The novel was dedicated to fellow NCCL activists Dudley Collard and Neil Lawson.

Bruce Hamilton, *Traitor's Way* (Cresset, 1938)
Fast, anti-Fascist period thriller which begins with the death of a Party member at an anti-Fascist demonstration; Hamilton was the older brother of the novelist and playwright Patrick Hamilton.

Margot Heinemann, *The Adventurers* (Lawrence and Wishart, 1960)
Study in the rise and fall of the British Left from 1943-56. Includes portraits of Arthur Horner and the young E.P. Thompson.

Harold Heslop, *Last Cage Down* (Wishart, 1935)
Late Third Period novel inspired by the 1929 dispute at Dawdon Colliery, dramatising the clash between opportunist lodge officials and rank-and-file Communist leadership inside the DMA.

Jack Hilton, *Laugh at Polonius* (Jonathan Cape, 1942)
The political education of a young weaver in Rochdale.

Barry Hines, *The Heart of It* (Michael Joseph, 1994)
Successful scriptwriter returns to his native Yorkshire after the 1980s miners' strike to face the memory of his father, a lifelong Party member.

William Holt, *Backwaters* (Nicholson and Watson, 1934)
Young Lancashire weaver emigrates to Canada where he works in lumber camps before returning home and joining the CP; includes a comic account of the Party in Todmorden (where Holt was a CP councillor).

Gwyn Jones, *Times Like These* (Gollancz, 1936)
1926 Lockout in a South Wales pit village.

Jack Jones, *Rhondda Roundabout* (Hamish Hamilton, 1934)
Affectionate satire on life in Merthyr, including a comical account of the Party in the Rhondda.

Lewis Jones, *We Live* (Lawrence and Wishart, 1939)
Sequel to Jones's *Cwmardy* (1937) representing events in the South Wales coalfield from the early 1920s to 1936 and the War in Spain; set in the 'Little Moscow' of Mardy in the Rhondda.

Mervyn Jones, *Today the Struggle* (Quartet, 1978)
Among the many characters in this cross-section of British society from the 1930s to the 1970s is Alf Saunders, a railway signalman and a lifelong Party member.

Dave Lambert, *He Must So Live* (Lawrence and Wishart, 1956)
Young foundry worker joins the Party in Glasgow in the late 1930s.

Dave Lambert, *No Time for Sleeping* (Lawrence and Wishart, 1958)
Sequel to *He Must So Live*, a study in Clydeside politics in the late 1930s, representing the Communist Party as a unifying force against sectarianism and sectional interest in industry and politics. Includes a brief appearance by Willie Gallacher.

John le Carré, *The Spy Who Came in from the Cold* (Gollancz, 1963)
Idealistic young British Communist is used in a cynical Cold War operation in the GDR; the novel includes a grim portrait of Party life in Bayswater.

Doris Lessing, *The Golden Notebook* (Michael Joseph, 1962)
Complex study in fictional autobiography which addresses, in the 'Red Notebook', the intellectual crisis in the British Party in the 1950s.

Jack Lindsay, *We Shall Return* (Dakers, 1942)
The Phoney War, the fall of France and the evacuation at Dunkirk seen through the eyes of a British communist in the BEF.

Jack Lindsay, *Hullo Stranger* (Dakers, 1945)
The politicisation of women working in industry during the War.

Jack Lindsay, *Betrayed Spring* (Bodley Head, 1953)
Set in London, Lancashire, Tyneside and the West Riding during the winter of 1946-7, the first of Lindsay's nine linked 'British Way' novels shows the Party valiantly trying to prevent the betrayal of wartime hopes by the Labour Government.

Jack Lindsay, *Rising Tide* (Bodley Head, 1953)
The CP's leadership of the Squatters' Movement and the 1949 Dock Strike.

Jack Lindsay, *Moment of Choice* (Bodley Head, 1955)
Communists fighting losing battles in industry, in the Peace Movement and in the campaign against the war in Korea.

Ian McEwan, *Black Dogs* (Jonathan Cape, 1992)
The high hopes of communists in 1946 and their defeat in 1989 are linked by the experiences of an ex-Party member.

Ethel Mannin, *Comrade O Comrade* (Jarrolds, 1947)
Satirical portrait of the London literary Left in the late 1930s, particularly scathing about the Party's attitude to events in Spain.

Naomi Mitchison, *We Have Been Warned* (Constable, 1935)
Study in the relationship between the Labour Left and the CP (including a Communist character called Donald McLean who defects to the Soviet Union).

Iris Morley, *Nothing But Propaganda* (Peter Davies, 1946)
Left-wing London during wartime, including a picture of work in a Communist Party bookshop.

Leslie Paul, *Men in May* (Gollancz, 1936)
General Strike in Lewisham, including sympathetic account of the role of Party members.

Jim Phelan, *Ten-a-Penny People* (Gollancz, 1938)
Violent political melodrama set in Manchester.

Zina Rohan, *The Small Book* (Bright Pen, 2010)
A family is obliged to confront its radical past, including an aunt who was Harry Pollitt's secretary. Includes an extremely fond portrait of Pollitt and a good picture of events at the *Daily Worker* in 1956.

A.P. Roley [George Chandler], *Revolt* (Arthur Barker, 1933)
Third Period novel in which a Liverpool Communist (based partly on Jim Phelan) is incriminated in an IRA raid on a post office.

Herbert Smith, *A Field of Folk* (Lawrence and Wishart, 1957)
Work and politics in a West London engineering factory, including workers who stayed in the Party after 1956.

Herbert Smith, *A Morning to Remember* (Lawrence and Wishart, 1962)
Work, health and safety, union politics and a Party branch in an electric power station.

John Sommerfield, *May Day* (Lawrence and Wishart, 1936)
Experimental, cinematic account of three days in the life of London, culminating in a May Day demonstration led by the London District CP.

John Sommerfield, *Trouble in Porter Street* (Key Books/Fore Publications, 1938)
Novella about a Party-led rent strike in working-class Chelsea (where the author was Branch Secretary).

John Sommerfield, *The Imprinted* (London Magazine Editions, 1977)
Fictional autobiography of ex-member of the International Brigade, including portraits of John Cornford, Stephen Spender and Jean Ross.

Philip Toynbee, *The Savage Days* (Hamish Hamilton, 1937)
Youthful fantasy about a bloodthirsty and successful Soviet Revolution in Britain.

Geoffrey Trease, *Missing from Home* (Lawrence and Wishart, 1937)
Adventure story for children about two middle-class runaways who are befriended by YCL hikers and help miners win a local strike.

Edward Upward, *Journey to the Border* (Hogarth, 1938)
Kafkaesque satire on 1930s Britain in which the only rational course of action is to join the Party.

Edward Upward, *In the Thirties* (Heinemann, 1962)
Autobiographical novel, which ends with the decision to join the Party.

Edward Upward, *The Rotten Elements* (Heinemann, 1969)
The second in Upward's trilogy *The Spiral Ascent*, in which Alan Sebrill leaves the CP in 1949, believing it to be 'Revisionist'; includes portraits of Pollitt, Dutt and Mahon.

Gordon Wardman, *Crispin's Spur* (Secker and Warburg, 1985)
Hard-boiled thriller set in the near future when Britain is on the edge of civil war and the Party has turned 'left'.

Ray Waterman, *A Family of Shopkeepers* (WH Allen, 1973)
Autobiographical story of Polish Jewish family in Stepney in the 1920s and 1930s, including picture of local CP.

Raymond Williams, *Loyalties* (Hogarth Press, 1989)
The overlapping stories of a group of friends from 1936 to the 1980s, including two characters (one possibly based on Margot Heinemann) who remain Party members.

T.C. Worsley, *Fellow Travellers* (London Magazine Editions, 1971)
Roman à clef set during the Spanish Civil War and including portraits of Stephen Spender and Giles Romilly.

The Communist Party on the Stage

Unsurprisingly there are few plays that deal with the CP or CP members. There is nothing as significant as Trevor Griffiths's *The Party*, which is based on Gerry Healy and the Workers' Revolutionary Party. There is room – though limited – for some research here, but most plays will be covered by two key comprehensive books on left-wing theatre: Colin Chambers's *The Story of Unity Theatre* and Steve Nicholson's *British Theatre and the Red Peril: The Portrayal of Communism, 1917-1945*, though the former only deals with one theatre company and the latter is not limited to portrayal of Communists in Britain. Nicholson is very interesting on censorship in the theatre, and Chambers is useful for actors who were in the CP.

Adrienne Scullion's *Glasgow Unity Theatre*, an article in *Twentieth Century British History*, covers a couple of plays just located in Scotland.

Arnold Wesker's *Chicken Soup With Barley* is based on Wesker's own Communist family members (though Piratin in *Our Flag Stays Red* claims it's based on his book).

Simon Blumenfeld, better known as a novelist, wrote two unpublished plays, *The Battle of Cable Street* (1987) and *No Pasaran* (1998); each is a reassessment of the CP's position of the 1930s and features members of a CP branch. A lengthy extract was published in *Remembering Cable Street: Fascism and Anti-Fascism in British Society*.

Communist Party Films

Bert Hogenkamp

The CPGB only commissioned a handful of films, including two election broadcasts that it was allowed to transmit on television during the 1966 and 1970 campaigns. But from the catalogue of films listed below it can be gathered that the Party was instrumental in the production of a much greater number. The majority of these were produced by organisations that were established at the instigation of the CPGB or at least endorsed by it. Without fail, their first aim was to secure the distribution and exhibition of films from communist countries. British-made films were generally seen as an extra. Thus, Atlas Film produced its own newsreel *Workers' Topical News* as a supplement to the Soviet feature films that it was distributing. This film company was established in 1929 to cater to the needs of the workers' film societies, affiliated to the Federation of Workers' Film Societies, which were emerging in London and a number of other industrial centres. Only three issues of *Workers' Topical News* were produced, in 1930 and 1931, as the movement petered out when the supply from the Soviet Union temporarily dried up and societies were faced with increasing interference by local authorities. The answer was the use of non-inflammable substandard (16mm) film, as the 1909 Cinematograph Act only applied to inflammable film. The flourishing of the left film movement in the second half of the 1930s was largely due to this anomaly. A crucial role was played by Kino, a film group set up in the autumn of 1933 by some members of the Workers' Theatre Movement. After waging numerous battles with the authorities Kino won the right to screen a 16mm print of *Battleship Potemkin*, Eisenstein's famous film that had been banned by the British Board of Film Censors for its revolutionary content. Like its predecessor, Kino produced a number of *Workers' Newsreels* (1934-5), but it also had a try at fiction, resulting in the 'featurette' *Bread*. In the course of 1934, Kino's production department merged with the Workers' Camera Club to form the Workers' Film and Photo League (WFPL). Adapting the Comintern's Popular Front policy, the League dropped the epithet 'Workers'' by the end of 1935. In the second half of the 1930s, a rift would develop between Kino, which adhered strictly to the Party line and believed in professionalism, and the Film and Photo League, which advocated the political unity of the Left and cherished amateurism. By that time another organisation had made its presence felt: the Progressive Film Institute (PFI). Set up by the well-known Communist zoologist/journalist/film maker Ivor Montagu as an outfit that would pick up the crumbs left by Kino and the commercial distributors, the PFI not only distributed 35mm prints of Soviet films but it also started producing films. *Defence of Madrid* (1936), a film record of Republican Madrid under siege, turned out to be the campaign film the Left had been waiting for. It was screened all over Britain, raising some £6000 for Spanish relief. Montagu would return to Spain in 1938, resulting in another batch of films on the war. In 1939 Montagu made an election film for the CPGB, entitled *Peace and Plenty*, after Harry Pollitt's main report at the 15th Party Congress. The film was a brilliant indictment of the policies of the Chamberlain government, but first the Molotov-Ribbentrop Pact and then the outbreak of the Second World War made it redundant.

During the war (which for the CPGB only started in July 1941, after the entry of the Soviet Union), both Kino and the PFI ceased to be active. The role of the Soviet Film Agency, set up in 1941 by the indefatigable Montagu, was limited. It left the Party ill-equipped for the post-war situation and it was not until 1951 that another body was established to provide the Left and in particular the Communist movement with films from the communist countries. This was Plato Films Ltd. Its managing director was Stanley Forman, who had previously had a career with the YCL, the British-Soviet Society and the Civil Service Union. Among Plato's shareholders were such Communist luminaries as Eva Reckitt, trade union official Bill Ellerby, secretary of the British-Soviet Friendship Society Bill Wainwright, composer Alan Bush and singer Martin Lawrence; British-Soviet Friendship Houses Ltd made a substantial investment of £500. Montagu donated a number of British left-wing films to Plato, both PFI productions and films made by Kino and the Workers' Film and Photo League. After the 22nd Party Congress in 1952, when Party organisations were urged 'to develop the cultural struggle as a part of the political struggle', film shows proliferated. Plato and Contemporary Films (a company founded by Charles Cooper, a British Communist who had been forced to leave the USA because of the McCarthy witch-hunt) provided most of the films.

Contemporary Films worked closely with the New Era Film Club, a revival of the idea of a workers' film society. New Era had been established in 1950 by a group of youngsters, including Anthony Simmons, Walter Lassally and Peter Brinson, who would all eventually make their mark in the British film industry. Their first success was the production of a newsreel, sponsored by the London Trades Council, of the 1950 May Day procession in London, which had been banned by the Labour government and which ended in clashes between police and demonstrators. The New Era Film Club produced films on youth festivals in Berlin (1951), Sheffield (1952) and Bucharest (1953), before it was disbanded in the mid-1950s. From 1954 another Communist film unit was active in Glasgow, the Dawn Cine Group. In 1957 one of the local New Era film societies, based in Ilford, premiered a particularly ambitious film (partly in colour, with a musical score written especially for this production) on the past, present and future of Ilford. Films were also made by individual Party members or sympathisers such as Beverley Robinson in Kent and William McQuilken in Paisley, who felt it their duty to put the film camera they owned to good use. But the most consistent chronicler of the British Communist movement was Plato Films. The unveiling of the Marx Memorial, the funerals of Communist leaders, Party Congresses, Festivals, demonstrations: from the mid-1950s to the late 1980s cameramen Lewis McLeod, Manny Yospa, Jeff Perks and others covered these events on behalf of Plato and its sister company ETV. In 1959 Plato was hit by a libel suit issued by British lawyers on behalf of the NATO General Speidel, who contested his portrayal in the GDR documentary *Operation Teutonic Sword*, which was distributed by Plato. The court battle went all the way to the House of Lords and lasted more than three years. A new company was set up, Educational & Television Films Ltd (ETV). As a result of the case Plato/ETV forged strong links with the GDR, resulting in co-productions with the DEFA film company and with East German Television. ETV, moreover, was responsible for the production of the election broadcasts mentioned above. In the 1970s it made a major contribution to the Chile Solidarity Campaign with films like *Compañero*. Its library has been used by many television companies and has enriched a great number of historical documentaries. Its archives are now held by the BFI; they can also be viewed at JISC MediaHub via an academic institutional subscription.

The following list contains films that have some link with the British Communist movement: because they were made for or by the CPGB or produced by an organisation that was established or endorsed by the Party. This is therefore *not* a list of any documentary or feature film in the making of which Communist film technicians were involved. All films are in the collections of the BFI National Archive or the Moving Image Collection at the National Library of Scotland, unless stated at the end of the entries in square brackets. A brief summary is provided on each of the ninety odd titles listed below. Unless indicated the films are black and white. The running times are approximate.

Action against the Means Test (1935)
A silent film (10 mins) made by the Film & Photo League, of demonstrations against the Means Test.

Against Imperialist War – May Day 1932 [Workers' Topical News No.4]
A 15 minute newsreel of the 1932 May Day demonstration, showing marchers from various parts of London, speakers in Hyde Park (among them Pollitt) and the march towards the Japanese Embassy

Anti-Fascist Demonstrations (1937)
A silent film (2 mins) composed of footage of various anti-fascist demonstrations in Paris, Great Britain and the Soviet Union.

Behind the Spanish Lines (1938)
Twenty minute film by the PFI showing how democracy works in Spain and how Italy and Germany are making a farce of Non-Intervention.

Bread (1934)
Fiction film (12 mins) about an unemployed man who is imprisoned for stealing a loaf of bread, while students arrested for spilling fruit off a cart are let off with a warning; the film, produced by Kino, ends with documentary footage of the 1934 Hunger March.

Britain 1935 – Jubilee Year
Silent film (10 mins) made by the brothers H.A. and R. Green, contrasting the royal East End tour, covered by batteries of newsreel cameras, with the slums, poverty and dole queues that the newsreel cameras never showed.

Busmen's Holiday (1937)
Silent colour footage (7 mins) of the London busmen's contingent in the May Day parade. Bert Papworth is shown. Followed by a black and white reportage of a busmen's outing to a seaside resort where they are entertained by Tom Mann.

Cine Holiday (1955)
A film shot by Hugh Dunlop showing members of the Glasgow-based Dawn Cine Group discussing scenes of their unrealised film *Lost Treasures* and acting them out.

Claude Berridge Funeral (13 July 1966)
Silent footage shot by Manny Yospa showing the crowd assembling, the cortege and people entering the crematorium; among the palbearers are Wolf Wayne, Bill Jones, Dennis Goodwin, Bill Alexander, John Mahon and Pat Devine.

Collet's Advert for Soviet Union magazine (early 1960s)
A five-minute colour advert for the *Soviet Union*, shot at Forman's North London home by Peter Robinson and Peter Weingreen.

Construction (1935)
(10 mins) Directed by building worker Alf Garrard, about the various activities on the Exeter House building site in Putney, including the re-enactment of a strike.

CP Congress (1963)
Silent footage (10 mins) of the Congress held at St Pancras Town Hall shot by Manny Yospa showing Willie Gallacher and Bob Stewart, with Frank Stanley in the chair and John Gollan delivering the main report.

CP Election Film (1963)
(10 mins) Also known as *Our Life in Our Hands* this was made by ETV Ltd as a party political broadcast for the 1964 elections but never transmitted as the CPGB was unable to field the required 50 candidates; it features Gollan, who discusses party policies and introduces the candidates Gladys Easton, Frank Stanley, Julian Tudor-Hart and Jimmy Reid.

CP Election Film (1970)
John Gollan addresses the nation in a party political broadcast (5 mins) made by ETV Ltd for the 1970 elections.

CP 15th Congress 1938 [XVth Congress Film]
A silent film (10 mins) made by the PFI. Pollitt, Hannington, Gallacher, Mann and Gollan are shown on the stage. *A Plant in the Sun* is performed by Unity Theatre and Tom Mann leads the community singing.

CP Home Policy [*The Housing Problem*] (1955)
A silent film (8 mins) exposing Tory and Labour housing policies, to be screened by the Communist Party cinema van.

CPGB Demonstration c.1953
Colour footage (10 mins) shot by Lewis McLeod showing the London District contingent leaving Hyde Park. Pollitt addresses the crowd on Trafalgar Square.

CPGB Demonstration, London 13 June 1971
Silent colour footage (10 mins) of a demonstration against the policies of the Heath Government. Gollan speaks in Trafalgar Square.

Crime against Madrid (1937)
A CNT film (30 mins) re-edited with other material.

Daily Worker Editorial Board (1948)
Footage (5 mins) shot by Pathé News but never shown. Shows *Daily Worker* staff (incl. Sheila Lynd and Florence Keyworth) in their new building.

Daily Worker Trailer (1938)
(3 mins) A silent advertising film for the *Daily Worker*.

Decision (1977)
On the 1977 Congress; made by Roger Graef for Granada Television.

Defence of Madrid (1936)
Silent film (50 mins) made in Madrid in November 1936 by Montagu and Norman McLaren as the PFI's contribution to Spanish Aid.

Dinner for Ambatielos (1964)
Silent footage (10 mins) of a dinner held to celebrate the release from jail and arrival in the UK of Greek Communist Tony Ambatielos.

Election (1966)
Gollan addresses the nation in a party political broadcast (5 mins).

Election (1966)
John Gollan introduces three CPGB candidates: Irene Swann, Frank Stanley and Tony Chater; this party political broadcast (10 mins) was not transmitted.

Fascists defeated at Cable Street (1936)
Silent footage (5 mins) of anti-fascist campaign.

Fiftieth Anniversary of Labour Monthly (1971)
Silent footage (10 mins) of the party to celebrate the 50th anniversary of *Labour Monthly* in 1971; with shots of R.P. Dutt and R. Page Arnot.

Fifty Fighting Years (1972)
A sound film (45 mins) on the history of *Labour Monthly* and the British Labour movement. Written by Forman, Montagu and Roger Woddis, co-directed by Forman and Roland Bischoff. It features Dutt and Page Arnot.

Free Thaelmann (1935)
Silent film (18 mins) edited from a longer American film by Ivor Montagu's Progressive Film Institute in support of the campaign of the Relief Committee for the Victims of German Fascism.

Gallacher's Funeral (1965)
Silent footage (10 mins) filmed by Manny Yospa in Paisley; among those paying their last respect are Bob Stewart, Dutt, D.N. Pritt, Hugh McDiarmid, Frank Stanley, John Platts-Mills, the Gollans; among the pallbearers are Frank Stanley, G. McLennan and P. Kerrigan. Shots of the crowd at the funeral; the nameplate on the door of Gallacher's house.

Glimpses of Modern Russia (1931)
A compilation film (10 mins) edited by Ralph Bond from footage on the Soviet Union.

Harry Pollitt's Funeral (1960)
Silent footage (7 mins) shot by Manny Yospa for ETV Ltd, showing well-known Communists assembling; among the crowd are Hewlett Johnson (the 'Red' Dean of Canterbury), Paul Robeson, a Chinese delegation and Soviet ambassador, Majorie Pollitt in the car, which is followed by Gollan, Gallacher, Kerrigan, Annie Powell and Brian Pollitt.

Harry Pollitt in Australia (1960)
Silent footage (20 seconds) of Harry Pollitt talking to reporters on his arrival in Australia; the film was sent as a fraternal gift by Australian comrades.

Harry Pollitt in China (1955)
A sound reportage (9 mins) of the visit by Pollitt and Stewart. They meet Mao and join the May Day celebrations; commentary by Alan Winnington.

Harry Pollitt in Manchester (1959)
Silent footage (3 mins) of the meeting on Sunday 22 February 1959 against Tory policies. Shot by Lewis McLeod for Soviet newsreel.

Harry Pollitt in the 1950s (date unknown)
Silent colour footage (10 mins) by Lewis McLeod of demonstration in Hyde Park with J. Jacobs, S. Kaye and George Bridges; silent colour footage of a May Day demo with Pollitt; black and white footage of CP petition to 10 Downing Street.

Harry Pollitt 1955 Election
A sound film (3½ mins) shot by Ralph Bond in the United Motion Pictures studios

in London; Bond (off screen) introduces Pollitt who exhorts the audience to vote Communist; this film which was made to be shown by the Communist cinema vans may possibly already have been shot in 1951.

[*The Housing Problem*] see CP Home Policy

Hunger March (1934)
Film record (15 mins) starting with an explanation by NUWM leader Wal Hannington of the purpose of the March, showing preparations in Glasgow and Cambridge where students and clergy demonstrate their solidarity and ending with the arrival in London.

Ilford (1957)
This fifty-minute 16mm sound film, produced over three years by the Ilford New Era Film Society, offers an ambitious 'people's history' of Ilford; a number of characters of humble origin are shown in different historical periods: in the fourteenth century they are exploited by the church, in the eighteenth by aristocracy and in the present day by big business and small profiteers; the film ends with a sequence in colour showing the future when Socialism will prevail.

International Brigade (1937)
Silent film (12 mins) made by Vera Elkan with support of the PFI; unique material on the day-to-day activities of the International Brigade; including shots of *Daily Worker* correspondent Claud Cockburn ('Frank Pitcairn'), Haldane, Jock Cunningham, George Nathan, Koltsov, Kahle, di Vittorio and Renn.

International Brigade – Empress Hall Rally (1939)
Silent footage (10 mins), shot by ACT members, of the meeting to celebrate the return of the British International Brigaders.

Jubilee see Britain 1935 – Jubilee Year

June 29th Demonstration (1954)
(10 mins) CPGB National Demonstration shot by M. Yospa.

King Street (1948)
Silent footage (5 mins) shot by Pathé News but never used; Piratin and Gallacher in discussion with Pollitt; Gollan working in his office; staff at 16 King Street, incl. Beattie Marks.

Lawrence Bradshaw Interview (1956?)
The artist is interviewed (5 mins) by GDR cameraman Dieter Kratz on his Karl Marx sculpture.

LDCP Garden Party and Coach Outing (1935)
A silent film (5 mins).

Let Glasgow Flourish (1956)
Produced by the Dawn Cine Group, this fifteen-minute silent film presents the problems of slum housing as seen through the eyes of ordinary Glaswegians; it ends with a demonstration against a Tory attempt to sell council houses at the Merrylee estate.

London Workers' Outing, Easter 1935
A silent film (4½ mins) of sports and other amusements at High Beech, organised by the London District of the CPGB.

May Day 1937
A silent film (9 mins) of the Communist demonstrations at May Day 1937.

May Day 1950
A silent film (10 mins) by the New Era Film Society, with support from the London TC, of May Day demonstration, banned by the Labour Government which ends in violence between police and marchers. Only extracts of the original film have survived. [Platform Films]

McQuilken Film One (1973-5)
8mm footage of strikes and demonstrations against the stationing of Polaris submarines in Scotland shot by William McQuilken.

McQuilken Film Two (c.1960)
8mm footage of strikes shot by William McQuilken.

A Message from Vietnam (1966)
Appeal on behalf of the people of Vietnam for money to buy medical supplies; this twelve-minute film was produced by Stanley Forman.

Mr Attlee in Spain (1937)
A five-minute newsreel of the visit to Republican Spain.

Never Again (1955)
A silent film (8 mins) about the horrors of Nazism and the campaign against nuclear arms; this film was made to be screened by the Communist Party cinema van during the 1955 local and Parliamentary election campaigns.

News Magazine; Daily Worker Outing (1951-6)
(10 mins) A compilation of protest marches in Glasgow including the Gorbals Tenants' Rents Protest and mass deputation to Edinburgh. Silent footage (black and white and colour) shot by Charlie Bukelis.

1953
A fifteen-minute colour newsreel of a Communist demonstration starting near the Angel Underground Station and ending in Harlesden, including Solly Kaye and George Matthews. [TUC Library]

One Great Vision (1953)
A lengthy (50 mins) report, produced by the New Era Film Club, of the World Youth Festival in Bucharest, presented with a love angle between a Scottish worker and a London bookshop assistant.

Our Life in their Hands see *CP Election Film* (1963)

Palme Dutt interview 28 June 1966
For GDR Television (20 mins).

Peace and Plenty (1939)
CP election film (sound; 23 mins) by PFI; an audiovisual adaptation of Pollitt's report at XVth Congress calling for the election of a democratic government. The puppet of Chamberlain was made by the mother of actress Elsa Lanchester, and the music was written by bandleader Van Phillips. Embodying the Popular Front policy, the film became obsolete in September 1939, while the election for which it was made did not take place until 1945.

Peace Demonstration, Clydebank (1952)
A report (16 mins) of the Youth Festival on 28 September, showing crowds gathering for a demonstration.

People's Jubilee (1977)
Colour footage (10 mins) shot by Jeff Perks of the alternative jubilee festivities in Alexandra Palace.

People's Scrapbook 1938
A newsreel (6 mins), filmed with 9.5mm equipment by local CPGB members and sympathisers, of various events in Sussex such as the Sussex People's History March and unemployed demonstrations.

[*People's Scrapbook* 1939] see Sussex 1939

Primrose Alley Gets Its Way (c.1958)
A film (16 mins) about the pollution by cement of the hop gardens of Kent, shot by amateur film maker Beverley Robinson.

Prisoners Prove Intervention in Spain (1938)
Interviews with Italian and German prisoners in Spain, filmed with a hidden camera by Montagu. This is an abridged version (5 mins) of *Testimony of Non-Intervention*.

Procession in Commemoration of Calton Weavers 1787 (1957)
A report (6 mins), produced by the Dawn Cine Group, of the commemoration by the Glasgow Trades Council.

Rhondda Depression Years (1935)
Incomplete print (11 mins) of a silent film shot by Donald Alexander and Judy Birdwood in the Rhondda Fach; scenes of housing conditions; miners on their way to a protest meeting.

Robert Smillie Centenary Demonstration (1957)
A report (6 mins), produced by the Dawn Cine Group, of the demonstration and park naming on Saturday 8 June.

Russian Dancers in London/Folk Festival 1935
Silent film of Russian folk dancers; originally this was an item in *Workers' Newsreel No. 4*, produced by the WFPL.

Scottish CND Protest (early 1960s)
Colour footage (2 mins) by Hugh Dunlop of CND marchers during a protest against Polaris.

St. Pancras Tenants' Demonstrations (1950s)
Footage (10 mins) of tenants' demonstrations and meetings at St Pancras Town Hall.

Smith, Our Friend (1948)
A silent film made by Walter Lassally and Derek York, telling the story of a demobilised soldier who, after returning to his bombed-out slum house and getting nowhere with the housing authorities, joins the squatters of the Ivanhoe Hotel in Bloomsbury. [Private collection]

Spanish ABC (1938)
Sound film (18 mins) made by the PFI for the Spanish Republican Government. Directed by Sidney Cole.

Stop Fascism (1937)
Silent footage (3 mins) of anti-fascist demonstrations.

Sussex 1939 [*People's Scrapbook* 1939]
A newsreel (10 mins), filmed with 9.5mm equipment by local CPGB members and sympathisers, of various events in Sussex such as May Day 1939 and the second Sussex People's History March.

Testimony of Non-Intervention (1938)
Interviews (33 mins) with Italians and Germans taken prisoner in Spain, filmed with a hidden camera by Ivor Montagu, proving conclusively that the Non-Intervention agreement was violated by Germany and Italy. An abridged version was released as *Prisoners Prove Intervention in Spain*.

Tom Mann's 80th Birthday 1936
A silent film shot by J.E. Richardson.

The UAB Film see Workers' Newsreel No.3 (1935)

Unveiling of the Karl Marx Memorial (1956)
Sound film (10 mins) produced by Plato Films but never released in Great Britain. It was financed by the Socialist countries through the services of Andrew Rothstein, who appears alongside Pollitt, Horner and J.D. Bernal to speak at the occasion of the unveiling of the memorial in Highgate Cemetery.

Visit to Soviet Union (1959-60)
Report (5 mins), possibly made by Charlie Bukelis, of a British delegation, including a display of a national dance and the laying of flowers on a memorial.

We Are the English (1936)
A film record (8 mins) of the History Pageant organised by the London District of the CPGB on Sunday 20 September 1936, showing the procession and its banners covering events from the Magna Carta to the Spanish Civil War.

We Speak for Our Children (1952)
A film made by Beverley Robinson in support of a campaign against the closure of day nurseries in Kent.

We Who Are Young (1952)
A report (32 mins) in black and white and colour, produced by the New Era Film Club, of the Youth Peace Festival in Sheffield.

Willie Gallacher and Funeral (1961-5)
8mm footage shot by William McQuilken of the eightieth birthday celebrations of Willie Gallacher in St Andrew's Halls, Glasgow, followed by shots of the funeral procession for Gallacher in Paisley.

Workers' Newsreel No.1 (1934)
Silent newsreel (10 mins) produced by Kino, showing the *Daily Worker* Gala in Plumstead, the building of a new Co-op store, the Hendon Air Display, the Youth Anti-War Congress in Sheffield and anti-war demonstration in Hyde Park in August.

Workers' Newsreel No.2 (1934)
Silent newsreel (15 mins) by Kino, showing the anti-fascist demonstrations in Hyde Park on 9 September, the removal by the police of a 'Free Thaelmann' banner on the Strand, the Gresford Colliery Disaster and anti-fascist sports rally in Paris.

Workers' Newsreel No.3 [The UAB Film] (1935)
Silent newsreel (15 mins), produced by WFPL of a demonstration in Hyde Park against the Unemployed Assistance Boards.

Workers' Newsreel No.4 (1935)
Silent newsreel (15 mins) by the WFPL, with items on the ILP Summer School in Letchworth, the 1935 May Day March, Soviet Folk Dancers in London and Tom Mann's visit to a Pioneers' camp.

Workers Topical News No.1 (1930)
Silent newsreel (5 mins), produced for the Federation of Workers' Film Societies, showing a demonstration on Tower Hill by the NUWM on the occasion of Unemployment Day 1930.

Workers Topical News No.2 (1930)
Silent newsreel (12 mins), produced for the Federation of Workers' Film Societies, showing the Hunger Marchers on their way to London and the 1930 May Day demonstration including close shots of Charlotte Despard and Shapurji Saklatvala.

Workers' Topical News No.4 see Against Imperialist War – May Day 1932

You Are the Lion (1957)
A film protesting at the rearmament of the Federal Republic of Germany, made by Beverley Robinson.

Youth Peace Pilgrimage (1939)
Silent film (9 mins) of march and meeting in Trafalgar Square by members of the Labour Party League of Youth, the Co-operative Societies and various youth groups; among those shown are Gollan, Charles Gibson, Bill Carritt, Denis Healey and Ted Willis.

Artists and The Communist Party

Some notable artists and graphic designers were involved in producing material for the CPGB. A comprehensive study of the relationship between the Party, its artists and those close to it, remains to be written (but see the chapters by Radford and Wallis in *A Weapon in the Struggle* for fascinating studies of the 'Three Jameses' – Boswell, Holland and Fitton – and political pageants respectively). This is not the place for such a work, but I have taken advantage of the time spent studying the contents of thousands of pamphlets and journals to try to identify some of the artists who designed and illustrated them. In this project, I was helped immensely by Paul Hogarth and others. These are tentative first steps, but they may encourage others, who are better qualified, to follow this up.

The first problem is that most designers of the pamphlets are anonymous, as were a lot of the authors themselves. They were published under pressure, often to fit in with a topical campaign, and not intended to be works of art or collectors' items. Even if the designers were well-known artists, their work would be seen as a political task, a contribution for which they would receive neither payment nor recognition, nor even, sometimes, thanks. But this contribution would no doubt be given gladly; the artist would be part of a collective on equal terms with the author, printer, literature secretary and branch activist who sold the final product. If a striking cover helped sales, the artist was satisfied. It would be interesting to know if there were ever any clashes between artists and the Party over credits, copyright or similar issues: there would never have been arguments over payment, which was always out of the question.

In the early days of the Party, the role of the artist was played down – the best contribution any intellectual or artist could make was to become a proletarian and work in a factory. With the advent of the Popular Front and the end of the worst period of sectarianism in the early/mid 1930s, the artists came into their own. They began to be appreciated as artists and were asked to work politically among other artists. In the pre-war period the CP artists formed the Hogarth Group (named after William not Paul), which became the Communist Artists' Group in 1947, a subgroup of the Cultural Committee.

This was the period of the Artists' International (later called the Artists' International Association), in which CP artists worked with many of the country's leading artists on a progressive, anti-fascist platform. The divisions between 'fine artists' and designers, critics and lecturers, disappeared in the exhibitions and journals of the AIA. Many artists and designers worked on banners for trade unions, for the International Brigade (James Lucas did two – a new version when the first one was captured), for pageants and for congresses. There were traditional exhibitions of watercolours and oils, but many turned their hand to quicker, more ephemeral styles that reflected the urgency of the political situation. Publicity material from all left-wing organisations became more imaginative in general, and this is reflected in the pamphlets, where cartoonists in particular produced much outstanding work.

It was with the onset of the Cold War that the CP turned in on itself more, and the broad alliances of the 1930s and war period fell apart. In 1956 many artists left the Party and it was only in the mid-1970s that the Party leadership again began to make use of the creative abilities of some of its members.

Even during the best period of the 1930s, probably a majority of the designers or illustrators of pamphlets were not only anonymous, but they also deserve to stay that way. The 1950s to 1970s saw a mass of poor and unimaginative designs, with some exceptions. Perhaps the YCL in the mid to late 1960s provided such exceptions to the drabness of these decades, but these were a minority of those produced. The final period of the CP was characterised by a huge variety of artistic styles, of widely differing quality.

The best pamphlets in the 1920s are characterised either by superb typography with small but high quality abstract detailing, or by Soviet inspired cartoons. Francis Meynell, an early editor of *The Communist* for a short period in the early 1920s, was a key figure in the design world. The Communist printing presses – Pelican Press and Dorrit Press – continued a tradition of fine printing and design from an earlier period. These pamphlets and journals have a traditional, serious, even slightly bourgeois, look about them; even the quality of the paper is high – one has the impression that no attention was given to cost ('Moscow gold' may have helped here) and that they were produced in a rather rarefied atmosphere. Later, the work of the Communist typographer Allen Hutt at the *Daily Worker* would receive national recognition.

The two major cartoonists of the 1920s were Will Hope, who used the pen name 'Espoir', and Michael Boland, who signed his work for many years as 'Michael'. Here I must thank Kevin Morgan for noting, while working in the Moscow archives, a passing reference, in the Political Bureau minutes from June 1928, to the appointment of Michael Boland as official cartoonist for the CPGB papers. 'Michael's' cartoons are like the early Soviet ones, with strong proletarian figures sweeping away the clergy and capitalists; they are similar to Kustodiev's stirring depiction of a worker – male, inevitably – smashing his chains, that appear on the cover of the *Communist International*. They appear dated and stereotyped now, but they combine a vigour and even a hint of violence with a lightness of touch, which also lent itself to the caricature of individual politicians. They are among the best of this style by any British artist. Will Hope's cartoons are more subtle, more humorous, but still on the dark side; they rely more on text and are more British in tone. J.F. Horrabin was in the CP till 1925 and drew some material for the Party; after he left, he continued to draw cartoons and maps for many left-wing journals, notably *Plebs*, and had a very distinguished career.

The second half of the 1930s was something of a golden age for Communist artists. The 'Three Jameses' provided some of the best political cartoons and drawings of the century. James Boswell, James Holland and James Fitton all became very successful commercial artists in the advertising industry, and there are still periodic exhibitions of their work, especially that of Boswell. Boswell has been described by the critic William Feaver as 'one of the finest graphic artists of the twentieth century'. There were two other Jameses as well: James Friell, who was the famous *DW* cartoonist under the pen name of 'Gabriel' from 1936, and James Lucas. Lucas was apparently the most modest of this group, and perhaps the most political. He hardly ever signed his work, making identification extremely difficult. His large engraving for the cover of the earliest copies of *The Country Standard* is a masterpiece, even if the occasional figure is a bit wooden. His work is dramatic and original.

Like William Gropper in the US, the caricatures of Boswell and Fitton are strongly influenced by George Grosz, and their best work equals that of the famous German satirist. But they could vary their styles, and never wholly adopted the Socialist Realism that some CP functionaries, following the line from the Soviet Union, expected of them. Artists and literary critics give no indication of automatically following a Comintern line. They were flexible and independently minded. All three Jameses could also incorporate an abstract geometric style, in imitation of the Russian Constructivists if required. They all did work for *Left Review* (not strictly speaking a CP journal), Martin Lawrence and the AIA. Boswell (who also signed some of his drawings 'Buchan') did more covers and cartoons for Party pamphlets than the others.

Cliff Rowe was another leading Communist artist of this period. He had worked in Moscow designing covers and dust jackets for the Foreign Languages Publishing House, and he too made a career in advertising back in England. He worked in a more figurative tradition, but was dismissive of Socialist Realism – he was more influenced by Leger's modernism. His subject matter largely consisted of factories and men and women at work in specific industries. There are series of his oil paintings in York's National Railway Museum and in the Science Museum. Tom Poulton, who was taught by Henry Tonks at the Slade, was another well-known artist in the 1930s, who produced at least three covers (scraperboard) for CP pamphlets, all of very high quality. Poulton was invited by Francis Meynell to provide illustrations for the Nonesuch Press, one of the finest small presses in the country. One of these illustrations, for Plutarch's *Lives*, shows his wife Diana (who was at one time the manager of Lawrence and Wishart) and another comrade, Eleanor Singer, as nymphs fondling the benevolent satyr's head of Meynell. On Poulton's death, it was discovered that he had produced an enormous amount of erotic drawings.

Ronald Horton was a founder member of the Party in Brighton and brother of the more famous Percy (himself a pacifist during the First World War and a long-standing sympathiser of the CP). Ronald produced material for the labour movement in Brighton, for the Spanish Medical Aid Committee and he drew cartoons for *Workers' Life*, *Workers Weekly* and *Young Comrade*, but I cannot trace any pamphlet covers by him. This is surprising given his lifelong commitment to the CP, his recognition as an artist and his role in the art world in general (trainer of art teachers, collector, AIA organiser, and someone who developed links with artists from the Socialist countries).

The quality of some of these artists was noted at the time by Howard Wadman in an article in the summer 1937 issue of *Typography*. One designer Wadman picked out was Alec Anderson, who designed the Peace Library series. Anderson also designed *The Eye*, until he went to fight in Spain in 1936. This irregular broadsheet journal, subtitled the *Martin Lawrence Gazette* (and then the *Lawrence and Wishart Gazette*) appeared for eight issues and is, stylistically, one of the most innovative publications the CP was associated with. Characterised by a superb range of typography, dramatic use of space and photomontage, it was also a serious review magazine of left-wing books.

Other notable artists included Pearl Binder, a pupil of Fitton, who also drew for *Left Review*, as well as becoming a prolific book illustrator, specialising in life in the East End of London. Binder was active in the AIA and a member of the CP, together with Misha Black, Viscount (Jack) Hastings (who painted the mural in the Marx Memorial Library) and Peggy Angus. I can find no credited illustrations by any of these artists in the CP pamphlets, but Angus produced cartoons for the women's page of the *Daily Worker*. It is quite possible that Black did some of the photomontage designs on the pamphlets, judging by the style of, for instance, the dustwrapper of John Sommerfield's *Mayday*, published by Lawrence and Wishart.

The *Daily Worker* provided many artists with the opportunity for publication. Pat Carpenter produced some excellent cartoons under the name of 'Patrick' in the late 1930s. During the war, Bill Bland was another artist who produced some equally effective cartoons, and there were also some good ones by 'Richards', whom I have not been able to identify.

Challenge asked readers to send in cartoons in the early years of the war and this provided the opportunity for Priscilla Thorneycroft and Elizabeth Shaw to be published, possibly for the first time. Shaw produced some unusual cartoon posters for the CP during the war in a rather whimsical style reminiscent of nineteenth century children's books by Lear and Belloc, and she went on to have a successful career in book illustration in the GDR. Al Jackson was another very competent artist who sent in his drawings and he became the regular cartoonist for the paper.

One artist, signed 'Miles', deserves mention. This is almost certainly Arthur Miles, RA. He designed half a dozen covers for the Party in Wales between 1937 and 1948 – some of the most striking graphic work of the period. A pamphlet published in October 1942 describes the South Wales District premises in Cardiff: 'A glass-roofed conservatory has been converted into a studio for the poster-artist' – was this for Miles?

The only photographer I have identified who features on a pamphlet cover is Howard Coster, with his striking portrait of Pollitt on *Forward* in 1936, which portrays him almost as a film star with its dramatic lighting. Coster also did some work for *The Eye* – a similar photo exists of T.A. Jackson in *The Eye* (No.5, 1936). There were a few good quality photomontages in the 1930s, all anonymous. Edith Tudor Hart, one of the best photographers of the period, did work for the CP publishing house, but none of her work can be identified in the pamphlets. Another photographer in the CP at this time was Helen Muspratt (later married to Jack Dunman), also widely recognised as a key photographer of the period; unfortunately, again, there is no evidence of her work in Party material.

The war dispersed many of these artists. A younger generation came through after the war, including Paul Hogarth, Francis Minns (these two artists worked together at Shell when Boswell was art director there), Ray Watkinson, Ern Brooks, Barbara Niven and Ken Sprague. All these artists produced covers for pamphlets (and other work) for the Party; and most were also active in the AIA (Niven, Brooks and Hogarth in Manchester before moving to London). Hogarth went on to enjoy a very successful international career as a book illustrator and became a member of the RA. Watkinson, Brooks and Sprague produced material for the Party for decades, including posters, while Barbara Niven gave up a promising artistic career to work for the CP, for many years as fundraiser for the *Daily Worker* (another artist, Clive Branson, had, briefly, made a similar move in the 1930s). The dilemma that most left-wing artists faced – of not being able to make a living from their left-wing art and not wanting to produce luxury goods for rich collectors – did lead some to stop painting, or to concentrate on agit-prop work.

Reg Turner, who was taught by Lucas at Plymouth, was another painter (like Brooks and others) who did dustwrappers for Party publishing firms but did not sign any pamphlet covers. He had done some covers for *Challenge* in January 1938 and one of his artworks does appear on the cover of an issue of *Daylight* in 1952. He may be the artist who signed himself 'RT'.

Recognition of the importance of some of these artists is reflected in Alan Horne's *The Dictionary of Twentieth Century British Book Illustrators* (Antique Collectors' Club, 1994), the standard reference work. Binder, Boswell, Paxton Chadwick, Fitton, Hogarth, Holland and Poulton all have entries, some with reference to their political views. In passing, it is worth noting the high number of

Communist artists who turned to book illustration as a career: this must reflect some political hostility from the art establishment. Indeed, it is only in recent years that Tate Britain has started displaying works by artists such as Branson, Peri and Boswell, even if they have been in the national collection for many years.

There were some cartoonists from the *Daily Worker* who have remained anonymous until now. 'Dyad' was popular during the war, and continued drawing for many years afterwards, but not even responsible figures at the newspaper knew his name – his cartoons arrived daily in an unmarked envelope. He was Wilfrid Paffard, a BBC engineer who was probably not in the CP, and who apparently did not want his links with the paper known. (The late Sid Brown was the source of this information.) The other regular cartoon feature during the war was by 'Hob-Nob': according to the wartime journals of Charles Brasch (a leading figure in New Zealand's literary world who was in Britain at this time), the artists were Cliff Rowe and Fred Manner. (Thanks to Andrew Parsloe, currently editing these journals, for this identification.)

In the post-war period, there was a stylistic move away from the harshness of the 1930s with its strident, and sometimes wonderful, class caricatures. In Hogarth's work, for example, while there was no lowering in the level of political commitment, the subjects were often positive images of workers in the communist countries. And in his career he remained true to his vocation of artist as reporter. The debate on Realism which echoed in CP and AIA material for many years was calmer, and the traditionalists got the upper hand – especially with the stronger line from the CPSU in the late 1940s and the establishment of the CPGB's National Cultural Committee in 1947. There was much less work of an experimental nature. It is the Cold War period that saw artists turn inwards to the aesthetic and political security of the Soviet worldview, and by this time it was a dull and conservative approach that dominated in the Soviet Union. The Cold War helped to create a distortion of national politics and culture within the countries on both sides of its front line, and it even had an effect on the psychology of its victims, encouraging a siege mentality and a hardening of views and closing of minds.

Many post-war pamphlets reflect the style associated with the Festival of Britain: crisp, light, attractive and inoffensive, 'modern' in a way that was not too challenging. But, given the hardships of the war years, and indeed of the post-war years, this was not surprising. In fact, three key members of the AIA had leading roles in the Festival design team: Holland, Black and Henrion, though only Holland was in the CP.

1956 dealt a heavy blow to the CP's influence among artists and many left, including Hogarth and Friell. The artist who dominated CP visual materials from this time was David Caplan, who usually signed himself 'Davy'. At times he appeared to have a monopoly, and between roughly 1950 and 1970 it was difficult for younger artists to get a look in. He was competent, his work was sometimes dull, occasionally very good – a safe pair of hands – but not as inspiring as his predecessors'. The *Daily Worker* cartoonist 'Eccles' (Frank Brown – one of three brothers who worked for the paper) first drew cartoons for *Challenge* in 1948 and was the Party's main cartoonist for many years, replacing 'Gabriel' after 1956. There were no illustrators of note in the final years of the CP as far as national pamphlets were concerned. Locally, the skills of members might be used – for instance in Liverpool most journals and pamphlets from the mid-1970s onwards have cartoons by Pete Betts.

Historiography of the CPGB

Kevin Morgan

The most immediately striking feature of this bibliography is its size. At the CPGB's low point in 1930 you could have assembled its entire membership in one end of a small-town football ground. Even its electorate did not quite match a cup-final crowd. Few populations outside of the country's social and political elites can nevertheless have generated so many printed words per member. As is amply demonstrated here, the party itself was a prolific disseminator of printed material. From the earliest factional rival or scandalised newspaper editorialist, outside observers have also made their contribution to a formidable stream of comment, invective and analysis. The level of interest seems incommensurate with any purely empirical measure of the party's standing, and some historians – A.J.P. Taylor was one of the first – have doubted its justification. The commonest alibi, not without foundation, was that the CPGB's influence was 'out of all proportion to its size'. In any case, the fascination it has exercised has been; within the field of British labour history, possibly only the Fabians, whom Eric Hobsbawm accredited with a similar flair for self-promotion, have so compensated for lack of numbers with such abundance of documentation.

The bibliography also shows how unevenly the interest in communist history has developed over time. Not only has the level of interest ebbed and flowed, so has its basic character, with partisan motivations increasingly giving way to, or taking the form of, professedly scholarly agendas. Long predating any such academic interest, the historiography of British communism begins with the party's own concern to affirm its role as self-designated vanguard of the British working class. As early as 1931, R. Page Arnot, later better known as a historian of the mining unions, took part in discussions in Moscow regarding a textbook of party history for use at the International Lenin School. This was a more politically sensitive matter than one might have imagined. Not only were there key issues and personalities to be avoided, but the presentation of any sort of acceptable narrative was conditional on a general party line that was always liable to be overturned in the time that it took to produce a decent history book. The first history of the CPGB, published by Tom Bell in 1937, was both an example in itself and a warning to others. Though Bell was a veteran functionary and sometime tutor at the Lenin School, his pioneering effort was immediately withdrawn and its alleged deficiencies detailed at length in Palme Dutt's *Labour Monthly*. 'The Secretariat desires to advise', the party pronounced, as if empowered to declare a pipe not a pipe, 'that this book should not be considered as a history of the Party'.

The result was a singular oversight and paradox. It was from just this point that one can begin to trace the contribution of British communists to a wider radical historiography. Through those who passed through its post-war Historians' Group – Hill, Saville, Hilton, Kiernan, Hobsbawm himself – this was certainly an influence disproportionate to the party's size. Nevertheless, as Hobsbawm later recorded, political constraints meant that the party's own history formed no real part of this activity. Indeed, post-1914 history as a whole was a subject they thought it safest to leave undisturbed. For some two decades after Bell's effort, just about the only available narratives of the CPGB's history were autobiographies of variable quality (Bell's *Pioneering Days* was one of the best) and official commemorative brochures of invariable lack of quality (Arnot's *Twenty Years*, published during the Nazi-Soviet Pact, was one of the worst). When Henry Pelling ventured onto this territory as its first academic historian in 1958, he described it as a sort of forbidden no-man's-land.

It was 1956 that changed all that. As long as powerful collective disciplines remained intact, no serious reckoning with the CPGB's past was to be anticipated. The first precondition of a critical communist historiography was therefore defection, a challenge from within or a crisis of the party itself. All three were irrepressibly in evidence in the communist *annus terribilis*, which also saw the emergence of a new left defined by its anti-Stalinism. Malcolm MacEwen, until then the *Daily Worker*'s foreign editor, would later refer to 1956 as the day that 'the party had to stop'. By the same token, it was the day the party's history could at last begin to be written. Rocked by the revelations about Stalin at the Soviet party congress in February 1956, the CPGB set up a history commission initially chaired by its departing general secretary Harry Pollitt. Participating historians included Hobsbawm and Brian Pearce, while Arnot was there as a reminder of political imperatives that were not simply to be thrown aside. Other issues must have seemed more pressing, as the party lost a quarter of its members and an even greater proportion of its historians. Minds were nevertheless concentrated by the challenge which such defections posed to the old taboos and sense of conformism. Writing as 'Joseph Redman', Pearce himself published essays on early communist history under the auspices of the Trotskyist Socialist Labour League. Pelling's *British Communist Party: a historical profile*, appearing shortly afterwards, claimed the assistance of 'some present and many former members of the party'. In the *New Reasoner*, organ of the anti-Stalinist revolt, Pelling's treatment occasioned pithy reflections by one of the CPGB's earliest leading defectors, J.T. Murphy. This wasn't a no-man's-land, and the party had no heavy guns to keep people off. If it failed to contest this territory itself, it was clear that this meant leaving it to those who were prepared to reconnoitre.

The initiation of an official party historiography had therefore something of the character of a bureaucratic rearguard action. Even those historians who remained loyal to the party were loath to have any part in it. Frank Jackson, the King Street librarian, reported irascibly of the first eighteen months of the history commission: 'Up to date we have had NO support from the Historian comrades in regard to this ...'. Probably Arnot was sufficiently occupied with his mining histories. The task of writing an official history consequently fell upon James Klugmann, a full-time party worker of brilliant but wasted intellect. Klugmann's *From Trotsky to Tito* was (and is) notorious, and he frankly referred to rival productions as 'enemy' histories. With the likes of Arnot and Dutt still around to read his drafts, it is perhaps surprising that he produced his first two volumes as quickly as he did, in 1968-9. Critically speaking, they mark little advance upon the commemorative brochure; Hobsbawm remarked on the impossibility of Klugmann being 'both a good historian and a loyal functionary'. But at the same time the no-man's-land was proliferating with independent histories. As Klugmann grumbled privately in 1966, 'dozens and dozens' of such histories were being written 'by people antagonistic to Marxism or by young people under their supervision'.

Klugmann had in mind an international phenomenon, with the American PhD industry to the fore. It is difficult to see that its British representatives were so hostile to communism. In other countries 'Cold War' or traditionalist versions of communist history were authoritatively expounded in works typically by former communists or close fellow travellers. Among them were Annie Kriegel (*Aux origines du communisme français*, 1964), Hermann Weber (*Wandlung des deutschen Kommunismus*, 1969) or, somewhat earlier, Theodore Draper in the USA. But there wasn't a British equivalent, unless it was Walter Kendall's painstaking but idiosyncratically teleological *Revolutionary Movement in Britain*, which concluded with the CPGB's foundation. In Britain ex-communists did not usually become anti-communists, and anti-communists (like Kendall) were not usually former party members. The historians who left in 1956-7 sought the fuller expression, not the abandonment, of the radical perspectives they had developed within the Historians' Group. Several now played their part in the emergence of a vibrant new school of British labour history. This was symbolised, on the one hand, by the formation in 1960 of the Society for the Study of Labour History, and on the other by the publication three years later of E.P. Thompson's *Making of the English Working Class*. It was from this ecumenical milieu – in which communists past, present and not-at-all, cheerfully intermingled – that the first serious academic treatments of British communist history emerged. If British communist history was a sub-specialism, it was of labour history, not of Cold War history.

Even Pelling, despite his unabashed hostility, came to the party as a recognised labour history specialist. Other accounts, like L.J. Macfarlane's study of the party's formative years or Roderick Martin's history of the Minority Movement, registered Moscow's directing hand, but did not (unlike Pelling) underplay the indigenous experience of working-class activism, without which there was nothing to direct. Kenneth Newton's *Sociology of British Communism* was explicitly framed as a rejection of the Cold War pathologies of the *Appeals of Communism* type, which had also flourished far more in America than in Britain. There was, in fact, no 'Cold War' narrative of British communism comparable in quality or scope with those produced in other countries. Whatever the insights or deficiencies of Pelling or Brian Pearce, they did not remotely represent the sort of sustained scholarly engagement of a Weber or a Kriegel.

With the exception of its first decade of activity, there was not much of a party history at all. At the time of Klugmann's death in 1977, the official history remained suspended in 1927. Neither Kendall, Martin, Macfarlane, Pearce or Pearce's fellow Trotskyist Michael Woodhouse had taken the story very much further. For the 'Stalinised' CPGB of the early 1930s onwards there was therefore almost nothing but Pelling's extremely slight and tendentious narrative. On the one hand, there was no chance of seeing any party archives, which was the one real control the party had over its historical no-man's-land. On the other hand, why should anybody want to disinter the skeletons in King Street cupboards? As every history undergraduate read their Hill or Hobsbawm, and as the 'new' social history swept all before it, interest shifted from the party as institution to the diverse social and cultural milieux in which communists had made their famously disproportionate contributions.

Geoff Eley in 1986 described this as the inexorable march of historiographical progress into 'previously recalcitrant fields of study'. At the head of the British contingent was the temporarily expatriated Australian Stuart Macintyre, who in the single year of 1980 published the classic texts *A Proletarian Science*, on working-class intellectuals, and *Little Moscows*. Other significant contributions included Sue Bruley's work on women and gender; Richard Croucher's *Engineers at War* and the South Wales miners' histories of Hywel Francis and Dai Smith. Some of these historians, like Macintyre and Francis, were CPGB members, reflecting the Gramscian, 'eurocommunist' perspectives of younger British communists. This was also reflected in the CP History Group, successor to the Historians' Group, whose irregular productions included inputs from several well-known exponents of the new social history. One hardly knows now whether they were in the CP or not, nor did it really matter.

Most of them would have agreed with Gramsci that the best party history should represent the history of the wider society from a monographic perspective. In which case, you might have thought, one might as well get straight into the history of the wider society itself. Implicitly, this was the principle on which the new historical cohort mainly worked. No history of the CPGB itself was produced according to Gramsci's dictum, and a projected collection of essays by the younger historians never saw the light of the day. Within the party itself, a mission to fill in what he later called the 'blank spots' of its history was more or less single-handedly the work of Monty Johnstone. Intruding a personal note, this was the state of British communist historiography when I stumbled across it as a student in 1980. Wanting to find out about the war years, the only accounts I could find were Pelling's, whose small 'c' conservatism immediately repelled, and the Trotskyist commentaries of Dewar and Black, which seemed respectively wispy and manic. There was no real need to have read anything else: if the insights of labour and social history were also applicable to communism and its forms of activism, then these arid rehearsals of the party line were just as clearly inadequate as any other variant of the 'old' institutional history. Focusing on the party itself, my own book *Against Fascism and War* was thus intended as a marriage of history 'from above' and 'from below', combining grassroots perspectives with recognition of the problems posed by its increasingly wayward political direction. Almost the only real model for such a study, to which I duly made acknowledgement, was James Hinton's *History Workshop* essay on Coventry communism.

Eley was right; this was simply the incursion of methods already pioneered elsewhere. By 1989, when my book was published, it nevertheless seemed an inauspicious time to have undertaken such work. The syndicalist Sorel once wrote that there can be no epic treatment of a 'thing which the people cannot picture to themselves as reproducible in the near future'. Histories of British communism had not exactly had an epic character. They were, even so, primarily the work of historians who, at however sublimated a level, had some commitment to the future as well as the past of such forms of mobilisation. For many of them, it might not much have mattered that the CPGB itself was a manifestly declining force, had it not been so apparent – in contrast to 1956 – that this was merely symptomatic of a wider malaise.

These were the years of Thatcherism, de-unionisation and Labour 'modernisation'. If the halcyon years of the post-war labour movement were clearly passing, so too were those of a radical historiography conceived as reproducible in some not-too-distant future. When Hinton and Richard Hyman published *Trade Unions and Revolution* in 1975, it was using communist history as the proverbial Leninist guide to action. Now, by contrast, it was its irrecoverable pastness that generated indifference or else a sort of revolutionary nostalgia. If the CP History Group established a more regular pattern of activity, it was as the vehicle of veteran party members engaged in a sort of collective retrospection. The official party history, now in Noreen Branson's capable hands, had something of the same character. The outstanding historiographical contribution of the 1980s, Raphael Samuel's essays on the CPGB's 'lost world', drew on the innovations of the History Workshop movement, but had an intensely personal and almost elegiac quality. Independently pursuing disparate PhD projects on communist history were Andy Croft, Nina Fishman and Steve Parsons as well as myself. But there were no networks, conferences or edited collections, nor any other significant collaboration or communication. With the fall of the Berlin wall at the end of 1989, this might have been the signal that the party history might as well stop.

Life itself, as Fishman's communist informants were wont to put it, saw to it that it was not. In 1956 the collapse of the Stalin myth had encouraged a first historical reckoning with the communist experience. In 1989-91 the collapse of the Soviet bloc itself held out the prospect, quickly shown to be an illusory one, of a sort of final balance-sheet. After 1956 the impetus to write histories had come from communists and others prepared to circumvent the lack of access to party archives. For the labour and social historians who followed, unofficial sources, notably including oral history, provided a bottom-up perspective that was definitely preferred to that of the party apparatus. But suddenly, with the collapse of the Soviet Union, it transpired that the Comintern archives in Moscow included over a thousand files relating to the CPGB, to say nothing of those relating to individual communists or to front organisations. Here in Britain, as the CPGB made way for the ill-fated Democratic Left, provision of access to the party's archives was formalised by their deposit in 1994 in Manchester's National Museum of Labour History, now the People's History Museum. In Moscow, meanwhile, though the extent and conditions of access have sometimes varied, nobody has ever returned from a research visit empty handed.

Between the documentation of the Comintern period in Moscow, and that primarily of the post-Comintern period in Manchester, historians of the CPGB were better provided for archivally than those of just about any other comparable political movement. For some periods, the practice of compiling full stenographic reports made for a closer parallel with a sort of King Street *Hansard*. No stranger to the cult of secrecy, the British state itself has lately assisted through the faltering release of MI5 files according to some utterly opaque and publicly unaccountable process. Compared to parties like those in France or the USA, the loyalty and longevity of the CPGB's leading cadre – even in 1956 – meant that few chinks of light had ever been provided by the personal papers and testimonies of defectors. In an article in 1993, I likened the impression to that of an old sepia photograph of party leaders suddenly animated by powers of speech and disputation.

A literature of shallow exposé was one of the first results internationally. In a less sensationalist register, academic discussion focused on the so-called 'centre-periphery' debate: that is, how far and by what means the 'centre' – Moscow – controlled and manipulated the 'periphery' – namely national parties like the CPGB. International conferences were convened, and by the middle of the decade important papers and monographs had appeared on several European communist parties, including some as marginal as Britain's. Nevertheless, the CPGB and its historians initially figured little in this debate. Whilst a reviving interest in communist history was demonstrated by the 'Opening the Books' conference in 1994, Hobsbawm observed how little the papers published from it actually used the newly accessible materials. Not until 1997 did Francis Beckett provide a first, avowedly journalistic account informed by the Moscow archives. Not until 2000 did a substantial contribution to the centre-periphery debate appear in the shape of Andrew Thorpe's

British Communist Party and Moscow. Two years later this was followed by Matthew Worley's study of the controversial Class Against Class period, using detailed notes made by Klugmann in the then inaccessible Comintern archives. Thorpe, unlike Worley, was not much interested in the 'new' labour history. He did, however, come to the subject as a practised historian of British political parties, alert to tensions and contingencies which Comintern controls never fully succeeded in stifling. Without any obvious ideological axe to grind, he contested what he called the 'slaves of Moscow' approach, though significantly the examples he cited were American ones. With the doubtful exceptions of Dewar and the now-distant Pelling, there simply weren't any British ones to speak of.

For reasons that are still unclear, a vigorous vindication of 'traditionalist' methodologies was now offered in a spate of overlapping articles by John McIlroy and Alan Campbell. Though both had hitherto expressed approval of recent developments in CPGB historiography, they not only targeted Thorpe and Worley but extended this to a putative revisionist school comprising practically all of the subject's principal practitioners. Bilious and unseemly in itself, the resulting controversy underlined the artificiality of the whole debate. As neither 'revisionist' nor traditionalist schools could be identified in the way suggested, there was little of substance to respond to, nor was any significant new account of CPGB history presented. Half a century after Pelling, the traditionalist view of CPGB history has still never been expounded in the traditionalist form of the scholarly research monograph, unless it is the Laybourn-Murphy volume *Under the Red Flag*. But the deficiencies, both general and particular, of their treatment were clearly identified in this case by McIlroy himself.

Polemical exertion will doubtless continue to fade with the receding of factional rivalries. The centre-periphery debate itself seems exhausted, for neither the cruder versions of Comintern control nor the supposed counterclaim of autonomous national party organisations are any longer entertained by any serious researcher. Even so, one feels confident that this bibliography will need a supplement a few years hence. Communism was one of the defining political movements of the twentieth century; the CPGB was both the primary expression of this phenomenon within a British context and a significant political actor raising crucial issues of culture, ideology, identity and the roots of political activism. More than most political movements, it presents us with the complex interactions of the personal, the sectoral, the local, the national and the international. As the vaunted 'end of history' proves just another beginning, and as the challenges of thinking global and acting local reappear as compellingly as ever, it would be odd if communist history did not continue to hold its more than proportionate interest.

Some of the possible lines of future research are already indicated in the listings here. Biography is one. In pre-archival days, only the MP Shapurji Saklatvala was the subject of a scholarly political biography, thanks to widely reported public utterances that were skilfully quarried by Mike Squires. Less dependent on institutional archives, important studies existed of communist writers and scientists, like those of Wendy Mulford and Gary Werskey, and recent additions to this body of work include the wonderfully empathetic lives of Randall Swingler (by Andy Croft) and Ewan MacColl (by Ben Harker). More difficult to imagine without the party archives are the biographies that appeared in quick succession of political figures like Pollitt, Dutt and Murphy. Most recently, and on a more imposing scale than any of these, the late Nina Fishman's study of the South Wales miners' leader Arthur Horner represented the culmination of a project undertaken by Hywel Francis some thirty years earlier. Already by 2001 there was enough work underway to generate the biographical symposium *Party People, Communist Lives*. Full-length studies of Willie Gallacher, Wal Hannington, James Klugmann and Dora Montefiore are among those that may be anticipated.

Interest in the wider social and cultural histories which they exemplify shows no sign of drying up. As well as the *Opening the Books* collection, this was vividly attested in 1997 by Andy Croft's edited collection on the 'cultural front', *A Weapon in the Struggle*. Croft's own interest in communist writers, earlier represented by his *Red Letter Days*, has recently been maintained by Philip Bounds, and further research is in progress or may be anticipated on such further key groups as communist scientists, architects and, it seems almost inexhaustibly, historians. On a broader scale, the Manchester-based CPGB Biographical Project combined insights from the newly accessible archives with oral sources, including a substantial project of life-history interviews. The resulting volume *Communists in British Society* employed a prosopographical methodology, and through the attempt at a synoptic social history did, within its limits, seek to provide a monographic perspective on the wider social framework by which the specificities of British communism were shaped.

To the extent that it depended on original interviews, a project of this type focusing on the CPGB's vaunted 'heyday' of the 1930s and 1940s is already more or less inconceivable. Nevertheless, significant bodies of oral testimony are accessible to historians at locations like the South Wales Miners' Library, the Imperial War Museum and the National Sound Archive. There are also signs of historians' interest moving on from the dominant preoccupation with the inter-war period, and therefore potentially of new cohorts of interviewees to be contacted. Though books by Neil Redfern and Thomas Linehan confirm the earlier period's enduring fascination, the belated completion of the 'official' party history, by the expressly non-official historians John Callaghan and Geoff Andrews, already indicates the scope for further exploration of the CPGB's final four decades. Biographically, this is also evident in Seifert and Sibley's recent volume on Bert Ramelson, which focuses more on the labour unrest of the Wilson-Heath-Callaghan years than on Ramelson's formative decades in the party. Mick McGahey for one would certainly merit a similar treatment. With increasing interest in the diverse ramifications of the Cold War, and in the militancies and contestations of the 1960s and 1970s, there is a history here which, in contrast to the earlier period, has hardly yet begun to be written.

There will therefore be no shortage of material for future instalments of this bibliography. At the same time, one may anticipate that the sub-specialism of British communist history will increasingly merge into broader fields of historical study. In part this will reflect the rationale of the 'new' social historians, for whom there was only so much institutional party history that could be written, and who rightly saw the CPGB as a way of exploring wider issues of conflict and identity. At the same time, it should reflect a continuing recognition of the CPGB's international links, and of how active party commitments at some level always represented a sort of intersection between the national and the international. Given current preoccupations with the writing of a transnational labour history, one may perhaps anticipate much more in the way of comparative and cross-border studies, and not just the monographic focus on a single party like the CPGB. If that is so, the boundaries of a CPGB bibliography will be even more difficult to define than they already are. Which would mean that this might turn out to have been a particularly timely moment to take stock of this literature.

Sources and Locations

This bibliography does not give locations for the items listed. However the vast majority of the CP material is located in three libraries, all easily accessible. These are: the Labour History and Archive Centre at the People's History Museum, Left Bank, Spinningfields, Manchester, M3 3ER (formally the National Museum of Labour History); Marx Memorial Library, 37a Clerkenwell Green, London, EC1R 0DU; the Working Class Movement Library, Jubilee House, 51 Crescent, Salford, M5 4WX. These libraries also contain much material about the CP. The William Gallacher Collection, the Scottish CP's library, now in Glasgow Caledonian University Library, is a major source of Scottish material. All these libraries have most of their collections on computerised databases. I was fortunate in being given free access to all four before computerisation started. I am deeply indebted to those responsible for this freedom, and this bibliography would not have been possible without it. This opportunity to search systematically through material that was not at the time properly catalogued was invaluable – many items turned up in unexpected places.

My own collection built up over many years was another source. Other important collections are in the Bodleian Library in Oxford, the Modern Records Centre at Warwick University, The South Wales Miners' Library at University of Wales Swansea, Methil Public Library and the British Library.

I list here the collections that I consulted, all of which revealed some useful material, in the hope that this will not only point researchers in the right direction for obtaining access to items in this book, but may indicate – through absence – sources that I have missed.

British Library

British Library of Political & Economic Science at the London School of Economics

East Sussex Record Office, Lewes: Archive of Ernie Trory; Papers of Percy Horton; Papers of Ronald Horton

Edinburgh University: MacDiarmid Papers

Glasgow Mitchell Library

Glasgow Caledonian University: Taylor Collection

Glasgow Strathclyde University, Andersonian Library: Aldred Collection

Glasgow University

Hull University, Brynmor Jones Library: DCP – Hull CP Records; DAR – Page Arnot Papers; DHH – Howard Hill Papers; DJH – Jock Haston Papers; DBN – Reginald Bridgeman Papers

Methil Public Library, Fife: David Proudfoot Papers; Hutt Collection (a rich collection of letters and early pit papers in a small urban branch library)

Modern Records Collection, University of Warwick: Miscellaneous Papers (MSS 21); London Busmen's Rank & File Movement (MSS 62); Tarbuck Papers (MSS 75); Militant Miners Newsheets (MSS 88); Purdie Papers (149); National Union of Seamen (Rank & File Organisations) (MSS 175); Reg Groves Papers (MSS 172); J. Askins Papers (MSS 189); Etheridge Papers (MSS 202); Michaelson Papers (MSS 233); *Times* Labour Editor's Papers (MSS 271); L. Daly Papers (MSS 302); R. Croucher Papers (MSS 180); TUC Papers (MSS 292)

National Library of Scotland

National Library of Wales, Aberystwyth: Dept of Manuscripts and Records; Papers of: Idris Cox; Benjamin Davies; Selwyn Jones; Gwenffrwd Hughes; Ty Cenedl

Oxford, Bodleian Library: John Johnson Papers; Douglas Garman Papers

Oxford County Library

Oxford, Ruskin College Library: Abe Lazarus Collection

Sheffield Central Library

Sheffield University: Lazar Zaidman Collection

Stirling University: Watson Collection; Tait Collection

Swansea University College: From *Guide to South Wales Coalfield Archive*, 1980: Papers of: NUM; J. Davies (Neath); David Francis; W. Eddie Jones (Cwmbran); H. Morgan (Abertillery). From *Supplementary Guide*, 1983: Papers of Jim David (Seven Sisters); Glyn Evans (Garnant); David Francis (2nd Deposit); J.S. Williams (Dowlais). From *Web Page Guide*: papers of Amos Mouls; Selwyn Jones. Special Collections. Also the South Wales Miners' Library – strong collection on CP

TUC Library, London Metropolitan University.

It is hoped that any omissions noted, and any corrections, will be forwarded to the author or publisher (see p.6). The aim has been to be as comprehensive as possible, but given the vast amount of material available and the ephemeral nature of much of it, the picture is bound to be incomplete. There may well be more university and local libraries and Record Offices with donations of CP and left-wing material that will come to light.

In many cases, the survival of the pamphlets and papers is due to the diligent work, over a long period, of a limited number of individuals. The creation of the Working Class Movement Library itself was down to the work of just two individuals; the papers in the various libraries just listed are the personal collections of the people they are named after. Sometimes a strong CP history group in an area helped raise the level of awareness of the value of ephemeral material – this was certainly the case in the North West and Yorkshire, which consequently have a much greater representation in this bibliography than, say, the North East. The collection of London District material in the national Archives is excellent, but there was never, unfortunately, any systematic attempt to get other District material sent to London for cataloguing or storage. The collection of nationally published pamphlets in the CP Archives is, however, nearly complete.

Bibliographies and Reference Works

Some of the following studies have entries in this bibliography, but for the sake of clarity, the most important ones are listed here.

────── *Northern Labour History: A Bibliography* Library Association, 1982 124pp
Covers Cleveland, Cumbria, Northumberland, Durham, Tyne and Wear.

Barberis, P; McHugh, John; Tyldesley, Mike
Encyclopedia of British and Irish Political Organizations Pinter, 2000 562pp
Entries on CPGB, YCL plus others with references to CP (NUWM, People's Convention, Maoist groups etc).

Bellamy, J. & Saville, J. (eds)
Dictionary of Labour Biography Macmillan/Palgrave Macmillan Vols. 1-13.

Bennett, John
Tom Mann: A Bibliography University of Warwick Library, Occasional Publications No.22, 1993 31pp

Boothroyd, David
The History of British Political Parties Politico's, 2001
2 pages on CPGB, plus entries for all the breakaways.

Buitekant, Barry
Bibliography of Trotskyist Books, Journals and Pamphlets Published in Britain in 1932-1976 Located in the Archives of Socialist Platform Ltd Diploma of Independent Studies, North East London Polytechnic, 1988-9   214pp

Burnett, John et al (eds)
Autobiography of the Working Class Vol.2 1900-45 and *Vol.3 Supplement* Harvester, 1987
Includes published work and unpublished typescripts.

Elwell, Charles
Tracts Beyond the Times: A Brief Guide to the Communist or Revolutionary Marxist Press Social Affairs Unit, 1983   32pp
Includes frequency, pagination, price, address and some notes.

Frow, E. & R.
Pit and Factory Papers Issued by the CPGB, 1927-34 s.p. 1996   29pp

Gulick, Charles et al
History and Theories of Working-Class Movements: A Select Bibliography Bureau of Business & Economic Research/Institute of Industrial Relations, Univ. of California, 1955   364pp
30 author entries on CPGB: all magazine articles, mostly from *Labour Monthly*.

Hammond, Thomas
Soviet Foreign Relations and World Communism: Selected, Annotated Bibliography Princeton, 1965   1240pp
Only about two dozen entries on CPGB.

Harrison, R.; Woolven, G.; Duncan, R. (eds)
Warwick Guide to British Labour Periodicals, 1790-1970 Harvester, 1977   685pp

Kahan, Vilem (ed.)
Bibliography of the Communist International Brill, 1990 Vol.1   400pp

Le Dreau, Christophe
Parti Communiste de Grande Bretagne: Essai Bibliographique in *Communisme 87: Regards sur le Communisme Britannique* L'Age de L'Homme, 2006   224pp
This book is in French, but the Bibliography consists almost entirely of English language works. Annotations are in French. With over 460 entries, laid out chronologically and thematically it is the most important of the works listed here. In two areas it goes further than this Bibliography – Spies and Anti-Communism. Another

very useful feature is on Historiography – it covers all the contributions up to the time of publication.

Libraries Association
Subject Index to Periodicals (later *British Humanities Index*). Annual.

Mackenzie, Alan J.
Communism in Britain: A Bibliography in *Society for the Study of Labour History Bulletin* No.44, 1982 20pp
This was a useful start, despite some spelling errors. 100 entries on the CP.

MacDougall, I. (ed.)
A Catalogue of Some Labour Records in Scotland Scottish Labour History Society, 1978 598pp
Includes 12pp on CPGB.

McDougall, I. (ed.)
An Interim Bibliography of the Scottish Working Class Movement Scottish Committee, Society for the Study of Labour History, 1965 142pp

Spiers, John; Sexsmith, Ann; Everitt, Alastair (eds)
The Left in Britain: A Checklist and Guide Harvester, 1976 168pp.

Sullivan, A. (ed.)
British Literary Magazines: The Modern Age, 1914-84 (Part 2) Greenwood, 1986 628pp
Has entries on *Arena, New Writing, Left Review* and *Our Time*.

Sworakowski, Witold
The Communist International and Its Front Organisations Hoover Institution, Stanford, 1965 493pp
Very few in GB.

Worley, Matthew
Reflections on Recent British Communist Party History in *Historical Materialism* No.4, Summer 1999 21pp
Over 80 entries, mostly from 1980s/1990s.

Worley, Matthew
The British CP, 1920-45 in *The Historian*, Autumn, 1997 3pp

For comparative interest, it is worth consulting:

────── *Labour Party Bibliography* Labour Party, 1967 (?) 96pp

Woolven, Gillian B.
Publications of the Independent Labour Party, 1893-1932 Society for the Study of Labour History, 1977 38pp

The following English-language bibliographies of other Communist Parties are worth consulting.

Corker, Charles (ed.)
Bibliography on the Communist Problem in the United States Fund for the Republic, 1955 474pp c.5000 entries.

Haynes, John Earl
Communism and Anti-Communism in the United States: An Annotated Guide to Historical Writings Garland, 1987 321pp

Narkiewicz, Olga A.
Eurocommunism 1968-1986: A Select Bibliography Mansell, 1987 188pp

Seidman, Joel (ed.)
Communism in the United States: A Bibliography Cornell UP, 1969 526pp 6600 entries.

Sharma, Jagdish Savan
Indian Socialism: A Descriptive Bibliography Vikas Publishing House, 1975 340pp Large section on Indian Communism.

Symons, Beverley (ed.)
Communism in Australia: A Resource Bibliography National Library of Australia, 1994 281pp c.3400 entries.

Haynes' work has been expanded and is online with a slightly altered title: *American Communism and Anticommunism: A Historian's Bibliography and Guide to the Literature*. This is a huge enterprise with over 9000 entries, 33 chapters and hundreds of sub-divisions which make it very useful. It does cover Trotskyism, Maoism etc. This was last updated in February 2009.

There are an increasing number of bibliographies appearing online.

Internet Sites

The development of the worldwide web and social media are causing significant changes in the way information is recorded, stored and accessed as well as in the way politics is experienced. The digitisation of printed texts is proceeding at a phenomenal rate. It is likely that in the future any pamphlet or book printed will be available online or print on demand – perhaps apart from recent material, due to copyright issues. Already the earliest key documents of CPGB history can be found, as can many of the articles listed here and some of the most recent academic works. I have just come across freely downloadable copies of *In Search of Revolution* edited by Matthew Worley and *The CPGB Since 1920* by James Eaden and Dave Renton; these were both very expensive books when first published. The websites for academic institutions, for individual academics and for activists usually now have bibliographies of their works. Journal websites usually contain contents pages of every issue and the option of downloading individual issues or articles. At the moment this is often at considerable cost, but there are often free sample articles and the journals are often freely accessible via academic libraries. Publishers often provide the same opportunity with books, offering free sample chapters from longer texts. E-readers are increasingly widespread but they are linked to ruthless, profit-making corporations like Amazon and Apple. Corporations such as these are generally slower in making available the sort of material listed in this bibliography, and the costs are not necessarily cheaper than the equivalent printed book where this is available.

A very recent development precipitated by the internet is the availability of some new texts solely as print on demand texts. This raises interesting questions of access, as the books will not be printed unless they are paid for, and so they cannot be freely viewed in a library – unless libraries start purchasing these POD items, which goes against the existing trends of movement away from the printed book. The print on demand industry has, however, made available some very rare titles at very reasonable cost. For example most published books of Chartist poetry were not previously available in the antiquarian book trade nor even in many libraries, and they are now available through POD. Book publishers now print much of their back list in POD versions – Lawrence & Wishart keep the set of histories of the CPGB available this way.

What follows is a tentative suggestion of some sites worth looking at for those researching the CPGB. Libraries (the main ones have been listed above in 'Sources and Locations') and organisations are generally excluded from this list, but these can generally be easily traced. This is a rapidly changing world, so not only may interesting new sites emerge, but existing ones may disappear or, more likely, not be updated, especially if the site is the work of one individual. Further suggestions welcomed.

Academia: http://www.academia.edu/People/Communist_Party_of_Great_Britain
Details of academics researching CP history. Has some downloadable articles.

Amiel-Melburn Trust: http://www.amielandmelburn.org.uk/archive_index.htm
The Archive has digitised copies of *Marxism Today,* from 1980; Our History Group pamphlets; *Universities & Left Review/New Reasoner*; plus other material including an earlier version of this Bibliography.

Archives Hub: http://archiveshub.ac.uk
Papers and archives relating to CP can be searched here.

British Library Sound Archives: http://www.bl.uk/reshelp/findhelprestype/sound/ohist/ohcoll/ohpol/politics.html
CPGB is well represented here.

Chronicon: An Electronic History Journal http://www.ucc.ie/chronicon/robfra.htm
Has Geoff Roberts' article The Limits of Popular Radicalism: British Communism and The People's War, 1941-1945.

Communist History Network Newsletter: http://www.socialsciences.manchester.ac.uk/chnn
22 issues from 1996 to 2008. It was then incorporated into the journal *Twentieth Century Communism* with its associated blog: http://c20c.wordpress.com.

Communist Party Archive – Microform Academic Publishers: http://www.communistpartyarchive.org.uk
Selection of digitalised key documents from the CP Archives. The site is worth browsing but full access is by payment.

Communist Party of Britain: http://communist-party.org.uk/
The back issues of their new series of *Our History* are of particular interest.

CPGB Scottish Committee Archive: http://www.gcu.ac.uk/archives/cpgb/history

Graham Stevenson: http://www.grahamstevenson.me.uk
Includes a list of over 1000 CP biographies; an extensive article on two decades of the YCL etc.

Marxists Internet Archive: http://www.marxists.org/history/international/comintern/sections/britain/index.htm
Includes Index of *Labour Monthly* (to 1947) and early copies of other CP journals, with digitalised copies.

Merseyside International Brigades Network: www.mibnet.org.uk
Has list of all Merseysiders who fought in the I.B., with address, trade and political affiliation.

Political Studies Association, Communism Specialist Group: http://psacommunism.wordpress.com
Not limited to Britain.

Socialist History Society: www.socialisthistorysociety.co.uk
The successor to the CP History Group.

Associated Publishers

All are pamphlets unless stated.

A. Direct or very close CP control

Caledonian Books Ltd 68 West Regent Street, Glasgow

J.R. Campbell *Burns The Democrat* 1945 40pp.

Arthur Brady *Poles Apart* 1946 16pp. Post war problems with demobilisation of Polish army and rise of Cold War attitudes; refers to rightwing actions of sections of Anders' army in Scotland. Cover by Frank McKenna.

John Gollan *Scottish Prospect: An Economic, Administrative and Social Survey* 1948 266pp hb.

Labour Monthly 6 Tavistock Square, WC1 to December 1923; 162 Buckingham Palace Road SW1 to December 1928; 79 Warren St, W1 to c.July 1931; 7 John St, Theobalds Road, WC1 to June or July 1938; 43 Museum St, WC1 to October 1940; 134 Ballards Lane, N3 to end.

All of the following are published by *Labour Monthly* or Trinity Trust (the official name of the company that produced *Labour Monthly*).

Tien Sen Shiao *Face Pidgin: The Chinese*, 1925? 8pp. Reprinted from *LM*.

P. Braun *Problems of the Labour Movement*, 1925 16pp Reprinted from *LM* June 1925, with a new preface by A.J. Cook.

'U.D.C.' *The Diplomacy Of Mr. Ramsay Macdonald* 1925 19pp From articles in *LM* January and February 1925. A biting critique by an anonymous former colleague.

R. Palme Dutt *Marxism After Fifty Years* 1933 30pp Pamphlet No.1.

L. Rudas *Dialectical Materialism and Communism* 1933 30pp

N.K. Krupskaya *How Lenin Studied Marx* 1933 12pp

Sean Murray *Ireland's Path To Freedom: Manifesto of the CP of Ireland* 1933 8pp Published with the CPI.

William Rust *Mosley and Lancashire* 1935 12pp Pamphlet No.5.

J.D. Bernal *Engels and Science* 1936 16pp

'British Resident' *Who is Prosperous in Palestine?* 1936 44pp

E. Varga *The Imperialist Struggle For a New Redivision Of The World* 1940 11pp War Pamphlet No.1.

R. Page Arnot et al *Forging The Weapon: The Struggle of The Labour Monthly 1921-1941* 1941 32pp

R. Palme Dutt *The New Order In Britain* 1941 16pp Reprinted from *LM*, March 1941. War Pamphlet No.2.

Maurice Dobb *Production Front!* 1941 24pp

Ivor Montagu *Roll On, Mississippi!* 1941 24pp

R. Palme Dutt & Ivor Montagu *Ruby Star* 1941 16pp On the 24th Anniversary of the Russian Revolution.

R. Palme Dutt *25 Years* 1942 10pp. On 25th Anniversary of the Russian Revolution.

J.B.S. Haldane *Dialectical Materialism and Modern Science* 1942 16pp

R. Palme Dutt *India: What Must Be Done* 1942 16pp

W.H. Andrews *The Nazi Danger in South Africa* 1942 20pp Author was founding member and leader of the South African CP.

R. Page Arnot *Japan* 1942 23pp

Roy Pascal *Karl Marx: His Apprenticeship To Politics* 1942 31pp

---- *Organised Discussion: The Formation, Function and Conduct of Political Groups* 1942 16pp *LM* organised these groups during WW2.

A. Marty *Patriots Of France: An Account Of The Martyrdom Of 27 French at Chateaubriant and Execution Of P. Semard* 1942 12pp

D.N. Pritt *Revolt in Europe* 1942 40pp Early accounts of resistance and sabotage in occupied Europe. With Appendix *German Call for Revolt* signed by 57 German writers, politicians, artists and trade unionists.

Tom Balmer (ed.) & Ivor Montagu (Preface) *The War Comes First: A Selection of Articles From the Soviet Press Depicting the Mobilisation of the Civilian Front in the War of Defence Against Hitlerite Germany* 1942 64pp

Ivor Montagu *Zero Hour Second Front* 1942 15pp

Roy Pascal *Karl Marx: Political Foundations* 1943 31pp

G. Adhikari & Ben Bradley (Foreword) *Pakistan And Indian National Unity* 1943 32pp

R. Palme Dutt *The Road To Labour Unity* 1943 48pp On CPGB affiliation to the LP.

Clemens Dutt (ed.) *The Soviet Worker Looks at the War* 1943 88pp From the Moscow magazine *War and the Working Class*.

R. Page Arnot *There Are No Aryans* 1943 32pp Cover by Theyre Lee-Elliott.

D.N. Pritt *The Mosley Case* 1944 32pp

---- *War Criminals* 1944 32pp

William Gallacher *What Is Democracy?* 1946 16pp

Arthur Horner *Trade Unions and Communism* 1948 11pp

---- *China Stands Up, Being the Common Programme of the Chinese People's Political Consultative Conference* 1950 10pp Reprinted from *LM* Dec 1949

R. Palme Dutt *Empire War Plans* 1949 15pp

R. Palme Dutt *Whither India?* 1949 12pp Reprinted from *LM* June 1948.

Agnes Smedley & D.N. Pritt et al *Korea Handbook* 1950 96pp

R. Palme Dutt *Mr Bevin's Record* (1950?) 15pp

R. Palme Dutt *George Bernard Shaw: A Memoir and 'The Dictatorship Of The Proletariat' The Famous 1921 Article By Shaw* 1951 30pp

D.N. Pritt *Light On Korea* 1950? 16pp

D.N. Pritt *Oppression in India* 1950 12pp Originally appeared in *LM*.

Mao Tse-Tung *Concerning Practice* 1951 16pp

D.N. Pritt *New Light On Korea* 1951 32pp

R. Page Arnot (ed.) *Unpublished Letters of William Morris* 1951 16pp

D.N. Pritt *The Truth About The USSR* 1951 15pp

J.D. Bernal *The Way To Peace.* 1951 23pp

Arthur Horner *The Right To Strike* 1955? 4pp

D.N. Pritt *Socialism and Civil Liberty* 1956? 12pp

---- *The British Empire and its Colonies: Information Document for Labour Monthly Discussion Conference* 1958 8pp

R. Palme Dutt *Britain's Colonies and the Colour Bar: Opening Report to LM Delegate Conference* 1958 11pp lf

R. Palme Dutt *Storming Heaven* 1961 16pp

R. Palme Dutt *The Rise and Fall Of The Daily Herald* 1964 17pp Includes some reproductions of cartoons from the *Daily Herald* of 1913.

D.N. Pritt *Neo-Nazis: The Danger Of War* 1965 55pp

R. Palme Dutt *India In Travail* 1967 16pp Originally appeared in *LM*.

R. Palme Dutt et al *Labour Monthly Golden Jubilee Souvenir* 1971 31pp Large format Tributes to *Labour Monthly*; includes cartoons from 1921 and pieces by Dutt.

Marx House / Workers' School / Marx Memorial Library 37a Clerkenwell Green, EC1

The library was set up in 1933, and in 1943 it temporarily moved to 1 Doughty Street. It published CP educational material for the Workers' School (see Prospectus for various years in the late 1930s/1940s) including syllabuses and tutors' notes; some were published in conjunction with the *Daily Worker* and some with Lawrence & Wishart. Serial publications included *The International Book Review* (two double issues in 1938 and 1939), various catalogues (now online), and from October 1941 a regular (monthly/bi-monthly/quarterly) *Bulletin* (currently annually, titled *Theory and Struggle* (initially *Praxis*) and a more professional publication than any previous MML journals). *Educational Commentary* (then *Educational Commentary on Current Affairs*) was published fortnightly from 4 November 1942 to October 1956 in association with the *Daily Worker* (from 4 May 1946 the publishers were inverted – it was 'Issued by the *Daily Worker* in Association with the MML'). 9th Series No.8 of the *Commentary* was not issued.

There had been an earlier version (*A Commentary on Current Political Events for the Supporters of the DW Defence Leagues*) published while the *DW* was banned (listed in main text).

There were four-page *Educational Leaflets* reprinted for sale from this *Educational Commentary*, 'published by A Massie for Marx House'. Massie produced the 'Educational Commentary' until his death in 1947.

A brief description of the Library, its activities and publications can be found in the last chapter of Andrew Rothstein *A House on Clerkenwell Green* (L&W, 1972).

Publications include (up to 1991, mainly):

---- *What Every Worker Wants to Know: A Syllabus of Current Economic and Political Problems* 1934 19pp (MML & Workers' School)

R. Page Arnot *An Introduction to Political Economy* 1940 28pp

Joan Thompson *Scientific Socialism* 1941 32pp (L&W for MML)

M. Dobb *Economics of Capitalism* 1941? 29pp (L&W for MML)

G. Allen Hutt *Problems of Trade Unionism* 1942 24pp (L&W for MML)

---- *Railways and Railwaymen in the USSR* 1942 41pp (L&W for MML)

Peter Kingsford *Problems of the Building Industry* 1941 47pp (L&W for MML, in conjunction with *The New Builders Leader*.)

H. Palmer *India* 1942 39pp (L&W for MML.)

R. Palme Dutt *Syllabus For A Course of Five Study Classes on 'India Today'* 1942 9pp lf

---- *Marxism and War* 1943? 30pp (L&W for MML)

---- *Books Against Barbarism* 1943 30pp

J. Kucszynski *Are the Workers Better Off?* 1945 22pp. (L&W for MML) (The introduction to the second edition of *A Short History of Labour Conditions under Industrial Capitalism.*)

F. Lambert *Labour's Case For The Forty Hour Working Week* 1945 16pp

A. Massie *Labour's Case For Public Ownership and Control* 1945 23pp

---- *Marx House: Its History and Traditions* 1956 7pp

A. Rothstein *Marxism After Eighty Years* 1963 24pp

J. Mahon & R. Scotter *Marx, Engels & the London Workers: Annual Memorial Lecture* 1964 20pp lf

---- *The Social Consequences of Automation* nd 13pp

E. Hobsbawm (misspelt as Hobsbaum) *The Dialogue on Marxism: Opening Speech at Discussion Conference, Oct 1965* 9pp lf

Sam Lilley *Marxism and the Technological Revolution: Opening Speech at Discussion Conference, May 1965* 11pp lf

Lionel Munby *Marxism and Democracy: Opening Speech at Discussion Conference, Jan 1966* 9pp lf

C. Desmond Greaves *Connolly, Socialism and Nationalism* 1968 15pp

J. Woddis *Opening Speeches at Discussion Conference on Who Will Lead the Struggle for Socialism? December 1968* 1969 13pp lf

Georges Cogniot *Karl Marx and the Paris Commune* Marx Memorial Lecture 1971 10pp

Mary Rosser et al *Marx Library: 75 Years of Enlightenment* 2008 64pp pb lf

Thames Publications 15 Greek Street, London W1.

Thames Publications was directly under CP control, and was linked to the chain of bookshops, Thames Books, set up by the London District.

J.D. Bernal et al *The Communist Answer to the Challenge to Our Time* 1947 85pp pb Printed by Farleigh Press.

Derek Kartun *This is America* 1947 89pp pb

Phil Piratin *Our Flag Stays Red* 1948 91pp pb

George Armstrong (ed.) *London's Struggle for Socialism* 56pp pb

Thames Publications 149 Coventry Rd. Ilford, Essex.

Jack Woddis *The Mask is Off: An Examination of the Activities of Trade Union Advicers in the British Colonies* 1954 48pp Printed by Narod Press.

The Workers' Bookshop/The Workers' Bookshop Ltd 38 Clerkenwell Green; later 49 Farringdon Road & 16 King Street

Linked to the CP literature distribution centre. It was the nominal publisher, for a period, of the Comintern's *International Press Correspondence* (listed).

T.H. Wintringham *Air Raid Warning!* 1934 16pp Printed by Western Printing Services, Bristol.

William Ferrie *The Banned Broadcast* 1934 16pp Printed by Marston Printing Co.

Anna Seghers *Ernst Thaelmann: What He Stands For* 1934 30pp

Dimitrov *Dimitrov Accuses: His Final Leipzig Speech* 1934 24pp

M N *The Role of the Communist Party in the Proletarian Revolution* 1934 19pp

---- *The Red Army* 1934? 14pp

---- *The Sedition Bill Exposed* 1934 21pp

---- *The Great 'Scales of Diet' Scandal* 1934 14pp

Vladimir Lenin *Marx* 1934? 48pp

Ivor Montagu *Blackshirt Brutality: The Story of Olympia* 1935 29pp

---- *The Jews and Fascism* 1935 16pp

---- *Elementary Economics* 1936/7 16pp

D.R. Davies *Elementary Historical Materialism* c.1937 16pp

---- *Pamphlet Guide* 1938 12pp Interestingly, this includes quite a number of Labour Party pamphlets.

V. Adoratsky *Dialectical Materialism* 96pp pb Title page imprint is Modern Books, front cover is Workers' Bookshop Ltd.

See also:

A. Hutt *Crisis on Clydeside* Workers' Bookshop, Glasgow and *Weithwyr Cymru! (Workers of Wales!)* Workers' Bookshop, Aberystwyth (both listed).

Victor Gollancz jointly with The Workers' Bookshop

John Strachey *Social Credit: An Economic Analysis* 1936 24pp

The Workers' Press Cayton Place, Cayton Street EC1.

Printers: Marston Printing Co. Linked to *The Daily Worker*.

W. Rust *Finland: Press Lies* 1940 8pp

B. Informal links with CP

Birch Books Southampton Street, Strand, WC1

Printers: Farleigh Press

T.D. Lysenko *Soviet Biology* 1948? 51pp pb

Arthur Clegg *New China, New World* 1949 73pp pb

J.D. Bernal & M. Cornforth *Science for Peace and Socialism* 1949? 86pp pb

S. Sarafis *Greek Resistance Army: The Story of ELAS* 1951 324pp pb

Various *Changing Epoch Series* was the title of four journal-type paperbacks on economic, cultural and political topics from both East and West Europe. All were published in 1947 in conjunction with Lawrence & Wishart. Each 72pp.

Cobbett Press / Cobbett Publishing 2 Southampton Place, London WC1

Established in 1943; sometime in 1944 the name changed to Cobbett Publishing and moved to 45 Great Russell Street, WC1.

---- *History of the CPSU (Bolsheviks): Short Course* 1943 345pp hb

Stanley Evans *The Churches in the USSR* 1943 160pp hb

Anna Louise Strong *The Russians are People* 1943 202pp hb

J.R. St John *To See Ourselves: A Contribution to Post War Sense* 1943 22pp

Fernand Grenier *Francs-Tireurs And Guerillas Of France* 1944 30pp

Mick Bennett *The Story of the Rifle* 1944 51pp pb

V. Gordon Childe *The Story of Tools* 1944 44pp

W. Cobbett; G.D.H. & Margaret Cole (ed.) *The Opinions of William Cobbett* 1944 340pp hb

B.L. Coombes *Those Clouded Hills* 1944 72pp Miner/writer describes the miner's life.

E.K. Fedorov *The Red Army: An Army of the People* 1944 48pp hb

Ralph Fox; Anand, Mulk Raj (Preface) *The Novel and the People* 1944 172pp hb

Hyman Levy *Social Thinking* 1945 174pp hb

Sam Lilley *Science and Progress* 1944 68pp

A.L. Morton *Language Of Men* 1945 93pp Essays on ballads, Swift, Bacon, Defoe, E.M. Forster, G.K. Chesterton, Negro Spirituals etc hb

M. Anderson (ed.) *Reformers And Rebels: A Calendar Of Anniversaries.* 1946 146pp hb A wide-ranging selection of radical quotes, poems etc for every day of the year.

Grahame Clark *From Savagery to Civilization* 1946 122pp hb

E.C. Curwen *Plough and Pasture* 1946 122pp hb

T.A. Jackson *Ireland Her Own: An Outline History Of The Irish Struggle For National Freedom And Independence* 1946 443pp hb

A.C. Moorhouse *Writing and the Alphabet* 1946 110pp hb

Roy Pascal *The Growth Of Modern Germany* 1946 145pp

V. Gordon Childe *History* 1947 86pp hb

Frank W. Walbank *The Decline Of The Roman Empire In The West* 1946 97pp hb

Charles Duff *No Angel's Wing* 1947 271pp hb Quite a bit of these memoirs concern Spain.

Victor Alba *Sleepless Spain* 1948 207pp hb

Ralph Fox; Jack Beeching (Preface) *The Novel And The People* 1948 172pp hb

Marion Gibbs *Feudal Order* 1948 149pp hb

Sam Lilley *Men, Machines and History* 1948 240pp hb

Collets

The publishing activities of Collets (they specialised in travel, reference, art and technical books) were extensive and are beyond the scope of this work. They produced very little on British politics. One exception was Konni Zilliacus *Why I Was Expelled* (1949). Collets and the Workers' Bookshop co-published an edition of *No Pasaran*, the novel by Upton Sinclair (1937). Post-war Collets imported and distributed books from the USSR and other socialist countries; they split this business with Central Books, each dealing with different publishers or subjects (with occasional overlap and conflict).

Fore Publications Great James Street; Henrietta Street (from July 1941); 28-29 Southampton Street (from 1942 to Nov 1956)

Fore Publications purchased these last premises at Southampton Street, which included a first floor office, three rooms on the second floor and four on the third floor. Some of these were rented out and were an important source of income.

Fore Publications had a strained, semi-independent relationship with the CPGB. Despite its broad approach, high literary quality and partnerships with Communist and non-Communist literary figures it was only partially successful. Although *Our Time* (initially) and the Key Books series fared quite well, Fore Publications was ignored (or criticised) by both the CP and the literary establishment.

Salme A. Dutt *When England Arose: The Centenary of the People's Charter* 1939 64pp Key Books No.6.

Richard Goodman *Britain's Best Ally* 1939? 64pp Key Books No.5.

J.B.S. Haldane *Science and You* 1939 64pp Key Books No.1.

Egon Erwin Kisch *The Three Cows* 1939 62pp Key Books No.8.

Jack Lindsay *England My England* 1939 64pp Key Books No.2.

Steven MacGregor *Truth and Mr Chamberlain* 1939 64pp Key Books No.7.

John Sommerfield *Trouble in Porter Street* 1939 64pp Key Books No.3. Short story. Illustrated by Molly Moss, the author's wife.

Hymie Fagan *England For All* 1940 64pp Key Books No.12.

Edmond Paul *Warning to Europe: The Story of Poland* 1940 64pp Key Books No.10.

Desmond Ryan *Ireland, Whose Ireland?* 1940 62pp Key Books No.9.

Geoffrey Trease *North Sea Spy* 1940 64pp Key Books No.4.

Wilfred Willett *British Farming* 1940? 64pp Key Books No.11.

Patrick Sloan *A Country With a Plan: A Key To the Soviet Union* 1941 72pp Key Books No.13.

Anna Louise Strong *China's New Crisis* 1941 62pp Key Books No.14.

Geoffrey Trease *Undercover Army* 1942? 72pp Key Books No.15.

Ted Willis *Buster* 1943 52pp pb Play.

Jack Lindsay *Perspective for Poetry* 1944 32pp Key Essays No.1.

John Manifold, Hubert Nicholson, David Martin *Trident* 1944 32pp Three poems: 'A Hat in the Ring' (Manifold); 'Song of the Little Town' (Nicholson); 'The Burning River' (Martin).

David Martin (ed.) *Rhyme and Reason: A Collection of Poetry* 1944 32pp Collection of political poems, includes J. Lindsay, Miles Carpenter, Idris Davies, H. MacDiarmid, R. Swingler, William Soutar and Phyllis Shand Alfrey.

A.L. Lloyd (ed.) *Corn on the Cob: Popular Traditional Poetry of the USA* 1945 66pp pb

---- *Speedway Stars: Past, Present and Future* 1948 Apparently a series.

Roy Pascal *The German Revolution of 1848* 1948 32pp

Albert Soboul *The French Revolution of 1848* 1948 36pp

---- *The Young Hero: Thrilling Stories for Boys and Girls* nd (1940s) By the 'Children's Editorial Committee, Fore Publications'.

Jack Beeching *Aspects of Love: Poems* 1950 23pp Key Poet No.9.

John N. Cameron *Forgive Me, Sire & Other Poems* 1950 24pp Key Poet No.10.

Maurice Carpenter *Gentle Exercise and Other Poems* 1950 24pp Key Poet No.8.

Dorian Cooke *Fugue For Our Time and Other Poems* 1950 22pp Key Poet No.6.

J.M. Denwood *Twinter's Wedding: A Poem* 1950 45pp Key Poet No.4.

Stanley Evans *East of Stettin-Trieste* 1950 84pp pb Illustrated by Paul Hogarth. Key Book No.4 (New Series).

Zdenek Hrdlicka; J. Needham; H. Empson *Contemporary Chinese Woodcuts* 1950 pb Unpaginated.

Jack Lindsay *Three Letters to Nikolai Tikhonov* 1950 24pp Key Poet No.7.

Jack Lindsay *A World Ahead: Journal of a Soviet Journey* 1950 164pp pb

Vitezslav Nezval *Song of Peace* c1950 16pp Translated from the Czech by Jack Lindsay & Stephen Jolly (who also wrote the brief foreword).

K. Pruszynski *Adam Mickiewicz: The Life Story of The Greatest Polish Poet* 1950 76pp hb Foreword by Jack Lindsay.

Jozsef Revai *Lukacs and Socialist Realism* 1950 37pp Intro. by E. Hobsbawm.

Edith Sitwell *Poor Men's Music: Poems* 1950 24pp Key Poet No.1.

Stanley Snaith *The Common Festival: Poems* 1950 24pp Key Poet No.5.

Neil Stewart *Background to the New Hungary* 1950 29pp pb

Randall Swingler *The God in the Cave: Poems* 1950 23pp Key Poet No.3.

Pierre Courtade *Albanian Travel Notebook & Documentary, with a Short Novel by the Albanian Writer Alecs Caci* 1951 68pp pb Key Books No.3 (New Series).

Julius Fucik *Report From the Gallows* 1951 97pp Key Books No.2 (New Series).

Rena Moisenko *Realist Music: 25 Soviet Composers* 1951 32pp

Zaharia Stancu *Barefoot* 1951 272pp pb Intro. by J. Lindsay. A novel.

A.H. Evans *I Face the Sun: A Book of Verse* 1952 110pp pb

Mihail Sadoveanu *Mitrea Cocor* 1953 178pp pb

Harold Watkins *The Dove and the Sickle* 1953? 125pp pb Author was Vice-President of British Peace Council & member of the World Peace Council.

Leonard Cassini *Music in Rumania* 1954 72pp pb Drawings by James Boswell.

Together, Fore and Illustrated Periodicals, London SE1 co-published the following book. (Illustrated Periodicals was a CP printing company):

Philip Fortyman *Men of Brit* nd (1945?) Cover by 'Kes'.

Fore Publications also published several journals.

Our Time (February 1941 to August 1949 but only owned by Fore between 1943 and 1947 – prior to those dates it was owned by Newport Publications, and afterwards by Our Times Publications) was edited by Vernon Beste then by Arnold Rattenbury et al. Klingender, Swingler, Sear and Slater were involved in editorial work. The impressive list of contributors included: Cunard, Aragon, Lindsay, Sommerfield, Priestley, Jennings, Willis, Phelan, Townsend Warner, Jameson, Fuller, E.P. Thompson etc. *Our Time* had covers and cartoons by many important left-wing artists – Paul Hogarth was art editor.

Theatre Today launched in 1946 and was sold on in the following year.

Fore Publications – or rather Randall Swingler personally – bought the magazine *Seven* in 1941.

Arena, in paperback format, 1949-51; edited by J. Davenport, Jack Lindsay & R. Swingler for the first four issues, then for final four issues by Lindsay with an Editorial Board of A. Kettle, M. Slater, R. Swingler and A. West. These last four issues had more direct CP input and reflected the cultural atmosphere of the Cold War. There were three special issues based on the CP's National Cultural Committee conferences:

Britain's Cultural Heritage 1952 64pp pb.

Essays on Socialist Realism and the British Cultural Tradition 1953 86pp pb.

The Transition from Feudalism to Capitalism 1954 75pp pb.

See Andy Croft 'The Boys Round the Corner: The Story of Fore Publications' in *A Weapon in the Struggle*.

Junior Press Ltd 2-4 Parton Street, WC1

Charles S. Segal (ed.) *The Junior Annual* 1945 104pp hb
   A large format children's illustrated annual, with a socialist orientation. Mix of fiction and non-fiction, with features such as *Soviet Song Scene, Unconquerable Russia, Sabotage in the Mine* and one on anti-fascism. This is similar to *Martin's Annual*, published in the 1930s by Martin Lawrence – a tradition of socialist writing for children that was never strong in Britain.

Charles S. Segal (ed.) *World Wonder Book* 1946 144pp hb
   The second, and apparently last, of his children's annuals. Less overtly pro-Soviet and socialist but still progressive. Contributors include: H.G. Wells; Amabel Williams-Ellis; W. Glynne-Jones; Vera Leff; J.B.S. Haldane; Geoffrey Trease; Hubert Phillips; H.G. Sear; Harold Goldman and J. London. The printer was David S. Smith who had links with the CP.

---- *Hero of the Air and Other Thrilling Tales for Boys and Girls* 1945 18pp

---- *Masters of the Sky: Thrilling Tales for Boys and Girls* 1945 18pp

Mary Frances Flack et al *Bruce of Scotland and Other Thrilling Stories* 1946 27pp

---- *Smuggler's Road and Other Stories* 1946? 24pp

---- *The Speed Demon and Other Thrilling Stories* 1946? 38pp

Left Review 2 Parton Street

Editors included T. Wintringham, R. Swingler and E. Rickword.
Printers included Workers' Bookshop, Fore Publications and Progress Publishing.

Alpha Group *It's Up To Us!* 1936 30pp Square format; outstanding design and art work.

C. Day Lewis *We're NOT Going to Do Nothing* 1936 31pp

S. & B. Webb *Soviet Communism: Dictatorship or Democracy?* 1936 32pp

S. & B. Webb *Is Soviet Communism a New Civilisation?* 1936 30pp

G. Dimitrov *The People's Front Against Fascism and War* 1937 16pp Nominally published by Tom Wintringham.

---- *Authors Take Sides on the Spanish War* 1937 30pp

Jack Lindsay *Who Are the English?* 1936? 7pp Poem.

London May 1st Committee (Wholesale Supplies from Workers' Bookshop Ltd)

John A. Mahon *The Meaning of May 1st* 1937? 15pp

People's Books 28/29 Southampton Street

People's Books Co-operative Society was a book club set up by Hyman Levy in 1953 from one of the rooms in the suite of offices owned by Fore Publications; it published two titles in 1954, before folding in 1955.

Cheddi Jagan *Forbidden Freedom: The Story of British Guiana* 96pp hb Published by arrangement with L&W.

Ralph & Nancy Lapwood *Through the Chinese Revolution* 216pp hb

Progress Publicity Co. Ltd 2-4 Parton Street

Vera Leff *Going Our Way? A Short Novel* 1946? 48pp Communist short story.

Progress Publishing Company Ltd 2-4 Parton Street and 1 Doughty Street, WC1

---- *People's Theatre: The Story of Unity Theatre* 1945? 11pp Published for Unity Theatre.

Peggy McIlvern *Two Loves: A Short Novel* 1945 79pp

William Peters *In Germany Now: The Diary of a Soldier* 1946 115pp pb

Charles Poulsen *Episode: A Tale of the Peasants' Revolt of 1381* 1946 279pp hb
Dustwrapper by A. Games.

Gwyn Thomas *Where Did I Put My Pity? Folk Tales from the Modern Welsh* 1946 193pp Card with dw.

William Sansom *Choice (Collection of Short Stories & Fine Writing)* 1946 191pp hb Contributors include: Elizabeth Bowen; William Plomer; Anna Kavan; P.H. Newby and Frank O'Connor. Illustrated by Leonard Rosoman.

Norman Dodds; Stanley Tiffany; Leslie Solley *Tragedy in Greece* 1946? 63pp By three Labour MPs who visited Greece. Published in conjunction with the League for Democracy in Greece.

Hubert Nicholson *No Cloud of Glory* 1946 224pp hb A novel.

Sid Chaplin et al *Saturday Saga: A Collection of Contemporary Short Stories* 1946 119pp hb

Senior Press 37 Grays Inn Road, WC1 (From 1957 this was the building used by Central Books.)

There appear to be only two titles published.

Jack Woddis *Under the Red Duster: A Study of Britain's Merchant Navy* 1947 160pp hb

---- *It Can Happen Again* 1947? 36pp Large format pamphlet on fascism.

Workers' Publications Ltd 254 Grays Inn Road.

Printers: London Caledonian Press or Dorrit Press.
Linked to *The Sunday Worker*.

A.J. Cook *Coal: The Next Round* 1926 17pp

A.J. Cook *Is It Peace?* 1926 12pp

'Socrates' *An Oration Over the Dead Body of a Miner* 1926 16pp

George Lansbury (Foreword) *Anti-Soviet Forgeries* 1927 141pp pb

A.J. Cook *Mond's Manacles* 1928 16pp

A.J. Cook *Mond Moonshine* 1928 12pp

A.J. Cook & J. Maxton *Our Case for a Socialist Revival* 1928 24pp

Discography

William Gallacher *An Appeal for Unity (Souvenir Record)* Celebrates his election in 1935.
The United Front Song (Hans Eisler) Daily Worker Choir
Issued by The Workers' Bookshop, 38 Clerkenwell Green. EB193-1 (EB1216); EB194-1 (EB1217)

London Labour Choral Union conducted by Alan Bush
Song of the Hunger Marchers (words Randall Swingler; music Alan Bush).
Patrol & Speech
Issued by The Workers' Bookshop 1936 L2150; L2151

London Labour Choral Union conducted by Alan Bush
May Day Song
The Red Flag
Issued by The Workers' Bookshop, 38 Clerkenwell Green. c1936

Harry Pollitt *Extract of Speech* Mass Rally, Empress Stadium, London 6 Nov 1938
Unity Male Voice Choir conducted by John Goss. *Red Cavalry Song* (D. & D. Pokrass) Same Rally.
Russia Today Society Ltd. GC24; GC23

Factory Papers – Not Traced

Some of these will be single sheet leaflets, rather than periodicals; some not produced for sale, but given away; some will be by the UMS or NMM. But even if only issued once, many will be proper factory papers. A few will be local street papers.

Abertillery Searchlight	**Wales**	Miners
Anti-Jelco	**NW**	Manchester YCL?
Bedwas Rebel	**Wales**	Miners
Bell	**London**	1933 (*PF*)
Bellerton Lamp	**?**	Miners 28 May 1932 (*PO* July/Aug 1936; Frow)
Blaenclydach Bomb	**Wales**	Miners
Blantyre Ferme	**Scotland**	Lanarkshire Pit Group No.1 (Sept?) 1925
Bobbin	**Scotland**	Dundee, jute workers (*WL* 26.7.29)
Bowhill Searchlight	**Scotland**	West Fife Miners (*PO* July/Aug 1932)
Bullcroft Searchlight	**Yorks**	Pit nr. Doncaster (*WW* 6.3.26; *WL* 25.2.27; *WL* 30.12.27)
Buzzer	**Northern**	Harraton Communist Pit Group, Durham (*WL* 25.3.27)
Cadby Ripper	**Yorks**	Miners Sheffield (No.1 June 1930) (Frow)
Colwick Call	**East Midlands**	Colwick Rail Depot (No.1 Jan 1931) (Frow)
Cortonwood Critic	**Yorks**	Cortonwood Militant Miners' Pit Group (June 1931). (Frow – where it is described as Cottonwood, surely a mistranscription from the archives in Moscow).
Courage	**London**	Idris Communist Group (No.1, 8.4.25) (Frow; JK)
Cowlair's Worker	**Scotland**	Cowlair's Railwaymen's Factory Cell, Glasgow (Dec 1930) (Frow)
Crawpicker	**Scotland**	Glencraig, Fife (*WL* 27.5.27)
Crystal, The	**NW**	Ward and Goldstone's, Salford. (*The CP in Manchester, 1920-26*)
Cwmparc Chipper	**Wales**	Miners
Cymmer Bomb	**Wales**	Miners
Dawn	**Scotland**	Parkhead Group CP (Frow; JK)
Dowble Unit or *DOUBLE*	**Scotland**	Kelby Pit Group (April 1928) (Frow)
Dry Hatch	**National**	Seamen, monthly (J. Mahon 1926)
Dumb Mill Loudspeaker	**Yorks**	Shipley (*WW* 26.2.26)

Farsley Mill Worker	**Yorks**	Farsley (*WL* 25.11.27)
Ferranti Spark	**NW**	Ferranti Works, Hollinwood, nr. Manchester (Frow)
Flame	**Scotland**	East Fife Issued by Michael Militant Miners 1932 (*PO* July-Aug 1932; *Militant Miners*; Frow)
Flash	**Wales**	
Force	**YCL**	
Forge	**NW**	Communist Group, Pearson & Knowles Ltd (1925) (Frow; JK)
Fryston Star	**Yorks**	Communist Pit Group Paper, Castleford (*WL* 25.3.27; *WW* 4.3.27 & Wilde)
Gas Appliance	**NW**	Manchester (*The CP in Manchester, 1920-26*)
Gillespie Torch	**London**	1933 Gillespie Road Group of the CP (*PF*)
Glasshoughton Dog & Chain	**Yorks**	Castleford (Wilde)
Glebe Torch	**London**	1933 (*PF*)
Gorton Tank	**NW**	Manchester (*The CP in Manchester, 1920-26*)
Gun	**Northern**	Communist Group at Armstrong Whitworths, Newcastle (Frow; *WL* 27.5.27; *WW* 2.7.26)
Hammer	**Scotland**	West Fife c1930? (*Militant Miners*)
Harrington Buzzer	**Northern**	Communist Pit Group, Durham (*WL* 25.3.27)
Headlamp	**Scotland**	Militant Group of Priory Miners, Blantyre, Lanarkshire (Frow)
Heatherington's Searchlight	**NW**	6/7 issues in edition of c300 produced by David Ainley (*The CP in Manchester, 1920-26*)
Huddersfield Millworker	**Yorks**	(*WL* 25.11.27)
Keighley Millworker	**Yorks**	(*WL* 25.11.27)
Lamp	**Scotland**	Cowdenbeath Local (*WL* 30.12.27)
Lamp	**Scotland**	East Fife Miners c1930? (*Militant Miners*; Frow)
Lewis Merthyr Bulletin	**Wales**	1925? Miners
Listers Rebel	**Yorks**	Listers' Communist Group, Bradford (*WL* 30.12.27)
Live Wire	**NW**	Metro-Vick, Manchester Engineering (*WL* 9.12.27)
Llanbradach Liberator	**Wales**	Miners

LMS Rebel	**Midlands**	Derby (Frow; *DW* 8.6.32; *WG* 1657)
Lochee Mill Worker	**Scotland**	Cox Brothers' jute works, Dundee (*WL* 17.6.27; *WW* 4.3.27)
Lump	**Scotland**	Cowdenbeath, Fife (*WL* 27.5.27)
Malvern Rebel Shuttle	**?**	(No.1, July 1931) (Frow)
Manningham Red Comet	**Yorks**	Communist Mill Group, Bradford (*WL* 25.11.27 & 30.12.27)
Mash	**Scotland**	West Fife Miners c1930? (*Militant Miners*)
Midland Red Star	**Yorks**	Midland Busmen, Bradford (*WL* 25.11.27)
Mell	**Northern**	Tyneside (*WL* 2.7.29)
Mersey Docker	**NW**	(Frow)
Mitchell's Main Weigh	**Yorks**	Wombwell Communist Group (Frow)
Money Wage Slave	**?**	(Frow)
Mount Street Rebel	**Yorks**	Bradford (*WL* 25.11.27)
Naval Pilot	**Wales**	Penygraig
Newton Slave Pen	**Scotland**	Glasgow (Frow)
North London Worker	**London**	1933 (*PF*)
North Star	**West**	Swindon CP Railwaymen (Frow; *WG* 2454)
Patricroft Firebox	**NW**	Rail/Engineering (*Edmund Frow* by R. Frow)
Pegswood Searchlight	**Northern**	Pegswood Communist Pit Group, Northumberland (*WL* 8.4.27)
Pet	**Yorks**	Allerton Communist Pit Group, Castleford (*WL* 25.3.27; Frow)
Platt Worker	**NW**	Platt Communist Group, Oldham (Frow)
Projectile	**London**	Communist Cell (Frow)
Rag Fair Star	**London**	1933 (*PF*)
Railway Rebel	**Midlands**	Birmingham (*WL* 30.12.27)
Railwaymen's Special	**NW**	Liverpool (*WL* 26.7.29)
Rawlings Truth	**SW ?**	(Frow; JK)
Rebel	**Wales**	Miners
Red Star	**Midlands**	Birmingham (*WL* 5.8.27)
Rebel Miner	**Scotland**	Rosehill Pit, Lanarkshire (No.9, 20.11.25) (Frow)
Risehow Rebel	**North West**	CP Pit Group, Risehow, Cumberland (*WL* 8.7.27)
Rolls Royce Rebel	**?**	(Frow)
Searchlight	**Scotland**	Imperial Tube Works Communist Group 1929? (JK)

INTRODUCTION

Searchlight	**Scotland**	Bowhill Militant Miners' Group (8.4.32) (Frow)
Siddick Cetawayo	**Cumberland**	(*WL* 8.7.27, which explains the unusual name)
Shipley Millworker	**Yorks**	Shipley (Frow; *WL* 25.11.27)
Shot Box	**Northern**	Blackhall, Durham Miners (*WL* 30.12.27)
Shotton Purger	**Northern**	Durham (*WL* 1.4.27; Frow)
Shovel	**Scotland**	Fauldhouse Militant Miners' Group (Dec 1930) West Lothian (Frow – where wrongly called Fauldhousey)
Six Bells	**Wales**	Miners
Spark	**NW**	Crookbottom Textile Workers 1932 (*DW*)
Spark	**Durham**	Ryhope Miners' Group Aug 1929 (Frow)
Spondon Star	**East Midlands**	Derby. Aug 1929 (Frow)
Spring To For Better Conditions	**NW**	Spring & Axle Workers, W.E. Carey's Works, Red Bank, Manchester No.2, 26.2.32 (Frow; *WG*)
Stannersgate Star	**Scotland**	Dundee shipyard workers (*WL* 26.7.29) Was this a continuation of *Brass Check* ? And must be a misspelling of Stannergate.
Sugar Factory Workers' Guide	**London**	North Woolwich (Frow; JK) Possibly not CP
Sunbeam Spark	**Midlands**	Sunbeam Communist Group, Wolverhampton (Frow)
Sunbeam Speed	**Midlands**	Ditto (*WL* 22.7.27)
Taff Merthyr Star	**Wales**	
Transport Worker	**NW**	Liverpool Communist Docks Group (No.6 in *WL* 30.12.27)
Underworld	**Scotland**	Kirkcaldy Pit Group 1925 (*Militant Miners*)
Upton Wedge	**Yorks**	Upton Miners' Militant Group (No.2 Feb 1932) (Frow)
Wedge	**Northern**	Easington, Durham March 1927 (*WL* 1.4.27; Frow)
Wolsely Special	**London**	1933 (*PF*)
Wormholt Floodlight	**London**	1933 (*PF*)
Young Rebel	**London?**	YCL? (1925) Young Workers at the General Gas Appliances Co. (Frow; JK)
Young Woodworker	**YCL**	

Source:

DW Daily Worker

Frow R. & E. Frow *Pit & Factory Papers Issued by the CP, 1927-34* s.p. 1996

JK J. Klugmann *History of the CPGB, Vol.2* (p341)

MacColl E. MacColl *Journeyman*; Sidgwick & Jackson 1990

J. Mahon 1926 John Mahon *Report to Factory Group Dept.* 1926

Militant Miners I MacDougall (ed.) *Militant Miners*; Polygon 1981

PF *Party Fighter* LDCP, October 1933 – Article by C.B. *Why Do We Publish Street Papers?*

PO *Party Organiser*

WG *Warwick Guide to British Labour Periodicals*

Wilde Arthur Wilde *The Biggest Battle is Yet to Come*; B. Lewis & D. Prudhoe 1980

WL *Workers' Life*

WW *Workers' Weekly*

Some Foreign Language Material

FRENCH:

Journès, Claude *L'Extrême Gauche en Grande-Bretagne* Librairie Générale de Droit & de Jurisprudence, 1977 229pp.

Courtois, Stéphane *L'Internationalisme Prolétarien à l'Epreuve: le PCGB Face au Pacte Germano-Soviètique* in *'Prolétaires de Tous les Pays, Unissez-Vous?'* Publications de L'Université de Bourgogne, 1993.

Johnstone, Monty *Le Parti Communiste Britannique vu de Moscou ou de Londres au Temps du Komintern* in *Une Histoire en Révolution? Du Bon Usage des Archives de Moscou et d'ailleurs* ed. S. Wolikow; Editions Universitaires de Dijon 6pp.

Salles, René *Le PCGB et les Elections* in *Revue Française de Science Politique* No.3, 1977.

Salles, René *Structures, Implantation et Influence du Parti Communiste en Grande Bretagne* 2 vols. Also published by Klincksieck 1981 (?).

Various *Communisme* 87, 2006; L'Âge de L'Homme, Lausanne. Special edition of this journal dedicated to CPGB. Articles by A. Croft, N. Fishman, K. Morgan etc.

RUSSIAN:

Matkovsky, N. *William Gallacher* Moscow 1990 158pp.

Undasinov, I.N. *The Communists and the Labour Party, 1919-1923* Moscow 1979 270pp.

GERMAN:

Hill, Roland *Grossbritanniens Gesellschaft der Freunde* in 'Kommunistische Parteien im Westen' Fischer Bucherei 1968 211pp.

Shaw, Elizabeth *Irish Berlin* Aufbau Verlag, Berlin 1990.

Callaghan, John *Die Marxistische Linke Grossbritanneiens: Ruckzug und Verfall* in P. Moreau et al (eds) 'Der Kommunismus in Westeuropa' Landsberg am Lech 1998.

HUNGARIAN:

Havas, Peter *Nagy-Britannia Kommunista Partjanak Helyzete Es Politikaja A Masodik*

Vilaghaboru Utan (1945-57) Budapest 1981 352pp.

Abbreviations

A&U	Allen & Unwin
AAM	Anti-Apartheid Movement
AEU/AUEW	Amalgamated Engineering Union / Amalgamated Union of Engineering Workers
AIA	Artists' International Association
ARP	Air Raid Precautions
Autob.	Autobiography
BICO	British & Irish Communist Organisation
BJOIR	*British Journal of Industrial Relations*
BL	British Library
BRS	*British Road to Socialism*
BSISLP	British Section, International Socialist Labour Party
BSP	British Socialist Party
BWSF	British Workers' Sports Federation
CAWU	Clerical and Administrative Workers' Union (later APEX)
CC	Central Committee
CCG	Communist Campaign Group
CEC	Central Executive Committee
CHNN	*Communist History Network Newsletter*
CI	Communist International (organisation and journal)
CND	Campaign for Nuclear Disarmament
COBI	Communist Organisation in the British Isles
contrib.	contributor/s; contributions

CPB	Communist Party of Britain
CPI	Communist Party of India **OR** Communist Party of Ireland
CPI(M)	Communist Party of India (Marxist)
CPS	Communist Party of Scotland
CPSU	Communist Party of the Soviet Union
CR	*Communist Review*
cttee	committee
CUL	Communist University of London
CUP	Cambridge University Press
d	duplicated
DC/DPC	District Committee / District Party Committee
Dept.	Department
DL	Democratic Left
DLB	*Dictionary of Labour Biography*
DMA	Durham Miners' Association
doc.	document
dw	dustwrapper
DW	*Daily Worker*
EC	Executive Committee
ECCI	Executive Committee of the Communist International
ed.	editor/edited/edition
EEPTU	Engineering, Electrical and Plumbers' Trade Union
EIS	Educational Institute of Scotland
esp.	especially
ETU	Electrical Trades Union
FBU	Fire Brigades Union
FSU	Friends of the Soviet Union
Gen Sec	General Secretary
GLC	Greater London Council
gov.	government
hb	hardback
HSIR	*Historical Studies in Industrial Relations*
HWJ	*History Workshop Journal*
IB	International Brigade
IBA	International Brigade Association
ICWPA	International Class War Prisoners' Aid

ILEA	Inner London Education Authority
ill.	illustrated/illustrator
ILP	Independent Labour Party
ILWCH	*International Labor & Working Class History Journal*
IMG	International Marxist Group
Incl.	Includes
Intro.	Introduction
IPD	*Inner Party Democracy*
IRD	Information Research Department
IRIS	Industrial Research Information Service
irreg.	Irregular
IRSH	*International Review of Social History*
IS	International Socialists (org.)/*International Socialism* (journal)
ISJ	*International Socialism Journal*
IUS	International Union of Students
JOCH	*Journal of Contemporary History*
JOCS	*Journal of Communist Studies (JOCS & Transition Politics)*
KFAT	Knitwear, Furniture & Allied Trades Union
L&W	Lawrence and Wishart
LBC	Left Book Club
LCC	London County Council
LCDTU	Liaison Committee for the Defence of Trade Unions
LDCP	London District CP
lf	large format
LHASC	Labour History Archive and Study Centre (at the People's History Museum, Manchester – formerly the National Museum of Labour History)
LHR	*Labour History Review* (previously *SSLH Bulletin*)
lib.	library
lit.	literature
LP	Labour Party
LPC	Labour Publishing Company
LRD	Labour Research Department (organisation and journal)
LSE	London School of Economics
LT	London Transport
MFGB	Miners' Federation of Great Britain
MFNT	*Manifesto for New Times*
MM	Minority Movement (also NMM)

MML	Marx Memorial Library
MS	*Morning Star*
MSF	Manufacturing, Science & Finance Union
MT	*Marxism Today*
MUP	Manchester University Press
na	not applicable
NALGO	National Association of Local Government Officers
NC	National Committee (YCL)
NCCL	National Council for Civil Liberties
NCP	New Communist Party
nd	no date
NEC	National Executive Committee
NEGSLH	North East Group for the Study of Labour History
nfs	not for sale
NLB	New Left Books
NMM	National Minority Movement
NUDAW	National Union of Distributive & Allied Workers
NUM	National Union of Mineworkers
NUPE	National Union of Public Employees
NUS	National Union of Seamen **OR** National Union of Students
NUT	National Union of Teachers
NUWM	National Unemployed Workers' Movement
NW	North West
NWGSLH	North West Group for the Study of Labour History
NWLHS	North West Labour History Society
OIOC	Oriental and India Office Collection (of the British Library)
orgs	organisations
OUP	Oxford University Press
p.	pamphlet
p.a.	per annum
pb	paperback
PB	Political Bureau (or Politbureau)
PCF	Parti Communiste Français (French Communist Party)
POUM	Partido Obrero de Unificación Marxista (Spanish Trotskyist-leaning party)
PPFF	People's Press Fighting Fund (*Daily Worker*)
PPPS	People's Press Printing Society (*Daily Worker*)
pref.	preface
prob.	probably

publ.	publisher/published/publication
RA	Royal Academy
RCG	Revolutionary Communist Group
RCP	Revolutionary Communist Party
RCT	Revolutionary Communist Tendency
refs	references
RPC	Revolutionary Policy Committee (ILP)
rev.	revised
RILU	Red International of Labour Unions (both the organisation and publication)
RKP	Routledge and Kegan Paul
RSSF	Revolutionary Socialist Students' Federation
SCR	Society for Cultural Relations with the Soviet Union
SDF	Social Democratic Federation
SDP	Social Democratic Party
sec.	secretary
sf	small format
SHS	Socialist History Society
SLHR	*Scottish Labour History Review*
SLHS	*Scottish Labour History Society Journal* (Renamed *Scottish Labour History* from 1998)
SLL	Socialist Labour League
SLP	Socialist Labour Party
SOAS	School of Oriental and African Studies
s.p.	self published
SPGB	Socialist Party of Great Britain
SS	Shop Stewards
SSLH	*Society for the Study of Labour History Bulletin*
STUC	Scottish Trades Union Congress
SU	Soviet Union
SWP	Socialist Workers' Party
TASS	Technical & Supervisory Section (of AUEW)
TC	Trades Council
TGWU	Transport and General Workers' Union
tr.	translated
TU	Trade Union
TUC	Trades Union Congress (occasionally Trades Union Council – a local body)
UCATT	Union of Construction and Allied Trades Union

UCL	University College London
UCS	Upper Clyde Shipbuilders
UMS	United Mineworkers of Scotland
UP	University Press
USF	University Student Federation
WCML	Working Class Movement Library (Salford)
WFTU	World Federation of Trade Unions
WIR	Workers' International Relief
WMA	Workers' Music Association
WMR	*World Marxist Review*
WSF	Workers' Socialist Federation
YCI	Young Communist International
YCL	Young Communist League

1. National Publications

This chapter includes all pamphlets (but not journals) published by the CP nationally, in chronological order by year; within each year they are in alphabetical order. If there is uncertainty about the year, then '(?)' appears at the end of the entry for each record (in general, throughout the bibliography, the year does not necessarily refer to the first edition but to the edition consulted). In some cases, usually in the 1940s and early 1950s, several editions of a pamphlet were published in the same year or in following years; rarely were there significant changes.

Excluded are pamphlets and books published by the BSP, SLP etc. prior to the formation of the CP that have stickers stating 'Communist Party, Temporary Address, 21a Maiden Lane, Strand, London WC2'. This was stock transferred to the new party.

A word needs to be said about Congress material. I have tried to be as inclusive as possible, as these are important documents. I have listed as many draft documents, Branch/District amendments etc, as I have traced; there are some missing, especially in earlier years. It can be assumed that in post-war years there would always be a draft resolution or document (e.g. on *IPD*, the *BRS*, *New Times*), and there would be amendments from branches and Districts. Any collection of CP material will include a lot of extra Congress material produced in advance – agendas, standing orders, changes to rule, Branch Resolutions, District Resolutions or – during the course of each Congress – composite resolutions and reports from committees, plus confidential financial statements and personal details of candidates standing for the Executive Committee as well as disciplinary material. After the Congress, a *Guide to Reporting Back* was sometimes produced for delegates.

One of the most important documents (important for historians that is, rather than for delegates, who probably treated it as a formality) was the Executive Committee's report of work since the previous Congress, referred to here as *EC Report of Work*, even if occasionally it had a slightly different title. These contain a wealth of material on membership, finance, activity, publications etc.

A *Congress Report* was also always produced in one form or another, and these are also important records; if, usually in later years, a separate Report was not published, I have indicated where it can be found (e.g. in *Comment* in 1979 and in *Focus* in 1983 and 1985).

Another interesting publication produced for Congresses was the document containing pre-Congress discussion. In traditional democratic centralist practice, in the period leading up to a Congress, any member could express any view. After Congress had decided on a 'line', all members, in theory, had to publicly follow it whatever reservations they might have had. The wide range of opinions – and even animosity – expressed in this discussion may come as a surprise to some people. Contributions were generally of a high level and are useful for gauging contemporary trends in the CP. In the pre-war period this discussion was printed in *Workers' Weekly, Communist Review* and later the *Daily Worker*; then it appeared in the more internal journals (*World News and Views, Comment* etc), and in the later period special journals, of perhaps half a dozen issues, were published. The latter appear in the chapter of National Magazines.

A word of warning about the date of some Congress material. If a Congress was held at the end of a year, then the report may actually have been published at the very beginning of the following year, but to avoid confusion I have occasionally listed them in the year of the Congress itself. For instance, the Report for the 8th Congress of 1926 came out in 1927, but could be confused with the Report of the 9th held in 1927 which also was published in 1927.

Material published by any CP department or advisory committee will be indicated, e.g. the Education Department (known as the Agit-Prop Department till the early 1930s). Each Department of the CP would produce a mass of material for internal distribution; most of that done by the Education Department was for sale, but had practically no circulation outside the Party (at least until the 1970s). Most produced by other departments was strictly internal, and some of it could be substantial and important. For instance, the Dominions Committee of the International Department produced some interesting *Information Documents*. These can be found in the CP Archives.

From August 1942 to August 1944 there was a series of 14 pamphlets which consisted of what in effect were articles that would normally appear in an internal journal. They appeared in this format because the paper shortage meant there was not enough paper that could be allocated to a journal. They don't have a journal title (but the word 'Organise' or 'Organisation' appears in most of them). Hence they appear in this chapter, but to identify them, the world 'Journal' plus month of issue appears in the entry for each of them.

Occasionally, pamphlets will be published by a named individual though they are obviously official CP publications. This was generally to avoid legal action against the Party – it was not so bad for an individual to be charged with libel, incitement to disaffection or treason if the chosen individual had no money!

1920

1 **Fundamental Tasks of the C.I.** 16pp Also in 'Theses of the C.I. as Adopted at 2nd Congress'.

2 **Left Wing Communism** Lenin 95pp pb First ed.

3 **National and Colonial Questions** 16pp Also in 'Theses of the C.I. as Adopted at 2nd Congress'.

4 **Official Report: Communist Unity Convention, London July 31 & Aug. 1** 72pp pb

5 **Parliamentarism, Trade Unionism and the C.I.** 16pp Also in 'Theses of the C.I. as Adopted at 2nd Congress'.

6 **Role of the CP in the Proletarian Revolution** 12pp Also in 'Theses of the C.I. as Adopted at 2nd Congress'. This was reprinted by Workers' Bookshops in 1934 – with some passages deleted for legal reasons.

7 **Statutes and Conditions of Affiliation of the C.I.** 12pp Also in 'Theses of the C.I. as Adopted at 2nd Congress'.

8 **The Agrarian Question** 16pp Also in 'Theses of the C.I. as Adopted at 2nd Congress'.

9 **The Dictatorship of the Proletariat** Kamenoff, L. 16pp

10 **The Life and Work of F. Engels** Coates, Zelda 51pp pb

11 **The Proletarian Revolution and Kautsky the Renegade** Lenin 128pp pb

12 **The Soviet System at Work** Williams, Robert 27pp

13 **Theses of the C.I. as Adopted at 2nd Congress, Aug.** 88pp pb Contains 6 items.

1921

14 **Annual Party Conference, Oct. 7-8** 15pp

15 **Communism or ILPism? – Verbatim Report of Debate in Glasgow, Aug. 30, Between A MacManus & R.C. Wallhead** 12pp

16 **Constitution and Rules as Adopted by the Special Conference at Manchester, April 23 & 24** 8pp

17 **Decisions of the Third Congress of the C.I., July** 134pp pb

18 **Draft Constitution and Rules for Special Delegate Conference, Manchester, April** 24pp

19 **Lenin: His Life and Work** Zinovieff, G. 48pp

20 **'Re-establishing' the Second International** MacManus, Arthur & Inkpin, Albert 8pp

21 **Russia Today: A Survey of Facts and Figures** 16pp

22 **The Communist Party and the Labour Party: All the Facts and Correspondence** 16pp

23 **The Doom of a Coalfield** Newbold, J. Walton 16pp

24 **The Economic Organisation of Soviet Russia** Miliutin, V. 36pp pb

25 **The International Situation: A Study of Capitalism in Collapse** Trotsky, L. & Varga, E. 20pp

26 **The Irish Crisis** Paul, William 14pp Cover by 'Espoir'.

27 **The Land Grabbers** Tanner, Frank 15pp 10,000 sold according to Report of EC.

28 **The Secrets of Menshevik Georgia** Shaphir, J. 100pp pb

29 **Third Congress of the C.I.: Report of Meetings Held at Moscow, June-July** 166pp pb

30 **To Working Women! A Communist Message** Y.J. 12pp

31 **What Are a Few Churchills?** Malone, C.J.L. (MP) 16pp Speech from the dock, Jan. 17 – he was charged with sedition for a speech during the 'Hands Of Russia' Campaign.

32 **What is This Communist Party?** McLaine, William 16pp 20,000 sold according to EC Report.

33 **Why this Unemployment?** Bell, Tom 12pp 2nd impression has cartoon on cover by 'W'.

34 **Workers of all Countries Unite: Twelve Days in Germany** Zinoviev, G. 80pp

1922

35 **A Straight Talk to the Miners: A Communist Policy for the MFGB** 12pp

36 **Agenda and Resolutions for Policy Conference (March)** 8pp lf

37 **Agenda for Annual Party Conference, Oct.** 15pp

38 **Between Red and White** Trotsky, L. 104pp pb

39 **Communism and Society** Paul, William 198pp hb

40 Communist Cartoons: Cartoons from 'The Communist' 1921-22 52pp pb lf Cartoons by 'Espoir' et al. from the early CP mag. This was re-issued by the CP in 1982, with an intro. by E. Hobsbawm, under the imprint of J.K. Pictorials (an unsuccessful attempt to market some items from James Klugmann's huge collection).

41 Communist Industrial Policy: New Tasks for New Times 10pp

42 Communist Parliamentary Policy and Electoral Programme: Conference Copy 16pp

43 Fourth Congress of the C.I.: Abridged Report 296pp pb

44 Labour's New Charter 124pp

45 Report of EC to Policy Conference, March 16pp

46 Report of NEC to Annual Party Conference, Oct. 12pp

47 Report on Organisation Presented by the Party Commission to the Annual Conference, Oct. 80pp pb

48 Resolutions and Theses of 4th Congress of the C.I. 124pp pb

49 Statutes and Rules As Adopted by Battersea Conference, Oct. 12pp sf

50 The ABC of Communism Bukharin, N. & Preobrazhensky, E. 428pp hb Tr. by E.&C. Paul.

51 The British Empire Jackson, T.A. 36pp

52 The Communist Parliamentary Policy and Electoral Programme 15pp

53 The CP, the Labour Party and the United Front 12pp

1923

54 A Short Course of Economic Science Bogdanoff, A. 391pp pb Further eds followed in 1925 and 1927.

55 Against the War-Mongers Newbold, J. Walton 8pp Print run 5,000.

56 Formation of Work and Factory Groups 8pp sf 'For the use of Party Locals & members NOT for general distribution'. ?

57 General Election: CP Manifesto 4pp

58 Handbook for Party Members No.1: Organisation 20pp Print run 5,000.

59 How a Trade Union Nucleus Works 12pp sf

60 How an Area Group Works 8pp sf

61 Japan in the Far East 68pp

62 Nikolai Lenin: A Brief Biographical Sketch of a Great Leader Bell, Tom 16pp

63 Snowden's Socialism Riddled Newbold, J. Walton (MP) 10pp Photo on cover.

64 The International Outlook: Speech at ECCI, June Radek, Karl 26pp

65 Towards a Communist Programme: C.I. Documents from the 4th Congress 40pp

66 Unemployment and How to Deal With It Newbold, J. Walton (MP) 8pp

67 Wake Up Mrs Worker: Are You Satisfied? Rothwell, Peggy 8pp Cartoon by 'Michael'.

68 What is the United Front? 20pp Print run of 5,000.

1924

69 5th Congress of C.I.: Abridged Report of Meetings Held at Moscow June, July 1924 294pp pb

70 Anti-Labour Legislations Colyer, W. T. 22pp Cover photo of author.

71 Can Labour Govern? Gallacher, W. 16pp

72 Fight the Slave Plan: Dawes Report Arnot, R. Page 15pp The Dawes Plan concerned German reparations.

73 From the 4th to the 5th World Congress: Report of ECCI 122pp pb

74 How to Organise the CP: Documents from 5th Congress C.I. 130pp pb

75 Is It a Labour Government? 31pp

76 Lenin and Britain Lepeshinsky, A. (ed.) 86pp pb

77 Lenin's Lash for 'Pacifist' Hypocrites 4pp ?

78 Manual of Party Training: Principles of Organisation 54pp pb Probably prepared by Tom Bell; the CP's first training manual, published after pressure from the C.I.

79 My Case Campbell, J.R. 15pp The famous sedition case that some still maintain brought down the Labour Government.

80 Neutrality and War at the Co-operators' Congress, Ghent 24pp lf

81 Party Training Syllabus: 'Historical Synopsis' Pack of 5 large fold out sheets.

82 Programme of the C.I. Adopted at 5th Congress 80pp pb

83 **Report of CEC to 6th National Party Congress** 32pp

84 **Report of Control Commission to Congress, May** 8pp Marked 'Confidential – For Party Members Only'.

85 **Speeches and Documents of the 6th Congress** 80pp pb

86 **The CP and the Labour Government** 8pp

87 **The Decline of Capitalism** Varga, E. 70pp pb Different from book of same title publ. 1928.

88 **The Labour Movement at the Crossroads: Open Letter to the LP Conference** 8pp

89 **The Path to Power** Paul, William 22pp Cover photo. New ed. in 1925 of 32pp.

90 **The Record of the Labour Government** 32pp

91 **The Workers Against War: Appeal from 5th Congress C.I.** 28pp

92 **Towards T.U. Unity! Speech to 5th Congress C.I.** Zinoviev, G. 22pp

93 **What is the Use of Parliament?** Campbell, J.R. 24pp

94 **Work Among Women** 78pp pb On USSR.

1925

95 **Annual Party Congress 1925: Theses on International Trade Union Unity** 7pp

96 **Bolshevising the C.I.: Report of ECCI, March/April** 205pp pb

97 **Communism and Nationalism** 10pp On the 'Bolshevik Conspiracy Case' in India.

98 **Communist Work in the Factories** 18pp Possibly by A. Rothstein.

99 **Empire 'Socialism'** Dutt, R.P. 20pp Ill. cover.

100 **History of the Zinoviev Letter** 48pp pb Commentary by A. McManus (sic).

101 **International Trade Union Unity** 12pp

102 **Labour Pocket Diary 1925 'Special Communist Edition'**

103 **Lenin As a Marxist** Bukharin, N. 64pp pb

104 **Lenin on Co-operatives** 24pp

105 **Murder! An Indictment of British Imperialism in China** 20pp

106 **Organising Report of the CEC to 7th Congress** 24pp

107 **Political Report of CEC to 7th Congress** 12pp

108 **Report of Seventh National Congress** 208pp pb

109 **Report of the Control Commission to the Party Congress** 8pp

110 **Resolution on Trotskyism (7th Congress)** 2pp

111 **Russia's Path to Communism** Zinoviev, G. 70pp pb

112 **State and Revolution** Lenin 158pp pb 2nd ed.

113 **The Class Struggle in Parliament: Speeches** Saklatvala, S. 12pp

114 **The Communist Bookshop Catalogue** 32pp

115 **The CP in Parliament: Second Series of Speeches** Saklatvala, S. 4pp lf Print run: 15,000. Interesting adverts.

116 **The CP on Trial: Harry Pollitt's Defence and Judge Swift's Summing Up** Pollitt, H. 32pp 12 leading Communists (incl. 8 out of 10 PB members) were arrested & charged with sedition in the build up to the General Strike.

117 **The CP on Trial: J.R. Campbell's Defence** Campbell, J.R. 32pp

118 **The CP on Trial: W. Gallacher's Defence** Gallacher, W. 24pp

119 **The Errors of Trotskyism: A Symposium** 392pp pb Contrib. include Trotsky, Zinoviev, Bukharin, Stalin, Kamenev – it was a real debate.

120 **The Reds and the Labour Party: Towards a Left Wing Policy** 30pp

121 **The Role and Tasks of the YCL** 12pp sf 'For the use of Party locals & members – NOT for general distribution'.

122 **The Theory and Practice of Leninism** Stalin, J. 130pp pb

123 **Thesis on the Colonial Question and the British Empire (7th Congress)** 4pp

124 **Wage-Labour and Capital** Marx, K. 32pp Cover by 'Savage'.

125 **What is the British Empire to You?** Jackson, T.A. 12pp

126 **What the YCL Stands For** Rust, W. 24pp

127 **Who Are the War-Makers?** 10pp

128 **Women in the Class Struggle** 8pp Cover drawing by 'Michael'.

1926

129 An Elementary Course of CP Training 24pp Preface by 'T.B.' – almost certainly Tom Bell.

130 And Now For Power! Bell, Tom 8pp Optimistic opening speech at 8th Congress.

131 Bolshevism: Some Questions Answered Stalin, J. 67pp pb

132 Brief Summary of District Organisation Reports 8pp Possibly submitted to 8th Congress. ?

133 Building Up Socialism Bukharin, N. 66pp pb

134 Communism is Common Sense 24pp Published in July. There was a 2nd ed. in 1927.

135 Draft Statutes and Rules to Be Submitted to Battersea Congress (8th) 16pp sf

136 Factory Groups: Organisation and Function 10pp ?

137 Fraction Work: for 8th Congress 8pp

138 Imperialism: The Last Stage of Capitalism Lenin, V.I. 160pp pb 1st UK ed.

139 On the Road to Insurrection Lenin, V.I. 132pp pb Pictorial cover.

140 Orders From Moscow? Brown, E.H. [Ernest] & Ferguson, A. 61pp

141 Organising Report of CC for 8th Congress 16pp

142 Party Structure: for 8th Congress 6pp

143 Political Report of CC to 8th Congress 20pp

144 Songs of the Revolution 8pp One of the rare fiction or poetry items the CP published – usually this task was left to the publishing house. This pamphlet went into a 2nd ed.

145 Statutes and Rules Adopted by 8th Congress 16pp sf

146 Ten Days That Shook the World Reed, John 344pp hb 1st UK ed. in book form – originally published in instalments in 'The Communist'.

147 The 8th Congress: Reports, Theses and Resolutions 82pp pb

148 The Aftermath of Non-Co-operation: Indian Nationalist and Labour Politics Roy, M.N. 136pp pb

149 The General Council and the General Strike Bennet, A.J. 21pp

150 The Industrial Crisis and the Co-operators Harrison, J. 16pp Cover by 'Savage'.

151 The International Situation: Report to 8th Congress 20pp

152 The Meaning of the General Strike Dutt, R.P. 36pp Reprinted from 'Communist International', June.

153 The Political Meaning of the Great Strike Murphy, J.T. 138pp pb

154 The Reds and the General Strike C.B. 32pp Probably by 'Bennet', alias 'Petrovsky', alias 'Lipec' born as Goldfarb (probably!); he was the C.I.'s man in Britain and headed the Anglo-American Secretariat in Moscow, 1928-9, where he was usually known as Petrovsky. Some info. on him in Kahan's article in 'IRSH' 1976 Part 2.

155 The Reds and the Labour Party [new ed.] 31pp

156 The Soldier's Conscience Dunstan, Robert 10pp Cover cartoon by 'Espoir'.

157 Thesis on the General Strike (8th Congress) 12pp

158 What Margate Means Pollitt, H. 14pp

159 Where Is Britain Going? Trotsky, L. 178pp pb

1927

160 A Defence of Communism: In Reply to H. Laski Fox, Ralph 96pp

161 A Short Course of Economic Science Bogdanoff, A. 475pp pb 2nd ed.

162 CC Political Report (9th Congress) 32pp

163 China: A Survey Fu, Seng Sin 104pp pb Cover by 'Espoir'.

164 CP Training 130pp pb Much expanded version of 1926 ed.

165 Handbook on Local Organisation 30pp

166 Is India Different? The Class Struggle in India Saklatvala, S. & Gandhi, M. 36pp Correspondence.

167 Lenin: Information Bulletin for the Use of Propagandists and Party Training Groups 12pp

168 Modern India Dutt, R.P. 174pp pb

169 Organising Report of CC: 9th Congress 24pp

170 Problems of the Chinese Revolution Bukharin, N. 50pp

171 Resolution of the Plenum of the ECCI on the Situation in GB (9th Congress) 12pp

172 **Resolution on the YCL (9th Congress)** 4pp

173 **Socialism and the Living Wage** Dutt, R.P. 240pp pb

174 **Stand by Workers' Russia! The Truth About the Break** 16pp

175 **Ten Years of Workers' Rule** 16pp Manifesto of Central EC of Congress of Soviets.

176 **The Bill to Smash Trade Unionism** 16pp

177 **The Future of Indian Politics** Roy, M.N. 118pp pb One of the rare CP publications officially published by an individual (R. Bishop) – probably for legal reasons.

178 **The Ninth Congress of the CPGB: Reports, Theses and Resolutions** 126pp pb

179 **The Red Star: Illustrated Souvenir of the Building Up Of Socialism** 16pp lf

180 **The Soldiers' Programme** 20pp

181 **The War on China** 24pp

182 **Thesis on the International and National Battle Front (9th Congress)** 20pp

183 **War: The C.I.'s Position** Bennet, A.J. 40pp

1928

184 **At the Parting of the Ways: Results of 9th Plenum of C.I.** Braun, P. 130pp pb Incl. chapter on CPGB.

185 **Brief Summary of District Organisation Reports: for Congress** 6pp

186 **Class War or Imperialist War? Information Bulletin for Propagandists and Party Training Groups** 16pp

187 **Communism and Coal** Horner, Arthur & Hutt, G.A. 316pp pb Lengthy analysis of the coal industry, in UK and worldwide, and the position of British miners and their organisation.

188 **Communism and Industrial Peace** Campbell, J.R. 21pp

189 **Communism is Commonsense [new ed.]** 24pp

190 **Communist Policy in GB: Report of British Commission of 9th Plenum of C.I.** 195pp pb

191 **Imperialism [3rd ed.]** Lenin, V.I. 150pp pb 1,000 print run.

192 **Is Labour Lost?** Campbell, J.R. 20pp On the new LP Programme.

193 **Left Wing Communism** Lenin, V.I. 95pp pb Print run of 1,500. 2nd ed. A hb ed. was also produced.

194 **Leninism** Stalin, J. 472pp pb

195 **Mondism and MacDonaldism** Gallacher, W. 16pp

196 **Peterloo** 16pp

197 **Red and White Terror** Krylenko, N. 40pp pb

198 **Red Politics in the T.U.s** Campbell, J.R. 18pp

199 **Report of the 15th Congress of the CPSU** 416pp pb

200 **Sailors' and Marines' Programme** Massie, A. 21pp Cover drawing by 'Savage'. Massie is named as the publisher (presumably so the CP would avoid prosecution) not credited as author.

201 **Socialism and Labouralism** Saklatvala, S. 16pp Speech in Parliament.

202 **The Communist International: Between the 5th & 6th World Congresses 1924-28** 508pp pb

203 **The Decline of Capitalism** Varga, E. 127pp hb Different from book of same title publ. 1924.

204 **The March of the Women** 20pp Intro. by Beth Turner, CP National Women's Organiser. This pamphlet was reproduced in NWLHS Journal, No. 28, 2003.

205 **The Organisation of a World Party** Piatnitsky, O. 94pp pb

206 **The Red Army** 16pp

207 **The Workers' State: Lies About Soviet Russia** Stalin, J. 26pp

208 **The Young Communist International Between the 4th and 5th Congresses, 1924-28** 250pp pb

209 **Where is Trotsky Going? Facts and Figures on the Discussion in the CP of Russia** 128pp pb Lengthy replies to points from the Platform of the Opposition in USSR from Soviet source.

210 **With the CP in Parliament** Saklatvala, S. 14pp Speech in Parliament, Nov. 7.

211 **Women in Russia: Report of Delegation** 32pp Beth Turner, Rose Smith, Lily Webb, Fanny Deakin, Florence Maxwell.

1929

212 **A Revolutionary Workers' Government** Murphy, J.T. 16pp

213 **Class Against Class: General Election Programme** 32pp

214 **Communism and the Co-operatives** 15pp

215 **Economic Struggles and the Tasks of the Party: Draft Resolution** 6pp lf

216 **Facing Both Ways: The ILP and the Workers' Struggle** Wintringham, Tom 16pp

217 **Fight the War Danger! Manifesto of the CPGB** 8pp

218 **Four Years of Labour 'Opposition'** Groves, Reg 15pp

219 **How Britain Rules India** Arnot, R. Page 36pp

220 **Labour and the Empire** Dutt, Clemens 16pp

221 **Make Way for the Women** 14pp lf Contrib. incl. Lily Webb, Beth Turner, M. Pollitt.

222 **Only Communism Can Conquer Unemployment** Campbell, J.R. 24pp Reply to Lloyd George.

223 **Organising Report of the CC for 10th Congress** 4pp

224 **Our Platform of the Class Struggle** 46pp

225 **Party T.U. Policy: Draft** 16pp

226 **Political Report of CC to 10th Congress** 28pp

227 **Resolutions of the 11th Congress CPGB** 48pp pb

228 **Russia's Socialist Triumph** Rothstein, Andrew 26pp

229 **Tasks of the CPGB: The 10th Plenum and the International Situation** 10pp lf For Congress.

230 **The Coming War** Dutt, R.P. 24pp

231 **The Election and the Coming War** Dutt, R.P. 16pp

232 **The Fight Against the War Danger in Britain: Draft Resolution** 6pp lf

233 **The New Line: Documents of 10th Congress** 130pp pb

234 **The Present Situation and the Tasks of the Party: Draft Thesis** 32pp

235 **The Record of the Labour Government** Williams, Bert 16pp

236 **The Struggle Against War and the Tasks of the Communists** 58pp

237 **The World Situation and Economic Struggle: Theses of 10th Plenum ECCI** 51pp pb

238 **Young Workers and the General Election** Cohen, Jack 22pp

1930

239 **A 6 Lesson Outline for Local Party Training Groups** *Agit Prop Dept* 61pp ?

240 **Building the Party in the Factories** 34pp

241 **Four Lesson Courses for Workers No.1: Socialist Construction in the Soviet Union** *Agit-Prop Dept* 40pp sf

242 **Four Lesson Courses for Workers No.2: Industrialisation of the Country and the Five Year Plan** *Agit-Prop Dept* 40pp sf

243 **Four Lesson Courses for Workers No.3: Socialist Reorganisation of Agriculture** *Agit-Prop Dept* 40pp sf

244 **Four Lesson Courses for Workers No.4: The Soviet Union and the Capitalist World** *Agit-Prop Dept* 40pp sf

245 **Tariffs and Starvation** Gallacher, W. 22pp

246 **The Fight of the Miners** 62pp

247 **The Labour Government** Murphy, J.T. 96pp pb 'Published by Modern Books for the CP'.

248 **What's Wrong with the Cotton Trade?** Utley, Freda 40pp

249 **Women on the March** Elias, Sid 10pp Women only NUWM march.

1931

250 **Capitalism or Socialism in Britain?** Dutt, R.P. 34pp

251 **Central Committee Resolutions, Dec.** 22pp

252 **Crisis-Tariffs-War** Dutt, R.P. 20pp

253 **Down With the National Government** Rust, W. 15pp

254 **For a Marxist Leninist School – Lesson Outline No.7: The Soviet as the Form of the Proletarian Dictatorship** 14pp

255 **For Marxist Leninist Education, District School Material – Outline No.2: The Era of Imperialsm** 24pp

256 **For Marxist-Leninist Education, District School Material – Outline No.1: The Origin**

and Development of Modern Capitalism 24pp

257 **For Marxist-Leninist Education, District School Material – Outline No.3: The Imperialist War and the Crisis of Capitalism** 15pp

258 **For Marxist-Leninist Education, District School Material – Outline No.4: The Period of Temporary Stabilisation of Capitalism** 14pp

259 **For Marxist-Leninist Education, District School Material – Outline No.5: The Transition Period** 16pp

260 **For Marxist-Leninist Education, District School Material – Outline No.6: The Tasks of the Proletariat after the Conquest of Power** 23pp

261 **The Colonial Question: A Study Syllabus for Workers** 14pp

262 **The CP Shows the Way Out: A Manifesto** 8pp

263 **The Workers' Answer to the Crisis** Dutt, R.P. 16pp

264 **The Workers' United Front and the ILP** 16pp

265 **To Fascism or Communism** 39pp

1932

266 **A Six-Lesson Outline for Local Party Training Groups** 61pp Contains revised eds of the separate pamphlets headed 'For Marxist-Leninist Education, District School Material …'

267 **An Open Letter to All Members of the YCL from the Political Bureau of the CP and the National Bureau of the YCL** 4pp lf ?

268 **China** Rathbone, Harry 16pp

269 **Draft Resolution on the Independent Leadership in Economic Struggles (12th Congress)** 8pp

270 **Immediate Tasks Before the Party and the Working Class** 16pp

271 **India's Fight for Separation and Independence** Rust, W. 16pp

272 **Lessons of Economic Strikes and the Struggle of the Unemployed, Adopted by 12th Plenum of ECCI** 12pp Subtitled 'Material for 12th Congress CPGB'.

273 **Report on the Crisis Policy of the Labour Party (for 12th Congress)** 20pp

274 **The C.I. Answers the ILP** 36pp Originally written 1920.

275 **The Capitalist State** Bell, Tom 16pp

276 **The ILP and the Labour Party** Rust, W. 8pp Reprint from Aug. issue of 'Communist Review'.

277 **The International Situation and the Tasks of the Sections of the C.I.: 12th Plenum ECCI (12th Congress)** 15pp

278 **The Revolutionary Way Out: Resolutions Adopted by 12th Congress** 28pp

279 **The Road to Victory** Pollitt, H. 93pp pb

280 **The Second Five Year Plan** 12pp Fine illustrated cover.

281 **The Way Out for the Cotton Workers** 24pp 'Written by a group of militant weavers on behalf of the textile operatives'. Probably written by R. Page Arnot. Printed in the North West, it has the appearance of a district publication – it is possibly by the NW District but just states 'published by the CP'.

282 **War and Intervention and the Tasks of the CPs: 12th Plenum ECCI (12th Congress)** 8pp

283 **War! And The Way to Fight Against It** Wintringham, Tom 24pp

284 **What Next in Germany?** Rathbone, Harry 16pp

285 **Which Way for the Workers? Pollitt v Brockway** 32pp Debate, April 18.

286 **Working Women and the Capitalist Crisis** Smith, Rose 16pp

1933

287 **A Workers' Enquiry** Marx, K. 16pp

288 **Communist Political Education: A Manual for Workers' Study Groups** 95pp

289 **Democracy and Fascism** Dutt, R.P. 23pp

290 **How to Work in the Factories and Streets** Cox, Idris 48pp sf

291 **How's It All Going to End ?** Robson, R.W. 16pp

292 **Hunger!** Hutt, Allen 16pp

293 **Meerut Conspiracy Case** Glading, Percy 20pp

294 **Pollitt's Election Special: Clay Cross** 4pp lf

295 **The Co-operative Movement and the Class Struggle** Henrotte, Esther 24pp

296 **Tom Mann and the ILP** 12pp

297 **What is the CP?** Burns, Emile 16pp

298 **Women, Into the Ranks!** Smith, Rose 24pp

1934

299 **Into Action** Pollitt, H. 15pp CP's Proposals for National Unity Congress, Feb.

300 **Labour and War** Pollitt, H. 24pp

301 **Pensioners of Capitalism** Gallacher, W. 38pp 'An exposure of Trotsky & the Social Democrats'.

302 **Sedition Bill Exposed** 22pp

303 **September 9: Drowned in a Sea of Working Class Activity** 14pp Anti Fascist rally in Hyde Park. Good cover.

304 **Slavery or Socialism** Arnot, R. Page 16pp Superb cover by Cliff Rowe.

305 **The Role of the CP in the Proletarian Revolution (Thesis of 2nd Congress of C.I., 1920)** 19pp Reprint.

306 **The Truth About Trotsky** 'Andrews, R.F.' 70pp

307 **Towards Soviet Power: Report on 13th Plenum ECCI** Pollitt, H. 48pp

308 **United Action: The Only Way** Mahon, John 19pp Criticism of 1934 TUC Congress.

309 **What Lenin Said About the Jews** 'Andrews, R.F.' (ed.) 16pp

310 **What the CP is and What it Means to the Workers** Gallacher, W. 31pp

1935

311 **A Hell of a Business: Memorandum to Arms Inquiry Commission** Pollitt, H. 16pp Ill. cover.

312 **Abyssinia Special** 4pp lf Published in name of A. Ferguson.

313 **Decisive Days Ahead** Dutt, R.P. 24pp

314 **Draft Resolution on Building a Mass CP (13th Congress)** 9pp

315 **Draft Resolution on the CP and Economic Struggles (13th Congress)** 9pp

316 **Draft Resolution on the CP and the United Front (13th Congress)** 11pp

317 **Dynamite in the Dock: H. Pollitt's Evidence Before Arms Inquiry Commission** 16pp Superb cartoon cover by J. Boswell.

318 **For a United CP: An Appeal to ILPers and to ALL Revolutionary Workers** Dutt, R.P. 20pp

319 **For Soviet Britain: Programme Adopted at 13th Congress** 32pp Period cover.

320 **For Soviet Power: Draft Programme of CP for 13th Congress** 31pp

321 **Gresford** 24pp Mining disaster.

322 **Harry Pollitt Speaks: A Call to All Workers** Pollitt, H. 80pp Incl. Resolutions of 13th Congress.

323 **Heartbreak Homes: An Indictment of the National Government's Housing Policy** 'Best, Michael' 14pp

324 **How the CP Works** Robson, R.W. 29pp

325 **Jubilee and How** Jackson, T.A. 30pp Superb cover by J. Boswell.

326 **Light on Lucas** 16pp Cartoon cover probably by James Boswell.

327 **Massacre of the Innocents** Smith, Rose 16pp sf On child health.

328 **Memorandum to the Royal Commission on the Private Manufacture of Arms** 16pp

329 **Men and Motors** 23pp Intro. by Jack Tanner.

330 **Socialist Democracy Advances: Speech to 7th Congress of the Union of Socialist Soviet Republics.** Molotov, V. 31pp Printed & Published by Marston Printing Company for the CPGB.

331 **Spotlight on Fascism** Douglas, J.L. 24pp Cover by J. Boswell. Unusually there were 2 versions of this pamphlet and both had superb covers – one by Boswell the other by Fitton.

332 **The CP and the General Election** 12pp lf d

333 **The Fight for Peace: Report of a Speech to the Special National Conference of the CPGB** 24pp

334 **The Food Racket** Robson, R.W. 15pp

335 **The Labour Party and the CP** Pollitt, H. 15pp

336 **The Labour Party and the Menace of War** 'Andrews, R.F.' 24pp

337 **The Poison Gas Government** 4pp ?

338 **The Price of a Dinner** Smith, Rose 8pp sf On miners' pay demand.

339 **Towards Revolution: The Party and the Workers** 31pp

340 **Unity Against the National Government: Speech to 7th Congress C.I.** Pollitt, H. 32pp

341 **We Can Stop War** Pollitt, H. 12pp

342 **What is the CP?** Robson, R.W. 14pp

1936

343 **A War Was Stopped** Pollitt, H. 14pp On 'The Jolly George' and the Hands Off Russia Campaign, 1920.

344 **Arms for Spain** Pollitt, H. 28pp

345 **Colonies, Mandates and Peace** Bradley, Ben 16pp 'Peace Library' series.

346 **Communism and Cotton** Rust, W. 8pp

347 **Communism and the Building Workers** 12pp

348 **Communism and the Co-ops** Gallacher, W. 15pp

349 **Communism and the Railways** 13pp Cover by Lloyd. ?

350 **Communist Affiliation** Burns, Emile 24pp

351 **Corruption: Speech on Budget Leakage** Gallacher, W. 14pp

352 **Difficulties Facing Peace** Burns, Emile 14pp 'Peace Library' series.

353 **For Unity and Peace: Manifesto of the CPGB, May 1st** 8pp

354 **Forward: Report of CC, Jan.** Pollitt, H. 16pp Interesting, and rare, cover photo of Pollitt by Howard Coster presenting him as film star rather than working class hero.

355 **I Accuse Baldwin** Pollitt, H. 16pp 'Peace Library' series.

356 **Indian Politics** Dutt, R.P. & Bradley, Ben 24pp Officially published by B. Bradley.

357 **Peace: But How?** Campbell, J.R. 31pp 'Peace Library' series.

358 **Safety in Mines: Memorandum to Royal Commission** 21pp

359 **Save Spain from Fascism** Pollitt, H. 16pp

360 **Spain** Burns, Emile 16pp

361 **Spain and the TUC** Pollitt, H. 16pp

362 **The Communist Party** Robson, R.W. 16pp

363 **The CP and Labour Party Affiliation** Bell, Tom 4pp Unpriced pamphlet printed for wide distribution in the Labour movement to win the argument for CP affiliation. ?

364 **The Irish Revolt** Murray, Sean 16pp Ill. cover.

365 **The Miners' Case** Francis, Ben 24pp

366 **The Moscow Trial** Shepherd, W.G. 16pp

367 **The Path to Peace** Pollitt, H. 31pp 'Peace Library' series.

368 **The People Can Save South Wales** Cox, Idris 24pp Cover by S.H.

369 **The Stay-In Strikes in France** 16pp

370 **The World's First Socialist Constitution** 14pp

371 **Towards a Popular Front** Horner, Arthur 15pp

372 **Trade Unionism and Communism: An Open Letter** Mahon, John 16pp

373 **Unity and Peace** Dimitrov, G. 13pp 'Peace Library' series.

374 **Unity Is The Watchword** 10pp lf d Report of extended CC meeting, Jan. 4 & 5. Largely Pollitt's report on impact of 7th Congress of C.I. on CPGB. Not for sale but distributed to CP organisations.

375 **Unity, Peace and Security** Pollitt, H. 16pp

376 **War And Culture** Rickword, Edgell 16pp

377 **War is Terribly Profitable** Owen, Henry 15pp 'Peace Library' series.

378 **What Next for the Labour Party?** Dutt, R.P. 16pp

379 **Zinoviev Trial Showed Fine Legal Tradition** Pritt, D.N. 4pp Reprinted from 'DW' 3.9.36.

1937

380 **Answer If You Dare! Youth Challenges the National Government** Gollan, J. 16pp ?

381 **Catering Scandal** 16pp

382 **China Fights for Freedom** 16pp

383 **Clean Up the Shops** 11pp

384 **Communist Theory Series: Four Lesson Course No.1: For the Use of CP Branches & Training Groups** 16pp sf

385 **Communist Theory Series: Four Lesson Course No.2: Course for New Members** 16pp sf

386 **Communist Theory Series: Four Lesson Course No.3: The Development of Socialist Thought** 20pp sf

387 **Communist Theory Series: Four Lesson Course No.4: The Party and Its Work** 16pp sf

388 **Co-operatives and N.D.C.** Gallacher, W. 12pp National Defence Contribution.

389 **Defeat of Trotskyism** Pollitt, Marjorie 24pp

390 **Draft Resolution (14th Congress)** 18pp

391 **Free the Harworth Prisoners** 16pp Cover by Cliff Rowe.

392 **Friday Night Till Monday Morning** 14pp On the 40 hour week.

393 **It Can Be Done: Report of 14th Congress** 320pp pb

394 **Labour and Armaments** Rust, W. 16pp

395 **Labour's Way Forward** Pollitt, H. 16pp Speech at Battersea.

396 **Milk** 15pp

397 **Notts United** 16pp On the fusion of the two Nottinghamshire miners' unions into the MFGB after the split of 1926.

398 **Pasionaria** 23pp Short biog., includes parts of her speeches and writings.

399 **Report of CC to 14th Congress** 26pp Incl. Roll of Honour of British Battalion in Spain.

400 **Rose Smith Tells You Why You Pay More Now** Smith, Rose 24pp Reprinted in Nov. as 'Why We Pay More' by R. Smith, (priced 1d. instead of 2d.!). The first print in April was 10,000 – there were 2 reprints in Nov. of 10,000 each time.

401 **Salute to the Soviet Union** Pollitt, H. 30pp

402 **Save Peace: Aid Spain** 16pp Print run: 40,000.

403 **Spain Organises for Victory: Policy of the CP of Spain** Hernandez, Jesus & Comorera, Joan 88pp

404 **Spain's Left Critics** Campbell, J.R. 16pp

405 **Stop Rents Going Up** 24pp

406 **The Plain Man's Guide to the Coronation No.1: Parade of War** 16pp Covers of this series by J. Boswell.

407 **The Plain Man's Guide to the Coronation No.2: One Happy Family** 16pp Illustrated.

408 **The Plain Man's Guide to the Coronation No.3: How is the Empire?** 16pp Illustrated.

409 **The Truth About Trotskyism** Pollitt, H. & Dutt, R.P. 36pp

410 **Trade Unions and Unity** Horner, Arthur 16pp

411 **Why We Pay More** Smith, Rose 16pp

1938

412 **A.R.P. Act Now** 16pp

413 **A.R.P. The Practical Air Raid Protection Britain Needs** 16pp

414 **Agenda and Draft Resolutions for 15th Congress** 12pp

415 **Austria** Pollitt, H. 15pp

416 **Books and Pamphlets: How to Sell Them** Pollitt, H. *Literature Commission* 40pp Intro. by Pollitt.

417 **Britain's Millions Against Britain's Millionaires: May Day** 16pp Cover by J. Boswell.

418 **Communist Crusade for the People** 4pp lf

419 **Czechoslovakia** Pollitt, H. 16pp

420 **Czechoslovakia and Britain** Pollitt, H. 16pp

421 **Czechoslovakia Betrayed** Pollitt, H. 16pp Print run: 105,000, 2nd printing 30,000.

422 **Fascist Agents Exposed in the Moscow Trials** Arnot, R. Page & Buck, Tim 23pp

423 **For Peace and Plenty: Report of Fifteenth Congress** 192pp pb

424 **Forging Ahead: A Song of the People: Words & Music by Rufus Hogg** 4pp lf

425 **Hitler's Friends in Britain** 18pp

426 **How Chamberlain Helped Hitler** Campbell, J.R. 16pp

427 **How the Rich Live** 16pp

428 **Palestine: Terror or Peace?** 34pp

429 **Plan for Britain's Agriculture** Cornforth, Maurice 20pp

430 **Rebuild Our Countryside** 4pp lf ?

431 **Report of the CC to 15th Congress** 144pp hb

432 **Spain Fights for Victory** Rust, W. 16pp

433 **The Final Victory of Socialism in the Soviet Union: Stalin's Reply to Ivanov** 8pp

434 **William Gallacher, M.P.** Bishop, Reg 16pp

NATIONAL PUBLICATIONS

435 **William Gallacher's Speeches in Parliament (Second Series)** 57pp

436 **William Gallacher's Speeches in Parliament: First Series** Gallacher, W. 54pp

437 **Women Take a Hand** 12pp lf Interesting pamphlet making good use of photos.

1939

438 **Can Conscription Save Peace?** Pollitt, H. 31pp Published May 6, withdrawn May 24.

439 **Crusade for the Defence of the British People: For Work, Wages and Peace** 4pp lf Free broadsheet issued on Jan. 25 in ed. of 250,000.

440 **Defence of the People** Pollitt, H. 16pp

441 **Draft Constitution for 16th Congress** 10pp The 16th Congress was never held because of the War.

442 **Draft Programme for 16th Congress** 70pp

443 **How to Get It: Better Housing** *Women's Dept* 16pp

444 **How to Win the War** Pollitt, H. 32pp Published the very day the C.I. telegram arrived instructing the CP to oppose the war; the pamphlet, which called for a 'war on two fronts' incl. a vigorous fight against fascist Germany, was withdrawn & Pollitt & Campbell dismissed from their posts.

445 **Mass Murder or Planned Protection** 16pp

446 **Parliament and the War: Speeches by W. Gallacher, MP** 21pp

447 **Rally Programme: July 22** 14pp

448 **Report of CC to Sixteenth Congress** 72pp This was the Congress cancelled because of the war.

449 **Spain: What Next?** Pollitt, H. 15pp

450 **The CP Presents a Policy for the Land and the People** 12pp lf

451 **The War and the Workers** Gallacher, W. 32pp War Library No.2. Published Nov. 1; print run 50,000.

452 **They Fought in Franco's Jails** 16pp

453 **Trade Unions Forward** 15pp

454 **Why This War?** Dutt, R.P. 32pp War Library No.1. Published Nov. 1; print run 50,000.

455 **Will It Be War?** Pollitt, H. 30pp

1940

456 **A.R.P. Safety Now** 16pp

457 **Bombers Over London** Bramley, Ted 14pp

458 **End the Railway Fares Robbery** 16pp

459 **Fair Play for Servicemen and their Families** Springhall, Dave 16pp Communist Policy series No.3.

460 **How to Defend Yourself: A Practical Legal Guide for Workers** 54pp

461 **Is There a Way Out for the Working People of Britain?** 4pp lf Cover by 'Buchan'/Boswell? Print run: 100,000.

462 **John Maclean** McShane, Harry 30pp

463 **The CP in War Time** 48pp Record of Activities & Documents Issued up to March 15.

464 **The Empire and the War** 16pp War Library No.10.

465 **The Federal Union Myth** Montagu, Ivor 22pp War Library No.6.

466 **The Meaning of the French Trial** Dutt, Clemens 16pp War Library No.9.

467 **The Men Behind the Myth** Johnson, James 16pp War Library No.5.

468 **The New Stage of the War** Kerrigan, Peter 16pp War Library No.8.

469 **The Soviet Union and Finland** Burns, Emile 16pp War Library No.3.

470 **The War and the Labour Movement** Pollitt, H. 12pp

471 **The War and the Workshop** Pollitt, H. 12pp sf 'Letters to Bill'.

472 **Trade Unions and the War** 16pp War Library No.4.

473 **Twenty Years** Gallacher, W. 16pp On CP.

474 **Wages: A Policy** Pollitt, H. 24pp

475 **Wanted: £5,000** 16pp On fundraising.

476 **We Fight for Life** Dutt, R.P. 30pp Communist Policy series No.1.

477 **What is Russia Going to Do?** Pollitt, H. 16pp sf 'Letters to Bill' No.2.

478 **Women and the War** Brown, Isabel 14pp War Library No.7.

1941

479 **A Call For Arms** Pollitt, H. 16pp

480 **Army Pay and Allowances** 16pp

481 **Britain's Chance Has Come** Pollitt, H. 16pp

482 **Coal: A Policy** 16pp Communist Policy series No.5.

483 **Course for New Members** 16pp Communist Theory series No.2. A new ed. appeared later in the year, and a reprint the following year.

484 **Daily Worker Debate: Speech of W. Gallacher, Jan. 28** 8pp Print run: 100,000. There was also an abbreviated duplicated foolscap ed. of 4pp.

485 **Dimitrov Accuses the Nazis** 32pp Cover by 'Davy'.

486 **Doing Well out of the War?** Campbell, J.R. 16pp sf 'Letters to Bill' No.3.

487 **'DW' Debate: W. Gallacher's Speech, Jan.** 4pp lf d An abbreviated, duplicated version published quickly.

488 **Food: What Must be Done** 16pp Communist Policy series No.6.

489 **In Freedom's Cause** Bennett, Mick 16pp On USSR.

490 **India** Carritt, Michael 24pp Author was senior civil servant in India, secretly liaising between CP & the nationalist movement.

491 **Ireland: Can It Remain Neutral?** Gallacher, W. 24pp

492 **Marxism and Industrial Workers [new ed.]** 12pp sf

493 **Russia's Story Told in Pictures** 50pp

494 **Scorch the Earth** Redmond, Patrick 24pp Cover by 'Buchan' [Boswell]. On Soviet Guerrillas.

495 **Smash Hitler Now** Pollitt, H. 16pp July 9. Over 100,000 sold.

496 **Stalin Speaks** 32pp

497 **The Army: Weapon for Victory** 16pp

498 **The CP and the National Front: Syllabus for 4 Session School** 24pp

499 **The Keynes Budget** 16pp

500 **The Role and Character of the YCL** 16pp sf

501 **The Second Front** Wainwright, William 16pp

502 **The Worker Special, Oct. 13** 2pp Duplicated foolscap sheet – officially published by the CPGB, otherwise could be one of the 'DW' Specials.

503 **Tom Mann: A Tribute** Pollitt, H. 8pp

504 **Twenty Four Years of Soviet Power** Rust, W. 16pp sf

505 **Why We Talk Politics** Robson, R.W. 16pp

506 **Women Against Hitler** Pasionaria & Brown, Isabel 16pp

507 **Women and War Work** 16pp ?

1942

508 **A Guide for Treasurers** 16pp

509 **A Soldier Writes to His Wife** 8pp

510 **Africa – Europe – Victory!** Dutt, R.P. 16pp

511 **America and the Second Front** 8pp

512 **An Urgent Memorandum on Production** 40pp

513 **Britain's Health Services: A Memorandum** 40pp

514 **Britain's Schools: A Memorandum** 40pp

515 **China the Unconquerable: 5 Years Against Japan** Clegg, Arthur 17pp

516 **Clear Out Hitler's Agents** Wainwright, William 16pp On Trotskyists in the Labour Movement!

517 **Communism: An Outline for Everyone** Robson, R.W. 32pp Another ed. in 1943.

518 **Communist Organisation for Victory** 16pp Journal – Aug. Printed in pamphlet form because of paper restrictions for magazines.

519 **Deeds Not Words!** Pollitt, H. 16pp

520 **Dieppe and the Don** 8pp

521 **Food and Farming for Victory** Cornforth, Maurice 14pp

522 **From People's Front to National Front** Fischer, Ernst 12pp

523 **Gabriel Peri** Rust, W. 16pp Leading French Communist and member of the Resistance shot by the Nazis in Paris in 1941.

524 **Hints on Public Speaking** Winnington, Alan 16pp

525 **How I Joined the CP** 24pp

526 **How to Organise Education** 16pp On internal CP education classes.

527 **How to Organise Public Meetings** 24pp

528 **How to Sell Literature** 12pp

529 **India: What We Must Do** Bradley, Ben 16pp Author was former Vice President of All-India TUC.

530 **India's Problems** 32pp From CPI's 'People's War'. Foreword by B. Bradley. Cover by 'AF'.

531 **Into Battle: The Call of May Day** Pollitt, H. 18pp

532 **Italians Against Mussolini** 'Ercoli' 16pp

533 **Labour's Way Forward** Burns, Emile 16pp

534 **Mighty Russia** Gallacher, W. 16pp

535 **Miners' Plan for Victory** Moffat, Abe 16pp

536 **Mobilising the Party for the Second Front** 28pp Journal – Oct.

537 **Mrs Bradshaw's Tommy [Invade Europe Now]** Johnson, Vera 16pp sf Cover by Barbara Niven.

538 **Organising to Win the Offensive** 48pp Journal – Dec.

539 **Parliamentary Debate: On the African Offensive** Gallacher, W. 4pp

540 **Political Letter on the Daily Worker, Dec. 2** 4pp

541 **Proud Record** Robson, R.W. 16pp On CPSU.

542 **Sevastopol** Montagu, Ivor & Ehrenburg, Ilya 8pp

543 **Soviet Leaders: Kalinin** Montagu, Ivor 16pp sf

544 **Soviet Leaders: Molotov** Montagu, Ivor 16pp sf

545 **Soviet Leaders: Stalin** Arnot, R. Page 16pp sf

546 **Soviet Leaders: Timoshenko** Montagu, Ivor 16pp sf

547 **Soviet Leaders: Voroshilov** Montagu, Ivor 16pp sf

548 **Speed the Second Front** Pollitt, H. 16pp

549 **Stalin: A Biographical Sketch** Montagu, Ivor 32pp

550 **Stalin's Speech** 16pp Nov. 6.

551 **Steel** 16pp

552 **The Case for The Second Front** 8pp

553 **The CP and the National Front: Syllabus for 4 Lesson School** 24pp New ed.

554 **The CP on the Way to Win: Decisions of National Conference, May** 64pp

555 **The CP: Its Theory and Practice No.1** 16pp Revised ed. in 1943.

556 **The CP: Its Theory and Practice No.2** 16pp Revised ed. in 1943.

557 **The CP's Memorandum on Agriculture** 40pp

558 **The CPSU: Syllabus on 'History of CPSU'** 32pp

559 **The Indian CP** Joshi, P.C. 34pp

560 **The Libya Debate: The Second Front and Mr Churchill** Gallacher, W. 8pp Speech in Parliament July 1.

561 **The Russian Glory** Gallacher, W. 16pp

562 **The World in Arms** Pollitt, H. 16pp

563 **Today not Tomorrow** 8pp On Second Front.

564 **Trade Union Policy in the War Against Fascism** 24pp

565 **Two Letters from Germany** Bell, Tom 16pp Intro. by Bell.

566 **Victory This Year** Rust, W. 16pp

567 **Wages and Income Tax** Kerrigan, Peter 12pp Cover by 'Jax'.

568 **Why You Should be a Communist** Wainwright, William 32pp

569 **Women at War: Received from His Majesty's Ships** 8pp

570 **Women at War: Safeguard Your Health** 8pp

571 **Women at War: Tanya, the Story of a Soviet Heroine** 8pp

572 **Women! Man the Factory Front** Brown, Isabel 16pp

1943

573 **Anti-Semitism: What it Means to You** Gallacher, W. 24pp

574 **Britain Today and Tomorrow** Dutt, R.P. 16pp

575 **British Agriculture** 40pp Revised Memorandum.

576 **Ceux de Chateaubriant** Grenier, F. 30pp In French.

577 **Clear the Lines: Better Conditions, Better Service** 16pp

578 **Clear the Ports** 16pp

579 **Coal** 8pp

580 **Coal and the Nation** Horner, Arthur 22pp Cover by Ern Brooks.

581 **Communism and Education** Bramley, Ted 16pp

582 **Communist Policy Statements Between June 1942 & April 1943** 40pp

583 **Discussion Notes: Why You Became a Communist** 16pp

584 **Discussion Statement for 16th Congress** 8pp

585 **Discussion Statement on the Colonies for 16th Congress** 8pp

586 **Draft Resolutions for 16th Congress** 12pp

587 **Draft Rules of the CPGB** 4pp For Congress.

588 **Farm and Food** 8pp lf

589 **Food and the Nation** Matthews, George 24pp Cover by E. Brooks.

590 **France's Hour Has Struck** Marty, André 20pp English version of 'L'Heure de la France a Sonné'.

591 **Hints on the Organisation of Press Work** Norton, Maire 16pp

592 **Hitler's Agents Exposed!** Mahon, John 20pp On Trotskyists.

593 **Hitler's Death Sentence: Three Power Conference** Dutt, R.P. 16pp

594 **Income and Expenditure Account of the CP for Year ended Dec. 31 1942 (For 16th Congress)** 4pp

595 **India's Famine: The Facts** Bradley, Ben 16pp

596 **Invade Now in the West** 8pp

597 **Italy Now Smash On!** Pollitt, H. 8pp

598 **Keep Mosley in Prison** 8pp

599 **L'Epopée de la Corse** Rochet, Waldeck & Cossoneau, E. 16pp In French – on Corsica.

600 **Letters on Affiliation** 8pp 4 letters between LP & CP, March/April.

601 **L'Heure de la France a Sonné** Marty, André 20pp An English ed. was published in the same year – 'France's Hour Has Struck'.

602 **Material for Delegates at 16th Congress** 8pp Agenda, Political Resolution, Emergency Resolution on India.

603 **Memorandum on a National Medical Service** 12pp

604 **Memorandum on the Beveridge Report** 26pp Cover by 'AF'.

605 **Men and Ships** 16pp

606 **Miners' Target** Pollitt, H. 16pp

607 **Organise to Mobilise Millions** 24pp Journal – March.

608 **Organising for Offensive Action** 28pp Journal – Feb.

609 **Organising for Victory in 1943** 24pp Journal – May.

610 **Party Organisation: Weapon for Victory** 24pp Journal – March.

611 **Put Mosley Back in Prison** 8pp

612 **Road Passenger Transport** 16pp

613 **Sharpening Our Weapons** 24pp Journal – July.

614 **Sicily: Stepping Stone to Victory** Wainwright, William 8pp

615 **Speed the Campaign** 24pp Journal – Oct.

616 **Square Deal for Miners** Gallacher, W. 8pp sf

617 **Sur L'Afrique du Nord: Documents** Grenier, F. 16pp One of a short range of pamphlets the CP produced for the PCF in French.

618 **The Case for Affiliation** Burns, Emile 16pp

619 **The CP and the Labour Party: Correspondence** 16pp Foreword by H. Pollitt.

620 **The CP: Its Theory and Practice No.3** 16pp

621 **The Fate of Europe** Ehrenburg, Ilya 6pp

622 **The Stench of Nazism** 8pp On Russian town of Rhzev.

623 **The Voice of Free Poland** 8pp

624 **This is the Enemy: A Book of Facts, Figures and Pictures About Fascism** 34pp

625 **Unity and Victory: Report of Sixteenth Congress** 64pp

626 **Victory and After** Stalin, J. 16pp

627 **What is Common Wealth?** Arnot, R. Page 12pp This was withdrawn from sale.

628 **Where Does Britain Stand?** Pollitt, H. 24pp

629 **Why Britain Needs a Strong Labour Movement** Reid, Betty 16pp

630 **Workers of Britain, Unite!** Pollitt, H. 20pp

1944

631 **17th Congress: Discussion Statement** 4pp From EC.

NATIONAL PUBLICATIONS

632 **A Memorandum on Housing** 40pp

633 **A National Health Service: Memorandum Issued by the CP** 30pp

634 **Agenda and Resolutions Submitted to 17th Congress** 16pp

635 **Agriculture After the War: Prosperity or Slump?** Cornforth, Maurice 16pp I believe this was never distributed.

636 **Agriculture and the World Today** 24pp

637 **Britain for the People: Proposals for Post War Policy** 24pp lf Programme adopted at 17th Congress; it marked an important change in CP's attitude to Parliament which could now be changed to help build socialism – previously Parliament was part of the state machine to be smashed.

638 **Britain's Young Citizens** 20pp

639 **British Soldier in India: The Letters of Clive Branson** 119pp pb Artist, poet; fought in Spain. Intro. by H. Pollitt gives brief biog. Some poems included. Described by J. Saville as 'one of the great classics of the anti-imperialist struggle'.

640 **Chemicals and the Future** 16pp

641 **D-Day** Pollitt, H. 8pp sf

642 **Demobilisation: How Should it be Done?** 16pp

643 **Documents for Congress: Political Statements Issued Between July 1943 & Aug. 1944** 48pp

644 **Electoral Reform** 16pp

645 **Equal Pay for Equal Work** 8pp

646 **Essentials of Communist Theory** Robson, R.W. 20pp

647 **Farm Workers' Wages: The Case for £4.10.0** Dunman, Jack 8pp

648 **French Workers Fight Fascism** Roubaud, R.A. 12pp

649 **Good Health For All** 16pp

650 **Higher Wages and Full Employment** 24pp

651 **How to End Muddle on the Railways** A Group of Communist Railway Workers 16pp

652 **How to Win the Peace** Pollitt, H. 96pp

653 **Improve Our Party Organisation** 24pp Journal – Aug.

654 **Jobs, Homes and Security** Burns, Emile 16pp

655 **Notes For Burns' Anniversary (1759-95)** 8pp

656 **Our Forces in India** Olorenshaw, A. 14pp

657 **Party Organisation and the Invasion** 24pp Journal – June.

658 **Party Organisation and the Offensive** 24pp Journal – May.

659 **Pollitt Answers Qestions on Communist Policy** Pollitt, H. 16pp

660 **Report of EC to 17th Congress** 16pp

661 **Salute to the Co-ops, 1844-1944** 8pp lf

662 **Seamen It's Up to You!** Evans, H. 24pp

663 **Service Pay Allowances and Pensions** Lesser, Frank 16pp

664 **Strengthen Our Organisation** 24pp Journal – Feb.

665 **Take Over the Mines!** Pollitt, H. 24pp

666 **The 'Multilateral' (or Common) School: A Memorandum** Educ. Advisory 4pp

667 **The Colonies and the Future: Study Syllabus** Bradley, Ben 12pp Author not credited. Based on 'Colonies – The Way Forward'.

668 **The Colonies: The Way Forward – A Memorandum** 64pp

669 **The Communist Party** Kerrigan, Peter 10pp

670 **The Co-operatives Against the Combines** 32pp

671 **The CP of France: Manifesto** 32pp

672 **The Final Offensive** Wainwright, William 16pp

673 **The Future of Rent Control** 32pp

674 **The Future of Ship Building: A Memorandum** 34pp Cover by Maxwell.

675 **The Germans: What Shall We Do About Them?** Montagu, Ivor 24pp

676 **Time For a Change** 8pp lf Communist Special.

677 **Tom Mann: His Life and His Work** 16pp

678 **Towards a Greater Trade Union Movement** 24pp

679 **Transport for the People: Proposals for Post-War Policy** 24pp

680 **Tune Up Our Organisation** 24pp Journal – Jan.

681 **Victory, Peace, Security: Report of 17th Congress** 64pp

682 **Wages and the Cost of Living: Sir John Anderson Answered by W. Gallacher** 16pp

683 **What's the Answer? 12 Questions that Country Workers and Farmers are Asking** 16pp

684 **Winning the Peace: Syllabus on 'How to Win the Peace'** Burns, Emile 12pp

685 **Woman's Place?** 24pp

1945

686 **18th National Congress: Guide for Reporting Back** 4pp lf

687 **A Busman Appeals to You: Join the CP Today** Papworth, Bert 8pp

688 **Agriculture Planned and Prosperous** 72pp

689 **Answers to Questions** Pollitt, H. 48pp K. Morgan in 'Harry Pollitt' calls this the most extreme example of Pollitt's 'orientation towards a constructive engagement with pogressive capitalism' in this period immediately before the end of the war.

690 **Communist Election Policy** 72pp For July General Election.

691 **Communist M.P.** 32pp On Gallacher.

692 **Communist Policy for Britain: Report of 18th Congress** 80pp

693 **Congress Discussion Statement** 2pp lf

694 **Crisis in Greece** 16pp

695 **Engineering Prospects and Wages** 34pp

696 **Equal Pay: Evidence Submitted to the Royal Commission** 24pp

697 **Fascist Murderers: Pictures of the Concentration Camps You Must Never Forget** 8pp

698 **France Today and Tomorrow** Thorez, Maurice 26pp

699 **Health Centres and the NHS: A Memorandum** Health Advisory 4pp lf

700 **Houses for the Millions** Rust, W. 16pp

701 **Italy's New Path** Togliatti, Palmiro 26pp

702 **Liberate Spain from Franco** Ibarruri, Dolores 16pp

703 **May Day 1945** Arnot, R. Page 16pp sf Attractive cover with typography by Francis Minns.

704 **Memorandum of EC on Party Organisation** 4pp lf For 18th Congress.

705 **No More Depressed Areas** 32pp

706 **Nurseries After the War** 12pp

707 **Over to Peace: CP Policy for the Reconversion of Industry** Campbell, J.R. 16pp

708 **Poland Liberated** Howard, R. 16pp

709 **Pollitt Answers Foot: The Coalowners' Plan Examined** Pollitt, H. 16pp

710 **Post-War Housing Problems** Housing Advisory Cttee 16pp

711 **Report of EC to 18th Congress** 32pp

712 **Resolution on Demobilisation** 4pp

713 **Resolutions and Agenda (18th Congress)** 72pp This was the first Congress agenda that included branch resolutions.

714 **Socialism: What? Why? How?** Jackson, T.A. 72pp

715 **The BBC** Arts Advisory Cttee 24pp

716 **The Crimea Conference: Safeguard of the Future** Pollitt, H. 16pp

717 **The Future of Britain's Mercantile Marine** 27pp

718 **The Way Forward for Miners** Moffat, Abe 16pp

719 **Trade Unions and the General Election** Campbell, J.R. 16pp

720 **Truth About the Tories** Dutt, R.P. 16pp

721 **Why Politics?** 4pp sf

722 **Why Professional Workers Should be Communists** Haldane, J.B.S. 4pp

723 **Why You Should be a Communist** Pollitt, H. 32pp

1946

724 **A Guide for Tutors** Education Dept 4pp

725 **A Wage Based on Human Needs: Metal, Engineering, Ship Building & Allied Trades** Birch, Reg 12pp

726 **Atomic Energy and Social Progress** Paul, William 30pp

727 **Britain Will Make It** Pollitt, H. 30pp

728 **Britain's Young Citizens: What They Expect from Labour** 16pp

729 **Capitalist Society: Elements of Political Economy** 32pp sf Marxism – Introductory Course.

730 **Communism in Russia: What it Has Achieved** 4pp lf CP Special.

731 **Daily Herald Poison Pens** Pollitt, H. 4pp lf

732 **Essentials for a Health Service** 12pp

733 **European Jewry and the Palestine Problem** 16pp

NATIONAL PUBLICATIONS

734 **For Peace in Palestine** Piratin, Phil 4pp lf

735 **Freedom for India** Dutt, R.P. 34pp

736 **Full Speed Ahead to the Britain We Want** 8pp lf 'Communist Special'.

737 **Give Us the Wages: We'll Do the Job** Rust, T. 4pp lf Women & Work News-Sheet.

738 **Hands Off Indonesia** Clegg, Arthur 16pp

739 **Impressions of Czechoslovakia** Pollitt, H. 48pp

740 **Inside the Soviet Zone** 4pp lf

741 **Jersey Looks Forward** Le Brocq, Norman 96pp Author, leading Communist in the Channel Islands, was elected to Jersey's 'parliament' – the States Assembly.

742 **Labour's Foreign Policy** Pollitt, H. 4pp lf

743 **Laski's Mistake** Dimitrov, G. 16pp

744 **Local Government Reorganisation: A Memorandum** 4pp lf

745 **No British Jobs for Fascist Poles** 4pp 'CP Folder'.

746 **Nursery Schools** Women's Advisory Council 12pp

747 **Our Maternity Services** Lynd, Sheila 16pp

748 **Our Villages As They Are and As They Ought To Be** 8pp lf

749 **Professional Workers** Pollitt, H. 12pp

750 **Report of EC to 19th Congress** 48pp

751 **Russia at the Peace Conference** Piratin, Phil 30pp

752 **Stalin, Wallace and Bevin** Rust, W. 4pp lf

753 **Steel: Take it Over Now!** 14pp

754 **The Aims of the CP: Marxism Introductory Course Part 1** 30pp sf

755 **The Communists Were Right!** 15pp Covers questions on the possibility of preventing WW2, the Second Front, etc.

756 **The CP and the Coal Crisis** Horner, Arthur 8pp

757 **The CP Today** Bolsover, Phil 16pp

758 **The Fight for Labour's Programme** Burns, Emile 16pp

759 **Towards a People's Army** 26pp Based on a discussion forum, chaired by J. Gollan; accepted military service as long as the army was democratised.

760 **Up With the Houses: Down With the Rents** 4pp lf

761 **Up With Wages: Cut Down Profits** 4pp lf

762 **Why the Food Shortage?** Gollan, J. 16pp

763 **Why Your Rates are Going Up** 24pp

764 **Work for the Development Areas: H. Pollitt Writes to Sir S. Cripps** Pollitt, H. 4pp lf

1947

765 **A Plan for Science** Science Advisory Cttee 32pp

766 **American Spider** Clegg, Arthur 16pp On U.S. economic imperialism.

767 **Break With Franco Spain** 4pp lf

768 **Bring the Men Home** 4pp lf

769 **Britain's Plan for Prosperity** 112pp pb

770 **Britain's Problems Can Be Solved** Pollitt, H. 32pp

771 **Egypt and the Labour Party** Audit, George 32pp

772 **Goods for Us: How to Get Them** 6pp lf 'Communist Special'.

773 **Guide for Reporting the 19th National Congress** 4pp

774 **Higher Education: A Memorandum** 4pp lf

775 **How to Plan Local Elections** 32pp

776 **Humanise The Hospitals** 4pp lf

777 **Klement Gottwald: A Biography** Necasek, F. 36pp

778 **Looking Ahead** Pollitt, H. 128pp pb Important document for development of CP programmes/strategies.

779 **Main Resolutions (19th Congress)** 28pp

780 **New Deal for Transport** 16pp

781 **Office Workers: Programme for Progress** 4pp lf

782 **Plan for Coal** Pollitt, H. 16pp

783 **Political Resolution Proposed by EC for 19th Congress** 4pp lf

784 **Prices: Where Your Money Goes** 8pp lf 'Communist Special'.

785 **Report of EC for 19th Congress** 70pp

786 **Report of EC to 20th Congress** 70pp

787 **Resolution on Youth Proposed by the EC for 19th Congress** 4pp lf

788 **Resolutions and Proceedings: 19th Congress** 32pp

789 **Strengthen the Government: And Put Things Right in Britain!** 4pp lf

790 **Successful Open-Air Meetings** 4pp

791 **The Best Education: Free For All** Chadwick, Lee 4pp lf

792 **The Fascist Threat to Britain** Thompson, E.P. 16pp

793 **The Film Industry: A Memorandum** 4pp lf

794 **The Future of Ship Building** 24pp

795 **The Small Farmer: Defence and a Policy** 8pp lf ?

796 **Uncle Sam** 16pp Cover by J. Boswell.

797 **We Speak for Freedom: Report of Conference of CPs of the British Empire, Feb./March** 96pp

798 **Women Can Make It** 4pp lf Calls for employment of women to reduce labour shortages.

1948

799 **A Communist Policy for the Theatre** 4pp sf

800 **A Confidence-Trick Budget** Piratin, Phil 4pp lf Speech in House of Commons.

801 **A Socialist Solution to the Crisis** Campbell, J.R. 12pp

802 **A Study Guide to the Communist Manifesto** 30pp sf

803 **Catholics and Communism** Gallacher, W. 16pp

804 **Communist Leadership: 2 Lesson Syllabus** 32pp sf

805 **Czechoslovakia: The Facts** 4pp lf

806 **Dialectical and Historical Materialism: Marxism: An Introductory Course Part 5** 36pp

807 **Evidence to Working Party on Building** 80pp lf d

808 **For Britain Free and Independent** Pollitt, H. 12pp Report to 20th Congress & Reply to Discussion.

809 **Full Steam Ahead: A Programme for Railway Men** 16pp

810 **Gallacher's Challenge to Bevin** 4pp lf

811 **Guide for Reporting the 20th National Congress** 4pp lf In 'Information', Propaganda Dept weekly for Feb. 26. Generally these 'Guides' were not for sale.

812 **Higher Education for the People** Meredith, Christopher 88pp pb Foreword by G.C.T. Giles.

813 **How to Save the Peace** Dutt, R.P. 16pp

814 **Palestine: A Background to the Conflict** Fagan, Hymie 4pp lf

815 **Party Initiative and the Mass Movement: Political Letter to All Members** Pollitt, H. 4pp lf

816 **Peace and Homes** Gallacher, W. 4pp lf

817 **Political Report to 20th Congress** Pollitt, H. 48pp

818 **Resolutions and Proceedings: 20th Congress** 16pp

819 **Stop the War in Malaya** 4pp lf

820 **The Battle of Ideas: 6 Speeches on the Centenary of the Communist Manifesto – 20th Congress** 20pp

821 **The Communist Manifesto: Centenary Edition** 38pp Cover by Tom Poulton.

822 **The Co-operative Movement: A Study Guide** 32pp sf

823 **The CPSU: Syllabus for 6 Lessons** 40pp sf

824 **The Future of Local Government** 4pp lf

825 **The Marshall Plan** Kartun, Derek 16pp Cover by 'Davy'.

826 **The Miners' Next Step** Pollitt, H. 16pp

827 **The State and Democracy: Marxism: An Introductory Course Part 3** 32pp sf

828 **The Story of the English Revolution** Morton, A.L. 16pp sf

829 **The Transition to Socialism: A 3 Lesson Syllabus** 30pp sf

830 **The Triumph of Communism** Burns, Emile 16pp

831 **The Witch Hunt Exposed** Gallacher, W. 4pp lf Speech in Parliamentary Debate on Communists and the Civil Service, March 25.

832 **Trade Unionists: What Next?** Pollitt, H. 16pp

833 **Wages and Homes: A Pamphlet for Farm Workers** Dunman, Jack 16pp

834 **Wages, Prices and Profits** Stevens, Walter 16pp

835 **Where Is Labour Going?** Pollitt, H. 4pp lf

836 **Which Way to Socialism?** Gollan, J. 16pp

837 **Women and the World Today: 3 Lesson Course** 20pp sf

1949

838 **A Memorandum on Building** 40pp

839 **After the Elections: Political Letter to All Members** 4pp lf

840 **American Communists on Trial: Speech by Eugene Dennis** 32pp

841 **Capitalist Society: Elements of Political Economy – Marxism: An Introductory Course Part 2** 32pp

842 **Communism and Labour: A Call for United Action** Pollitt, H. 48pp

843 **Communism and Liberty** Gallacher, W. 16pp

844 **Communist Information Bureau Resolutions** 30pp sf

845 **Communist Policy to Meet the Crisis: Report of 21st National Congress** 64pp

846 **Corruption: Comments on the Lynskey Tribunal** Bolsover, Phil 16pp

847 **Cut Arms Not Houses: Raise Wages Not Profits** Piratin, Phil 4pp lf

848 **Deakin Exposed** 4pp lf

849 **Defend Trade Union Rights** 28pp

850 **Devaluation: What it Means to You** 4pp lf 'Communist Special'.

851 **Facts and Figures for Local Elections** 24pp sf

852 **For Homes Not Bombs** 4pp lf

853 **Guide for Reporting the 21st National Congress** 4pp lf

854 **Political Report to 21st Congress** Pollitt, H. 38pp

855 **Protection at Work** Piratin, Phil 16pp

856 **Report of EC for 21st Congress** 52pp Good list of CP shops at end.

857 **Resolutions and Proceedings of 21st Congress** 16pp

858 **Stop Purging Communists: Watch Your Wages** Papworth, Bert & Jones, Bill 4pp lf On TGWU.

859 **The Aims of the CP: Marxism: An Introductory Course Part 1** 32pp sf

860 **The Communist Party** Lauchlan, William 16pp

861 **The Communists Fight for Peace** Gallacher, W. 4pp lf Speech in House of Commons.

862 **The Great Film Lock-Out** A Group of Communist Film Makers 24pp

863 **The Labour Movement in Britain: Marxism: An Introductory Course Part 4** 32pp

864 **The Socialist Road for Britain: Draft General Election Programme** 32pp For 21st Congress.

865 **The Socialist Road for Britain: General Election Programme Adopted at 21st Congress** 32pp

866 **The Tactics of Disruption** Pollitt, H. 4pp lf Answer to TUC p. of same title.

867 **Those Russians** Pollitt, H. 16pp

868 **Wages – Homes – Peace** 4pp lf 'Communist Special'.

869 **Why the Slump?** Kerrigan, Peter 16pp

1950

870 **30 Years of Struggle** Gollan, J. 26pp On history of CP.

871 **Election Facts: For Speakers and Canvassers** 32pp sf New ed. in 1951.

872 **Farmworkers for Peace and Higher Wages** Dunman, Jack 16pp

873 **Fight for Wages, Homes, Peace!** 4pp lf 'Communist Special'.

874 **Forward With Confidence: Political Letter to All Members** 4pp lf

875 **Into the Fight For Peace: Political Letter to All Members** 4pp lf

876 **Local Election Facts: For Speakers and Canvassers** 24pp sf New ed. in 1955.

877 **On the Thirtieth Anniversary of the CP** 32pp

878 **Peace Depends on the People** Pollitt, H. 36pp

879 **Stop the War in Malaya** Woddis, Jack 16pp

880 **The Communist Party: Unity and the Fight for Peace – Marxist Study Themes No.1** 20pp

881 **The Fight for Peace and Working Class Unity: Pollitt's Report to EC, July** Pollitt, H. 24pp

882 **The Gravest Crisis Since the War: Political Letter to All Members** 2pp lf

883 **The Meaning of Socialism** Burns, Emile 16pp

884 **The Soviet Transition from Socialism and Communism** Burns, Emile 16pp

885 **Three Talks for Socialists** Propaganda Dept 14pp

886 **Wall Street's Drive to War** Klugmann, James 20pp

887 **Women's Place in Society** Educ. Dept 24pp lf d ?

888 **Work, Wages and the Atlantic War Pact: Discussion Statement** Economic Sub Cttee 28pp lf d

1951

889 **After the Election: A Fighting Policy for Labour – Report to EC, Nov.** Pollitt, H. 8pp lf

890 **America: Go Home!** Kartun, Derek 16pp

891 **An Appeal to Members of the Labour Party** Pollitt, H. 4pp

892 **An Open Letter to a Trade Unionist** Pollitt, H. 16pp

893 **Coal and the Miners** Allison, George 16pp

894 **Communist Policy for Peace: Negotiate Now** Pollitt, H. 16pp Cover by 'Gabriel'.

895 **Election Facts for Speakers and Canvassers** 32pp

896 **Is There a Co-operative Way to Socialism?** 12pp

897 **National Independence and Fraternal Association: Marxist Study Themes No.3 BRS – Part 2** 8pp

898 **No War with China** Clegg, Arthur 16pp

899 **On People's Democracy in Eastern Europe and China** Minc, Dimitrov et al. 52pp

900 **Peace and Friendship with all Peoples: Marxist Study Themes No.3 BRS – Part 1** 8pp

901 **People's Democracy: The Path to Socialism – Marxist Study Themes BRS No. 3 Part 3** 8pp

902 **Political Letter on the BRS** 4pp lf

903 **Prices: Stop Them Rising!** 4pp lf

904 **Social Democracy and the Fight for Working Class Unity: Marxist Study Themes No.2** 16pp

905 **Social Services: Marxist Study Themes No.3 BRS – Part 5** 8pp

906 **Socialist Nationalisation: Marxist Study Themes No.3 BRS – Part 4** 8pp

907 **Study Year 1951-2: Special Syllabuses for Day Schools No.1 – People's Democracy in Eastern Europe** Educ. Dept 8pp lf

908 **The Big Lie About Russia** Matthews, George 16pp Cover by 'Eccles'.

909 **The British Road to Socialism** 22pp First ed. of what was to be the CP's Programme for 40 years.

910 **The CP and the Way Forward: Marxist Study Themes No.3 BRS – Part 6** 8pp

911 **The Disruptive Role of the Titoites: Marxist Study Themes No.4** 8pp

912 **The Political and Economic Situation in the Empire Countries During 1951** 35pp Presumably published by the International Dept; appears to be for internal use.

913 **The Tories and How to Beat Them** Heinemann, Margot 12pp

914 **Unite Now to Defeat the Tories** Pollitt, H. 4pp Based on Report to April EC.

915 **Which Way for Students?** 20pp

916 **Why Britain Needs the CP Today More Than Ever** Pollitt, H. 4pp Reprinted in 1952.

917 **World Greetings to Harry Pollitt on his Sixtieth Birthday** 22pp

1952

918 **A Policy for Distributive Workers** 8pp sf

919 **An Open Letter to Students** Pollitt, H. 4pp

920 **Britain Arise: Political Report to 22nd Congress** Pollitt, H. 52pp pb

921 **Coal: For War or Peace?** Moffat, Alex 4pp

922 **Draft Rules for 22nd Congress** 6pp

923 **Furniture: Production and Wages** 8pp sf Reprinted from 'World News'.

924 **Guide to Reporting Back From 22nd Congress** 4pp lf

925 **Hands Off the Schools** Morris, Max 4pp

926 **Malaya: Stop the War** Pollitt, H. 12pp

927 **Out With the Tories** Lauchlan, William 12pp

928 **Peace Means Jobs for Clothing Workers** Ackerman, Mick 8pp sf

929 **Peace Means Jobs for Furnishing Workers** 8pp sf

930 **People's Democracy for Britain** Gollan, J. 24pp Report introducing the 'BRS' to Congress.

931 **Political Economy: 6 Months' Reading and Study Programme – Intermediate** 4pp sf

932 **Political Economy: Marxist Study Themes No.6** 20pp

933 **Report of EC to 22nd Congress** 60pp

934 **Resolutions and Proceedings of 22nd Congress** 16pp

935 **Revised Draft of the BRS for 22nd Congress** 20pp

936 **The British Road to Socialism** 20pp New ed. agreed at 22nd Congress in April.

937 **The CP and the Fight for Unity: Marxist Study Themes No.5** 20pp

938 **The Engineer Looks Ahead** Hitchings, Gilbert 12pp

939 **The Issues Before Our 22nd Congress: Political Letter to all Members** 4pp

940 **The Nazis Shall not Pass** Pollitt, H. 12pp

941 **The Outlook for Railway Men** 4pp

942 **The Outlook for Steel** Hill, Howard 4pp

943 **The Transport Sell-Out** 8pp

944 **The Truth About Moral Re-armament** Hilson, Frank 20pp

945 **Towards Communism** Gollan, J. 20pp

946 **We Must Have Higher Wages** Kerrigan, Peter 12pp

947 **Who Is for War?** 4pp

1953

948 **A Comprehensive Occupational Health Service** 12pp lf d

949 **A Policy for Labour** Pollitt, H. 16pp

950 **Bring Down Food Prices!** Jeffery, Nora 8pp

951 **Britain and the Colonies** Dutt, R.P. 8pp lf Reprinted from 'World News & Views'.

952 **Concert Programme: 10 Oct.** *National Cultural Cttee* 4pp Interesting programme: Birmingham Workers' Choir, A.L. Lloyd, E. MacColl, L. Fung, songs by F.B. Silvester & Elisabeth Thomson; Indian & W. Indian groups; produced by A. van Gyseghem.

953 **Coronation** 12pp

954 **Crisis of Britain and the British Empire: Marxist Study Themes No.7** 24pp

955 **Five Women Tell Their Story** 12pp

956 **Foundations of Leninism: 6 Months' Reading and Study Programme – Elementary** 4pp

957 **In Memory of Joseph Stalin and Klement Gottwald** Pollitt, H. 16pp

958 **Introduction to Marxism: 6 Months' Reading and Study Programme (Elementary) Jan.-June 1953** 4pp sf Based on 'Introduction to Marxism' by E. Burns.

959 **Kenya What are the Facts?** Bolsover, Phil 12pp

960 **Labour: What Next?** Pollitt, H. 12pp

961 **More Wages, More Jobs: 15% for Shipyard Workers** Hart, Finlay 12pp

962 **Not a Penny on the Rent** 4pp lf

963 **Problems of Leninism: 6 Months' Reading & Study Programme** *Educ. Dept* 4pp sf

964 **Put the Children First** Morris, Max 12pp

965 **Right Away for Railway Wages** Ahern, Tom 8pp

966 **Socialism for Trade Unionists** Campbell, J.R. 12pp

967 **The Tories' Secondary School Swindle** 4pp lf Supplement to 'Educational Bulletin'.

968 **U.S. Spies in Socialist Countries** Gallacher, W. 12pp

969 **Wage Increase for Miners** Moffat, Alex 12pp

970 **Wages Increase for Building Workers** 8pp

971 **Wages Increase: 15% for Engineering Workers** Abbott, Syd 8pp

972 **What Do Miners Need?** Pollitt, H. 12pp

1954

973 **A Call to Co-operators** Burns, Elinor 20pp

974 **Allies for Freedom: Report of 2nd Conference of CPs Within the Sphere of British Imperialism** 148pp pb

975 **Distributive Workers and the Fight for Increased Wages** Roche, Peter 8pp

976 **Draft of New Members' Syllabus** *Central Education Dept* 14pp lf d ?

977 **Farming to Feed Britain: A Policy for Farm Workers, Farmers and Consumers** 23pp

978 **Food for Thought** 4pp lf Written by Communist food workers; about food processing. ?

979 **Freedom Outlawed in the USA** Bolsover, Phil 16pp Cover by 'Gabriel'.

980 **Guide to Reporting Back 23rd Congress** 4pp

981 **In Defence of Peace: The Case Against Rearming the Nazis** Pollitt, H. 16pp

982 **Indian Diary** Pollitt, H. 32pp

983 **Memorandum on National Insurance** 20pp

984 **No Arms for Germany** 4pp lf

985 **Nothing is Lost: Ann Lindsay 1914-54: Memorial Pamphlet** *Rickword for CP Writers' Group* 16pp Actor with Unity Theatre.

986 **Report of EC to 23rd Congress** 36pp

987 **Resolutions and Proceedings: 23rd Congress** 12pp

988 **Socialism and the British Labour Movement Part 1: Marxist Study Themes No.8** 32pp

989 **Socialism and the British Labour Movement Part 2: Marxist Study Themes No.8** 24pp

990 **Syllabus on the 23rd Congress of the CP** *Educ. Dept* 12pp lf d

991 **The British Labour Movement: 6 Months' Reading and Study Programme – Elementary** 4pp sf

992 **The British State: Marxist Study Themes No.9** 28pp

993 **The Challenge to Labour: Political Report to 23rd Congress** Pollitt, H. 56pp

994 **The People on the March** Pollitt, H. 16pp

995 **The State: Six Months' Reading and Study Programme – Intermediate** 4pp sf

996 **This Good Life: The Socialist Road for Britain** 4pp lf

997 **When the Whistle Blows: Economics for Trade Unionists** Ainley, Ted 12pp

998 **Your Insurance Benefit** 8pp

1955

999 **A Policy for Britain: General Election Programme** 16pp

1000 **A Policy for Health** 36pp

1001 **Build the CP** Gollan, J. 8pp lf Report to EC.

1002 **Communists Show the Way** 4pp lf

1003 **Forging the Weapon: A Handbook for Members** 30pp

1004 **Freedom and the Communists** Kartun, Derek 16pp

1005 **Literature as a Political Weapon** 16pp

1006 **Local Election Facts for Speakers and Canvassers** 24pp sf

1007 **Mr Bevan: An Issue of Policy** 4pp lf

1008 **No Colour Bar for Britain** Bolsover, Phil 12pp

1009 **Our Aim is Socialism** 24pp

1010 **Productivity: For Whom?** Cannon, Les 16pp The Electricians' leader shortly to be a leading anti-CP figure.

1011 **Rents Must Not Go Up** MacEwen, Malcolm 12pp

1012 **Searchlight on the Tories** Lauchlan, William 16pp

1013 **The CP and the Labour Party** Pollitt, H. 12pp

1014 **The CP and the Role of the Branches: A Course for Branch Secretaries and Officials** 12pp

1015 **The Fight Goes On!** 4pp lf 'Communist Special'.

1016 **The Future for Miners** Ellis, Les 16pp

1017 **The Party of Socialism** Mahon, John 16pp

1018 **The Role of the CP: Marxist Study Themes No.10** 20pp

1019 **Time For More in the Pay Packet** Henderson, Sam 16pp

1020 **Vote for Life: Communist Policy, General Election May 1955** 4pp lf

1021 **Win the Local Councils** 24pp 2 eds in 1955 – Feb. and Nov.

1022 **Women in the British Labour and Democratic Movement: Part 1 – 1770-1850** 20pp lf d ?

1023 **Women in the British Labour and Democratic Movement: Part 2 – 1850-1900** 28pp lf d

1024 **Women in the British Labour and Democratic Movement: Part 3 – 1900-1921** 22pp lf d

1956

1025 **Automation: Friend or Foe?** Campbell, J.R. 16pp

1026 **CP 24th National Congress: Guide to Reporting Back** 4pp

1027 **End the Bans** Gollan, J. 16pp On orgs proscribed by the Labour Party (so-called Communist front orgs), and about the ban on Communists attending LP Conferences if delegated by their union.

1028 **Facts on Hungary** 8pp lf

1029 **Hungary: Some Notes on the Background** *Propaganda Dept* 26pp lf d

1030 **Marxist and Near-Marxist Historical Work Available in English** Holley, N. (ed.) *Historians' Group* 20pp lf

1031 **Political Report to 24th Congress** Pollitt, H. 32pp

1032 **Political Resolution for 24th Congress** 8pp lf Incl. Discussion Statement on 'The CP and Young People'.

1033 **Questions Posed by the 20th Congress of the CPSU** Togliatti, P. 12pp lf Published by 'World News'.

1034 **Rent Rebate Schemes Exposed** Fagan, Hymie 16pp

1035 **Report of EC for 24th Congress** 20pp

1036 **Resolutions and Proceedings: 24th Congress** 20pp

1037 **Rules** 12pp sf

1038 **Suez Crisis Special** 4pp lf

1039 **The CP and the Local Councils** 26pp

1040 **The People Will Decide: Speeches at the 24th National Congress** 56pp Speeches by Pollitt, Gollan, Matthews.

1041 **The Role of the CP: Reading and Study Programme** 4pp sf

1042 **Two-Session Syllabus on the 24th Congress of the CP** *Educ. Dept* 6pp lf d

1043 **Wanted! Homes at Lower Rents!** 4pp lf Local Election Special.

1044 **What Price Bread?** 4pp

1957

1045 **About Socialism: A Book for Women** Leigh, Bessie 40pp

1046 **Amendments Submitted by Party Organisations: Report of the Commission on IPD** 20pp lf

1047 **Amendments to Political Resolution: 25th Congress** 25pp lf Submitted by Branches and DCs.

1048 **Amendments to Rules** 24pp lf

1049 **Amendments to the 'BRS'** 34pp lf For 25th Congress.

1050 **An Introduction to Marxism: A 4 Months' Reading & Study Programme** 4pp sf

1051 **An Introduction to Marxism: Advanced Course** 4pp

1052 **British Railways** 12pp

1053 **BRS: New Text Prepared by EC After 25th Congress** 32pp

1054 **Draft Political Resolution (25th Congress)** 20pp

1055 **Draft Revised Text of BRS (25th Congress)** 34pp

1056 **For Peace! For Socialism! Statement of the World's CPs** 20pp Adopted in Moscow, Nov.

1057 **H Bomb Tests: End Them Now** Wainwright, William 12pp

1058 **Inner Party Democracy** 32pp

1059 **More on the Historical Experience of Proletarian Dictatorship** 60pp From 'People's Daily', Peking.

1060 **Now for Top Level Talks: Satellite Special** 4pp lf

1061 **On the Correct Handling of Contradictions Among the People** Mao Tse-Tung 16pp lf

1062 **Political Report to 25th Congress** Gollan, J. 24pp John Gollan worked full-time for the CP from 1932; he was General Secretary from 1956-76.

1063 **Repeal the Rent Act** 8pp lf

1064 **Report of 25th Congress** 78pp Incl. Gollan's 'Political Report', Matthews' on 'BRS', Mahon on 'IPD' plus Resolutions etc.

1065 **Report of Commission on Inner Party Democracy (25th Congress)** 60pp The Commission set up to produce this report included a wide range of views, but was inevitably weighted towards producing a safe pro-leadership line; a famous Minority Report was allowed – Christopher Hill introduced it to the 1957 Special Congress though it was mainly drafted by M. MacEwen. The whole episode was indicative of the limited amount of change that the leadership would or could accept after the trauma of the preceding 12 months.

1066 Report on BRS (25th Congress) Matthews, George 18pp

1067 Report on Inner Party Democracy (25th Congress) Mahon, John 14pp

1068 Some Hints for Party Tutors Klugmann, James *Educ. Dept* 15pp lf

1069 Study Outline on the 25th Party Congress *Educ. Dept* 13pp lf d

1070 Summary for Reporting, 25th Congress 4pp lf

1071 Syllabus on the Class Struggle *Educ. Dept* 28pp lf d Revised in 1962.

1072 The Rent Bill: What it Means to You 6pp lf

1073 The Role of the CP: Marxist Study Themes No.10 24pp An expanded ed. of the 1955 version.

1074 The Soviet Union and Socialism Rothstein, Andrew 100pp pb

1075 Why Not Nationalise? Gollan, J. 16pp Reply to Labour's 'Industry & Society' on public ownership.

1076 World News Discussion Supplement *World News* 24pp lf 3 issues, Jan.-March, of this supplement which consists of discussion contributions for 25th Congress.

1077 Your Chance to Get the Tories Out 8pp lf May elections.

1078 Your Child at School Morris, Max 14pp

1958

1079 A Lecture by Alan Bush on his Opera 'The Sugar Reapers (Guyana Johnny)' Bush, Alan *Music Group* 4pp Event held in the Purcell Room, South Bank Centre. ?

1080 Berlin: The Facts 4pp lf 'World News' Report, March 28.

1081 Build the Factory and Pit Branches *Org. Dept* 10pp lf d

1082 Close All U.S. Bases Wainwright, William 16pp

1083 Crisis in Aircraft: What Can be Done? 16pp

1084 Education: CP Policy 24pp

1085 Hands Off the Middle East! Jeffery, Nora 8pp

1086 Lecture Notes on the BRS *Educ. Dept* 8pp lf d

1087 Our Aim is Socialism: Syllabus for New Members *Educ. Dept* 19pp lf d Further eds in 1959 & 1962.

1088 Outlook for Mining Paynter, Will 16pp Intro. A. Horner.

1089 Syllabus on Political Economy *Educ. Dept* 34pp lf d Revised in 1960.

1090 Syllabus on Problems of the Advance to Socialism *Educ. Dept* 28pp lf d This was a draft syllabus, revised in 1962.

1091 The British Road to Socialism [new ed.] 30pp

1092 The CP and the Trade Unions Hart, Finlay 24pp Intro. A. Moffat.

1093 The Great All-Britain March: Souvenir Pictorial 4pp lf A rare event – a march solely organised by the CP to mobilise its members. June 29 1958.

1094 Which Way for Socialists? Gollan, J. 16pp

1959

1095 About Wages, Strikes, Stewards Crane, George 16pp

1096 Aims and Constitution 16pp sf

1097 All-African Peoples' Conference, Accra, Dec. 1958 *International Dept* 12pp lf

1098 Amendments to the Draft Political Resolution (26th Congress) 10pp lf

1099 Bibliography of Historical Writing in the Light of Marxism *Historians' Group* 31pp lf d New ed. of Marxist & Near-Marxist Historical Work Available in English. There had also been an ed. in 1958.

1100 Draft Aims and Constitution 4pp lf For 26th Congress.

1101 Draft Aims and Constitution with Amendments and Recommendations by the EC 16pp lf For 26th Congress.

1102 Draft Political Resolution 4pp lf For 26th Congress.

1103 Draft Standing Orders 4pp lf For 26th Congress.

1104 Higher Education in the Nuclear Age 24pp

1105 It's a Family Affair 4pp lf For local elections.

1106 **Men and Motors: A Policy for the Industry** 20pp

1107 **Millions Like Us: Mainly for Women** 4pp lf

1108 **Nyasaland Special: Tory Lies and Fake Plots Blown to Pieces by Commission** 4pp lf Reprinted from 'World News' Aug. 1.

1109 **Our Aim is Socialism: Syllabus for New Members** 12pp New ed.

1110 **Peace or H-Bomb War?** 4pp lf

1111 **Reading and Study Programme on 'Marxist Philosophy'** *Educ. Dept* 8pp d

1112 **Report of 26th Congress** 72pp

1113 **Report of EC for 26th Congress** 20pp

1114 **Resolutions from Branches and DCs** 4pp lf For 26th Congress.

1115 **Robert Burns Bi-Centenary Celebration: Programme** 4pp

1116 **Standing Orders for the Convening and Conduct of the National Party Congress** 2pp lf Adopted at 26th Congress, Easter 1959.

1117 **Syllabus on 'Marxism versus Reformism': Sessions 1-3** *Educ. Dept* 14pp lf d

1118 **Syllabus on Imperialism** *Educ. Dept* 25pp lf d

1119 **The Future for Dockland** 12pp

1120 **The Future in Your Hands** 16pp lf 'Communist Pictorial'.

1121 **What Next?** Gollan, J. 16pp

1122 **Your Vote Can Help Ban the Bomb** 4pp lf

1960

1123 **36 Million Communists Say... (Statement and Appeal of the World's CPs, Moscow)** 40pp

1124 **40 Fighting Years 1920-60** Campbell, J.R. 24pp History of CP.

1125 **40th Anniversary: Celebration Meeting, Illustrated Programme** 8pp

1126 **Africa: 1960** 4pp lf

1127 **Beware Sharks: Tory Rent and Housing Policy Exposed** Falber, Reuben 16pp

1128 **Freedom** Simon, Brian 24pp

1129 **Gaitskell or Socialism?** Gollan, J. 16pp

1130 **Harry Pollitt: A Tribute** 32pp

1131 **Homes and Rents: The Communist Answer** 4pp lf

1132 **Labour and the Bomb** Gollan, J. 10pp

1133 **London Landmarks (Marx, Engels, Lenin, Stalin)** 8pp Reprint of 1948 ed.; there was an enlarged one in 1963.

1134 **Notes on Trotskyism** *Educ. Dept* 22pp lf d

1135 **Report of EC to 27th Congress** 24pp

1136 **Shipbuilding: Looking Forward** Hart, Finlay 16pp

1137 **Spotight on Coal** Kane, Jock 16pp

1138 **Stand by the Congo** Dutt, R.P. 12pp

1139 **Standing Orders: Adopted at 26th Congress** 16pp lf

1140 **Syllabus on 'Marxism versus Reformism': Session 4 – The 1959 General Election and the Way Forward** 14pp lf d

1141 **Syllabus on 'Peace or War'** *Educ. Dept* 28pp lf d

1142 **The Communist Answer** 4pp lf

1143 **The German Menace: A Damning Exposure** Gollan, J. 8pp

1144 **The Money Game: Or How Much Do You Make for Your Boss?** Brown, Alan 8pp

1145 **Tutors' Guide to 'Syllabus on Peace or War'** *Educ. Dept* 4pp lf d

1146 **Woman Today** Keith, Molly 16pp

1961

1147 **A Six Months' Personal Study Programme on 'Fundamentals of Marxism-Leninism'** *Central Education Dept* 8pp ?

1148 **A World of Difference** 20pp lf Illustrated magazine format.

1149 **Amendments by Branches and DCs to the Draft Resolution on 'The CP and Young People'** 4pp lf For 27th Congress.

1150 **Amendments to the Aims and Constitution Submitted by Party Organisations to 27th Congress** 4pp lf

1151 **Draft Resolutions (for 27th Congress)** 12pp lf

1152 **End Terrorism in Iraq** Cox, Idris 12pp

1153 **For Your Family's Sake** 4pp lf

1154 **Independence from USA** 4pp lf

1155 **Let Nothing Divide Us** Holland, B. 8pp On TGWU.

1156 **No War Over Berlin** 4pp lf

1157 **Notes For Branch Classes and Discussions on the Meeting of the 81 CPs, Nov. 1960** *Educ. Dept* 18pp lf d

1158 **Notes on Fundamental Principles of Marxism** *Educ. Dept* 35pp lf d

1159 **Notes on Nationalisation** *Educ. Dept* 14pp lf d

1160 **Report of 27th Congress** 76pp

1161 **Resolutions from Branches** 6pp lf For 27th Congress.

1162 **Select Bibliography of the History of the British Labour Movement,1760-1939** *History Group* 24pp lf d A 2nd ed. was published in 1968 (36pp) ed. by E. Frow.

1163 **Sport: A CP Plan** Levenson, Stan 16pp

1164 **Syllabus on Fundamental Principles of Marxism** *Educ. Dept* 4-8pp lf Reprinted/revised in 1963 & 1966.

1165 **The Alternative to the Common Market** Bowman, Dave 16pp

1166 **The Development of Higher Education in Britain – Evidence to the Robbins Cttee** 30pp

1167 **The Money You Wear** Cohen, Hymie 12pp Fashion industry.

1168 **The Role of the CP: Syllabus** 24pp

1169 **The Strategy of Revenge: The Unceasing Aim of German Militarism** Henri, Ernst 36pp

1170 **The TV Tie Up** Baker, Bert 16pp

1171 **To British Jewry: A Call to Act** 4pp lf

1172 **Together Say No to Discrimination** Moss, John 16pp

1173 **Wages: The Tory Attack** 4pp lf

1962

1174 **A New Deal for Our Children** Wiles, Maurice 16pp

1175 **Britain Needs Coal** Taylor, Sam 16pp

1176 **Common Market: The Truth** 4pp lf

1177 **Co-ops: The Way Ahead** Ainley, David 16pp

1178 **Handbook For Members of the CP** 38pp sf

1179 **It's Time for a Change** 4pp lf

1180 **Moral Rearmament** *Press & Publicity Dept* 6pp lf d

1181 **More Pay for Engineers** Kerrigan, Peter 12pp

1182 **Our Aim is Socialism: Syllabus for New Members** 20pp New ed.

1183 **Say 'No' to the Common Market** Ainley, Ted 16pp

1184 **Smash the Pay Pause** Moffat, Abe 12pp

1185 **Study Guide to 'The British Labour Movement' by Tate & Morton** 32pp Based on Morton & Tate 'The British Labour Movement'. There was an earlier ed. in 1957, shortly after the book appeared.

1186 **Syllabus and Guide for Tutors on the New Programme adopted by 22nd Congress CPSU** *Educ. Dept* 18pp lf d

1187 **Syllabus on 'Communism and the World Today'** *Educ. Dept* 37pp lf d

1188 **The Dockers' Next Step** Kirby, Ted 12pp

1189 **The Railways and the People** Ahern, Tom 16pp

1190 **Who is to Blame?** Wainwright, William 16pp Nuclear weapons.

1191 **Your Vote is Worth Something When You Vote Communist** 4pp lf

1963

1192 **A Good Life: That's What We Want** 4pp lf

1193 **Amendments to Draft Political Resolution** 42pp lf For 28th Congress.

1194 **Beeching Answered** 4pp lf

1195 **Britain's Future (Speech to 28th Congress)** Gollan, J. 20pp

1196 **Communism and the World Today** 56pp

1197 **Communism: Your Questons Answered** Burns, Emile 4pp

1198 **Don't Be a Donkey** Etheridge, Dick 4pp lf On productivity in industry.

1199 **Draft Resolutions (for 28th Congress)** 16pp lf

1200 **Food and Farming** Dunman, Jack 18pp

1201 **London Landmarks: Where Marx, Engels and Lenin Lived and Worked** 12pp

1202 **New Days, New Ways: Communist Policy for Trade Unions** Campbell, J.R. 8pp

1203 **Notes and Guide for Tutors for Use with the Syllabus 'Communism and the World Today'** *Educ. Dept* 9pp lf d

NATIONAL PUBLICATIONS

1204 **Report of 28th Congress** 98pp

1205 **Report of EC to 28th Congress** 20pp

1206 **Restore the Unity of the International Communist Movement: EC Statement** 4pp lf

1207 **Sin, Security and the Tories** 4pp lf On the Profumo scandal.

1208 **Syllabus on 'The CP and the Labour Movement'** *Educ. Dept* 36pp lf d

1209 **The Case for Higher Wages** Campbell, J.R. 16pp

1210 **The Councils Need Communists** 28pp

1211 **The Future of Trade Unionsim** Kerrigan, Peter 14pp

1964

1212 **Britain '64: The Case for Socialism** 12pp lf Election manifesto.

1213 **Campaign Facts: General Election 1964** 52pp lf d

1214 **Communist Policy for Britain** 48pp Election manifesto.

1215 **Higher Pay and a Six-Hour Day: The Miners' Case** 4pp lf

1216 **How Will You Vote?** Falber, Reuben 16pp

1217 **Shakespeare: 400th Anniversary: Lecture** Kettle, Arnold *Cultural Cttee* 28pp lf d Kettle was a leading cultural spokesperson for the CP and a respected Marxist literary critic.

1218 **Syllabus on Capitalism and Socialism** *Educ. Dept* 6pp lf Reprinted from 'Comment'.

1219 **The Centenary of the First International: Speaker's Notes** 8pp lf d

1220 **The Councils Need New Policies, New People: Vote Communist** 4pp lf

1221 **The CP and Science** 4pp lf

1222 **Which Road?** Gollan, J. 48pp Reprint from 'MT', July.

1223 **Women and the General Election** 4pp lf

1965

1224 **8 Session Course: Introduction to Marxism-Leninism** *Educ. Dept* 22pp lf d

1225 **8 Session Course; Political Economy** *Central Education Department* 19pp lf d ?

1226 **A Future for the Miners** 8pp lf

1227 **A New Deal for Women** 8pp lf

1228 **Britain's Crisis: The Communist Solution** 16pp lf

1229 **'British Capitalism Today': Tutor's Guide & Notes** *Educ. Dept* 10pp lf d

1230 **Changing Britain: The Need for the CP** Matthews, Betty 16pp

1231 **Conference of Communist and Workers' Parties in European Capitalist Countries** 12pp lf

1232 **Draft Resolutions for 29th Congress** 14pp lf

1233 **Engineering Wages: An Analysis and Exposure** 10pp lf d

1234 **Hands Off the Trade Unions** Campbell, J.R. 16pp

1235 **Outlines for 8 Session Course on Marxist Philosophy** *Educ. Dept* 11pp lf d

1236 **Pre-Congress Discussion** 4pp lf For 29th Congress. Supplement to 'Comment' (insert) – 8 issues.

1237 **Racialism: Cause and Cure** Bourne, Harry 14pp

1238 **Report from Vietnam** Mahon, John 12pp

1239 **Report of 29th Congress** 72pp

1240 **Report of EC to 29th Congress** 24pp

1241 **Report of the Committee on Party Organisation** 24pp

1242 **Syllabus on 'British Capitalism Today'** *Educ. Dept* 28pp lf d

1243 **The Communists and TV** Baker, Bert 12pp

1244 **The International Communist Movement: EC Statements** 28pp

1245 **The Role of the CP: Syllabus** 26pp

1246 **Tutor's Guide to 'British Capitalism Today'** *Educ. Dept* 10pp lf d

1247 **William Gallacher: A Great Working Class Leader** 16pp

1966

1248 **Campaign Facts: General Election 1966** 48pp lf d

1249 **Documents for Electoral Schools** 18pp lf d

1250 **Electoral Reform: Proposals Submitted by CP to the Speaker's Conference on Electoral Reform** 16pp lf d

1251 **Give the Girls Their Due ... Equal Pay No Less!** 4pp lf

1252 **Incomes Policy: The Great Wage Freeze Trick** Ramelson, Bert 22pp

1253 **New Britain, People's Britain: General Election Manifesto** 16pp

1254 **Notes on How the Councils Work** *Electoral Dept* 36pp lf d

1255 **Problem of British Motors** 32pp lf d

1256 **Syllabus 'The CP, The Labour Movement and the Way Forward'** *Educ. Dept* 29pp lf d

1257 **The Case for Socialism in the Sixties** Gollan, J. 98pp

1258 **The Future of NATO** 4pp lf

1259 **We Want Forty: The Case for the Seamen** Coward, Jack 12pp

1967

1260 **A Communist Plan to Safeguard Jobs and Wages** 8pp lf

1261 **A Reader's Guide to the Study of Marxism** Cohen, Jack & Klugmann, James 82pp ?

1262 **Amendments and Resolutions from Branches and Districts for 30th Congress** 74pp lf

1263 **Congress Discussion** 4-81pp lf For 30th Congress. Supplement to 'Comment' (insert) – 6 issues.

1264 **Draft of BRS (for 30th Congress)** 44pp

1265 **Draft Resolutions for 30th Congress** 8pp lf

1266 **Keep Out of the Common Market** 16pp

1267 **Motor Industry Special: Insecurity for Car Workers** Aaronovitch, Sam 4pp lf

1268 **Questions of Ideology and Culture: EC Statement** 12pp

1269 **Report of 30th Congress** 36pp

1270 **Report of EC to 30th Congress** 20pp

1271 **Revolution 1917-67** Ogden, Dennis 24pp

1272 **The Background to the Middle East Crisis** 8pp lf

1273 **The Middle East: Crisis, Causes, Solution** Ramelson, Bert 42pp

1274 **Tutor's Guide for Discussion on 50th Anniversary of the October Revolution** *Educ. Dept* 12pp lf d

1275 **Vietnam: Stop America's Criminal War** Montagu, Ivor 18pp

1276 **What Socialism Offers Key People** 12pp lf d Addressed to 'foremen & technicians in British Industry'.

1277 **Whither China?** Dutt, R.P. 42pp

1968

1278 **BRS: Draft as Amended Following 30th Congress** 44pp

1279 **Communist Unity Convention, 1920: Official Report – Reprint** 72pp pb

1280 **Crisis: The Communist Answer** Gollan, J. 22pp

1281 **Donovan Exposed** Ramelson, Bert 16pp

1282 **For Democracy and Advance in Higher Education** 4pp lf ?

1283 **From Rebel to Revolutionary** 4pp On the radicalisation of students.

1284 **Homes, Jobs, Imigration: The Facts** Bellamy, Joan 16pp

1285 **Select Bibliography of the History of the British Labour Movement, 1760-1939** Frow, Ruth (ed.) 36pp lf Enlarged version of 1961 ed.

1286 **The British Road to Socialism** 72pp The revised ed. which was published in Oct.

1287 **The Case for Higher Wages** McGahey, Mick 18pp

1288 **The Royal Commission on Trades Unions and Employers' Associations: A Memorandum** 44pp lf d

1289 **The Socialist Revolution** Klugmann, James & Jacques, Martin 32pp Articles from MS.

1290 **Tutor's Guide and Study Material for Discussion of BRS** *Educ. Dept* 36pp lf d

1969

1291 **Amendments and Resolutions from Branches and Districts for 31st Congress** 64pp lf

1292 **Co-ops: The Future** Dunman, Jack 18pp

1293 **CP May Day Special: Kill the Bill** 4pp lf

1294 **Documents of the World Communist Conference** 48pp

1295 **Draft Resolutions for 31st Congress** 8pp lf

1296 **Keep the Unions Free** Ramelson, Bert 16pp

1297 **Nationalism and Internationalism: Part 1** *Educ. Dept* 30pp lf Based on 2 lectures by J. Klugmann.

1298 **Nato – No! Defence or Danger!** Montagu, Ivor 12pp

1299 **Northern Ireland: Civil Rights and Political Wrongs** Greaves, C. Desmond 12pp

1300 **Official Report of the Socialist Unity Conference (1911)** 32pp Reprint.

1301 **Pay Up Now!** 4pp lf On equal pay for women.

1302 **Red Bases in the Colleges** Woddis, Jack 7pp lf Reprinted from 'Comment'.

1303 **Report of 31st Congress** 40pp Reprint, spiral bound, of 2 issues of 'Comment' (Nov. 29 and Dec. 6).

1304 **Report of EC to 31st Congress** 20pp

1305 **Speech to the World Communist Conference** Gollan, J. 12pp

1306 **The Common Market: Why Britain Should not Join** Gollan, J. 28pp

1307 **The Communist View** Costello, Mick 18pp

1308 **The First Annual Conference of the BSP (1912)** 72pp Reprint.

1309 **The National Future of Scotland and Wales (Speech to 31st Congress)** Wyper, Hugh 4pp lf

1310 **The Victims of Whiggery, etc.** Loveless, George *London* 32pp Reprint of 1838 ed.

1311 **Ultra-Leftism in Britain** Reid, Betty 58pp

1312 **Vietnam and Peace Appeals from the World Communist Conference** 10pp

1970

1313 **Carr's Bill and How to Kill It** Ramelson, Bert 24pp

1314 **December 8th: National Day of Action: Kill the Bill** 4pp lf Industrial Relations Bill.

1315 **Election '70: Campaign Guide** 45pp Detailed political analysis of domestic politics and some material on key international issues,

with CP's position and proposals. Probably not produced for sale.

1316 **Lenin in Britain** Rothstein, Andrew 32pp

1317 **Notes for Those Introducing New Members Discussions** *Educ. Dept* 5pp lf d

1318 **Notes for Tutors: Challenging the Tories and Right Wing Labour** *Educ. Dept* 4pp lf d

1319 **Notes for Tutors: Socialism or Managed Capitalism** *Educ. Dept* 4pp lf d

1320 **People Before Profits: General Election Manifesto** 16pp

1321 **Productivity Agreements** Ramelson, Bert 24pp

1322 **Speeches and Documents of 6th Conference, May 1924: Facsimile Edition** 80pp pb

1323 **The Future of Man** Klugmann, James 40pp

1324 **The Menace of the Monopolies** Jacques, Martin 1970 20pp

1325 **What is the Socialist Way Forward?** Gollan, J. 16pp

1971

1326 **Amendments by Branches and District Cttees. for 32nd Congress** 86pp lf

1327 **Bangladesh, Pakistan, India: What Next?** Rahman, Syedur 8pp

1328 **Britain and the Socialist Revolution** Matthews, Betty 24pp

1329 **Common Market: For and Against** 4pp lf

1330 **Common Market: The Tory White Paper Exposed** Bellamy, Ron 24pp

1331 **Draft Resolutions for 32nd Congress** 12pp lf

1332 **Fraternal Greetings to 32nd Congress** 20pp These generally formal messages and speeches from other parties were occasionally enlivened by a message from a CP or liberation movement involved in crucial struggles (e.g. Vietnam or S. Africa).

1333 **Further and Higher Education in the 1970s** *Higher Education Cttee* 34pp lf d

1334 **Ireland: A Communist View** 4pp lf

1335 **Kill the Bill: National Industrial Action! The TUC Must Lead** 4pp lf Articles by Ramelson & Chater.

1336 **No Sackings, No Closures** 4pp lf

1337 **No to the Common Market Sell Out** 4pp lf

1338 **Report of 32nd Congress** 44pp Special spiral bound ed. of 'Comment' Dec. 18.

1339 **Report of EC to 32nd Congress** 16pp

1340 **Rhodesia: A Communist View** 4pp lf

1341 **Science and Technology, Marxism and Society: Report of Science & Technology Section of 3rd CUL** Chater, Tony et al. 20pp lf d

1342 **State Monopoly Capitalism: Part 1** *Educ. Dept* 8pp lf

1343 **State Monopoly Capitalism: Part 2** *Educ. Dept* 16pp lf

1344 **The International Firms and the European Working Class** 95pp Speeches at Conference of CPs of capitalist countries of Europe.

1345 **The Paris Commune: A Study Outline** Ainley, Ben *Educ. Dept* 6pp lf d

1346 **UCS: The Fight for the Right to Work** Murray, Alex 20pp

1347 **Unite Against Racialism: Defeat the Immigration Bill** Bellamy, Joan 12pp

1348 **Zionism: A Socialist View** Kaye, Solly 10pp

1972

1349 **'Britain and the Socialist Revolution': How to Open a Discussion** *Educ. Dept* 8pp lf d

1350 **Nationalism and Internationalism** Woddis, Jack 28pp

1351 **No Rent Rises** 4pp lf

1352 **Northern Ireland: Branch Study Theme** *Educ. Dept* lf d

1353 **Papers Presented to the Peace Consultative Committee** Chater, Tony & Woddis, Jack 16pp lf d

1354 **Stop the Trial: Free Angela Now!** 4pp lf Angela Davis.

1355 **Take a Pill: The Drug Industry – Private or Public?** Robson, John 50pp

1356 **The International Monetary Crisis** Menell, W. *Economic Cttee* 26pp lf Occasional Paper that took the place of 'Economic Bulletin' No.21.

1357 **The James Report on Teacher Education and Training** 8pp lf d ?

1358 **The Miners' Victory: A Victory for All** 4pp lf

1359 **The NHS Co. Ltd.: Notes on the Health Service Re-organisation** 14pp lf

1360 **The NHS in England and Wales** Hart, Julian Tudor *Health Sevices Advisory Cttee* 32pp Reprinted from 'MT' Nov. 1971.

1361 **Why Unemployment? Discussion Theme for Branches** *Educ. Dept* 10pp lf d

1362 **Women: The Road to Equality and Socialism** Small, Rosemary 22pp

1363 **Women's Status: Part 2 – Family; Equal Pay** 12pp lf d

1364 **Women's Status: Provision for Under Fives; Family Planning; Education and Training** 10pp lf d In effect, this is Part 1.

1973

1365 **A Guide to Opening Discussions on 'Time to Change Course'** *Educ. Dept* 8pp lf d ?

1366 **Amendments to Draft Resolutions for 33rd Congress** 62pp lf

1367 **Britain and the Irish Crisis** McLennan, Gordon 20pp

1368 **Chile: Solidarity with Popular Unity** 24pp

1369 **Draft Amendments for 33rd Congress** 12pp lf

1370 **Draft Resolutions for 33rd Congress** 12pp lf

1371 **Heath's War on Your Wage Packet** Ramelson, Bert 22pp

1372 **Inflation: Study Theme** *Educ. Dept* 20pp lf Cover by 'Eccles'.

1373 **Public Ownership and Control** Chater, Tony 20pp

1374 **Report of EC to 33rd Congress** 20pp

1375 **Resolutions from Branches and DCs for 33rd Congress** 38pp lf

1376 **Smash Phase 3** Ramelson, Bert 20pp

1377 **Stop the Slaughter of the British Steel Industry** 4pp lf

1378 **Students** Cook, Dave 24pp

1379 **The Environmental Crisis** Robinson, Pauline 22pp

1380 **The Way Out of the Crisis** 4pp lf

1381 **Time to Change Course** Woddis, Jack 150pp pb

1974

1382 **About Marxism** *Educ. Dept* 34pp lf ?

1383 **Challenge Big Business: Build a New Britain – Election Manifesto** 16pp

1384 **Class Structure** 40pp lf Articles from 'MT'.

1385 **Marxism and the Family** *Educ. Dept* 20pp lf Articles from 'MT'.

1386 **Marxist Reader's Guide on the Revolutionary Role of the CP** *Educ. Dept* 2pp lf d

1387 **Marxist Reader's Guide on the State** *Educ. Dept* 2pp lf Very basic, only lists 24 items.

1388 **Political Economy: A CP Study Course** *Educ. Dept* 28pp lf

1389 **Questions and Answers About Capitalism** Purton, John *Educ. Dept* 8pp lf d Reprinted from 'MS'.

1390 **Questions and Answers About Racialism: Branch Discussion Theme** 4pp lf

1391 **Social Contract: Cure-All or Con-Trick?** Ramelson, Bert 28pp

1392 **Some Thoughts on Gramsci** Riva, S. *Educ. Dept* 10pp lf

1393 **The 1859 'Preface to a Contribution to the Critique of Political Economy' by Karl Marx** Gunn, Richard *Philosophy Group* 10pp lf Paper No.1 by the Philosophy Group.

1394 **The Role of CP Branches** 50pp sf

1395 **There is a Way Out** 4pp lf

1396 **Which Way for Labour?** Cohen, Gerry 26pp

1975

1397 **34th Congress: Report Guide** 8pp lf

1398 **Amendments to Draft Resolutions plus Resolutions from Branches and DCs (34th Congress)** 96pp lf

1399 **Amendments to Rules for 34th Congress** 8pp lf

1400 **Britain's Crisis: Cause and Cure** Matthews, George 30pp

1401 **Discussion Theme on the Struggle for a Democratic Press** *Educ. Dept* 10pp lf d Based on 'Poor Men's Guardian' by S. Harrison.

1402 **Draft Resolutions for 34th Congress** 14pp lf

1403 **Inner Party Democracy** 32pp

1404 **Leisure and Recreation in Britain Today** Bushell, Terry 18pp

1405 **Marxism as a Science** Jones, Howard *Philosophy Group* 14pp lf d

1406 **Northern Ireland: A Programme for Action** Brennan, Irene 30pp

1407 **Official Report of 34th Congress** 44pp lf Double issue of 'Comment' in spiral binding.

1408 **Out of the Common Market** 4pp lf

1409 **Political Economy** *Educ. Dept* 26pp lf

1410 **Portugal: Support the Revolution** Woddis, Jack 12pp

1411 **Quit the Market: Join the World** McLennan, Gordon 34pp Cover by 'Eccles'.

1412 **Racialism At Work** 4pp lf

1413 **Report of EC to 34th Congress** 20pp

1414 **The Fight Against Racialism in Britain** Bellamy, Joan *Educ. Dept* 22pp

1415 **The Rates Explosion: How to Defuse it** Falber, Reuben 16pp

1416 **Universities and Capitalism: The Present Crisis** Jacques, Martin *National University Staffs Advisory Cttee* 12pp lf Reprinted from 'MT', July.

1417 **Victory in Vietnam** Gollan, J. 32pp

1976

1418 **Britain Needs Socialism** Falber, Reuben 28pp

1419 **CP Guide to the Conduct of Local Elections** 22pp lf d

1420 **Democracy and the Fight for Socialism** Matthews, Betty *Educ. Dept* 22pp lf d Reprint of articles from 'MS'.

1421 **Discussion on Socialist Democracy** 34pp lf Contributions to the debate initiated by Gollan's article in 'MT' Jan. 1976 'Socialist Democracy: Some Problems', and not published in 'MT' due to lack of space.

1422 **Electoral Bulletin No.2, Nov.** 6pp lf d

1423 **Farming to Feed Britain** Page, Wilf 28pp

1424 **For Peace, Security, Co-operation and Social Progress in Europe: Document Adopted by 29 Communist and Workers' Parties of Europe** 42pp 7 statements on the conference by EC, July.

1425 **Into Action: The Campaign on Teacher Unemployment** Bloomfield, Jon 16pp

1426 **One Race, The Human Race** 8pp lf

1427 **Socialist Democracy: Some Problems** Gollan, J. 38pp lf Important document in the history of CPGB's analysis of Soviet Union.

1428 **Southern Africa: Which Side is Britain On?** Woddis, Jack 12pp

1429 **The Economics of Capitalism** Harrison, Mark *Educ. Dept* 42pp lf Cover & design by Richard Hill.

1430 **The Motor Industry** 4pp lf

1431 **The Soviet Union: State Capitalist or Socialist?** Purdy, David 48pp sf Critique of I.S. position. Reply in 'I.S.' Sept. 1976.

1432 **Women, Oppression and Liberation: Part 1 – The Beginning** *Educ. Dept* 30pp lf An attractively produced booklet reflecting the impact of feminism on the CP & a glimmer of awareness of the importance of design after years of duplicated material from the Educ. Dept.

1977

1433 **Amendments to the Draft of the 'BRS'** 445pp For 35th Congress. 4 vols.

1434 **BRS Draft** 36pp lf

1435 **Bury the Social Contract** Ramelson, Bert 36pp

1436 **How October 1917 Changed the World** Woddis, Jack 24pp Uncritical celebration of Russian Revolution at height of Eurocommunist influence in CP.

1437 **Northern Ireland** *Educ. Dept* 14pp lf d

1438 **October Revolution: 60th Anniversary** *Educ. Dept* 12pp lf d

1439 **Official Report of 35th National Congress** 28pp lf 2 issues of 'Comment' in spiral binding.

1440 **Report of EC to 35th Congress** 26pp

1441 **The Communist Party's Evidence to the Royal Commission on the NHS: What Kind of Health Service?** *Health Advisory Committee* 28pp ?

1442 **The CP and Unity: An Interview with G. McLennan** 26pp

1443 **The Revolutionary Party** *Educ. Dept* 16pp lf

1444 **The West German Face of McCarthyism** Latham, Hugh *West European Cttee* 18pp

1445 **Trotskyist Organisations in Britain** *Trotskyism Study Group* 20pp lf Various groups, advisories & sub-committees flourished in the mid 1970s-early 1980s, but usually did not publish much.

1446 **Women At Work** 8pp

1447 **Women, Oppression and Liberation: Part 2 – Struggle Today** *Educ. Dept* 28pp lf

1978

1448 **A Building Industry for the People** 4pp lf

1449 **A Knife at the Throat of Us All** Cook, Dave 32pp On the rise of the extreme right.

1450 **Class, Unity and Alliance** *Educ. Dept* 16pp lf

1451 **Cut the Dole Queues** Costello, Mick 18pp

1452 **Long Term Strategy for Energy Policy** *Science & Technology Sub Cttee* 24pp lf d

1453 **People's Festival Programme, Alexandra Palace June 18** 20pp lf

1454 **Racism: How to Combat It** *Race Relations Cttee* 10pp lf

1455 **Reformism and Revolution** Gollan, J. 82pp pb

1456 **Report of EC Sub-Committee on 'Morning Star'** 24pp The 1977 Congress had voted for a commission to look at all aspects of the 'MS', against the wishes of ed. T. Chater; the implication of the vote was a deep dissatisfaction with the contents & style of the paper but the Report's criticisms were mild.

1457 **The British Road to Socialism** 62pp The final version.

1458 **The Common Market Fraud** Pocock, Gerry 28pp

1459 **The Comprehensive School** 8pp lf

1979

1460 **16-19 ... The Age of Opportunity? The Education and Training of the 16-19's** *Educ. Sub Cttee* 8pp lf

1461 **36th Congress Report** SEE 'COMMENT' DEC. 1.

NATIONAL PUBLICATIONS

1462 **A Charter of Democratic Rights** 12pp lf

1463 **Amendments to EC Resolutions for 36th Congress** 124pp

1464 **Amendments to Report of Commission on IPD for 36th Congress** 134pp

1465 **Amendments to Rules Submitted to 36th Congress** 10pp

1466 **Draft Resolutions & EC Amendments on IPD for Congress** 16pp lf

1467 **End the Ban** 14pp 'Published by a group of Communist EETPU members'. ?

1468 **Higher Education: A New Perspective** *Educ. Sub Cttee* 10pp lf

1469 **No Racist Immigration Laws** Sharma, Vishnu 20pp

1470 **People Before Profit! Communist Election Manifesto** 4pp lf

1471 **Report of EC to 36th Congress** 24pp

1472 **Report of the Commission on IPD with Alternative Proposals and Comments of the EC** 62pp lf The 1977 Congress set up a new Commission on internal structure and democracy; its Report to the 1979 Congress, together with alternative, more radical suggestions, did not lead to any major changes.

1473 **Stop the Tory Wreckers** 4pp lf

1474 **The Case For Trade Unions** Halpin, Kevin 20pp

1475 **The Right to Choose? CP Discussion Pamphlet on Abortion** 24pp lf

1980

1476 **A Policy Statement on Secondary Education** 24pp ?

1477 **A Real Future for Steel** 12pp ?

1478 **Act Now to End Mass Unemployment** Bolton, George 26pp

1479 **All For the Cause: The Communist Party, 1920-80** Matthews, George 32pp lf

1480 **Defeat the Anti-Union Laws** Costello, Mick 26pp

1481 **Dismantling the Health Service: A Reply to 'Patients First'** *Social Services Cttee* 8pp

1482 **Money Matters: How CP Branches Raise Money for Poltical Campaigning** *National Finance Cttee* 22pp ?

1483 **Power and Prejudice = Racism – Discussion Pack** *Educ. Dept* 40 loose pages. ?

1484 **Revolutionary Strategy in the 80s – Discussion Pack** *Educ. Dept*

1485 **The Case for Peace and Disarmament** Chater, Tony 32pp

1486 **The Common Market: Let's Get Out** *EEC Study Group* 60pp

1487 **Town Hall Democracy: NALGO and the Local State** 12pp

1488 **Women, Oppression and Liberation – Part 3: Women, Liberation and Socialism** *Educ. Dept* 18pp lf

1981

1489 **37th Congress Report** SEE 'COMMENT' DEC. 5.

1490 **Amendments to Rules and Standing Orders for 37th Congress** 12pp

1491 **Black and Blue: Racism and the Police** 32pp Based on transcript of a conference; contrib. include S. Hall, T. Bunyan, V. Sharma et al.

1492 **Draft Resolutions from EC for 37th Congress** 13pp lf

1493 **Engineering: The Way Forward** 4pp lf

1494 **Food for Thought: Discussion Document on Food and Agriculture** *Science & Technology Sub Cttee* 24pp ?

1495 **Introduction to Feminism – Education Pack** *Educ. Dept*

1496 **It's Our Future** 4pp lf ?

1497 **Local Politics and Revolutionary Strategy – Education Pack** *Educ. Dept*

1498 **Marxism and Britain Today – Introductory Discussion Pack** *Educ. Dept*

1499 **Oppose Tory Policies** McLennan, Gordon 36pp

1500 **Pre-Congress Discussion Journal No.1** Sept; No. 2 Oct. (37th Congress) 10pp/53pp lf

1501 **Railways for the People** 4pp lf

1502 **Reading Marxism (CP Education Notes)** *Educ. Dept* 12pp lf d

1503 **Report of EC for 37th Congress** 26pp

1504 **South Africa: Time Runs Out for the White Laager – Education Pack** ?

1505 **The Road from Thatcherism – Education Pack** *Educ. Dept* Based on S. Aaronovitch's book of same name. ?

1506 **We're on the March** 4pp lf The People's March for Jobs.

1507 **When the People Arose** Morton, A.L. 32pp On Peasants' Revolt 1381.

1982

1508 **British Print: Victim of Marauders** 4pp lf

1509 **Childcare: A Question of Choice? – A CP Discussion Document** 28pp ?

1510 **Communications for the Community** *Industrial Dept* 16pp On privatisation of BT & the Post Office. ?

1511 **Condition Critical: Private Medicine and the NHS** Iliffe, Steve 40pp

1512 **Education For Adults** *Educ. Sub Cttee* 20pp

1513 **Health Matters! Policy Statements on Dismantling the Health Service etc.** *Health Advisory Committee* 20pp ?

1514 **On the Road: Activities for Branch Development – Education Pack**

1515 **Poland – Education Pack** *Educ. Dept*

1516 **Racism in Britain – Discussion Pack** *Educ. Dept* Same text as 'Power & Prejudice = Racism'.

1517 **Racism in Britain: Tutor's Notes** *Educ. Dept* 6pp lf

1518 **Tebbit's Bill: Kill It!** Costello, Mick 20pp

1519 **The 'Don't Care' Tories** 4pp lf

1520 **The Battle for the Town Hall** 4pp lf ?

1521 **The Middle East … In the Eye of the Storm** 4pp ?

1522 **The SDP: Centre Forward – Education Pack** ?

1523 **Their Fingers on the Button** 4pp lf

1524 **Two-Way Street: Arts and the Community** *Arts & Leisure Cttee* 16pp lf

1983

1525 **38th Congress Report** SEE 'FOCUS' NO.14, DEC. 1983.

1526 **Britain Needs Jobs not Bombs** 4pp lf Election broadsheet. ?

1527 **Britain's Housing Scandal** 4pp lf ?

1528 **Bullying the Backyard** 6pp lf US in Latin America.

1529 **Communist Party 'Star' Campaign Guide** 10pp lf ?

1530 **Discussion 38: Pre-Congress Journal (38th Congress)** 12pp/45pp lf 2 issues.

1531 **Draft Congress Resolutions from the EC (38th Congress)** 16pp lf

1532 **Higher Education: Survival or Transformation?** *Educ. Advisory Sub Cttee* 20pp

1533 **Report of EC for 38th Congress** 33pp

1534 **The Co-operative Movement: Problems, Solutions and the Way Ahead** Hodgson, Geoff *Co-op Advisory Cttee* 20pp lf

1535 **The Primary School** *Educ. Advisory Cttee* 31pp lf

1984

1536 **Cable and Satellite TV** Landis, Harry *Industrial Dept* 10pp lf ?

1537 **Common Cause: Trade Unionists and Ireland** Myant, Chris *Irish Advisory/Industrial Department* 10pp lf

1538 **Primary Care and the Crisis in the Cities** *Social Services Advisory Cttee* 4pp ?

1539 **Proportional Representation** Peck, John 18pp

1540 **Solidarity with the Miners** 4pp lf ?

1541 **The Education and Training of the 16-19 Age Group: A Discussion Statement** *Education Advisory* 8pp lf Completely different document to '16-19 … The Age of Opportunity? The Education and Training of the 16-19s' ?

1542 **War and Peace** Cox, John 16pp lf

1543 **William Morris Now: Socialism by Design** Simon, Roger 28pp lf One of the most attractive pamphlets produced by the CP.

1544 **Work for Peace** Cox, John 4pp lf Reprint of article from 'MS' & Congress Resolution.

1985

1545 **39th Congress Report** SEE 'FOCUS' 23 MAY 1985.

1546 **40 Years After the Defeat of Fascism** 4pp lf

1547 **Amendments to Resolution 'Unite the Party Around the BRS': For 39th Congress** 4 vols – 377pp in total.

1548 **Britain's Sexual Counter-Revolutionaries and Infertility: A Suitable Case for Treatment** 8pp lf Reprint of 2 articles from 'MT'.

1549 **CPVE: Certificate of Pre-Vocational Education** *Educ. Advisory Cttee* 20pp

1550 **Document from Congress Appeals Committee for 39th Congress** 55pp lf 'Confidential: For Delegates Only'. Documents submitted by those disciplined since 38th Congress.

1551 **Draft Resolution from EC: 'Unite the Party Around the BRS' – For 39th Congress** 4pp lf

1552 **International Bulletin [2]** *International Dept* 14pp Sept. Very short-lived publication (maybe 2 issues?) produced by Gerry Pocock.

1553 **Life on the Margins: The Politics of Mass Poverty** Booth, Alan 32pp lf

1554 **Pre-Congress Discussion Bulletin** 9pp lf Only 1 issue. Other discussion contributions in 'Focus'.

1555 **The Miners' Strike Assessed** 16pp lf Reprinted from 'MT', April.

1986

1556 **Defend Comprehensive Schools** 38pp

1557 **Guidelines For Men** *National Women's Advisory* 4pp lf This pamphlet was issued free, unlike practically all the others in this bibliography, but is so unusual for any organisation that it merits an entry.

1558 **Guidelines on Childcare** *National Women's Advisory* 4pp lf ?

1559 **Spain** Burns, Emile 16pp Reprint of 1936 pamphlet.

1560 **The Roots of Thatcherism** Priscott, Dave 10pp lf ?

1561 **The Threat to Higher Education** 8pp

1562 **The Way Forward on the Railways** *Rails Advisory Group* 18pp

1563 **Trade Unions: The New Reality** Carter, Pete 52pp lf Carter, a well-known Birmingham building worker activist, became the CP Industrial Organiser; he was viewed with suspicion from some on the 'hard left' because of his openness to new social forces & new thinking.

1987

1564 **40th Congress Report** SEE 'NEWS AND VIEWS' DEC.

1565 **40th Congress: Pre-Congress Discussion – Longer Contributions** 8pp lf

1566 **A Guide to Money Making for Political Purposes** 16pp Published by '7 Days'. ?

1567 **Amendments to 'The New Challenge Facing Britain's Labour and Democratic Movements' (40th Congress)** 100pp

1568 **Amendments to Rule by EC: 40th Congress** 15pp

1569 **Branch and District Amendments for 40th Congress** 55pp/100pp 2 parts.

1570 **Branch and District Resolutions for 40th Congress** 48pp/63pp 2 parts.

1571 **Document from Congress Appeals Committee (40th Congress)** 23pp Details of disciplinary action and in some cases appeals against expulsion. 'Confidential' – for delegates only.

1572 **Fallout With the Tories** 4pp lf Post Chernobyl. ?

1573 **How to Beat the Tories and Go One Better: Election Manifesto** 4pp lf

1574 **Lessons in Elitism** Simon, Brian 4pp lf Reprint from 'MT'. This pamphlet was also reprinted by Midlands District.

1575 **Palestine** 8pp lf

1576 **Racism and Schools** Ebbutt, Keith & Pearce, Bert (ed.) 60pp pb ?

1577 **Report of EC for 40th Congress** 22pp

1578 **Statements on International Situations and Campaigns: For 40th Congress** 8pp lf

1579 **The CP and the PPPS & 'MS': Amendments for Congress** 55pp

1580 **The CP's Response to the Consultative Papers of the Secretary of State for Education & Science** *Educ. Advisory Cttee* 8pp

1988

1581 **A Health Service for the Nineties** 14pp lf Published by 'Medicine In Society'. ?

1582 **Forward to Freedom: The Politics of Apartheid** Hudson, Kate (ed.) *International Cttee* 32pp

1583 **Love in a Cold Climate** 4pp lf Gay & Lesbian rights.

1584 **Mick's Story** McGahey, Mick 4pp lf Very short autobiog. pamphlet. ?

1585 **Palestine: A Communist Party Broadsheet – The Uprising in the Occupied Territories** 4pp lf ?

1586 **Poll Tax: Thatcher's Flagship: How to Sink It** 8pp lf

1587 **Post Office Privatisation – Behind the Hype** Richards, Peter 10pp lf 1,000 printed.

1588 **Speeches at the Memorial Meeting for Leslie Morton** History Group 50pp

1589 **Trade Unions into the Nineties** 14pp lf ?

1989

1590 **41st Congress Report** SEE 'NEWS AND VIEWS' DEC.

1591 **Draft of 'Manifesto For New Times'** 40pp lf

1592 **For Fair Votes** 4pp lf On Proportional Representation.

1593 **Redraft of 'Manifesto For New Times'** 36pp lf

1594 **Report of Work of EC for Congress** 24pp

1990

1594a **42nd Congress Report** SEE 'CHANGES' Dec. 22 1990 & Jan. 8 1991. Preceding issue also has material on this Special Congress.

1595 **Amendments to Draft Resolution (for 42nd Congress)** 106pp

1596 **Congress Views** 4 issues: Sept. to Dec. 12-24pp. Pre-Congress discussion.

1597 **Draft Resolution: For 42nd Special Congress** 12pp lf

1598 **Looking to the Future?** McKay, Ian 4pp lf

1599 **Manifesto For New Times: A Strategy For The 1990s** *CP in association with L&W* 96pp pb The CP's final programme. 7,000 printed. 22,000 copies of 'MT' Oct. 1988 had also been printed – which was a special issue of 'New Times'.

1600 **Notes on Local Income Tax** 4pp lf

1991

1601 **43rd Congress Report** SEE 'NEW TIMES' NO.1, NOV. 30.

1602 **A War Too Far** 16pp lf On Gulf War. The final pamphlet from the CP.

1603 **Amendments (to Draft Constitution) for 43rd Congress** 53pp lf

1604 **EC Comments on Amendments to Rule: For 43rd Congress** 12pp lf

2. Local Publications

This chapter includes all pamphlets published by local CP organisations – Districts, Areas, Branches etc. Scotland and Wales are treated as they were within the CP, i.e. basically as Districts, but with more importance.

All are published by the District Committee unless stated (or in very rare cases this may not be known); when published by Areas or Branches, I have listed the name that appears on the pamphlet. In some early cases, up to 1936, the organisation is called 'local' or 'group' rather than branch.

Areas (or Boroughs in London's case) consisted of groups of branches (both local and factory) within a District and had a more advisory status than the formal Districts. Areas did have biennial Conferences that elected Area Committees and accepted Reports of Work and passed resolutions, but these could not affect Party policy in the way the biennial District Congresses could. Most District Secretaries, certainly of the larger Districts, would automatically be expected to be on the Executive Committee. This did produce some anomalies where Areas, especially in industrial regions, could have more members and be more influential than Districts. Regional identity clashes and rivalries were not unknown.

For clarity, I have only used the District names that were in existence from the later period of the CP's existence. As in local government, there were organisational changes at various times: for instance, the Lancashire and Cheshire District became the North West District, and in the late 1980s Merseyside finally achieved its long-sought District status, breaking free from the North West District. For the purposes of this book, I have only used the North West District. These Districts do correspond to the period when most pamphlets were produced and also to area boundaries that will be widely understood by any reader. Where I have 'reclassified' a pamphlet by a smaller District into a larger one I have always given the original District as publisher followed by the branch, if applicable.

The Districts affected are as follows: Lancashire and Cheshire; West Middlesex (included in London); South Yorkshire (Yorkshire); South Essex (Eastern); South Midlands (Berkshire, Buckinghamshire, Oxfordshire and North Wiltshire included in Midlands). The Channel Islands are included in West of England.

Any reference to 'Congress' will, of course, refer to District Congress not National Congress. The points made in the Introduction to Chapter 1 about National Congress publications apply also to District ones – which were smaller versions of the national ones in their format.

Unfortunately, there are fewer surviving District Committee Reports, District Congress Reports and very few draft documents, political statements and branch amendments, with the exception of London District (though even here there are many gaps). There would still always have been some sort of report of the Congress, however minimal, but these were rarely printed for sale. The NE District *Congress Reports* in the 1970s consisted more or less of four pages of typed minutes for internal use – and to satisfy King Street that all due formalities were adhered to. The report of the 17th Yorkshire District Congress in 1974 is just eight typed sheets. Some Districts reported their congresses in their regular bulletins, e.g. Hants and Dorset. Some Districts produced substantial *Discussion Statements* for Congresses (e.g. Scotland from 1970 onwards). Reports (and Resolutions) of London District Congresses were carried in the *Bulletin* (e.g. Oct. 14 1955; March 3 1960). London DC *Reports to Congress* were usually 16pp in the 1950s and 1960s – longer than the *Congress Reports* and more informative of the level of activity and organisation. London District published *Information and Draft Resolutions* (4pp) in the 1960s for sale, but these are not listed – at other periods they would be issued free to delegates.

A standard procedure for District, Scottish and Welsh Congresses was set up between 1943 and 1945. Initially, they were held every year, but from 1953 changed to every two years, alternating with the National Congress.

I have included all *Reports of Congresses*, but not all *DC Reports to District Congresses*, together with *Resolutions*, even though occasionally they were printed and for sale, and despite the fact that they are important sources of information. It is safe to assume that they were produced in some form for every Congress (and the same applies to Area and borough Conferences); but they turn up very infrequently and most extant copies will be in the three major collections.

More District material, of all kinds, will doubtless turn up over the coming years, in the collections of individuals and in archives as more gets listed.

Occasionally, a CP District or local members were involved in setting up small publishing houses: the Welsh set up Gwasg y Seren Goch (Red Star Press) in the late 1930s, aiming at a wider audience and author base than that of the CP.

As in the previous chapter, a question mark at the end indicates uncertainty about the year.

West of England

1943

1605 **Increased Pay and Pensions for the Fighting Forces** Manning, Mick & Manning, Hilda *Gloucester Branch* 10pp

1606 **Your Water: How? When?** *Cinderford Branch* 12pp Water shortages in East Dean Rural Council.

1944

1607 **West Country Forward** 8pp lf

1945

1608 **A Soldier's Dream of Home: Bristol CP's Housing Proposals** *Bristol City Cttee* 8pp ?

1609 **A Town Plan for Gloucester** *Gloucester Branch* 16pp ?

1610 **Chard's Chance: CP's Post War Proposals** Wallis, Peter *Chard* 18pp Good example of a CP branch (or at least an individual) rooted in the community; has various specific proposals e.g. turning the local reservoir into a 'People's Lido'.

1611 **The New Swindon** *S Midlands* 4pp lf

1946

1612 **Congress Resolves: Report of 4th District Congress** 8pp lf d

1613 **Our Bristol** *Bristol City Cttee* 20pp

1614 **Our States' Constitution** *Jersey CP (?)* 8pp ?

1948

1615 **A People's Plan for Bath** *Bath CP* 20pp ?

1950

1616 **Our Fight in Totnes Division: The Story of Devon and Cornwall CP's First Parliamentary Contest** Goodman, Dave *Cornwall & Devon CP* 18pp lf d

1951

1617 **A Festival History of Plymouth** *Plymouth Branch* 20pp

1618 **TB Can Be Conquered** 8pp

1955

1619 **Plymouth: Fight for Your Future** Harper, Bob *Plymouth Branch* 8pp lf d

1957

1620 **Full Employment in the Dockyard** *Plymouth Branch (?)* 4pp lf d

1961

1621 **Jersey's Way to Socialism: Programme of the Jersey CP** *Jersey* 8pp

1970

1622 **V.I. Lenin Centenary: Its Relevance to Cornwall** 17pp d Incl. reflections on Cornwall by R. Green. Probably free.

1979

1623 **Reach Out to the People: Report of 20th District Congress** 10pp lf d

1982

1624 **Drawing the Threads Together: Report of 22nd District Congress** 18pp lf d

1984

1625 **What is the Duchy of Cornwall?** Green, Royston *Cornwall Branch* 8pp ?

Hampshire & Dorset

1940

1626 **Make Southampton Safe For All!** Hooper, Bill *Southampton Branch* 16pp On A.R.P.

1944

1627 Backing the Attack 8pp On Second Front.

1628 May Day Special Print run of 6,700.

1629 Who Was Who in Ramsay's Book? Ramsay, notorious anti-semite and pro-fascist, was the only MP to be interned during WW2. The title refers to a ledger he kept of members of The Right Club. ?

1945

1630 Portsmouth's Future *Portsmouth CP* 16pp Cover by R. Pick.

1946

1631 5th District Congress 8pp lf This states that the District produced its own publications for the very first time in the preceeding year.

1948

1632 7th District Congress: Report of Proceedings etc., Oct. 1948 22pp

1949

1633 Into Action Now! Report of District Conference 20pp lf d

1953

1634 Report of 9th District Congress 24pp lf d

1954

1635 Southampton Dock Strike 1890 Young, Eric 10pp lf d

1955

1636 Report of 10th District Congress 19pp lf d

1958

1637 Report of 11th District Congress 14pp lf d

1983

1638 David Guest and the CP: A Reminiscence Cornforth, Maurice & Branson, Noreen 12pp lf d Contains interesting memoir of Southampton CP in the 1930s by Fred Ward. ?

Sussex

1938

1639 The Other Hastings *Hastings CP* 16pp

1939

1640 A.R.P. Eastbourne *Eastbourne* 8pp

1641 A.R.P. The CP Plan for Real Protection of Brighton *Brighton CP* 12pp

1642 Sussex for the People Trory, Ernie 20pp Report to 2nd Sussex County Congress, Feb. Interesting on local economy and CP activity. 1st impression (March): 2,000 copies, 2nd (May): 3,000.

1643 Sussex People's March of History: Souvenir Programme 8pp Contains a song, plus history of Sussex.

1946

1644 Brighton Today and Tomorrow *Brighton CP* 16pp lf Well illustrated. On planning and reconstruction. Contains interesting adverts. ?

1953

1645 A Socialist Policy for Crawley Grove, David *Crawley CP* 6pp Author not credited.

1953

1646 Memorandum on the Rents Problem Grove, David *Crawley CP* 8pp lf d Author not credited.

1954

1647 Crawley: The Way Forward Grove, David 6pp

Surrey

1944

1648 **A New Mitcham** Jarrett, Louise *Mitcham Branch* 16pp

1945

1649 **A Better St Helier** *Carshalton, Merton & Morden Branches* 4pp lf ?

1946

1650 **Our Town: The Future of Dorking** *Dorking* 4pp lf Jack Clark's election pamphlet.

1651 **Wake Up Horley and District!** *Horley CP* 8pp lf Election pamphlet. ?

1949

1652 **Housing Plan for Surrey** *Surrey Area Cttee* 26pp ?

1958

1653 **Sack the Surrey Tories!** 8pp lf ?

1959

1654 **Education in Surrey: The Way Forward** 12pp

1974

1655 **Housing Prospects** *Croydon Borough* 14pp ?

1656 **Merton's Housing: The Truth** French, Sid *Merton Branch* 12pp d Author was to break from CP & found the NCP in 1977.

1976

1657 **Education in Kingston** *Kingston Borough* 12pp d

1978

1658 **Report of District Congress** 10pp lf d

1659 **Understanding History** Rothstein, Andrew 8pp

1986

1660 **1986+ ... Education in Britain** 6pp

Kent

1944

1661 **Food From Kent: A Plan for Agriculture** 16pp

1945

1662 **Kent in the Fight for Victory and Progress: Report of 5th Congress, Feb.** 30pp

1663 **The Bromley We Want** *Bromley CP* 12pp ?

1946

1664 **Plan for Kent**

1958

1665 **Keep the Main Gate Open: The CP's Proposals on the Dockyards and the Admiralty Cuts** 10pp ?

1980

1666 **Special on Peace** 8pp Special issue of Kent Party News (usually free).

1983

1667 **Bromley Communists in the Thirties: A Personal Reminiscence** Belsey, Harry John 20pp Author in CP 1934 to 1956. Published anonymously.

London

1924

1668 **Saklatvala in Parliament** *s.p.* 4pp Text reprinted from Hansard. Almost a regular publication – No. 4 is dated April-May 1925 (and it has some great adverts ranging from local garage to Indian silk merchant, chimney sweep & private piano lessons). ?

1926

1669 **London County Council Trams and the Traffic Combine: The Coming Struggle** *Tramwaymen's Cttee* 8pp

1929

1670 **May-Day Talk on the Closing Parliament and the Coming Election** Saklatvala, S. *E Pountney* 4pp lf Not official LDCP publication – part of Saklatvala's election campaign.

1931

1671 **The CP: A Few Notes to Assist New Members** 8pp lf d ?

1672 **The Party of Lenin** 18pp lf d

1673 **Resolutions of the London District Congress** 26pp lf

1934

1674 **Paddington Housing Scandal** Smith, H. *Paddington CP* 16pp ?

1675 **Programme of the Great All London Communist Rally, Shoreditch Town Hall, Jan.** 8pp Good cover; adverts incl. 'New Plan Books'.

1676 **Rent Acts Explained** *North-West Sub-District* 10pp lf

1677 **Tenant Versus Landlord** *North-West Sub-District* 30pp

1678 **The Royal Wedding** 4pp lf

1679 **The Situation and Tasks of the Party in London: Resolution Adopted at District Congress, May** 4pp

1935

1680 **For United Working Class Action in London: Resolution of London District Congress, June** 16pp

1681 **The Royal Jubilee: 25 Years of War and Starvation** 4pp lf

1682 **What's Wrong with the Building Industry?** *Building Trades Group, London District Council CP* 4pp 'Communist Industrial Series'. ?

1683 **What's Wrong with the Clothing Industry?** *Clothing Trades Group, London District Council CP* 4pp 'Communist Industrial Series'. ?

1936

1684 **Healthy Happy Homes: Plan for Paddington** Wheeler, Peter & Lynd, Sheila 16pp ? Authors not credited.

1685 **Hollybush Gardens Strike Victory** Graves, Bob *Bethnal Green CP* 8pp ?

1686 **New London** Bramley, Ted 60pp Cover by Tom Poulton. ?

1687 **Spotlight on Local Affairs** *Chiswick Branch* 9pp lf d

1688 **The London Transport Scandal** Downton, Arthur 30pp

1689 **The March of English History** 12pp

1690 **Workers Rejoice** *West London CP/Paddington CP* 12pp lf d ?

1937

1691 **A People's Charter for Slough** *Slough CP, West Middlesex District* 15pp ?

1692 **Communist Plan for Life in Acton** *Acton CP* 16pp ?

1693 **Communist Plan for Life in Bethnal Green** *Bethnal Green CP* 16pp ?

1694 **Communist Plan for Life in Ealing** *Ealing CP* 16pp ?

1695 **Communist Plan for Life in Edmonton** *Edmonton CP* 16pp ?

1696 **Communist Plan for Life in Finchley** *Finchley CP* 16pp ?

1697 **Communist Plan for Life in Finsbury** *Finchley CP* 16pp ?

1698 **Communist Plan for Life in Fulham** *Fuham CP* 16pp ?

1699 **Communist Plan for Life in Hackney** *Hackney* 16pp ?

1700 **Communist Plan for Life in Hampstead** *Hampstead CP* 16pp ?

1701 **Communist Plan for Life in Holborn** *Holborn CP* 16pp ?

1702 **Communist Plan for Life in Islington** *Islington CP* 16pp ?

LOCAL PUBLICATIONS

1703 **Communist Plan for Life in Kensington** *Kensington CP* 16pp ?

1704 **Communist Plan for Life in Lambeth** *Lambeth CP* 16pp ?

1705 **Communist Plan for Life in Marylebone** *Marylebone CP* 16pp ?

1706 **Communist Plan for Life in Paddington** *Paddington CP* 16pp ?

1707 **Communist Plan for Life in Poplar** *Poplar CP* 16pp ?

1708 **Communist Plan for Life in Southall** *Southall CP* 16pp ?

1709 **Communist Plan for Life in St Pancras** *St Pancras CP* 16pp ?

1710 **Communist Plan for Life in Stepney** Piratin, Phil *Stepney CP* 16pp

1711 **Communist Plan for Life in Stoke Newington** *Stoke Newington* 16pp ?

1712 **Communist Plan for Life in Tottenham** *Tottenham CP* 16pp ?

1713 **Communist Plan for Life in Walthamstow** *Walthamstow CP* 16pp ?

1714 **Communist Plan for Life in Wandsworth** *Wandsworth CP* 16pp ?

1715 **Communist Plan for Life in Wanstead & Woodford** *Wanstead & Woodford CP* 16pp ?

1716 **Communist Plan for Life in Wembley** *Wembley CP* 16pp ?

1717 **Communist Plan for Life in Westminster** *Westminster CP* 16pp ?

1718 **Communist Plan for Life in Willesden** *Willesden CP* 16pp ?

1719 **Communist Plan for Life in Wood Green** *Wood Green CP* 16pp ?

1720 **Sixteen Bob a Day for Dockers: Abolish Casual Labour** 16pp ?

1721 **The Communist Way to Make London Gay, Healthy, Happy** 16pp lf For LCC elections. Many illustrations.

1722 **The London Bus Strike: What Next? Our Reply to Mr Bevin** 16pp

1723 **To the People of London: Manifesto of London District Congress, April** 12pp

1938

1724 **A.R.P. A Plan for Hendon** 16pp

1725 **For Unity in London Speeches of T. Bramley and H. Pollitt at London District Congress, June, & Resolution & Statement** Bramley, Ted & Pollitt, H. 34pp

1726 **More Fares Please** 16pp

1727 **Prepare Now! Air Raid Precautions for Stepney** *Stepney CP* 16pp

1728 **Quinn Square Tenants' Rent Strike Victory** 14pp 10,000 print run.

1939

1729 **A.R.P. for Hampstead** *Hampstead CP* 16pp ?

1730 **A.R.P. For Londoners** 16pp

1731 **Programme for Communist Rally, July** 14pp Includes Pageant of Chartism.

1732 **Souvenir Programme, Conway Hall Rally, Oct. 30** 4pp

1733 **The Co-operative Movement in London** 20pp lf d

1734 **We Can Get Those Deep Shelters** Beauchamp, Kay *Finsbury Branch* 16pp ?

1940

1735 **Beating the Bombs** 4pp ?

1736 **Fight for Life in Lambeth** *Lambeth CP* 12pp On A.R.P.

1737 **Make Battersea Safe: A.R.P.** *Battersea CP* 16pp ?

1738 **We Are Many!** Bramley, Ted 16pp Cover by Cliff Rowe.

1739 **Workers Against the War: Resolution of London District Congress, Jan.** 16pp sf

1941

1740 **London Blitz** 4pp lf

1741 **London's Way Forward: Resolutions of District Congress, Jan.** 16pp

1742 **Ward Groups: The Way Forward** Grandjean, Duke 16pp ?

1942

1743 **London Docks** Aylward, Bert & Coleman, Pat 16pp ?

1744 **Study While You Struggle** *Educ. Dept, LDCP* 20pp lf d

1745 **The Fighting Bennetts** 16pp ?

1746 When We Make Again: The Furnishing Trade in War and Peace Hurst, D. 28pp

1943

1747 Her First Pay Packet 4pp On pink paper. ?

1748 Opportunity: Dare We Miss It ? 8pp lf ?

1749 Speakers' Notes 4pp

1750 What Are the Proposals of the CP on … Policy Adopted at District Congress, Sept. 20pp

1751 Women for Victory 4pp lf ?

1752 Workers' Pictorial: London Special 8pp lf ?

1944

1753 CP Special: 8 Pages About the Britain We Fight For 8pp lf ?

1754 Eire and the War Keehan, Jim 8pp ?

1755 Examination of the County of London Plan 16pp ?

1756 'Fellow Workers' *Cossor Group* 8pp Contributors incl. Ted Warr, Hazel Crooks, V. Stubbens, Nigel Kelsey, Pearl Foles. ?

1757 Gallacher Speaks for the People *Hornsey* 6pp Programme for rally in Hornsey Town Hall. Has words to 3 agitprop songs (performed by Kay Birbeck's Songsters).

1758 Hornsey Forward: CP Policy for Victory and Peace *Hornsey CP* 4pp lf

1759 Houses for Marylebone *Marylebone CP* 16pp ?

1760 How to Speed up Repairs Shapiro, Michael 12pp

1761 Lin: A Short Novel McIlven, Peggy 24pp Fiction.

1762 London Clothing Industry: Resolutions Adopted by Conference of Communist Clothing Trade Workers, Nov. 1944 8pp sf

1763 London Engineering: Resolutions Adopted by Conference of Engineering and Metal Workers, Oct. 8pp sf

1764 London Engineers: The Epic Story of the Longest Battle Owen, Jack 8pp ?

1765 London Railway Workers Owen, Jack 16pp ?

1766 London Special: What 1944 Will Bring? 8pp lf

1767 Post-War Rail Problems: Communist Policy for Victory and Peace – Resolutions of Conference of Rail Workers, Nov. 8pp sf

1768 Royal Arsenal Co-operative Society: The Shops that Give Their Profits Back to You Hardy, Albert 16pp

1769 The Building Industry in London: Resolutions Adopted by Conference of Building Workers, Nov. 8pp sf

1770 The Future of Passenger Transport in London: Statement Adopted by Conference of Communist Transport Workers, Dec. 8pp sf

1945

1771 A Hornsey Man *Hornsey CP* 4pp G.J. Jones.

1772 A Policy Discussion Statement on Electricity, Gas and Water Supply in London 8pp sf

1773 A Stepney to be Proud Of: Plans and Prospects *Stepney Branch* 16pp lf Interesting adverts.

1774 Acton Communists Fight for Unity *Acton CP* 16pp

1775 Balham and Tooting CP Special *Balham & Tooting CP* 4pp lf

1776 Build Now! 4pp lf London Special.

1777 Campaign Guide to the Borough Council Elections 16pp Marked 'Not For Sale' but deserves an entry as it's a substantial item on an important topic.

1778 Canvassing Beauchamp, Kay 16pp

1779 Chelsea New Citizen *Chelsea CP* 8pp lf For 1945 election.

1780 CP Proposals on Housing in East Ham *East Ham CP* 8pp lf ?

1781 Decisions of Congress, Jan. 16pp

1782 Edmonton Forward *Edmonton CP* 8pp lf

1783 Europe's Jews: Relieve Their Suffering! *East London Cttee* 4pp

1784 Greece: Our Friend 4pp lf ?

1785 Hackney for the People *Hackney Borough Cttee* 8pp lf For General election. Incl. M. Mindel on clothing industry.

1786 How To Get New Homes in Hampstead *Hampstead CP* 8pp ?

1787 **I.C.I. Factory Closes Down: Will Hayes Become Another Jarrow?** Foster, Frank *Hayes CP* 8pp sf ?

1788 **Islington Pictorial (The Future is His!)** 8pp lf ?

1789 **Jones for Hornsey: One Candidate to Beat the Tory** McIlvern, Peggy *Hornsey CP* 12pp

1790 **Life Depends on Food, Shelter, Clothing ... And Clothing Depends on You** 12pp sf Addressed to clothing trade workers.

1791 **London's Arsenal** Job, Charles *Woolwich Branch* 36pp Foreword by W. Hannington; cover by Cliff Rowe.

1792 **London's Education in Danger** 4pp lf ?

1793 **Meet Your S.I.** 8pp On sanitary inspectors.

1794 **Mile End Election Special! Vote Piratin** H.W. Carver 4pp lf Broadsheet election publication. Substantial document with a lot of text, but also photos and cartoons. Superbly written; sections on housing, women, Catholic workers, Jewish workers, Tories' national campaign, appeal to Labour Party members – and only 3 passing refs to the Soviet Union. Would be considered too wordy today, but one of the best pieces of election literature I have ever seen.

1795 **Mile End Has a Memory** *Stepney*

1796 **Our Borough** *Hendon CP* 16pp lf

1797 **Our Hounslow: Hounslow CP Plan** *Hounslow CP* 8pp

1798 **Plan and Policy for Hayes & Harlington** *Hayes CP* 16pp

1799 **Plan Your Publicity** Beauchamp, Kay (ed.) 36pp Cover by P. Hogarth, but plain! Contains good lists of addresses of shops, papers, Labour Movement orgs etc. ?

1800 **Post-War London: Railways** 8pp

1801 **Railway Clarion: An Illustrated Booklet for All Railway Workers** *West London Sub-District* 8pp lf ?

1802 **Redundant: Why?** *North London Cttee* 4pp

1803 **St Pancras: Homes or Slums?** *St Pancras Branch* 16pp

1804 **Sutton Housing Special** *Sutton Branch* 8pp lf ?

1805 **The Battle for Homes** Bramley, Ted 64pp Light on London series No.1 ?

1806 **The Future of the Furnishing Trades in London: Statement Adopted by Conference of Communist Furnishing Trade Workers, Feb.** 8pp sf

1807 **The Rise of Paris** Ballanger, Robert 16pp Speech at District Congress, Jan.

1808 **The Town Hall** Carver, H.W. 12pp Cover by Dorothy Chapman.

1809 **Wandsworth Tomorrow** *Wandsworth Borough* 8pp ?

1810 **Wanstead and Woodford Clarion** *Wanstead & Woodford CP* 6pp lf

1811 **We Can Do It! Westminster Election Special** J. Gaster (Election Agent) 8pp lf Bill Carritt election pamphlet – one of the more useful and impressive ones.

1812 **Where's That Fact?** 20pp

1813 **Why We Must Put Labour in Control of the Borough Council** *Woodford CP* 8pp

1814 **Win Holborn for the People** *Holborn Branch* 16pp Cover by Norman Pugh. ?

1815 **Wood Green Housing: Proposals for Discussion** Clarke, A.T. & Levitt, Vic *Wood Green Branch* 12pp

1816 **Your Vote: How Will You Use It?** 8pp lf London Communist Special.

1946

1817 **Ban the Fascists** 4pp lf London Communist Special.

1818 **Bramley's Speech at the Old Bailey, Sept. 1946** Bramley, Ted 16pp 'Trial of London Communists Arrested for Action on Behalf of London's Homeless'.

1819 **Communist Proposals for Twickenham** Bateman, Angus (ed.) *Twickenham Borough* 12pp

1820 **Communist Spotlight on Willesden** *Willesden CP* 8pp lf ?

1821 **Direction: Socialism: May Day** Mahon, John 16pp Cover by P. Hogarth.

1822 **Franco Spain: Danger to Britain** 4pp lf

1823 **Hayes & Harlington Illustrated** *Hayes* 20pp lf Feb. 1946. Ed. Arthur Davis.

1824 **Labour and Communist: Achieve It Together** 8pp lf London Communist Special.

1825 **London's Fares: Going Up?** 8pp ?

1826 **London's Gas** 8pp ?

1827 **Office and Administrative Workers** 8pp ?

1828 **Our Borough** Beauchamp, Kay 22pp

1829 **Peace is in Danger! Stop the Fighting in the East** 4pp lf On Indonesia & India.

1830 **R. Palme Dutt in India** 12pp

1831 **St Pancras Challenge** *St Pancras CP* 4pp lf Largely on housing issues.

1832 **The Squatters** Pollitt, H. 4pp lf

1833 **They Fight for You: London's Communist Councillors in Action** 8pp lf

1834 **What We Are Fighting For: Decisions of London District Congress** 20pp

1947

1835 **Britain's Crisis: The Way Out** 8pp lf London Communist Special; print run of 100,000.

1836 **Building Workers! 500,000 Families Look to You!** 4pp lf

1837 **Communist Appeal to All Building Trade Workers** Weaver, Harry 4pp

1838 **Communist Leadership in the Factories: Syllabus for Branch Discussion** 16pp ?

1839 **Communist Leadership: A Four-Session Syllabus for Branch Committee Members** 16pp ?

1840 **Communists at Paddington Council: Statement on Housing** *Paddington CP* 6pp

1841 **Engineers on the Move Again** 4pp lf Communist Special.

1842 **How To Get Houses in Hendon** *Hendon Borough* 12pp ?

1843 **London's Answer – Programme for Rally** 8pp ?

1844 **Mighty City: Report of District Congress** 8pp lf

1845 **Pay Your Way: Guide for Branch, Industrial Group and Borough Treasurers** Cotton, Bob 62pp

1846 **Report to London's Engineers** 4pp lf

1847 **Staffing London's Hospitals** Bramley, Ted *London Health Advisory Cttee* 18pp Print run of 3,000.

1848 **Stepney Anniversary News** *Stepney CP* 4pp lf 5,000 printed – 4,000 sold.

1849 **The CP Programme for Distributive Workers** 4pp

1850 **The Social Needs of London's People** 4pp lf

1851 **Why I Am a Communist** Keehan, Jim 16pp sf Cover by Paul Hogarth. ?

1948

1852 **Communist Manifesto – Centenary Meeting and Pageant, March 30: Programme** 12pp

1853 **Defend Your Living Standards** *Acton* 4pp lf

1854 **Home Sweet (?) Home: A Statement on Repairs and Rents** *Kensington CP* 4pp

1855 **How to Produce a 'Special'** 8pp lf d Detailed instructions for publishing local pamphlets. ?

1856 **Lightermen: Today and Tomorrow** 16pp ?

1857 **Municipal Workers and the Crisis** 8pp

1858 **Report to London's Housewives** 4pp lf Print run of 20,000.

1859 **The Future of Electricity Supply** 4pp ?

1860 **Three Communist Councillors Report to the People of Westminster on Their Second Year's Work** *Westminster* 8pp lf Joan & Bill Carritt, Joyce Alergant. Free pamphlet.

1949

1861 **Day of Struggle: Souvenir of London's May Day** 16pp

1862 **London Communists and the Crisis: A Political Letter to Every Member and Friend** Pollitt, H. 8pp lf

1863 **London's Engineers: What Now?** 4pp lf

1864 **Report of the Stepney Borough EC to AGM** *Stepney Borough* 21pp

1865 **The New Battle for London** Mahon, John 16pp

1950

1866 **1920-50: Episodes from the CP's 30 Years of Struggle** 16pp lf

1867 **Marxism and War** 8pp ?

1868 **Stop the Increase in Fares** Beauchamp, Kay 16pp

LOCAL PUBLICATIONS

1869 **The Story of May Day: Highlights of Great May Day Actions by London Workers** 14pp lf ?

1951

1870 **For an Immediate Advance in the Factory and Public Work of Our Party in London** Mahon, John 10pp lf d

1871 **London's Development Plan 1951** 14pp lf

1952

1872 **An Attack on You** 4pp d

1873 **Cultural Conference Programme** *West Middlesex District* 8pp Interesting Programme of Entertainment and Exhibition (included Guttuso, Herman, Binder, Hogarth and a Rembrandt!)

1874 **LCC Elections: Information for Speakers and Canvassers** *Propaganda Dept* 4pp lf d

1875 **London's Education in Danger: Memorandum to LCC** 4pp

1876 **The Camden Clarion** *Camden Rail Branch* 4pp lf d No sign of being a regular journal. ?

1877 **The Clothing Workers of London in the Fight for Peace and Full Employment** Mahon, John 10pp lf d

1878 **Tory Housing Policy: What It Means for London** 10pp lf d

1953

1879 **America: The Facts** 8pp lf

1880 **How to Get the Homes We Need** 16pp lf d

1881 **In Defence of Our Children: Education Policy for the Local Elections** 12pp lf d ?

1882 **London's Youth: The Facts** 8pp lf

1883 **The Fight for Lower Fares** *Propaganda Dept* 4pp lf d

1884 **The Poplar Story, 1921** CP Historians' Group *East London Area Cttee* 22pp lf d

1885 **The Thomson Battle: NATSOPA Takes Up the Challenge** *Westminster & City* 4pp Supporting printers on strike at D.C. Thomson. ?

1886 **The Tory Attack on Health** 14pp lf d

1954

1887 **A Perspective for the Branch** *North Middlesex Area Cttee* 12pp lf d

1888 **American Big Business Threatens Britain** 6pp lf d

1889 **Brothers in the Fight for a Better Life** 16pp lf d On 'Colonial workers' in London. ?

1890 **But Why MY Child?** 8pp lf On Education. 5,000 printed.

1891 **Deptford's Tribute to Kath Duncan** 26pp lf

1892 **Engineering Workers' Wages** 8pp lf d

1893 **For a Home of Our Own [Draft ed.]** 16pp lf d

1894 **Guatemala: The Facts** 8pp lf d ?

1895 **Have Hornsey Children a Chance?** *Hornsey CP* 12pp lf d ?

1896 **Let the Old Folk Live** ?

1897 **London Labour and Colonial Freedom: Two Centuries of Struggle** 16pp

1898 **London Transport** 8pp lf

1899 **London Women** 8pp lf ?

1900 **London's Battle for Homes** 16pp lf

1901 **Socialist Power** 6pp lf d On electrical supply industry. ?

1902 **Taxi!** *London Cab Branch* 4pp lf ?

1903 **The Story of Joe Vaughan: First Labour Mayor of Bethnal Green** Grant, Betty *East London Area Cttee* 28pp lf d

1955

1904 **An Outline of Communist Policy for London's Young People** *LD CP & YCL* 6pp lf d

1905 **Beckton's Struggles** Grant, Betty *Beckton Gas Works Branch* 36pp lf d

1906 **British Railways** 8pp lf

1907 **Building!** 8pp lf

1908 **Clothing Today and Tomorrow** *East London Area Cttee* 8pp lf ?

1909 **Communist Policy for Health: Speakers' Notes** 10pp lf d For LCC elections.

1910 **Communist Policy for LCC Finance** 8pp lf d

1911 **Homes for Our People: A Policy for Housing** *Chiswick CP* 14pp lf d ?

1912 **Homes for Our People: A Policy for Housing** *Hayes CP* 14pp lf d ?

1913 **Homes for Our People: A Policy for Housing** *Uxbridge* 14pp lf d ?

1914 **No Arms for Germany** 8pp lf

1915 **Rents: Stop Them Rising** 8pp lf ?

1916 **The Needs of London's Children** 6pp lf d

1917 **Turning the Key to the Future: A Policy Statement by CP Members Working in Hoovers (Perivale)** *W Middlesex DC* 16pp lf d ?

1956

1918 **Cyprus** 8pp lf

1919 **Finsbury's Future: Communist Candidates for the Council and A Programme for Improvements** *Finsbury CP* 10pp lf d ?

1920 **Homes for Hampstead** *Hampstead CP* 8pp lf

1921 **Homes for Hornsey: How to Get Them** *Hornsey CP* 16pp

1922 **Homes for Willesden** *Willesden CP* 9pp lf d

1923 **May Day: Specially for Children** 8pp lf Contributors include Judith Todd, Jill Howard, Vera Leff. Poems, stories, cartoons, crosswords – in a rare item for children.

1924 **Our London – Great Communist Rally, Oct. 6: Programme** 12pp

1925 **Prices, Monopolies, Socialism: What the London Co-operative Society Can Do** Ainley, David 12pp ?

1926 **Put the Children First: A Statement on Uxbridge Education** *Uxbridge CP, West Middlesex District* 12pp lf d

1927 **St Pancras People Need Homes** *St Pancras CP* 4pp lf

1928 **Suez Special** Bent, Joe *South West London Area* 6pp lf d

1929 **The Communist Campaign in the Municipal Elections** 16pp lf d

1930 **The New Tory Threat to Jobs and Earnings** 6pp lf d

1931 **The Truth About Wages** 8pp lf ?

1932 **United We Stand ... 100 Years of Struggle in the Docks** 32pp

1957

1933 **Change Here! Policy Statement** *Acton Works Branch* 12pp lf d 300 copies sold.

1934 **Homes for Our People: A Policy for Housing** *Slough Branch, West Middlesex District* 12pp ?

1935 **Problems of Unity and the London Labour Movement** Goodwin, Dennis 16pp lf d ?

1936 **Some Notes on Trotskyism: Past and Present** Beauchamp, Kay 7pp lf d Based on Statement at DC, June. 'I do not know to what extent the Trotskyists became fascist agents, but we all know that objectively they aided the fascists and used almost identical propaganda during the war'.

1937 **The British Aircraft Industry** Foster, Frank *West Middlesex DC* 12pp lf d

1958

1938 **British Airlines: A Policy for Civil Air Transport** *London Airport Branch, West Middlesex District* 14pp lf d ?

1939 **Denny Hurst: A Tribute** 12pp Hurst was President of National Union of Furniture Trade Operatives, and for a time on the London DC.

1940 **Education: LCC Elections** 6pp lf d

1941 **Elect Communist Councillors, April 16** 6pp lf d

1942 **Housing: LCC Elections** 4pp lf d

1943 **London's Old People: LCC Elections** 6pp lf d

1959

1944 **Crisis in Building** 16pp ?

1945 **Fascism and How to Defeat It** 14pp lf d

1946 **Outlook in Engineering** Stanley, Frank (ed.) *Hayes CP* 16pp lf ?

1947 **Sholom Aleichem: Champion of the Jewish People** West, Alick *East London Area Cttee* 10pp

1948 **Which Way?** Foster, Frank *West Middlesex DC* 12pp lf d

1960

1949 **40 Proud Years 1920-60 – Souvenir Programme** 12pp lf Ill.

1950 **A New Willesden** *Willesden CP* 8pp lf d For local elections.

1951 **Campaign Points for 1960 Municipal Elections** 10pp lf d

1952 **Electoral Work in London: Discussion Article for Congress** Matthews, Betty 8pp lf d

1953 **End the Crisis in the Motor Industry** 8pp lf d

1954 **Festival of Socialism: Programme** 8pp Organised jointly with London YCL.

1955 **London Rhymes No.1** *London Communist Poets Group* 2pp Poems. ?

1956 **The CP and Youth: Summary of Joe Bent's Opening Statement to District Meeting** 4pp lf d

1957 **The London Labour Movement: Discussion Article for Congress** Goodwin, Dennis 8pp lf d

1958 **The Printing Industry: What is Its Future?** Woolley, George 16pp

1959 **This Southwark Housing Problem** Bent, Joe *Southwark* 18pp lf d ?

1961

1960 **Cuba's Struggle For Freedom** 8pp lf d

1961 **Defend British State Airlines** *London Airport Branch, West Middlesex District* 8pp d ?

1962 **The Odhams Takeover and What It Means** *Central London Print Branch* 6pp d

1963 **What Next?** *Bus Branch* 4pp d

1962

1964 **Hands Off Cuba** 8pp lf

1965 **Homes Not Bombs** Nicholson, Jock *St Pancras CP* 12pp ?

1966 **London Transport: The Way Out of the Crisis** 6pp lf

1967 **London's Homeless** Cornforth, Kitty 18pp lf

1968 **The Growth of Unemployment in London: And How to Stop It** 10pp lf d

1969 **Welfare Services for Old People** 10pp lf d

1970 **Who is to Live in Hampstead?** *Hampstead CP* 8pp ?

1963

1971 **End Islington's Housing Scandal** Moss, John *Islington CP* 10pp ?

1972 **The Alternative to Beeching** 6pp lf d

1973 **The Beeching Report** 12pp lf d

1974 **The Case for a Rail Strike** 6pp lf d

1975 **The Story of May Day: Highlights of Great May Day Actions by London Workers** 10pp lf d

1976 **Willesden Housing: A New Look** Harper, Bob *Willesden* 8pp lf d For May election campaign.

1964

1977 **A Word to Office Workers from a Communist** Hayes, Eddie 10pp d

1978 **London District Congress (Report)** 4pp

1979 **London Transport: The Case for Ending Fare Increases** 10pp lf d

1980 **Print Workers and Monopoly** *Central London Area Cttee* 8pp lf d ?

1981 **Resolutions: District Congress** 4pp lf

1982 **Shakespeare and Our World: Narration Written, and Extracts Compiled, by Ruth Burns & Sidney Cole** *West Middlesex DC* 76pp lf d Script of a celebration of 400th anniversary of Shakespeare's birth 'Sponsored & organised by West Middlesex DC'. A curious cultural publication.

1983 **Your Voice in the Council: The Record of Stepney's Councillors** *Stepney* 4pp lf

1965

1984 **Against Racial Discrimination and Incitement: Memorandum** 10pp lf d

1985 **Children's Service and the Borough Councils** *Social Services Cttee* 6pp lf d

1986 **Old People's Welfare** 8pp lf

1987 **The Battle Against the Pay Pause** 10pp lf d

1988 **The Menace of Anti-Trade Union Legislation** 8pp

1989 **Welfare Services for Old People** *Social Services Cttee* 12pp lf d

1966

1990 **Borough Council Health Services: Memorandum** *Social Services Cttee* 10pp lf d ?

1991 **Comprehensive Schools for Kingston? Plan for State Education in the Kingston Borough** *Kingston CP* 10pp lf d

1992 **Hands Off the Scheme: Nationalise the Docks!** 16pp lf d Evidence to Public Enquiry.

1993 **Hands Off Trade Union Rights** 8pp lf d

1994 **London District Congress (Report)** 6pp lf

1995 **Resolutions: District Congress** 4pp lf Incl. names of new DC members.

1996 **The Challenge of Equal Pay** 4pp lf

1997 **The Screw Tightens: Prices and Incomes Board on Rail Wages** 10pp lf d

1998 **Tower Hamlets' Housing Crisis: How to Tackle It!** Kaye, Solly *Tower Hamlets* 8pp ?

1967

1999 **1967 Greater London Elections: CP Policy Statement** 12pp lf d

2000 **A Policy for the Exhibition Industry** Communist workers in the exhibition industry 8pp lf d ?

2001 **How to End the Housing Crisis** 8pp lf

2002 **London's Social Services** 20pp lf d

2003 **Marxist Education: 1967 Programme of Marxist Education** 8pp lf d

2004 **Memorandum to the GLC on Passenger Transport** 5pp lf d

2005 **Race Relations: Why New Legislation is Needed Now – Memorandum** 10pp lf d

2006 **Your Health** *Hillingdon Borough CP* 18pp lf d

1968

2007 **Building Workers: What Communists Have Got to Say About the Industry** 8pp lf ?

2008 **Haringey Needs Homes** Morris, Margaret *Haringey CP* 12pp

2009 **London's Housing Problem** *Social Services Cttee* 12pp lf d New ed. in Nov. 1968. Further ed. in March 1970.

2010 **London's Schools** *Social Services Cttee* 14pp lf d

2011 **Report of London District Congress** 6pp lf

2012 **Resist the Attacks on London's Social Services** 4pp lf d

2013 **Your Borough Health Services** 8pp lf d

1969

2014 **Greater London Development Plan** 14pp lf d

2015 **London Transport** 14pp lf d

2016 **Stop Rates Going Up** 10pp lf d

2017 **The Public Scandal of the Notting Hill Housing Crisis** *Kensington & Chelsea CP* 8pp d

1970

2018 **Co-op Wages, Prices, Socialist Policies** 8pp lf d ?

2019 **District Congress Report** 6pp lf

2020 **Housing – Jobs: Evidence to Public Inquiry on Greater London Development Plan** Kaye, Solly 10pp lf d

2021 **London Co-operative: The Next Steps** 8pp lf d

2022 **London's Transport: End the Chaos** 14pp lf d

2023 **Old People's Welfare Concerns You** 8pp lf d New ed. in 1972.

1971

2024 **A Home is a Human Right** 10pp lf d

2025 **Comprehensive Education in the ILEA Area** 6pp lf d

2026 **Health Cuts** 10pp

1972

2027 **Black Citizens** Beauchamp, Kay 14pp

2028 **Docks: The Fight for Jobs** Dunn, Bill 8pp

2029 **Now Let's Flush the Tories Out!** 4pp lf

2030 **Report of District Congress** 14pp lf d

2031 **The History of May Day** 10pp lf

2032 **The Real Voice of London – Rally Souvenir Programme** 8pp lf ?

1973

2033 **Printers' Charter** 10pp Printed by Briant Colour Work-In. ?

2034 **The London We Want** 4pp lf Local elections, April.

2035 **Watch Out! Tory Speculator About!** *Kensington & Chelsea CP* 12pp d

1974

2036 **A Communist Manifesto for Lambeth** *Lambeth Borough Cttee* 16pp lf ?

2037 **Act Now to Save London** 10pp lf ?

2038 **Angela Davis Speaks Out!** 8pp Reprinted from 'African Communist'. ?

2039 **London Communists Campaign: Souvenir Programme** 8pp lf Rally at Royal Festival Hall.

2040 **Northern Ireland: Report of a Delegation** 12pp lf

2041 **Report of District Congress** 12pp lf d

2042 **Stop Bussing 3,000 Children** *West Middlesex DC* 6pp lf d On Ealing Borough.

1975

2043 **Barbados: The End of 'Little England'** Biggs, Ken *Haringey CP* 8pp d Reprinted from 'Comment'.

1976

2044 **Carnival '76** *W11 Branch* 22pp lf d Critical of policing at the Notting Hill Carnival.

2045 **Dock Work or Dole Queue** 8pp ?

2046 **Hackney Needs Socialism** *Hackney Borough* 36pp This pamphlet was re-issued on several occasions over the next few years in different formats.

2047 **Report of District Congress** 28pp lf d

2048 **Stop the Slump: A CP Building Workers' Broadsheet** 6pp lf

2049 **The Plight of Cyprus** Mitchell, Hambis 26pp ?

1977

2050 **A Conversation with Tony Chater** Baxter, Malcolm 30pp d About the 'MS'.

2051 **Poems on My Mind** Ward, Bert *Lewisham Borough* 21pp lf

2052 **Report of the Working Party** 10pp lf d On internal structure.

2052a **Women, A New Social Force: Discussion Document** *Lewisham CP* 12pp Cheaply produced for internal use but interesting.

1978

2053 **Hackney Needs Socialism** *Hackney* 16pp For local elections.

2054 **Parliamentary Elections and the British CP 1920-78** Ravden, Colin *Hackney South Branch (?)* 44pp lf d Excellent research.

2055 **Report of District Congress** 16pp lf d

2056 **The GLC and London's Housing** *River Branch* 20pp lf

2057 **Towards a Broad Alliance in London: Discussion Document and Campaign Proposals for Congress** 12pp lf

2058 **What We Say ...** *Lambeth CP* 32pp

1979

2059 **London for the People** 64pp lf

2060 **London People's Festival, June 17 – Programme** 16pp

2061 **Seize the Chance: Falling Rolls = Higher Standards** *London CP Teachers* 8pp ?

2062 **United Against Racism** *Hackney CP* 4pp lf ?

1980

2063 **Deptford's Tribute to Kath Duncan** 26pp Reprint of 1954 ed.

2064 **Islington: The Fight for Survival** *Islington CP* 14pp lf

2065 **Report of District Congress** 24pp lf

2066 **The General Strike: Deptford Official Strike Bulletins, May 1926** *Lewisham ?* 17pp lf Reprint of the 8 bulletins. Intro. by S. Williams and J. Attfield states this is the work of Communists working on local labour movement history. Does not appear to be an official CP publication.

1981

2067 **Fight for the People of London** 4pp lf Broadsheet for GLC elections, May.

2068 **GLC Election Manifesto** 24pp lf

2069 **Guide to the Politics of Money** 14pp d

2070 **Inside Out: Scenes from 'Women in the Rag Trade'** *Hackney Women's Group* 34pp

2071 **Which Way for Wandsworth?** *Wandsworth CP* 32pp ?

1982

2072 **Day School on Ireland: Background Papers** 12pp lf

2073 **Finance Working Party Report** 14pp d

2074 **Hackney Needs Socialism: Our Future** *Hackney Borough* 32pp lf

2075 **Report of 17th District Congress: W Middlesex** 10pp lf d

2076 **Report of Congress** 6pp lf

1983

2077 **No Euroshima** 4pp lf ?

1984

2078 **Cyprus 1984** 4pp lf

2079 **Hands Off London: Save the GLC** 4pp lf ?

2080 **Ireland: A Question for Us All – Report of Delegation to Belfast** 32pp

2081 **Now We Can Win** 6pp lf

2082 **Report of the Working Party on Branch Life** 12pp lf

2083 **Report of Work: London District Congress '84** 23pp lf

2084 **Save London** 6pp lf

1985

2085 **Miners' Strike: Experiences and Impressions** *Camden CP* 24pp ?

1986

2086 **Capitalist Crisis in Britain: A Communist Response** *Camden Borough* 20pp A 'hard line' Borough producing material for the inner-Party struggle as much as for a wider audience.

1987

2087 **Thatcher's Third Term: A Comment on the General Election** 4pp lf

1988

2088 **Don't Help Thatcher Wreck the Councils** 4pp ?

Eastern

1943

2089 **Essex in the Front Line** Keehan, Jim *Essex Sub-District Cttee* 12pp Cover by Forster. ?

1945

2090 **Fords: Today, Tomorrow** *Ford Group CP* 8pp

2091 **Ilford's Future** *Ilford CP* 8pp lf ?

2092 **The Immediate Programme of the CP in Dagenham** *Dagenham CP* 6pp ?

1947

2093 **Southend Buses** Watson, Harry *Southend Branch* 4pp ?

1952

2094 **Essex Education** *South Essex CP* 8pp ?

2095 **Their Profits, Your Loss: The Facts on 12 Firms in South Essex** *South Essex CP* 4pp ?

1956

2096 **Health Services in Basildon** *Basildon Branch* 8pp lf d

1963

2097 **Dagenham: Who Will Decide Its Future?** *Dagenham Branch* 8pp

1964

2098 **Fords and the Motor Car Industry** Halpin, Kevin & Aaronovitch, Sam *South Essex DC* 4pp lf

LOCAL PUBLICATIONS

1965

2099 **Fords: Whose Hands on the Wheel?** *South Essex DC* 8pp

2100 **Plessey Profile** *South Essex DC* 4pp lf ?

1971

2101 **Ford Britain Strike 1971** *South Essex DC* 4pp lf

1972

2102 **The Tory Housing Finance Bill** *South Essex DC* 12pp d

1973

2103 **Maplin: Jumbo Threat to Britain's Future** Samson, Peter *South Essex DC* 4pp lf ?

1977

2104 **Economic Crisis: Public Spending Cuts – An Alternative Policy** *Harlow CP* 12pp lf d Text largely same as one by Becontree CP.

2105 **Public Spending Cuts: An Alternative Policy** *Becontree CP* 12pp lf d ?

2106 **Strategy For Revolution: A Discussion** *Walthamstow* 12pp lf

2107 **Workers Are Parents Too! A Communist Policy for the Under Fives** *South Essex Women's Advisory* 18pp lf d Covers Barking, Harlow, Redbridge. ?

1979

2108 **Dagenham Needs Socialism OK!** *Becontree CP* 6pp lf d

1985

2109 **Thatcher's Britain: The Waste of a Nation** *Eastern District* 8pp lf

East Anglia

1935

2110 **Busmen versus Combines in East Anglia** 8pp

1939

2111 **Memorandum on Air Raid Precautions for the Town of Cambridge** 7pp

1944

2112 **A Policy for Engineering in East Anglia** Parish, Dan 12pp

2113 **The Future of Ipswich** *Ipswich Branch* 18pp

2114 **The Railways: The Front Line on the Home Front** 4pp ?

1945

2115 **Cambridge Today and Tomorrow** *Cambridge Branch* 30pp lf ?

2116 **Lincoln for the People** *Lincoln Branch* 24pp

1946

2117 **Our City: Norwich** Carey, Neville *Norwich CP* 8pp

2118 **The New Ipswich: A Plan for the Development of the Town with Comments on the Official Proposals** *Ipswich CP* 28pp lf d Contains extraordinary gatefold architect's drawings. ?

1947

2119 **Ipswich and the Crisis** Pipe, Richard 8pp Produced for local elections.

2120 **Norwich and the Crisis** Carey, Neville *Norwich CP* 10pp

1953

2121 **Get Out!** Morton, A.L. 12pp US bases. Cover by 'Gabriel'. ?

1973

2122 **The Sainsbury File** *Norwich & Univ. of East Anglia CP* 18pp ?

1979

2123 **Cambridge Into the Eighties: A Draft Programme** *Cambridge Branch* 18pp d ?

1982

2124 **History of Ipswich Branch** Pipe, Richard 52pp An unfortunately rare example of a branch history.

1984

2125 **Guidelines on NATO, Alternative Defence, Non Violent Direct Action** *District Peace Advisory Cttee* 11pp lf A document prepared for a District school, internal and not for sale. Interesting in how it reflects activities of the peace movement influencing CP.

South East Midlands

1938

2126 **Communist Policy for Life in Letchworth** *Letchworth Branch* 6pp ?

1939

2127 **A.R.P. Plan for Watford** *Watford CP* 14pp

1942

2128 **Corby for Victory!** *Corby Branch* 10pp

1943

2129 **1,200 in Search of a Home: Dunstable's Housing Problem** *Dunstable Branch* 12pp ?

1945

2130 **Report of the DC Presented to the 3rd District Congress** 8pp
2131 **The Future of the Boot and Shoe Industry** 20pp
2132 **Your Letchworth** 16pp lf

1946

2133 **Bridge Special** *Bedford CP* 4pp lf On a public campaign for a bridge! ?

1962

2134 **Tomorrow's Victors** 12pp lf d

1974

2135 **Report of 17th District Congress** 10pp lf d

1976

2136 **Report of 18th District Congress** 10pp lf d

Midlands

1924

2137 **Why I Joined the CP** Dunstan, Robert *Birmingham District Propaganda Cttee* 8pp Portrait on cover.

1926

2138 **The Plot in West Birmingham** Dunstan, Robert *Miss M.D. Clarke* 8pp Not an official CP publication. Dunstan was a member of the CP and LP and stood as the official Labour candidate before the right-wing split the local LP branch, forcing Dunstan to stand as a broad left 'Workers' Candidate'. He was expelled from the LP in 1928 when it banned dual membership.

1927

2139 **What Price Glory** *Birmingham DPC* 1,000 copies at Birmingham Air Pageant (Workers' Life July 29 1927)

1928

2140 **Hanley Election 1928: To the Workers of Hanley** 4pp For by-election, though little local information.

1936

2141 **The Legacy of Joseph Chamberlain** *Birmingham CP* 14pp ?

1938

2142 **49,000 Tenants Say No Rent Increase! No Means Test!** 16pp

1939

2143 **Real A.R.P. for Wycombe** *South Midlands; High Wycombe Branch* 16pp ?

1941

2144 **All Out For Victory: Programme for Coventry CP Rally, Sept.** 8pp

2145 **Birmingham Today: The Role and Record of Neville Chamberlain and Others** Blackwell, Sam 48pp

2146 **For Life, Peace and Socialism** *S Midlands DC* 16pp

1942

2147 **Coventry: What Now?** Blackwell, Sam 12pp

1943

2148 **13 Questions and Answers on the Aston By-Election** Blackwell, Sam *Birmingham CP* 8pp

2149 **The Coventry Evening Telegraph and the Second Front** *Coventry CP* 24pp

2150 **The Housing Problem: A Plan for Birmingham** Stevens, Phyllis *Birmingham CP* 20pp Pictorial cover.

2151 **The People's Needs: A Fighting Policy for the Midlands** 12pp lf

1944

2152 **A Policy for Farm-Workers and Farmers in Oxon, Bucks & N. Wilts** *S Midlands DC* 4pp

2153 **Birmingham Against Hitler** Blackwell, Sam 16pp ?

2154 **Birmingham Past, Present and Future** Blackwell, Sam 28pp

2155 **Forward!** *S Midlands DC* 4pp lf d

2156 **Production Proposals** *CP Aero Factory Group, Birmingham* 4pp Pictorial cover by S.R.V.

2157 **Some Guiding Points for Strengthening Party Organisation** Blackwell, Sam 32pp ?

2158 **Some Guiding Points on the Work of Branch Committees** 18pp ?

1945

2159 **Coventry Citizen, The** 8pp lf April 1945; No.7 Aug. 1946. Ed. J. Singer.

2160 **For Prosperity and Social Advance in the Midlands: Report of Midlands District Congress** 28pp

2161 **Homes for Birmingham: The CP Plan** *Birmingham CP* 12pp lf

2162 **Mr Amery's Record** Dutt, R.P. 16pp Sparkbrook election.

2163 **Our Black Country: Its Past and Future** Westwood, James 20pp ?

2164 **Speed Victory, Win the Peace** *S Midlands DC* 4pp lf Could be an ed. of the District Bulletin.

2165 **The Future of the Small Trader** Blackwell, Sam 16pp ?

1946

2166 **8th District Congress** *S Midlands DC* 16pp lf d Resolution & Report.

2167 **Pots and Plans** Marshall, Lily *Potteries Branch* 14pp ?

2168 **You Live Here! A Practical Guide to Sparkbrook and Balsall Heath** Barrow, N. 18pp

1947

2169 **A Plan for the Motor Car Industry** Warman, W. 8pp Author was Chair, Standard Motors S.S. Cttee

2170 **Report of 9th South Midlands District Congress** *S Midlands* 8pp lf d

1953

2171 **Jobs For All Midland Workers** Pearce, Bert 8pp

1954

2172 **A Man's A Man: A Study of the Colour Bar in Birmingham** Gunter, Henry 14pp ?

1955

2173 **Men and Motors** 16pp

1956

2174 **Forward Birmingham: A Policy for the City** *Birmingham City Cttee* 20pp

1962

2175 **Your Birmingham Needs Communist Councillors** 8pp lf ?

1963

2176 **The Midland's Case Against the Common Market** 16pp

1965

2177 **Franks Commission: Communist Evidence** *S Midlands* 8pp lf d Commission of Inquiry on Oxford Univ.

1968

2178 **Who Is Enoch Powell?** 8pp d 'Written by members of the Cultural Cttee of Birmingham CP'.

1971

2179 **The Battle of the Bulge** Panes, Andrew *Oxford*

1972

2180 **A History of Education in Wolverhampton 1800-72** Barnsby, George *Wolverhampton CP* 34pp lf d

1977

2181 **British Leyland: Save It!** Bloomfield, Jon 16pp lf Foreword by Derek Robinson. ?

2182 **Coventry in Crisis: A Socialist Solution** 32pp ?

1978

2183 **Whose City? A Policy for the People** Bloomfield, Jon & Murray, Roger 12pp lf On Birmingham. ?

1980

2184 **For a Multicultural Britain** 8pp lf ?

1981

2185 **People's March for Jobs … The Next Steps** *Birmingham* 8pp lf

2186 **Picking Up the Pieces** *Birmingham CP* 8pp lf ?

1982

2187 **Feminism and Socialism** *Birmingham CP* 8pp lf Material from 1982 Midlands District Congress.

2188 **Hands Off Our City** 8pp lf Birmingham. ?

2189 **Introducing Gramsci** Simon, Roger 12pp lf Reprint from 'MT'. ?

2190 **It's Your City** *Birmingham CP* 8pp ?

2191 **Poland: A Background to the Crisis** 8pp lf d

1984

2192 **Communists and Peace** 8pp lf ?

2193 **Comprehensive Education: A Death Sentence?** *Coventry & Warwickshire CP* 4pp lf ?

2194 **Spectre Haunting Education** Simon, Brian 8pp lf Reprint from 'MT' Sept.

East Midlands

1934

2195 **Revolutionary Unity: Answers by Leading Members of the C.I. to Questions**

Raised by the ILP Rank & File Delegation, May 1934 Edwards, R. & Whalley, E. *Progressive Bookshop, Nottingham* 20pp

1937

2196 **Harworth Men Make History: A Story of the Fight Against Spencerism** *Nottingham CP* 14pp

1938

2197 **A.R.P. A Plan for the Safety of the People of Nottingham** *Nottingham CP* 16pp

2198 **Let's Be Proud of Our City** *Nottingham CP* 8pp

2199 **Notts Miners Forward** 12pp Pictorial cover. No publisher – could be national pamphlet.

1939

2200 **A.R.P. A Plan for Rugby** *Rugby CP* 14pp ?

1943

2201 **13 Questions and Answers on the Newark By-Election** Blackwell, Sam 8pp

1944

2202 **Nottingham: Plan or Sprawl** *Nottingham CP* 8pp

1946

2203 **Derby: Your Town** *Derby CP* 22pp

1949

2204 **500 Years of Struggle: A People's History of Nottingham** 16pp

2205 **500 Years of Struggle: Souvenir Programme (March and Meeting)** 4pp

1962

2206 **Nottingham For You** Peck, John *Nottingham Area* 18pp

1972

2207 **Report of 18th District Congress** 10pp lf d

North West

1923

2208 **6th Anniversary of Russian Workers' Soviet Republic: Great Demonstration – Programme** *Manchester District Party Committee* 4pp Platform included Tom Bell, Ellen Wilkinson, Saklatvala, Phillips Price. Interesting list of names and addresses of Manchester CP contacts.

1933

2209 **An Industrial Town Under Capitalism: What Soviet Power Would Do in Ashton-under-Lyne** *Ashton CP* 12pp

2210 **Souvenir Programme: Lenin, Liebknecht and Luxemburg Commemoration, Jan. 22** *Rochdale Local* 4pp

1935

2211 **Special Congress Number: Party Life** *Lancs District* 8pp lf d Usually not for sale?

1936

2212 **What's Wrong With Lancashire?** Rust, W. 12pp

1937

2213 **Manchester and Salford Annual Conference** 10pp lf

2214 **The Hope Hospital Scandal** *Salford CP* 12pp

2215 **This Our City: A Programme for Modern Manchester** *Manchester & Salford DC* 16pp Foreword by H. Pollitt.

1938

2216 **100 Years of Struggle: Manchester's Centenary: The Real Story** *Manchester & Salford DC* 26pp

2217 **Birkenhead For Labour** *Birkenhead CP* 16pp

2218 **Liverpool for Labour** *Merseyside CP* 16pp

2219 **Make Liverpool Fit To Live In: A Municipal Programme** Bright, Frank *Merseyside DC* 12pp

2220 **The March of History: A Message to You From the CP** *Lancs District* 12pp

2221 **To Our Comrades** *Merseyside* 8pp d No publisher, address, date; probably CP or Aid Spain campaign. Letters from Merseysiders in I.B. plus messages from wives supporting them. ?

2222 **What Next for Manchester?** Jenkins, Mick *Manchester & Salford DC* 16pp 4,000 sold.

1939

2223 **Better Times for Lancashire** *Lancs District* 13pp

1940

2224 **Birkenhead and the Bombers** 14pp A.R.P. ?

2225 **Blitzkrieg on Manchester** Jenkins, Mick *Manchester & Salford DC* 16pp Cover probably by Manchester Group AIA and 'Gabriel'.

2226 **Lancashire Forward** Whittaker, Bill *Lancs & District DC* 32pp

1941

2227 **Cotton: How Lancashire Workers Can Save Their Homes and Livelihood** Devine, Pat & Kershaw, Harry *Lancs DC* 16pp 5,000 printed. Devine was CP councillor in Motherwell in 1922 and later left for the US where he became Secretary of the National Textile Workers' Union.

2228 **It's Up To You and Me: The Real Story of the Manchester and Salford Bombing** Jeffrey, Nora *Manchester & Salford DC* 10pp

1942

2229 **Lancashire Fights to Win** Devine, Pat 15pp Important list of local addresses on back page. Cover by Sheila Greenhalgh. ?

1943

2230 **Lancashire for Luck** Johnson, Vera 14pp Fiction. ?

2231 **Shorten the War: Attack the Nazis Now!** *Lancs & Cheshire District* 8pp lf ?

1944

2232 **All Into the Attack!** Devine, Pat *Lancs & Cheshire DC* 4pp

2233 **Co-op Centenary Special** *Lancs & Cheshire District* 4pp lf Ill. by P. Hogarth & E. Brooks.

2234 **Cotton for Victory** Dickenson, Harold *Lancs District* 12pp ?

2235 **Cotton Workers Advance** Whittaker, Bill & Dickinson, Harold *Lancs & Cheshire CP* 6pp ?

2236 **Manchester for the People** *Manchester Area* 20pp ?

2237 **We Pledge the Lads: The Sabre** *CP Group at Napiers (Sabre Engines), Liverpool* 8pp

1945

2238 **180,000 Houses for Lancashire and Cheshire: Communist Policy for Lancs No.1** Jenkins, Mick *Lancs & Cheshire District* 16pp

2239 **Communist Councillor** *Merseyside CP* 4pp lf Election broadsheet. ?

2240 **Forward to a New Preston** 16pp Contrib. incl. Pat Devine, Edgar Riley, D. Archer, Tessa Worswick, Eleanor Harvey, Percy Robson.

2241 **Stockport Tomorrow** 18pp

2242 **The Future for Lancashire and Cheshire Coal Miners: Communist Policy for Lancs, No. 2** Hammond, Jim *Lancs & Cheshire District* 14pp

1946

2243 **A New Chance in Life for the Children: The Fight for the Carrying Through of the**

1944 Education Act in Lancs and Cheshire Whittenbury, Joan 16pp ?

2244 Cotton: Memorandum Submitted to the Working Party for the Cotton Industry 24pp ?

2245 May Day Programme *Lancs & Cheshire District* 4pp lf

2246 Report to District Congress October 1945-September 1946 *Lancs & Cheshire DC* 16pp

1947

2247 A Charter for the North West *Lancs & Cheshire District* 18pp Cover (signed 'PH') possibly by Percy Higgins. ?

1948

2248 Centenary of the Communist Manifesto *Merseyside Area* 8pp Souvenir Programme for rally at Philharmonic Hall, June.

2249 Drive Out the Spectre from Merseyside Alexander, Bill *Merseyside CP* 6pp On unemployment. ?

2250 Lancashire 1848-1948: Communist Manifesto Centenary 30pp

2251 Merseyside CP Presents Little Humpback Horse and The Forgotten Village: Programme *Merseyside Area* 4pp Programme for cultural event. ?

2252 Report of District Congress: Sweep Away the Warmongers! *Lancs & Cheshire DC* 34pp

2253 Report of the Lancashire and Cheshire District 1947-8 16pp

2254 Spotlight on Cotton Whittaker, Bill 12pp ?

1951

2255 Frederick Engels in Manchester Jenkins, Mick *Lancs & Cheshire CP* 24pp

1952

2256 The Truth About Cotton *Lancs & Cheshire DC* 4pp

1953

2257 Ernest Jones (Chartist): A Fighter for Manchester's Working Class *Lancs & Cheshire History Group* 6pp lf d

2258 Lancashire and Cheshire Look Ahead: Report of District Congress *Lancs & Cheshire DPC* 42pp Incl. Report by Syd Abbott. Much on cotton industry.

2259 Report of Industrial Conference, Oct. 4 *Lancs & Cheshire DC* 14pp lf Main contributors are Tom Rowlandson & P. Kerrigan. ?

1954

2260 A Programme for Manchester *Manchester & Salford Area Cttee* 4pp lf ?

2261 Report of Industrial Conference, Oct. 16/17 *Lancs & Cheshire District* 27pp lf

1958

2262 District Congress Discussion Statement *Lancs & Cheshire District* 4pp lf

1959

2263 Housing in the Hugh Oldham Ward *Collyhurst & Platting Branch, Manchester* 8pp d

1960

2263a Harry Pollitt Memorial Meeting, St. George's Hall, Liverpool 4pp lf

2264 Heartbreak Houses: An Outline of Communist Housing Policy for Hugh Oldham Ward Cohen, Manny *Platting Branch* 4pp

1966

2265 Report of Resolutions of District Congress *Lancs & Cheshire DC* 22pp lf

1968

2266 Make the Grey Areas Red: Report of Lancs and Cheshire District Congress, Nov. *Lancs & Cheshire District* 42pp

1969

2267 **Peterloo** *Lancs & Cheshire DC* 8pp

2268 **Proposed Central Lancashire New Town** Cohen, Gerry *Lancs & Cheshire DC* 8pp lf Statement on behalf of the DC to Enquiry.

1970

2269 **1920-70 'Battling' Merseyside Communists Celebrate 50 Glorious Years – Souvenir Programme** *Merseyside Area* 4pp Incl. some useful snippets of local CP history.

2270 **Congress Report** 10pp lf

1972

2271 **A Biographical Sketch of the Life of Jim Gardner** *NW History Group* 36pp lf d Gen. Sec. Amalgamated Union of Foundry Workers; EC of CP. ?

2272 **Congress Report** 6pp lf

1973

2273 **1973 Merseyside Elections: Communist Policy Statement** *Merseyside Area Cttee* 16pp lf

1974

2274 **Improvement Grants** Taylor, George *Salford CP* 22pp lf d ?

1975

2275 **Merseyside on the Dole** O'Hara, Roger *Merseyside Area* 18pp

1976

2277 **Which Way for the North West? Report of District Congress** 6pp lf

1977

2278 **George Brown: Portrait of a Communist Leader** Jenkins, Mick *NW History Group* 30pp Brown was Manchester Organiser for CP and Political Commissar of I.B. ?

2279 **The North West: Technological Relic or Modern Industrial Region ?** 16pp ?

1978

2280 **About the CP: A Study Guide in 4 Parts** 32pp lf d ?

2281 **Congress Report** 22pp lf

2282 **Merseyside in 1980s: Report of Merseyside Area Conference** O'Hara, Roger *Merseyside Area* 21pp Lengthy Secretary's Report, election results to Area Cttee, Resolutions, Credentials Report.

2283 **People's Festival '78, Belle Vue, Nov. 26: Programme** *Greater Manchester Area* 24pp

1979

2284 **Frank Bright: Miner, Marxist and Communist Organiser 1891-1944** Frow, Ruth & Eddie *History Group* 10pp lf

2285 **The CP in Manchester, 1920-1926** Frow, Ruth & Eddie *History Group* 80pp Includes short biogs of 126 members.

1980

2286 **Conference Report** *Manchester Area* 14pp lf d Incl. Report by P. Salveson, the Area Sec.

2287 **People's Festival Programme** *Greater Manchester Area Cttee* 24pp

1983

2288 **Karl Marx and Harry Pollitt Souvenir Brochure** *Greater Manchester Area* 10pp lf

2289 **Liverpool's State of Health** Gardner, Katy & Munby, Steve *Merseyside Area* 40pp lf A shorter version had been published in 1980.

2290 **Police: Accountable to Whom?** O'Hara, Roger (ed.) *Merseyside Area* 20pp lf ?

1986

2291 **District Congress: Discussion Statement; Report of Work; Plan of Work** 20pp lf

1988

2292 **Merseyside Out of the Crisis** Munby, Steve (ed.) *Merseyside Area* 34pp lf ?

1989

2293 **The Mancunian Way: A CP Approach to the Regeneration of Manchester** Quigley, Mark *Manchester Area* 20pp ?

Yorkshire

1923

2294 **Souvenir Programme: Rally at AEU Institute, Sheffield, October** 4pp Contains words of Internationale, Red Flag and extract from a Commons speech by Newbold.

1927

2295 **The 'Anti-Trade Union Bill': Special Bulletin** *Sheffield DPC* 4pp lf d In form of factory paper, dated May 4.

1932

2296 **The Handrags of 'Law and Order'** Murphy, J.T. *Sheffield* 16pp On NUWM's conflicts with Sheffield TC and LP Branch.

1933

2297 **Sheffield Week Special** 4pp lf d

1936

2298 **The March of English History: Rally Programme** *North Midlands DC* 10pp

2299 **Wharncliffe Woodmoor Colliery Disaster** *North Midlands CP (Sheffield)* 14pp

1938

2300 **A.R.P. A Complete Plan for Sheffield** *Sheffield Branch* 16pp ?

2301 **Leeds Has a Plan for Health and Happiness** *Leeds Branch* 20pp

2302 **Sheffield: The People's Policy for the City** *Sheffield Branch* 12pp

1941

2303 **The 'Blitz' and Leeds** *Leeds* 12pp

1943

2304 **Your Health and the Factory** *Yeadon Branch* 14pp ?

1944

2305 **All For the Front: Yorkshire to France!** 8pp

2306 **Miners: Victory and After** 8pp lf

2307 **Your Leeds** *Leeds Area Cttee* 16pp

1945

2308 **Calling All Bevin Boys** Moss, Bob 4pp

2309 **Municipal Special: Vote Communist** *Sheffield CP* 4pp lf Candidates for local elections – incl. Herbert Howarth, Minnie Atkin, Bas Barker.

2310 **Redundancy: Some Questons Asked** *Leeds Area Cttee* 4pp On the forthcoming changeover from war to peace time production, especially in engineering.

2311 **Wool: A Memorandum on the Future of the Wool Textile Industry** 16pp ?

1946

2312 **1946: Miners Year** 4pp lf On pit communities, not just the mines.

2313 **Report of District Congress** 25pp lf d

2314 **Wool Workers** 4pp lf ?

2314a **Year of Battle: Report of Yorkshire Committee to 2nd Annual Congress** 12pp

1955

2315 **Memorandum on Housing in Leeds** *Leeds Area Cttee* 6pp lf d

1962

2316 **Syllabus on Right-Wing Labour and the Ruling Class** *Education Cttee* 17pp lf

1967

2317 **Rents, Housing and the Sheffield People** *Sheffield CP* 8pp d

1976

2318 **Zionism: A False Philosophy Which Adds to Confusion** Kaye, Solly *Leeds CP* 8pp ?

1978

2319 **Turn Leeds Left** *Leeds Area* 16pp Manifesto for Council Elections.

Northern

1937

2320 **Crusade for the People: CP Plan for Teeside** *Teeside CP* 16pp

2321 **The North East Marches On: History of Socialism in the N.E. From the Industrial Revolution** 15pp

1940

2322 **Make the North East Safe: A Practical Programme for A.R.P.** Gollan, J. 14pp

1942

2323 **How to Run Marxist Education** 34pp sf d

2324 **Unity For Victory: Programme for Rally Feb. 1** 8pp Incl. songs. Pictorial cover. List of local premises.

1943

2325 **Clear the Ways! Tyneside's Case for a Square Deal and More Ships** MacEwen, Malcolm 16pp ?

2326 **Ships for Victory** *Newcastle* 4pp lf

2327 **Spotlight on Tyneside** Owen, Jack 16pp Reprinted from 'DW'. Intro. by Joe Waters, North East District Sec.

2328 **Steel: A Call to Tees-Side Steel Workers** 26pp

2329 **The People Against Mosley**

2330 **The People's Health: Report of Conference, Oct. 9** 16pp

1945

2331 **Congress Report** 24pp lf d Incl. DC Report.

2332 **Resolution and Report of 2nd Annual Congress** *NW District* 14pp lf d This early 'NW' District was Cumberland and Westmorland, plus Furness. Published under the aegis of the Northern District.

1948

2333 **100 Years of Working Class Struggle in the North-East** 4pp Brief chronology of Labour movement history in the North East.

1949

2334 **The North-East Marches On** 16pp

1955

2335 **Report of Proceedings of 8th District Congress** *Teesside District* 6pp lf d Teesside was a District at this point.

1976

2335a **District Congress Report** 4pp

1982

2336 **Strategy of Resistance: Congress Report** 14pp lf

1986

2337 **From the Tees to the Ebro: My Road to Spain** Goodman, Dave *Middlesbrough* 28pp

1987

2338 Newcastle's Crisis: A Communist Solution *West Central Branch* 34pp ?

1988

2339 Northern Comment 8pp lf District Congress Report/News.

1989

2340 From Middlesbrough to Manchuria: The Story of the Haruna Maru Clegg, Arthur *Teesside CP* 36pp Teesside dockers support for China against Japan. ?

2341 I'll See Socialism in My Time: Teesside Politics in the 1950s Ward, Bert *Teesside CP* 46pp Autobiog. of leading local CP member. ?

Wales

1921

2342 The Last Speech of Comrade Hewlett Delivered to Delegates of 3rd International Congress, Moscow, July *Abertillery Branch* 8pp Bill Hewlett played important role in the formation of CP. This pamphlet includes a foreword, a report of his burial in the Kremlin wall as well as his speech. Also in 'C.R.' Aug. 1921.

1934

2343 District Congress Discussion Bulletin 3pp lf d No.1, 18 October 1934 – the only one?

1935

2344 Merthyr Royal Commission Special *Merthyr Borough Sub-District* 4pp lf

2345 Rhondda East Special 4pp lf For Election in Nov.

1937

2346 A Programme of Life, Health and Work for South Wales *South Wales District* 24pp

2347 Make Cardiff a Capital City *Cardiff Branch* 18pp Cover by Miles. ?

2348 South Wales in the March of History *Rhondda CP* 12pp

1938

2349 'A Town on the Dole' *Brynmawr CP* 24pp

2350 Llwybr Rhyddid Y Werin (People's Road to Freedom) Williams, John Roose 18pp In Welsh, published from King Street. Author was active Christian and Communist. ?

2351 TB: The White Scourge *South Wales District* 12pp

2352 The Lore of the People *South & North Wales Districts* 16pp On the Eisteddfod. In English & Welsh. ?

2353 Weithwyr Cymru! (Workers of Wales!) Nicholas, T.E. *Workers' Bookshop, Aberystwyth* 4pp 5 songs in Welsh, incl. 'The Red Flag' (Y Faner Goch) translated by Nicholas. ?

1939

2354 Congress Report 10pp lf d Summary of Reports by Glyn Jones & W. Paynter.

1940

2355 South Wales and the Bombers! Cox, Idris 12pp On A.R.P.

2356 Tuberculosis: The White Scourge, The War and Wales *South Wales District* 20pp Updated ed. of 1938 pamphlet.

1941

2357 Communists in South Wales: Policy and Aims *South Wales DC* 32pp Summarised speeches & resolutions from District Congress. Pictorial cover.

2358 Information Special 4pp lf d On German attack on USSR.

1943

2359 **The Swansea Plan and YOU** *Swansea CP* 4pp lf ?

2360 **The Way Forward for South Wales** *South Wales DC* 16pp Resolutions from District Congress.

1944

2361 **A Great Welshman: T. Gwynn Jones – Symposium of Tributes** 24pp Unusual pamphlet: contains more about Jones's cultural writing than his radical politics.

2362 **Communists and Welsh Self-Government** 4pp

2363 **Forward to a New Life for South Wales** Cox, Idris *South Wales DC* 16pp 18,000 sold. Cover by Miles.

2364 **The Flame of Welsh Freedom** 20pp On the Eisteddfod.

2365 **Wales in the New World** 32pp Cover by Miles. Useful list of CP addresses/shops. 10,000 print run.

2366 **When War Jobs Finish!** *Mid-Glamorgan CP* 32pp

1945

2367 **A Brighter Future for Abertillery and District** 16pp ?

2368 **Beware! The Enemy in Our Midst** Thomas, Alun *West Wales Area Cttee* 8pp On Trotskyism & the Neath by-election.

2369 **Communist Plan for Cardiff** *Cardiff & Barry Area Cttee* 32pp Cover by Miles.

2370 **Communist Policy for the People of Wales: Report of the 1st All-Wales Congress, Jan.** 32pp

2371 **Siartr Y Chwarelwr (Quarrymen's Charter)** *Wrexham CP (?)* 12pp In Welsh. Cover by A. Miles. ?

2372 **The People Demand Houses!** 8pp About Women's National Housing Deputation to House of Commons, Dec 1944.

2373 **Tinplate: New Merger, Old Policy** Duckworth, R. 14pp

2374 **Young Wales and the Future** Williams, John Roose 24pp

1946

2375 **Bridgend Looks to the Future** *Bridgend* 16pp

2376 **Drive the Spectre from Wales** Cox, Idris 8pp Cover by Miles.

2377 **Make 1947 a Real New Year in Wales** 8pp

2378 **Over the Hills** *Aberdare CP* 14pp

2379 **Report and Resolutions of 2nd Welsh Congress** 8pp lf d

2380 **The Future of the Ogmore Valley** *Ogmore Valley CP* 16pp ?

2381 **Where We Stand: The CP and the Neath Rural District Council** *Neath Rural District Group of CP* 8pp ?

1947

2382 **Fighters for the People: A Record of the Activities of Communist Councillors in Wales** 8pp

2383 **The Battle for Coal** 4pp lf

1948

2384 **The Fight for Socialism in Wales 1848-1948** Cox, Idris 24pp Cover by Miles.

2385 **Y Maniffesto Comiwnyddol** Marx, Karl & Engels, Friedrich 48pp 'The Communist Manifesto' in Welsh, intro. & trans. by W.J. Rees. 3,000 printed. First ed.

1949

2386 **A Oes Heddwch? (Is There Peace?)** Cox, Idris 8pp In Welsh.

2387 **Annual Conference, Jan.** *Rhondda Area Cttee* 26pp lf d

2388 **The Socialist Road for the Neath Constituency** *Neath CP* 10pp

1964

2389 **The New Way for Wales** 4pp lf Set of 5 slightly different election broadsheets for the 5 candidates in Wales: Annie Powell, Jim David, Eddie Jones, Julian Tudor Hart & Bob Hitchon.

1965

2390 **'Daily Worker' Rally, Cory Hall, Cardiff: Souvenir Programme** 4pp

1968

2391 **Communist Policy on the National Question in Wales** 14pp lf d Reprint of Speech to Congress by Bob Hitchon & article by Bert Pearce.

1970

2392 **Constitutional Reform and the Future of Wales: Evidence to the Commission on the Constitution** 24pp lf d

2393 **Devolution, Democracy and Socialism: Policy Statement** 13pp lf d Resolution Adopted at Welsh Congress, Nov.

2394 **Let Wales Lead: Election Manifesto for Wales, June** 12pp lf d

1971

2395 **T.E. Nicholas: Proffwyd Sosialaeth a Bardd Gwrthryfel (Prophet of Socialism and Anti-War Poet)** Williams, John Roose (ed.) 46pp In Welsh. Published on behalf of the Welsh Committee by J.R. Williams ?

1972

2396 **The Communist Party Welsh Congress 1972** 16pp lf d Incl. Discussion Statement & Draft Resolution.

1974

2397 **A Parliament with Power for Wales: Comments Submitted on Government Discussion Paper 'Devolution Within the UK'** 15pp

2398 **Opportunity For Wales To Give Britain A Lead: Election Manifesto For Wales, Feb.** 12pp lf d

2399 **Wales Needs Communist Policy: Power to the People – Election Manifesto For Wales, Oct.** 12pp lf d

1975

2400 **The Communist Party Welsh Congress 1975** 18pp Incl. Discussion Statement & Draft Resolution.

1977

2401 **A Welsh Assembly: Policy Statement** 13pp lf d

1978

2402 **Which Way for North Wales?** 32pp lf d Largely the work of Manny Cohen.

1979

2403 **Communists Care: For A Better Life For Wales – Election Manifesto For Wales, May** 12pp lf d

1980

2404 **Communist Party Welsh Congress 1980** 17pp lf d Incl. Discussion Statement & Draft Resolution etc.

2405 **Cyffro Broadsheet** 12pp lf

1983

2406 **Communists Want: A Real Future For Wales, Jobs Not Bombs – Election Manifesto For Wales, June** 14pp lf d

Scotland

1924

2407 **Celebration Meeting: 7th Anniversary of the Russian Revolution, City Hall, Nov. 7 – Souvenir Programme** *Glasgow Local Party Cttee* 8pp

1927

2408 **Secret Documents of the CP** *Fife Sub Cttee* 4pp lf d Reply to 'secret documents' scare in local press about CP activity in mines.

1928

2409 Gala Day Special, June 1 *Fife Sub-District* 6pp d

1934

2410 Crisis on Clydeside Hutt, Allen *Workers' Bookshop, Glasgow* 32pp pb Intro. by Hugh Hinshelwood. Reprinted from 'The Condition of the Working Class in Britain', Martin Lawrence 1933.

1935

2411 Jubilee Special *Glasgow District* 8pp lf Pictorial. Scathing attack.

1936

2412 Communist Crusade for the People *Glasgow Cttee* 4pp lf ?

2413 For a Brighter and Happier Glasgow: A Real Live Municipal Programme *Glasgow Cttee* 16pp

2414 Socialism and Peace: A Reply to the ILP – Speeches by W. Rust & J.R. Campbell, May Rust, W. & Campbell, J.R. 20pp

1937

2415 Programme of the Pageant of Scottish History 16pp ?

2416 Scotland Ferguson, Aitken 32pp ?

2417 Scotland and Its Bus Service 16pp ?

1938

2418 Let's Spend a Million: The Communist Plan for Building a Better Edinburgh Douglas, Fred *Edinburgh Branch* 18pp

2419 The Protestant Movement X-Rayed Douglas, Fred *Edinburgh Branch* 16pp ?

2420 Whose Edinburgh? Douglas, Fred 12pp Not officially a CP publication – self-published.

1939

2421 2nd Annual All-Scottish CP Rally, Stanley Village, Perthshire, Aug. 20 – Programme 4pp

2422 A.R.P. Scheme of Protection for Glasgow Cowe, William 16pp ?

2423 Scotland's March to Peace and Progress Kerrigan, Peter 16pp Report to Scottish District Congress, Feb.

1940

2424 20th Anniversary Celebration Meeting, St Andrew's Halls Aug. 11 4pp lf Programme & songs.

2425 Five Speeches Gallacher, W. 20pp

2426 Scotland and the War Cowe, William 16pp Speech to Scottish Congress, Jan.

1941

2427 Scottish District 21st Anniversary Meeting, August – Souvenir Programme 8pp Includes 5 songs.

1942

2428 India Week Special, June *Glasgow* 4pp lf In effect, this is almost an ed. of the 'DW' which was banned at this time – it is not just about India.

2429 Scotland For the Offensive 12pp

2430 Scottish District Congress Report, Oct. 8pp

2431 Socialism Through Victory: A Reply to the Policy of the ILP Campbell, J.R. 16pp

2432 Spotlight on the Clyde Owen, Jack 24pp ?

2433 Women in War Special *Glasgow* 4pp lf In effect, an ed. of the banned 'DW'.

2434 Your Part in Victory: An Appeal to Workers in the Mining, Shipbuiding, Engineering & Building Industries Campbell, J.R. 16pp ?

1943

2435 An Intelligent Socialist's Guide to World War No. 2 Fraser, Hamish 36pp

LOCAL PUBLICATIONS

2436 **Dundee Social Problems** Annan, Alexander *Dundee Area* 16pp ?

2437 **Glasgow Wants: Houses in a Hurry** McShane, Harry 8pp

2438 **Guilty Men of the Clyde!** Gollan, J. 20pp

2439 **Health and Housing in Aberdeen** *Aberdeen* 8pp ?

2440 **Health for the People: Memorandum on Scotland's Health Services** 24pp

2441 **Houses for Lanarkshire** *Lanarkshire Area Cttee* 16pp

2442 **Housing: An Immediate War Emergency Programme for Scotland** McCourt, B. 12pp

2443 **Nazi Atrocities Special** 4pp lf As well as subject matter indicated in the title, this journal-type pamphlet has interesting page on CP response to Beveridge Report.

2444 **Put Mosley Back In Prison** 8pp

2445 **Report of the Scottish Congress, Sept.** 16pp

2446 **Scotland's Electric Power: A Report of a Debate on the Hydro-Electric Development (Scotland) Bill** *Clyde Books* 12pp

2447 **Scottish Agriculture** 16pp

2448 **United Action for Victory and Progress, Regal Cinema Paisley, July – Programme** 4pp

1944

2449 **Fighting France Special** McShane, Harry et al. 4pp lf

2450 **Glasgow's Housing Disgrace** McShane, Harry *Glasgow Cttee* 14pp ?

2451 **Glasgow's Housing Hunger** McShane, Harry *Glasgow* 16pp

2452 **Housing: Lanarkshire Must Act** McCourt, B. *Lanarkshire Area Cttee* 16pp Author was a local councillor. ?

2453 **Invasion Special** 4pp lf

2454 **Scotland's Fishing Industry** 16pp

2455 **Scotland's Schools** 32pp

2456 **Searchlight on the Foundry** *Stirling Area Cttee* 20pp ?

2457 **Unity For the General Election: Report of Conference on Working Class Unity, Glasgow Nov. 18 – Speeches by W. Gallacher & H. Pollitt** Gallacher, W. & Pollitt, H. 16pp

1945

2458 **A Modern Tale of Two Cities: Communist Housing Policy for Edinburgh** 8pp ?

2459 **A People's Plan for Scotland** 38pp

2460 **Dundee Needs Houses** Barclay, W. *Dundee Area Cttee* 16pp

2461 **Future of Jute** Bowman, Dave *Dundee CP* 16pp

2462 **Labour Must Lead** 8pp lf Incl. H. McShane on housing.

2463 **Lanarkshire Prospect Special** *Lanarkshire Cttee* 4pp lf

2464 **Motherwell Election Special** *Lanarkshire Cttee* 4pp lf

2465 **People's Plan for Scotland: 4 Course Syllabus of Study** *Educ. Dept, Scottish Cttee* 8pp

2466 **Post War Policy For Aberdeen** *Aberdeen CP* 12pp ?

2467 **Prefabrication: Demarcation and the Shipyard Trades** Hart, Finlay 16pp Preface by H. Pollitt. ?

2468 **Prestwick Airport: Alex Sloan's Speech in House of Commons, March** *Ayrshire Cttee* 14pp

2469 **Rent Rocket: Communist Special** *Motherwell* 4pp lf ?

2470 **Scotland's Road to Victory, Peace and Security: Resolutions of Scottish Congress, April** 20pp

2471 **Scottish Students**

2472 **The Ayrshire We Want** *Ayrshire Cttee* 8pp lf ?

2473 **The Dodgers: An Exposure and Criticism of the ILP** Gallacher, W. 20pp

2474 **The Fight for a Full Life: A Social Plan and Programme for the People of West Lothian** Reid, David *West Lothian County Cttee* 16pp ?

2475 **The Scottish Tories** Douglas, Fred 94pp

2476 **Towards a People's Lanarkshire** *Lanarkshire Cttee* 16pp ?

2477 **Towards the New Falkirk** *Falkirk* 24pp

2478 **Whither Scotland?** 36pp Pictorial.

2479 **Your Irvine** Smith, Alex 16pp Author was Secretary of CP in Ayrshire. Self-published. ?

1946

2480 **Build a Better Gorbals** McShane, Harry *Gorbals Branch* 16pp ?

2481 **Glasgow's Transport** *Glasgow City Cttee* 16pp ?

2482 **Hamilton Fights for the Future** Nicholson, J. *Hamilton Branch* 16pp ?

2483 **Houses: Rents and Racketteers** Smith, Alex 16pp ?

2484 **Our Plan for Prosperity: Fife** *Fife Area Cttee* 22pp ?

2485 **Rent Rocket** *Dumbarton Area*

2486 **Report of Sottish Committee and Resolutions of Scottish Congress, Sept.** 20pp

2487 **Scotland Needs 150,000 Jobs** Gollan, J. 32pp

2488 **Spain Special** Gollan, J. et al. 4pp Broadsheet.

2489 **The Battle for Houses in Glasgow** McShane, Harry *Glasgow* 16pp

2490 **The Housing Subsidy: Rents and Rates** Gollan, J. 32pp ?

2491 **What Next in Glasgow?** McIlhone, Bob *Glasgow Cttee* 16pp

2492 **Your Kilmarnock** *Kilmarnock Branch* 16pp

1947

2493 **Housing and Rent**

2494 **Let Lanarkshire Help Solve Britain's Crisis: CP Special** 4pp lf

2495 **Scotland – And Its Future: A Short Term Plan Adopted by Scottish Congress, Oct.** 8pp lf

2496 **Scotland and the Crisis** Lauchlan, William 20pp

2497 **Scotland Demands** 4pp lf Communist Special.

2498 **Scotland: An Economic Survey** 36pp

2499 **Steel: The Next Step** *Lanarkshire Area Cttee* 4pp lf

1948

2500 **Rents Racket** 4pp lf

2501 **Searchlight on Wages, Prices, Profits** 4pp lf

1949

2502 **Mr Brogan Opens Wide His Mouth** Gallacher, W. 12pp Brogan wrote 'The Case Against Gallacher' attacking Gallacher & CP from right-wing Catholic viewpoint.

1950

2503 **Children First** 16pp

2504 **Pals and Other Verses** Gallacher, W. 24pp lf No publisher or date given. ?

1951

2505 **70th Birthday Greetings to W. Gallacher: Souvenir Programme** 8pp lf Incl. poetic tributes!

1952

2506 **Housing Swindle: CP Special** 4pp lf Incl. article by H. McShane. ?

2507 **Poems From Clydeside** 20pp Includes poems by F. Anderson. ?

2508 **Poems of a Glasgow Worker** Anderson, Freddy 16pp No publisher stated. Printed by Caledonian Press.

1953

2509 **A Future for Scotland and Her People: Report to Scottish Congress** Lauchlan, William 20pp

2510 **'But They Shall Be Free': Scottish Affairs – Memorandum by Scottish Cttee to Royal Commission** 16pp lf d

2511 **Higher Wages Now** 4pp lf ?

1954

2512 **The Great Rent Swindle** 4pp lf ?

1956

2513 **Tory Rent Racket Exposed** 4pp lf ?

1958

2514 **Burns Belongs to the People** 24pp ?

1959

2515 **Glenrothes: A Better Place to Live and Work** *Glenrothes Branch* 12pp

2516 **Robert Burns 'The Democrat'** Campbell, J.R. 40pp

1960

2517 **Demand a Future for Scotland** McLennan, Gordon *Glasgow Cttee* 18pp

2518 **Glasgow's Prospect** Clark, Alex *Glasgow Cttee* 16pp

1961

2519 **Keep Out the Polaris Peril!** McLennan, Gordon 4pp lf ?

1962

2520 **Out With the Tories: CP Special** 4pp lf

2521 **Scotland's Economy: Memorandum to Secretary of State for Scotland** 12pp lf d

1965

2522 **Scotland's Children** 4pp Election broadsheet.

1966

2523 **Congress Report** 15pp lf d

1974

2524 **For a Scottish Parliament** 8pp ?

1977

2525 **Glasgow: A Call to Action** *Glasgow Cttee* 20pp lf

1980

2526 **A Discussion Document on Child Care** *Glasgow Women's Advisory* 12pp lf ?

2527 **Weirs: Don't Let Them Run It Down!** *Glasgow* 4pp lf ?

1982

2528 **Make OUR Council FIGHT The Cuts** *Glasgow* 4pp lf For Strathclyde Regional elections.

1986

2529 **Congress 1986: Decisions and Resolutions, Congress Report** 18pp lf d

1988

2530 **Power in People's Hands ... Services for People's Needs** 4pp lf For District council elections.

2531 **Scotland's Future** 16pp lf ?

1989

2532 **A People's Plan for Govan** *Govan* 24pp lf

1990

2533 **Scottish Politics in the 1990s ... Meeting the Challenge: Ending Minority Rule** 4pp lf

3. National Magazines

This chapter lists all magazines and journals published nationally in title order. A surprising discovery was the lack of national industrial journals – though this would be compensated for by the numerous rank and file papers which lie outside the scope of this bibliography e.g. those produced by the NMM, and later papers like *Flashlight, Building Workers' Charter, Seamen's Charter* etc. In all of these papers individual CP members and organisations would have played crucial roles from writing to printing and selling.

Editors are listed when known.

There are cases of titles being used more than once (e.g. *Communist Review*) – these have been distinguished by a number in square brackets. Sometimes these titles might be in different chapters e.g. *Live Wire* [2] is in this chapter and *Live Wire* [1] is in Chapter 4. The journals published by Advisory Committees (of which there was an upsurge in the 1970s) varied in size and quality depending on the individuals involved; when there was continuity of editor, or editorial group, these journals could be both long lasting and influential, e.g. Historians' Group, Education Advisory Committee. Others were more topical and short lived, e.g. *Portugal Information Bulletin* and the journals associated with the 'Eurocommunist' period (*Socialist Europe* and *Euro Red*). After the Historians' Group publications, the cultural journals are worth highlighting, as the artists and writers concerned were often of national importance.

There was a group of duplicated journals in the late 1940s and early 1950s which reflected the CPGB's activity in anti-colonial concerns; some were directly published by the Party (the *West Indies Newsletter* and the *Africa Newsletter*) but others were produced by national groups of foreign Communists often in close collaboration with King Street (the *Malayan Monitor* and the *Ceylon Newsletter*). The Greek Cypriot Communist community published its own Greek language weekly, *Vema*, for many years.

Although in each entry I have indicated, where relevant, which journal preceded and succeeded a specific journal, listing them alphabetically means that the relationship between the papers is not clear, so below is a list of the main national publications showing continuity.

Newspapers/official organs:

Communist, The [1]	1920-3	(weekly)
Workers' Weekly, The	1923-7	(weekly)
Workers' Life	1927-9	(weekly)
Daily Worker	1930-66	(daily)
Morning Star	1966-	(daily)
Seven Days	1985-90	(weekly)
Changes	1990-1	(fortnightly)

Reviews (primarily internal):

International Press Correspondence	1921-37	(at least weekly) [CI rather than CPGB]
World News and Views	1937-53	(weekly)
World News	1954-62	(weekly)
Comment	1963-82	(weekly/fortnightly)
Focus	1982-5	(monthly)
News and Views	1986-90	(monthly)

Internal organisational journals:

Communist Organiser (1)	March 1932-December 1932	(monthly)
Communist Organiser (2)	July 1938-June 1940	(monthly)
Untitled (see below)	August 1942-August 1944	14 issues

Theoretical Journals:

Communist Review [1]	1921-7	(monthly)
Communist, The [2]	1927-8	(monthly)
Communist Review [2]	1929-35	(monthly)
Discussion	1936-8	(monthly)
Modern Quarterly [1]	1938-9	(quarterly)
Modern Quarterly [2]	1945-53	(quarterly)
Communist Review [3]	1946-53	(monthly)
Marxist Quarterly	1954-7	(quarterly)
Marxism Today	1957-91	(monthly)

Women's Journals:

Woman Worker [1]	1926-7	(monthly)
Working Woman	1927-9	(monthly)
Woman Worker [2]	1929-30?	(monthly/bimonthly)
Woman Today	1938-59	(monthly/bimonthly)
Link	1973-84	(quarterly)

A couple of these were not strictly CP publications – see the entry for each item's status.

Labour Monthly (1921-79) was also not an official journal. Edited for most of its existence by Palme Dutt, it was influential in the labour movement and had many non-communist contributors. Its editorials (the famous 'Notes of the Month') reflected CP policy, though in later years, notably in 1968 over the invasion of Czechoslovakia, it distanced itself from the CP line.

Between August 1942 and August 1944 there was a set of 14 pamphlets that constituted a run of journals dealing with internal and organisational matters, but presumably paper restrictions meant they had to be published as 'one-offs'. These are listed individually in National Publications (but to identify them, the world 'Journal' plus month of issue appears in the entry for each of them):

Communist Organisation for Victory	Aug 1942
Mobilising the Party for the 2nd Front	Oct 1942
Organising to Win the Offensive	Dec 1942
Organising for Offensive Action	Feb 1943
Organise to Mobilise Millions	March 1943
Party Organisation – Weapon for Victory	March 1943
Organising for Victory in 1943	May 1943
Sharpening Our Weapons	July 1943
Speed the Campaign	Dec 1943
Tune Up Our Organisation	Jan 1944
Strengthen Our Organisation	Feb 1944
Party Organisation and the Offensive	May 1944
Party Organisation and the Invasion	June 1944
Improve Our Party Organisation	Aug 1944

Inevitably there were some difficult decisions to make concerning inclusion. Generally, as indicated already, I have excluded magazines of 'front organisations'. Similarly, I have not included the cultural journal *Our Time* (which incorporated *Poetry and the People*): the editors included many CP members (Rickwood, Swingler, Slater, Willis etc) but the policy of the magazine (occasionally to the chagrin of some CP officials) was resolutely wider than that of the Party. Also, *Our Time* did not contain articles specifically on CP policy (hence it also never appears in the 'Magazine Articles' Chapter) even though it would not have existed without CP members' input. Another magazine not included is *Red Rag* (1971-8), published by a feminist collective that included some CP women such as Bea Campbell; this journal was criticised by the EC but the women involved were left to continue their work in it. Some bulletins published by Advisory Committees were not for sale, so have been excluded (*Psychological Transactions, Middle East Newsletter*).

If a year appears on its own after an entry, this indicates the year of the first known issue. First and last known issues are given, or the dates of the only ones traced. Pagination is occasionally omitted if there was great variation. The national organisation that produced the journal is given in italics, if relevant.

2533a Africa Newsletter 16pp Started 1947. Monthly/bi-monthly in early 1950s. Became 'Africa Bulletin' (no longer CP) Sept. 1954, published by Association For African Freedom from 1955. Monthly, till Feb. 1957. Reduced to 8pp. Ed. D. Buckle (from 1950).

2534 Anchors Aweigh *Seamen's Cttee* 8pp No.3, Nov. 1948; prior to this issue the paper was London based.

2535 Architects and Allied Technicians Group Bulletin 14pp d No.1, March 1950: 'Marxism and Modern Architecture'.

2536 Artists' Group Bulletin 8pp lf d No.1 (no date) ed. Robert Palmer; No.3 Feb. 1955, ed. Godfrey Rubens.

2537 Books for Progress *Central Books* 4pp No.1, July (?) 1950 to No.38, 1958. Monthly, then quarterly, review of books. Produced for many years after this for the book trade, but not for sale.

2538 Changes 8pp No.1, Oct. 1990 to No.28, Nov. 1991. Fortnightly. Ed: Simon Barrow then Mike Power. The CP's last periodical. The final issue had R. Falber's revelations on 'Moscow gold'.

2539 Colonial Information Bulletin *Colonial Information Bureau* Started 1937. Available on subscription only? Ed. Ben Bradley. Became 'Inside the Empire' in 1940 (8pp).

2540 Comment 16pp No.1, Jan. 5 1963 to Vol.20 No.16, Aug. 7 1982. Successor to 'World News'. Weekly, fortnightly from 1971. Eds: (not initially named): Dennis Ogden, Arthur Jordan, Alex McDonald, Gladys Brooks, Paul Olive, Sarah Benton, Ian McKay.

2541 Communist Daily 4pp 3 issues Nov. 13-15 during General Election campaign of 1922. There was also a Scottish ed.

2542 Communist Review [1] 50-100pp Vol.1 No.1, May 1921 to Vol.7 No.9, June 1927. Monthly. Ed: Tom Bell, W. Paul. Theoretical journal. Became 'The Communist'.

2543 Communist Review [2] 20-50pp Vol.1 No.1, Jan. 1929 to Vol.8 No.8, Aug. 1935. Monthly. From Aug. 1933 thinner, but wider format. Followed on from 'The Communist [2]'.

2544 Communist Review, The [3] 32pp March 1946 to Dec. 1953. Monthly. Ed. E. Burns. Dealt with political analysis & strategy; not as theoretical as 'Modern Quarterly' which came out at the same time.

2545 Communist, The [1] 8-12pp Vol.1 No.1, Aug. 5 1920 to No.131, Feb. 3 1923. 'An Organ of the Third (Communist) International – Published by the EC CPGB'. Weekly. Ed: Fred Willis, F. Meynell (for first 6 months of 1921), R. Postgate (July 1921), T.A. Jackson (May 1922). Incorporated 'The Call', the paper of the BSP. Interesting cartoons by 'Espoir', 'Westral' et al. Circulation reached high point of 60,000 after Black Friday.

2546 Communist, The [2] 50pp Vol.1 No.1, Feb. 1927 to Dec. 1928. Monthly pagination varied. Followed on from 'Communist Review' [1] – changed name same time as 'The Woman Worker' & 'Worker's Weekly'.

2547 Counter Attack *Workers' Bookshops of London, Glasgow, Newcastle* 8pp Started 1931(?); March 1933 (no.6?). There was a supplement to one issue – 'The Historical & Working Class Associations of Clerkenwell Green' lf, 16pp.

2548 Country Standard Started 1935. Originally ed. and published by William Savage from Essex, with a pro-Labour line, from Jan. 1948 it became 'The Rural Crusader & Clarion' and from Aug. 1949 'The Rural Crusader & Country Standard'. It was ed. by Jack Dunman from the CP's national office while remaining a genuine broad left paper. Published in a variety of formats. Astonishingly long-lived, it survived to the end of the CPGB and even has a contemporary incarnation under the CPB.

2549 Daily Worker No.1, Jan. 1 1930. Ed: W. Rust, 1930; J. Shields, 1932; I. Cox, 1935; R. Palme Dutt, 1936; W. Rust, 1939; J. Campbell, 1949; G. Matthews, 1959; T. Chater, 1974. Re-named 'Morning Star' in 1966. Earlier trial runs: during the Election of 1922, the Dockers' Strike of July 1923 and the Election of 1923. Banned Jan. 22, 1941 till Aug. 26 1942; re-appeared on Sept. 7, even though the printing press had been bombed and 12 of the 18 journalists were in the forces.

2550 **Daylight** 16pp Published as a supplement to 'World News & Views', but also sold separately. Vol.1 No.1, Autumn 1952 to Vol.2 No.3, 1954. Very interesting cultural journal; art work by D. Chittock, C. Rowe, P. Hogarth, R. Turner, F. Millett. Poems by R. Swingler, E.P. Thompson, N. Buchan, E. McColl, J. Beeching. Stories by D. Lessing, L. Doherty, H. Smith etc.

2551 **Discussion** 26-32pp No.1, Jan. 1936 to April 1938. First issue d, rest printed; monthly from No.2; larger format from June 1937. No issue Oct. 1936.

2552 **Economic Bulletin (New Series)** 28-60pp No.1, Spring 1977 to last issue: No.11, Spring/Summer 1984. Biannual then annual. Ed. John Fairley. The 1st series started as a quarterly internal bulletin in Jan. 1952, then more widely available on subscription; eventually single copies were sold.

2553 **Education Today And Tomorrow** *Education Advisory Cttee* 12-24pp Started in 1955; 4 or 5 issues a year till 1990, then irregular (but continued in existence with links to DL after demise of CP). Ed: Frank Gubb till 1957, then Ian Gunn till ousted in 1984 – the paper had always been virulently anti-Trotskyist and had become a focus for the traditionalists in the Party & its politics had long been criticised by most CP teachers. Apart from its politics it was famous for the strange paper it was printed on and & its archaic design.

2554 **Educational Bulletin / Education Today** *Education Advisory Cttee* 8-12pp lf Vol.1 No.1, Nov. 1948. Changed name to 'Education Today' from Nov./Dec. 1953, though numbering continued. Bi-monthly. From Mar/April 1955 became 'Education Today And Tomorrow'. First named ed.: F. Gubb (1955). Followed by Pat Allen, R. Thomas. Ed. board incl. some high profile educationalists: M. Morris, R. & S. Fisher, H. Rosen, C. Giles.

2555 **Esperanto Group Bulletin** 8pp No.1, Sept. 1972; No.12, May 1980. In English, though the Group did publish material in Esperanto.

2556 **Euro Red** *West European Sub Cttee of International Dept* 16-26pp No.1, Summer 1976 to No.11 1979. Quarterly. Reflected the growing interest in Eurocommunism.

2557 **Eye, The** *Martin Lawrence (later Lawrence & Wishart)* 4-8pp No.1, Sept. 1935; No.8 1937. Broadsheet review of left-wing books; stunning design by Alec Anderson.

2558 **Focus (or Communist Focus)** 16pp No.1, Nov. 1982 to Oct. 1985. Monthly. Succeeded 'Comment'. From No.26 (Jan. 1985) it went weekly (tabloid format, 4pp – but longer for Congress discussion and reports). The intention was to distribute it to every member to counter the 'Morning Star'. Ed. P. Olive.

2559 **Inside The Empire** *Colonial Information Bureau* 8-20pp Vol.1 No.1, Feb. 1940. Monthly. Suspended publication after Nov. 1940 (due to the Blitz) till March 1943. Last issue Vol.5 No.3, Oct. 1946. From April sf, quarterly. Not claimed as CP publication, but address was 16 King St. Replaced the 'Colonial Information Bulletin'. For information on CP's Colonial Cttee, see Chapter 6 in 'History of the CPGB, 1941-51'; also Adi 'Forgotten Comrade?'.

2560 **International Affairs Bulletin** *International Dept* 18-26pp Vol.1 No.1, April 1966 to Vol.6 No.1, May/June 1972. 4/5 issues p.a. till 1970 then 2 or 3 (26 issues in total).

2561 **International Press Correspondence** 12pp Sept. 1921 to Vol.18 No.32, June 25 1937. Weekly, plus special CI Congress/Plenum issues. Commonly known as 'Inprecorr', it was the journal of the CI and came out in several languages (published in Britain by CPGB). Succeeded by 'World News and Views'. Published in Berlin till 1933, then in London: better quality and longer (20pp) till the war.

2562 **Ireland Information Bulletin** *Ireland National Advisory Cttee* 10-20pp lf No.1, April 1983; last issue: No.12, July 1985. Bimonthly/quarterly.

2563 **Jewish Clarion** *National Jewish Cttee* 4-10pp No.1, Dec. 1945 to No.89, Feb. 1955. Monthly. New Series: No.1, March 1955 to No.12, Mar 1957; monthly then bi-monthly and finally quarterly (8pp). Publisher changed from CP to Abe Lazurus (Dec. 1949) & R. Bernard (July 1952). There had been an ed. published by Fred Stone in April 1945 (12pp), and, in identical style and length, 'The Jewish Opinion' Feb. 1945. Both are very similar to 'Jewish Forum' May/June 1945 from the Workers' Circle, Branch No.9.

2564 **Link** *CP Women's Journal* 16-20pp lf No.1, Spring 1973; last issue: No.44, Summer/Autumn 1984. Quarterly. Editor: Rosemary Small, till 1981 then collectively.

2565 **Live Wire [2]** *Rails Advisory* 12pp No.1 1983. Intended to be quarterly. Surprisingly, this was one of the few national industrial newsletters attempted by the CP and it was not a success.

2566 **Marxism Today** 32-58pp No.1, Oct. 1957 to Dec. 1991/Jan. 1992. Monthly. 'Theoretical & Discussion Journal of the CP' (till 1989). Ed: J. Gollan till August 1962; J. Klugmann till September 1977; M. Jacques till end. In its early form, 'MT' was especially interesting for traditional Marxist academic cultural analysis & debate. Under M. Jacques, it became the most influential magazine the CP ever had, though moving away from direct CP control, to the disapproval of some.

2567 **Marxist Quarterly** *L&W* 60-70pp No.1, Jan. 1954 to Jan. 1957. Ed. E. Burns. Published to replace 'Modern Quarterly' and 'Communist Review'.

2568 **Medicine In Society** *Marxists in Medicine – The Research Group of the London Health Students Branch* 40pp Vol.1 No.1, Autumn 1973; last issue Vol.13 No.3, 1988 after which it transformed into 'Health Matters'. Duplicated then printed from Vol.3 No.1. Initially ed. by John Robson; longer serving members of ed. board: Jane Bernal, Iraina Clarke, Steve Iliffe, Sue Lewis, Wendy Sims & J. Robson.

2569 **Modern Quarterly** [1] *Gollancz and L&W* 100pp Vol.1 No.1, Jan. 1938 to Vol.2 No.3, July 1939. Quarterly. Published jointly so not an official CP journal but it fulfilled the function of a theoretical journal for the CP after 'Discussion' till the outbreak of the war. Contributors incl. Dobb, Bernal, Hill, Cornforth etc. Editors incl. D. Garman.

2570 **Modern Quarterly** [2] *L&W* 66-96pp No.1, Dec. 1945 to Autumn 1953. Quarterly. Ed. J. Lewis. More obviously an official CP journal than its pre-war predecessor with the same title. Concentrated on theoretical problems of culture & science.

2571 **Morning Star** No.1, April 25 1966. Daily. See 'Daily Worker'.

2572 **Music And Life** *Music Group of the CP* 10-20pp lf d No.1, April 1956. Quarterly to 1973 then bi-annual, then irregular. There was a Special Issue in Autumn 1969: A. Bush 'National Character an Essential Ingredient in Musical Art To-day', 10pp. Last issue: No.55 1978. Editors: H. Sear, Alfred Corum (c1958-69), Frank Stokes, George Burn. Alan Bush was on Editorial Board.

2573 **News and Views** 16-24pp No.1, Feb. 1986 to No.61, Aug. 1990. No.49 misnumbered as another No.48. Monthly. Ed. G. Pocock. Followed by 'Changes'.

2574 **Our History Journal** *History Group* No.1, Dec. 1977 to No.18, 1991. To No.13 it was

d. pamphlet of 8-20pp, irregular – sometimes a year between issues. Then it was in smaller printed format of 40-60pp. From No.19, May 1992 it became 'The Socialist History Journal' (Socialist History Society), from Autumn 1993 'Socialist History' published by Pluto Press then Rivers Oram Press and now L&W. The Journal was preceded by a free Newsletter to members of the History Group (No.1 Oct. 1973 to No.11 Feb. 1977), approx. quarterly 8-14pp. There had been an earlier monthly bulletin,

2575 **Party Life** [1] *Organising Dept* 6pp lf d Nos 7 & 9 1929. No indication of regularity; apparently free. This was called 'New Series', but no trace of earlier copies.

2576 **Party Life** [2] 16pp Vol.1 No.1, Oct. 1962 to No.7, Oct./Nov. 1963. Bi-monthly.

2577 **Party Organiser** [1] 32-48pp No.1, March 1932 to No.8, Dec. 1932. Monthly/bi-monthly.

2578 **Party Organiser** [2] 20-32pp New Series. Vol.1 No.1, July 1938 to June 1940. Monthly/bi-monthly. Contains Congress discussion, District Congress Reports, lit. sales, & much internal information. During the war years it was replaced by magazine format pamphlets (e.g. 'Communist Organisation For Victory').

2579 **Portugal Information Bulletin** *International Dept* 10-20pp lf No.1, 1975 to last issue: No.14, Summer 1977. Also 'Special Issue – Documents from 8th Congress of Portuguese CP' Nov. 1976. 24pp. Initially monthly then bi-monthly & quarterly. Reflects the Left's great interest in the Portuguese revolution.

2580 **Proceedings of the Sigerist Society** 8-32pp Theoretical and social discussion of medicine from a Marxist view. Founded 1947; No.37, July 1956. Subscription only?

2581 **Realism** *Journal of the Artists' Group of the CP* No.1, June 1955 to last issue No.6, Nov./Dec. 1956. Quarterly/Biannual. lf 16/20pp, later broadsheet of 6pp. Editor: Godfrey Rubens.

2582 **Red Letters** 16-80pp No.1 1976; No.28 last as paper of CP's Cultural Cttee Initially lf , Nos 6-9 were smaller with spine, then larger. Collective ed. board, but D. Margolies was main ed.

2583 **Roadway** *Communist Road Haulage Workers* 6pp d May 1954.

2584 **Science Bulletin** 16pp No.1, Spring 1972 to last issue: No.23 1978(?). Quarterly then more irregular. Ed. Richard Clarke. There had been a 'Science Bulletin' in mid-1950s, not for sale: address was C/o L&W.

2585 **Seven Days** 12pp No.1, Oct. 1985 to Vol.2 No.48, Oct. 1987. Weekly. Ed. C. Myant. Officially published by JK Pictorials.

2586 **Socialist Europe** *Cttee For the Study of European Socialist Countries* 20-32pp No.1, 1976 to No.4, 1978. Grew out of sessions at the Communist University of London.

2587 **Soldiers' Voice** 4pp No.1, Sept. 1929 – only issue?

2588 **The Discussion Starts** 22-28pp lf Pre-Congress discussion journal. 4 issues, Jan. – April, 1969

2589 **Transactions of the Engels Society** *Science Group* 16pp No.1 in 1949 to No.7 July 1952. Theoretical articles. There was also a Bulletin from 1948 for members. The Science Group was divided into Psychology, Physics, Chemistry, and Biology groups. Sec. and Assistant Sec.: M. Cornforth and Barbara McPherson.

2590 **University Newsletter** *University Staffs Advisory* 8pp No.1, Spring 1962 to No.4, Summer 1963. Ed. Lionel Munby & Arnold Kettle.

2591 **West Indies Newsletter** *West Indies Cttee (International Cttee)* 8pp d Vol.2 No.1, Jan. 1950; No.11, Nov. 1950. Monthly. Available on subscription. Circulation c300.

2592 **Woman Today** *Women's Cttee Against War & Fascism; later Women's Cttee For Peace & Democracy* 12-24pp A curiously complicated history. In March 1942 it appeared as 'Home Front – The World of Women Today & Tomorrow': it took the wartime paper allowance of 'The Home Front' the monthly paper of the National Federation of Tenants & Residents Associations as well as its name. It appeared monthly/bi-monthly in varying formats & covers (incl. colour from Sept. 1943 – the same time as ed. changed from Eileen Murray to Tamara Rust). Name reverted to 'Woman Today' in July 1944 (though there are issues of 'Home Front' AND 'Woman Today' in July which are identical apart from cover and first page) and it came out monthly in 8pp. Larger format from Nov. 1950 to final issue in June 1959. At its peak, circulation was 12,000. Not to be confused with paper of same name by British Section of Women's World Cttee v. War & Fascism (Sept. 1936 – Feb. 1940), though this also had very high CP input but no refs to the Party (Charlotte Haldane was ed., T. Rust publisher, from 27 Bedford Street).

2593 **Woman Worker [1]** *Women's Dept* 4pp lf No.1, March 1926 to No.10, Jan. 1927. Monthly. Ceased publication when 'Workers' Weekly Publishing Company' was placed in hands of receiver. Replaced by 'Working Woman'.

2594 **Woman Worker [2]** 6pp lf d No.1, July 1929; No.5, Dec. 1929. Monthly/bi-monthly.

2595 **Workers' Bulletin [1]** 2pp No.1, May 4 1926; 10 issues. Daily. Published by M. Pollitt.

2596 **Workers' Daily [1]** 4pp lf No.1, Dec. 2 to No.3, Dec. 4 1923. This was a special election ed. of 'The Workers' Weekly', published from 196 St Vincent St, Glasgow.

2597 **Workers' Daily [2]** May 3 1926 – only 1 issue: 'General Strike ed. of the Workers' Weekly'. 40,000 copies.

2598 **Workers' Illustrated News** *Workers' Publications Ltd* 16pp Vol.1 No.1, Dec. 13 1929. 3 issues, though there had been a dummy. A poor imitation of the German 'AIZ', but used best technology for the period; distribution through the newstrade was successful but payment was slow and there wasn't enough capital to pay the printers for a further issue. Ed. Walter Holmes.

2599 **Workers' Life** 6pp No.1, Jan. 1927 to No.151, Dec. 1929. Weekly. This replaced 'Workers' Weekly' which went bankrupt after legal proceedings (see details under 'Woman Worker' [1]). Again, last page was 'Miners' Page'. Ed. J.R. Campbell 1928-9; also R.P. Dutt & A. Rothstein.

2600 **Workers' Weekly** 8pp No.1, Feb. 1923 to No.205, Jan. 1927. Last page was called 'Miners' Supplement' – devoted to the coal industry. Ed. R.P. Dutt, J.R. Campbell 1924-5, T.A. Jackson (during General Strike).

2601 **Working Woman** *Alice Holland* 4pp lf d No.1, Feb. 1927 to No.26, March 1929. Monthly. Some issues had 'Anti-War Supplement', making it 6pp.

2602 **World News** 12-24pp Vol.1 No.1, Jan. 2 1954 to Vol.9 No. 51, Dec. 22 1962. Successor to 'World News and Views'. Weekly. Ed. 1957-62: Ted Ainley.

2603 **World News and Views** 12-24pp No.1, July 2 1937 to Dec. 19, 1953. Weekly. Successor to 'International Press Correspondence' (continued pagination & numbering); more articles on British politics – no longer the official organ of the C.I. Ed: A. Clegg, J. Klugmann, M. Heinemann.

2604 **World Youth Review** 24pp Jan. – Sept. 1939. Monthly. Published by H.R.G. Jefferson. Supplement to 'World News and Views' but sold separately.

4. Local Magazines

These are classified first by District, then by title. Bulletins intended for internal distribution are not listed if they were not published for sale. This does mean that some longstanding and significant 'magazines' are excluded (e.g. *High Wycombe Branch Bulletin*, which ran to 224 issues between 1949 and 1972); some of the priced bulletins were really internal (e.g. *East Midlands DC Bulletin*) but these have been included. Every District, Area and Borough produced, at some time or other, a bulletin or newsletter that was usually free to members, even if it was just an irregular sheet. Larger Districts might run to a bulletin for women members (e.g. *London Communist Women's Bulletin*).

There are many occasions when the numbering and dating of papers was erratic. Sometimes the phrase 'New Series' is used after a gap of years, sometimes after weeks and sometimes even after a change of title! This is particularly the case with the early factory papers, which are a law unto themselves. It is possible that some of them listed here were intentionally one-offs and should be listed in the 'Local Publications' chapter, but other issues of some titles may turn up in the future. Several aspects of these factory papers can be difficult to identify: the District is often not evident (I have had to resort to guessing with a couple of them), and the same applies to the year. The industry may not be clear; this is partly because they were sometimes produced in response to national calls for campaigns (e.g. on the perceived threat of war in 1929, or on unemployment): in these cases the content may be national and not refer to a specific industry. It is also worth noting that occasionally factory papers from different branches could be almost identical in content – there were some attempts to co-ordinate them. On the other hand, there was a series of papers on the textile trades in July 1929 issued in Lancashire towns and all with different content; they were called, for example 'The Accrington Millworker' and were produced for Manchester, Preston, Oldham, Nelson, Burnley, Bar'Lick and Haslingden – at least. Some definitely ran to two editions; they were probably all free.

In some extreme cases, Communist papers were produced by non-members – John Mahon in his *Report of Factory Groups Conference* in November 1926 said one paper was produced by contacts who were not yet in the Party. Other problems include the loose use of titles (*The Ringer* or *The Rossington Ringer*) and the not infrequent change of name.

These early factory or pit papers constituted one of the most difficult areas of research. Historians have always been interested in them, though their quality and importance vary considerably. It is often unclear whether they were published by CP organisations, by individuals, or by other organisations (e.g. the Minority Movement or United Mineworkers of Scotland). An article by Hal Wilde in *Communist Review*, March 1931, noted: 'Even when a Party cell exists, some papers are published in the name of the militant workers of the enterprise ... which is certainly a mistake'. In the 1920s and 1930s especially, it was difficult for CP members to openly proclaim their identity in a workplace – the risk of victimisation was always present. Sometimes the content of these papers was personal and highly inflammatory as well.

The same article by Wilde claimed there were forty-six papers in existence at the time. The 9th National Congress Report of 1927 stated that there were fifty-four factory papers. The previous year John Mahon's Report says there were twelve London papers in rail depots and stations alone. Eleven of these twelve are almost certainly identified here, but in the case of Wilde's article and the 1927 Congress Report not even half have been found.

There are very few copies extant of most of these papers, which would have been printed in small quantities, and only consisted of one, two or occasionally four or more pages. They were also often short-lived, many probably not running to a second copy. A list of papers that almost certainly existed, together with the source of information, but that I have not been able to trace, is provided below. I have found two local papers (*The Laddie* and the *Ward and Goldstone Spark*) that were published by industrial branches of the YCL – see in 'YCL Magazines'.

The pit based papers, which form the bulk of the workplace papers, were often found in clusters – in 1927 there were five in the Castleford area of Yorkshire and five in the Wheatley Hill district of Durham (*Workers' Life*, April 1 1927). *The Biggest Battle is Yet to Come* very briefly describes the distribution of some in part of the Yorkshire coalfield; this short book also shows how more than one were edited by the same person, in this case Jack Johnson, and would therefore be very similar in content. Johnson also wrote an article in *Workers' Life* (August 23 1929) describing sales of *The Rossington Ringer* and mentioning the Pit Paper Department at Castleford. In the same paper the previous week, Wilde stated that circulation of these pit papers was 300 to 600.

The General Strike saw a proliferation of local papers supporting the miners and the strike. The 8th Congress in October 1926 was informed that at least 1200 members had suffered at the hands of the law, and the majority of those were fined or imprisoned for production or even possession of strike bulletins or leaflets, probably mainly these pit papers. Many pit papers were suspended during and following the strike. *Workers' Life* (June 17 1927), for example, reported that in South Wales there were sixteen pit papers before the lock-out and by June 1927 ten of these had been revived. This can add to the problems in identifying numbers and dates. There is a fascinating, and probably unique, account of the production and sale of some of these papers in one small area, Fife, in *Militant Miners*.

First and last known issues are given, or the dates of the only ones traced.

As with national magazines there where instances of titles being used more than once. Branches in different parts of the country might choose a popular revolutionary title (*The Spark, The Torch*).

West of England

2605 Bristol Rails Worker *Bristol Rails Branch CP* 4pp lf d 1952 At least 10 issues till July 1955. Approx. quarterly.

2606 Critical Times *Rosa Luxemburg Group of Post Office Communists, Bristol* 4pp pb lf 1935 Ed. by John Currie & Tom Lewis. George Massey describes distributing this in 'Grasshopers, Stonkers and Straight Eights ... '

2607 Jersey Communist *Jersey CP* 8pp lf d 1957 Quarterly.

2608 West of England District Bulletin 4pp lf Jan. 1953

Hampshire & Dorset

2609 Hants and Dorset Bulletin 4pp Special eds were produced for District Congresses in Oct. 1943 & Feb. 1945. Usually this bulletin was monthly and for sale only to members.

2610 Hants and Dorset District News 4pp 1960s Issued regularly – occasionally priced.

Sussex

2611 Bulletin of the Mugsborough Communist Party 12pp No.2, Sept. 1982 has a substantial article by F. Ball on 'The Tressell Mural', plus an obit. of Peter Blackman, a window cleaner, T.U. activist and one of the group who bought the manuscript of 'The Ragged Trousered Philanthropists' (not the poet Peter Blackman). Mugsborough is of course Hastings.

2612 East Brighton Worker 6pp Formerly called 'The Hereford Street News'. No.4, July 1934 Much on anti-Fascist activity; also includes lyrics to 'Song of the Sickle and Hammer', and 'Bye Bye Blackshirts'.

2613 Punch, The *Railway Communist Group (or Southern Railway Workers)* 4pp lf

No.33, Dec. 10 1926 Fortnightly. Published from Brighton.

Surrey

2614 Epsom & Ewell Citizen 12pp d No.1, May 1948

Kent

2615 Kent Party News 4-8pp 3 issues in 1969; Winter 1980 issue, unusually, was for sale.

London

2616 Action Keynote *Communist Group, Herrburger Brooks (Piano Manufacturer)* 1-2pp 1926 4 issues (?) incl. General Strike issue. Weekly? Each issue was subtitled 'Chord' No.1, instead of Number 1, etc. Logo was a crossed hammer hitting a drum and piano keyboard sickle. This must be the wittiest bannerhead of any CP journal, though perhaps the title is beaten by the Bulletin of Mugsborough CP. Probably all issues were free.

2617 Agitation and Propaganda Bulletin 4pp 1927 Internal – not for sale.

2618 Anvil, The *Dorman & Long Branch* 6pp d No.1, Sept. 1954 to May 1961 Early issues for sale, not clear if later ones were.

2619 Battersea Garage Bulletin *Battersea Bus Group* 6pp lf d 1956/7

2620 Battersea Loco Bystander *Clapham Railway Shed Group* 1926? 2 issues? Ed. by Jack Blunt.

2621 Battersea News 6pp lf d No.8, Oct. 1959.

2622 Battersea Worker *Battersea CP* 4pp lf No.1, Dec. 1977; No.2, Spring 1978; No.7, Dec. 1979 (last?) Quarterly.

2623 **Bell, The** *Hendon CP* 8pp No.1, Dec. 1932 'Published by A Banerji'.

2624 **Bermondsey Beagle** *Bermondsey Branch* 4pp 1988 Undated, no number; apparently sold in newsagents but given to supporters.

2625 **Boreham Wood Bulletin** *Boreham Wood Branch* 2pp lf d 2 issues in 1953

2626 **Builder's Whistle, The: Organ of the Croydon & District Building Workers Communist Group** 4pp lf No.13, 1926 Fortnightly.

2627 **Bus Worker** *Communist Busmen* 4pp lf d No.1, June 19 1926; No.12, Dec. 1926 Fortnightly. A pilot issue was issued on June 11 1926 called 'Bus'. Circulation of 1,200.

2628 **Busman's Punch** 4-8pp lf d No.4, Nov. 1931 From 1932 starts at No.1 again! No.3, Sept. 1932. From No.2 in 1932 this was published by 'Militant Busmen From Cricklewood' and from Nov. 1932 ('New Series') it was 'The Official Paper of the London Busmen's Rank & File Movement' i.e. no longer a CP publication. NB first issues spelt 'Busmen's Punch'. Monthly.

2629 **Camberwell Worker** *Camberwell CP* 4pp lf No.1, March/April 1949

2630 **Camden and Granby Street Spark** 2-4pp 1925-6 Over 30 issues. Last issue Aug. 19 1926, then merged with 'LMS Worker'. Another paper officially produced by CP and the NMM.

2631 **Camden Star** *Camden CP* 8pp d Nov. 1969

2632 **Chalk Farm Steering Wheel** *Depot Paper of the Chalk Farm CP Cell* 4pp lf d No.1, Aug. 1931; No.3, Oct. 1931 Monthly.

2633 **Chalker, The** *Chalk Farm* 8pp d No.1, Oct. 1933; Sept. 1935 Monthly/quarterly.

2634 **Chelsea Citizen** 8pp d 1949 2 issues.

2635 **Clarion** *Finsbury CP* 4pp No.1, 1946 to No.53, June 4 1948 Then from No.54 called 'Finsbury Clarion'. Fortnightly/monthly.

2636 **Communist Report: Bulletin of London Trades Councils Advisory** March 1986

2637 **Croydon Leader** 4pp lf No.1, Feb. 1949; No.3, April 1949

2638 **Dock and River Worker** *Communist Docks Group* 4pp lf d No.1, July 1926; No.2, Aug. 1926 'New Series'. Replaced 'Waterside Worker' (no trace).

2639 **Dockers' Searchlight** *Dockers' Communist Group* Referred to in 'Workers' Weekly' July 21 1926

2640 **East End Worker** *Joint Cttee of West Ham, East Ham, Walthamstow, Leyton* 4 issues Oct. to Nov. 1926 Campaigned against Board of Guardians in West Ham.

2641 **Eighth Notch** *M.E.T. Communist Groups* 4pp lf d Dec. 1926 Circulation 500 according to Report by J. Mahon to Factory Groups Conference, Nov. 21 1926. Fortnightly.

2642 **Election Bulletin** 2pp lf No.1, Feb. 21 1964; about 5 issues. Fortnightly.

2643 **Feltham Tatler** *Feltham Communist Group* 6pp lf d 1925 6 issues. Fortnightly. 'Issued by the Feltham Reds'.

2644 **Fifth Light At Crypto** *The Communist Group* 4pp lf d No.1, Dec. 1931; No.9, May 1932 Fortnightly. Factory that made electric light bulbs. Followed by 'Cryptogram': No.1, March 1934, No.2, June 1934 (4pp); introduction states that this paper, unlike its predecessor, is not a 'political party paper' but 'fights for stronger trade union organisation'.

2645 **Finsbury Clarion** 4pp lf Previously 'Clarion' (Nos.1-53); No.54, July 1948 Fortnightly/monthly. Became Finsbury & Shoreditch Clarion, then from No.67, Dec. 1949 became Shoreditch & Finsbury Clarion. Monthly.

2646 **Flash, The** *Croydon & District Railwaymen's Communist Group* 4pp 1925? – 1929? At least 28 issues. Publisher also sometimes given as: Croydon Railworkers, Croydon Local CP.

2647 **Fleet News** 6pp lf d No.1, Feb. 1955 Busworkers.

2648 **Gas Worker, The** *G.L. & C.C. Communist Group* 1pp lf d At least 15 issues in 1926. Fortnightly.

2649 **Goswell Road Megaphone** *Goswell Road Group of the Holborn & Finsbury Local* 6pp lf d No.6, June/July 1933 Bi-monthly. Still in existence in Oct. Appeal 'to the workers of Gee Street and Bastwick Street'.

2650 **Great Western Star** *GW Group of Communist Railwaymen* Successor to 'Paddington Star'. No.8, June 1927

2651 **Hackney Woman Worker** *Hackney Local* 4pp No.28, Nov. 1 1927 Weekly. Initially published by Hackney Trades Council; by No.23 it is published by the CP.

2652 **Hackney Worker** 4pp lf Vol.1 No.1, Dec. 1948; June 1949 Monthly then bi-monthly.

2653 **Hammer, The** *Workers at Hoe's* 2pp No.1, April 16 1926 'Fortnightly' (but not known if any others appeared). Engineering factory in Walthamstow.

2654 **Hammersmith Outlook** *Hammersmith CP* 4-8pp lf d 1947-8 Monthly. Vol.2 No.11, Nov. 1948.

2655 **Hammersmith People** 4pp No.1, March 1949; No.2, April 1949 Monthly.

2656 **Harrow Life** 4pp lf Vol.1 No.1, July 1948; March 1949

2657 **Headlight, The** *St Pancras* 4pp lf d 'The CP Paper for St Pancras & Somers Town Goods Workers'. No.1, Nov. 1929.

2658 **Hendon Leader** 4-8pp lf No.3, July 1948; No.7, March/April 1949 Monthly/ bi-monthly.

2659 **Holborn Calling** 4-6pp lf No.22, May 1948; Vol.5 No.2, 1950 Monthly.

2660 **Holloway Bus Worker** 4pp No.1, Jan. 1930 Continued into 1931 at least. Some published by 'Holloway Concentration Group, CPGB'.

2661 **Hornsey Rise Estate Express** 6pp lf d No.4, Sept. 1933 (?). With large children's section.

2662 **Hornsey Star [2]** 2pp lf d No.2, Feb. 1963.

2663 **Hornsey Star [1]** *Hornsey Group of Communist Railwaymen (or Hornsey Rail Depot)* 4pp lf No.43, April 1927 Fortnightly. New monthly series a few years later: Vol.3 No.1, Jan. 1934 (6pp).

2664 **Hunger Marcher** *St Pancras Local* 4pp lf d Feb. 1929 'Produced on the Occasion of the March to Trafalgar Square'.

2665 **Idris Ginger** *St Pancras Local* 4-8pp lf d No.2, April 1925; No.7, July 1925 Curious numbering: Vol.2 started in Nov. 1926 and No.1 (presumably of a new series) in Aug. 1929. Idris Factory in Camden; in 1925 initially publ. by Works Cttee of this soft drinks factory, then taken over by CP.

2666 **Indicator** *London Bridge & New Cross Communist Railwaymen* 4pp New Series: 2 issues July & Aug. 1926.

2667 **Islington Woman Worker** *Islington Local* 4pp 4 issues July 1927 to Oct. 1927 There was an 8pp special issue. Printed & published by Dora Savage then J Murray. First issue was free.

2668 **Islington Worker** 4-10pp lf Vol.1 No.4, July 1948; Vol.2 No.6, Aug. 1949 Monthly.

2669 **Islington Worker's Bulletin** *Islington CP* 2pp lf d No.3, Friday 7th May, 1926

2670 **Jogger, The** *Euston Rail Group CP* 4pp lf d No.1, Nov. 1927; No.20, March 1930 'The CP Paper for Clearing House Clerks'. Sales averaged c150 according to accounts book. Monthly. Ed. Stuart Purkiss & Billy Williams.

2671 **Juice** *Organ of the 'Underground' Workers* 4pp 12 June 1926

2672 **Kensington Bulletin** 8pp d Nov. 1946

2673 **Kensington Clarion** 4pp lf No.1, Jan. 1949; No.6, Aug. 1949 May issue has short biogs of 5 local election candidates.

2674 **Kidbrooke Pilot** 2pp lf d No.1, July 17 1925 (though there was a 'pilot' issue on July 3); No.7, Sept. 18 1925 'Issued by the Depot Reds', later 'Depot Communist Group', Kidbrooke aircraft factory. Fortnightly.

2675 **King's Cross Star [1]** *King's Cross Communist Cell/Group of Communist Railwaymen* 4pp lf d No.6, July 1925; No.68, April 1933 Various series. Fortnightly/quarterly. In 1927 published by Islington Local.

2676 **King's Cross Star [2]** 4pp lf d Jan. 1955

2677 **Lambeth Leader** 4pp lf Feb./March 1975; Jan./Feb. 1977 Bi-monthly.

2678 **Lambeth Searchlight** 8-12pp lf No.4; Nov./Dec. 1939; No.7, May 1940

2679 **Leasider** *Clapton Branch, Hackney* 4pp lf Spring 1982 For local election.

2680 **Leyton Citizen** 4pp lf March 1949; Sept./Oct. 1949

2681 **Leyton Worker** 4pp lf d Sept. 1948

2682 **Lit News** 4pp 1946? Published by Thames Bookshops (chain of CP bookshops in London region) for London District. by 1948 it was no longer a pamphlet for sale, but a smaller 2 sided fortnightly leaflet. Contains reviews, plus interesting details on literature sales. In an earlier incarnation, in 1942, it was published, probably fortnightly, as a supplement to the London District Bulletin.

2683 **Live Rail [1]** *LCC Tramway Workers Communist Group/Holloway Road Tram Depot Workers* 4pp lf d No.3, June 1925; No.39, Dec. 1926 Circulation up to 1,400 according to J Mahon's Report. Fortnightly.

2684 **Live Rail [2]** *Earl's Court Branch CP* 2pp lf d Jan. 1952

2685 **Live Rail [3]** *L.T.E. Rails Group* 6pp lf d May 1960 There was also a free journal called

'Live Rail' in 1973 by 'CP members in Signals Dept of London Transport'.

2686 LMS Railway Worker *Communist Railway Group* 4pp 8 issues in 1926 'The Paper of the St Pancras & Kentish Town Railway Workers'. Merged with 'Camden & Granby Street Spark' in Aug. 1926. There was also 'LMS Camden Town Goods Depot' paper (undated and un-numbered, probably free).

2687 London Bulletin: Teachers 6pp lf d No.1, June 1939 Almost certainly the only issue.

2688 London Campaigner 4pp lf d 1974 Fortnightly.

2689 London Communist Bulletin 8pp 1983-mid 1986 Approx. every 2 months.

2690 London Communist Women's Bulletin 6-12pp lf No.4, Sept./Oct. 1977; March 1985 Every 2 months?

2691 London Communists 2-6pp lf 1977-83 Irregular – every 2,3,4 weeks.

2692 London District Bulletin 4pp lf 1941 Initially 'London District': weekly, for members only, duplicated (later printed but not dated or numbered!). From June 1941 became 'London District Bulletin' then from Feb. 1944 'The Bulletin'. Weekly to 1953. Late 1950s became 'Bulletin' and ranged from weekly to monthly. Mid 1960s: 'GLC Bulletin' (lf d). Early 1970s: 'London Bulletin' weekly then fortnightly (internal only); May 1976: 'London Communists'; 1979: 'London District Bulletin'. Jan. 1981: 'The London Bulletin'; April 1986-Autumn 1991: 'Capital Communist' (every 2 months).

2693 LT Worker *London Transport Communists* 8pp No.1, 1974; irregular to 1984(?) Reduced in size and eventually given out free.

2694 Market Worker *Markets Group CP* 8pp lf d No.2, 1959

2695 Monthly Record of the London & Home Counties District Council of the CPGB 4-8pp lf No.3, June 1921; No.10, March 1922 Monthly?

2696 Napiers Searchlight *Napier's Communist Group [Acton]* 4pp lf d No.1, April 8 1925; No.4, June 29 1925 New series: No.1, Jan. 1928; No.4, June 1929

2697 New Crossed Lines *Deptford & Brockley CP* 12pp lf d No.1, 1977

2698 Oak Fighter, The *Gospel Oak CP* 8pp lf d July 1934 Monthly ?

2699 Old Oak Star 2pp No.3, June 1931; No.17, Jan. 1932

2700 Organising Bulletin 4pp lf Jan.-Aug. 1939

2701 Paddington Star *Paddington, Westbourne Park & Old Oak Common Railwaymen of All Grades* 4pp lf d At least 20 issues 1926-7. Fortnightly. From No.18: 'Xmas Greetings to All Workers, Felix and the Scabs Excepted'. Succeeded by 'Great Western Star'.

2702 Paddington Worker *Paddington Borough* 4-8pp lf No.18, July 1948; No.28, July 1949 Bi-monthly. No.28 has list of 10 branches in the Borough.

2703 Party Fighter, The: Bulletin of LDCP & YCL 12-24pp No.1, May 1933; No.4, Jan. 1934 Bi-monthly/quarterly.

2704 Party News *W Middlesex DC* 6pp Monthly. 1981-6 at least. Priced for sale, but internal. Probably a direct continuation of 'West Middlesex Party News'.

2705 Penge Discussion *Penge CP* 6-10pp No.1, May 1938 to No.4, Sept. 1938 No.2 entitled 'Beckenham & Penge Discussion'; No.4 'Beckenham & Penge Discussion & Labour News'. Monthly.

2706 Piano Worker *Communist Piano Workers* No.1, June 1925 General Strike issue July 1926.

2707 Power *Communists in the London Supply Undertakings* 4pp lf d No.1, Sept. 1926; March 1927 (this issue published by 'Communists in the ETU')

2708 Railway Special 2pp lf d July 12, 1925.

2709 Ranelagh Worker *Communist Group at George Glovers Ltd* 2pp No.1, April 1925; No.20, Dec. 1925. Some by Minority Movement.

2710 Red Letter *Postal Workers' Communist Group* 2-6pp lf d No.1, Oct. 1931; No.10, Aug. 1933 Irregular.

2711 Red Phone-Call *CP Paper For Standard Telephone Company Workers* 4pp lf d No.1, Oct. 1931; No.10, Aug. 1933 Monthly.

2712 Revolt: Chelsea Workers' Weekly 6pp d Vol.2 No.1, 1933?

2713 Shepherd's Pie *Batoum Gardens Group CP, Shepherd's Bush* 4pp d No.3, Jan. 1933

2714 Ship Repair Worker *Ship Repair Branches [then Branch]* 8pp Aug. 1956; Nov. 1957 Monthly.

2715 Spark [1] / Nine Elms Spark *Nine Elms Reds* or *Nine Elms Communist Railwaymen* 2-6pp lf d No.1, March 10 1925 From No.2 titled 'Nine Elms Spark'. 35 issues at least. Weekly.

2716 Spark [3] *Communist Group, Bishopsgate & Broad Street* 4pp No.12, June 25 1926

2717 **St Pancras Forward** 4pp lf No.8, April 1948; No.9, May 1948 Monthly.

2718 **St Pancras News** *St Pancras* 4pp March 1957

2719 **St Pancras Woman Worker** 2pp No.2, Dec. 1925

2720 **St Pancras Worker** *St Pancras Local* 10pp lf d 1932-4 Bi-monthly. There were earlier free journals with this title.

2721 **Stepney Leader** *Stepney Branch* 10pp lf No.30, Feb. 26 1940 There was another series from Oct. 1947 to April 1948 – not clear if this was for sale. Replaced by 'The Stepney People'.

2722 **Stepney People** Monthly. Dec. 1948 to May 1949 Replaced 'The Stepney Leader'. Average sales were 2,500-3,000 but it still lost money and sales interfered with the 'DW' so it was suspended.

2723 **Stoke Newington Socialist** *Stoke Newington Branch* 4pp lf No.4, Jan. 1982 Quarterly.

2724 **Stratford Railway Worker** *Stratford Communist Rail Group* 4pp lf No.1, Dec. 1931 There was another series with no publisher and no date but CP line: 4 issues all c1945 but with different titles: Stratford Rail Special, Railwayman, Railway Clarion, Railway Worker.

2725 **Streatham Outlook** *Streatham* 8-16pp d No.12, Nov. 1959

2726 **Themes: Discussion Journal of Lewisham Borough CP** 16-46pp lf 1975-6 8 issues. Last issue (?) was No.8 – titled 'There's Nane Ever Feared ...': attractive A5 format printed collection of poems from the Lewisham Festival of the Left, 1978. A 'Themes' Special issue (Bert Ward's poetry 'Poems On My Mind') was published in 1977 (listed separately).

2727 **Torch** [1] *Talbot's Engineering* 4pp No.9, July 1926 District uncertain.

2728 **Tottenham Town Hall Crier No.1, March** *Town Hall Group* 4pp lf No.1, March 1933

2729 **Transport News** *Transport Cttee* 8pp No.1, 1973 3 issues till late 1974. Replaced by 'LT Worker'.

2730 **Unity** [1] *Communist Group on the Downham Estate, Lewisham* 2-4pp lf d 13 issues in 1926. Fortnightly. Building workers' paper.

2731 **Victoria Signal** *Signal Communist Group, Victoria Station* 4-8pp lf d No.1, April 1925; No.37, Aug. 1926 Fortnightly.

2732 **Vision** [2] *Hendon* 8pp lf d No.3, Feb. 1956

2733 **Wandsworth Searchlight: The CP Election Bulletin** *Wandsworth* 4pp d No.1, Oct. 8-15 1934.

2734 **West Middlesex Party News** *West Middlesex DC* 6pp lf No.1, April 1950; Vol.7 No.17, May 1956 Started when District set up in 1950. Printed then duplicated. Sold 630 per week in 1951.

2735 **Westminster Clarion** *Westminster CP* 4pp No.1, July 1947; No.6, Sept. 1948

2736 **Wood Green Women's Sentinel** 4-8pp lf d No.1, June/July 1937; Oct. 1938 Monthly/bi-monthly. Published by Mrs Clarke, then Mrs Gates.

2737 **Workshop News & Views** *Factory Group, Southwark; South West Area* 8pp lf d 1956?

Eastern

2738 **Chingford Pioneer** *Chingford CP* lf First appeared in 1945? 8pp. Later series: No.6, Oct. 1950; New Series No.2, Nov./Dec. 1955

2739 **Coryton Star** *Essex Refinery CP* 4pp lf Feb. 1981

2740 **Ford Bulletin** *Fords CP* 8pp lf No.2, Feb. 1981

2741 **Ford Worker** *Communist Group at Fords, Dagenham* 2-6pp No.1, April 1933; monthly to No.12, March 1934 Note in No.2: 'will be published by a group of militant Trade Unionists and the Works Cttee will no longer be responsible for it'.

2742 **Live Wire** [1] *'Western' Communist Group* 3pp lf d No.5, June 11 1925 Re-appeared as an irregular free publication in 1935, in Southend, not specifically CP.

2743 **Redbridge Star** *Redbridge Borough* 8pp d No.1, March 1972

2744 **South Chingford Review** 8pp d No.6, June 1948

2745 **South Essex Bulletin** *South Essex DC* 2-6pp d No.1, 1952 to last issue early 1980s Started when South Essex DC was set up. Incl. reports of District Congresses.

2746 **The Beacon** *Southend* 4pp Vol.2 No.9; Vol.4 No.6, Oct. 1956 'Southend Monthly Newsletter'.

East Anglia

2747 **Anglia Action** 34pp lf d Dec. 1977 Quarterly.

2748 Cambridge Red Front *Cambridge Local* 6pp lf d April 1935

2749 Leiston Leader 6-10pp lf d No.1, Jan. 1936; No.248, Oct. 1957 One of the most enduring & influential local papers. Monthly.

South East Midlands

2750 Bedford Clanger *Bedford CP* 8pp lf No.2, March 1933; No.13, 1934

2751 Luton – Dunstable Newsletter 6pp lf d No.8, 1977

2752 North Berkshire Bulletin 4pp lf d No.1, Sept. 1944 to Aug. 1947 Monthly/bi-monthly. More an internal bulletin – free to members but was sold to non-members.

2753 Peterborough Leader *Peterborough Branch* 10pp Jan. 1940 to June 1944 Monthly. Ed. Will Granger. Circulation: 3,500.

2754 Reading Communist Review *Reading Branch* 30pp No.1, Aug. 1988; No.2, Winter 1988/9; No.3, Spring 1989 (last issue?)

2755 Seed, The *Watford Women's Cttee* 3pp No.9, April 1926 Published by P.A. Neal.

2756 Wellingborough Digger 26pp d No.1, Winter 1980

Midlands

2757 Birmingham Red 16pp lf No.3, 1980; No.11, Spring 1983 Quarterly.

2758 Bright Sparks 12pp lf 1978? Sparkhill, Sparkbrook, Balsall Heath, Fox Hollies. At least 4 issues – none with dates or numbers.

2759 Ko-Ko-Kick *Cadbury Communist Cell* 6pp lf d No.5, May 1925; referred to in 'Workers' Life' Jan 27 1928. No.1 (new series) Nov. 1931 – with NMM.

2760 Morris Spark *S Midlands; Morris Group (Oxford)* 10pp lf Vol.3 No.9, 1937? An 'Election Special' was published for Oxford (1937?).

2761 South Midlands District Bulletin *S Midlands* 4pp lf Nov. 1942 Monthly. 'For Party Members Only' though priced. This issue incl. article on 'Communist Shock Brigade' in Morris Radiators Factory.

2762 Swindon Broadsheet *Swindon CP* 10pp lf d No.1, Oct. 1968 to June 1971 Monthly/bi-monthly.

2763 Vision [1] *Oxford* 8pp lf No.1, 1969? to Vol.1 No.11, Aug. 1971

East Midlands

2764 Bulletin 4pp d 1965 (?) to 1968/9 at least. Priced for sale, but really of internal interest (and production quality!).

2765 Gleam, The *The Gleam Cttee, Annesley Pit, Nottingham* 4pp lf d 1936?

2766 New Hucknall Standard *New Hucknall Group CP* 2pp No.1, July 1929 Ed. F Smethurst. Mining.

2767 Pleasley Star *Pleasley Pit Group CP* 4pp No.7, April 1925

2768 Rufford Star *Rufford Pit Communist Group (Mansfield)* 4pp lf d No.12, Feb. 1926

2769 Shirebrook, Langwith and Warsop Miner 4pp lf d No.56, Jan. 29 1930 Not explicitly CP paper, but strongly pushes CP line. Fortnightly/monthly. Re-appears fortnightly in 1936 (No.17, July 10), though even less explicitly CP.

2770 Summit Butty *Kirkby Group of the CP* 2-4pp lf d 1929?

North West

2771 Ashton News Special *Ashton-Under-Lyne CP* 4pp lf 1949 Only one issue?

2772 BDC Worker 4pp British Dyestuffs Corporation (later ICI), Blackley, Manchester. Fortnightly. 3 issues (?) 1931-2

2773 Carr Lane Salt Box *Carr Lane Communist Building Group, Liverpool* 4pp lf d No.6, Nov. 1927 Monthly; sales reached 600. 'Salt box' was a term used describe back-to-back council houses. Leo McGree responsible for this paper.

2774 Cotton Strike Leader 4pp lf 1932 Officially publ. by Cotton Strikers' Solidarity Movement, but articles by Rose Smith and subjects like W.I.R. indicate full CP control.

2775 Crossley Motor *Crossley Motor Works; Gorton, Manchester* 1929 There was also possibly a version called 'The Motor' by Crossley Motor Lads Group.

2776 Haslingden Election Special 6pp 1928 Referred to in J Garnett's 'My Autobiography'.

2777 Hump, The *Liverpool CP Joiners' Group, Cammell Lairds* 2pp lf d July 1929 Monthly.

Leo McGree was mainly responsible for this publication.

2778 Lancashire News *Lancs DPC* 4pp lf Started 1938 Weekly. 'For members only'. Became Lancashire & Cheshire News. Still in existence in 1947.

2779 North West *Manchester District Cttee* 2-4pp lf d No.1, Aug. 14 1929; No.2, Aug. 16 1929

2780 North West News: Bulletin of Lancs & Cheshire District 8pp Vol.2 No.5, May 20 1968

2781 Rawlings Truth No.1, 12 March 1925 District uncertain.

2782 Salford Docker *Workers in the Port of Manchester* 4pp 52 issues July 1932 to Sept. 1934 Ed. E. Frow. Fortnightly.

2783 Save Merseyside *Merseyside Area* 12pp lf No.3, Feb./March 1979 Very well produced with good balance of internal info. & campaigning news.

2784 Shop Steward *Barrow Local* 5pp lf d April 1927

2785 Spark [4] *Manchester DC* 8pp No.1, Jan. 1925; No.2, Feb 1925. Ed. Arthur McManus.

2786 Sprinker, The *Communist Group, Mather & Platts, Manchester* No.1, Nov. 1925

2787 Under the Bed *Merseyside Area* 10-12pp lf No.1, Nov. 1978; No.3, Feb./March 1979 Monthly/bi-monthly.

2788 Who Cares? *Merseyside Area* 16pp Irregular mag. by Merseyside CP Health Group; at least 7 issues 1983 (?) to 1986. Circulation reached 600.

2789 Wigan Red *Wigan Branch* 8pp lf d No.1, June 1971; No.2, Aug. 1971

2790 Workers' Bulletin [2] *Barrow Local* 4pp lf d 1926 Daily during General Strike – at least 4 issues to May 12.

Yorkshire

2791 Askern Turn Point *Askern Communist Pit Group* 4pp lf Nos 1-3 all July 1929; No.12, Nov. 15 1929 to last issue Dec. 1931? Circulation claimed of c500.

2792 Barnsley Main Spark/Barnsley Spark *Militant Miners at Barnsley Main* 4pp lf d No.4, Dec. 12 1930; No.13, April 4 1931

2793 Bentley Turnplate *Militant Miners at Bentley Pit* 4pp lf d No.1, Dec. 12 1930;

No.15, March 27 1931 Still produced in 1932 acording to 'DW' 20 May. Weekly.

2794 Bradford Herald 6pp lf d 1970? No. 65, Dec./Jan. 1976-7 Ed. Mike Squires.

2795 Burton's Red Leader *Burton's Communist Group, Leeds* 6pp No.1, May 1932 Fortnightly to about Oct. 1933. Benson [3915] says it lasted about 2 years and that one issue sold 1,200 copies. Ed. Jim Roche. It became 'Garment Workers' Voice' (Rank & File Clothing Workers' Movement, Leeds) then 'Garment Workers' Leader'.

2796 Canklow Buzzer *Rotherham CP* 2pp March 1929 Free?

2797 Darfield Main Drifter 2pp 1929

2798 Denaby and Cadeby Rebel *Militant Miners of Denaby and Cadeby Pit* 2-4pp No.1, Jan. 1931 (free); No.3, Feb. 27 1931

2799 Dog and Chain *Briggs Communist Pit Group, Shipley* Referred to in 'Workers' Weekly' 6 March 1926 and 'Workers' Life' 25 March 1927.

2800 Edlington Lamp *Edlington Militant Miners* 4pp lf d 1930-31 At least 10 issues. Weekly.

2801 Featherstone Bank-Bar *Featherstone, South Kirkby & Ackton Hall Joint Communist Pit Group* 2pp lf d Aug. 30 1929

2802 Flying Shuttle *Textile Advisory Cttee, Yorkshire District* 12pp d No.1, Dec. 1950 to No.4, 1951 last issue. From late 1951 incorporated into 'The Woolworker', issued free.

2803 Harworth Spark *Militant Miners at Harwarth* 4pp lf d No.2, Dec. 1930; No.9, Sept. 5 1931

2804 Maltby Flatsheet Guide *Maltby Communist Group* 4pp lf d 7 issues in 1929; more in 1930? Weekly/fortnightly.

2805 Manver's Main Stop Block *Wombwell Communist Pit Group* 4pp lf d No.2, Feb. 23 1929 Sheffield. Same pit group published 'Mitchell's Main Weigh'.

2806 Mitchell's Main Weigh *Wombwell Communist Pit Group* 2pp lf d No.1, Feb. 15 1929

2807 Nunnery Flat Sheet *Nunnery Communist Pit Group* Aug. 1929

2808 Prince Smith's Comb *Prince Smith's Communist Group* 4pp No.2, May 1927 Occasionally titled 'Prince Smith Comb'. 2nd series: No.1, Sept. 1933; No.17, May 1934 Published by Keighley Local; Prince Smith and Stells Factory Group.

2809 **Rebel, The** *The Lister's Communist Group, Bradford* No.11, April 1928

2810 **Ringer, The** *Rossington Communist Pit Group* or *Rossington Militant Miners* 4pp lf d No.7, April 1929; No.17, Aug. 1929 New series: No.11, Sept. 4 1931 – and then called 'The Rossington Ringer' and NMM/CP. Fortnightly/weekly.

2811 **Ripper, The** *Glasshoughton Communist Pit Group, Castleford* 2pp lf d Probably started 1927. Aug. 28 1929.

2812 **Saltaire Searchlight** *Salts Communist Group, Shipley* 4pp No.24 referred to in 'Workers' Life' Oct. 21 1927 – published by Salt Mills Group.

2813 **Sheffield Red** 4pp d No.1, Oct. 1979 – only issue? 'Industrial Bulletin of Sheffield & Rotherham CP'.

2814 **'Sheffield Star' Lads' Strike Sheet** *Street Sellers Cttee* Aug. 18 1932 A strike bulletin, but with very strong CP element.

2815 **Sheffield Workers' Gazette** 4pp No.1, Jan. 1949; No.6, Sept. 1949 May have been free mag.

2816 **Special Strike Bulletin** 2pp No.2, May 6 1926. Published by the 'District Party Committee' – contents indicate Yorkshire.

2817 **Sylvester Rebel** *Stainforth Communist Pit Group, Sheffield* 4pp lf d No.1, July 27 1929; No.55, Sept. 4 1931 Weekly. Publisher's name was sometimes Hatfield Pit Group.

2818 **Textile Battle Front** *CP Textile Group, Shipley* 2pp lf d 1 issue n.d. – 1929?

2819 **Thorne Butty Squasher** *Thorne Communist Pit Group* 4pp lf d No.9, June 1929; No.97, Aug. 1931 Weekly. Pit near Doncaster. 'Butty' was an unpopular method of paying wages by group.

2820 **Wheldale Buzzer** *Communist Pit Group, Castleton* 1927-8?

2821 **Yorkshire Woman: District Women's Newsletter** 6pp lf d No.2, 1978? Child Care Issue.

2822 **Briggs Pollitt Buzzer** *Woollen Textile Group* No.1, Sept. 1929

Northern

2823 **Billingham Workers' Banner** *Billingham Branch* 6pp lf d No.1, Sept. 1946 Incorporating 'The Workers' Voice'. Monthly.

2824 **Crane, The** *Palmer's Shipyard Communist Group* 1927

2825 **Durham Miners' Monthly Journal** 8pp Northern District Congress Report calls this 'our popular miners' paper', so it appears to be CP. 6 issues sold 30,000 copies in 1944.

2826 **Gateshead Branch Bulletin** 2pp lf d 1952-3 'For members'. Monthly.

2827 **Lamp, The** *Dawden Communist Pit Cell* Several issues in 1930.

2828 **Midgie, The** *Communist Group at New Hartley Pit, Blyth* 4pp No.2, May 22 1926

2829 **Miners' Marro** *Wheatley Hill, Durham* Started Feb. 1927 Sometimes referred to just as 'The Marro'.

2830 **Northern Searchlight** *Spen and Chopwell Reds* 4pp 1927 Presumably a continuation of 'The Workers' Seachlight'.

2831 **Steel Point** *South Durham Iron & Steel Works* 4pp No.2, Oct. 5 1934 Not overtly CP.

2832 **Synthetic Workers' Voice** *Billingham Factory Cell* 1931

2833 **Tyneside Red** *Newcastle & Area CP* 16pp No.2, 1978 ?

2834 **Wear Valley Worker** *Bishop Auckland CP* 4pp lf 1975?

2835 **Winch, The** *Communist Group at Clarke-Chapmans, Gateshead* 4pp lf d No.1, June 20 1925

2836 **Workers' Searchlight** *Spen and Chopwell Reds* 4pp lf d No.1, May 30 1926; No.8, July 18 1926. Weekly.

Wales

2837 **Abertillery Communist Special** *Abertillery* 4pp No.2, Aug. 1947; No.5, Feb. 1948

2838 **Cambrian X Ray** *Cambrian Pit Group (Clydach Vale)* 2pp lf d Started 1925; erratic. Revived March 1927; 2 issues in July 1929, printed & published by Lewis Jones. (These are examples of the widespread production of anti-war 'papers' in 1929.)

2839 **Cardiff Vanguard** 10pp lf d No.2, 24 June 1978 Not priced but very substantial.

2840 **Cwmtillery Searchlight** *Organ of the Militant Workers of Cwmtillery* 4pp lf d No.26, Dec. 12 1930 Not claimed as a CP paper but has CP application form. 2nd Series: no.1, 10 Jan. 1936; No.16, 24 July 1936. By this time it was 'Organ of the Communist Pit Group'.

2841 Cyffro 50-60pp lf No.1, Summer 1969 to last issue Summer 1982 17 issues. 1/2 issues per year, though irregular – no issues in 1980. Title means 'Change'. Changed to 'Moving Left in Wales'. 1st ed. was Alistair Wilson. 'Initiated by Welsh Cttee, CP' – always tried to have broad approach. Articles in English & Welsh.

2842 Cymmer Searchlight *Cymmer Colliery Group of CP* 4pp lf d No.6, Oct. 23 1925 Fortnightly. There is a reference to a paper called 'Cymmer Bomb' (untraced).

2843 Gilfach Rebel *Trone Pit Group* 1927 At least 6 issues. See 'Workers' Life' May 20 1927 – 3 militants died just before due to start production.

2844 I'r Chwith (To the Left) 16pp No.1, Autumn 1984 Probably only issue. In Welsh.

2845 Llais Rhyddid (The Voice of Freedom) *North Wales Area Cttee* 1941-46? Bilingual. Ed. John Roose Williams.

2846 Llais y Werin (The Voice of the People) *N. Wales District* 8-12pp Nos 1-3: July, Oct., Dec. 1937 Bilingual. T.E. Nicholas was the main person behind this publication and it includes some of his poems.

2847 Llwynypia Searchlight *Llwynypia Pit Group* 2pp 1925? Special anti-war issue July 1929.

2848 Mardy Leader *Mardy Local CP (later: Mardy Communist Colliery Groups)* 4pp lf d No.4, July 1925; No.17, Oct. 1925 Weekly.

2849 Miners' Voice 4pp lf 1977 One issue?

2850 Moving Left in Wales 24pp lf No.1, Summer 1983; No.3, Summer 1984 Replaced 'Cyffro'. Mainly in English, a few articles in Welsh.

2851 New Broom *Organ of the South Wales DPC* 4pp lf d No.3, Aug. 1 1929; still appearing in 1931 Some issues marked 'Confidential/For Party Members Only'. Very good cartoon.

2852 New Dawn *Ferndale Communist Pit Group* 2pp No.1, July 29 1929

2853 Party News *Welsh District* 6pp lf d 1952 Priced for a short period in 1952/3, otherwise free. Monthly. Larger, Congress ed. in Oct.

2854 People's Welfare Bulletin 10pp lf d No.1, Spring 1971; No.2, Summer 1971 Ed. by Tony Simpson.

2855 Red Challenger *Merthyr Local* 4pp 1928. At least 5 issues. Fortnightly.

2856 Red Dawn *Ferndale Communist Pit Group* 4pp No.7, Oct. 16 1925; No.9, Nov. 20 1925 Fortnightly/monthly. Revived March 1927.

2857 Red Miner *Cwmdu Pit Group, Maesteg* 4pp July 19 1929 'Printed and published by Ben Francis'.

2858 Red Observer *Tylorstown Communist Colliery Group* 4pp lf No.1, Aug. 1925; No.4, Oct. 1925 Fortnightly. Rare printed factory mag.

2859 Red Star *Lady Lewis Pit Group of the CP* 4pp lf d No.2, Jan. 17 1925; No.10, 1925 Fortnightly?

2860 Rhondda Vanguard *Rhondda* 4pp No.1, June 1935 to No.8, April 1936 Properly printed; incl. reports of work of the 7 CP councillors. Monthly sales of 4,500 according to 'Report of CC to 14th Congress'. There had been earlier duplicated versions (e.g. a local election special in March 1935).

2861 Seren y Gogledd (Northern Star) *North Wales Area Cttee* About 10 issues in early 1970s. Unpriced, but while free to CP members was sold to others.

2862 Steam *Railway Communist Group, Cardiff* No.3, Nov. 1925

2863 Treharris Searchlight *Treharris Pit Group* 4pp lf d No.1, Sept. 28 1934

Scotland

2864 Advance, The *Communist Rail Group, Dundee* 1927 Fortnightly.

2865 Black Squad, The *Govan Communist Group* 5pp No.2, June 1927 NMM/CP.

2866 Bogie *Brighills Miners' Pit Group* No.7, Nov. 1931; May 28 1932.

2867 Brass Check, The *Shipyard Communist Group, Caledon and Stannergate; Dundee* No.1, April 10 1925 6 issues ? Weekly. Also supposed to be NMM Metalworkers' Section paper!

2868 Buzzer, The *Militant Miners of Glencraig, Fife* 4pp No.3, April 1930; Aug. 15 1930 Fortnightly. Abe Moffat involved in production.

2869 CP Town Council Bulletin 4pp lf No.3, Sept. 1946

2870 Daily Communist [Scottish Edition] 4pp 4 issues: Nov. 11-14 1922 for election campaign. Ed: H Pollitt. There was also a London ed.

2871 Dundee Worker *Dundee Ctte.* 2-4pp lf No.1, Sunday Oct. 19 1924; just for election? New series: No.19, July 18 1929.

2872 Fan, The [1] *Militant Miners of South Lanarkshire* 4pp lf d No.1, March 8 1930;

No.37, Nov. 22 1930 Bannerhead slogan: 'To Ventilate Grievances and to Fan the Flame of Revolt'. Weekly. 'Published by James Hunter'. CP/UMS.

2873 **Fan, The** [2] *Militant Section, Muiredge Mineworkers (Fife)* 4pp d 1930 6 issues in 1931? Weekly.

2874 **Hutch, The** *Kirkcaldy Pit Group CP* 4pp No.1, Dec. 1925; No.9, April 1926 Probably issued in May also (see 'Militant Miners' p 281.) Replaced 'The Underworld' which appeared for a few issues earlier in 1925 (p256).

2875 **Jigger, The** 4pp lf d No.7, Aug. 1930; No.13, Nov. 14 1930 Fortnightly. Mining. Published by Frank Moore in Hurlford (East Ayrshire) who also published 'The Kenneth's Hawk' at same time.

2876 **Justiceman, The** *Bowhill Pit Group CP* 4pp No.1, April 17 1926 Unusually, this paper was printed not duplicated.

2877 **Kenneth's Hawk** 4pp lf d No.2, Sept. 12 1930 For Highhouse and Barony pits.

2878 **Links Reflector** *Prestonlinks Communist Cell, Edinburgh* 4pp 3 issues 1930 (one dated Aug. 23) Weekly/fortnightly.

2879 **Lookout, The** *Communist Railway Group, Perth* 4pp 1927-1930? See 'Workers' Life' June 17 1927 & Dec. 30 1927.

2880 **Northern Light** *North East Scotland Area* lf d No.1, March 1946; No.2, May 1946

2881 **Old Torch** *Cowdenbeath Pit Group CP* 2 issues 1927 Successor to 'The Torch'?

2882 **Our Street** *Organ of the Muirhead Street Cell of the CP* or *Organ of Partick East Branch* 6pp lf d 1935-7(?) Vol. 4 No.15, 1937 Several issues each week. Probably the most substantial 'street' newspaper produced by a local CP Branch – and all under the bannerhead slogan of 'For Soviet Power'.

2883 **Pan Bolt** *Peeweep Communist Pit Cell* 4pp Most issues in 1930? Ed. Abe Moffat.

2884 **Picket, The** *Lochgelly Group* 4pp No.1, 1926; No.22, Feb. 1927 Ed.'s nom de plume was 'Joyful Kicks' (Home Secretary at time was Joynson-Hicks).

2885 **Red Flag** *Edinburgh Local* No.1, Feb. 1927

2886 **Red Guard** *Mary Colliery, Fife* 4pp lf d No.1, Aug. 17 1929 Ed. B Selkirk. See 'Opening the Books' p56. In Selkirk's autobiog. he says that in Fife there were 8 pit papers, with sales between 200 and 500.

2887 **Sawdust** *Aberdeen CP & YCL* No.8, Oct. 1925 For woodworkers at Fiddes & Sons.

2888 **Scottish Bulletin** 4pp Series 3 No.7, Jan. 1954 Weekly. 'Members only'.

2889 **Scottish Marxist** No.1, June 1972 to No.29, 1984 Up to No.21: sf, av. 54pp; afterwards: lf 16pp. Quarterly/bi-annual. Ed. Willie Thompson, Martin Myant (last issues).

2890 **Searchlight** *Clydebank* 4pp lf 2 issues in 1947?

2891 **Spark** [2] *Methil Local, Fife* 4pp lf d No.1, July 1925; Vol.3 No.22, June 1931 Last issue Dec. 1931. Fortnightly then weekly from 1927. Published by 'Methil Communist Pit Group' then 'Methil CP and YCL' & finally as 'Wellesley Spark' in 1932 for at least 4 months by 'Militant Section Wellesley Workers'. Initially, largely the work of David Proudfoot. First issue sold 240 copies; one year later 1,000. Possibly the most influential pit paper.

2892 **Specials** 4pp While the 'DW' was banned, Jan. 1941 to Aug. 1942, a series of 'papers' with titles like 'Unity Campaign Special', 'Allied Offensive Special', 'Stalin Birthday Special', 'Production Special', 'Greenock Election Special' etc. were issued by the Scottish DC to replace the Scottish ed. of the 'DW'; only on rare occasions were the names used for more than one issue (did this avoid declaring them as a newspaper?). Undated and un-numbered.

2893 **Sprag, The** *Shotts CP/Shotts Miners Militant Group/U.M.S.* 4-6pp First series 1927? (see 'Workers' Life' Feb. 25 1927). Another series: No.2, April 1930; No.23, Oct. 1930. New series: No.1, May 29 1935; No.4, Aug. 23 1935. Weekly. Organ of both CPGB and U.M.S.

2894 **Squatter** *Aberdeen* 1946?

2895 **Textile Picker** *Dundee Textile Communist Group* No.1, June 1925; Vol.2 No.1, June 1926

2896 **Torch, The** [2] *Militant Section, Frances Colliery Workers* 4pp lf d No.1, Oct. 1930; 6 issues to 1931? Fortnightly/Monthly. Kirkcaldy/Buckhaven.

2897 **Torch, The** [3] *Cowdenbeath Communist Pit Group* 4pp No.1, 1925

2898 **Unity** [2] *Cambuslang Branch* 6pp lf d No.29, May 13 1938

2899 **Viewpark Clipper** *Viewpoint Militant Miners or Bellshill Communist Pit Paper, Uddington* 4pp No.5, July 1930; No.17, Nov. 1930 Existed in 1927 (Workers' Life Oct. 21 1927 refers to No.4).

5. Our History

Our History pamphlets, published by the Historians' Group (which was called the CP History Group after 1957), are listed here in chronological order. Though not strictly speaking a journal, they comprise a unique series of works of some interest which deserve individual listing. They qualify for BL categorisation as a serial. They were duplicated up to No. 51 and then printed in a smaller format. Some, especially the earlier pamphlets, were anonymous. Some earlier duplicated copies were re-issued in printed format.

2900 **1. The Class Struggle in Local Affairs** 1956 30pp

2901 **2. Luddism, 1779-1830** 1956 26pp

2902 **3. The Struggle for Educational Opportunity** 1956 27pp

2903 **4. Some Dilemmas for Marxists, 1900-14** 1956 32pp

2904 **5. Labour – Communist Relations, 1920-39** 1957 37pp Expanded in 1990/1991 into 3 substantial eds – see Nos.83 & 84/5.

2905 **6. The Tradition of Civil Liberties in Britain** 1957 24pp

2906 **7. Enclosure and Population Change** 1957 20pp

2907 **8. Land Nationalisation in Britain** 1957 35pp

2908 **9. Cromwell in the English Revolution** 1958 24pp

2909 **10. Social Conditions in the Early 19th Century** 1958 16pp

2910 **11. Town Privileges and Politics in Tudor and Stuart England** 1958 20pp

2911 **12. The Working Week** 1958 24pp

2912 **13. The Historical Novel** Lindsay, Jack & St John, Diana 1959 20pp

2913 **14. Africa in World History** Buckle, Desmond 1959 24pp

2914 **15. Party Politics in the 19th Century: 'Namierism'** 1959 18pp

2915 **16. John Burns' Library** Kapp, Yvonne 1959 21pp

2916 **17. Chartist Literature** Kovalev, Y.V. 1960 19pp

2917 **18. Sheffield Shop Stewards, 1916-18** Moore, Bill 1960 18pp Reprinted in c.1970.

2918 **19. An SDF Branch, 1903-06** Rothstein, Andrew 1960 19pp

2919 **20. The Common People, 1688-1800** 1960 19pp

2920 **21. Diary of Ernest Jones, 1839-47** 1961 21pp

2921 **22. The General Strike in the North East** Arnot, R. Page et al. 1961 19pp

2922 **23. Pages From a Worker's Life, 1916-26** Davies, Bob 1961 18pp

2923 **24. The Lancashire Cotton Famine, 1861-65** 1961 18pp

2924 **25. Thomas Bewick, 1753-1828: Artist, Naturalist, Radical** Watkinson, Ray 1962 19pp

2925 **26/27. Tom Mann, 1890-92** Torr, Dona & Thompson, E.P. 1962 38pp

2926 **28. The Lesser Fabians** Hobsbawm, Eric 1962 14pp

2927 **29. Transition from Feudalism to Capitalism** Dobb, Maurice 1963 12pp

2928 **30. Songs of the Labour Movement** Miller, John 1963 21pp

2929 **31. Chartism and the Trade Unions** 1963 17pp

2930 **32. The World of Homer** Willetts, R.F. 1963 13pp

2931 **33. Shakespeare's Idea of History** Morton, A.L. 1964 18pp

2932 **34. Houses of the People** Mercer, E. 1964 32pp

2933 **35. Slave Society: Some Problems** Browning, R. 1964 15pp

2934 **36/37. Prints of the Labour Movement** 1965 40pp

2935 **38. Tom Mann in Australasia, 1902-09** Torr, Dona 1965 18pp

2936 **39. The Organisation of Science** 1965 24pp

2937 **40. Chartism in the Black Country, 1850-60** Barnsby, George 1965 24pp

2938 **41. Problems of the German Anti-Fascist Resistance** Merson, Allan 1966 30pp

2939 **42. Class and Ideology in Bath, 1800-60** Neale, R.S. 1966 24pp

2940 **43. The Easter Rising as History** Greaves, C. Desmond 1966 19pp

2941 **44/45. History and Social Structure on the East African Plateau** 1966 43pp

2942 **46. A Contemporary View of the Napoleonic Wars** Knight, Frida 1966 23pp

2943 **47. The Second Reform Bill** 1967 19pp

2944 **48. Alexander Macdonald and the Miners** Challinor, Ray 1967 34pp

2945 **49/50. The Revolt in the Fields in East Anglia** Peacock, Alf 1968 37pp

2946 **51. Leveller Democracy: Fact or Myth?** Morton, A.L. 1968 22pp

2947 **52. German Imperialism and its Influence in GB** Rothstein, Andrew 1968 16pp

2948 **53. The Nations of Britain: The Making of the Union** Ruheman, Barbara 1970 17pp

2949 **54. The Nations of Britain: Since the Industrial Revolution** Jenkin, Alfred 1970 19pp

2950 **55. Social Control in the 19th Century** Barnsby, George 1972 10pp

2951 **56. Europe's 17th Century Crisis: A Marxist Review** Parker, David 1972 22pp

2952 **57. Nazis and Monopoly Capital** Merson, Allan 1973 19pp

2953 **58. The Miners of Kilsyth and 1926** Carter, Paul & Carol 1974 24pp

2954 **59. The SDF and the Boer War** Baker, Bill 1974 24pp

2955 **60. Time and Motion Strike, Manchester 1934-7** Jenkins, Mick 1974 34pp

2956 **61. Middle Class Opinion and the 1889 Dock Strike** Cronje, Gillian 1974 24pp

2957 **62. 1945: Year of Victory** Barnsby, George 1975 37pp

2958 **63. On the Origins of Capitalism** Chistozvonov, Alexander 1975 28pp

2959 **64. Imperialism and the British Labour Movement in the 1920s** Macintyre, Stuart 1975 24pp

2960 **65. The 1926 General Strike in Lanarkshire** McLean, John 1976 25pp

2961 **66. Feudalism, Capitalism and the Absolutist State** Hobsbawm, Eric & Bourn, Douglas 1976 18pp

2962 **67. Spain Against Fascism, 1936-9** Green, Nan & Elliot, A.M. 1976 30pp

2963 **68. Workers' Newsreels in the 1920s and 30s** Hogenkamp, Bert 1977 36pp

2964 **69. Rank and File Building Workers' Movements, 1910-20** Latham, Peter 1977 27pp

2965 **70. The Struggle Against Fascism and War, 1931-9** Power, Mike 1978 28pp

2966 **71. From Radicalism to Socialism: Paisley Engineers, 1890-1920** Brown, James 1978 20pp

2967 **72. People's Theatre in Bristol, 1930-45** Tuckett, Angela 1979 28pp

2968 **73. T.A. Jackson: A Centenary Appreciation** Morton, Viven & Macintyre, Stuart 1979 27pp

2969 **74. The National Question in Cornwall** Green, Royston 1980 28pp

2970 **75. The 1842 General Strike in South Wales** Jordan, Heather 1982 23pp

2971 **76. Armed Resistance and Insurrection: Early Chartism** Baxter, John 1984 38pp

2972 **77. Appeasement** Moore, Bill 1985 24pp

2973 **78. The Making of a Clydeside Working Class: Shipbuilding and Working Class Organisation in Govan** Campbell, Calum 1986 32pp

2974 **79. 1688: How Glorious was the Revolution?** Morton, A.L. 1988 33pp

2975 **80. London Squatters, 1946** Branson, Noreen 1989 28pp

2976 **81. The Anti-Fascist People's Front in the Armed Forces: The Communist Contribution, 1939-46** Moore, Bill & Barnsby, George 1990 40pp

2977 **82. Labour – Communist Relations, 1920-51 Part 1: 1920-35** Branson, Noreen & Moore, Bill 1990 72pp Much extended version of No.5.

2978 **83. Labour – Communist Relations, 1920-51 Part 2: 1935-45** Branson, Noreen & Moore, Bill 1991 48pp

2979 **84/85. Labour – Communist Relations, 1920-51 Part 3: 1945-51** Moore, Bill 1991 68pp

6. YCL Publications

The YCL was always a very small organisation, but it mirrored its parent body in publishing a wide range of material, and also in its structure, which meant there had to be District Congresses with the usual formal publications.

The leading body changed its name several times, so it may appear as the National Committee, the Executive Committee, or the General Council.

Listing is alphabetical, within each year.

All are national publications unless stated – the name of the publishing body (YCL Branch, District or other) will be in italics.

1921

2980 **Draft Constitution & Rules** 8pp Adopted at Conference of Reps of Young Workers' League and International Communist School Movement, Birmingham

1922

2981 **Amendments & Resolutions to be Submitted to the 1st Annual Conference** 12pp
2982 **Draft Statutes and Rules** 12pp sf
2983 **No More War?** Young, Harry 12pp
2984 **The Hope of the Future: An Appeal to Young Workers** Stewart, James 16pp ?
2985 **Thesis on Anti-Militarism Adopted by 3rd World Congress of YCI** 12pp

1923

2986 **Resolutions of the Second National Conference of the YCL** 36pp Incl. Constitution.

1924

2987 **Draft Programme of the YCI** 84pp pb
2988 **January 15: The Murder of K. Liebknecht and R. Luxemburg – Manuals for** **Proletarian Anniversaries No.1** 72pp pb Pictorial cover by 'Michael'.
2989 **Resolutions Adopted at 4th Congress of YCI** *EC of YCI* 120pp pb See 'Tasks of YCL of GB'.

1925

2990 **Bolshevisation of the YCL of GB** 12pp
2991 **Highroads to Progress: Minutes of 3rd Congress**
2992 **League Training Syllabus** 61pp pb
2993 **Lenin and the Youth** *YCI/YCL* 80pp pb
2994 **Resolutions of the Enlarged EC of the YCI, March** 62pp
2995 **Young Miners Awake!** 'Pit Lad' 12pp

1926

2996 **A Call to the Youth: Opening Speech to 4th Congress** Rust, W. 16pp
2997 **A Congress of Young Fighters: Report of 4th Congress of YCL** 36pp
2998 **A Short History of the Working Class Children's Movement of GB** 12pp Mainly on Young Comrades' League. The status & publisher of this poorly duplicated pamphlet are unclear (internal? YCL?) but it is one of the few items on the subject.

2999 **A Welcome to New Members and A Useful Guide** 12pp sf

3000 **Report of EC to 4th National Congress** 31pp

3001 **Resolutions of the Enlarged Executive of the YCI, Nov.** *YCI* 42pp

3001a **The Crisis in GB and the Organisation of the Working Youth** 20pp Presumably for the 4th Congress.

3002 **The United Front of the Youth** 10pp Pictorial cover.

3003 **The Young Workers and the General Strike** 20pp Ill.

1927

3003a **After Twenty Years** *Publishing House of the YCI* 20pp Foreword by W. Rust.

3004 **Baden-Powell Exposed!** 16pp

3005 **Report of Second British Youth Delegation to the USSR** 20pp The first Delegation's report, 'Youth in Red Russia' 1926, was published by the National Campaign Committee. This second one, though published by the YCL, had more members from the ILP than the YCL.

3006 **Statutes and Rules Adopted at 4th National Congress, Dec. 1926** 12pp

1928

3007 **EC Report to (Fifth) Congress** 19pp

3008 **Report of Fifth National Congress, March** 32pp

3009 **Resolutions for 5th Congress** 16pp

3010 **Results of Two Congresses: Abridged Report of 6th Congress of CI and 5th Congress of YCI, Sept.** 18pp

3011 **The Case for the YCL** Rust, W. 20pp Cover illustration by Savage.

3012 **The Scout Special** *Glasgow District* 4pp lf d ?

3013 **A Short History of the YCI** 40pp pb ?

1929

3014 **'Be Prepared' for War!** Douglas, John L. 22pp

3015 **Programme of the YCI** 83pp pb

3016 **Stand Ready! The Call of the 1st International Children's Congress to All Proletarian Children** 32pp Ill.

3017 **YCL Song Sheet** *Liverpool* 2pp lf d 'Selections will be sung at the Youth Demonstration on Sept. 9th at Islington Square'. Words to 6 songs – 4 are lesser known. ?

1930

3018 **Dead Fish or Alive: A Word to All Workers** 4pp ?

3019 **Manifesto to All Young Workers** *Fife Cttee* 1pp ?

3020 **Next Steps on the Road to a Mass YCL**

3021 **The Chartist Youth Programme** Massie, Alex 16pp

3022 **The Road to Mass Organisation of Proletarian Children: Decisions of 4th International Conference of Leaders of Communist Children's Leagues** 32pp Meeting held in Moscow, Sept. 1929; also incl. Resolution of Enlarged Plenum of YCI, Moscow Dec. 1929.

3023 **Where Shall We Start?** 22pp Perhaps the most sectarian YCL pamphlet of the Third Period. 'Our principal enemy is the Social-Democratic youth organisation'. ?

3024 **Working Lads of the Scouts** *Glasgow* 4pp 'Scout Special'. ?

1931

3025 **Young Workers and the More Loom System** *Burnley* 8pp

1933

3026 **For Youth Unity: Reply to ILP Guild of Youth** 12pp ?

3027 **Report of CC and the Tasks of the YCL: 7th National Congress, July** 10pp lf d

3028 **Special Supplement: 7th National Congress** 4pp lf

3029 **The Young Communist International: Report and Decisions of Plenum, Dec. 1932** 20pp

1934

3030 **10 Answers to Arguments Against Affiliation (to the Guild of Youth)** 10pp lf d ?

3031 **10 Points Against Fascism** 16pp

3032 **Lenin and the Youth Movement** 8pp ?

3033 **Struggle or Go Down: The Right of Youth Independence in the Fight for Socialism** Chemodanov, V. 16pp

3034 **We Are For the United Front** Chemodanov, V. 16pp Reprint from 'Communist International' No.17.

3035 **Young Workers Advance! Report of the Meeting of the Representatives of the ILP Guild of Youth and the YCI, Paris, May** 20pp Published by Youth Press – joint ILP/YCL.

1935

3036 **Defend the Rising Generation** Gollan, J. 12pp

3037 **London's Youth March Forward in Unity Against the National Government** London 6pp Fold out Pamphlet.

3038 **The Day Is Ours! Report to 6th World Congress YCI** Woolf, M. 37pp No publisher stated, but printed by Marston and adverts on back are by YCL; could conceivably be by Modern Books.

3039 **The Tasks of the United Front of Youth: Resolutions Adopted at 6th Congress of YCI** 15pp

3040 **The YCI: Report of 1st Congress, Berlin, Nov. 1919** *International Proletarian School Movement (Glasgow) & YCL* 32pp ?

1936

3041 **An A1 Nation** Goss, Joe 10pp 'The Youth Library' No.2.

3042 **Clean Up the Factories** Douglas, J.L. 10pp 'The Youth Library' No.1.

3043 **Everything is Going Up … What About Our Wages? We Want More!** 4pp ?

3044 **For Life With a Purpose** London 8pp d

3045 **Give Us Jobs** Burke, David 10pp 'The Youth Library' No.3.

3046 **Mass Youth Rally, Feb. 7: Programme** 4pp

3047 **Raise High the Banner: Speech to 6th World Congress of the YCI, Oct. 1935** Gollan, J. 16pp

3048 **We Ask for Life** 24pp Based on Gollan's Report to 8th National Congress of the Communist Youth Movement, Feb.

1937

3049 **'Challenge' Festival and Sports Rally Programme** 36pp ?

3050 **Clydeside Apprentices Strike: The Full Story** 12pp

3051 **Constitution of the YCL Adopted at 9th National Conference** 8pp This was amended in 1939, after a vote in 1938.

3052 **Draft Constitution** 6pp For 9th Congress.

3053 **Five Lesson Course for Use of Youth League Education Groups** London 18pp Probably London YCL.

3054 **Report to the 9th National Conference of the YCL** 24pp

3055 **The Defence of Madrid** Gillan, Phil 12pp

3056 **The Development of Trotskyism from Menshevism to Alliance with Fascism and Counter Revolution** Gollan, J. 19pp d Special Information Report of J Gollan to Enlarged National Council Meeting, Jan. 30 & 31.

3057 **We March to Victory: Report of National Council to 9th National Conference** 24pp Cover by Tom Poulton.

3058 **Why Youth Strikes** Gollan, J. 12pp ?

3059 **Youth of Britain Advance! Report & Resolutions of 9th National Congress, June** 38pp

1938

3060 **A Plan For Hammersmith's Youth** *Hammersmith* 12pp lf d

3061 **Defend the People: Report to 10th National Conference** Gollan, J. 24pp

3062 **Songs For Socialism** 8pp lf Words to 17 songs. ?

3063 **The Road to Life** Bennett, Mick 8pp

3064 **What London's Youth Will Do! Discussion Pamphlet for Annual Conference of London District YCL** 14pp

3065 **Youth Will Serve for Feedom** Gollan, J. 16pp

1939

3066 **Building the YCL: Report, Resolution on Building the YCL; Other Resolutions** 96pp Interesting resolution on organising girls;

others on Education, Industry, Unemployed, Fitness, Rural Areas, etc. Also Speech by Fred Heath on 'Challenge' with detail on its finances.

3067 Handbook for Branch Education Secretaries 2nd ed.

3068 Report of 11th National Conference 96pp pb See also special ed. of 'Our Youth' April 1939 (47pp) which has resolutions plus Report of National Council for 1938/9.

3069 The YCL and 'Fitness for Democracy' London 22pp lf d A Compendium of Material for YCL Branch Education & study on the question of 'Fitness for Democracy' ?

1940

3070 Make Life Worth While! What the YCL Stands For 20pp

3071 Songs for Conscripts and Others Challenge 2pp Uncommon collection of witty lyrics to well-known tunes on conscription, air raid shelters, 'Hitler's pals in Downing Street', Hitler and Mussolini etc. in the period before the German attack on the USSR. ?

3072 Youth and the War Bennett, Mick 16pp

1941

3073 An Introduction to Communism: Course for New Members of the YCL 16pp ?

3074 For Life and Liberty: Our Way to Win 16pp ?

1942

3075 A Handbook of League Organisation 20pp ?

3076 Battle for Youth Bennett, Mick 12pp

3077 Conquer Your Future Now Bennett, Mick 16pp

3078 Fitness and the Great Summer Campaign 14pp d

3079 Memorandum on the Service of Youth 8pp ?

3080 Shock Brigade: A Guide – How to Start Them, How They Work 4pp

3081 Shock Brigades for Victory Sussman, Jack 16pp sf ?

3082 The Progress of Man: A 4 Lesson Course for New Members of the YCL Claydon, Cyril 20pp

3083 We Young Communists Jones, Gladys 12pp

3084 What of the Future? A Course for New Members of the YCL 16pp ?

3085 YCL Rally Sept. 5: Souvenir Programme Swansea 4pp 'Speakers, Rhythm Orchestra, Community Singing & a One-Act Play'.

3086 Youth and the Trade Unions Eastwood, Fred 20pp

3087 Youth for Victory Bennett, Mick 16pp

1943

3088 1943! A Year of Unity of Youth for Victory and A Happy Future: Report of National Council, Jan. 4pp lf

3089 A Guide to the YCL 12pp lf d ?

3090 A Memorandum on the Health & Fitness of the Young Worker in Industry 20pp

3091 Constitution and Principles 24pp sf Adopted at 12th National Congress, June 1943.

3092 Cultural Week, April 12-18: Programme S E London 4pp

3093 Dues: A Guide 5pp Internal, free, organisational document about membership subscriptions. ?

3094 Get Fighting Fit for Victory: Policy for a Healthy Youth 4pp ?

3095 Hitler's Slave Drive Bennett, Mick 8pp

3096 Manifesto: To All Who Are Young 4pp lf ?

3097 Service for Victory: Policy and Programme Adopted by 12th National Conference, June 32pp

3098 Socialism Claydon, Cyril 14pp ?

1944

3099 Education Handbook No.1: June London Education Cttee 13pp

3100 Make Life Worth While: Course for Members Based on Constitution & Principles of the YCL 24pp Different from 1940 title of same name. ?

3101 Our Most Glorious Year: Special Conference of YCL, Jan. 8pp 2 main speeches by Gladys Jones & Murdoch Taylor.

3102 The British Empire: What It Is 4pp ?

1945

3103 **Fight and Win a Labour Majority** 7pp d

3104 **Fight and Win: 13th National Conference** 16pp

3105 **How to Organise a Debate, A Dutch Parliament etc.** 14pp sf ?

3106 **Hull for Youth: Memorandum on the Hull Youth Charter** Hull YCL Club 8pp ?

3107 **When the Fire Burns: Booklet of Poems** Crossland, Vincent Edwin *Challenge* 16pp

1946

3108 **14th National Conference: Main Report, Resolutions, Commissions** 26pp lf d

3109 **Discussion Statement for 14th National Congress** 12pp lf d

3110 **What is Socialism?** 12pp lf d ?

1948

3111 **For Peace and Socialism: Speech to 15th National Congress, March** Brooks, Bill 16pp

3112 **London Landmarks** Shields, J. 8pp d Places associated with Marx, Engels & Lenin. Probably YCL but not stated.

3113 **Report of National Committee to 15th National Congress** 16pp lf d

3113a **Report of the District Committee to the District Congress** North West 6pp lf d

3114 **Save Britain From War: Speech to 15th Congress** Pollitt, H. 4pp lf

1949

3115 **Build the YCL: For Peace and Socialism – Report of 16th National Congress** 28pp

3116 **Report of the National Committee to 16th National Congress** 8pp lf d

3117 **The Progress of Man: 4 Lesson Course for Members of YCL** 24pp

3118 **The Way to the Future: Discussion Statement for 16th National Congress** 4pp lf

1950

3119 **Into Action for Peace and a Better Life: Discussion Statement for 17th National Congress** 4pp lf

3120 **National Committee Report to 17th National Congress** 10pp lf d

3121 **We Fight for Peace: Report of 17th Congress of YCL, May** 30pp Incl. Main Report by B. Brooks.

3122 **Young Miner: Challenge Special** 4pp lf Another with same title June 1954. ?

1951

3123 **Annual Report of National Committee to 18th Congress** 6pp lf d

3123a **Colonial Youth Day: Speakers' Notes** 9pp lf d Unpriced.

3124 **Unity for Peace and a Better Life: Report of National Cttee to 18th National Congress** Moss, John 20pp

3125 **We Accuse the Tories** Moss, John 8pp

3126 **Youth! Win Your Future** Bridges, George 8pp

1952

3127 **A Letter to All Members** Moss, John 4pp

3128 **Free Britain's Youth: Branch Nite Notes No.3** 6pp lf d

3129 **Free Britain's Youth: Report to 19th National Congress, Oct.** Moss, John 22pp

3130 **National Committee Report of Work: 19th National Congress** 6pp lf d

1953

3131 **A Letter to All Members** 4pp

3132 **A Policy for London Youth: Main Political Report for Congress** 24pp lf d

3133 **Give Youth a Sporting Chance: Branch Nite Notes No.13** 8pp lf d

3134 **Socialism? The Future for Youth** Cohen, Gerry 8pp Author was National Organiser of YCL. ?

3135 **Stalin's Youth** 8pp lf d ?

3136 **The General Strike** 16pp

3137 **The General Strike: 9 Days That Shook Capitalism!** 16pp lf

3138 **Youth and Crime: Branch Nite Notes No.9** 12pp lf d

1954

3139 **Africa: The Stark Truth** 4pp lf

3140 **Announcing the 20th National Congress** 8pp lf d

3141 **Britain's Youth Assembly: For a Happy Life** 10pp lf d

3142 **For Friendship and Solidarity With Colonial Youth: Branch Nite Notes No.2** 10pp d

3143 **Lenin: Youth's Friend and Teacher – Branch Night Notes No.1** 6pp lf d

3144 **Let's Go to the Pictures: Branch Nite Notes No.3** 8pp lf d

3145 **Malcolm Jepps Exhibition: A Tribute and an Example** *London* 8pp Exhibition of his art at Holborn Library. ?

3146 **No Nazi Army: Cut the Call-up** 2pp

3147 **Parliament and the People: Branch Nite Notes** 8pp lf d

3148 **Political Report of the National Cttee to 20th Congress** 24pp lf d

3149 **Report of the Work of the National Cttee to 20th Congress** 12pp lf d

3150 **Sex Equality: Branch Nite Notes** 6pp lf d

3151 **The 12th Congress of the Lenin YCL of the Soviet Union** 12pp d

3152 **The Challenge to Labour: CP Congress – Branch Nite Notes** 8pp lf d

3153 **Youth Speaks Out** 4pp lf

1955

3154 **Tomorrow's Citizens Speak Out: Memorandum for Discussion** 12pp ?

1956

3155 **Learn and Enjoy Life: Report of 21st National Congress, Oct.** Moss, John 16pp

3156 **The Call-Up Must Be Cut** 4pp lf ?

1958

3157 **Report of 22nd National Congress, Nov.** 22pp lf d Mainly J. Reid's Report.

3158 **Report of Work of National Cttee to 22nd National Congress** 8pp lf d

1959

3159 **Time to Hit Back** 4pp lf

3160 **Youth in the Space Age** *Kent* 15pp ?

1960

3161 **All Together Now: The Challenge Song Book** 40pp Collated by E. Winter.

3162 **Political Report to 23rd Congress, Oct.** 30pp lf d

3163 **Report of Twenty-Third National Congress** 28pp lf

3164 **'We Are On the Winning Side': Main Report to 23rd National Congress** Reid, Jimmy 12pp lf d

1962

3165 **Aims and Principles of the YCL: New Members Course Syllabus** 16pp lf d ?

3166 **Report of 24th National Congress, Nov.** 28pp lf d

3167 **Report of Work of National Committee** 8pp lf d

3168 **Report to 24th National Congress** 28pp lf d

1963

3169 **District Congress Discussion Statement** *Scottish Cttee* 8pp lf d

3170 **Report of District Congress** *London* 12pp lf d

1964

3171 **Report of 25th National Congress** 27pp

3172 **Report to 25th National Congress** 18pp lf d

3173 **Tutor's Guide to the Syllabus for New Members of the YCL** 24pp lf d

1965

3174 **Memorandum on Votes at 18** 8pp lf d

3175 **Report of District Congress** *London* 18pp lf d

3176 **What is the Prices & Income Policy?** 6pp lf d ?

1966

3177 Branch Guide 18pp lf New ed. issued in 1967.

3178 Report of Work to 26th Congress 6pp lf d

3179 Who is Wrong: Youth or Britain? 4pp lf d ?

1967

3180 International Youth Festival, May 27 – June 3: Souvenir Programme 40pp

3181 Resolutions of 26th National Congress, May 14pp lf d

3182 Young Workers Reject Racialism *Surrey* 10pp lf d ?

1968

3183 Wanted for Intent to Fool the People: An Anti-Racialist Broadsheet 8pp lf On Enoch Powell. ?

3184 YCL Discussion Document Yardley, Colin & Davis, Barney 14pp lf

1969

3185 Give The Boss Some Agro: The Rate With the Vote 8pp lf

3186 May Day Special *Yorkshire* 4pp lf d

3187 Pre-Congress Discussion Bulletins Like the CP, the YCL issued cheaply produced collections of contributions to pre-Congress debates. The first traced is for the April 1969 Congress: 4 issues monthly. For 1971 see 'Cogito – Pre Congress Disc. Bulletin'. 1973 Congress: only 1 issue? (lf d 14pp). 1975: only 1 issue? (lf d 16pp). 1977: 2 issues? (lf d 36pp/42pp); 1979: 1 issue (lf d 20pp).

3188 Report of Work of the National Committee 37pp lf d

3189 Resolutions, Amendments etc. for 27th National Congress 37pp lf d

3190 Vietnam Extra: Vietnam Will Win 8pp lf ?

1970

3191 1870-1970: A Party of a New Type – Centenary Publication of Selected Writings of Lenin *Kent* 15pp lf d

3192 A Party of a New Type *Kent* 16pp lf d

3193 Education: Work and Technical Training for Young People 7pp lf d

3194 Ireland in Crisis *Surrey* 8pp ?

3195 It's Our Future ... Vote Communist 6pp lf ?

3196 The Middle East *Surrey* 8pp ?

1971

3197 28th National Congress Report 34pp lf d

3198 Challenge Special: Tories Out 4pp lf

3199 Challenge UCS Special 8pp lf

3200 Cogito: Pre-Congress Discussion Bulletin 16–22pp lf d 1971. 3 issues.

3201 National Congress Report, April 36pp lf d

3202 Report of District Congress *London* 26pp lf d

3203 Young Workers and Training 10pp lf d

1972

3204 Challenge Young Workers' Special 8pp lf

3205 Dimitrov Lives On! Geldart, Dick *Surrey* 18pp d

1973

3206 Challenge Special 4pp lf Fold out poster.

3207 London YCL Congress Report, Dec. 18pp

3208 YCL Congress, April 57pp lf Incl. Speeches, Resolutions, Rules, Report of Work of National Cttee, analysis of Congress delegates etc.

1974

3209 Petrol and War *Surrey* 12pp d

3210 The Communist Case 8pp d

3211 The Fascist Threat Power, Mike 12pp lf

3212 The Socialist Revolution and After 6pp d

1975

3213 **30th National Congress Report** 54pp

3214 **A Future for Scotland: Socialism** *Scottish Cttee* 8pp lf

3215 **Challenge: Reader's Guide** 12pp lf d

3216 **It's Our Future: Say 'No' on June 5** 4pp lf Common Market Referendum.

3217 **London YCL Congress Report** 28pp lf d

3218 **The Shrewsbury Two** *Surrey* 16pp sf d ?

3219 **Young Communists' Branch Guide Campaign** 8pp lf d

1976

3220 **Branch Education Notes No.1: The General Strike** 12pp lf d

3221 **Branch Education Notes No.2: Women** 14pp lf d

3222 **Red Festival (Programme)** 16pp May.

3223 **Unemployment and the Crisis of Capitalism** *Surrey* 18pp ?

1977

3224 **A Socialist Song Book** *Harrow* 48pp sf

3225 **Against War: The Soviet Union Leads the Way** 14pp d ?

3226 **Discussion Document on Gay Rights** *Glasgow Cttee* 14pp ?

3227 **Official Report 31st Congress** 42pp

3228 **Red Festival (Programme)** 25pp Oct.

3229 **Young People and Industry in the Seventies** 22pp

1978

3230 **Activist's Handbook** 18pp lf 600 printed. ?

3231 **Branch Builders Kit** Pack of current pamphlets & leaflets.

3232 **Challenge Festival (Programme)** 12pp d

3233 **London YCL Congress Report** 32pp lf d

3234 **What Happened in Czechoslovakia 1968** Sling, Jan 24pp lf d ?

1979

3235 **Amendments & Resolutions for 32nd National Congress** 118pp

3236 **Our Future: Draft for Discussion at Congress** 16pp lf 2,000 printed.

3237 **Our Future: Programme of the YCL** 30pp

3238 **Report of Work from EC for 32nd National Congress** 22pp lf d

3239 **The YCL** 14pp ?

1981

3240 **Congress Report** 40pp lf d

3241 **YCL Congress '81 (33rd)** 31pp lf

1983

3242 **Congress Document** 24pp lf

3243 **Congress Resolutions** 68pp lf d

3244 **Marxism After 100 Years** Rothstein, Andrew *Tyneside* 22pp Reprint from 'African Communist', No.93.

1984

3245 **London YCL Congress Report** 20pp lf d

3246 **Support the Miners** 4pp lf

1985

3247 **YCL Congress Report** 20pp lf

7. YCL Magazines

National and local YCL magazines are listed together in chronological order; entries will be national unless stated otherwise (the publisher is in italics). Included are papers by the Young Pioneers, and the Young Comrades' League (short-lived children's organisations). There are certainly more local magazines to be unearthed, though many never got beyond one or two issues.

As with early YCL pamphlets, there were some cases of magazines being officially published by the Young Communist International, often from the YCL office in London: these are included.

I have tried to list the internal bulletins, from 1950, as one item – generally they were not for sale (see *Internal Bulletin*).

Each issue of *Cogito*, the YCL's theoretical and discussion journal, was usually devoted to a particular topic and is, exceptionally, listed separately, as it is more like a series of separate pamphlets. I have also listed authors here, something not done anywhere else in chapters on Magazines. The numbering and dating of *Cogito*, as with some other YCL journals, was extremely erratic and at times non-existent – and there were several series as well as Supplements.

3248 **100 Lines** *Bristol YCL Schools Magazine* 12pp d 1971 ?

3249 **Aberdeen Young Worker** *Aberdeen YCL* 4pp lf 1982 ?

3250 **Alive: Cultural Magazine** 20-36pp lf d No.1, Feb. 1940 to No.3, April 1940. Probably the only issues. Was supposed to be a monthly mag. of stories & poems. Ed. Maurice Carpenter.

3251 **Bulletin For Leaders of Communist Children's Groups** *YCI* 30pp Vol.2 No.3/4, Jan. 1925; Vol.2 No.5, Sept. 1925. Also called 'Bulletin for Teachers of Communist Children's Groups'.

3252 **Challenge** The YCL's main paper for 50 years. Vol.1 No.1, March 1935 lf. Monthly till 1938 then weekly (12pp then 8pp). 1941: smaller format (16pp). 1942: lf (8pp). 1943: smaller till 1950. 1951: lf (4pp). 1955: Monthly, smaller (12pp). 1960: lf (6pp then 8pp). From Nov. 1967: New Series, smaller (20pp). From Oct. 1971: New Series lf (4pp); more or less monthly. By 1977: bi-monthly then irregular till last issue No.87, 1985. Eds incl. Ted Willis, Richard Kisch, Stan Jacques, Monty Cohen, Sid Kaufman, Monty Johnstone, Gerry Pocock, Trevor Hyett, Anne Devine, Colin Yardley, George Bridges, Paul Bradshaw, Steve Munby, Chris Horrie.

3253 **Club News (Incorporating Our Youth)** 12-16pp March 1944 Then monthly. Last issue Jan. 1947.

3254 **Cogito No.1 (Second Series?): Time for Change** 20pp lf d 1971 Eds of Cogito: Colin Yardley & Peter Lowe; Ron Vizard; Laureen Mason; Jackie Bridges; Ian Findlay; Nick Guy.

3255 **Cogito No.3 (Second Series?): Trends Among Youth in the 70s** Bradshaw, Paul 32pp lf d June 1976

3256 **Cogito No.4 (Second Series?): Aspects of the Ideological Struggle** 34pp April 1977 Smaller format.

3257 **Cogito No.5 (Second Series?): Socialism in the Colours of France** 30pp Oct. 1977 Smaller format.

3258 **Cogito No.6: Czecho Cogito** 20pp lf d 1968 On the intervention in Czechoslovakia.

3259 **Cogito No.7: Czechoslovakia's Struggle for Socialist Democracy** Johnstone, Monty 38pp lf d 1969

3260 **Cogito Supplement No.1: YCL Discussion Document** Yardley, Colin & Davis, Barney 20pp lf d May 1968

3261 **Cogito Supplement No.2: Yugoslavia and World Youth Festival Reports** 10pp lf d 1968

3262 **Cogito Supplement No.3: The YCL and 'Challenge'** 16pp lf d 1968 ?

3263 **Cogito Supplement No.4: Czechoslovakia** Bridges, George 22pp lf d 1968 ?

3264 **Cogito Supplement No.5: Socialism and Democracy** Davis, Barney 8pp lf d 1968

3265 **Cogito Supplement No.6: Marxist Ideas for Change** 14pp lf d 1969 ? 500 printed.

3266 **Cogito: Black Power** Thompson, Willie 18pp lf d 1969

3267 **Cogito: Britain's Road to Revolution** Cook, Dave 22pp lf d Feb. 1976

3268 **Cogito: China** Woddis, Jack 28pp lf d 1968

3269 **Cogito: Class and Politics in Britain** Squires, Mike 24pp lf d May 1972

3270 **Cogito: Democracy in Chile** Myant, Chris & Chater, Tony 26pp lf d 1974 ?

3271 **Cogito: Revolution** 22pp lf d 1968

3272 **Cogito: Role of Communist Youth Movement** Bell, Tom 16pp lf d August 1973

3273 **Cogito: Schools and Education Discussion Document** 12pp lf d 1971

3274 **Cogito: The Youth Movement in Britain 1780-1971** 16pp lf d 1971 ?

3275 **Cogito: Trotsky – Part 1** Johnstone, Monty 36pp lf d 1969

3276 **Cogito: Trotsky and World Revolution** Johnstone, Monty 16pp lf May 1976

3277 **Cogito: With God on Our Side** Sloan, Pat 22pp lf d May 1967

3278 **Cogito: Women's Lib** Small, Rosemary 14pp lf d 1971

3279 **Comanaiche** *Scottish YCL* 12pp lf d No.1, Oct. – Resolutions & Speeches of 1972 Congress; No.2, Dec.

3280 **Communist Youth Information: New Series** 8pp lf No.17, 1935. Weekly. For sale but really internal.

3281 **Communist Youth: Theoretical & Organisational Bulletin of the CC of the YCL** 16-22pp lf d Vol.1 No.1, April 1934. 4 issues in 1934. Monthly?

3282 **Correspondence of the Young International: English Edition** *British Section of the YCI* 8pp lf No.10, Oct. 1 1921.

3283 **Drum, The** *Young Pioneers of GB* 8pp No.2, March 1932. 6 issues in 1932?

3284 **East End Challenge** *Tower Hamlets (North)/Newham YCL* 8pp lf No.1, April 1985. Supposedly issued every 2 months, alternating with 'Challenge', but there may only have been a single issue. Ed. Dewi John (later expelled from CP).

3285 **For a Life with a Purpose** *Magazine of the Mile End Communist Youth* 14pp Vol.1 No.2, May 1937.

3286 **Format: Journal of YCL's National Schools Campaign** 10pp No.1, Jan. 1969. This was probably the only issue.

3287 **Internal Bulletin** 4-16pp Jan. 1950: 'YCL Bulletin'; Aug. 1950: 'League Life'; 1958: 'Fortnightly Letter'; 1967: 'Internal Bulletin'; 1968 (late): 'Once A Fortnight'; 1969: 'Communist'; 1972: 'Young Communist'; 1979-86: 'YCL Informer' (13 issues); 1986: 'Young Communist Bulletin' (2 issues?). Generally these were not for sale – though 'Communist' was free to members of the NC, DCs and Branch Secs and sold to others. Initially fortnightly, usually monthly, sometimes quarterly. There was also a 'Newsletter' (1972-8).

3288 **International Bulletin [1]** 30pp; 16pp lf d No.1, Nov. 1968 to No.2, March 1969. Probably the only 2 issued. Possibly n.f.s.

3289 **International of Youth** *YCI* 40pp 1921? Vol.4 No.1, 1924. No publisher, printed in Sweden. Graphic cover. Another series: No.2 1925 or 1926 (graphic cover). New Series No.1, March 1927 (pb 42pp) – bi-monthly. No.1, Nov. 1929 (pb 70pp), April/May 1930 also No.1(!); 1934: Oct.

3290 **Internationale** *Northolt YCL* 32pp lf d No.2, 1967. Ed. Keith Veness.

3291 **Laddie, The** *Marro YCL Pit Group, Wheatley Hill, Durham* 2pp No.2, Feb. 19

1927. This was a supplement to 'The Miners' Marro'.

3292 **League Organiser** 16pp No.1, March 14 1930. This was probably the only issue.

3293 **Leeds Red** *Leeds YCL* 22pp lf d 2 issues, early 1968.

3294 **Monthly Bulletin for Girl Members** Not traced, but the YCL issued a circular in July 1936 announcing this as forthcoming for sale in August.

3294a **National Campaign Guide to Action For YCL Branches** 6pp April-May 1949 Bi-monthly; probably not for sale.

3295 **Our Youth: Discussion Magazine of the YCL** 24-32pp No.1, April 1938 then more or less monthly to March 1940. Appears to have been replaced by 'YCL News' – but I have only seen one issue from 1943 – before the regular 'Club News' appeared in 1944.

3296 **Partick Young Worker, The** *Partick Branch* 6pp Only one issue appeared, July 1964.

3297 **Permanent Red: Journal of Yorkshire Young Communists** 14pp lf d First 5 issues free. No.6 1970.

3298 **Pioneer News: Organ of the Young Comrades' League** 4pp lf Vol.1 No.6, 1929. Followed on from 'Young Comrade'.

3299 **Real Life: Theoretical & Discussion Journal of the YCL** 12-24pp lf None dated. 1981? Last issue No.6 Winter 1983/4.

3300 **Red Action News** *Dundee YCL* 2pp No.3 1989.

3301 **Red Barrel** *Merseyside YCL* 8pp lf d 2 issues in 1975.

3302 **Red Flag** *Merseyside YCL* 10pp Vol.1 No.1, April 1969; Vol.3 No.1 (nd – early 1970s). First copy duplicated, then printed. Monthly. Became journal of NW YCL not just Merseyside.

3303 **Red Rag** *Wembley YCL* 4pp d No.1, no date.

3304 **Red Thistle** *Partick YCL* No.1, 1968?

3305 **Red Work** *Hemel YCL* 6pp No.15, 1976. Hemel Hempstead.

3306 **Spark: Discussion Journal of Tufnell YCL** 1967

3307 **Street Sheet** *Aberdeen YCL* 8pp d 1981

3308 **Threshold** *Wembley YCL* 12pp No.2, 1963. Quarterly.

3309 **Tolpuddle: School Students' Journal** 8-16pp lf No.1, 1971 (?); No.2, 1971, plus 2 more undated/unnumbered issues.

3310 **Under the Bed** *Dundee YCL* 10pp No.1, Sept. 1979. Probably just internal.

3311 **Ward and Goldstone Spark** *Ward and Goldstone Group YCL, Salford* 4pp No.1, July 1 1930; No.3, July 24 1930. Factory paper.

3312 **Worker's Child: An International Magazine With Illustrations** *YCI* 60-70pp No.1, Sept. 1926; No.2, Jan. 1927.

3313 **YCL News (Incorporating Our Youth)** 4pp April 1943.

3314 **Yorkshire Challenge** *Yorkshire Young Communists* 4pp lf Only 1 issue 1987?

3315 **Young Communist: Organ of Theory & Practice of the YCL** 8pp lf d New Series? No.2 1929.

3316 **Young Communist: The Organ of the YCL** 8pp lf No.1, Dec. 1921 to Vol.2 No.8, 1923. Replaced by 'Young Worker'.

3317 **Young Comrade: Official Organ of the Young Comrades' League** 4pp lf No.1, April 1924 to May 1928. Possibly new series for a while (see 'Warwick Guide'). Monthly. In 1925 it claimed a circulation of 4,000.

3318 **Young Mancunian** *Greater Manchester YCL* 10pp lf d Sept. 1983; another issue 1984.

3319 **Young Striker** 2pp 1926 Published daily in London during General Strike (Klugmann 'History of the CPGB' Vol.2). George Miles was one of the publishers.

3320 **Young Worker Bulletin** 38pp lf No.1, Nov. 1971. There was a new series called Young Workers' Bulletin with an issue in 1980 and a second in Spring 1981 (8pp).

3321 **Young Worker [1]** 4-24pp lf Replaced 'Young Communist' after July 1923. No.37, early Dec. 1934. Monthly, then fortnightly and weekly from New Series No.1, May 1st 1926 till at least 1928; monthly in early 30s. 1926-7 titled 'Weekly Young Worker'. In 1926 contained Young Miners' Supplement. Early issues had cartoons/drawings by 'Michael'. Incl. some fiction and poetry; also sports activities (BWSF).

3322 **Young Worker [2]** *Glasgow West Young Communists* 8pp Only 1 issue 1984?

8. Students

Again, national and local publications are listed together, and magazines are also included. These could have had a separate section in the Magazine chapter, but the CP student branches had more in common with each other than with local CP branches in same District. In some cases, both pamphlets and magazines were published by more than one student branch. As with the YCL, an element of disorganisation is common in the dating of publications. I have not listed the internal *Reports of Annual Conference of Communist Students*, apart from 1951 which is substantial and was priced for sale.

Not surprisingly, the vast majority of entries date from 1968 and the following decade. Branch or District is indicated in italics; otherwise they are National publications or unknown. This chapter only includes material produced by student organisations; there are some pamphlets addressed to students in the National CP chapter (e.g. *An Open Letter to Students*).

'?' at the end of an entry indicates query over year of issue or of first issue in the case of a journal.

1921

3323 **Free Oxford** *Oxford* 40pp lf Journal. 6 issues 1921-2. 'A Communist Journal of Youth'. Initially not CP but by No.6 it had a slogan by Trotsky across the bannerhead. It has been described as 'the un-official Communist journal for the universities'. Ed. Arthur Reade was expelled from Oxford – the Vice-Chancellor describing the paper as 'obscene licentiousness & the bitterest class-hatred … being pushed into the hands of ladies coming out of church'. Reade worked at 'LM' as Business Manager.

1932

3324 **Student Vanguard** 32pp Journal. Vol.1 No.1, Nov. 1932 to Vol.3 No.2, Nov./Dec. 1936? Monthly/bi-monthly. Format varied. CP dominated.

1945

3325 **The Fee Rise in Oxford** *Oxford* 4pp

1946

3326 **Memorandum on Student Problems: Special Reference to LSE** 4pp lf d

3327 **Oxford: A Future for Our University – A Statement for Discussion** *Oxford* 36pp Foreword by H. Pollitt.

1951

3328 **Win Students for Peace to Save Britain: Communist Students' Annual Conference, Sept. 1951** 24pp lf d

1956

3329 **Student Today** *National Student Cttee* 8-16pp Journal. 1956?-1959? Quarterly.

1961

3330 **Communist Student [1]** *National Student Cttee* 20pp Journal. 1961?-1963? At least 8 issues. First issue published by Manchester Univ. Com Soc. An ed. appears to have been produced with slight differences by Univ. of London Union Com Soc. Their issue No.1 is dated April 1962. Initially the journal appears to have been edited by different student branches in turn.

1962

3331 **Communist Student International News Bulletin** *Univ. of London Communist Society* 76pp d Journal. No.1, April. 'On the 22nd Congress'. Probably only issue.

1963

3332 **Mainstream** *National Student Cttee* 16pp lf Journal. Nov. 1963 – Oct. 1965. Termly. Well produced.

1964

3333 **Intercom [1]** *Oxford* 24pp lf d Journal. Jan. 1964; Jan. 1966.

1966

3334 **Penny Red [1]** *Leeds* 2pp lf Journal. 1966-1970. Publication erratic – occasionally weekly. There was a 22pp issue in 1968. Incorporated into 'Red Star' but not for sale.

1968

3335 **Agitprop** *Communist Club, Oxford* Journal. 2 issues 1968-9.

3336 **Ideological Digest: Student Movement Unity** Thompson, Willie (ed.) *National Student Cttee* 36pp lf d Papers from CUL, 1968.

3337 **Revolution in Africa: Report of Seminar** 16pp lf d

3338 **Students, Society and Revolution** Pearce, David & Thompson, Willie et al. *Sheffield Students Union Communist Society* 34pp lf

1969

3339 **Agitart** 8pp Journal. 'The first national art & design students' newspaper'; no number or sign of further issue. Ed. D. Jacks et al. No publisher, probably CP. ?

3340 **Penny Red [2]** *Scotland* 4pp Journal. 6 issues during this year.

3341 **The Future for Art and Education** 6pp lf d ?

3342 **Thrust: Theories of Revolution** 30pp lf d Includes Letter to R.S.S.F. from National Student Cttee. ?

1970

3343 **Greece: Class War Against Fascism** *Cambridge* 4pp

1971

3344 **Agro** *Strathclyde* 8pp Journal. Dec. 1971.

3345 **Free Angela** 8pp lf d On Angela Davis.

1972

3346 **Jimmy Reid Speaks to All Students** *Wales* 8pp d ?

3347 **Leicester Red** *Leicester* 12pp lf Journal. Oct. 1972.

3348 **Marxism and Anarchism** Hobsbawm, Eric *Birkbeck College & London Univ. Communist Students* 6pp lf d ?

3349 **Red** *Manchester Univ. Students* 8pp lf Journal. Also described as 'Manchester Red' (Warwick MRC). Supposed to be fortnightly. Last issue Vol.2 No.3?

3350 **Socialism, Democracy and the One-Party System** Johnstone, Monty *South Bank Poly* 28pp Reprinted from 3 issues of 'MT', 1970. ?

3351 **'Take A Pill ... ' The Drug Industry: Private or Public?** Robson, John *Marxists in Medicine – Health Section of the Central London Students Branch* 50pp

3352 **The Communist** *Kent* Journal. Early 1970s. ?

1973

3353 **I.S. and the Student Movement** *London Central Students Branch/National Student Cttee* 14pp 'Written by CP Students in Leeds'. ?

3354 Forging the Weapon: Student Unions 10pp lf d

3355 Lessons From the LSE 26pp

3356 Occupation at the LSE *LSE* 4pp lf

3357 On Art and Art Education *Gloucester College of Art & Design* 12pp lf d ?

3358 Red Lead *Essex* 16pp lf Journal. No. 8 1975. There was a 'Special' issue in 1976 on 'Lysenko: A Theoretical & Historical Analysis' by Colin Beardon (18pp). ?

3359 Revolutionary Perspectives Hobsbawm, Eric *London Central Student Branch* 10pp lf d

1974

3361 Breaking the Barriers: Ideology and Post-School Education 28pp

3362 Community in Conflict *Essex* 36pp ?

3363 Essex: Background to the Dispute – A Strategy to Win *CP Student Cttee* 4pp lf d A version was also produced by Essex Students Branch.

3364 Grants Campaign: The Time is Now *Student Committee* 4pp lf

3365 The Fight Against Victimisation: Essex, Kent – A CP Broadsheet *CP Student Cttee* 4pp lf d A national, unpriced pamphlet. Contains accounts of events at the 2 universities – at Kent the trouble started when a CP member, Joe Cotter, was sent down.

3366 Women in the Student Movement *Central London Students* 14pp

1975

3367 Althusser and Marxist Theory Macintyre, Stuart & Tribe, Keith *Cambridge* 32pp Actually published by the authors, but based on their opening contribution at a Cambridge Student Branch meeting.

3368 The Challenge of Marxism: A Guide to Reading *LSE* 57pp lf

3369 The Crisis and the Outlook Hobsbawm, Eric 16pp

3370 The Education Cuts in Oxfordshire *Oxford Student Branch* 10pp lf d

3371 The Little Red Struggler: A Handbook for Student Militants 56pp sf

1976

3372 Privilege and Ideology: Action Against Reaction in Oxford University *Oxford* 40pp

3373 Problems and Advances in the Theory of Ideology Hirst, Paul *Cambridge* 20pp Talk at 1st Communist University of Cambridge.

3374 Red Shift *Cambridge Univ. CP* 28pp Journal. At least 4 issues 1976-7.

3375 Socialism and Democracy *Essex* 24pp lf d Contains papers by M. Johnstone & G. Bridges.

3376 The Althusser/Lewis Debate *South Bank Poly Student Branch* 36pp lf Reprint of 5 articles from 'MT' 1972 & 1974.

1977

3377 Consent *Essex* 34pp lf Journal. I isssue in 1977. Substantial theoretical journal; typical of the Eurocommunist period.

3378 Revolting Students *Bristol* 4pp lf d Journal. ?

1978

3379 Top Marx *York* Journal. ?

1979

3380 Commpress *National Student Cttee* 12pp lf Journal. Winter Term. ?

1980

3381 Communist Student [2] *National Student Cttee* 4-28pp lf Journal. Early 1980s to 1984? Some were given away. Not numbered, some not dated. Followed by 'CP Student Bulletin'.

1983

3382 Spectre, The *National Student Cttee* 30pp Journal. No.1, 1983.

1984

3383 Communist Student Bulletin *National Student Cttee* 8pp lf Journal. 1984-1989? Perhaps quarterly. At least 12 issues appeared, though some were given away at NUS Conferences.

3384 Student Bulletin *National Student Cttee* 4pp Journal. 3 issues (1 dated Nov. 1984). Replaced 'Communist Student'.

1988

3385 Intercom [2] 24pp lf Journal. Oct. 1988.

9. Daily Worker/Morning Star

This chapter consists, in chronological order, of all publications by the *Daily Worker* and then the *Morning Star*, plus associated organisations – the Daily Worker League, the People's Press Printing Society etc. (These organisations' names appear in brackets.) It includes one journal (the *Stepney DW Defence League Monthly Bulletin*). The entry for the *Daily Worker* itself appears in Chapter 3.

From 22 January 1941 to 26 August 1942, the *Daily Worker* was banned. I have listed the eleven 'alternative' issues that appeared during this time: the titles are followed by an asterisk. According to an article by Bert Baker in the *Morning Star* on January 4 1993, there was supposed to be one of these issued each month in the latter half of 1941. They were printed by Dorchester and City Newspapers which had been bought in 1940 in case of production problems in London, including the possibility that the printing presses would be closed down and the Party declared illegal.

There are a couple of items from this period when the paper was banned that may not have been for sale – or may have been given away for a donation, or obtained on subscription – but I have listed them for their importance (e.g. *Commentary on Current Political Events for Supporters of the DW Defence Leagues*).

I have, rather reluctantly, only listed a couple of the programmes from national *Daily Worker* rallies and anniversary celebrations, simply for reasons of space. I have seen nearly all of them and they form a curious collection and, in their own way, say a lot about Communist culture – through the adverts; the iconography; the financial support from the USSR and Eastern Europe; the musicians, actors and comedians who appeared; the cartoons; the speakers and the very agendas. The 16th, in 1946, is not only an attractive publication, but has a wealth of photographs of the premises and staff. These rallies were an annual event, certainly through the 1940s to the 1980s, with a programme for sale (of which 2000 copies could be printed). They were often in large halls, including the Royal Albert Hall. There were some in other cities (e.g. Cardiff) and I have listed a few I have come across.

I have given one collective entry each to other annual publications – *DW Diary*, *DW Children's Annual* and *DW Football Annual*.

One source of information, excluded because not published for sale, is the Annual Report of the PPPS – especially interesting in the later years during the struggle for control over the *Morning Star*.

'?' at end indicates uncertainty about date.

1935

3386 **Press Barons' Teeth Drawn** 16pp

1938

3387 **8th Annual 'DW' Bazaar Programme** 36pp

3388 **Cartoons** 'Gabriel' 80pp lf Cartoons from 1936-8 with commentary by P. Bolsover.

3389 **Souvenir Programme of the 'DW' Gala and Fete, Abbey Wood, Aug.** 24pp

1939

3390 **Back From the Dead** Coward, Jack 32pp The gripping account of IB member Coward's escape from Franco's Spain. Cover portrait by 'Gabriel'. The reprint by Merseyside Writers, 1985, has a lengthy introduction with much biog. material on Coward. ?

3391 **'Daily Worker' Leagues Grand Picnic, Co-operative Woods, Abbey Wood: Souvenir Programme and Song Sheet** DW Leagues 4pp lf Programme includes sports, boxing and wrestling, bathing beauty contest, ankle contest, prize distribution by Tom Mann, Community singing, dance. Speakers include Elsy Borders ('The Tenants' K.C. who puts the wind up the landlords') and Charlie Wellard ('Hero of the Siemens' Strike').

3392 **'DW' Gala and Fete, Newcastle, Souvenir Programme, Aug.** 6pp

1940

3393 **Hands Off the 'DW'** Haldane, J.B.S. et al. 16pp Prior to the ban on the 'DW' (Jan. 1941 to Aug. 1942), the government discussed action against the paper for a leaflet 'The People Must Act', only to issue a warning in July 1940, which this pamphlet attacks. Cover by 'Gabriel'.

3394 **It's Your Paper: The Story of the 11th Year of the 'DW'** Rust, W. 26pp

3395 **The Inside Story of the 'DW'** Rust, W DW Readers' League 24pp ?

1941

3396 **A Commentary on Current Political Events for the Supporters of the 'DW' Defence Leagues** 8pp No.1, July 1941 to No.55, Aug. 26 1942 (when the ban was lifted). Weekly. Published by DW Defence Leagues/ League, then by the PPFF. Replaced by 'Educational Commentary' [5462].

3397 **British Worker** * DW Defence League 8pp Sept. ?

3398 **Campaign Notes** DW Defence Leagues 2pp March 1941 – Sept. 1942 (when ban ended). Weekly, but not for sale.

3399 **Daily Worker Jan. 22-24** * 2-4pp These are duplicated leaflets rather than newspapers, produced to defy the ban, but effort was put into rescinding the ban rather than producing token illegal isues.

3400 **For Victory Over Fascism** * DW Defence League 4pp July ?

3401 **Free Press Campaign Special** * DW Defence League 4pp Early March. 42,500 sold.

3402 **Industrial and General Information** Daily news sheet of 2 or 4pp produced during the ban on the 'DW' by W. Holmes and other staff. Issued daily, incl. Sat. after about 6 weeks and was available on subscription. No.1 (Feb. 11? 1941) to 474 (Sept. 4 1942). Proprietor: George Jones.

3403 **People's Press Special** * PPFF 4pp May ?

3404 **Press Freedom Rally, Nov. 30** 4pp

3405 **Russia and the 'DW'** Rust, W. DW Defence Leagues 12pp

3406 **'Russia Today' News Letter – Specially Issued For the PPFF** 4pp lf Not strictly speaking a 'DW' publication. Not for sale. Only appeared during the ban.

3407 **The 'DW' and its Machine-Men** DW Defence Leagues 8pp

3408 **The 'DW' and the War** DW Defence Leagues 70pp March. Reprint of 30 selected leading articles from June 15 1940 to Jan. 21 1941.

3409 **The Case for the 'DW'** DW Defence Leagues 20pp Articles by Haldane, O'Casey, Owen & Arnot – Members of the former Ed. Board.

3410 **The Stepney Worker: Stepney 'DW' Defence League Monthly Bulletin** 10pp d Vol.3 No.5, 1942. ?

3411 **The Worker** * DW League 8pp Nov. There were 2 eds of this paper.

3412 **The Workers' News** * DW League 8pp Nov. 'Produced by members of the 'DW' Staff'.

3413 **We're in the Army Now** 'Gabriel' *DW Defence Leagues* 16pp Cartoons. ?

3414 **Workers' Gazette** * *DW Defence League* 8pp Aug.

1942

3415 **Daily ...** * *DW Defence League* 4pp 'This specimen copy of a newspaper showing what the "DW" would have looked like if issued on July 27, has been prepared for the information of MPs, it is not for public circulation.'

3416 **Lift the Ban on the 'DW'** Rust, W. *DW Defence League* 26pp Incl. correspondence, resolutions of support etc. Cover by Ern Brooks.

3417 **Report of Scottish 'DW' Conference, Dec. 13 1941** *DW Defence League* 4pp

3418 **Strike Now in the West! May Day** * *First of May Demonstration Cttee* 8pp In effect, this was just like all the other 'alternative DWs', though nominally not by a CP organisation.

3419 **The 'DW': Weapon of Victory: Report of London 'DW' Conference, March 21** *DW League* 8pp

3420 **The New Year Clarion** * *J. Crossley* 8pp Jan.

3421 **The Second Front: 6 Objections Answered by the 'DW'** *DW Defence League* 12pp sf

1943

3422 **'DW' Reborn** Rust, W. 16pp

3423 **13 Years of Anti-Fascist Struggle** 36pp lf Many cartoons.

3424 **Daily Worker in the Fight for Victory: Report of Delegate Conference, Feb. 27** *DW League* 24pp

3425 **Professor J B S Haldane** Phillips, Peter *DW League* 8pp ?

3426 **The Most Terrible Place in the World** Gibbons, John *DW League* 10pp 'DW' Moscow Correspondent on Kiev & Babi Yar.

3427 **Where France Begins: What I Saw in Algiers** 'Pitcairn, Frank' *DW League* 12pp Cockburn's visit as 'DW' correspondent was controversial – the authorities tried initially to send him back and ban his reports.

1944

3428 **'DW' Cartoons by Gabriel and Our War Babies** 'Gabriel' & 'Dyad' *DW League* 36pp lf 'Dyad', Wilfred Paffard, was never known to staff at the 'DW'; the cartoons that he produced for the paper, from 1943, being posted in each day: he was an engineer at the BBC who had worked on deflection of radar beams during WW2 before working for Radio Moscow. Probably not in CP.

3429 **Gagged by Grigg** Rust, W. *DW League* 12pp Plea for the lifting of the ban, apparently on Churchill's direct instructions, on the appointment of a 'DW' war correspondent.

3430 **Information Notes of Daily Worker League** Day, William (ed.) *Daily Worker League* 8pp

3431 **More Power to the Land** An Agricultural Worker 8pp sf Cover by B. Niven better known for her fundraising activities for the paper.

3432 **Report of Unity Conference, London April 2** *DW League* 12pp Cover by E. Brooks.

3433 **The Case of Captain Ramsay** *DW Defence League* 4pp Ramsay was a Pro-German, anti-Semitic MP.

3434 **The Death Factory Near Lublin** Simonov, Konstantin *DW League* 32pp ?

3435 **The Epic of Leningrad** Gibbons, John *DW League* 24pp

3436 **The General Election: Unity for Victory** *DW NW Regional Office* 12pp Report of Conference on Working Class Unity held in Manchester, Nov. 11.

3437 **The Little Tuskers' Own Paper** Niven, Barbara & Brooks, Ern *DW League* 16pp Children's cartoon story. One of the few pamphlets illustrated by Barbara Niven. ?

3438 **Voice of the People** Rust, W. *DW League* 16pp

1945

3439 **'DW' Fund Broadsheet** 2pp lf ?

3440 **Daily Worker on the Atom Bomb** Haldane, J.B.S. et al. *DW League* 8pp Reprint of 3 articles from 'DW', Aug.

3441 **Greece: The Facts** *DW League* 4pp ?

3442 **India and You** Dange, S.A. *DW League* 12pp Reprint of articles from 'DW' in Jan.

3443 **Post War 'Daily Worker'** Campbell, J.R. *DW League* 16pp Report of Conference, May 12; 500 delegates attended.

3444 Report on Plans for the Post-War 'DW' 4pp lf Good cover by B. Niven and E. Brooks.

3445 Spotlight on the Channel Islands Russell, Sam *DW League* 32pp

3446 Transport Workers: Your Fare – The Daily Worker Jones, Bill et al. 16pp sf ?

1945

3447 Victory Year: 1945 Rust, W. *DW League* 12pp This is about the 'DW', not about the war. Cover by 'C.T.'

1946

3448 'DW' 16th Birthday Festival Souvenir Programme 16pp lf Incl. 'Meet the Staff' – photos & short biogs.

3449 'DW' Bazaar and Social News *PPPS* 4pp lf

3450 'DW' Football Annual 1946-7 200pp pb Annual publication, probably up to 1952-3. Apparently the 'DW' was very successful with these handbooks. Ed. A.A. Thomas (Sports Ed. at 'DW'), E. Butler, F. Geddes, W. Deards.

3451 'DW' Gala Programme: Tottenham, Aug. 5 12pp Cover by E. Brooks. Incl. Boxing (Harry Davis, 'a great supporter of the DW'), Wrestling, Shapely Ankles/Lovely Legs/Beach Beauties Competition, 'Unity Dance Band' & politics!

3452 Gabriel's 1946 Review *PPPS* 48pp pb Cartoons by the 'DW' cartoonist.

3453 Grand Fun Fair: Programme *DW Defence League* 5pp lf To celebrate the anniversary of Phil Piratin's election; includes photos of the 10 CP Councillors in Stepney.

3454 Here Are the Facts About the Potsdam Agreement *PPPS* 4pp Reprint of an issue of Educational Commentary on Current Affairs.

3455 The Forces Speak: Report of Conference of Demobilised Men and Women 20pp Cover by 'Gabriel'.

3456 The Pope, The People and Politics McShane, Harry et al. *PPPS* 8pp Reprint of 3 articles from the 'DW'. ?

3457 Truth Behind the News *DW League* 24pp sf Cartoons by 'W. Storm'. ?

3458 Where is Germany Going? Rust, W. *DW League* 16pp Based on Rust's tour of British Zone in Feb.

1947

3459 32 Questions on Press Freedom 16pp The 'DW''s response to the questionnaire from the Royal Commission on the Press. ?

3460 'DW' Fair Programme, Tottenham, May 8pp Cover by 'Davy'.

3461 Open the Door, Britain! *PPPS* 8pp lf Reprint of 6 leading articles. ?

3462 Royal Festival Hall Programme Owen, Jack 16pp lf Very attractive design by (Ern) Brook(s). One page of programme (Bush, Lindsay, music dramatic tableaux etc) but the rest is about the 'DW' and its staff – useful biogs and photos. ?

3463 Science in the Atomic Age Huxley, J. et al. 24pp Reprint of articles from 'DW'. Cover by Ern Brooks.

1948

3464 'DW' Central London Christmas Bazaar, Prince of Wales Baths, Kentish Town 2pp Fold out poster.

3465 'DW' Christmas Bazaar: St Pancras Town Hall 2pp

3466 'DW' Cricket Handbook Thomas, A.A. (ed.) *PPPS* 144pp There was at least one more of these, published in 1949.

3467 Inside Free Greece Joannides, Evdos 16pp Incl. General Markos' first interview with a Western journalist.

3468 Pools: A Battle You Can Win 112pp pb Companion to the Football Annual. Annual publication (?) – only traced 1948/9 & 1951. Ed. Jack Silver.

3469 'The People's Paper' *DW Fighting Fund* 4pp Song-sheet; music by Alan Bush. ?

3470 The People Rule in Yugoslavia Rust, W. 16pp ?

3471 The People Want Peace 20pp Speeches from 'Conference for World Peace' organised by 'DW', July.

3472 What's Up With the Russians? Campbell, J.R. 14pp

1949

3473 Daily Worker Diary 130pp sf Issued annually for a short period.

3474 **The Story of the Daily Worker** Rust, W 128pp hb Ed. & completed by A. Hutt. 16pp of photos.

3475 **William Rust 1903-49: A Fighter for the People** 24pp Collection of Rust's articles & Tribute by J.R. Campbell.

3476 **Wreckers!** Sinfield, George 16pp On the break up of the WFTU.

1950

3477 **A-Z for 'DW' Bazaars** 32pp sf ?

3478 **I Saw the Truth in Korea** Winnington, Alan 16pp

3479 **Relaxation: A Collection of Satirical Verse** Gallacher, W. *DW Bazaar Cttee* 20pp

3480 **Welfare State or Warfare State?** Pollitt, H. et al. 16pp Articles reprinted from 'DW' in Aug.

1951

3481 **21st Birthday of the 'Daily Worker': Souvenir Programme** 8pp lf Cover design by Baron Moss.

1952

3482 **Stop This Horror in Malaya** 4pp lf Contains the infamous photos of British soldiers with decapitated heads of Malayans.

3483 **The Struggle for a Free Press** Thompson, E.P. 24pp

1953

3484 **USA '53: The Truth Behind Eisenhower** Kartun, Derek 96pp pb

1954

3485 **'DW' Children's Annual** *PPPS* 48-64pp lf At least 4 eds – initially called Children's Book.

1955

3486 **25 Fighting Years: 'Daily Worker' Silver Jubilee** 16pp lf Illustrated celebratory pamphlet. Cover by 'Gabriel'.

1957

3487 **Eye-Witness in Hungary** Coutts, Charlie 32pp

1961

3488 **International Exhibition of Children's Art** 16pp

3489 **Press Lords v Press Freedom** Matthews, George 16pp

1964

3490 **The Rise and Fall of the Daily Herald** Dutt, R.P. *DW and LM* 16pp

1965

3491 **Eye-Witness in Vietnam** Burchett, Wilfred 12pp

1970

3492 **No Chains For the Unions** 4pp lf Reprinted from 'MS' Oct. 16.

1978

3493 **The British Road to Socialism: A 'MS' Supplement** 4pp lf An illustrated broadsheet introducing the new BRS.

1980

3494 **1930-1980** 16pp lf Illustrated history of the 'DW'/'MS'.

1982

3495 **A Land With People: A Report From Occupied Palestine** Whitfield, David 58pp lf ?

1987

3496 **Afghanistan: Grasping the Nettle of Peace** Trask, Roger 24pp lf

1996

3497 **A Popular Paper: A Fighting Paper** Dywien, Jack *PPPS* 20pp History of 'DW'/'MS'.

2001

3498 **Is That Damned Paper Still Coming Out? The Very Best of the 'DW' and 'MS'** Howe, Mark (ed.) *PPPS* 254pp pb Collection of articles, and some cartoons. The brief notes accompanying entries are of interest.

10. Modern Books

Modern Books was the small company set up by the CPGB in 1929 to publish material by the Communist International in the UK. Most items were published between 1929 and 1936, but the imprint was resurrected in 1939 and 1940, mainly for Comintern views on the war before the German invasion of the USSR.

It was managed by Henry Parsons, who also ran Martin Lawrence. The preceding period had seen several legal problems concerning CP publishing companies, so this may be why a separate company was created – or it may have been a condition of funding from the Soviet Union. This chapter contains very few books by CPGB members and even fewer about the CPGB (four are listed in Chapter 11). Modern Books published mainly pamphlets, some by Lenin, Stalin and leading figures of the C.I. (the CPGB also published some by these authors). It also published many official documents by the C.I. – reports of Executive Committee meetings and Congresses. References to congresses in this chapter are thus to C.I. Congresses not those of the CPGB.

This chapter may therefore appear slightly extraneous to the main bibliography. However, it does show the extent of the publishing empire of the CPGB. The Party considered itself an integral part of the international communist movement at this time; there was nothing anomalous about such an enterprise, and, under different circumstances, these titles might have been published under the imprint of the Party. There was definitely some overlap. For instance, the CPGB published Pollitt's speech to the 7th Congress of the C.I., while Modern Books published all the other speeches; the CPGB published the *Theses of the 10th Plenum of the ECCI*, but later ones came from Modern Books. And, at one stage, Modern Books had their office in King Street. However, as these titles are not about the CP, they are not generally annotated and they are not given index entries, unless the authors were CPGB members.

There are some complications with Modern Books. To start with, very few of their publications are dated. The lists of other titles often found at the back of them are not necessarily published by Modern Books, despite being advertised as such. Titles occasionally differ between the cover and the inside of the publication, as well as in the lists. Some are printed in the US, in the style and format of the Labor

MODERN BOOKS

Research Association's series of 'International Pamphlets'; these are by American authors and aimed at an American audience, but are published in the UK (e.g. *Soviet China; Chemical Warfare*). There is some overlap with the Co-operative Publishing Society of Foreign Workers in the USSR – some titles were published by both this body and Modern Books.

All titles are pamphlets unless stated.

Titles are listed alphabetically within each year.

1929

3499 **Communism and the International Situation (Theses Adopted at the 6th World Congress of C.I., 1928)** 46pp pb

3500 **Heading for War** Bell, Tom 54pp pb

3501 **Labor and Automobiles** Dunn, Robert W. 224pp

3502 **Labor and Silk** Hutchins, Grace 192pp ?

3503 **Manifesto of the Communist Party** Marx, K. & Engels, F. 55pp pb

3504 **Marxism** Lenin, V.I. 49pp pb

3505 **Preparing for Revolt** Lenin, V.I. 289pp pb

3506 **Reminiscences of Lenin** Zetkin, Clara 78pp pb

3507 **Revolutionary Lessons** Lenin, V.I. 86pp pb

3508 **Ten Years of the C.I.** Komov, I. 46pp pb

3509 **The CPSU** Molotov, V. 80pp pb

3510 **The Proletarian Revolution and the Renegade Kautsky** Lenin, V.I. 160pp pb

3511 **The Revolutionary Movement in the Colonies (1)** 63pp pb Thesis adopted at 6th Congress.

3512 **The Twenty-One Points of the C.I.** Piatnitsky, O. 32pp ?

3513 **Women in the Soviet Union: With Impressions by G G L Alexander and F Niurina** 67pp pb Includes contribution by Rose Smith, in discussion.

1930

3514 **Anti-Soviet Sabotage Exposed** Krzhyzhanovsky, G.M. 40pp ?

3515 **Chemical Warfare** Cameron, D. 31pp ?

3516 **In Soviet Russia, Autumn 1930** Dobb, Maurice 30pp

3517 **Political Report to 16th Congress, CPSU** Stalin, J. 223pp hb

3518 **Russian Women in the Building of Socialism** Razumova, Anna 23pp ?

3519 **The Developing Crisis of World Capitalism: Report of Delegation of the CPSU in ECCI** 56pp

3520 **The Five Year Plan and the Cultural Revolution** Kurella, A. 48pp ?

3521 **The Immediate Tasks of the International Trade Union Movement** Piatnitsky, O. 40pp Contains 2 articles: 'On the Eve of the 5th Congress of the RILU & All Sections of the C.I.' & 'RILU Must Become Really Mass Organisations'.

3522 **The Life of Stalin: A Symposium** Kaganovitch, L. et al. 96pp pb

3523 **The New Phase in the Soviet Union** Molotov, V. 55pp

3524 **The Red Army** Alfred, A. 40pp ?

3525 **The Rise of the Soviets and the Decline of Capitalism** Stalin, J. 8pp ?

3526 **The Soviet War on Religion** Sherwood, M. 46pp ?

3527 **What is the Five Year Plan?** 24pp ?

3528 **Working Women! War is Coming!** 16pp ?

3529 **World Communists in Action** Piatnitsky, O. 64pp

3530 **World-Wide Unemployment: 20,000,000 Unemployed** 30pp ?

1931

3531 **50,000,000 Unemployed** 16pp ?

3532 **Building Collective Farms** Stalin, J. 191pp pb

3533 **Chapei in Flames** 18pp ?

3534 **Chinese Toiling Women** 32pp ?

3535 **Co-Report of the YCI at 11th Plenum of ECCI** 80pp

3536 **From the February Revolution to the October Revolution, 1917** Ilyin-Genevsky, A. 122pp pb

3537 **German Miners in the Donbas** 20pp

3538 **New Conditions: New Tasks** Stalin, J. 21pp

3539 **That 'Forced Labour' Lie** 40pp ?

3540 **The Communist Parties and the Crisis of Capitalism** Manuilsky, D. 121pp pb 11th Plenum.

3541 **The Menshevik Trial** Molotov, V. 88pp pb

3542 **The October Revolution and the Triumph of Socialism** Molotov, V. 32pp ?

3543 **The Revolt on the Armoured Cruiser Potemkin** Matushenko, A. 28pp Pages From Bolshevik History.

3544 **The Strike of the Dredging Fleet, 1905** Nikiforov, P. 46pp Pages From Bolshevik History.

3545 **The Success of the 5 Year Plan** Molotov, V. 77pp

3546 **The Tasks of the Working Class in Mastering the Technique of Production** Stalin, J. 12pp

3547 **The War of Intervention Against the Soviet Union and the 2nd International** Dietrich, P. 46pp

3548 **The World Crisis and the International Class Struggle: An Outline of Debates & Decisions of 11th Plenum** 18pp

3549 **The Wreckers Exposed (Industrial Party)** Holmes, Walter 24pp

3550 **Theses, Resolutions and Decisions of the 11th Plenum ECCI** 32pp

3551 **Towards the World October** Dietrich, P. 24pp

3552 **Trade Unionism in India** Bradley, Ben 64pp ?

3553 **Unemployed Councils in St Petersburg in 1906** Malyshev, S. 51pp Pages From Bolshevik History.

3554 **Unemployment and the Tasks of the CPs** Piatnitsky, O. 48pp

3555 **Urgent Questions of the Day** Piatnitsky, O. 43pp 11th Plenum.

3556 **War Preparations Against the Soviet Union** Cachin, M. 80pp 11th Plenum.

3557 **Wreckers on Trial: A Record of the Trial of the Industrial Party** Rothstein, Andrew (ed.) 214pp pb

1932

3558 **Assault on China** Dietrich, P. 32pp

3559 **Behind the Scenes of the Disarmament Conference** Lippay, Z. 60pp

3560 **Bolshevik Smugglers** Shaumyan, B. 35pp ?

3561 **Bolsheviks on Trial** Tchernomordik, S. 46pp Pages From Bolshevik History.

3562 **Book Publishing Under Tsarism** 40pp Pages From Bolshevik History.

3563 **Escape From the Gallows** Kuhn, F. 47pp Pages From Bolshevik History.

3564 **Free Soviet Labour Versus Capitalist Forced Labour** Farkash, G. 44pp ?

3565 **Fulfill the Decisions** Piatnitsky, O. 80pp 12th Plenum.

3566 **Guide to the 12th Plenum** 120pp

3567 **Hell Over Shanghai: Eye Witnesses' Reports** 16pp ?

3568 **In a Ring of Fire** Ovcharenko, I. 135pp pb ?

3569 **Ivan Babushkin: A Friend of Lenin** Bobrovskaya, C. 32pp Pages From Bolshevik History.

3570 **Japan in Manchuria** Dashinsky, S. 48pp

3571 **Japanese Imperialism Stripped** 38pp

3572 **Kamo: The Life of a Great Revolutionist** Obolenskaya, R. 39pp ?

3573 **Karl Marx** Perchik, L. 63pp pb ?

3574 **Kuznetskstroi: The Birth of a Gigantic Socialist Steel Plant** Bakhtamov, I. 54pp ?

3575 **Leninism Vol.1** Stalin, J. 472pp Vol.2 was published in 1933 (468pp).

3576 **Lenin's Road to the October Revolution** Bobrovskaya, C. 48pp

3577 **Marxism: The Doctrine of Proletarian Dictatorship** Manuilsky, D. 48pp

3578 **Meerut 1931: The Prisoners' Reply** 46pp ?

3579 **Prepare for Power** Kuusinen, O. 160pp pb 12th Plenum

3580 **Preparing for October: The Historic 6th Congress of the Bolshevik Party** 71pp

3581 **Provocateurs I Have Known** Bobrovskaya, C. 35pp Pages From Bolshevik History. ?

3582 **Religion in the USSR** Yaroslavsky, F. 66pp pb

3583 **Soviet China** James, M. & Doonping, R. 32pp

3584 **The Agent Provocateur in the Labour Movement** Buchner, J. 56pp ?

3585 **The Attitude of the Proletariat to War** 80pp

3586 **The Bolshevisation of CPs by Eradicating the Social Democratic Traditions** Piatnitsky, O. 23pp

3587 **The First President of the Republic of Labour: Sverdlov** Bobrovskaya, C. 32pp ?

3588 **The Fulfilment of the First Five Year Plan** Molotov, V. 88pp

3589 **The Next Step in Britain, Ireland and America** Gusev, S. et al. 88pp 12th Plenum.

3590 **The Programme of the C.I.** 72pp pb

3591 **The Soviet Union and the World's Workers** Manuilsky, D. 48pp 12th Plenum

3592 **Theses and Resolutions of 12th Plenum** 64pp

3593 **War in the Far East (1)** Hall, H. 32pp ?

3594 **War in the Far East (2) & The Tasks of the Communists in the Struggle Against Imperialism** 'Okano' 52pp 12th Plenum

1933

3595 **Four Weeks in the Hands of Hitler's Hell-Hounds: The Nazi Murder Camp of Dachau** Beimler, Hans 48pp ?

3596 **Germany: Hitler and the Trade Unions** 24pp sf

3597 **Germany: Hitler or Lenin** 32pp

3598 **Lenin on Ramsay MacDonald** 20pp ?

3599 **Lenin on the ILP** 55pp Intro. W. Rust. ?

3600 **Marx, Engels, and Lenin on Ireland** Fox, Ralph (ed.) 36pp pb ?

3601 **Marxism Versus Social-Democracy** Kun, Bela 73pp Address to EC of YCI.

3602 **Poland on the Road to Revolutionary Crisis** Bratkovski, J. 220pp pb

3603 **Results of the First Five Year Plan** Stalin, J. 64pp

3604 **Social Democracy: Stepping Stone to Fascism** Manuilsky, D. 64pp Address to EC of YCI.

3605 **Some Urgent Problems of the Indian Labour Movement** Basak, V. 43pp ?

3606 **The CP of Germany Lives** 32pp

3607 **The Far East Ablaze** Safarov, G. 48pp ?

3608 **The Moscow Trial** 8pp

3609 **The Moscow Trial: Authentic Report** 64pp Based on Bulletins issued by the Anglo-Russian Parliamentary Committee.

3610 **The Present Situation in Germany** Piatnitsky, O. 44pp 2nd ed. (48pp) incl. C.I. Resolution.

3611 **The Second International in Dissolution** Kun, Bela 84pp

3612 **The Work in the Rural Districts** Stalin, J. 24pp

3613 **The World Economic Crisis** Piatnitsky, O. 122pp pb ?

3614 **War Again Tomorrow!** 'Nemo' 33pp ?

3615 **Why Hitler in Germany?** Heckert, Fritz 48pp

3616 **Wrecking Activities at Power Stations in the Soviet Union: The Case of L C Thornton et al... Heard Before the Special Session of the Supreme Court of the USSR, Moscow, April 12-19, 1933 – Verbatim Report** 800pp hb 3 vols in 1.

1934

3617 **Fascism, Social-Democracy and the Communists** Knorin, V. 52pp 13th Plenum.

3618 **Fascism, The Danger of War and the Tasks of the CPs** Kuusinen, O. 120pp pb

3619 **From the First World War to the Second** 'Nemo' 75pp

3620 **Natasha: A Bolshevik Woman Organiser** Katasheva, L. 63pp

3621 **Problems of the International T.U. Movement** Piatnitsky, O. 20pp Reprinted from 'C.I.'.

3622 **Revolutionary China Today** Ming, Wang & Sing, K. 128pp pb 13th Plenum.

3623 **Revolutionary Crisis, Fascism and War** Manuilsky, D. 44pp 13th Plenum.

3624 **The Civil War in Austria** Schonau, A. 48pp

3625 **The CPs in the Fight for the Masses** Piatnitsky, O. 100pp pb 13th Plenum.

3626 **The Most Burning Question: Unity of Action** Kun, Bela 64pp

3627 **The Toilers Against War** Zetkin, Clara 128pp hb

3628 **Theses and Decisions of 13th Plenum of ECCI, Dec. 1933** 120pp pb

3629 **Verbatim Report of Negotiations Between 2nd & 3rd Internationals on Spain** 40pp

3630 **We Are Fighting for a Soviet Germany** Pieck, W. 100pp pb 13th Plenum.

1935

3631 **Engels in the Struggle for Revolutionary Marxism** Manuilsky, D. 30pp 7th Congress.

3632 **For International T.U.Unity: Official Texts of Proposals for United Acton by RILU and Its Rejection by Amsterdam** 28pp

3633 **Marx, Lenin** 48pp No publisher or date; could be published by MB or Martin Lawrence. Printer: Marston Printing Co. ?

3634 **Report of the ECCI, with Reply to Discussion** Pieck, W. 86pp 7th Congress

3635 **Report to the Active Members of Moscow Organization on 7th Congress** Manuilsky, D. 63pp

3636 **Resolutions and Decisions of 7th Congress** 40pp

3637 **Resolutions of the 7th World Congress of the C.I.** 30pp

3638 **Seventy Million Co-operators** Finch, George 16pp May not be Modern Books – no publisher stated.

3639 **The Colonial Peoples** Ming, Wang 48pp 7th Congress.

3640 **The Fascist Dictatorship in Germany** Piatnitsky, O. 144pp pb

3641 **The Fight for the People's Front in France** Cachin, M. 15pp 7th Congress.

3642 **The First of May: Day of Struggle for Proletarian Unity** 24pp

3643 **The Future is the Workers': Concluding Address** Dimitrov, G. 16pp 7th Congress.

3644 **The Great Crisis and Its Political Consequences** Varga, E. 177pp pb

3645 **The Movement of theYouth and the Struggle Against Fascism and the Danger of War** Kuusinen, O. 16pp 7th Congress

3646 **The Preparation for War** 'Ercoli' 78pp 7th Congress.

3647 **The Revolutionary Movement in the Colonies (2)** Ming, Wang 48pp 7th Congress

3648 **The Successes of the Anti-Fascist United Front** Thorez, M. 40pp 7th Congress.

3649 **The Truth About the Murder of Kirov** Shepherd, W.G. 32pp

3650 **The Victory of Socialism in the USSR** Manuilsky, D. 46pp 7th Congress.

3651 **The Working Class Against Fascism: Reply to Discussion** Dimitrov, G. 32pp 7th Congress.

3652 **The Working Class in the Struggle Against Fascism: Report** Dimitrov, G. 79pp 7th Congress.

3653 **Unity Will Conquer** Dimitrov, G. 40pp

3654 **What You Can Do Against Fascism and War** Dimitrov, G. 32pp From speeches at 7th Congress

1936

3655 **Busmen on Strike** Marsh, Fred 72pp ?

3656 **China's Struggle for Freedom: 15th Anniversary of CP of China** Miff, P. 100pp

3657 **National Defence Against Fascist War Plans** Gottwald, K. 16pp

3658 **Peace or War** Lang, P. 30pp ?

3659 **Report of the 7th World Congress of the C.I.** 678pp hb Incl. pamphlets listed separately plus several other speeches & index.

3660 **Soviet Peace Policy** 'Andrews, R.F.' 12pp ?

3661 **The Spanish People's Struggle** 16pp

3662 **Unite Against Fascist War** Hart, Heinrich 36pp

3663 **Youth in the Soviet Union** 12pp

1939

3664 **After Munich** Dimitrov, G. 48pp sf

3665 **Citrine and Others v. Pountney: The 'DW' Libel Case** 48pp

3666 **Communism and The War** Dimitrov, G. 24pp

3667 **For Socialism and Peace** Dimitrov, G. 16pp

3668 **Lenin** Manuilsky, D. 16pp

3669 **Lessons of the Spanish Civil War** Diaz, J. 24pp ?

3670 **Molotov's Statement on the Soviet-German Pact** 14pp

3671 **Russia and the War** Molotov, V. 19pp Speech, Oct. 31.

3672 **Russia's Way to Victory** Campbell, J.R. 32pp

3673 **Speech to Supreme Soviet, March** Molotov, V. 20pp

3674 **Statement in the Supreme Soviet on the Ratification of the Soviet-German Pact of Non-Agression** Molotov, V. 14pp

1940

3675 **Czechoslovakia's Guilty Men** 16pp

3676 **Freedom in Europe** 32pp Articles in English, German, Polish & French.

3677 **The Epic of the Black Sea** Marty, André 40pp pb ?

3678 **The Fall of France** Ehrenburg, Ilya 32pp

3679 **What is Happening in Finland?** Eriksson, I. 48pp

11. About the CP – Books and Pamphlets

This chapter includes pamphlets, books and chapters from books in author order (those entries without known authors come first). In many ways this was the most difficult section of the bibliography. The criteria for inclusion had to be flexible. Several autobiographies and biographies of CP members have been omitted if there are not enough references to the Party to justify inclusion (e.g. Tom Wintringham's *English Captain* and Bob Clark's *No Boots To My Feet*, both important books about CP members who fought in the Spanish Civil War). Another example is *Power in a Trade Union* by L. James: this has a long analysis about a strike involving Benny Rothman's victimisation – but no mention of his being in the CP (and this was not the reason for his victimisation). But other biographies are included even if the subject was not a member but if there are sufficient references to the Party, e.g. *Zilliacus: A Life for Peace and Socialism*.

There are snippets about the CPGB in many of the reports of Plenums and Congresses of the C.I. – only major items are included.

I have listed all entries from the *Dictionary of Labour Biography* (up to Volume 13) of members of the CPGB, but as this reference work is so accessible, I have rarely annotated the entries. Entries on non-members are included if there are enough references to the CP.

Pseudonymous authors are put in inverted commas.

3680 A Challenge to Guiding: The Menace of Communism *Girl Guide Association* 1951 12pp

3681 A Challenge to Scouting: The Menace of Communism *Boy Scout Association* 1951 12pp On Scouts, see Sarah Mills article 'Be Prepared'.

3682 A Survey of Left Wing Plans For Transforming Education *Common Cause* 1980 102pp lf Contains chapter on CP. Well researched info. on CP activity/organisation in all fields of education – lists of branches in universities, of leading student/academic activists, of CULs etc.

3683 A World War on All Religions *Christian Protest Movement* 1933 ? 20pp

3684 All About the Campbell Case *National Unionist Association* 1924 14pp sf Reprinted from the 'Morning Post' Oct. 14.

3685 Annual Reports *TUC* 1948 Civil Service purge. See also 1949; 1959 (for ETU).

3686 Anti-Apartheid Movement in the Red *Britain & South Africa Forum* 1967 8pp Brief notes on CP influence on the AAM.

3687 Appeal No.2: Programme and Rules *Appeal Group* 1972 ? 8pp

3688 Bread or Batons? Trial of Bailey, Parker and Webber *International Labour Defence (Bristol Section)* 1931 18pp

3689 Britain: Aspects of Political and Social Life *VEB Verlag Enzyklopädie, Leipzig* 1985

147pp hb One chapter specifically on CPGB & other refs. Text book produced in GDR.

3690 British Labour and Communism *LP* 1936 12pp

3691 Citrine and Others v. Pountney: The 'Daily Worker' Libel Case: Full Summary with Extracts from Verbatim Evidence *Modern Books* 1940 48pp

3692 Class War on the Home Front! Brief History of the Anti-Parliamentary Communist Federation *Wildcat Group* 1986 92pp lf

3693 Clem Beckett: Hero and Sportsman *Manchester Dependents' Aid Cttee* 1937 12pp Beckett died in Spain. He was a well-known speedway racer in Manchester; involved in Workers' Sports Federation. Incl. speech by his wife at Memorial Meeting.

3694 Cold War and Class Collaboration: Red Baiting and Witch-Hunts in the Civil Service Unions *Socialist Caucus* 1984 20pp Published by 'the left opposition in the civil service trade unions'.

3695 Communism and British Youth: An Analysis of the Plans for the CP for the Penetration and Capture of Certain British Youth Organisations *Economic League* 1936 12pp lf

3696 Communism in the Schools in *'Common Cause'* 64 1957 4pp

3697 Communism Unmasked *Unionist Workers' Handbooks/National Unionist Association* 1924 48pp Reprint of articles from 'Morning Post'.

3698 Communism, the Labour Party and the Left *Proletarian Pamphlet No.1, COBI* 1974 ? 24pp lf

3699 Communist Grip on ETU Exposed: A Summary of the Judgement of Mr Justice Winn *IRIS* 1961 36pp

3700 Communist Influence on the Campaign for Nuclear Disarmament *Common Cause* 1983 18pp

3701 Communist Papers: Documents Selected from those Obtained on the Arrest of the Communist Leaders on 14 & 21 October 1925 *HMSO* 1926 135pp pb

3702 Communist Party of Britain: Re-establishment Congress *CPB* 1988 30pp lf

3703 Contemporary British History, Vol.15 No.3, Autumn – Special Issue: The British Left and the Cold War 2001 173pp 2 chapters largely on CP, plus many refs.

3704 Contemporary Communism *Conservative Political Centre* 1963 64pp Mainly general,

international with one chapter by Aidan Crawley MP on 'Communism in the Unions'.

3705 Course in Modern Communism *Anti-Socialist & Anti-Communist Union* 1927 ? 132pp Chapter on CP, YCL, ICPWA, NMM etc.

3706 Czechoslovakia and the CP: A Letter to a CP Militant *Militant* 1968 13pp

3707 Dear Comrade: A Contribution to the YCL Congress by Young Members of the LP *Ted Knight/Keep Left* 1956 7pp lf d

3708 Decision: British Communism – A Three-Part Study of the Party and Democracy *Granada Television* 1978 23pp Pamphlet that accompanied Roger Graef's 3 part TV documentary into the debate and decisions around the 1977 BRS. Probably the first time any CP had given the outside media unrestricted access to its meetings.

3709 Documents Illustrating the Hostile Activities of the Soviet Government and the Third International Against GB *HMSO* 1927 32pp

3710 Down With Hitler Justice *International Labour Defence* 1933 16pp Title may be 'Trial of Welsh Communists' (different title inside & outside). On the trial of L. Jefferies, C. Stead, S. Paddock, & E. Whatley (miners) for conspiracy. Covers role of agents provocateurs in CP.

3711 Essays in Honour of William Gallacher *Humboldt University, Berlin* 1966 355pp pb 80pp of this book are reminiscences of Gallacher – incl. by Abe Moffat, W. Hannington, H. MacDiarmid. The book also contains articles on socialist musicians, with some refs to the CP & H. Henderson, A. Bush, etc.

3712 Expose the Agents of the Fascist Bourgeoisie Within the Working Class Movement! *Workers' Institute of Marxism-Leninism-Mao-Tsetung Thought* 1976 Deals with '"CPE(ML)", Trade Unions, "CPGB", IS & other Trotskyist Miscreants'.

3713 Fight for a Marxist Policy for the YCL *Militant* 1967 10pp

3714 Fight Revisionism: The Most Dangerous Enemy in the Working Class Movement *Revolutionary Communist League of Britain* 1978 ? 8pp Maoist.

3715 Fighting For Socialism *NCP* 1987 46pp Critique of BRS and CPGB in general.

3716 Five Hundred Leading Communists – The Strategy and Tactics of World Communism *US Congress Cttee on Foreign Affairs, Subcttee. No.5* 1948 130pp pb Section on

CPGB lists 19 names with brief biogs; not very original information, but it does inform us that Ted Bramley was 'son of former charwoman at Russian Embassy'.

3717 Getting the Balance Right: An Assessment of the Achievements of the CPGB *SHS* 1996 36pp lf Papers from Conference at London Univ; on solidarity movements, economists, cinema, writers, anti-fascism in 1930s, trade unions etc. Contrib. incl. Hobsbawm, Forman, Moore, Branson, Fishman, Croft, Bellamy etc.

3718 Go Home Yankee: 'Daily Worker' Demonstration, Harringay Arena, 15th Feb. – Programme of Songs *WMA* 1953 4pp lf Includes 'Ballad of the Daily Worker', 'Go Home Yankee' (John Hasted) 'It's My Paper' (Bob Claiborne/Hasted) & 'This is no' my Ain Hoose' (E. MacColl) – songs about the CP and its campaigns.

3719 Harry Wicks – A Memorial *Socialist Platform* 1982 54pp

3720 Hello, Are You Working? *Strong Words* 1977 94pp See Hilda Ashby's chapter.

3721 Hindering National Defence *Economic League* 1937 20pp lf Detailed analysis of CP work relating to armed forces and fight against rearmament.

3722 History and Perspectives of the Communist Movement in Britain: Papers from Conference at University of London Union. 1991 29pp Incl. 'The CP's First 25 Years' N. Branson; 'Communist Campaigns in E London' S. Kaye; 'Peace, Democracy & National Liberation 1945-75' J. Cox.

3723 Hungary and the Crisis in the CP *Revolutionary Socialist League/Workers' International News* 1956 8pp Of some interest as the only publication officially published by the RSL, i.e. The Militant Tendancy – they always publicly denied the existence of the RSL.

3724 In Perspective: Concerning the Role of the CP and its Effectiveness *IRIS* 1972 14pp

3725 In Proud Memory of the St Pancras Men Who Died Fighting in the British Battalion of the I.B. *St Pancras Section, I.B. Dependants Aid Cttee* 1938 ? 4pp Short biogs of 10 men – 9 in CP/YCL (A Katsaronas, J.F. Stevens, Johnnie Stevens, E. Julius, W. Seal, S. Yates, G. Bright, A. Yates).

3726 Industrial Subversion: Background to the Future *Economic League* 1972 ? 54pp

3727 Ireland and British Revolutionary History: A New Interpretation *Mosquito Press* 1982 24pp lf d Maoist (or Kim Il Sungist); section on CP, curiously praises William Rust's analysis of Irish situation.

3728 Ireland: British Labour and British Imperialism *Revolutionary Communist Group* 1976 35pp Mostly a Trotskyist critique of the CP's policy on Ireland.

3729 James Boswell: Drawings, Illustrations and Paintings: Exhibition Catalogue *Nottingham Univ. Art Gallery* 1976 32pp Incl. short articles by P. Hogarth, John Lucas, M. Slater, R. Cork, Ruth Boswell, plus autobiographical notes.

3730 Jerry Dawson, 1912-88: A Celebration of His Life and Work 1988 12pp Liverpool teacher, activist, local historian & organiser of Merseyside Unity Theatre.

3731 Joan McMichael-Askins: Her Life and Work *Medical and Scientific Aid for Vietnam, Laos and Cambodia* 1959 44pp In CP from 1937 to 1988. Communist councillor in Westminster. Known for her work for Medical Aid for Vietnam.

3732 Labour and the Popular Front *LP* 1938 8pp

3733 Labour Re-affirms Opposition to Communist Affiliation *LP* 1943 2pp

3734 Labour Side of the Motor Industry in *'Common Cause Bulletin' 125* 1969 32pp CP positions in engineering unions.

3735 Left-Wing Unity: A Critical Analysis *Economic League* 1945 12pp Looks at left organisations criticising each other.

3736 Let Labour Say No! *Fighting Facts/Catholic Worker* 1946 4pp

3737 London Trades Council 1860-1950 *L&W* 1950 160pp pb

3738 Mark Ashton in *'Walking After Midnight: Gay Men's Life Stories' Hall Carpenter Archives/Gay Men's Oral History Group; Routledge* 1989 20pp pb Memories of Mark Ashton, YCL Gen. Sec. Material on support for miners in 1984.

3739 National Hunger March *Economic League* 1934 12pp 'Counter Communist Campaign' Feb./March.

3740 No United Front with Communism: Report of Speeches at Plymouth TUC *TUC* 1936 24pp Reprint from Annual Report; incl. Statement by National Council of Labour.

3741 Notes and Comments No. 792: Subversive Activities in the Building Industry *Economic League* 1967 6pp

3742 Old Chrysanthemum: J.D. Bernal in *'New Statesman Profiles'; Phoenix House* 1957 6pp hb From March 6 1954.

3743 On the British CP's Policy *CPI* 1948 34pp Very interesting no-holds barred correspondence between CCs of Australian & British CPs published by Indian CP, apparently not published elsewhere. Australian CP criticises CPGB on: post-war coalition, exaggerated hopes of Labour Gov., fighting for a left Labour gov., supporting Marshall Plan etc.

3744 Our Willie: Willie Gallacher Centenary Souvenir *Scottish Miner Supplement; NUM Scottish Area* 1981 8pp lf

3745 Out of Apathy: Voices of the New Left 30 Years On *Verso* 1989 172pp hb Papers from Conference organised by Oxford Univ. Socialist Discussion Group.

3746 Parliamentarism and Communist Strategy *Proletarian Pamphlet No.3, COBI* 1975 ? 46pp lf Material on 1974 General Election campaign.

3747 Pioneering Mistakes *Appeal Group* 1973 ? Originally published by Bexley Branch CP. The Appeal Group were Brezhnevites led by Eddie Jackson in Bexley Branch; they were finally expelled in 1971. They produced a monthly paper which apparently lasted 5 issues.

3748 'Poems' by C. Caudwell: Biographical Note (Introduction) *L&W* 1949 3pp

3749 Political Resolution Without Politics *Forum for Marxist-Leninist Struggle* 1965 12pp lf d Maoist. On 'Draft Political Resolution for 29th Congress'.

3750 Potted Biographies: A Dictionary of Anti-National Biography *Boswell* 1930 127pp Right-wing but useful; among Labour, pacifist and trade union figures, it includes Wilkinson, Arnot, Malone, Mann and Saklatvala from CP.

3751 Radical and Revolting: The English Working Class *Revolutions per Minute* 2003 56pp Short chapter by Reg Weston, Sec. of Southgate Branch, on Cable Street.

3752 Raphael Samuel 1934-1996: Tributes and Appreciations *No publisher stated* 1996 104pp pb Collection of obits and tributes, with photos.

3753 Red Octopus *Economic League* 1950 16pp lf

3754 Reds Under the Bed? *Aims of Industry* 1974 16pp

3755 Report of 24th Annual Conference *LP* 1924 Incl. 'The LP and the CP' in Report of EC (3pp) and the debate on CP affiliation (9pp) with speeches by W. Paul, A. Gossip, H. Pollitt and Saklatvala among others.

3756 Report of a Court of Inquiry into the Cause and Circumstances of a Dispute at Briggs Motor Bodies Ltd. (The Cameron Report) *HMSO* 1957 35pp pb Fords, Dagenham.

3757 Report of a Court of Inquiry Into the Causes and Circumstances of a Dispute at London Airport (the Jack Report) *HMSO* 1958 40pp

3758 Report of Annual Conference of Trade Councils *TUC* 1949 Debate on 'Disruptive Bodies'; also in 1950 ed.; more minor material in Reports for 1952 and 1953.

3759 Report of Annual Labour Party Conference *LP* 1921 10pp pb Many subsequent reports contain refs to CP, esp. attempts at affiliation. The most important years are: 1922-6, 1930 (on banned organisations), 1936, 1942 ('DW'), 1943, 1946, 1948. Most inter-war years have a 1 page update resolution on banned orgs.

3760 Review of the British Docks Strikes *HMSO* 1949 47pp From the Foreword: 'These strikes had one aim only – to restore the fortunes of the Communist dominated Canadian Seamen's Union'.

3761 Revisionism and 'Peaceful Coexistence' or How to Increase the Danger of War *Forum for Marxist-Leninist Struggle* 1965 9pp lf Maoist attack on CP's position on Vietnam.

3762 Revisionism and the Women's Liberation Movement *Union of Women for Liberation* 1972 68pp lf Maoist. Used in the attempts to disrupt national Women's Lib. conferences.

3763 Revolutionary Communist Papers No.1 *Revolutionary Communist Tendency* 1977 56pp lf On the split from the RCG, but a lot on CP as it was attitudes towards the CP that were behind this split.

3764 Royal Commission on the Private Manufacture of and Trading in Arms – Minutes of Evidence *HMSO* 1935 18pp lf Pollitt's evidence to the Commission – published by the CP as 'Dynamite in the Dock' & CP's Memorandum, published as 'A Hell of a Business'.

3765 Russian Banks and Communist Funds: Report of Enquiry into Certain Transactions of the Bank for Russian Trade and the Moscow Narodny Bank *HMSO* 1928 58pp

3766 **Security Procedures in the Public Service (The Radclffe Report)** *HMSO* 1962 46pp 'We regard this presumably deliberate massing of Communist effort in the Civil Service unions as most dangerous to security, however one defines it.'

3767 **Socialism and Class Struggle** *NCP* 1980 30pp

3768 **Something in Common: A Group Autobiography** *Institute of Advanced Studies, Manchester Polytechnic* 1975 64pp 'Frank' and 'Dolly' – members of CP in Manchester.

3769 **Stalin's Men: 'About Turn!'** *LP* 1940 24pp

3770 **Stalin's War Against Britain: No.1: The Civil Service** *Common Cause* 1952 4pp Lists CP members in Civil Service Clerical Association & other unions, incl. quoting one CP membership card number.

3771 **Subversion in British Industry** *Economic League* 1958 48pp

3772 **Suppression Of 'The Daily Worker' & 'The Week'** in *'Parliamentary Debates' Jan. 28; HMSO* 1941 18pp pb

3773 **The 'Popular Front' Campaign: Declaration by NEC** *LP* 1939 2pp

3774 **The Agitators** *Economic League* 1975 ? 75pp There was a shorter ed. in 1964, and a longer one in 1981.

3775 **The Art of Wogan Philipps** *Oriel Contemporary Art* 1995 20pp Wogan Philipps (Lord Milford) was an artist, active in the AIA, who drove an ambulance for the Republicans during the Civil War; as the CP's sole member of the House of Lords, his maiden speech called for its abolition. This is a short exhibition catalogue with a brief intro. and a letter from John Berger.

3776 **The British CP** *SWP Training Series* 1977 ? 24pp lf

3777 **The British Road to Nowhere: A Critique of the Politics of the CPGB** *Workers' Action* 1977 16pp

3778 **The British Road to Stalinism: Communist Menace to Britain Exposed** *IRIS* 1958 65pp pb

3779 **The British Road ... To Where?** *Forum for Marxist-Leninist Struggle* 1965 14pp lf d On 29th Congress.

3780 **The Case for the NCP** *NCP* 1978 ? 14pp

3781 **The Common Market: The CPGB Exposed** *Communists for Europe* 1975 8pp Linked to BICO, who were pro-Common Market.

3782 **The Communist Menace: Exposure of 'Red' Action in GB** *Anti-Socialist & Anti-Communist Union* 1932 ? 16pp

3783 **The Communist Prosecutions** *National Union of Conservative & Unionist Associations* 1925 16pp

3784 **The Communist Solar System [2]** *IRIS* 1957 86pp

3785 **The CP and Affiliation** *LP* 1946 16pp

3786 **The CP and Labour** *Forum for Marxist-Leninist Struggle* 1965 16pp lf

3787 **The CP and the Atom Bomb** in *'A Socialist Review'; I.S.* 1965 2pp pb Reprint from 'Socialist Review' Oct. 1954.

3788 **The CP and the Left Book Club** *Economic League* 1938 4pp lf Incl. chart of CP influence in the cultural field.

3789 **The CP and the War: A Record of Hypocrisy and Treachery to the Workers of Europe** *LP* 1943 16pp

3790 **The CP and the War: Look at Their Record!** *Workers' International League* 1941 ? 8pp

3791 **The CP Today** *IRIS News Survey, Aug* 1966 28pp Whole issue on CP. The anti-Communist organisation IRIS was formed in 1956, and concentrated on engineering and electrical unions.

3792 **The CPGB, IS and IMG at the 1974 General Elections** in *'Parliamentarism & Communist Strategy'; COBI* 1975 4pp

3793 **The Crisis in the CP and the Way Forward** *CCG* 1984 ? 34pp

3794 **The Cult of the Individual: The Controversy Within British Communism 1956-58** *BICO* 1975 96pp pb

3795 **The ETU Case: A Study of Communism At Work in a T.U.** *Economic League* 1962 48pp

3796 **The Far Left Guide: Directory of Organisations and Supporters** *Common Cause* 1985 Lists c200 leading national & local leaders; not very original – obviously taken from Congress credentials among other sources, but useful as a biographical profile at a certain period.

3797 **The Labour Party and the So-Called 'Unity Campaign'** *LP* 1937 4pp

3798 **The Left and World War Two: Selections from the Anarchist Journal 'War Commentary' 1939-43** *Freedom Press* 1989 80pp pb

3799 **The LP and Communism** *Conservative Political Centre* 1978 16pp

3800 The LP and the CP: Statement by NEC *LP* 1943 8pp

3801 The Morning Star Celebrates Fifty Years of Stalinism *News Line* 1980 104pp

3802 The Next Step in Britain, Ireland and America *Modern Books* 1932 88pp Speeches & Reports from 12th Plenum, ECCI. Contains Pollitt's 'The CPGB in the Fight for the Masses', plus article by S. Gusev which covers Britain. All chapters are reprinted from 'C.I.'.

3803 The Political Theory of the Student Movement: Notes for a Marxist Critique *Student Publications, Liverpool* 1971 93pp lf d Publ. by individuals in the RSSF; has section on CP and other refs.

3804 The Press and the War *Press Freedom Cttee of NCCL* 1941 22pp On suppression of 'DW'.

3805 The Proposed 'United Front' *LP* 1934 3pp

3806 The Red Tide *Economic League* 1948 16pp lf

3807 The Revolutionary Aspect of the Miners' Strike *Duke of Northumberland Fund/Boswall* 1921 12pp

3808 The Spanish Civil War Collection: Sound Archive, Oral History Recordings *Imperial War Museum* 1996 324pp pb Incl. synopsis of each recording which is useful biographical source; a majority of the interviewees were in CP/YCL.

3809 The Tactics of Disruption: Communist Methods Exposed *TUC* 1949 11pp

3810 The Threat to Democracy: Communist Intrigues in the LP *Economic League* 1981

3811 The TUC and Communism *TUC* 1955 12pp

3812 Trade Unions and Communism *Conservative Political Centre* 1954 24pp sf

3813 Tribute to Alan Bush on his 50th Birthday: A Symposium *WMA* 1950 64pp pb

3814 Union Leaders Vindicated: A Full Account of the Hearing of the Libel Action Brought by W. Citrine et al. Against the Proprietors of the Daily Worker. *TUC* 1940 109pp

3815 Unity: True or Sham? *LP* 1939 16pp

3816 What Future for the Communist Party? *Militant* 1971 4pp lf d Produced to give to CP members on their national march and rally in June 1971.

3818 What Is To Be Done Now? *Marxist-Leninist Organisation of Britain* 1973 34pp lf

3819 What's Wrong with Our CP? *Forum for Marxist-Leninist Struggle* 1965 16pp lf d For 29th Congress.

3820 When the 'DW' was Suppressed in *'Common Cause' 90* 1960 4pp

3821 Why We Left the CP *Nottingham Marxist Group* 1957 8pp Group of 12 ex members, incl. Pat Jordan.

3822 William Gallacher: Centenary Commemorative Brochure *NUM Scottish Area* 1981 12pp

3823 William Holt, 1897-1977 *Estate of W. Holt* 1980 48pp Exhibition catalogue.

3824 Wogan Philipps, Lord Milford 1902-1993 *No publisher stated* 1993 8pp Memorial pamphlet to the Communist councillor, member of House of Lords, EC member of National Union of Agricultural Workers, painter.

3825 Yearbook on International Communist Affairs *Hoover Institution/Stanford Univ.* 1966 254pp This large annual publication always has an entry on the CPGB which serves as a brief but useful snapshot.

3826 Abbott, Thea Diana Poulton: The Lady With the Lute *Smokehouse Press* 2013 hb The well-known musician and musicologist was the manager of Lawrence & Wishart. She and her husband Tom, the artist, were early members of the CP; Diana left after 1956.

3827 Addison, Paul The Road to 1945 *Quartet* 1975 334pp hb Interesting on the government's attempt to limit CP influence in WW2.

3828 Adereth, Max Line of March: An Historical and Critical Analysis of British Communism and its Revolutionary Strategy *Praxis Press* 1994 153pp pb A traditional, CPB analysis.

3829 Adi, Hakim West Africans and the CP in the 1950s in *'Opening the Books'* G. Andrews et al. (eds) 1995 19pp pb

3830 Adi, Hakim West Africans in Britain, 1900-60: Nationalism, Pan-Africanism and Communism *L&W* 1998 224pp pb On students, especially the West African Students' Union and its links with the CP and the rest of the left in Britain.

3830a Adlington, Robert (ed.) Red Strains: Music and Communism Outside the Communist Bloc *OUP* 2013 320pp hb Incl. B. Harker 'Workers' Music: Communism and the British Folk Revival'; J. Bullivant 'Black, White and Red: Communism and Anti-Colonialism in Alan Bush's *The Sugar Reaper*s'; J. Tranmer 'Rocking Against Racism: Trotskyism, Communism and Punk in Britain'

3831 Aguirre, Chus & Klonsky, Mo **As Soon As This Pub Closes ... The British Left Explained** *Full Marks Bookshop* 1988 ? 40pp

3832 Ainsworth, Jim **Accrington 1926** *Hyndburn TC* 1994 219pp pb A few refs to CP. Similarly in the follow up vol. 'Accrington & District, 1927-34' 1997.

3833 Ainsworth, Jim **Accrington and District, 1927-1934: The Cotton Crisis and the Means Test** *Hyndburn & Rossendale TUC* 1997 460pp pb

3834 Aitken, Ian **Film and Reform: John Grierson and the Documentary Film Movement** *Routledge* 1990 246pp pb Some brief refs in Chap. 7.

3835 Aitken, Keith **The Bairns o' Adam: The Story of the STUC** *Polygon* 1997 328pp pb

3836 Alderman, Geoffrey **London Jewry and London Politics, 1889-1986** *Routledge* 1989 186pp Some useful bibliographical refs in the Notes.

3837 Aldred, Guy **Communism: The Story of the CP** *Strickland Press* 1943 126pp Critical.

3838 Alexander, Bill **British Volunteers for Liberty: Spain 1936-39** *L&W* 1982 288pp Among other details of CP's involvement in the Spanish Civil War, this is interesting on Political Commissars, who were appointed by the CP unlike the military leaders; and on work among prisoners when captured. Author was briefly commander of the British Battalion in 1938 before being wounded; after the war he worked full-time for the CP till 1967, becoming Assistant General Secretary.

3839 Alexander, Robert **International Trotskyism, 1929-1985: A Documented Analysis of the Movement** *Duke UP* 1991 1125pp hb Sixty-three detailed pages on GB.

3840 Alexander, Sally **Becoming A Woman** *Virago* 1994 329pp pb Chapter on Yvonne Kapp. Also some brief refs to CP women and Spanish Civil War.

3841 Ali, Abid **The Indian Communists Exposed** *Indian National TUC* 1965 44pp pb Quite a bit on CPGB.

3842 Allen, Steve **Thompsons: A Personal History of the Firm and Its Founder** *Merlin Press* 2012 470pp pb Harry (or W.H.) Thompson founded the famous Thompsons Solicitors in 1921, known for its close links with the labour movement. He was in the CP for probably 2 years, his wife, Joan Beauchamp, for much longer. For many years there was an organised CP group within the firm, John Bowden being one of the best known.

3843 Allen, Vic **The Militancy of British Miners** *Moor Press* 1981 337pp hb Mainly on 1960s/1970s.

3844 Allen, Vic **Trade Union Leadership** *Longman* 1957 349pp hb Anti-Communism in the TGWU.

3845 Allison, George & Shepherd, William **Penal Servitude for Politics** *International Labour Defence* 1931 18pp Defendants' speeches at trial relating to Invergordan Mutiny (they were set up by agents provocateurs).

3846 Almond, Gabriel **The Appeals of Communism** *Princeton UP* 1954 414pp hb Based on extensive interviews with former members of British & other CPs. From blurb: 'Especially revealing is the picture of the American CP as a refuge for neurotics & a stage of acculturation for foreign-born & first-generation Americans'!

3847 Alsop, George **A Kind of Socialism** in *'But the World Goes On the Same: Changing Times in Durham Pit Villages'; Strong Words* 1979 14pp pb

3848 Amis, Kingsley **Memoirs** *Hutchinson* 1991 346pp There is one paragraph on his joining the CP Students' Branch at Oxford in 1941 – very brief membership.

3849 Anderson, Gerald **Fascists, Communists and the National Government: Civil Liberties in GB, 1931-7** *Missouri UP* 1983 244pp hb Discusses legislation to control political violence and its effects on civil liberties.

3850 Anderson, Paul & Davey, Kevin **Moscow Gold? The True Story of the Kremlin, British Communism and the Left** *New Stateman Supplement 7 April* 1995 12pp lf Expanded in 2013 into online book.

3851 Anderson, Perry **Arguments Within English Marxism** *NLB* 1980 218pp pb Much on E.P. Thompson and 1956.

3852 Anderson, Perry **Communist Party History** in *'People's History & Socialist Theory'* R. Samuel (ed.); *RKP* 1981 12pp pb An important overview of approaches to CP history.

3853 Andrew, Christopher & Gordievsky, Oleg **KGB: The Inside Story** *Sceptre* 1991 847pp pb

ABOUT THE CP – BOOKS AND PAMPHLETS

3854 Andrew, Christopher **Secret Service: The Making of the British Intelligence Community** *Sceptre* 1986 859pp pb

3855 Andrew, Christopher **The Defence of the Realm: The Authorised History of MI5** *Penguin* 2010 1044pp Much on the Communists who became spies, and on state spying of the CP. The entry for the CPGB (let alone individual members) in the index is second in length only to that of Vernon Kell, security chief for 30 years. So there are more refs than for other figures in the security services, the KGB, India (and many of these refs are about the CPGB). Mosley has the same number as the SWP – and Betty Reid: 2.

3856 Andrews, Geoff **Endgames and New Times: The Final Years of British Communism** *L&W* 2004 264pp pb Final vol. in L&W's 6 part history of the CP. Author emphasises similarities between CP & wider labour movement.

3857 Andrews, Geoff &, Fishman, Nina & Morgan, Kevin (eds) **Opening the Books: Essays on the Social and Cultural History of the British Communist Party** *Pluto* 1995 275pp pb An important collection of essays covering many aspects of CP history based on a Manchester conference.

3858 Andrews, Geoff **Young Turks and Old Guard: Intellectuals and the CP Leadership in the 1970s** in *'Opening the Books' G. Andrews et al. (eds)* 1995 26pp pb

3859 Andrews, Geoff et al. (eds) **New Left, New Right and Beyond: Taking the Sixties Seriously** *Palgrave* 1999 207pp Interesting debates on CP and MT's influence into the 1990s. See especially the chapters by Steele, Andrews, Williams.

3860 Andrews, Molly **Lifetimes of Commitment: Ageing, Politics, Psychology** *CUP* 1991 229pp hb An academic approach combined with oral history; of the 10 key respondents, 8 were in CP at one time.

3861 Angus, John **With the International Brigade in Spain** *Dept of Economics, Loughborough University* 1988 20pp

3862 Arnison, Jim & Frow, E. & R. **And the New Paths are Begun: Manchester T.C. History Vol.2** *Manchester TUC* 1993 169pp pb Contains short biogs. of T.C.'s officials from 1939, of whom about half were in the CP.

3863 Arnison, Jim **Decades** *s.p.* 1991 134pp pb Autobiog. by 'MS' journalist who was active in the CCG & CPB.

3864 Arnison, Jim **Eurocommunism: The Historic Sell Out** *Peter Grimshaw* 1984 14pp lf

3865 Arnison, Jim **Hilda's War** *s.p.* 1996 62pp pb Hilda Froom campaigned against internment of anti-fascist Germans. She worked full-time for YCL during the war.

3866 Arnison, Jim **Leo McGree** *UCATT* 1980 95pp pb Hugely popular building worker and T.U. official on Merseyside, famous for his wit; he deserves a fuller and better biog.

3867 Arnison, Jim **Oliver's Work** *s.p.* 1996 71pp pb Brief history of the world, spies and the CP. Claims that 'MT' became 'a tool of the class enemy'.

3868 Arnison, Jim **Stop the Rot: The Crisis Within the CP** *J. Bowden* 1985 12pp

3869 Arnold, G.L. **The New Reasoners** in *'Revisionism: Essays on the History of Marxist Ideas' L. Labedz (ed.); A&U* 1962 14pp hb On the New Left of 1956.

3870 Arnot, R. Page **Twenty Years: The Policy of the CPGB from its Foundation, July 31 1920** *L&W* 1940 80pp pb

3871 Arthur, Dave **Bert: The Life and Times of A.L. Lloyd** *Pluto* 2012 432pp The singer, musicologist and broadcaster was a lifelong CP member. A charismatic man from a working class background, during the 1930s he was a key figure in left-wing cultural circles. His abilities ranged from producing occasional cartoons for the 'DW', writing short stories, translating Lorca and Kafka and helping found the AIA. Only later did he find his vocation in the world of folk music.

3872 Ashley, M.P. & Saunders, C.T. **Red Oxford** *Holywell Press, Oxford* 1930 44pp Interesting on the journal 'Free Oxford' and CP involvement in the University Labour Club.

3873 Ashman, Sam **The CP's Historians' Group** in *'Essays on Historical Materialism' J. Rees (ed.); Bookmarks* 1998 15pp pb

3874 Ashplant, T.G. **Fractured Loyalties: Masculinity, Class and Politics in Britain, 1900-30** *Rivers Oram* 2007 360pp General analysis with case studies, incl. of Alick West.

3875 Atienza, Tony **What the Papers Said** in *'Britain, Fascism and the Popular Front' J. Fyrth (ed.)* 1985 18pp pb Press reaction to 7th Congress of the Comintern.

3876 Atkinson, Katharine **The Communist Menace** *Bumpus* 1923 40pp Poor, unoriginal stuff but shows a curious level of panic – she refers to a campaign to write Communist propaganda in the margins of library books!

3877 Attallah, Naim (ed.) **Of a Certain Age** Quartet 1992 311pp hb Contains interview with Reuben Falber, a full time CP worker for many years; responsible for CP businesses, and handling secret Russian donations to the CP.

3878 Attfield, John & Williams, Stephen (eds) **1939: The CP and the War** L&W 1984 190pp pb Proceedings of Conference organised by the CP History Group. Includes papers, discussion and reproduction of documents.

3879 Aubry, Arthur **Field, Arthur** in *'DLB' 13* 2010 5pp

3880 Austin, Terry et al. (eds) **But the World Goes On the Same: Changing Times in Durham Pit Villages** Strong Words 1979 106pp pb See contributions by George Alsop & Maurice Ridley – Communist miners.

3881 Auty, Dave **The Trophy is Democracy: Merseyside, Anti-Fascism and the Spanish Civil War** Hegemon Press 2000 32pp

3882 Bagwell, Philip **The Railwaymen: The History of the N.U.R., Vol.2** A&U 1982 459pp hb

3883 Bailey, Jack **The Zig Zag 'Left'** Co-operative Party 1948 24pp

3884 Baker, Blake **The Far Left: An Exposé** Weidenfeld 1981 182pp pb Chapter on CP.

3885 Baker White, John **The Innocents' Club** s.p. [or Economic League] 1935 35pp Very useful right-wing pamphlet on 'Front' orgs. – W.I.R., ICWPA, League Against Imperialism, FSU, SCR, British Anti-War Council etc.

3886 Baker White, John (ed.) **The Red Network: The C.I. at Work** Duckworth 1939 93pp hb

3887 Baker White, John **The Soviet Spy System** Falcon 1948 133pp hb Mainly on Canada spy trials of 1946 but also on CPGB, esp. D. Springhall and P. Glading.

3888 Ballard, Daniel & Martin, David **Dash, Jack** in *'DLB' 9* 1993 4pp

3889 Banac, Ivo (ed.) **The Diary of Georgi Dimitrov 1933-1949** Yale UP 2003 495pp Some very minor refs, but an intriguing wartime ref. to 'Pollitt's strange behaviour …' on p219 merits its inclusion.

3890 Barker, Bas **Free But not Easy** Derbyshire County Council 1989 133pp pb Narrated by Barker to L. Straker.

3891 Barker, Martin **A Haunt of Fears: The Strange History of the British Horror Comics Campaign** Pluto 1984 228pp pb CP members played a large part in this interesting anti-American culture campaign of the 1950s.

3892 Barnsby, George **Socialism in Birmingham and the Black Country, 1850-1939** Integrated Publishing Services 1998 578pp hb Extremely useful.

3893 Barnsby, George **Subversive: Or One Third of the Autobiography of a Communist** s.p. 2002 50pp 1939-46; in the army he produces a Soldiers' Paper – 'Red Front'. Like many CP soldiers, he contacted Indian and Burmese communists.

3894 Barrett, Neil **The Anti-Fascist Movement in South-East Lancashire, 1933-1940: The Divergent Experiences of Manchester and Nelson** in *'Opposing Fascism' T. Kirk & A. McElligott (eds)*; CUP 1999 15pp Material on local CP in Nelson and YCL in Cheetham, Manchester (the latter with a largely Jewish composition).

3895 Baxell, Richard & Jackson, Angela **Antifascistas: British and Irish Volunteers in the Spanish Civil War** L&W 2010 123pp pb

3896 Baxell, Richard **British Volunteers in the Spanish Civil War: The British Battalion in the I.B., 1936-1939** Routledge 2004 240pp

3897 Baxendale, John & Pawling, Christopher **Narrating the Thirties: 1930 to the Present** Macmillan 1996 246pp

3898 Beauchamp, Joan (ed.) **Poems of Revolt** LRD 1969 9pp See Introduction by Page Arnot. Beauchamp was suffragette, conscientious objector, Guild Communist, stalwart of LRD – and a J.P.

3899 Beauman, Nicola **The Other Elizabeth Taylor** Persephone 2009 444pp pb This well respected novelist was a very active member of the CP between 1936 and 1948. She lived in High Wycombe and there are descriptions of the Communist Party premises and activities. She maintained her membership, despite a very bourgeois marriage, partly due to a longstanding relationship with another CP member.

3900 Beavis, Dick **What Price Happiness? My Life From Coal Hewer to Shop Steward** Strong Words, Whitley Bay 1979 88pp pb Autobiog. by Durham miner. Contains some poems.

3901 Beckett, Francis **Enemy Within** Merlin 1998 253pp pb Very readable and fair 'journalistic' history of CP that aroused some controversy on publication. This 2nd ed. has an extra chapter.

3902 Beckett, Francis **Stalin's British Victims** *Sutton* 2004 209pp hb British Communists who either perished under Stalin or whose husbands did: Rosa Rust, Rose Cohen, Freda Utley, Pearl Rimel.

3903 Beckett, Francis **The Rebel Who Lost His Cause: The Tragedy of John Beckett, MP** *London House* 1999 224pp hb Not in CP, but interesting refs e.g. to CP's relationship to National Union of Ex-Servicemen.

3904 Beckman, Morris **The 43 Group** *Centerprise* 1993 228pp pb CP not involved in this militant anti-fascist Jewish organisation, but couple of refs to CP's anti-fascist work in the post war period.

3905 Behan, Brian **With Breast Expanded** *MacGibbon & Kee* 1964 208pp hb Building worker, briefly on E.C.; later became Trotskyist. Brother of Brian.

3906 Behrend, Hanna **An Intellectual Irrelevance? Marxist Literary Criticism in the 1930s** in *'A Weapon in the Struggle' A. Croft (ed.)* 1998 17pp pb

3907 Bell, David **Ardent Propaganda: Miners' Novels and Class Conflict, 1929-39** *Univ. of Umea, Sweden* 1995 189pp pb On H. Heslop and Lewis Jones.

3908 Bell, P.M.H. **John Bull and the Bear: British Public Opinion, Foreign Policy and the Soviet Union, 1941-5** *E. Arnold* 1990 214pp hb

3909 Bell, Tom **The British CP: A Short History** *L&W* 1937 201pp pb This famous first attempt at a history of the Party was quickly criticised in 'Labour Monthly' and withdrawn.

3910 Bell, Tom **Pioneering Days** *L&W* 1941 316pp pb Readable account by respected CP elder statesman.

3911 Bellamy, Joyce **Ablett, Noah** in *'DLB'* 3 1976 3pp

3912 Bellamy, Joyce **Ganley, Caroline** in *'DLB'* 1 1972 2pp An addition in Vol.6 suggests she may have been in the CP.

3913 Ben Rees, D. **Nicholas, T.E.** in *'DLB'* 13 2010 10pp

3914 Bennett, John **Tom Mann: A Bibliography** *Warwick University* 1993 31pp

3915 Benson, Ernie **To Struggle is to Live** *People's Publications, Newcastle* 1980 280pp hb 2 vols; one of the most useful 'small press' autobiographies of CP members – the 2nd vol. is almost completely about his political activity:

NUWM, producing factory papers, opening one of the CP's most successful provincial bookshops in Hunslet, etc. Very little in Vol.1 – he joins CP on penultimate page. 'Deserves to become a classic of the genre' – J. Hinton.

3916 Benton, Sarah **Eurocommunism and the 'BRS'** in *'Socialist Strategies' D. Coates & G. Johnston (eds); Martin Robertson* 1983 32pp

3917 Berg, Leila **Flickerbook: An Autobiography** *Granta* 1997 240pp hb Active in London YCL. One of the most vivid descriptions of activity in the YCL & CP in late 30s.

3918 Bernard, Oliver **Getting Over it** *Peter Owen* 1992 159pp hb Brother of the more famous Jeffrey, Oliver was in the CP during the war and worked at Central Books.

3919 Berry, Joe **70 Years of Struggle: Britain's CP 1920-1990** *CPB* 1990 24pp lf

3920 Birch, Chris **My Life** *St Christopher Press* 2010 229pp pb Lifelong Communist journalist and activist. Notably involved in HIV/Aids politics.

3921 Birchall, Ian **Bailing Out the System** *Pluto* 1986 287pp pb

3922 Birchall, Ian **Workers Against the Monolith: The Communist Parties Since 1943** *Pluto* 1974 256pp pb

3923 Blaazer, David **The Popular Front and the Progressive Tradition: Socialists, Liberals and the Quest for Unity, 1884-1939** *CUP* 1992 247pp hb An historical analysis of 'popular frontism' that argues that it was not a CP manipulation but a genuine political response to crisis by sections of the Labour left.

3924 Black, Lawrence **The Political Culture of the Left in Affluent Britain, 1951-64** *Palgrave* 2003 263pp Much on CP (despite no ref. in index); looks at branch life, culture, organisation of the left in general.

3925 Black, Robert **Stalinism in Britain: A Trotskyist Analysis** *New Park* 1970 440pp hb

3926 Blackburn, Robin & Cockburn, Alexander (eds) **The Incompatibles: Trade Union Militancy and the Consensus** *Penguin* 1967 282pp pb Esp. P. Foot on 'The Seamen's Struggle' (1966 strike).

3927 Blackman, Peter **Footprints** *Smokestack* 2013 106pp Chris Searle's Introduction to this collection of poems by the pioneering Black British poet has much on the life of this Barbados born member of the CP. Former priest, engineer, friend of Paul Robeson, who worked on the 'Colonial Information Bulletin'

– he was later to assert his colour excluded him from advancement in the CP. Ignored, possibly banned, by the BBC, his poetry was 'discovered' late in his life.

3928 Bolt, Sydney **Pseudo Sahib** *Hardinge Simpole* 2007 269pp pb A few refs to CPGB/CPI relations by this CP member in his autobiog.

3929 Bone, Edith **Seven Years Solitary** *Bruno Cassirer* 1966 212pp hb Autobiog. of Hungarian born, British citizen sentenced to life imprisonment as 'English spy' in Hungary 1949 (released by uprising in 1956). She had worked for Comintern as a courier, came to Britain in mid-thirties and joined CP. Bit about CP and 'DW' – interesting for her view of CPGB as open to debate unlike other CPs she had been a member of and for CP's lack of support for her when imprisoned.

3930 Boothroyd, David **Politico's Guide to the History of British Political Parties** *Politico's Publishing* 2001 338pp hb Brief section on CPGB and various groups that split from it.

3931 Borkenau, Franz **European Communism** *Faber* 1953 564pp hb Passing refs to CPGB, especially on WW2.

3932 Borkenau, Franz **World Communism: A History of the C.I.** *Univ. of Michigan* 1963 443pp pb Especially on General Strike.

3933 Bornat, Richard **'Children of the Revolution' ed. P. Cohen – Review** in *'Oral History'* Spring 1998 2pp

3934 Bornstein, S. & Richardson, A. **Against the Stream: A History of the Trotskyist Movement in Britain 1924-38** *Socialist Platform* 1986 302pp hb Traditional Trotskyist analysis.

3935 Bornstein, S. & Richardson, A. **Two Steps Back: Communists and the Wider Labour Movement 1935-45** *Socialist Platform* 1982 143pp pb

3936 Bornstein, S. & Richardson, A. **War and the International: A History of the Trotskyist Movement in Britain 1937-49** *Socialist Platform* 1986 252pp pb

3937 Borovik, Genrikh **The Philby Files** *Warner* 1994 380pp pb

3938 Boulton, Walter (Rev.) **Communist Aims and Tactics** *Crisis Booklets; Diocese of Guildford* 1954 ? 32pp

3939 Bounds, Philip **British Communism and the Politics of Literature, 1928-1939** *Merlin Press* 2012 320pp Studies on the third period and popular front, a balanced account of the impact of Soviet cultural theory plus chapters on A. West, R. Fox and C. Caudwell. Among the lesser known figures discussed is P.R. Stephenson, a collaborator of Jack Lindsay. Useful Biographical Appendix, but lacks a bibliography. A monumental work.

3940 Bounds, Philip **Learning From his Enemies: George Orwell and British Communism** in *'Orwell Today'* R. Keeble (ed.); Abramis 2012 15pp pb

3940a Bounds, Philip **Notes from the End of History: A Memoir of the Left in Wales** *Merlin Press* 2014 200pp Searingly honest and memorable autobiographical account of politics in Swansea in the 1980s and 1990s. An original account of strengths and weaknesses of the CP (and other left groups).

3941 Bounds, Philip **Orwell and Marxism: The Political and Cultural Thinking of George Orwell** *I.B. Tauris* 2009 253pp pb Intro. contains a very broad analysis of CP's cultural politics, and the book, generally, pits Orwell and the CP in opposition but with some overlaps.

3942 Bounds, Philip **Orwell and Mass Communication: The Dialogue with British Marxism** in *'Recharting Media Studies: Essays on Neglected Media Critics'* P. Bounds & M. Jagmohan (eds); Peter Lang 2008 30pp pb

3943 Bowd, Gavin **Comintern Cadre: The Passion of Allan Eaglesham** *Socialist History Society* 2006 38pp Joined the CP in Edinburgh shortly after its formation; emigrated to New Zealand where he soon became General Secretary of the very small CP. Returned to Britain in 1929, went to the Lenin School but died shortly after his return to Britain. Author, a relative of Eaglesham, was also in YCL.

3944 Bowen, Roger W. (ed.) **E.H. Norman: His Life and Scholarship** *University of Toronto Press* 1984 206pp hb See V. Kiernan's chapter on CP activity in Cambridge where he knew Herbert Norman (future Canadian diplomat), esp. on work with Indian progressives.

3945 Boyle, Andrew **The Climate of Treason** *Hutchinson* 1980 574pp pb

3946 Braddock, Jack & Bessie **The Braddocks** *MacDonald* 1963 244pp Leading CP members in Liverpool till they left in 1924 – Bessie became a Labour MP in 1945.

3947 Bradford, Richard **Lucky Him: The Life of Kingsley Amis** *Peter Owen* 2001 432pp hb Briefly active in the CP at Oxford.

3948 Brand, Carl **The British Labour Party and the Communists** in *'British Labour's Rise to Power'*; Stanford UP/OUP 1941 55pp

3949 Branson, Noreen **History of the CPGB, 1927-41** *L&W* 1985 350pp hb An easier read than Klugmann's preceeding books, more open but still a bit 'official'.

3950 Branson, Noreen **History of the CPGB, 1941-51** *L&W* 1997 262pp pb

3951 Branson, Noreen **Myths From Right and Left** in *'Britain, Fascism and the Popular Front'* J. Fyrth (ed.) 1985 16pp pb On 7th Congress of Comintern.

3952 Braunthal, Julius **History of the International, 1914-43** *Nelson* 1967 596pp Brief refs Also in following vol. 1943-68, Gollancz 1980.

3953 Brett, Philip (ed.) **Benjamin Britten: Peter Grimes** *CUP* 1983 217pp See chapter 'Montagu Slater: Who Was He?'. Has annotated interview with Slater's widow, Enid (24pp). Slater wrote the libretto.

3954 Bridges, George & Brunt, Rosalind (eds) **Silver Linings: Some Strategies for the 80s – Papers from CUL 1980** *L&W* 1981 189pp pb Contains: 'Rocky Road Blues: The CP & The Broad Democratic Alliance' by Dave Cook and 'Popular Politics & Marxist Theory In Britain: The History Men' by Schwarz & Mercer.

3955 Bridges, George **The CP and the Struggle for Hegemony** in *'Socialist Register'; Merlin* 1977 12pp pb

3956 Briggs, Asa & Saville, John (eds) **Essays on Labour History 1918-39: Vol.3** *Croom Helm* 1977 292pp hb Esp. on 1930s.

3957 Brill, Kenneth **Groser, John** in *'DLB' 6* 1982 6pp

3958 Brockway, Fenner **Inside the Left** *A&U* 1942 352pp hb This autobiog. by the ILP leader has more on the CP than any of his other autobiogs.

3959 Brogan, Colm **Labour's Opportunity** *s.p., Glasgow* 1945 ? 16pp

3960 Brogan, Colm **Red Puppets** *s.p., Glasgow* 1944 16pp

3961 Brogan, Colm **The Case Against Gallacher** *s.p.* 1949 ? 20pp

3962 Brogan, Dennis **The Price of Revolution** *H. Hamilton* 1951 288pp hb

3963 Brooksbank, Mary **No Sae Lang Syne: A Tale of This City** *Dundee Printers* 1973 59pp Dundee mill worker, unemployed activist (imprisoned several times), songwriter; expelled from CP in 1934 for criticising Stalin, but not anti-Communist.

3964 Brotherstone, Terry **1956: Tom Kemp and Others** in *'History, Economic History & the Future of Marxism'* T. Brotherstone & G. Pilling (eds); *Porcupine Press* 1996 59pp pb Mainly on the better known CP members who left around 1956 and turned to Trotskyism (Kemp, Pearce, Fryer), plus Saville. See also the first chapter for more on Kemp, for whom this book is a festschrift.

3965 Brotherstone, Terry (ed.) **Covenant, Charter and Party: Traditions of Revolt and Protest in Modern Scottish History** *Aberdeen UP* 1989 128pp pb Bit on CP and John Maclean (revised version of article in 'SLHS Bulletin' No.23, 1988).

3966 Brown, Andrew **J.D. Bernal: The Sage of Science** *OUP* 2005 562pp hb

3967 Brown, F.J. **Journal of a Stranger** *Londinium Press* 1978 222pp Right-wing industrial correspondent. Some refs to 1956, CP Congresses etc.

3968 Brown, Gordon **Maxton** *Mainstream* 1986 336pp hb

3969 Brown, Michael Barratt **Seekers: A Twentieth Century Life** *Spokesman* 2013 724pp pb Autobiog. Author left CP in 1956.

3970 Bruley, Sue **Leninism, Stalinism and the Women's Movement in Britain, 1920-1939** *Garland Press, NY* 1986 324pp Reprinted by Routledge in 2012.

3971 Bruley, Sue **Women Against War and Fascism** in *'Britain, Fascism and the Popular Front'* J. Fyrth (ed.) 1985 26pp pb

3972 Bruley, Sue **Women and Communism: A Case Study of the Lancashire Weavers in the Depression** in *'Opening the Books'* G. Andrews et al. (eds) 1995 19pp pb

3972a Buchanan, Tom **East Wind: China and the British Left, 1925-1976** *OUP* 2012 250pp hb

3973 Buchanan, Tom **The Spanish Civil War and the British Labour Movement** *CUP* 1991 250pp hb

3974 Bullock, Ian & Carew, Anthony **Kendall, Walter** in *'DLB' 13* 2010 8pp

3975 Bullock, Ian **Sylvia Pankhurst and the Russian Revolution: The Making of a 'Left Wing' Communist** in *'Sylvia Pankhurst: From Artist to Anti-Fascist'* I. Bullock & R. Pankhurst (eds); *Macmillan* 1992 28pp

3976 Bunyan, Tony **The History and Practice of the Political Police in Britain** *Quartet* 1983 324pp pb Info. on removal of CP civil servants.

3977 Burke, David **The Spy Who Came in from the Co-op: Melita Norwood and the Ending of Cold War Espionage** Boydell 2009 209pp The last of the Communists who passed information to the USSR to be uncovered – in her case it was information that speeded up the Soviet atomic bomb. Unusually, she was also active in the CPGB.

3978 Burns, Maggie **George Thomson in Birmingham and the Blaskets** Birmingham Library Services 2000 20pp lf Academic and historian; short chapter on his membership of the CP.

3979 Bush, Alan **In My Eighth Decade and Other Essays** Kahn & Averill 1980 92pp pb Autobiog. & other articles on music from well-known composer; unfortunately little on CP of which he was a longstanding member.

3980 Bushell, Terry **Marriage of Inconvenience** Deutsch 1985 237pp hb Autobiog. by sports writer at 'MS'; some info. on YCL & 'MS'.

3981 Cadogan, Peter **The British CP in the Light of 1956** Imre Nagy Institute for Political Research, Brussels 1961

3982 Caesar, Adrian **Dividing Lines: Poetry, Class and Ideology in the 1930s** MUP 1991 248pp hb Esp. useful on Jack Lindsay & H. MacDiarmid, also 'Left Review', 'Poetry & the People' etc. Has one chapter on 'The Left'.

3983 Cairncross, John **The Enigma Spy: An Autobiography – The Story of the Man Who Changed the Course of World War Two** Century 1997 203pp hb Bit on Cambridge but plays down his links with CP.

3984 Cairns, David **Southampton Working People** Southampton City Museums/Southampton TUC 1990 ? 96pp pb

3985 Calhoun, Daniel **The United Front: The TUC and the Russians, 1923-28** CUP 1976 450pp hb

3986 Callaghan, John & Harker, Ben (eds) **British Communism: A Documentary History** MUP 2011 304pp A chronological and themed collection of extracts from texts, letters, reviews from members and ex-members that covers the whole range of CP activities and debate.

3987 Callaghan, John **British Trotskyism** Blackwell 1984 255pp hb

3988 Callaghan, John **Cold War, Crisis and Conflict: The CPGB 1951-68** L&W 2003 320pp pb 5th vol. in the L&W history of the CP. Written after the demise of the CPGB, and with better access to archives and interviews with members, it is more critical – and the first by a non-member. Contents are arranged thematically. A very interesting section of Biographical Notes (though one minor error: Arnold Kettle joined the CP in 1936 not 1956).

3989 Callaghan, John **Endgame: The CPGB** in 'Western European Communists and the Collapse of Communism' D.S. Bell (ed.); Berg 1993 18pp hb

3990 Callaghan, John **Rajani Palme Dutt: A Study in British Stalinism** L&W 1993 304pp pb The only full-length study of this key figure.

3991 Callaghan, John **Socialism in Britain** Blackwell 1990 279pp pb

3992 Callaghan, John **The British Road to Eurocommunism** in 'CPs in Western Europe: Decline or Adaptation?' M. Waller & M. Fennema (eds); Blackwell 1988 20pp

3993 Callaghan, John **The Communists and the Colonies: Anti-Imperialism Between the Wars** in 'Opening the Books' G. Andrews et al. (eds) 1995 19pp pb

3994 Callaghan, John **The CPGB and Local Politics** in 'Marxist Local Governments in Western Europe and Japan' B. Szajkowski (ed.); Pinter 1986 10pp pb A rare analysis of this aspect of the CP's activity that remained one of its weakest points.

3995 Callaghan, John **The Far Left in British Politics** Blackwell 1987 249pp hb

3996 Callaghan, John **Towards Isolation: the Communist Party and the Labour Government** in 'Labour's Promised Land' J. Fyrth (ed.); L&W 1995 13pp pb

3997 Campbell, Alan &, Fishman, Nina & McIlroy, John (eds) **British Trade Unions and Industrial Politics** Ashgate 1999 335; 389pp hb 2 vols covering periods 1945-1964 and 1964-1979 respectively. Very important; there are specific chapters on the CP, plus many more refs – even more than the extensive index shows. Particularly useful on engineering, docks, buses.

3998 Campbell, Alan & McIlroy, John **Miner Heroes: Three Communist Trade Union Leaders** in 'Party People, Party Lives' J. McIlroy, K. Morgan, Campbell, A. (eds) 2001 26pp Willie Allan, David Proudfoot, Abe Moffat – 3 successive Gen. Secs of the UMS.

3999 Campbell, Alan & Fishman, N. & Howell, D. (eds) **Miners, Unions and Politics 1910-47** Scolar 1996 307pp hb One chapter specifically on CP, but many other refs.

4000 Campbell, Alan **Moffat, Abe** in 'DLB' 12 2005 12pp

4001 Campbell, John **Nye Bevan: A Biography** Hodder 1994 430pp pb

4002 Campbell, Alan **The CP in the Scots Coalfields in the Inter-War Period** in *'Opening the Books'* G. Andrews et al. (eds) 1995 20pp pb

4003 Campbell, Alan **The Scottish Miners, 1874-1939 – 2 Vols** Ashgate 2000 416; 433pp More on CP in Vol.2 which deals with trade unions and politics.

4004 Campbell, William **Villi the Clown** Faber 1981 256pp hb Autobiog. of the stepson of J.R. Campbell; he was first secretary of Glasgow YCL, emigrated to the USSR in 1932 where he worked as a clown. First chapter has material on CP/YCL.

4005 Cannon, Olga & Anderson, J.R.L. **The Road From Wigan Pier: A Biography of Les Cannon** Gollancz 1973 323pp pb Prominent ETU official who left CP in 1956 and became leading anti-Communist.

4006 Capern, Amanda **Horrabin, Winifred** in *'DLB' 11* 2003 4pp With husband, Frank, she was in the CP 1921-4.

4007 Carpenter, Maurice **A Rebel in the Thirties** Paperbag Book Club 1975 ? 192pp pb lf On YCL, Cable Street etc.

4008 Carr, E.H. **Mr Gallacher and the CPGB** in *'Studies in Revolution'*; F. Cass 1962 16pp hb

4009 Carr, E.H. **The Twilight of the Comintern, 1930-1935** Pantheon 1982 461pp hb Chapter on CPGB.

4010 Carr, Frank **Municipal Socialism: Labour's Rise to Power** in *'Life and Labour in a Twentieth Century City: The Experience of Coventry'* B. Lancaster & T. Mason (eds); Cryfield Press 1987 32pp pb Much on LP/CP relations pre WW2.

4011 Carr, Griselda **Pit Women** Merlin 2001 174pp pb Intro. has brief ref. to the author and her husband's CP activities in Yorkshire.

4012 Carritt, Michael **A Mole in the Crown** s.p 1985 204pp pb Brother of CP full-timer Gabriel, Carritt was senior civil servant in India who acted as conduit between CPGB and Indian nationalists.

4013 Carritt, Michael **The Mole in the Crown: Memories of the Indian Underground, 1935-8** in *'Britain, Fascism and the Popular Front'* J. Fyrth (ed.) 1985 15pp pb

4014 Carruthers, Susan **Winning Hearts and Minds: British Governments, the Media and Colonial Counter Insurgency, 1944-60** Leicester UP 1995 307pp pb More on 'DW' than CP.

4015 Carter, Miranda **Anthony Blunt: His Lives** Pan 2001 590pp pb Cambridge students.

4016 Carter, Trevor **Shattering Illusions: West Indians in British Politics** L&W 1986 158pp pb Incl. interesting comments by Black CP members.

4017 Catterall, Stephen & Cohen, Gidon **Sandham, Elijah** in *'DLB' 11* 2003 16pp Not in CP, but much on the relationship between the CP and the ILP & Independent Socialist Party.

4018 Caute, David **The Fellow Travellers** Yale UP 1988 458pp hb Revised & updated ed.

4019 Cecil, Robert **A Divided Life: A Personal Portrait of the Spy Donald Maclean** William Morrow 1989 212pp pb

4020 Cecil, Robert **The Cambridge Comintern** in *'The Missing Dimension: Governments and Intelligence Communities in the Twentieth Century'* C. Andrew & D. Dilks (eds); Macmillan 1984 30pp

4021 Cesarani, David (ed.) **The Making of Modern Anglo-Jewry** Blackwell 1990 222pp

4022 Challinor, Ray **The Origins of British Bolshevism** Croom Helm 1977 290pp hb Important, controversial book; sees the SLP as more revolutionary than the CP.

4023 Chambers, Colin **The Story of Unity Theatre** L&W 1989 446pp hb Very detailed and includes much on CP and individual CP members.

4024 Chandler, F.W. **Political Spies and Provocative Agents** s.p. 1936 149pp pb Last chapter on Tom Mann & Emrhys Llewellyn jailed in 1932, and 4 Welsh miners (L Jefferies, E. Stead, S. Paddock & E. Whatley) imprisoned in 1933 following evidence from a police infiltrator into the CP & NUWM.

4025 Chapple, Dave **Grasshoppers, Stonkers and Straight Eights: George Massey and the Bristol Post Office Workers, 1930-1976** Somerset Socialist Library 2010 240pp One of the founders of the Rosa Luxemburg Group of Post Office Communists in 1935; in the 1950s he was on the union's EC. A fascinating mix of oral history, research and visual material.

4026 Chapple, Dave **Trowbridge Communist Councillors** in *'Wiltshire Industrial History: Working Class Episodes'*; Watermarx on Behalf of White Horse (Wiltshire) TC 2011 9pp Idris Rose was a councillor between 1961 and 1973 –

he was joined by his wife, Phyllis, between 1969 and 1973. See also the chapter by Derique Montaut, former Trotskyist and later Labour leader of Swindon Council, which has a few refs to CP.

4027 Chapple, Frank **Sparks Fly** *M. Joseph* 1985 239pp pb

4028 Charlton, John **Don't You Hear the H-Bomb's Thunder? Youth and Politics on Tyneside in the Late 'Fifites and Early 'Sixties** *North East Labour History/Merlin* 2009 202pp Includes refs to the CP – Dave Leigh, Ann Kane and others – among the whole range of CND activists and leftists. Generally an unsectarian approach, but author's politics evident when he describes CP members as 'an impressive and attractive core of political animals' but adds 'Their problem was the fundamentally rotten set of politics which underpinned their motivation and activity'. He may well be correct in his assessment that their influence was short-lived.

4029 Cherry, Steven **Our History: A Pocket History of the Labour Movement in Britain** *s.p.* 1981 120pp pb

4030 Chester, L. et al. **The Zinoviev Letter** *Heinemann* 1967 219pp hb

4031 Chun, Lin **The British New Left** *Edinburgh UP* 1993 230pp hb

4032 Church, Ray & Outram, Quentin **Strikes and Solidarity: Coalfield Conflict in Britain, 1889-1966** *CUP* 1988 314pp

4033 Citrine, Walter **Democracy or Disruption? An Examination of Communist Influences in the T.U.s** *TUC* 1928 32pp There was a 2nd ed. in the early 1930s. Originally appeared in 'Labour Magazine'.

4034 Citrine, Walter **Men and Work: An Autobiography** *Hutchinson* 1964 384pp hb Chapter on his libel case against Workers' Publications. Nothing on CP in his 2nd vol. ('Two Careers').

4035 Clark, J. et al. (eds) **Culture and Crisis in the 30s** *L&W* 1979 279pp hb Contains chapters on 'Left Review'; 'Left Book Club'; 'Film'; 'Agitprop' etc.

4036 Clark, Ronald **J.B.S.: The Life and Work of J.B.S. Haldane** *Hodder* 1968 286pp hb

4037 Clarke, Oliver Fielding **Unfinished Conflict: An Autobiography** *Citadel Press* 1970 368pp hb Anglican vicar in Kent who actively supported the CP during WW2 and in Cold War period – 'I used to attend meetings regularly though I never took a party card'.

4038 Clegg, H.A. **Labour Relations in London Transport** *Blackwell* 1950 188pp

4039 Clews, John **Communist Propaganda Techniques** *Methuen* 1964 326pp hb General study; very little on CPGB but does have appendix of 'Communist Publications in the UK in 1963' and list of LP proscribed orgs; also list of 'Front' orgs and lists of mags from the Socialist countries distributed in GB.

4040 Cliff, Tony & Gluckstein, Donny **Marxism and Trade Union Struggle: The General Strike of 1926** *Bookmarks* 1986 320pp

4041 Clinton, Alan **The Trade Union Rank and File: Trade Councils in Britain 1900-40** *MUP* 1977 262pp hb Excellent bibliography.

4042 Clunie, James **The Third (Communist) International: Its Aims and Methods** *SLP* 1921 61pp Author was delegate to the 3rd Congress of the C.I. (but his credentials were not accepted as he was from the part of the SLP that did not accept the formation of the CP, but he still went to all the meetings). Interesting on debates in the early Communist movement esp. about elections and affiliation to the LP.

4043 Clutterbuck, Richard **Britain in Agony: The Growth of Political Violence** *Faber* 1978 334pp hb Plays on fear of left-wing violence, but well researched and useful for CP's role in industrial disputes between 1971-7.

4044 Cockburn, Claud **I Claud …** *Penguin* 1967 454pp pb Autobiog. by 'DW' journalist and ed. of 'The Week', though not a CP member.

4045 Cockburn, Patricia **The Years of 'The Week'** *Penguin* 1971 293pp pb On Claud Cockburn's journal. Covers CP and 'DW'.

4046 Cohen, Gidon **From 'Insufferable Petty Bourgeois' to Trusted Communist: Jack Gaster, the Revolutionary Policy Committee and the CP** in *'Party People, Party Lives'* J. McIlroy, K. Morgan, Campbell, A. (eds) 2001 20pp

4046a Cohen, Gidon & Flinn, Andrew **In Search of the Typical British Communist** in *'Agents of the Revolution'* K. Morgan et al. (eds) 2005 20pp

4047 Cohen, Hilda **Bagels With Babushka** *Gatehouse Project* 1989 63pp pb Autobiog.; bit about YCL in Manchester.

4048 Cohen, Phil **Children of the Revolution: Communist Childhood in Cold War Britain** *L&W* 1997 189pp pb Includes interviews with 13 sons and daughters of Communists talking about growing up in the 1950s. Some joined CP/YCL: Jude Bloomfield, Pat Devine, Hywel Francis, Ann Kane, Jackie Kay, Martin Kettle, Mike Power, Brian Pollitt, Alexei Sayle and Nina Temple.

4049 Cole, G.D.H. **A History of the LP from 1914** *RKP* 1948 516pp hb Useful index.

4050 Cole, Margaret **Mellor, William** in *'DLB' 4* 1977 4pp

4051 Cole, Margaret **Postgate, Raymond** in *'DLB' 2* 1974 5pp

4052 Collette, Christine **The International Faith: Labour's Attitudes to European Socialism, 1918-39** *Ashgate* 1998 211pp hb Esp. for cultural activity; also Spain.

4053 Collins, Henry **The Founding of the British CP** in *'A Socialist Review'; I.S.* 1965 3pp pb Reprinted from 'Socialist Review', Sept. 1960.

4054 Collison, Peter **The Cutteslowe Walls** *Faber* 1963 194pp hb Sociological study with brief refs to CP's role in early days in Oxford.

4055 Common, Jack **Fake Left** *Working Press* 1992 12pp Reprint of article from 'Adelphi' March 19 1933. Also reprinted in 'Revolt Against an Age of Plenty' Strongwords, 1980.

4056 Connole, Nellie **The Leaven of Life: The Story of George Henry Fletcher** *L&W* 1961 212pp hb Sheffield master baker and member of Bakers' Union – probably the only person who led a strike against himself! Very active in BSP, then CP especially against unemployment.

4057 Connolly, Cressida **The Rare and the Beautiful: The Lives of the Garmans** *Fourth Estate* 2004 281pp Communism meets Bloomsbury. Much on Douglas Garman (ed. at L&W, Head of CP's Education Department), incl. his relationship with Peggy Guggenheim, the American heiress and art collector, who, the author claims, was persuaded to become a member of the CPGB 'albeit it a most half-hearted one'.

4058 Conrad, Jack **In the Enemy Camp** *November Publications* 1993 142pp pb On CP's electoral policy by publishers of the far-left 'Leninist'. Reprints some early CP documents.

4059 Conrad, Jack **Which Road? A Critique of 'Revolutionary' Reformism** *November Publications* 1991 268pp pb Critique of BRS, MFNT, CPB & Militant.

4060 Conradi, Peter **A Very English Hero: The Making of Frank Thompson** *Bloomsbury* 2012 432pp Recruited to the CP by his lover, Iris Murdoch, he was a great influence on his younger brother – E.P. Thompson.

4061 Conradi, Peter **Iris: A Life** *HarperCollins* 2001 706pp CP students in Oxford.

4062 Cook, Dave **Breaking Loose** *Ernest Press* 1989 204pp pb Cook worked for the CP for many years, incl. as National Organiser. This is an account of his round world bike trip (he was to die on a follow-up trip in 1993), but has a Foreword by P. Devine which looks at the life and ideas of this much loved activist.

4063 Cook, Judith **Apprentices of Freedom** *Quartet* 1979 149pp Based on interviews with members of the I.B., many of whom were CP members – George Atiken, Sam Wild, Will Paynter, Bob Cooney, Sid Quinn, Garry McCartney, Fred Copeman.

4064 Cookridge, E.H. **The Third Man: The Truth About Kim Philby** *Arthur Baker* 1968 283pp hb

4065 Coombes, John **British Intellectuals and the Popular Front** in *'Class, Culture and Social Change' F. Gloversmith (ed.)* 1980 31pp

4066 Cooper, Mike & Parkes, Ray **We Cannot Park On Both Sides: Reading Volunteers in the Spanish Civil War** *Reading International Brigades Memorial Committee* 2005 139pp pb

4067 Cooper, Wayne **Claude McKay: Rebel Sojourner in the Harlem Renaissance** *Schocken* 1987 441pp pb A couple of brief but tantalising refs to McKay's membership of CP – he was a founder member as part of Pankhurst's W.S.F., and he wrote regularly for her 'Workers' Dreadnought'.

4068 Cope, Dave **Central Books: A Brief History, 1939-99** *Central Books* 1999 80pp pb About the well-known CP business, based on the company's minutes and interviews with former members of staff. Respective managers of the business were: Charley Hall, Harry Bourne, Harvey Bagenal, Peter Wheeler, Margaret Mynatt, Iris Walker, Dave Wynn, Alan Brooks and Bill Norris.

4069 Cope, Phil **Wise and Foolish Dreamers: Wales and the Spanish Civil War** *Welsh Centre for International Affairs* 2007 148pp pb Many illustrations. Text in English, Welsh and Spanish.

4070 Copeman, Fred **Reason in Revolt** *Blandford* 1948 235pp hb Autobiog. by unemployed activist & I.B. Battalion Commander in Spain who defected to Moral Re-armament.

4071 Copsey, Nigel **Anti-Fascism in Britain** *Macmillan* 2000 229pp hb Refs to CP are mainly to 1930s and late 1940s, but there are some to 1970s.

4072 Copsey, Nigel & Renton, David (eds) **British Fascism, The Labour Movement and the State** *Palgrave Macmillan* 2005 209pp Notably, chapters by Thurlow and Mates.

4073 Copsey, Nigel & Olechnowicz, Andrzej **Varieties of Anti-Fascism: Britain in the Inter-War Period** *Palgrave Macmillan* 2010 275pp In particular, chapter by Thomas Linehan on the CP; and Copsey 'Every Time They Made a Communist, They Made a Fascist: The LP & Popular Anti-Fascism in the 1930s'.

4074 Corkill, David & Rawnsley, Stuart (eds) **The Road to Spain: Anti-Fascists at War** *Borderline* 1981 164pp pb Interviews with 17 members of I.B., 12 of whom were in CP.

4075 Cornford, John **Understand the Weapon, Understand the Wound: Selected Writings** *Carcanet* 1976 203pp hb

4076 Cornforth, Maurice **Communism and Philosophy** *L&W* 1980 13pp Intro. consists of brief autobiog. and account of his political & philosophical development – incl. setting up first CP branch at Cambridge.

4077 Cornforth, Maurice (ed.) **Rebels and their Causes** *L&W* 1978 224pp pb Contains: 'The Historians' Group of the CP' by Hobsbawm and 'A.L. Morton: Portrait of a Marxist Historian' by Cornforth.

4078 Corthorn, Paul **In the Shadow of the Dictators: The British Left in the 1930s** *I.B. Tauris* 2006 288pp

4079 Costello, John & Tsarev, Oleg **Deadly Illusions: The First Book from the KGB Archives** *Century* 1993 538pp hb

4080 Costello, John **Mask of Treachery** *Pan* 1989 664pp pb On the Cambridge spies. Much on CP in Cambridge, incl. Dobb & Roy Pascal. Good bibliography.

4081 Costley, Nigel **West Country Rebels** *Breviary Stuff Publications* 2012 212pp Well-illustrated and attractively produced book – surprisingly so since it is print on demand. Tantalisng refs to some Communists who surely deserve more research: Arthur Jordan and Jessie Waterman, hugely successful organisers of Dorset agricultural labourers; Doris Hatt and Margery Mack Smith, artists and activists who lived openly as lesbians in Clevedon, Somerset; Idris and Phyllis Rose, elected councillors in Trowbridge.

4082 Coward, Jack **Back From the Dead** *Merseyside Writers* 1985 56pp Reprint of 1939 ed. with extensive intro. by A. O'Toole & J. Nettleton on Coward (incl. his activities as a seamen's leader) and other Merseyside members of the IB. Also incl. photos.

4083 Cowden, Morton **Russian Bolshevism and British Labour, 1917-1921** *Columbia UP* 1984 238pp hb

4084 Craik, W.W. **Central Labour College** *L&W* 1964 191pp hb Has brief biogs of some former students of the College, incl. some CP members.

4085 Crail, Mark **Tracing Your Labour Movement Ancestors** *Pen & Sword Books* 2009 176pp Chapter on 'CPGB and Other Organizations'.

4086 Crawley, Aidan **The Hidden Face of British Communism** *Sunday Times* 1962 16pp lf

4087 Croft, Andy **'Left Book Club Anthology' ed. P. Laity – Review** in *'Socialist History'* 22 2002 3pp

4088 Croft, Andy (ed.) **A Weapon in the Struggle: The Cultural History of the CP in Britain** *Pluto* 1998 218pp pb Very important collection of essays incl. chapters on S.T. Warner, James Barke, J. Boswell, J. Fitton, J. Buchan, film, pageants, music, etc.

4088a Croft, Andy (ed.) **After the Party: Reflections on Life Since the CPGB** *L&W* 2012 159pp 8 members who stayed in CP to the end write about the political impact of the CP and their very different political lives since 1991. D. Cope, A. Croft, A. Findlay, S. Hill, K. Hudson, A. Pearmain, M. Perryman, L. Reith.

4089 Croft, Andy **Authors Take Sides: Writers and the CP, 1920-56** in *'Opening the Books'* G. Andrews et al. (eds) 1995 19pp pb

4090 Croft, Andy **Comrade Heart: A Life of Randall Swingler** *MUP* 2003 301pp hb One of the CP's most well-known poets, he also wrote plays, novels, songs; edited 'Left Review'; active in many areas of CP's cultural activity, incl. publishing. Left in 1956.

4091 Croft, Andy **Heslop, Harold** in *'DLB'* 10 2000 3pp

4092 Croft, Andy **Introduction to 'Last Cage Down' by Harold Heslop** *L&W* 1984 7pp pb Mining novel originally published 1935.

4093 Croft, Andy **Longden, John Miles** in *'DLB'* 10 2000 1pp Bohemian Teesside literary figure.

4094 Croft, Andy **Red Letter Days: British Fiction in the 1930s** *L&W* 1990 352pp hb

Much on Communist writers and CP cultural politics.

4095 Croft, Andy **The Boys Around the Corner: The Story of Fore Publications** in *'A Weapon in the Struggle' A. Croft (ed.)* 1998 21pp pb A cultural/political venture (involving R. Swingler, E. Rickword et al.) never strictly under CP control.

4096 Croft, Andy **The Young Men Are Moving Together: The Case of Randall Swingler** in *'Party People, Party Lives' McIlroy, J., Morgan, K., Campbell, A. (eds)* 2001 21pp

4097 Crossman, Richard (ed.) **The God That Failed** *H. Hamilton* 1950 272pp hb See Stephen Spender's unusual account of how he joined the CP, and then left after a few weeks.

4098 Croucher, Richard **Divisions in the Movement: The NUWM and its Rivals in Comparative Perspective** in *'Opening the Books' G. Andrews et al. (eds)* 1995 21pp pb

4099 Croucher, Richard **Engineers At War** *Merlin* 1982 400pp pb

4100 Croucher, Richard **We Refuse to Starve in Silence: A History of the NUWM 1920-46** *L&W* 1987 216pp hb

4101 Cummings, A.J. et al. **The Challenge to Democracy: A Popular Front For Britain** *News Chronicle* 1937 ? 80pp 4 speeches to Liberal Summer School; see chapter by Cummings.

4102 Cunningham, Valentine **British Writers of the Thirties** *OUP* 1989 530pp pb J. Lindsay, E. Rickword, M. Slater et al. Refs to 'Left Review' etc.

4103 Cunningham, Valentine **Neutral? 1930s Writers and Taking Sides** in *'Class, Culture and Social Change' F. Gloversmith (ed.)* 1980 25pp On 'Authors Take Sides on the Spanish War' published by 'Left Review' in 1937.

4104 Cunningham, Valentine (ed.) **The Penguin Book of Spanish Civil War Verse** *Penguin* 1980 507pp pb Intro. has lot of material on CP & individual members. See also John Saville 'Valentine Cunningham and the Poetry of the Spanish Civil War'.

4105 Curry, John **The Security Service, 1908-45: The Official History** *Public Record Office* 1999 442pp Originally written in 1946. Very official, does not give away much.

4106 Daffern, Eileen **Essays on a Life: Politics, Peace and the Personal** *B&M Publishing* 2007 245pp pb Peace activist and CP member in Brighton.

4107 Dalton, Alan **Turn Left at Land's End** *Red Boots Publ.* 1987 95pp pb A quirky but interesting survey, based on a walk, of left wing activists in Cornwall – incl. Alfred Jenkin.

4108 Daniels, John **Letter to a Member of the CP** *Labour Review* 1957 20pp Trotskyist.

4108a D'Arcy, Hugh **A Bible of Discontent: The Memoir of Hugh D'Arcy, Bricklayer and Trade Unionist** *University of Westminster* 2014 118pp pb Scottish building worker, UCATT official and long-standing CPGB member.

4109 Darke, Bob **The Communist Technique in Britain** *Collins* 1953 160pp One of a batch of autobiographies from this period by hostile ex-members. Darke was leading figure in London bus struggles. An American ed. was published the same year with the title 'Cockney Communist'.

4110 Darlington, Ralph & Lyddon, Dave **Glorious Summer: Class Struggle in Britain 1972** *Bookmarks* 2001 304pp

4111 Darlington, Ralph (ed.) **Molly Murphy: Suffragette and Socialist** *Institute of Social Research, Univ. of Salford* 1998 168pp Autobiog., ghost-written according to her son, by husband Jack. She was active alongside him and served as nurse in Spain.

4112 Darlington, Ralph **Murphy, J.T.** in *'DLB' 12* 2005 6pp

4113 Darlington, Ralph **Syndicalism and the Transition to Communism: An International Comparative Analysis** *Ashgate* 2008 333pp

4114 Darlington, Ralph **The Political Trajectory of J.T. Murphy** *Liverpool UP* 1998 316pp pb Important leader of engineers, on leading bodies of CP and Comintern, founder of RILU; left CP in 1932.

4115 Dash, Jack **Good Morning Brothers!** *L&W* 1969 190pp hb Leading figure in London dock struggles, then East End pensioners' movement.

4115a David, Wayne **Remaining True: A Biography of Ness Edwards** *Caerphilly Local History Society* 2006 118pp Passing refs to CP reflect its influence in South Wales mining communities.

4116 Davidson, Basil **Special Operations Europe: Scenes from the Anti-Nazi War** *Gollancz* 1980 288pp hb Included solely for the dazzling portrait of James Klugmann.

4117 Davidson, Michael **The World, the Flesh and Myself** *Quartet* 1977 393pp pb Journalist and translator; friend of Felicia Browne (whom he saved twice from suicide) and Charles Ashleigh. Joined the German CP in 1932 and worked clandestinely in Hitler's Berlin and briefly joined the CPGB on his escape to London. A finely-written and pioneering autobiog. of a gay man.

4118 Davies, Andrew **To Build a New Jerusalem: The Labour Movement from the 1880s to the 1990s** *M. Joseph* 1992 344pp hb One of the general histories of the left that gives a reasonable amount of coverage to the CP.

4119 Davies, Paul **A.J. Cook** *MUP* 1987 223pp hb

4120 Davies, Sam et al. **Genuinely Seeking Work: Mass Unemployment on Merseyside in the 1930s** *Liver Press* 1992 216pp pb Passing refs.

4121 Davis, Leonard **Luise Davis: Unsung Heroine** *s.p.* 1982 88pp pb She was Secretary of the Vegan Society.

4122 Davis, Mary **Fashioning A New World: A History of the Woodcraft Folk** *Holyoake Books* 2000 147pp pb YCL and CP members played a role, but not a preponderent one, in this progressive children's organisation.

4123 Davis, Mary **Sylvia Pankhurst: A Life in Radical Politics** *Pluto* 1999 157pp pb

4124 Davis, Tricia **What Kind of Woman Is She? Women and CP Politics, 1941-55** in *'Feminism, Culture and Politics' Brunt & C. Rowan (eds); L&W* 1982 24pp pb

4125 Deacon, Richard **The Greatest Treason** *Century* 1989 212pp hb More about the world of spies, but includes refs to two interesting CP members: 'Peter' Murphy, a confident of Lord Mountbatten, and Joyce White.

4126 Deakin, Arthur & McManus, T. **Chaos is Their Objective! Communist Tactics Spotlighted** *TGWU* 1951 14pp Reprint of 2 articles from 'The Record'. Docks' strike.

4127 Deakin, Arthur **Democracy Versus Communism** *TGWU* 1948 24pp Speeches.

4128 Deakin, F.W. et al. **A History of World Communism** *Weidenfeld* 1975 177pp hb Short chapter on formation of CPGB.

4129 Deegan, Frank **No Other Way: An Autobiography** *Toulouse Press* 1980 107pp pb Author fought in Spain, was active member of CP on Merseyside and was one of the leaders of the unofficial Merseyside Port Workers' Cttee

4130 Degras, Jane **The Communist International 1919-43: Documents** *F. Cass* 1971 1587pp New ed. of this 3 vol. standard work; incl. Theses, Resolutions, Instructions etc. with excellent introductory comments.

4131 Degras, Jane **United Front Tactics in the Comintern, 1921-8** in *'St. Anthony's Papers No.9' D. Footman (ed.); Chatto* 1960 14pp hb

4132 'Democritus' **Communist Circus** *Heston & Isleworth LP* 1946 16pp Ill. by Gow. Different from p. of same name published by Clarion Y.H.

4133 Desmarais, Ralph **Cook, Arthur James** in *'DLB' 3* 1976 7pp

4134 Dewar, Hugo **Communist Politics in Britain: CPGB From Origins to Second World War** *Pluto* 1976 159pp pb Trotskyist.

4135 Dickie, John **Geordie's Story: The Life of Jack Brent** *Azlan* 2012 148pp Jack Brent (real name George Dickie) was a British army deserter who joined the CP and fought in Spain. Author is his nephew.

4136 Dickinson, Bessie **James Rushton and his Times 1886-1956** *WCML* 1982 51pp lf Concentrates on the cotton industry in 1930s Lancashire.

4137 Dickinson, Margaret (ed.) **Rogue Reels: Oppositional Film in Britain, 1945-90** *British Film Institute* 1999 330pp hb See Chap. 1 and the Oral Histories section which includes interviews with Charles Cooper, Stanley Forman and Dave Douglass.

4138 Docherty, Mary **A Miner's Lass** *Cardendon Mining Archives* 1992 281pp pb Autobiog. Incl. memories of the 'Young Comrades'.

4139 Dodd, Kathryn (ed.) **A Sylvia Pankhurst Reader** *MUP* 1993 248pp hb Contains her articles in 'Workers' Dreadnought' on the formation of the CP and her later expulsion.

4140 Doherty, Mary (ed.) **Auld Bob Selkirk** *s.p.* 1996 194pp pb Selkirk was miner who became a Communist councillor in Cowdenbeath for 32 years. Book consists of a reprint of his autobiog. ('The Life of a Worker') plus other writings by and about him.

4141 Donnachie, Ian et al. (eds) **Forward! Labour Politics in Scotland, 1888-1988** *Polygon* 1989 184pp hb

4142 Dorril, Stephen **MI6: Fifty Years of Special Operations** *Fourth Estate* 2000 907pp Brief refs, but more than the index indicates.

4143 Douglass, Dave **Geordies – Wa Mental** *TUPS Books* 2000 309pp pb Better known as a syndicalist miner, this autobiog. of his early years describes his involvement with the YCL in Newcastle before he turned to pacifism and anarchism.

4144 Dowse, Robert **Left in the Centre** *Longman* 1966 231pp hb Study of the ILP.

4145 Doyle, Charlie **The BRS Draft: Revolutionary Path or Diversion?** *s.p.* 1977 19pp

4146 Drakeford, Mark **Social Movements and Their Supporters: The Green Shirts in England** *Palgrave Macmillan* 1997 248pp Describes CP members breaking up meetings organised by Social Credit.

4147 Driberg, Tom **Guy Burgess** *Weidenfeld* 1956 124pp hb

4148 Driberg, Tom **Ruling Passions** *Quartet* 1977 271pp pb Joined CP while at public school; Oxford during General Strike; expelled during the war – claims he never found out why.

4149 Drucker, H.M. (ed.) **Multi-Party Britain** *Macmillan* 1979 242pp Contains chap. on 'The Marxist Left' by Peter Mair.

4150 Druker, Janet **McBain, John** in *'DLB' 5* 1979 2pp

4151 Duncan, David **Mutiny in the RAF: The Air Force Strikes of 1946** *SHS* 1999 94pp pb Fascinating account of Communist activity in the forces. Arthur Attwood was court martialled for mutiny.

4152 Duncan, Rob & McIvor, Arthur (eds) **Militant Workers: Labour and Class Conflict on the Clyde 1900-50 – Essays in Honour of H. McShane** *J. Donald* 1992 197pp pb

4153 Duncan, Robert **Newbold, J.T. Walton** in *'DLB' 10* 2000 6pp

4154 Durham, Martin **The Early Years of the CP in Birmingham, 1920-24** in *'Worlds of Labour: Essays in Birmingham Labour History'* A. Wright (ed.); *Univ. of Birmingham* 1983 16pp pb

4155 Dutt, Salme **Lucifer and Other Poems** *Mitre Press* 1965 103pp hb R. Page Arnot's intro. has some brief details on the life of this interesting, shadowy and influential figure in the early days of the CP.

4156 Dworkin, Dennis **Cultural Marxism in Postwar Britain** *Duke UP* 1997 322pp Good on Historians' Group, also New Left. Much on E.P. Thompson and R. Williams.

4157 Dyson, B. **Liberty in Britain, 1934-1994** *Civil Liberties Trust* 1994 100pp pb NCCL was regularly accused of being used by CP – this official history sets the record straight.

4158 Eaden, James & Renton, David **The Communist Party of Great Britain Since 1920** *Palgrave* 2002 220pp hb

4159 Ebon, Martin **World Communism Today** *Whittlesey House/McGraw Hill* 1948 536pp hb Chapter on CPGB – 12pp.

4160 Edelstein, J. David & Warner, Malcolm **Comparative Union Democracy: Organisations and Opposition in British and American Unions** *A&U* 1975 378pp hb Esp. on engineering (incl. on Reg Birch) and mining industries.

4161 Eds of Labour Review **Congress Special** *Labour Review* 1957 lf d Daily foolscap newsletter of 2/4 pages issued by the SLL at the CP Congress, April 19-22.

4162 Edwards, Ruth **Victor Gollancz: A Biography** *Gollancz* 1987 782pp hb Obviously a lot on the LBC.

4163 Egbert, Donald Drew **Social Radicalism and the Arts: Western Europe from the French Revolution to 1968 – A Cultural History** *Duckworth* 1970 874pp hb Despite the huge scope of this book, it contains some valuable and unusual research on the CPGB.

4164 Eley, Geoff **A Crooked Line** *University of Michigan Press* 2005 301pp Part memoir, part analysis of academic history – the CP Historians' Group features prominently.

4165 Eley, Geoff **From Welfare Politics to Welfare State: Women and the Socialist Question** in *'Women and Socialism, Socialism and Women: Europe Between the Two World Wars'* H. Gruber & P. Graves (eds); *Berghahn* 1998 30pp Has a discussion on women in the CP.

4166 Elliott, Gregory **Hobsbawm: History and Politics** *Pluto* 2010 198pp First chapter assesses his membership of, and writing on, the CP.

4167 Ellis, C.H. **The New Left in Britain** *Common Cause* 1968 16pp

4168 Elwell, Charles **Tracts Beyond theTimes: A Brief Guide to the Communist or Revolutionary Press** *Social Affairs Unit Research Report* 1983 32pp Of some interest, as it names CP members/influence in various organisations & journals. Also a bit on 'Straight Left'.

4169 'Espinasse, Margaret **Hill, Howard** in *'DLB' 7* 1984 3pp

4170 'Espinasse, Margaret **Southall, Joseph** in *'DLB' 5* 1979 5pp Not in CP, but close and this entry has info. on CP in Birmingham.

4171 Evans, A.H. **Against the Enemy!** Cttee to Defeat Revisionism, For Communist Unity 1963 13pp Maoist.

4172 Evans, A.H. **On Khruschov and Others** David-Goliath Publications 1963 34pp Pro-Albanian.

4173 Evans, A.H. **Truth Will Out** Cttee to Defeat Revisionism, For Communist Unity 1964 70pp Collection of letters between Arthur Evans & the leadership of the CPGB 1947-53.

4174 Evans, A.H. **What's Wrong with Peter Seltman? An Analysis of Seltman's Pamphlet 'What's Wrong With the British CP'** Goliath Publications 1967 ? 24pp Maoist.

4175 Evans, Chris **History of Seven Sisters** Cymric Federation Press 1964 182pp hb Incl. small section on CP history in this part of Neath; author was CP Councillor.

4176 Evans, George Ewart **The Strength of the Hills: An Autobiography** Faber 1983 180pp Cambridge in the 1930s. Evans became a pioneer of oral history.

4177 Ewing, K.D. & Gearty, C.A. **The Struggle for Civil Liberties: Political Freedom and the Rule of Law in Britain, 1914-1945** OUP 2000 451pp hb Much on the CP.

4178 Exell, Arthur **The Politics of the Production Line: Autobiography of an Oxford Car Worker** History Workshop 1981 76pp Autobiog. Originally published in 'HWJ' Nos 6, 7 & 9.

4179 Falber, Reuben **The 1968 Czechoslovak Crisis: Inside the British CP** Socialist History Society 1996 36pp

4180 Feather, Victor **Defend Democracy: Communist Activities Examined** TUC 1948 12pp Author not credited.

4181 Feather, Victor **How Do the Communists Work?** Background Books, Batchworth 1953 64pp pb

4182 Feather, Victor **Trades Councils and Proscribed Organisations** TUC 1950 8pp Extract from Proceedings of the Annual Conference of Trades Councils.

4183 Felstead, Richard **No Other Way: Jack 'Russia' and the Spanish Civil War** Alun Books 1981 115pp pb Biog. of Jack Roberts, known as Jack 'Russia', by his grandson.

4184 Felstead, Richard **Roberts, Jack** in 'DLB' 7 1984 2pp

4185 'Ferguson, Alex' **Prospects for the CP** Communist Publications 1987 ? 8pp Previously in 'Communist' Sept. 1987.

4186 Fernbach, David **Wintringham, Tom** in 'DLB' 7 1984 9pp

4187 Ferns, Harry **Reading From Left to Right** Univ. of Toronto Press 1983 374pp pb Canadian in CP at Cambridge 1930s.

4188 Ferris, Paul **The New Militants** Penguin 1972 112pp pb

4189 Ferry, Georgina **Dorothy Hodgkin: A Life** Granta 1998 423pp hb Distinguished scientist; close to, but not member of CP though her husband was. Refs to other CP scientists.

4190 Fieldhouse, Roger **Adult Education and the Cold War: Liberal Values Under Siege, 1946-51** Univ. of Leeds, Dept of Adult Education 1985 111pp Reveals the extent of discrimination against CP members in the WEA and adult education in general (though see Goldman 'Dons and Workers' for a differing view).

4191 Fieldhouse, Roger **Anti-Apartheid: A History of the Movement in Britain** Merlin 2005 546pp pb

4192 Fieldhouse, Roger **Cold War and Colonial Conflicts in British West African Adult Education, 1943-1953** in 'History of Education Quarterly' Fall 1984 13pp Refs to David Wiseman, T.L. Hodgkin, J.A. McLean.

4193 Fielding, N. et al. (eds) **Active Citizens: New Voices and Values** Bedford Square Press 1991 108pp pb 6pp on Jane Saxby from Liverpool.

4194 Fishman, Nina **Arthur Horner: A Political Biography (2 vols)** L&W 2010 1134pp

4195 Fishman, Nina **Horner and Hornerism** in 'Party People, Party Lives' J. McIlroy, K. Morgan, Campbell, A. (eds) 2001 21pp

4196 Fishman, Nina **No Home but the Trade Union Movement: Communist Activists and 'Reformist' Leaders, 1926-56** in 'Opening the Books' G. Andrews et al. (eds) 1995 22pp pb

4197 Fishman, Nina **Tanner, Jack** in 'DLB' 11 2003 9pp Engineer's leader; only in CP for 8 months.

4198 Fishman, Nina **The British Communist Party and the Trade Unions, 1933-45** Scolar Press 1995 380pp hb Based on widespread interviews with activists, esp. in engineering & buses. Detailed examination of grass roots activity, shows how CP varied in different localities and unions, and gives weight to the view that there was much scope for initiative in the CPGB, within the line that came from Moscow.

4199 Fishman, Nina **The British Road is Resurfaced for New Times: From the British CP to DL** in *'West European CPs After the Revolutions of 1989'* M. Bull & P. Heywood (ed.); Macmillan 1994 33pp hb One of the better published accounts of the end of the CP.

4200 Fishman, Nina & Lloyd, J. **The CPGB Now** BICO 1979 30pp

4201 Fishman, William **A People's Journée: The Battle of Cable Street** in *'History From Below'* F. Krantz (ed.); Concordia Univ., Montreal 1985 14pp

4202 Flanagan, Richard **'Parish-Fed Bastards': A History of the Politics of the Unemployed in Britain, 1884-1939** Greenwood 1991 289pp hb

4203 Flett, Keith (ed.) **1956 And All That** Cambridge Scholars Publishing 2007 237pp Includes: D. Renton 'The CP Historians and 1956', T. Brotherstone 'History, Truth, Context and Meaning: Two Memories of the 1956-57 Crisis in the CPGB' (on B. Pearce and P. Fryer). Also other refs in chapters by N. Davidson (on Alasdair Macintyre), K. Flett and P. Blackledge.

4204 Flewers, Paul **Confronting the Unthinkable:The CPGB and the Molotov-Ribbentrop Pact** s.p. 1994 37pp lf BA Dissertation (London, School of Slavonic & East European Studies) – reproduced for sale.

4205 Flewers, Paul **The New Civilisation? Understanding Stalin's Soviet Union, 1929-1941** Francis Boutle 2008 299pp

4206 Flinn, Andrew & Morgan, Kevin **Hardy, George** in *'DLB'* 11 2003 11pp

4207 Flinn, Andrew **William Rust: The Comintern's Blue-Eyed Boy** in *'Party People, Party Lives'* J. McIlroy, K. Morgan, Campbell, A. (eds) 2001 24pp

4208 Fong, Gisella Chan Man **Shoulder to Shoulder: Rose Smith, Who Stood For 'Different but Equal and United'** in *'Party People, Party Lives'* J. McIlroy, K. Morgan, Campbell, A. (eds) 2001 20pp

4209 Fong, Gisela Chan Man **Smith, Rose** in *'DLB'* 11 2003 4pp National Women's Organiser, 1929-33; journalist on 'DW' and in China.

4210 Foot, Michael **Aneurin Bevan, 1897-1945** Granada 1982 528pp pb Very little in the second vol. on CP.

4211 Foote, Alexander **Handbook for Spies** Museum Press 1949 223pp hb Author fought in Spain, close to CPGB but not member; 'recruited' by Copeman & Springhall. Ran Soviet spy network in Switzerland during war before breaking with Communism. New ed. in 1964.

4212 Forbes, Duncan (ed.) **Edith Tudor Hart: In the Shadow of Tyranny** Hatje Cantz 2013 152pp Mainly on her photographic work, but places her in the context of her membership of the CP and work for the Comintern.

4213 Forbes, Duncan **Politics, Photography and Exile in the Life of Edith Tudor Hart** in *'Arts in Exile in Britain, 1933-1945: Politics and Cultural Identity, The Yearbook of the Research Centre for German and Austrian Exile Studies, Vol.6* S. Behr & M. Malet (eds); Rodopi, Amsterdam 2005 42pp

4214 Forbes, Duncan **The Worker Photography Movement in Britain, 1934–1939'** in *'The Worker Photography Movement (1926-1939): Essays and Documents'* J. Ribalta et al (eds); Museo Nacional Centro de Arte Reina Sofia, Madrid 2011 11pp

4215 Forbes, Duncan **Wolfgang Suschitzky and the British Documentary Tradition in the 1930s** in *'Photography and Research in Austria: Vienna, The Door to the European East – Proceedings of the Vienna Symposium'*; European Society for the Study of Photography/Dietmar Klinger Verlag 2002 10pp Some refs to Edith Tudor Hart, Suschitzky's sister, and her photography. If some of the CP novelists, poets and critics provide a link to Bloomsbury or Surrealism, Tudor Hart provides a link to the Bauhaus – even if she did abandon her modernism for the realist British documentary tradition, as is argued here.

4216 Forman, Charles **Industrial Town: Self Portrait of St Helens in the 1920s** Paladin 1979 272pp pb Incl. contributions from a couple of anonymous CP members.

4217 Foster, John **Willie Gallacher: A Paisley Communist in Parliament** in *'Essays on the Labour and Social History of Renfrewshire'* Renfrewshire Council/STUC/University of Paisley 1999 10pp lf

4218 Foulser, George **Seaman's Voice** MacGibbon & Kee 1961 192pp hb

4219 Foulser, George **Unholy Alliance: The 1966 Seamen's Strike, An Analysis** Direct Action 1967 ? 16pp Syndicalist; critical of CP esp. J. Dash & Gordon Norris.

4220 Fox, Colin **'Motherwell is Won for Moscow': The Story of Walton Newbold, Britain's First Communist MP** *Scottish Militant Labour* 1992 40pp

4221 Francis, Dai **Red Banner, Red Dragon** *Y Faner Goch Publications* 1979 24pp Mainly articles written by Francis but includes short tribute/biographical sketch.

4222 Francis, Hywel **Miners Against Fascism: Wales and the Spanish Civil War** *L&W* 2012 320pp New ed.

4223 Francis, Hywel **Rhondda and the Spanish Civil War** in *'Rhondda, Past & Future' K. Hopkins (eds); Rhondda Borough Council* 1980 18pp hb Much on CP. Annie Powell, the Communist Mayor of Rhondda, wrote the Foreword.

4224 Francis, Hywel **The Fed: History of the South Wales Miners** *L&W* 1980 530pp hb

4225 Fraser, Robert **Night Thoughts: The Surreal Life of the Poet David Gascoyne** *OUP* 2012 469pp Britain's most prominent Surrealist poet was briefly in the CP in Twickenham, and this book records the Party's ambiguous relationship with Surrealism. Other CP literary figures appear in the narrative incl. Romilly, Toynbee, Upward and, most importantly, Roger Roughton (ed. of 'Contemporary Poetry and Prose').

4226 Fraser, Ronald (ed.) **Work: Twenty Personal Accounts** *Penguin* 1968 299pp Very brief autobiographical entries follow each entry; 2 in CP. Also Vol.2, 1969, is similar – see P. Higgs and S.G. Turvey, but very little on the CP.

4227 Fraser, W. Hamish **A History of British Trade Unionism** *Macmillan* 1999 291pp

4228 'Frater Om-Soc' (Cosmo Trelawny) **The Conference of the Golden Spawn** *s.p.* 1943 16pp A very strange satire on the CP. Fiction.

4229 French, Sid **Reminiscences** *NCP* 1988 32pp lf Leader of NCP.

4230 Friend, Andrew **The Post War Squatters** in *'Squatting: The Real Story' N. Wates & C. Wolmar (eds); Bay Leaf Press* 1980 10pp pb

4231 Friguglietti, James **A Scholar 'In Exile': George Rudé as a Historian of Australia** in *'French History and Civilization: Papers from the George Rudé Seminar, Vol.1' Ian Collier et al (eds); George Rudé Society, Melbourne* 2005 10pp Reveals that Rudé was arrested and fined for his participation in the Battle of Cable Street.

4232 Frow, Ruth **Edmund Frow (Eddie): The Making of an Activist** *WCML* 1999 168pp pb NUWM activist, engineering shop steward and organiser, bibliophile. Co-founder of Working Class Movement Library.

4233 Frow, Ruth & Eddie **Beckett, Clem** in *'DLB'* 9 1993 3pp

4234 Frow, Ruth & Eddie **Bob and Sarah Lovell: Crusaders for a Better Society** *WCML* 1976 ? 26pp lf Active in NUWM, ICWPA, engineering struggles etc.

4235 Frow, Ruth & Eddie **Clem Beckett and the Oldham Men Who Fought in Spain, 1936-8** *WCML* 1980 26pp lf

4236 Frow, Ruth & Eddie **Finley, Lawrence** in *'DLB'* 4 1977 2pp

4237 Frow, Ruth & Eddie (eds) **Greater Manchester Men Who Fought in Spain** *Greater Manchester I.B. Memorial Cttee* 1983 ? 69pp pb Specifically on Syd Booth, Maurice Levine, and Sam Wild.

4238 Frow, Ruth & Eddie (eds) **Jack Askins 1919-1987** *TGWU, North West Region* 1987 30pp Full-timer and activist in North West.

4239 Frow, Ruth & Eddie **McGree, Leo** in *'DLB'* 9 1993 7pp

4240 Frow, Ruth & Eddie **Munro, Jack** in *'DLB'* 7 1984 2pp

4241 Frow, Ruth & Eddie **Peet, George** in *'DLB'* 5 1979 2pp

4242 Frow, Ruth & Eddie **Pit and Factory Papers Issued by the CPGB, 1927-34** *s.p.* 1996 30pp lf Important attempt to list these rare papers, though despite the title they range from 1924 to 1936. Unfortunately it excludes some mags that are in CP Archive collection, but lists some from the Moscow Archives for the first time. Research a bit rushed e.g. it confuses 'Workers' Life' and 'Workers' Weekly'. Locations given.

4243 Frow, Ruth & Eddie **The Liquidation of the CPGB** *s.p.* 1996 24pp A disappointing, one-sided 'contribution to discussion'.

4244 Fryer, Peter **Defend the ETU! Against Fleet Street and King Street** *Newsletter (SLL)* 1958 12pp

4245 Fryer, Peter **Hungarian Tragedy** *Index* 1997 192pp Incl. 'Hungary and the CP' published as a pamphlet in 1957.

4246 Fryer, Peter **Hungary and the CP: An Appeal Against Expulsion** *s.p.* 1957 46pp

4247 Fryer, Peter **The Battle for Socialism** *SLL* 1959 192pp pb Chapter on CP.

4248 Fryer, Robert & Williams, Stephen **Dix, Bernard** in *'DLB'* 13 2010 20pp

4249 Fyrth, Jim **An Indian Landscape, 1944-1946** *SHS* 2001 96pp pb Bit about CPGB/CPI links.

4250 Fyrth, Jim (ed.) **Britain, Fascism and the Popular Front** *L&W* 1985 261pp pb Most chapters have material on the CPGB. Important.

4251 Fyrth, Jim **Brown, Isabel** in *'DLB'* 9 1993 4pp CP women's organiser in 1930s. Article is followed by feature on Aid for Spain Movement.

4252 Fyrth, Jim (ed.) **Labour's Promised Land? Culture and Society in Labour Britain, 1945-51** *L&W* 1995 320pp pb

4253 Fyrth, Jim **The Signal Was Spain: The Aid Spain Movement in Britain 1936-39** *L&W* 1986 344pp pb

4254 Gadsby, Jack **Memoirs of a Worker in South Wales and Coventry** *CRIS Resource Centre, Coventry* 1975 ? 58pp

4255 Gale, Jack **Class Struggle in the Second World War: The 1944 Police Raid** *Workers' International League* 1991 60pp Trotskyist. Reprinted from 'Workers' Press' 1975.

4256 Gallacher, W. **Last Memoirs** *L&W* 1966 320pp hb

4257 Gallacher, W. **Revolt on the Clyde** *L&W* 1949 301pp pb One of several autobiographies by Gallacher.

4258 Gallacher, W. **The Case for Communism** *Penguin* 1949 208pp pb A general political & philosophical exposition, but has material on the CP; of interest for the very fact of being published as a Penguin Special, and a successful one, at this period during the Cold War.

4259 Gallacher, W. **The Rolling of Thunder** *L&W* 1947 229pp hb Autobiog. – carries on from 'Revolt on the Clyde'.

4260 Gallacher, W. **The Tyrants' Might is Passing** *L&W* 1954 104pp pb

4261 Gardner, Llew **The Fringe Left** in *'The Left'* G. Kaufman (ed.); A. Blond 1966 25pp pb

4262 Garside, W.R. **The Durham Miners, 1919-60** *A&U* 1971 544pp hb Brief but interesting comments on MM and CP in 1930s.

4263 Gascoyne, David **Journal 1936-37** *Enitharmon Press* 1980 144pp Page 1: '22.9.36 – I joined the CP Yesterday'; but this book is of much more literary significance than political.

4264 Ghose, Pramita **Meerut Conspiracy Case and the Left-Wing in India** *Papyrus, Calcutta* 1978 230pp

4265 Gibbs, Henry **The Spectre of Communism** *Selwyn & Blount* 1936 28pp hb About half the book is about Britain (& Empire); more substantial than most anti-Communist works, has some interesting potted biographies & details on anti-religious attitudes.

4266 Gildart, Keith **Braddock, Tom** in *'DLB'* 12 2005 9pp Several refs to CP in Wimbledon. The following article, 'Special Note on the Nenni Telegram' by D. Howell, also has several refs.

4267 Gildart, Keith **Lawson, Hugh** in *'DLB'* 11 2003 10pp Lawson was not in CP, but refs to J. Roose Williams & the CP in North Wales.

4268 Gildart, Keith **North Wales Miners – A Fragile Unity, 1945-96** *University of Wales Press* 2001 277pp hb Refs to CP miners (see Keith Hett) and CP in the wider N Wales community (incl. an attack on a CP meeting in Flint in 1952).

4269 Gillies, William **The Communist Solar System [1]** *LP* 1933 24pp

4270 Glasser, Ralph **Growing Up in the Gorbals** *Pan* 1986 207pp pb The CP has a brooding presence in this well written autobiog. of a working class youth in 1930s Jewish Gorbals; sometimes this extends to a sinister presence but it is not always convincing.

4271 Glees, Anthony **The Secrets of the Service: British Intelligence and Communist Subversion 1939-51** *Cape* 1987 447pp hb Very few refs to CPGB: the Blunts and Burgesses are there, plus a couple of tentative mentions of 'secret Communists'.

4272 Glover, Jonathan **Humanity: A Moral History of the Twentieth Century** *Cape* 1999 464pp Incl. analysis of CP change of policy on WW2 from a moral perspective.

4273 Gloversmith, F. (ed.) **Class, Culture and Social Change** *Harvester* 1980 286pp hb Contains 'Class Against Class: The Political Culture Of The CPGB, 1930-35' by A. Howkins (a rare defence of the 'Third Period'); 'John Sommerfield' by S. Laing; 'British Intellectuals and the Popular Front' by J. Coombes.

4274 Godden, Gertrude **Communist Attack on Great Britain** *Burns, Oates & Washbourne* 1938 109pp hb One of the more useful anti-Communist tracts; author very concerned by anti-religious propaganda of CP but well researched on CP publications, factory journals, cultural activities & she expresses regular admiration for the quality & quantity of written material e.g. 'the admirably produced publications inciting the native races of India and Africa to revolt'. This is enlarged ed. of book first published in 1935.

4275 Goldman, Lawrence **Dons and Workers: Oxford and Adult Education Since 1850** OUP 1995 375pp Disagrees with Fieldhouse on discrimination against CP WEA tutors in Oxford in 1940s ('Adult Education & the Cold War').

4276 Goldman, Leonard **Back to Brighton** s.p. 2002 192pp pb Sequel to 'Brighton Beach to Bengal Bay'. Became teacher, active on educational issues in London, then Brighton after some years in GDR. Much on CP activities.

4277 Goldman, Leonard **Brighton Beach to Bengal Bay** s.p. 1999 117pp pb Pedestrian autobiog.; Jewish London background, active in Unity Theatre in 1930s. India during WW2.

4278 Goldsmith, Maurice **Sage: Life of Bernal** Hutchinson 1980 256pp hb Joined CP in 1923: 'He lost his card in 1933 or 1934 and never rejoined'.

4279 Goldstein, Joseph **The Government of British Trade Unions** A&U 1952 300pp hb On the TGWU. Foreword by A. Deakin.

4280 Gollancz, Victor **Russia and Ourselves** Gollancz 1941 131pp hb Chapter on CP and WW2.

4281 Gollancz, Victor (ed.) **The Betrayal of the Left** Gollancz 1941 324pp hb Contrib. incl. J. Strachey, G. Orwell, H. Laski, & documents.

4282 Gollancz, Victor **Where Are You Going? An Open Letter to Communists** Gollancz 1940 40pp Published in May.

4283 Goodman, Geoffrey **The Awkward Warrior: Frank Cousins His Life and Times** Spokesman 1979 616pp hb Esp. on CP in TGWU. Also, Cousins' wife, Nance, was in CP.

4284 Goodwin, Dennis & Fryer, Peter **The Newsletter Conference and the CP: Two Attacks by Dennis Goodwin With Replies by Peter Fryer** Newsletter (SLL) 1958 32pp

4285 Gorman, John **Images of Labour** Scorpion 1985 192pp pb Interesting snippets on various artists, notably Cliff Rowe, Ken Sprague, Felicity Ashbee.

4286 Gorman, John **Knocking Down Ginger** Caliban 1995 260pp hb Autobiog. of labour historian who was active in CP in early 1950s – good picture of branch life in E London. Describes the design/print business he set up with Lionel Bart.

4287 Gorringe, Tim **Alan Ecclestone: Priest as Revolutionary** Cairns Publications 1994 167pp hb Biog. of the Christian Socialist priest, influenced by Conrad Noel; with his wife, Delia, he joined the CP in 1948 and remained a member for 40 years. Lived in Barrow, Cumberland and Sheffield always choosing working class parishes. Active WEA lecturer and leader of national peace campaigns. Author concludes that 'the Church authorities were far less comfortable with a Communist priest than the Party Headquarters were'.

4288 Gould, Julius **The Attack on Higher Education: Marxist and Radical Penetration** Institute for the Study of Conflict 1977 55pp lf Appendix on CP lists speakers and courses at CULs etc. Whatever the value of some of this pamphlet's arguments, it reeks of 'naming names' & witch-hunting.

4289 Grant, Ted **History of British Trotskyism** Wellred Publications 2002 pb

4290 Graubard, Stephen **British Labour and the Russian Revolution** Harvard UP 1956 305pp hb

4291 Graves, Pamela **Labour Women: Women in British Working-Class Politics, 1918-39** CUP 1994 270pp pb

4292 Gray, Daniel **Homage to Caledonia: Scotland and the Spanish Civil War** Luath Press 2009 223pp

4292a Green, John **Britain's Communists: The Untold Story** Artery Publications 2014 348p Very readable book that covers all the areas of social life (culture; work) and political arenas (peace, anti-fascism, LP, internationalism, youth, women) that the CP engaged in. Largely biographical approach. Has some of the strengths and weaknesses of the Introduction to this Bibliography.

4293 Green, John **Ken Sprague: People's Artist** Hawthorn Press 2002 137pp pb Attractive and profusely illustrated book about well known lifelong Communist artist.

4294 Green, Joseph **A Social History of the Jewish East End in London** E. Mellen Press 1991 552pp Beware of the strange double index!

4295 Green, Laurie **The Red Above the Green** s.p. 2007 315pp Like many of his generation, he was deeply influenced by his wartime experiences in the Far East. A headteacher, this autobiog. has info. on CP education policy; also on activity in the peace movement.

4296 Green, Nan **A Chronicle of Small Beer: The Memoirs of Nan Green** *Trent Editions* 2004 243pp Green went to Spain to work for the IB, in which her husband was already enrolled (he died on the very last day of the war). She returned to England to work for the IB Association. Excellent account of CP Branch life in London and the support she gets when she goes to Spain. Some good stories of selling literature, and second hand books, and the support from local community – other stall-holders when the fascists threaten to come, a local prostitute and a policeman.

4297 Greening, Edwin **From Aberdare to Albacete** *Warren & Pell* 2006 160pp pb Autobiog. of Welsh Communist miner.

4298 Gregory, Walter **The Shallow Grave: A Memoir of the Spanish Civil War** *Gollancz* 1986 183pp hb

4299 Greig, Ian **The Assault on the West** *Foreign Affairs Publ. Co.* 1968 357pp hb Wide-ranging right-wing attack on all aspects of Communism everywhere, but has quite a bit on CPGB – much from CP sources, so not very original.

4300 Griffiths, P. **The Changing Face of Communism** *Bodley Head* 1961 223pp hb Chapter on CPGB.

4301 Groves, Liane **The Life and Times of Alf Salisbury** *Cities of London & Westminster TC* 1993 30pp Unemployed campaigns, Spanish Civil War, rent strikes, Savoy picket, pensioners' movement etc.

4302 Groves, Reg **General Strike in Battersea: A Reassessment – Reminiscences by Jimmy Lane, Alf Loughton, H. Wicks** *Battersea LP* 1976 ? 16pp

4303 Groves, Reg **The Balham Group: How British Trotskyism Began** *Pluto* 1974 111pp pb

4304 Guest, C.H. (ed.) **David Guest: A Scientist Fights For His Freedom** *L&W* 1939 256pp pb

4305 Guggenheim, Peggy **Out of This Century** *A. Deutsch* 1983 396pp pb Autobiog. by famous art collector features material on Douglas Garman, one of her lovers. Through Garman she joined the CP. Garman himself worked for the CP after working for Ernest Wishart, his brother-in-law, who owned the publishing house which later merged to become part of L&W.

4306 Gupta, Parathi Sarathi **Imperialism and the British Labour Movement, 1914-64** *Macmillan* 1975 454pp Deals almost exclusively with LP – only a couple of passing refs to the CP, but interesting.

4307 Gupta, Sobhanlal **Comintern and the Destiny of Communism in India, 1919-1943** *Seribaan* 2006 329pp hb Many refs to CPGB.

4308 Hagger, Nicholas **Scargill the Stalinist? The Communist Role in the 1984 Miners' Strike** *Oak-Tree* 1984 128pp pb Foreword by F. Chapple. An awful book: half consists of quotes from Scargill to prove he is a revolutionary; the rest does have some useful biographical info., plus a little on the CP.

4309 Haithcox, John **Communism and Nationalism in India: M.N. Roy and Comintern Policy 1929-39** *Princeton UP* 1971 389pp Esp. on debates at 6th Congress of C.I.

4310 Haldane, Charlotte **Truth Will Out** *Weidenfeld* 1949 339pp hb She left the CP after working in the USSR as correspondent for the 'Daily Sketch' in 1941. Wife of J.B.S. Claims her son was youngest British volunteer in IB; she worked for Dependants Aid Cttee, so quite a bit on Spain.

4311 Hall, Christopher **'Disciplina Camaradas': Four English Volunteers in Spain, 1936-9** *Gosling Press* 1996 132pp pb M. Levine, B. McKenna, D. Goodman and S. Cottman were all in the YCL/CP at some time (Cottman, who fought with the POUM, for a short while). This book has quite a bit on the political background of the volunteers.

4312 Hall, Lesley **The Life and Times of Stella Browne** *IB Tauris* 2011 292pp Only a few, but interesting, refs to CP.

4313 Hallas, Duncan **The Comintern** *Bookmarks* 1985 184pp pb Especially on General Strike.

4314 Hallstrom, Bjorn **I Believed in Moscow** *Lutterworth* 1953 187pp hb A leading Swedish YCL member, at 18 he was involved in vetting all British YCL publications – because the YCI didn't trust the YCL, because Moscow saw the British YCL as 'the problem child of the YCL' and because they were short of English language speakers.

4315 Halpin, Kevin **Memoirs of a Militant** *Praxis Press* 2012 201pp pb Engineering activist (Fords) and Organiser for the LCDTU.

4316 Hamilton, Scott **The Crisis of Theory: E.P. Thompson, The New Left and Postwar British Politics** *MUP* 2011 293pp

4317 Hammond, Eric **Maverick: The Life of a Union Rebel** *Weidenfeld* 1992 214pp hb A few interesting comments on CP members in electricians' and printing unions by the anti-Communist Gen. Sec.

4318 Hanlon, Richard & Waite, Mike **Notes from the Left: Communism and British Classical Music** in *'A Weapon in the Struggle'* A. Croft (ed.) 1998 19pp pb

4319 Hann, Dave **Physical Resistance: A Hundred Years of Anti-Fascism** Zero Books 2013 407pp A comprehensive account that gives credit to all participants who fought fascism in Britain, though the author prioritises physical action. Much on the CP.

4320 Hannam, June & Hunt, Karen **Socialist Women: Britain, 1880s to 1920s** *Routledge* 2002 232pp Brief refs.

4321 Hannington, Wal **Never On Our Knees** *L&W* 1967 368pp hb

4322 Hannington, Wal **Tom Mann: A Short Biography** *Coventry Tom Mann Memorial Trades & Labour Hall Fund Cttee* 1947 8pp

4323 Hannington, Wal **Unemployed Struggles, 1919-36** *L&W* 1979 337pp pb Autobiog. that plays down his own role. This has index unlike the original ed. of 1936

4324 Hardy, George **Those Stormy Years** *L&W* 1956 256pp hb Slightly disappointing autobiog. by seaman and former Wobbly who joined CP and was leader of the MM.

4325 Harker, Ben **Class Act: The Cultural and Political Life of Ewan MacColl** *Pluto* 2007 348pp pb

4326 Harker, Dave **Fakesong: Popular Music in Britain** *Open Univ.* 1985 297pp pb Esp. on A.L. Lloyd.

4327 Harker, Dave **One For the Money: Politics and Popular Song** *Hutchinson* 1980 301pp pb Very brief refs to CP but interesting – 'The intervention of the CP … was absolutely crucial in the second folksong revival'.

4328 Harman, Claire **Sylvia Townsend Warner: A Biography** *Chatto* 1989 358pp hb

4329 Harries, M. & S. **A Pilgrim Soul: The Life and Work of Elisabeth Lutyens** *M. Joseph* 1989 324pp hb Disappointingly few refs to this composer's brief CP membership (though her husband, the interesting Edward Clark, was in much longer). Discusses the curious 1955 libel case between Clark and Ben Frankel, which involved CP members. Lutyens' autobiog. does not mention the CP – apart from a King Street offer to organise baby-sitting for her so she could attend a meeting.

4330 Harrison, Martin **Trade Unions and the Labour Party Since 1945** *A&U* 1960 360pp hb

4331 Harrison, Stanley **Good to be Alive: The Story of Jack Brent** *L&W* 1954 96pp hb Activist who was crippled following wounding in Spain.

4332 Harrison, Stanley **Poor Men's Guardians: A Survey of the Struggles for a Democratic Newspaper Press, 1763-1973** *L&W* 1974 256pp pb Harrison, who played an important role in the award-winning designs of the 'DW' and 'MS', includes the history of Communist newspaper production in this history.

4333 Hart, Richard **Rise and Organise: The Birth of the Workers' and National Movements in Jamaica, 1936-1939** *Karia Press* 1989 157pp Couple of pages in last chapter refer to contacts with CPGB.

4334 Hasted, John **Alternative Memoirs** *Greengates Press* 1994 204pp pb lf Professor of physics and musician; much on WMA and political songs in general.

4335 Hasted, John **It's my Paper!** *WMA* 1950 ? 4pp Song about the 'DW', music by Bob Claiborne.

4336 Hauser, Kitty **Bloody Old Britain: O.G.S. Crawford and the Archaeology of Modern Life** *Granta* 2009 286pp Crawford was a pioneer of aerial photography and archaeologist, and a pro-Soviet socialist who came close to British communism through archaeology – he knew and worked with Ralph Fox, Gordon Childe and Page Arnot, but he never joined the CP. He took millions of photographs – incl. series of Communist graffitti, and of every site in London associated with Marx, Engels and Lenin.

4337 Hayburn, Ralph **Purcell, Albert Arthur** in *'DLB'* 1 1972 4pp

4338 Hayburn, Ralph **The NUWM in Eccles, 1929-36** *Eccles & District History Society* 1972 15pp lf

4339 Healey, Denis **The Time of My Life** *Penguin* 1990 607pp pb Autobiog. by LP leader who never hid his short membership of YCL & who describes this period with some humour.

4340 Healy, Gerry **Revolution and Counter Revolution in Hungary** *New Park* 1956 14pp

4341 Heffer, Eric **Never A Yes Man** *Verso* 1991 251pp hb Autobiog. by activist &

Labour MP expelled from CP in 1948 for Trotskyism.

4342 Heinemann, Margot **'Left Review', 'New Writing' and the Broad Alliance Against Fascism** in *'Visions and Blueprints';* MUP 1988 24pp

4343 Heinemann, Margot **1956 and the Communist Party** in *'Socialist Register';* Merlin 1976 16pp

4344 Heinemann, Margot **The People's Front and the Intellectuals** in *'Britain, Fascism and the Popular Front'* J. Fyrth (ed.) 1985 30pp

4344a Henderson. Frank **Life on the Track: Memoirs of a Socialist Worker** Bookmarks 2009 123pp The CP crops up regularly in this autobiog. based on interviews with Matt Perry (as it does in the latter's Afterword). Includes an account of harrassment and violence by CP members when author was a 16 year old ILP member, after USSR entered the war.

4345 Henderson, Hamish **The Edinburgh People's Festival, 1951-54** in *'A Weapon in the Struggle'* A. Croft (ed.) 1998 8pp

4346 Henderson, H.W. **Communism in Industry** IRIS 1957 ? 8pp

4347 Henderson, H.W. **Spotlight on What British Communists Really Stand For** IRIS 1973 40pp

4348 Henderson, H.W. **This is Communism** s.p. 1946 ? 32pp

4349 Henderson, Stan **Comrades on the Kwai** Socialist History Society 1998 76pp Interesting account of trying to maintain CP organisation and political debate in Japanese P.O.W. camps.

4350 Hennessy, Peter **The Secret State: Whitehall and the Cold War** Penguin 2003 287pp

4351 Henning, Vida **Woman in a Shabby Brown Coat** Green Cottage Publishing; Bedhampton 2000 200pp Biog. of lifelong CP activist Ellen Cose (nee Cooper) by daughter, also in CP. Oxford, then Brighton postwar. Of interest especially for discussion on role of women, domestic violence.

4352 Hepburn, A.G. **Communism In Scotland** s.p. 1941 32pp Catholic, anti-Communist. In the interests of exposing CP influence in Scotland, author analyses all Scottish contributions to 'DW' Fighting Fund in April 1940! (Rutherglen came top).

4353 Heppell, Jason **A Question of 'Jewish Politics'? The Jewish Section of the CPGB, 1936-45** in *'Jews, Labour and the Left, 1918-48'* C. Collette and S. Bird (eds); Ashgate 2000 29pp

4354 Heppell, Jason **Party Recruitment: Jews and Communism in Britain** in *'Studies in Contemporary Jewry, Vol.XX: Dark Times, Dire Decisions – Jews and Communism';* OUP 2004 20pp

4355 Herbert, Michael & Taplin, Eric (eds) **Born With a Book in His Hand: A Tribute to Edmund Frow, 1906-97** NWLHG 1998 65pp Incl. obituaries and other articles on Frow,

4356 Herbert, Michael **Never Counted Out: The Story of Len Johnson, Manchester's Black Boxing Hero and Communist** Dropped Aitches Press 1992 123pp Johnson was born of an African father & an Irish Mancunian mother; he was barred from fighting for British titles because he was Black. Active in Black politics and in CP in 1940s & 1950s, regularly standing in elections.

4357 Heslop, Harold **Out of the Old Earth** Bloodaxe 1994 270pp Autobiog. of miner & one of the better CP writers of the 1930s, who was active in the MM. Edited by A. Croft & G. Rigby. R. Challinor calls this 'one of the finest autobiographies I have ever read' (LHR Spring 1995).

4358 Higgins, Jim **More Years For the Locusts: The Origins of the SWP** IS Group, London 1997 177pp Author was in CP till 1956 & describes his experiences in a Post Office Engineering factory branch; other refs to CP esp. 1956.

4359 Hill, Dennis **Seeing Red, Being Green** Iconoclast Press 1989 588pp Brighton activist.

4360 Hill, Denis ('Rocky') **Underdog Brighton: A Rather Different History of the Town** Iconoclast Press 1991 278pp

4361 Hill, May (ed.) **George Sinfield: His Pen a Sword – Memoirs and Articles** E. Sinfield 1988 106pp 'DW' journalist.

4362 Hill, May **Red Roses For Isabel** s.p. 1982 110pp Short uncritical biog. of CP National Women's Organiser in 1930s. Covers her role in Spanish Civil War.

4363 Hinsley, F.H. & Simkins, C.A.G. **British Intelligence in the Second World War** HMSO 1990 408pp Although a wide-ranging study, there is a lot of detailed information on CP.

4364 Hinton, James **Shop Floor Citizens: Engineering Democracy in 1940s Britain** E. Elgar 1994 222pp

4365 Hinton, James **The CP, Production and Britain's Post-War Settlement** in *'Opening the Books'* G. Andrews et al. (eds) 1995 16pp

4366 Hinton, James & Hyman, Richard **Trade Unions and Revolution: The Industrial Politics of the Early British CP** *Pluto* 1975 78pp 'From a revolutionary postion' looks at problems of a revolutionary party in a non-revolutionary situation, and criticises the 'non-revolutionary' positions of Martin and Macfarlane, the 'antiquarian' position of Klugmann and the 'orthodox Trotskyist' position of Pearce and Woodhouse'. Brief but important analysis.

4367 Hobbs, Sandy & Thompson, Willie **Out of the Burning: Political Socialization in the Age of Affluence** *Cambridge Scholars Press* 2011 175pp Thompson describes his transition from LP to CP.

4368 Hobday, Charles (ed.) **Communist and Marxist Parties of the World** *Longman* 1986 529pp 3 pages on CPGB.

4369 Hobday, Charles **Edgell Rickword: A Poet at War** *Carcanet* 1989 337pp Poet, critic, ed. of radical journals ('Left Review', 'Our Time').

4370 Hobsbawm, Eric **Afterword** in *'Opening the Books'* G. Andrews et al. (eds) 1995 3pp Discusses why CP history is important.

4371 Hobsbawm, Eric et al.(eds) **George Rudé 1910-93: Marxist Historian – Memorial Tributes** *SHS* 1995 24pp

4372 Hobsbawm, Eric **Interesting Times** *Allen Lane* 2002 447pp Autobiog. of the lifelong Communist historian; very useful on Cambridge students in 1930s.

4373 Hobsbawm, Eric **Maurice Dobb** Intro. to *'Socialism, Capitalism and Economic Growth: Essays Presented to M. Dobb'* C. Feinstein (eds); *CUP* 1967 8pp

4374 Hobsbawm, Eric **Politics for a Rational Left** *Verso* 1989 250pp Collection of articles, incl. from 'MT'. Does contain new translation of an interview from a German mag. dealing with CP.

4375 Hobsbawm, Eric **Revolutionaries** *Quartet* 1982 278pp Includes his famous critique of Klugmann's 'History of the CPGB', plus review of Newton and Kendall.

4376 Hodge, Herbert **It's Draughty in Front: The Autobiography of a London Taxidriver** *M. Joseph* 1938 286pp Hodge was in Soho branch in the 1920s and active in the NUWM; left CP for Mosley's New Party.

4377 Hodgkin, Dorothy **J.D. Bernal 1901-71** offprint from *'Biographical Memoirs of Fellows of the Royal Society'*, Dec. 1980 70pp pb Incl. extensive bibliography.

4378 Hodgson, Keith **Fighting Fascism: The British Left and the Rise of Fascism 1919-1939** *MUP* 2010 242pp

4379 Hogarth, Paul **Afterword** in *'A Weapon in the Struggle'* A. Croft (ed.) 1998 3pp pb Personal recollection of the contradictions facing a Communist artist.

4380 Hogarth, Paul **Drawing on Life: Autobiography** *David and Charles* 1997 192pp hb Incl. the activities of this world famous illustrator in Spain, in the AIA, in CP's cultural mags ('Our Time' etc.). Left CP in 1956. Many illustrations.

4381 Hogenkamp, Bert **Deadly Parallels: Film and the Left in Britain 1929-39** *L&W* 1986 240pp pb

4382 Hogenkamp, Bert **The Sunshine of Socialism: The CPGB and Film in the 1950s** in *'A Weapon in the Struggle'* A. Croft (ed.) 1998 15pp pb

4383 Hogenkamp, Bert **The Workers' Film Movement in Britain, 1929-39** in *'Propaganda, Politics and Film, 1918-45'* N. Pronay (ed.); *Macmillan* 1982 13pp hb

4384 Hogg, Douglas **The Communist Conspiracy** *Anti-Socialist & Anti-Communist Union* 1925 48pp From his speech at the trial of CP leaders in Nov. (He was Attorney-General at the time.)

4385 Høgsbjerg, Christian **Chris Braithwaite** *SHS* in association with Redwords 2014 118pp pb A shorter version appeared in 'Race & Class', Oct. 2011.

4386 Holford, John **Reshaping Labour: Organisation, Work and Politics: Edinburgh in the Great War and After** *Croom Helm* 1988 276pp hb One of the few studies of a locality in this period.

4387 Hollingsworth, Mark & Norton-Taylor, Richard **Blacklist: The Inside Story of Political Vetting** *Hogarth Press* 1988 258pp pb Quite a few refs to CP, but nothing in index.

4388 Hollis, Christopher **About Communism** *Conservative Political Centre* 1948 34pp

4389 Holt, William **I Haven't Unpacked** *Harrap* 1939 205pp hb Autobiog. by the eccentric artist, novelist, unemployed activist, broadcaster, inveterate traveller (on horseback) & one-time CP councillor in Todmorden.

4390 Holt, William **I Was A Prisoner** *J. Miles* 1934 155pp The first ed. was self published; this second ed. has illustrations by Wragg and a short biog.

4391 Hooper, Barbara **Cider With Laurie: Laurie Lee Remembered** *Peter Owen* 1999 207pp hb

4392 Hopkins, James K. **Into the Heart of the Fire: The British in the Spanish Civil War** *Stanford UP* 1998 475pp hb Wealth of material on many CP members.

4393 Horne, Robert **'Workers' Weekly': Vote of Censure Proposed** *HMSO* 1924 61pp Official Report of Parliamentary Debate, Oct. 8.

4394 Horne, Harold **All the Trees Were Bread and Cheese** *Owen Hardisty* 1998 74pp pb Engineering Shop Steward in Luton & London. Company Commander of British Battalion I.B.

4395 Horner, Arthur **Incorrigible Rebel** *MacGibbon & Kee* 1960 235pp hb Autobiog. by President of South Wales Miners Fed., and leading member of CP.

4396 Horner, Arthur **Trade Unions and Communism** *Labour Monthly* 1948 8pp Reprinted from 'LM', Feb.

4397 Hoskins, Katharine **Today the Struggle: Literature and Politics in England During the Spanish Civil War** *University of Texas Press* 1969 294pp hb Useful on the writers of the period and their attitude to the CP.

4398 Howard, Peter **Beyond Communism to Revolution** *Oxford Group* 1963 14pp

4399 Howarth, T.E.B. **Cambridge Between Two Wars** *Collins* 1978 258pp hb No index entry for CP but material can be found through name index.

4400 Howe, Antony **Torr, Dona** in *'DLB' 12* 2005 7pp

4401 Howe, Stephen **Anticolonialism in British Politics: The Left and the End of Empire, 1918-64** *OUP* 1993 389pp hb Much on CP.

4402 Howell, David **Casasola, Rowland** in *'DLB' 4* 1977 3pp

4403 Howell, David; Kirby, Dianne & Morgan, Kevin (eds) **John Saville: Commitment and History – Themes from the Life and Work of a Socialist Historian** *L&W* 2011 224pp pb

4404 Howell, David **Nicholas of Glais: The People's Champion** *Clydach Historical Society* 1991 50pp On T.E. Nicholas.

4405 Howell, David **Respectable Radicals: Studies in the Politics of Railway Trade Unionism** *Ashgate* 1999 446pp

4406 Howell, David **The Rise and Fall of Bevanism** *ILP* 1977 ? 43pp

4407 Howkins, Alun **Class Against Class: The Political Culture of the CPGB, 1930-1935** in *'Class, Culture and Social Change'* F. Gloversmith (ed.) 1980 18pp

4408 Hudson, Kate **Let's Face the Future: The Labour Party's Programme and Communist Co-operation** in *'The Democratic and Social Progress, 1942-1945'; Budapest* 1997 5pp pb Covers 1944-7.

4409 Hudson, Kate **Post-Communism: The Impact in Britain – Decline and Demise of the CPGB** in *'Questions of Ideology': Occasional Papers No.1, South Bank Univ., London* 1993 13pp lf Analysis of the end of the CP by a participant/academic.

4410 Hudson, Kate **The CPGB and the Labour Party, 1945-1948** in *'The Forward March of the Left and the Problems of Its Progess 1945-1948; Magyar Lajos Alapitvany'* 2001 5pp pb

4411 Hughes, Mike **Spies at Work: The Rise and Fall of the Economic League** *1 in 12 Publications* 1995 172pp Includes cases where this right-wing and anti-union organisation worked against the CP: Invergordon, the legal case against the 'DW', 1966 seamen's strike etc.

4412 Hunt, Karen **Dora Montefiore: A Different Communist** in *'Party People, Party Lives'* J. McIlroy, K. Morgan, Campbell, A. (eds) 2001 21pp

4413 Hunter, Bill **Lifelong Apprenticeship** *Index/Porcupine* 1997 440pp pb Lifelong Liverpool Trotskyist, active in engineering industry – much on CP.

4414 Hunter, Bill **They Knew Why They Fought: Unofficial Struggles and Leadership on the Docks, 1945-89** *Index Books* 1994 134pp pb

4415 Hunter, Ian **Ten Years for the Locust Reconsidered: An Essay on Trotskyism in Britain, 1938-49** s.p. 1989 22pp Reply to J. Higgins in 'I.S.' Autumn 1963; info. on Balham Group & CP. Revised ed.

4416 Hurd, Michael **Rutland Boughton and the Glastonbury Festivals** *OUP* 1993 415pp hb British composer who joined CP in 1925, left in 1929 because he felt the Party was not using him and his abilities; rejoined in 1945, left 1956.

4417 Hutt, Allen **This Final Crisis** *Gollancz* 1936 268pp hb

4418 Hutton, J.B. **The Subverters of Liberty** *W.H. Allen* 1972 266pp hb Awful – e.g.

claims that the Russians, through the CP, fermented the Notting Hill 'Race Riots' in 1958.

4419 Hyde, Douglas **Communism and the Home** *Catholic Truth Society* 1954 16pp

4420 Hyde, Douglas **Communism At Work** *Catholic Truth Society* 1953 20pp At least 30,000 printed.

4421 Hyde, Douglas **Communism from the Inside** *Catholic Truth Society* 1948 24pp

4422 Hyde, Douglas **From Communism Towards Catholicism** *Paternoster* 1948 22pp

4423 Hyde, Douglas **I Believed** *Reprint Society* 1952 285pp hb Hyde was News Ed. at the 'DW' when he resigned from the CP in a blaze of publicity, turning to Catholicism. Curiously, in his later years he moved closer again.

4424 Hyde, Douglas **The Answer to Communism** *Paternoster* 1949 70pp pb Mainly general, though some material on CPGB.

4425 Hyde, Douglas **The Peaceful Assault: The Pattern of Subversion** *Bodley Head* 1963 127pp

4425a Hyland, Bernadette (ed.) **Northern ReSisters: Conversations with Radical Women** *Mary Quaile Club* 2015 76pp pb See interviews with Betty Tebbs and Linda Clair.

4426 Hynes, Samuel **The Auden Generation: Literature and Politics in England in the 1930s** *Bodley Head* 1976 428pp hb Full coverage of the politics of writers of the period.

4427 Inglis, Fred **Raymond Williams** *Routledge* 1995 333pp hb A fine biog.

4428 Inglis, Fred **The Cruel Peace: Everyday Life in the Cold War** *Aurum* 1992 492pp Incl. chapters on E.P. Thompson and Frank Thompson, but little on CP.

4429 Ingram, Kevin **Rebel: The Short Life of Esmond Romilly** *Weidenfeld* 1985 252pp hb More on CP than appears from the index. Good on David Archer's Parton Street Bookshop.

4429a Jackson, Angela **For Us It Was Heaven: The Passion, Grief and Fortitude of Patience Darton, From the Spanish Civil War to Mao's China** *Sussex Academic Press* 2012 239pp

4430 Jackson, Ben **Equality and the British Left: A Study in Progressive Political Thought, 1900-64** *MUP* 2007 259pp pb Some refs to CP influence in the 1930s.

4431 Jackson, E. **Congress: An Appeal to Delegates** *Appeal Group* 1971 40pp lf d

4432 Jackson, T.A. **Solo Trumpet** *L&W* 1953 166pp hb Fascinating character: self taught intellectual, renowned for his dirty clothes and unkempt appearance and his oratory.

4433 Jackson, T.A. **The Communists: The Twelve of 1925** in *'Trials of British Freedom'*; *L&W* 1940 16pp hb

4434 Jacobs, Joe **Out of the Ghetto** *J. Simon* 1978 320pp pb Famous autobiog. by leading East End Jewish anti-fascist activist, who was expelled from CP, for second time, in 1952. He moved to Trotskyism then Syndicalism.

4435 Jameson, Derek **Touched by Angels** *Ebury Press* 1988 217pp hb This autobiog. has surprisingly affectionate memories of YCL (he was the only non Jewish member of Hackney YCL); Pollitt advised him to concentrate on a career in journalism rather than stay in the YCL when his employers at Reuters (where he was known as the 'Red Menace') forced him to choose. He went on to edit 3 tabloid newspapers, known for their soft porn.

4436 Jeffery, Keith & Hennessy, Peter **States of Emergency: British Governments and Strikebreakers Since 1919** *RKP* 1983 312pp hb Especially on governmental fears of CP in industry, late 1940s-early 1950s.

4437 Jenkins, Mark **Bevanism: Labour's High Tide** *Spokesman* 1979 323pp hb

4438 Jenkins, Mick **Brown, George** in *'DLB'* 3 1976 2pp

4439 Joannou, Maroula **Sylvia Townsend Warner in the 1930s** in *'A Weapon in the Struggle'* A. Croft (ed.) 1998 17pp pb

4440 Johns, Stephen **Reformism on the Clyde** *SLL* 1973 128pp pb Esp. on J. Reid.

4441 Johnson, Barry **Nine Days That Shook Mansfield** *The Ragged Historians* 2005 78pp pb General Strike. Very brief refs, incl. Rose Smith.

4442 Johnson, Buzz **'I Think of My Mother': Notes on the Life and Times of Claudia Jones** *Karia Press* 1985 194pp pb Unfortunately little on her membership of CPGB – more on her work in USA, then after her imprisonment and deportation to Britain, on her work in the West Indian community.

4443 Johnson, Stowers **Agents Extraordinary** *Hale* 1975 192pp hb Partly on Major Frank Thompson, a British agent who died fighting with the Bulgarian guerrillas in 1944.

4443a Johnston, Roy **Century of Endeavour: A Biographical & Autobiographical View of** the Twentieth Century in Ireland *Lilliput* 2003 576pp Incl. material on C. Desmond Greaves.

4444 Johnstone, Monty **Britain: Prospects for the Seventies** in *'Socialist Register'; Merlin* 1970 13pp

4445 Jones, Bob **Left-Wing Communism in Britain, 1917-21** *Pirate Press* 1991 14pp Argues that the Moscow imposed formation of the CPGB marginalised healthy anti-Parliamentary trends in British socialism and anarchism.

4446 Jones, Greta **Science, Politics and the Cold War** *Routledge* 1988 150pp Esp. on Haldane, Bernal and the Lysenko debate.

4447 Jones, Jack **Unfinished Journey** *H. Hamilton* 1937 318pp hb Welsh writer. Jones attended, and gives lively description of, founding Conference of CP in this autobiog. He left in 1923, joined Labour Party, then Liberal Party, New Party and ended up supporting the Tories.

4448 Jones, Jean **Ben Bradley: Fighter for India's Freedom** *SHS* 1994 40pp

4449 Jones, Jean **Bradley, Ben** in *'DLB' 10* 2000 5pp

4450 Jones, Jean **The League Against Imperalism** *Socialist History Society* 1996 43pp pb

4451 Jones, Stephen **Sport, Politics and the Working Class** *MUP* 1988 228pp hb Deals with British Workers' Sports Federation and much more.

4452 Jones, Stephen **The British Labour Movement and Film** *RKP* 1987 248pp hb Contains chapter on 'The Communist Movement & Film' & much other material.

4453 Jones, Stephen **Workers at Play: A Social and Economic History of Leisure, 1918-39** *RKP* 1986 286pp hb

4454 Joseph, Yvonne & Jean-Baptiste, Louisa **Claudia Jones 1915-64: A Woman of Our Times** *Camden Black Sisters Group* 1988 ? 16pp lf

4455 Joynson-Hicks, William **Communist Plotting: Lessons from the General Strike** *National Union of Conservative & Unionist Associations* 1926 12pp Reprint in pamphlet form of a rather flimsy letter by the Home Secretary.

4456 Jupp, James **The Radical Left in Britain 1931-41** *F. Cass* 1982 261pp hb

4457 Kadish, Sharman **'London Jews and British Communism' by H. Srebrnik – Review** in *'Studies in Contemporary Jewry, Vol. XIII: Fate of the European Jews, 1939-1945 – Continuity or Contingency'* 1997 2pp

4458 Kadish, Sharman **Bolsheviks and British Jews** *Cass* 1992 298pp hb Detailed information on the period preceeding the formation of the CP and its earliest years.

4459 Kane, Jock **No Wonder We Were Rebels: An Oral History** *Armthorpe NUM* 1994 122pp pb

4460 Kapp, Yvonne & Mynatt, Margaret **British Policy and the Refugees, 1933-1941** *Cass* 1997 152pp hb Foreword by C. Brinson has biographical material on Kapp and Mynatt; very little has been written on Mynatt – Austrian born, member of Brecht's circle, alleged Comintern courier, who became Manager of Central Books.

4461 Kapp, Yvonne **Time Will Tell: Memoirs** *Verso* 2003 296pp hb Active in anti-fascist refugee support in the 1930s, she became Chief Research Officer for the AEU. She was a writer, translator and historian playing a role in the Historians' Group. Contains some details about the life of Margaret Mynatt, her partner.

4462 Karat, Prakash (ed.) **Across Time and Continents: A Tribute to Victor G. Kiernan** *LeftWords Books* 2003 255pp hb Covers the Historians' Group (chapters by H. Kaye & E. Hobsbawm). Also India.

4463 Katz, Philip **The Long Weekend: Combating Unemployment During the Inter-War Years** *Hetherington Press* 2001 182pp pb Mainly on the NUWM.

4464 Kaye, Harvey & McClelland, Keith (eds) **E.P. Thompson: Critical Perspectives** *Polity* 1990 283pp Robert Gray's chapter is only one to refer in any detail to the CP.

4465 Kaye, Harvey **The British Marxist Historians** *Macmillan* 1995 316pp pb This 2nd ed. has new Preface, plus foreword by E. Hobsbawm.

4466 Kaye, Harvey **The Education of Desire: Marxists and the Writing of History** *Routledge* 1992 211pp pb Chapters on Rudé, Kiernan, Thompson, Morton etc.

4467 Keable, Ken (ed.) **London Recruits: The Secret War Against Apartheid** *Merlin Press* 2012 348pp pb Most of the young white people who went to South Africa on secret missions for the ANC from 1970 were recruited in London by Ronnie Kasrils, through the structures of the CP and YCL.

4468 Keating, Conrad **Smoking Kills: The Revolutionary Life of Richard Doll** *Signal*

Books 2009 495pp hb 'Perhaps Britain's most eminent doctor' (British Medical Journal), he was the world's leading expert on causes of cancer and was the first to publicly expose the role of tobacco in a scientific paper. As well as the tobacco industry, he took on the asbestos, nickel and gas industries over workers' health. Member of the CP, he was one of the individuals most singled out for vilification and attack by multinational companies in the 20th century.

4469 Keleman, Paul **The British Left and Zionism: History of a Divorce** *MUP* 2012 272pp

4469a Kelly, John **Rethinking Industrial Relations** *Routledge* 1998 177pp Only a few refs in this interesting study of industrial relations theory, but they direct the reader to some useful books.

4470 Kelly, Stephen **Idle Hands, Clenched Fists: The Depression in a Shipyard Town** *Spokesman* 1987 105pp pb On the unemployed riots in Birkenhead in 1932; much on Joe Rawlings.

4471 Kelly, Stephen **Rawlings, Joseph** in *'DLB'* 8 1987 4pp

4472 Kemp, Harry & Riding, Laura et al. **The Left Heresy in Literature and Life** *Methuen* 1939 270pp hb Strange anti-Communist book – a sort of cultural critique of Communist attitudes, mainly on Britain, by an ex CP member. Much on literature and the arts.

4473 Kemsley, Walter (ed.) **Martin Eve Remembered** *Merlin* 1999 108pp pb Cambridge. Left CP 1956, founder of Merlin Press.

4474 Kendall, H. **The Communist Crisis** *Vanguard Pamphlets* 1957 18pp

4475 Kendall, Walter **The Revolutionary Movement in Britain 1900-21:The Origins of British Communism** *Weidenfeld* 1969 453pp hb Important study that concludes the formation of the CP was an error, an artificial imposition on the British labour movement. This is a key debate in the historiography of the CPGB. Forcibly countered by Hinton in SSLH No.19.

4476 Kenefick, William **Red Scotland! The Rise and Fall of the Radical Left, c1872 to 1932** *Edinburgh UP* 2007 230pp Useful information on Dundee and Aberdeen.

4477 Kenny, Michael **Communism and the New Left** in *'Opening the Books'* G. Andrews et al. (eds) 1995 15pp pb

4478 Kenny, Michael **The First New Left: British Intellectuals After Stalin** *L&W* 1995 216pp pb

4479 Keyworth, Florence **Invisible Struggles: The Politics of Ageing** in *'Feminism, Culture and Politics'* R. Brunt & C. Rowan (eds); *L&W* 1986 11pp

4480 Kibblewhite, Liz & Rigby, Andy **Fascism in Aberdeen: Street Politics in the 1930s** *Aberdeen People's Press* 1978 48pp pb

4481 Kimber, Jane **Famous Women of Lewisham** London Borough of Lewisham, Leisure Services Cttee 1986 44pp Article on Kath Duncan.

4482 King, Francis & Matthews, George (eds) **About Turn: The CP and the Outbreak of the Second World War – The Verbatim Record of the Central Committee Meetings, 1939** *L&W* 1990 318pp hb The hard-hitting and tense debates took place behind closed doors at the end of Sept. and beginning of Oct. and show the CP coming to terms with the instructions from Moscow to reverse its support for the war. A key work for understanding the politics and psychology of British Communists. Intro. by M. Johnstone.

4483 Kingsford, Peter **The Hunger Marchers in Britain, 1920-1940** *L&W* 1982 244pp

4484 Kingsley, Isabel **Is Materialism the Basis of Communism?** *Hendersons The Bomb Shop* 1926 45pp Intro. explains how the author, a CP member, tried to argue for her unusual anti-materialist (Spiritualist?) views within the CP but in vain! Her real name was Iris Kingston. Expelled from CP in 1926 (having been expelled from the Labour Party in 1919).

4485 Kisch, Richard **The Days of the Good Soldiers: Communists in the Armed Forces in WW2** *Journeyman Press* 1985 179pp pb Based on many interviews, as official records minimised the importance of political activity in the armed forces; covers the Cairo Parliament, Heliopolis House of Commons and other activities incl. various mutinies.

4486 Klaus, H. Gustav **James Barke: A Great-Hearted Writer, a Hater of Oppression, a True Scot** in *'A Weapon in the Struggle'* A. Croft (ed.) 1998 21pp pb

4487 Klaus, H. Gustav **The Literature of Labour** *St Martin's Press, NY* 1985 210pp hb Esp. for 1930s – Heslop etc.

4488 Klaus, H. Gustav (ed.) **The Socialist Novel in Britain** *Harvester* 1982 190pp hb Esp. relevant for CP and novels in 1950s/1960s.

4489 Klugmann, James History of the CPGB: Vol.1 Formation and Early Years 1919-1924 L&W 1980 381pp pb The very official history of the CPGB. Klugmann only wrote 2 vols – it was just not possible then to deal with more controversial and recent events. It is still packed with useful information.

4490 Klugmann, James History of the CPGB: Vol.2 The General Strike 1925-6 L&W 1980 373pp pb

4491 Knightley, Philip Philby: KGB Masterspy Pan 1988 291pp pb Quite a bit about CP in Cambridge.

4492 Knowles, Kenneth Strikes: A Study in Industrial Conflict OUP 1952 330pp hb

4493 Knox, William (ed.) Scottish Labour Leaders 1918-39 Mainstream 1984 270pp hb

4494 Koditschek, Theodore Marxism and the Historiography of Modern Britain in 'History, Economic History & the Future of Marxism' T. Brotherstone & G. Pilling (eds); Porcupine Press 1996 46pp pb

4495 Koonin (or Kunin), A.W. & A.I. The Communist Party of Great Britain Gos. Uchebno-Pedagogicheskoe Izd., Moscow 1931 110pp pb A Russian school text book in English, with English-Russian glossary. Much on the General Strike; includes extracts from leaflets and CP statements.

4496 Kramnick, Isaac & Sheerman, Barry Harold Laski: A Life on the Left H. Hamilton 1993 669pp hb

4497 Kushner, Tony & Valman, Nadia (eds) Remembering Cable Street: Fascism and Anti-Fascism in British Society Vallentine Mitchell 2000 288pp pb Stimulating account of CP involvement in, and interpretation/ mythologising of, the battle of Cable Street incl. in fiction and drama. Originally appeared as Special Issue of Jewish Culture and History, Winter 1998.

4498 Kushner, Tony The Persistence of Prejudice: Antisemitism in British Society During the 2nd World War MUP 1989 257pp hb CP activity mentioned in passing, but important material & refs.

4499 Laing, Stuart John Sommerfield's 'May Day' and Mass Observation in 'Class, Culture and Social Change' F. Gloversmith (ed.) 1980 19pp

4500 Laity, Paul (ed.) Left Book Anthology Gollancz 2001 254pp hb See intro.

4501 Lane, Tony Some Merseyside Militants of the 1930s in 'Building the Union' H. Hikins (ed.); Toulouse Press 1973 198pp hb The ed. & publisher of this book, Harold Hikins (also a poet), will be of interest to those studying the cultural impact of the CP on Merseyside. Reminiscences of J. Fitzgerald, J. Byrne, B. Pinguey.

4502 Langton, Winifred & Jacobsen, Fay Courage: An Account of the Lives of Eliza Adelaide Knight and Donald Adolphus Brown s.p. 2007 166pp Knight was a working class suffragette and founder member of the CP; her husband, Brown, a seaman and union activist was the son of a freed slave from Guyana. Langton, their daughter, was a lifelong CP member, active in community politics in Sheppey then Ulverston where she was a local celebrity due to her peace campaigning; did much work for Medical Aid for Vietnam. Jacobsen, Langton's daughter, was also in the CP. See also Barry 'The Courage of Her Convictions: Win Langton'.

4503 Laporte, Norman; Morgan, Kevin & Worley, Matthew (eds) Bolshevism, Stalinism and the Comintern: Perspectives on Stalinization, 1917-53 Palgrave Macmillan 2008 319pp Contains one chapter comparing Thaelmann and Pollitt by Laporte and Morgan, and another comparing the CPs of New Zealand and Britain by Taylor and Worley.

4504 Lashmar, Paul & Oliver, James Britain's Secret Propaganda War Sutton 1998 223pp Many more refs than in index. Important for state activities against the CP.

4505 Laski, Harold The Secret Battalion: An Examination of the Communist Attitude to the LP LP 1946 30pp

4506 Laws, J.A. & Peacock, H.L. Political Parties: A Comparative Survey W. Heffer & Sons 1937 54pp pb CP gets same space as Tories, LP, Liberals, ILP, BUF.

4507 Laybourn, Keith Marxism in Britain: Dissent, Decline and Re-emergence, 1945-c2000 Routledge 2006 206pp Concentrates on CPGB, but also covers Trotskyism.

4508 Laybourn, Keith The Rise of Socialism in Britain Sutton 1997 198pp pb

4509 Laybourn, Keith & Murphy, Dylan Under the Red Flag: A History of Communism in Britain Sutton 1999 233pp hb Rather pedestrian one-vol. history with many minor errors of detail.

4510 Lazitch, Branko & Drachkovitch, Milorad Biographical Dictionary of the Comintern

Hoover Institution, Stanford Univ. 1986 532pp 19 entries on CPGB members – the usual suspects plus P. Spratt & J. Tanner. Some errors, incl. saying J.T. Murphy was Scottish (repeated in Beckett's 'The Enemy Within').

4511 Lee, Jennie **Tomorrow Is Another Day** *Cressett* 1939 264pp hb Relates bitter arguments between Lee (ILP) and CP in Cowdenbeath.

4512 Leeming, David **Stephen Spender: A Life in Modernism** *Henry Holt* 1999 304pp hb

4513 Lehmann, John et al. (eds) **Ralph Fox: A Writer in Arms** *L&W* 1937 253pp hb Mainly selection of his writings but incl. various tributes, bibliography etc.

4514 Lerner, Shirley **Breakaway Unions and the Small Trade Unions** *A&U* 1961 210pp hb Chapter on the United Clothing Workers' Union – a breakaway from the Tailors' Union – led by CP members notably Sam Elsbury.

4515 Lessing, Doris **Walking in the Shade** *HarperCollins* 1997 369pp hb This 2nd vol. of autobiog. describes her membership of the CPGB in the 1950s.

4516 Levine, Maurice **Cheetham to Cordova: A Manchester Man of the Thirties** *N. Richardson* 1984 54pp Author joined CP in 1931; describes anti-fascist activities, Kinder trespass etc. Fought in Spain.

4517 Lewenstein, Oscar **Kicking Against the Pricks: A Theatre Producer Looks Back** *Nick Hern* 1994 210pp hb Autobiog. of active CP member who achieved fame as impressario and film producer. Unity Theatre, Living Theatre, Artistic Director of Royal Court etc. In his youth he worked in the Workers' Bookshop. Index weak.

4518 Lewis, Brian & Gledhill, Bill **Tommy James: A Lion of a Man** *Yorkshire Art Circus* 1985 82pp pb Unemployed activist in Rotherham. Member of I.B. – second part of book is his account of his time in Spain. A 2nd editon was published in 2010 by the I.B. Memorial Trust, Rotherham Branch.

4519 Lewis, C. Day **Letter to a Young Revolutionary** in *'New Country'; Hogarth Press* 1933 17pp

4520 Lewis, C. Day **The Buried Day** *Chatto* 1960 244pp hb In CP, 1935-8, in Cheltenham area.

4521 Lewis, Joel A. **Youth Against Fascism: Young Communists in Britain and the United States, 1919-1939** *VDM Verlag Dr. Muller* 2007 224pp

4522 Lewis, John **The Left Book Club** *Gollancz* 1970 163pp hb CP members were involved at all levels in the Club.

4523 Lewis, John et al. **The Communist Answer to the Challenge of Our Time** *Thames Publications* 1947 88pp pb

4524 Lewis, Jon (ed.) **Raising the Flag: Trotskyism and the Neath By-Election** *Antidoto Press, Cardiff* 1990 20pp lf d Collection of docs on May 1945 by-election.

4525 Lewis, Richard (ed.) **For the Public Good: Studies to Commemorate the Centenary of Stockton & District T.C.** *Tesside Poly* 1990 75pp Chapter on CP & the T.C. – concentrates on post-war period. Also other refs.

4526 Lewis, Richard **Leaders and Teachers: Adult Education and the Challenge of Labour in South Wales, 1906-40** *Univ. of Wales Press* 1993 271pp

4527 Lewis, Richard **Starr, Mark** in *'DLB'* 9 1993 7pp

4528 'Lex' **Youth for Communism? Challenge to Socialist Students** *Solidarity Press, Glasgow* 1942 64pp Leftist.

4529 Lidderdale, J. & Nicholson, M. **Dear Miss Weaver: Harriet Shaw Weaver 1876-1961** *Faber* 1970 509pp hb Weaver was Literary Executrix of James Joyce and a dual member of CP & LP in Oxford in 1930s.

4530 Liddington, Jill **The Life and Times of a Respectable Rebel** *Virago* 1984 536pp pb This biog. of ILP feminist Selina Cooper has brief sketches of CP activity among women in 1930s Lancashire, incl. Rose Smith.

4531 Liddington, Jill **The Road to Greenham: Feminism and Anti-Militarism in Britain Since 1820** *Verso* 1989 340pp hb Quotes from Vera Leff's unpublished memoir – she played important role in the organisations leading to the formation of CND.

4532 Lieven, Michael **Senghennydd, The Universal Pit Village, 1890-1930** *Gower* 1994 387pp See last 2 chapters, esp. court case involving Edwin Pitt who upset his landlord, a fellow miner, by using his rented rooms for CP meetings – with up to 50 visitors a week he kept folding chairs in the pantry & under his bed.

4533 Lilleker, Darren **Against the Cold War: The History and Political Traditions of Pro-Sovietism in the British Labour Party, 1945-89** *I.B. Tauris* 2004 294pp

4534 Lindsay, Jack **Life Rarely Tells** *Penguin* 1982 826pp pb Contains his autobiographical trilogy; very little on CP (though more than appears from the index), mostly in Epilogue.

4535 Linehan, Thomas **Communism in Britain, 1920-39: From the Cradle to the Grave** *MUP* 2007 213pp hb Looks at Communist attitude to children's upbringing, home life, marriage, morality, behaviour, lifestyle and death. Section on CP's children's movement and YCL.

4536 Linehan, Thomas **East London for Mosley** *Frank Cass* 1996 316pp

4537 Litvinoff, Emanuel **Journey Through a Small Planet** *Robin Clark* 1993 158pp pb Member of YCL in East London.

4538 Livingstone, Sheila **Bonnie Fechters: Women in Scotland, 1900-50** *Scottish Library Association* 1994 50pp lf Incl. brief biogs. of Mary Brooksbank, Marion Henery, Annie Murray.

4539 Lockyer, Robert **What is a Communist?** *Background Books, Batchworth* 1954 38pp

4540 Lotz, C. & Feldman, P. **Gerry Healy: A Revolutionary Life** *Lupus* 1994 366pp pb Leader of WRP was in CP in Cardiff in his youth.

4541 Lowe, Bert **Anchorman: Autobiography** s.p. 1996 180pp pb Building workers' leader, active in Stevenage – interesting on new towns.

4542 Lowles, Nick (ed.) **From Cable Street to Oldham: Seventy Years of Community Resistance** *Searchlight* 2007 170pp Esp. on Cable Street and Stepney Tenants' Defence League.

4543 Lucas, John (ed.) **The 1930s: The Challenge to Orthodoxy** *Harvester* 1978 268pp hb Incl. interview with E. Rickword; chapter on C. Caudwell; reminiscences by A. Rattenbury; plus material on S. Swingler, M. Slater, J. Boswell. Much on CP.

4544 Lynch **Speech** in *'Co-Report of YCI at 11th Plenum of ECCI'*, *Modern Books (?)* 1931 3pp Report of YCL's work.

4545 MacColl, Ewan **Journeyman** *Sidgwick & Jackson* 1990 400pp hb Autobiog. by the famous political folk-singer.

4546 MacDiarmid, Hugh **Lucky Poet: A Self-Study in Literature and Political Ideas – Autobiography** *Cape* 1972 436pp hb

4547 MacDiarmid, Hugh **The Company I've Kept: Essays in Autobiography** *Hutchinson* 1966 288pp hb

4548 MacDonald, J. Ramsay **Free Speech in Danger: The Significance of the Communist Prosecution** *ILP* 1925 16pp A speech in Parliament against the trial of CP leaders.

4549 MacDougall, Ian (ed.) **Essays in Scottish Labour History** *J. Donald* 1978 265pp hb See chapters on General Strike and The New Left.

4550 MacDougall, Ian (ed.) **Militant Miners** *Polygon* 1981 352pp hb Biog. of John McArthur & letters of David Proudfoot to A. Hutt. Fife miners' leaders

4551 MacDougall, Ian (ed.) **Voices From the Hunger Marches Vol.1: Personal Recollections by Scottish Hunger Marchers of the 1920s & 1930s** *Polygon* 1990 218pp pb All contributors were in YCL or CP (except one): F. Hart, H. McShane, P. Gillan, T. Ferns, J. Allison, M. Beattie, W. McVicar, J. Reilly, D. Burns, F. McCusker, A. McInnes, W. Stevenson, M. Henery, E. & I. Porte, Rab Smith, John Brown.

4552 MacDougall, Ian (ed.) **Voices From the Hunger Marches Vol.2** *Polygon* 1991 443pp pb In CP: Emily Swankie, Mary Johnston, Thomas Davidson, John Lochore, James Henderson, Hugh Sloan, Tom Clarke, Guy Bolton, John Lennox, David Anderson.

4553 MacDougall, Ian (ed.) **Voices From the Spanish Civil War: Personal Recollections of Scottish Volunteers** *Polygon* 1986 369pp pb 16 of the 20 interviewed were in CP: D. Renton, G. Watters, F. McCusker, P. Gillan, T. Clarke, A. Murray, D. Anderson, G. Murray, E. Brown, J. Dunlop, J. Londragan, H. Sloan, G. McCartney, D. Stirrat, G. Drever, T. Murray.

4553a MacDougall, Ian **Voices of Scottish Journalists** *Scottish Working People's History Trust/ John Donald* 2013 633pp pb See chapters on Tom McGowran (not a member but close) and George MacDougall (Worked at Glasgow Herald, then at 'DW').

4554 MacEwen, Malcolm **The Day the Party Had to Stop** in *'Socialist Register'*; *Merlin* 1976 20pp pb

4555 MacEwen, Malcolm **The Greening of a Red** *Pluto* 1991 306pp pb Preface by E.P. Thompson. MacEwen was leading journalist at 'DW' – he signed Minority Report on Inner Party Democracy in 1957 but then left CP.

4556 Macfarlane, Leslie **The British CP: Its Origin and Development Until 1929** *MacGibbon & Kee* 1966 338pp hb Important study that counters the emphasis of Kendall's controversial 'Revolutionary Movement in Britain'.

4556a MacGregor, Rosie, **Angela Remembered: The Life of Angela Gradwell Tuckett** *WaterMarx* 2015 54pp pb The first woman solicitor in Bristol. She caused a diplomatic incident when, as a member of the England Hockey team in Germany in 1935 she refused to give the Nazi salute. Worked for the 'DW' and 'Labour Monthly'. Later active in Swindon. Also a peace activist and a folk musician.

4557 Machin, H. (ed.) **National Communism in Western Europe: A Third Way to Socialism?** *Methuen* 1983 232pp

4558 MacIntyre, Alasdair **'Communism and British Intellectuals' by N. Wood – Review** in *'Alasdair MacIntyre's Engagement with Marxism: Selected Writings, 1853-1974'; Historical Materialism Vol.19,* 2008 8pp Text of a BBC radio broadcast, originally published in 'The Listener', Jan. 7 1960.

4559 Macintyre, Stuart **A Proletarian Science: Marxism in Britain, 1917-1933** *CUP* 1980 286pp hb Interesting and well researched. Links CP educational work with an earlier tradition in the Labour Movement; also useful on geographical differences.

4560 Macintyre, Stuart **Little Moscows** *Croom Helm* 1980 213pp hb Important study of areas with strong CP presence: Mardy, Lumphinnans & Vale of Leven. Widely recognised as one of the best studies of local CP activity.

4561 Mackie, Robert (ed.) **Jack Lindsay: The Thirties and Forties** *Univ.of London, Institute of Commonwealth Studies* 1984 97pp lf

4562 Mackney, Paul **Birmingham and the Miners' Strike** *Birmingham TUC* 1987 148pp pb Chapter on Role of the CP – 3 times the length of chapter on the LP, due to author's interest in splits in the CP.

4563 MacLachlan, Alastair **The Rise and Fall of Revolutionary England: An Essay on the Fabrication of 17th Century History** *Macmillan* 1996 431pp pb Includes detailed analysis of Historians' Group.

4564 Macleod, Alison **The Death of Uncle Joe** *Merlin* 1997 269pp pb Description of Communists at the 'DW' reacting to Soviet invasion of Hungary. Vivid mix of the personal and political, and one of the best accounts of coming to terms with Stalinism – or not, in some cases.

4565 Macpherson, Don (ed.) **Traditions of Independence: British Cinema in the Thirties** *British Film Institute* 1980 226pp pb Much on Left films, especially CP involvement.

4566 Mahon, John **Harry Pollitt** *L&W* 1976 567pp hb Exhaustive but very official biog.

4567 Maitland, Frank & Tait, William **'Socialism Through Victory': Victory for Whom? – Reply to J.R. Campbell** *T. Tait Memorial Cttee* 1942 ? 8pp Authors were Trotskyists in ILP.

4568 Margolies, David & Joannou, J. (ed.) **Heart of the Heartless World: Essays in Cultural Resistance in Memory of Margot Heinemann** *Pluto* 1995 240pp pb Includes biog. & bibliographical details of Heinemann; also includes an essay on her novel 'The Adventurers' with much info. on CP cultural policies.

4569 Margolies, David (ed.) **Writing the Revolution** *Pluto* 1998 208pp pb See the Introduction rather than the bulk of the book which consists of extracts from 'Left Review', which don't refer to the CP but which are imbued by its cultural politics.

4570 Marks, John **Fried Snowballs** *Claridge Press* 1990 367pp hb General right wing critique of Marxism, USSR etc. but has section on CPGB at end.

4571 Marks, Peter **Art and Politics in the 1930s** in *'The Oxford Critical History of Modernist Magazines Vol.1' P. Brooker & A. Thacker (eds); OUP* 2009 25pp On 'Left Review' and 'Poetry and the People', with some refs to CP literary figures.

4572 Marriott, John **The Culture of Labourism: The East End Between the Wars** *Edinburgh UP* 1991 198pp pb

4573 Marsh, Kevin & Griffiths, Robert **Granite and Honey: The Story of Phil Piratin, Communist MP** *Manifesto Press* 2012 256pp First biog. of the Stepney MP. Much on anti-fascist activity of 1930s, especially Cable Street, and housing struggles of the 1940s; also on CP and Jewish politics. Interesting on how the CP 'managed', or more usually did not, its MPs.

4574 Martin, David **Fletcher, George** in *'DLB'* 9 1993 9pp Sheffield bakery owner.

4575 Martin, David **Malone, Cecil John L'Estrange** in *'DLB'* 7 1984 7pp

4576 Martin, Roderick **Communism and the British Trade Unions, 1924-33: A Study of the National Minority Movement** *OUP* 1969

209pp hb Important document; subtlely argued.

4577 Massey, Bill **Shepherds Bush Memories** *Shepherds Bush Local History Project* 1981 16pp Chairman of Hammersmith Trades Council.

4578 Masters, Anthony **The Man Who Was M: The Life of Maxwell Knight** *Grafton* 1984 253pp pb

4579 Mates, Lewis **Practical Anti-Fascism? The Aid Spain Campaigns in the North East of England, 1936-1939** in *'British Fascism, The Labour Movement and the State'* N. Copsey & D. Renton (eds) 2005 20pp

4580 Mates, Lewis **The Spanish Civil War and the British Left: Political Activism and the Popular Front** *I.B. Tauris* 2007 292pp Includes details of local campaigns.

4581 Mather, Graham **The CPGB: Freedom's Foremost Enemy** *Aims for Freedom* 1978 18pp

4582 Mathers, Helen **Barton, Alfred** in *'DLB'* 6 1982 3pp

4583 Matkovsky, N.V. **A True Son of the British Working Class (Harry Pollitt)** *Progress* 1972 115pp pb Short uncritical biog.

4584 Matkovsky, N.V. **Great Soviet Encyclopedia Vol.12** *Macmillan* 1976 1pp This translation from the 3rd Russian ed. (1974 – 1983) has one double columned page entry on the CPGB. There are other short entries on various leaders in other vols (see Index vol.) but these are perfunctory, perhaps of use for dates they may have edited journals. But the translation is not perfect – Dutt was apparently a member of the Independent Workers' Party and not the ILP!

4585 Mattausch, John **A Commitment to Campaign: A Sociological Study of CND** *MUP* 1989 192pp hb Contains couple of interviews with anonymous CP members, but the index is no help.

4586 Maxwell, D.E.S. **Poets of the Thirties** *Routledge* 1969 224pp hb Contains chap. on 'C. Caudwell and J. Cornford – Poets in the Party'.

4587 Mayhew, Christopher **A War of Words: A Cold War Witness** *I.B. Tauris* 1998 148pp CP student at Oxford, later Labour MP; key figure in IRD, professional anti-communist but with no bitterness – interesting.

4588 Mayhew, Christopher **Party Games** *Hutchinson* 1969 176pp hb First chapter has a lot about CP/LP relations at Oxford in mid-1930s.

4589 McCann, Gerard **Theory and History: The Politcial Thought of E.P. Thompson** *Ashgate* 1997 194pp The first chapter is startlingly titled 'The Origins of British Communist Libertarianism'.

4590 McCarthy, Mary **Generation in Revolt** *Heinemann* 1953 276pp hb Autobiog. of activist (YCL & CP) from Lancs textile industry. Sec. of Burnley NUWM; worked in Moscow for a while. Later very anti-Communist.

4591 McCreery, Michael **Destroy the Old to Build the New! A Comment on the State, Revolution and the CPGB** *Cttee to Defeat Revisionism, For Communist Unity* 1963 13pp Maoist.

4592 McCreery, Michael **Organise at the Place of Work** *Cttee to Defeat Revisionism, For Communist Unity* 1964 6pp Argues for concentrating on factory branches as opposed to the 'constitutional' road to socialism.

4593 McCreery, Michael **Some Basic Criticisms of the 'CPGB'** *Workers' Bookclub, Glasgow* 1976 16pp Reprint of 'The Way Forward' from 1964.

4594 McCreery, Michael **The Way Forward: The Need to Establish a CP in England, Scotland & Wales** *Cttee to Defeat Revisionism, For Communist Unity* 1964 16pp Reprinted in collection of his pamphlets, also called 'The Way Forward', by the Working People's Party of England in 1972.

4595 McCrindle, Jean & Rowbotham, Sheila **Dutiful Daughters** *Penguin* 1983 396pp pb See interview with Catherina Barnes.

4596 McDermott, Kevin & Agnew, Jeremy **The Comintern: A History of International Communism From Lenin to Stalin** *Macmillan* 1996 304pp pb

4597 McGinn, Matt **McGinn of the Calton** *Glasgow City Libraries* 1993 201pp pb Autobiographical excerpts, songs and stories by the well known Glaswegian political folk-singer. 'My reputation was of a man who had left the CP so often that King Street was thinking of issuing specially perforated cards to tear up'.

4598 McGovern, John **Neither Fear nor Favour** *Blandford* 1960 236pp hb Autobiog. of ILP leader; chapter on the CP plus many other refs.

4599 McGuire, Charlie **Sean McLoughlin: Ireland's Forgotten Revolutionary** *Merlin*

Press 2011 186pp pb Irish nationalist and Communist.

4600 McIlroy, John **Birch, Reg** in *'DLB'* 13 2010 11pp

4601 McIlroy, John & Campbell, Alan **Coalfield Leaders, Trade Unionism and Communist Politics: Exploring Arthur Horner and Abe Moffat** in *'Towards a Comparative History of Coalfield Societies'* S. Berger (ed.); Ashgate 2005 17pp

4602 McIlroy, John **Grooves, Reg** in *'DLB'* 12 2005 13pp

4603 McIlroy, John **Haston, Jock** in *'DLB'* 12 2005 13pp

4604 McIlroy, John **Healy, Gerry** in *'DLB'* 12 2005 10pp

4605 McIlroy, John **Hobsbawm and SDP Socialism** *Workers' Liberty* 1984 22pp

4606 McIlroy, John; Campbell, Alan & Gildart, K. (eds) **Industrial Politics and the 1926 Mining Lockout: The Struggle for Dignity** *University of Wales Press* 2009 333pp Has a chapter by McIlroy on the CP, plus other refs incl. an entertaining account of a young woman actvist in South Wales, Lil Price.

4607 McIlroy, John; Campbell, Alan **McGahey, Mick** in *'DLB'* 13 2010 15pp

4608 McIlroy, John; Morgan, Kevin & Campbell, Alan (eds) **Party People, Communist Lives: Explorations in Biography** *L&W* 2001 256pp pb Important collection of well researched essays generally on lesser known CP members, or as in the case of Rust and Smith who held leading positions, on whom there is no other published work. D. Montefiore, A. Reade, W. Rust, Rose Smith, A. Horner, R. Swingler, J. Gaster, Willie Allan, D. Proudfoot, Abe Moffat. One general chapter on Communist biog., plus another on British Communists in the USSR between the wars. The 'Who's Who' has very useful biographical comments.

4609 McIlroy, John **Reade, Arthur** in *'DLB'* 11 2003 6pp In CP in Oxford in early 1920s. Moved to Trotskyism.

4610 McIlroy, John (ed.) **Revolutionary History Vol.9 No.3** *Porcupine Press/Socialist Platform* 2006 276pp pb 4 articles in this issue are specifically about the CPGB and are listed separately, while others by McIlroy and Flewers also refer to it.

4611 McIlroy, John **Sara, Henry** in *'DLB'* 11 2003 12pp In CP for about 10 years from 1922 before becoming a Trotskyist.

4612 McIlroy, John; Campbell, Alan & Geldart, Keith (eds) **The Struggle for Dignity: Industrial Politics and the 1926 Lockout** *University of Wales Press* 2004 334pp

4613 McIlroy, John **The Young Manhead of Arthur Reade** in *'Party People, Party Lives'* J. McIlroy, K. Morgan, A. Campbell, (eds) 2001 27pp

4614 McInnes, Neil **The Communist Parties of Western Europe** *OUP* 1975 209pp hb

4615 McKibbin, Ross **The Evolution of the Labour Party, 1910-24** *OUP* 1983 261pp hb

4616 McKinlay, Alan & Morris, R.J. (eds) **The ILP on Clydeside, 1893-1932** *MUP* 1991 248pp

4617 McKnight, David **Espionage and the Roots of the Cold War** *F. Cass* 2002 226pp Includes brief survey of CP's anti-military activities. Also interesting material on work of George Hardy for Profintern in Asia.

4618 McLachlan, Kenny **One Great Vision: Memoirs of a Glasgow Worker** *s.p.* 1995 151pp pb Author active in CP in Glasgow from 1938 till expelled in 1966; became President of E.I.S.

4619 McLaine, Ian **Ministry of Morale: Home Front Morale and the Ministry of Information in World War 2** *A&U* 1979 325pp

4620 McLean, Iain **The Legend of Red Clydeside** *J. Donald* 1983 296pp hb Few refs to CP but useful on W. Gallacher and origins of CP in Scotland and also as the start of a long-running debate on 'Red Clydeside'.

4621 McLoughlin, Barry **Visitors and Victims: British Communists in Russia Between the Wars** in *'Party People, Party Lives'* J. McIlroy, K. Morgan, Campbell, A. (eds) 2001 21pp Incl. Margaret McCarthy, Jane Tabrisky (Degras), Freda Utley, Violet Lansbury, Rose Cohen and some lesser known activists and victims – all shameful episodes in Soviet and British communism.

4622 McNeish, James **The Sixth Man: The Extraordinary Life of Paddy Costello** *Quartet* 2008 414pp New Zealander who joined CPGB at Cambridge in 1930s and was accused of being a spy – wrongly, suggests this book.

4623 McShane, Denis **International Labour and the Origins of the Cold War** *OUP* 1992 324pp hb Esp. chap. on 'UK Metalworkers and Communism'.

4624 McShane, Harry & Smith, Joan **No Mean Fighter** *Pluto* 1978 283pp pb McShane was a leading Scottish Communist who left in the early 1950s and who moved close to Trotskyism.

4625 McShane, Harry **Three Days That Shook Edinburgh: Story of the Historic Scottish Hunger March** *AK Press* 1994 32pp This reprint of 1933 pamphlet has brief profiles of Aitken Ferguson & Harry McShane.

4626 Mercer, Paul **'Peace' of the Dead: The Truth Behind the Nuclear Disarmers** *Policy Research Publ.* 1986 465pp hb Right-wing but useful on CP relationship with CND.

4627 Meynell, Francis **My Lives** *Random* 1971 331pp hb Autobiog. of well known cultural figure who edited 'The Communist' for 6 months in 1920s.

4628 Middlemas, Keith **Politics in Industrial Society** *A. Deutsch* 1979 512pp Passing refs to CP and relations with TUC & LP.

4629 Miliband, Ralph **John Saville: A Presentation** in *'Ideology and the Labour Movement' D. Martin & D. Rubinstein (eds); Croom Helm* 1979 17pp hb

4630 Miliband, Ralph **Moving On** in *'Socialist Register'; Merlin* 1976 13pp pb Critique of all left parties/orgs. 20 years after Hungary – much on CP.

4631 Miller, Joan **One Girl's War** *Brandon* 1986 155pp hb Working for the secret services, she broke into R.P. Dutt's flat in search of a mysterious trunk only to find his marriage certificate!

4632 Milotte, Mike **Communism in Modern Ireland** *Gill and Macmillan* 1984 326pp Useful on relations between the CPs of GB and Ireland, esp. early years.

4633 Mirsky, Dmitri **The Intelligentsia of Great Britain** *Gollancz* 1935 237pp hb Passing refs.

4634 Mitchell, Alex **Behind the Crisis in British Stalinism** *New Park* 1984 128pp pb Trotskyist.

4635 Mitchell, David **The Fighting Pankhursts** *Cape* 1967 352pp

4636 Mitchell, Renate Zemke (ed.) **Children of Workers** *s.p.* 1999 44pp A document of family history, includes autobiographies of Johnny Mitchell and Lizzy Bain who married and were active in the YCL and CP in Glasgow. Plus some other writings on W. Gallacher and J. Maclean. Also accessible online.

4637 Mitford, Jessica **Faces of Philip: A Memoir of Philip Toynbee** *Heinemann* 1984 175pp hb An upper-class Communist in Oxford in the 1930s.

4638 Mitford, Jessica **Hons and Rebels** *Gollancz* 1960 222pp pb Together with its sequel, 'A Fine Old Conflict' 1977, this autobiog. contains some passing refs to the CPGB – incl. a wonderful story of how she tried to donate her share of a family owned Scottish island to the CP. Neither Jessica, nor her husband Esmond Romilly, actually joined the CPGB though they were 'staunch fellow travellers' in her words; she was to become very active in the CPUSA.

4639 Modin, Yuri **My Five Cambridge Friends** *Headline* 1994 282pp pb The Cambridge spies by their Soviet controller. Interesting on Klugmann.

4640 Moffat, Abe **My Life With the Miners** *L&W* 1965 324pp hb The most well-known of three brothers (with Alex and Dave) in Lumphinnans in Fife who became leaders of the miners' union, and long-sitting Communist county councillors in the case of Abe and Alex.

4641 Montagu, Ivor **The Youngest Son** *L&W* 1970 384pp hb Autobiog. by member of aristocracy who became leading cultural figure in the CP.

4642 Montefiore, Dora **From a Victorian to a Modern** *E. Archer* 1927 222pp Last chapter describes her attendance at CP's founding conference and then election to EC, and her going 'on the run' in 1921 disguised as a nurse in South Wales.

4643 Moore, Bill **All Out: The Story Of the Sheffield Demonstration Against Dole Cuts, Feb. 6 1935** *Sheffield City Libraries* 1983 ? 66pp lf

4644 Moore, Bill et al. **Behind the Clenched Fist: Sheffield's Aid to Spain, 1936-1939** *Holberry Society* 1986 22pp lf Material on Arthur Newsum, a Young Communist killed fighting in Spain.

4645 Moore, Bill **The Cold War in Sheffield** *Sheffield T.C. Peace Sub Cttee* 1990 30pp Brief appendix on his experience as a teacher when a local vicar tried to initiate a witch-hunt.

4646 Moore, Bill (ed.) **The General Strike in Sheffield** *Holberry Society* 1981 56pp pb lf Much on CP incl. reproduced bulletins & leaflets.

4647 Moorhouse, John **A Historical Glossary of British Marxism** *Pauper's Press* 1987 48pp Very brief section on CP but there are other refs.

4648 Morgan, Dave **A Short History of Dave Morgan** s.p. 1992 223pp pb Teacher and full-time CP worker in Bristol.

4649 Morgan, Dave **A Short History of the British People** VEB, Leipzig 1979 181pp hb A textbook written by a hardline British Communist for use in the former GDR, it hugely over-emphasises the role of the CP.

4650 Morgan, Dave **Looking Back to Look Forward** s.p. 1993 19pp Short, personal assessment of impact of Stalinism on CP.

4651 Morgan, Kevin **A Family Party? Some Geneaological Reflections on the CPGB** in 'Agents of the Revolution' K. Morgan et al. (eds) 2005 24pp

4652 Morgan, Kevin **Against Fascism and War: Ruptures and Continuities in British Communist Politics, 1935-1941** MUP 1989 328pp hb

4653 Morgan, Kevin & Cohen, Gidon (eds) **Agents of the Revolution: New Biographical Approaches to the History of International Communism in the Age of Lenin and Stalin** Peter Lang 2005 319pp pb Three chapters on CPGB, incl. one on W. Gallacher; one based on interviews that considers family links within the CP; final one analyses class, gender, age.

4654 Morgan, Kevin **An Exemplary Communist Life? Harry Pollitt's 'Serving My Time' in Comparative Perspective** in 'Making Reputations: Power, Persuasion and the Individual in Modern British Politics' J. Gottlieb & R. Toye (eds); I.B. Tauris 2005 13pp

4655 Morgan, Kevin **Bolshevism, Syndicalism and the General Strike: The Lost Internationalist World of A.A. Purcell – Bolshevism and the British Left, Part 3** L&W 2013 480pp pb Purcell was in CP till 1922.

4656 Morgan, Kevin & Cohen, Gidon **Cohen, Rose** in 'DLB' 11 2003 8pp

4657 Morgan, Kevin & Cohen, Gidon; Flinn, Andrew **Communists and British Society, 1920-1991** Rivers Oram 2007 356pp pb Based on a 3 year project on British communist biog. at Manchester University using thousands of questionnaires, and hundreds of taped interviews this book looks at the CPGB through its individual members and their social, as well as political, views and practices.

4658 Morgan, Kevin **Hannington, Wal** in 'DLB' 10 2000 8pp

4659 Morgan, Kevin **Harry Pollitt** MUP 1993 210pp hb Finely judged biog.

4660 Morgan, Kevin **Harry Pollitt, the British CP and International Communism** in 'Communism: National and International' T. Saarela & K. Rentola (eds); Finnish Historical Society 1998 24pp pb

4661 Morgan, Kevin **Hyde, Douglas** in 'DLB' 13 2010 14pp

4662 Morgan, Kevin **King Street Blues: Jazz and the Left in Britain in the 1930s-1940s** in 'A Weapon in the Struggle' A. Croft (ed.) 1998 19pp pb

4663 Morgan, Kevin **Labour Legends and Russian Gold: Bolshevism and the British Left, Part 1** L&W 2006 315pp pb

4664 Morgan, Kevin **Parts of People and Communist Lives** in 'Party People, Party Lives' J. McIlroy, K. Morgan, Campbell, A. (eds) 2001 20pp This introductory chapter is a thoughtful contribution to the problems of communist biographies – a theme taken up in the Afterword by David Howell who compares biographies of CP and LP members.

4665 Morgan, Kevin **The CP and the Daily Worker, 1930-56** in 'Opening the Books' G. Andrews et al. (eds) 1995 18pp pb

4666 Morgan, Marguerite **Part of the Main** People's Publications 1990 120pp pb Autobiog.

4667 Morris, Aubrey **Unfinished Journey** The Polemicist/Artery Publications 2006 207pp pb Cab driver who became a travel agent and briefly MD of Thomson Holiday Group; businessman who remained a long-standing member of the CP, standing in General Election in Stoke Newington in 1955.

4668 Morris, Max & Darke, Marion & Stevenson, Howard **Memories** in 'Education Today and Tomorrow' 1998 In this 50th Anniversary ed., three leading CP educationalists reflect on the Educational Advisory Committee and the journal itself.

4669 Morris, Max **Sam Fisher: A Life for Education – Obit** in 'Education Today and Tomorrow' Vol.44 No.2, Autumn 1992 1pp

4670 Mortimer, Jim **A Life on the Left** Book Guild 1999 533pp hb Many passing refs to the CP in this autobiog. by left-wing Labour Party Gen. Sec.

4671 Mortimer, John **Clinging to the Wreckage** Penguin 1983 256pp pb Short, but hilarious, ref. to his brief membership of CP as schoolboy at Harrow.

4672 Morton, A.L. **Morley, Iris** in *'DLB' 4* 1977 6pp Novelist.

4673 Morton, Vivien **Jackson, Thomas Alfred** in *'DLB' 4* 1977 9pp

4674 Moss, Les **Live and Learn: A Life and Struggle for Progress** *QueenSpark Books, Brighton* 1979 137pp pb Engineer activist in Brighton CP till 1947.

4675 Mulford, W. **This Narrow Place** *Pandora* 1988 276pp pb On Sylvia Townsend Warner & Valentine Ackland – two important and controversial literary figures from the 1930s, both in CP.

4676 Mulvihill, Margaret **Charlotte Despard: A Biography** *Pandora* 1989 211pp pb

4677 Munton, Alan & Young, Alan (eds) **Seven Writers of the English Left: A Bibliography of Literature and Politics, 1916-80** *Garland* 1981 365pp hb On A. West, E. Rickword, R. Bates, E. Upward, R. Warner & C. Caudwell. Incl. short biographies plus comprehensive bibliog. (newspaper articles, photos, adverts for 4 lectures, letters, translations etc.).

4678 Murphy, J.T. **New Horizons** *Bodley Head* 1941 352pp hb Important autobiog.

4679 Murphy, J.T. **Preparing For Power** *Pluto* 1972 296pp pb Originally published 1934, shortly after he left the CP. Intro. by J. Hinton.

4680 Murray, Andrew **The CPGB: A Historical Analysis to 1941** *Communist Liaison* 1995 106pp pb A traditional, Leninist viewpoint.

4681 Muthiah, Welsey & Wanasinghe, Sydney **The Bracegirdle Affair** *Young Socialist, Sri Lanka* 1997 576pp pb Australian who went to Ceylon to help the young revolutionary movement. Came to Britain in 1930s and worked in Collets bookshop, and was lifelong CP member.

4682 Nawrat, Chris & Roberts, Geoff **Every Cloud Has a Silver Lining? The CP, the LP and Representational Politics** in *'Politics and Power 2'; RKP* 1980 11pp pb

4683 Nazir, Pervaiz **The Life and Work of Rajani Palme Dutt** *School of Oriental & African Studies, Univ. of London* 1986 24pp Published in conjunction with an exhibition.

4684 Neat, Timothy **Hamish Henderson: A Biography** *Polygon* 2007 377pp A 2nd vol. appeared in 2007. Not a CP member (according to author), he was involved in left-wing socialist and cultural circles for his whole life and there are many refs to CP and members, especially in Scotland.

4685 Newman, Michael **Harold Laski** *Macmillan* 1993 438pp hb

4686 Newman, Michael **John Strachey** *MUP* 1989 208pp hb

4687 Newman, Michael **Ralph Miliband and the Politics of the New Left** *Merlin* 2002 368pp pb A key figure in the New Left; never in the CP, though close as a student.

4688 Newton, Kenneth **The Sociology of British Communism** *Allen Lane* 1969 214pp hb One of the major texts till the recent period; made use of questionnaires and interviews but no original conclusions.

4689 Newton, Ray **One Step Forward, Two Steps Back?** *Minerva Press* 1998 212pp pb Autobiog. of CP activist in Scotland; education, peace movement.

4690 Nicholas, W.J. **Settling Accounts: A Life Lived Through Bristol's Labour Movement** *Bristol TUC & South West TUC* 2008 43pp lf Well produced pamphlet on Bill Nicholas, NUDAW activist, Co-operator and Trades Council President.

4691 Nicholson, Steve **British Theatre and the Red Peril: The Portrayal of Communism, 1917-1945** *University of Exeter Press* 1999 195pp pb Excellent research uncovers many plays with a political content – covers portrayal of the USSR as well as British Communism.

4692 Nicholson, Steve **Montagu Slater and the Theatre of the Thirties** in *'Recharting the Thirties'* P. Quinn (ed.); *Associated University Presses* 1996 21pp Incl. excellent bibliography on Slater.

4693 Nicolson, Jock **A Turbulent Life** *Praxis Press* 2009 111pp pb Worked for the CP in Scotland; a railwayman in London he was elected to the Executive of the NUR. For many years a key Communist in the rail industry. There was an early version of this book published privately by his family in 2007 (lf, 82pp).

4694 Nield, Barbara **Saklatvala, Shapurji** in *'DLB' 6* 1982 5pp

4695 Nield, Keith **Rothstein, Theodore** in *'DLB' 7* 1984 9pp

4696 Nobes, Arthur **Faceless Men** *s.p.* 1986 ? 82pp lf Possibly not produced for sale.

4697 Nobes, Arthur **From Cambridge to Meerut: The Travail of Philip Spratt, An Idealist** *s.p.* 1986 64pp lf

4698 Nolan, Michael **Lessons of the 1966 Seamen's Strike** *SLL* 1967 22pp lf Virulent attack on CP and the TGWU.

4699 North, David **Gerry Healy and His Place in the History of the Fourth International** *Labor Publications, Detroit* 1991 123pp pb

4700 Northedge, F.S. & Wells, A. **Britain and Soviet Communism** *Macmillan* 1982 280pp pb

4701 O'Connor, Emmet **Larkin, James** in *'DLB' 13* 2010 15pp

4702 O'Connor, Emmet **Murray, Sean** in *'DLB' 11* 2003 5pp Irish Communist leader was in the CPGB during the General Strike. Useful on links between the Irish and British parties.

4703 O'Connor, Emmet **Reds and the Green: Ireland, Russia and the Communist Internationals 1919-43** *University College Dublin Press* 2004 260pp hb Much on CPGB and Ireland.

4704 O'Connor, Kristine Mason **Joan Maynard: Passionate Socialist** *Politico's Publishing* 2003 324pp Callaghan wrongly considered her a Communist. This book refers to her relationship with the CP, especially in Yorkshire and in the National Union of Agricultural Workers.

4705 O'Connor, Peter **A Soldier of Liberty: Recollections of a Socialist and Anti-Fascist Fighter** *MSF, Eire* 1996 44pp Irish activist at various times (sometimes simultaneously!) member of IRA, Revolutionary Workers' Group, Republican Congress, I.B., LP, CPI and, briefly in 1930s while working in London, CPGB.

4705a O'Dair, Marcus **Different Every Time: The Authorised Biography of Robert Wyatt** *Serpent's Tail* 2014 464pp It's not often a member of the CP turns into a 'national treasure', but musician Wyatt is one.

4706 O'Neill, A. **The CPGB and Trade Unions** *Cttee to Defeat Revisionism, For Communist Unity* 1964 Maoist.

4707 Osment, Rose **Experiences of a Jewish Communist** *Self-published* 1975 22pp Disappointing – mostly about her journey from Jewish Atheism to Christianity.

4708 Owen, Nicholas **The British Left and India: Metroplitan Anti-Imperialism, 1885-1947** *OUP* 2007 340pp hb

4709 Paananen, Victor N. (ed.) **British Marxist Criticism** *Garland Publishing* 2000 506pp Annotated bibliographies of A. West, C. Caudwell, J. Lindsay, A.L. Morton, A. Kettle, M. Heinemann, R. Williams (and T. Eagleton who was never a CP member). Each subject preceded by a short introduction – biographical and critical. A book not widely referenced in the UK.

4710 Page, Bruce et al. **Philby: The Spy Who Betrayed a Generation** *Deutsch* 1968 336pp hb CP activity in Cambridge.

4710a Palfreeman, Linda **Aristocrats, Adventurers and Ambulances: British Medical Units in the Spanish Civil War** *Sussex Academic Press* 2013 256pp pb

4710b Palfreeman, Linda **Salud! British Volunteers in the Republican Medical Service During the Spanish Civil War, 1936-1939** *Sussex Academic Press* 2012 296pp pb

4711 Palmer, Bryan **E.P. Thompson: Objections and Opposition** *Verso* 1994 201pp pb

4712 Palmer, Bryan **The Making of E.P. Thompson** *New Hogtown Press, Toronto* 1981 144pp pb

4712a Palmer, William **Engagement with the Past: The Lives and Works of the World War 2 Generation of Historians** *UP of Kentucky* 2001 372pp Includes the CP Historians.

4713 Parker, David (ed.) **Ideology, Absolutism and the English Revolution: Debates of the British Communist Historians 1940-1956** *L&W* 2008 285pp pb The substantial introduction has much on the CP Historians' Group.

4714 Parker, Lawrence **The Kick Inside: Revolutionary Opposition in the CPGB, 1945-1991** *November Publications* 2012 118pp Expanded ed. of a book that originally came out in 2007. A delight for anoraks of sectariana, published by The Leninist (aka CPGB Provisional CC, aka CPGB). The politics are all over the place, but it's a useful account of the Maoists, the Appeal Group and the NCP, and of course The Leninist group (never more than 30 strong). Covers opposition to the different BRS eds, and individuals like McShane, Heffer and Upward. Well researched and makes good use of interviews.

4715 Parry, Jane **A History of the Labour Movement in Neath** *Peter Hain* 1996 52pp

4716 Parsons, Steve **Communists in the Professions: 'Professional Workers' 1941-47** in *'The Forward March of the Left and the Problems of Its Progess 1945-1948; Magyar Lajos Alapitvany'* 2001 15pp

4717 Paynter, Will **My Generation** *A&U* 1972 172pp pb Miners' leader.

4718 Peacock, W. (ed.) **Tom Mann 80th Birthday Souvenir** *Tom Mann 80th Birthday Celebration Cttee* 1936 18pp lf

4719 Pearce, Brian & Woodhouse, Michael **A History of Communism in Britain** *Bookmarks* 1995 257pp pb Reprint of 'Essays on the History of Communism in Britain' with new intro.

4720 Pearce, Brian **Early History of the CPGB** *SLL* 1966 62pp Trotskyist.

4721 Pearce, Brian **Some Past Rank & File Movements** *Labour Review* 1959 40pp Also in 'Labour Review' Vol.4 No.1.

4722 Pearce, Edward **Dennis Healey: A Life in Our Time** *Little, Brown* 2002 634pp Students at Oxford.

4723 Pearce, Nikki **God Loves Communists Too** *New Wine Press* 1989 160pp pb 'She desired from an early age to serve the Lord. Confused how this could be achieved, she later succumbed to the attractions of Communism & joined the CP'. Before the Lord intervened and she left, she gives an unusually rare picture of branch life.

4723a Pearmain, Andrew **The Politics of New Labour: A Gramscian Analysis** *L&W* 2011 288pp Includes discussion of relationship between 'MT' and CP.

4724 Peck, John **Persistence: The Story of a British Communist** *s.p.* 2001 283pp Autobiog. by activist who, after many attempts, got elected as Communist councillor in Nottingham. Peck was a leading campaigner within the CP for participating in local politics and elections. He became the National Election Agent. Good descriptions of the life of a CP full-timer; also useful on the final years – as a member of the 'Eurocommunist' minority in the East Midlands he was removed from leading positions there. He joined the Green Party in 1990.

4725 Peet, John **The Long Engagement: Memoirs of a Cold War Legend** *Fourth Estate* 1989 242pp hb An interesting story: Peet was involved, as a public schoolboy, in 'Out of Bounds'. Involved in underground anti-fascist work in Vienna & Prague; wounded in Spain. He was Reuters chief correspondent in West Berlin when he defected to the east in 1950. His friends there included Stefan Heym, Alan Winnington and John Heartfield – and in Britain, Len Deighton. Briefly a member of the CPGB as a public schoolboy, he remained a non-card carrying communist but became critical of the GDR.

4726 Pelling, Henry **Great Britain, the CP and the Trade Unions** in *'The Strategy of Deception: A Study in World-Wide Communist Tactics' Jean Kirkpatrick (ed.); Hale* 1964 31pp hb

4727 Pelling, Henry **The British CP: A Historical Profile** *Black* 1975 204pp hb This re-issue of 1958 ed. has new short intro. The first history of the CP: readable, well researched but unremittingly negative esp. on 'infiltration' of T.U.s etc.

4728 Pelling, Henry **The Early History of the CPGB, 1920-29** *Transactions of the Royal Historical Society* 1958 17pp Incorporated into his 1958 book.

4729 Pentelow, Mike **Norfolk Red: The Life of Wilf Page, Countryside Communist** *L&W* 2009 176pp

4730 Perry, Matt **Marxism and History** *Palgrave* 2002 195pp Section on CP Historians' Group.

4731 Perry, Matt **The Jarrow Crusade: Protest and Legend** *University of Sunderland Press* 2005 264pp Refs to many local CP members.

4732 Perry, Roland **Last of the Cold War Spies: The Life of Michael Straight** *Da Capo Press* 2005 396pp Title proved a little premature – see 'The Spy Who Came in from the Co-op'. It's still unclear what this American actually did, and this book may overestimate his importance.

4733 Philips, Wogan (Lord Milford) **Maiden Speech** in *Hansard, House of Lords Official Report July 4* 1963 2pp 'My Lords, I have been warned that in a maiden speech one should never be controversial ... I and my Party are for the complete abolition of this Chamber'.

4734 Phillpott, H.R.S. **The Right Hon. J.H. Thomas: Impressions of a Remarkable Man** *Sampson Low, Marston* 1932 214pp Chapter on his libel case against 'The Communist' – contains more than his awful autobiog. 'My Story'.

4735 Piatnitsky, O. **World Communists in Action** *Modern Books* 1930 64pp 2pp on CPGB.

4736 Pile, Stephen **The Book of Heroic Failures** *Futura* 1985 216pp pb 'The Worst Protest March' (p53) – perhaps not the most serious entry in this bibliography, but one of the funniest.

4737 Pimlott, Ben **Frustrate Their Knavish Tricks: Writings on Biography, History and Politics** *HarperCollins* 1994 417pp hb See the chapter on 'The Strange Life of British Stalinism' – review of 'Harry Pollitt' by Morgan and 'Rajani Palme Dutt' by Callaghan. Also previous chapter – review of 'Proletarian Philosophers' by Ree.

4738 Pimlott, Ben **Labour and the Left in the 1930s** *A&U* 1977 262pp pb Very useful analysis of all left-wing organisations in the 1930s, incl. the CP.

4739 Pincher, Chapman **Their Trade Is Treachery** *Sidgwick & Jackson* 1981 240pp hb Some nonsense about the CP (secret files, 50,000 secret members etc.) but some useful information on the spies (plus some errors e.g. on Driberg).

4740 Pincher, Chapman **Too Secret Too Long** *Sidgwick & Jackson* 1984 646pp hb Sequel to 'Their Trade is Treachery'.

4741 Piratin, Phil **Our Flag Stays Red** *L&W* 1980 92pp pb Autobiog. by Stepney activist who was Communist MP from 1945-50. Originally publ. in 1948 by Thames Publications, this ed. has new preface by author. Important book on local politics, especially housing campaigns.

4742 Pirie, N.W. **J.B.S. Haldane** in *'Biographical Memoirs of Fellows of the Royal Society' Vol.12* 1966 31pp

4743 Pitt, Robert **John Maclean and the CPGB** *s.p.* 1996 48pp lf 2nd ed.

4744 Platts-Mills, John **Muck, Silk and Socialism: Recollections of a Left-Wing QC** *Paper Publishing* 2002 687pp hb Very few refs to the CP - only in Finsbury and the Haldane Society – from this pro-Soviet Labour lawyer and MP.

4745 Podmore, Will **Reg Birch: Engineer, Trade Unionist, Communist** *Bellman Books* 2004 308pp pb The only significant CP member to convert to Maoism.

4746 Pollitt, H. **Pollitt Visits Spain** *I.B. Dependants' Aid Cttee* 1937 30pp

4747 Pollitt, H. **Selected Articles and Speeches – 2 Vols** *L&W* 1953 180; 144pp pb 4 vols were planned but only 2 appeared – probably because of the difficulty of facing up to the policy changes over the nature of WW2.

4748 Pollitt, H. **Serving My Time** *L&W* 1941 292pp pb Very readable autobiog.; several commentators have remarked how much better it is than 'Son of the People' by M. Thorez, the leader of the PCF, which was published not long before.

4749 Pollitt, Marjorie **A Rebel Life** *Red Pen* 1989 134pp pb Autobiog. by Harry's wife, a teacher, who was active in her own right.

4750 Pooke, Grant **Francis Klingender, 1907-1955: A Marxist Art Historian Out of Time** *Gill Vista Marx Press* 2008 258pp

4751 Porter, Bernard **Plots and Paranoia: A History of Political Espionage in Britain** *Routledge* 1992 276pp hb Nothing original – summarises what's known on spies and the CP.

4752 Porter, Gerald **The World's Ill-Divided: the CP and Progressive Song** in *'A Weapon in the Struggle'* A. Croft (ed.) 1998 21pp pb

4753 Post, Ken **Revolution's Other World: Communism and the Periphery, 1917-39** *Macmillan/Institute of Social Studies* 1997 219pp CPGB in India in 1930s.

4754 Postgate, John & Mary **A Stomach For Dissent: The Life of Raymond Postgate – Writer, Radical Socialist and Founder of the Good Food Guide** *Keele UP* 1994 368pp hb Founder member, edited 'The Communist', left in 1922.

4755 Postgate, Raymond **How to Make a Revolution** *Hogarth Press* 1934 199pp hb General, but some refs to CPGB.

4756 Potter, Karen **British McCarthyism** in *'North American Spies'* R. Jeffreys-Jones & A. Lownie (eds); *Edinburgh UP* 1991 14pp

4757 Potts, Archie **Zilliacus: A Life for Peace and Socialism** *Merlin* 2002 227pp pb The left-wing Labour MP; author says Zilliacus was asked to be a secret member of the CP but refused.

4758 Poulsen, Charles **Scenes from a Stepney Youth** *THAP* 1988 128pp pb For more biographical details on Poulsen see Hobday in CHNN 14, Spring 2003.

4759 Pountney, Ernie **For the Socialist Cause** *L&W* 1973 80pp pb

4760 Powell, Glyn **Controlling the Fire: British Communism and the Post-War Consensus** in *'Consensus or Coercion: The State, the People and Social Cohesion in Post-War Britain'* L. Black et al; *New Clarion Press* 2001 26pp

4761 Preston, Paul **Doves of War: Four Women of Spain** *HarperCollins* 2002 469pp pb One of the subjects is Nan Green. Based partly on her then unpublished autobiog. (see 'A Chronicle of Small Beer').

4762 Pritt, D.N. **Autobiography** *L&W* 1965/1966 3 vols 319pp; 322pp; 228pp hb Most on CP in Vol.3.

4763 Purcell, Hugh **The Last English Revolutionary: Tom Wintringham 1898-1949** *Sutton* 2004 274pp hb Foundation member of the CP, imprisoned with 11 other leaders in 1925. Military expert, commanded British battalion in Spain; expelled from CP in 1938 over his relationship with American woman the party was suspicious of, he went on to found Common Wealth and nearly got elected as an MP. Played important part in development of the Home Guard and theory of a people's army; he was also a poet.

4763a Purdie, Bob **Hugh MacDiarmid: Black, Green, Red and Tartan** *Welsh Academic Press* 2012 145pp

4764 Purdy, Anthony & Sutherland, Douglas **Burgess and Maclean** *Secker* 1963 191pp hb

4765 Radford, Robert **To Disable the Enemy: The Graphic Art of the Three Jameses** in *'A Weapon in the Struggle'* A. Croft (ed.) 1998 20pp pb

4766 Rafeek, Neil **Communist Women in Scotland: Red Clydeside from the Russian Revolution to the End of the Soviet Union** *I.B. Tauris* 2008 294pp Based on interviews with 41 individuals, 34 of whom were women.

4767 Ram, Mohan **Indian Communism: Split Within a Split** *Vikas Publications* 1969 293pp hb Esp. post independence.

4768 Ramdin, Ron **The Making of the Black Working Class in Britain** *Gower* 1987 626pp hb Section on Saklatvala; also on CP and Indian Workers' Association.

4769 Rattenbury, Arnold **James Boswell: Artist Against Fascism** *Manchester City Art Gallery* 1986 4pp Exhibition catalogue.

4770 Rattenbury, Arnold **Literature, Lying and Sober Truth: Attitudes to the Work of Patrick Hamilton and Sylvia Townsend Warner** in *'Writing and Radicalism'* J. Lucas; *Longman* 1996 45pp pb A key text on writings by and about Communists in the 1930s and 1940s; covers much more than Hamilton and Warner.

4771 Reckitt, Maurice **As It Happened** *Dent* 1941 306pp Covers USF, sketches of CP leaders, Rose Cohen.

4772 Redfern, Neil **Class or Nation: Communists, Imperialism and the Two World Wars** *I.B. Tauris* 2005 256pp hb Criticises the CPGB for betraying its revolutionary role and subordinating itself to national interests.

4773 'Redman, J.' **The CP and the Labour Left, 1925-9** *Reasoner Pamphlet No.1* 1958 32pp Intro. J. Saville. See 'British Communist History' for a later version.

4774 Ree, Jonathan **Proletarian Philosophers: Problems in Socialist Culture in Britain, 1900-1940** *OUP* 1984 176pp hb Includes chapters on 'British Communists & Dialectical Materialism 1920-37', 'Dialetical Materialism & The Scientists' etc.

4775 Rees, Tim & Thorpe, Andrew (eds) **International Communism and the Communist International, 1919-43** *MUP* 1998 323pp pb Has 2 chapters specifically on CPGB – A. Thorpe 'The C.I. & the British CP' and Y. Sergeev 'The C.I. & A Trotskyite Menace to the British Communist Movement on the Eve of WW2'. Latter argues that Trotskyists in ILP & NCLC had some influence and that Stalin was worried they might hinder his plans to collaborate with Germany after Munich.

4776 Reid, Jimmy **Reflections of a Clyde-Built Man** *Condor* 1976 166pp pb Charismatic leader of Upper Clyde Shipbuilders work-in who was a political figure as well as an industrial one. Former leader of YCL; Communist councillor in Clydebank. He and the CP had high but unrealistic hopes of winning a seat in the 1974 General Election. He left the CP in 1976 and worked in journalism.

4777 Renton, Dave **Fascism, Anti-Fascism and Britain in the 1940s** *Macmillan* 2000 203pp hb Much on London.

4778 Renton, Dave **Red Shirts and Black: Fascists and Anti-Fascists in Oxford in the 1930s** *Ruskin College Library* 1996 54pp

4779 Renton, Dave **This Rough Game: Fascism and Anti-Fascism** *Sutton* 2001 235pp hb Especially on Cable Street and Spanish Civil War.

4780 Renton, Dave **When We Touched the Sky: The Anti-Nazi League, 1977-1981** *New Clarion Press* 2006 204pp The ANL was an SWP initiative, and the CP didn't feature prominently in it, but there are some refs.

4781 Renton, David **Sidney Pollard: A Life in History** *I.B. Tauris* 2004 214pp The economic historian was in the CP for a few months at the LSE.

4782 Reynolds, Reginald **My Life and Crimes** *Jarrolds* 1956 260pp Pacifist, Secretary of the

No More War Movement, he writes about the difficulties of working with CP members.

4783 Rhodes, Rita **An Arsenal for Labour: The Royal Arsenal Co-operative Society and Politics, 1896-1996** *Holyoake Books* 1998 298pp pb

4784 Richardson, Al **Frank Maitland – Obituary** in *'Revolutionary History' Vol.8 No.1* 2001 3pp Active in CP from 1930 in Edinburgh, left and joined the extremely small Revolutionary Socialist Party in 1936.

4785 Richter, Irving **Political Purpose in Trade Unions** *A&U* 1973 258pp hb Esp. on AUEW.

4786 Ridley, Maurice **Making A Contribution** in *'But the World Goes On the Same: Changing Times in Durham Pit Villages'; Strong Words* 1979 14pp pb

4787 Riley, Percy **The Life of Riley** *Yorkshire Art Circus* 1986 48pp pb Full-time YCL organiser during WW2, local councillor in Yorkshire, active in mining industry.

4788 Riordan, Jim **Comrade Jim: The Spy Who Played for Spartak** *Fourth Estate* 2008 223pp hb Autobiog. by the man trained as a British spy who converted to Communism, moved to Moscow – and played football for Moscow Spartak – before returning to Britain.

4789 Riordan, Jim **The Last British Comrade Trained in Moscow: The Higher Party School, 1961-1963** *Socialist History Society* 2007 34pp

4790 Roberts, B.C. **Trade Union Government and Administration in G.B.** *London School of Economics/G. Bell* 1956 570pp hb

4791 Roberts, Edwin **The Anglo-Marxists: A Study in Ideology and Culture** *Rowman & Littlefield* 1997 296pp pb Esp. on J. Lewis, J.D. Bernal, J.B.S. Haldane & M. Cornforth. Argues that a particularly Anglicised version of Marxism developed in CPGB. Original.

4792 Roberts, Ernie **Strike Back** *s.p.* 1994 302pp pb Autobiog. of engineering union leader and MP, who was on Executive of YCL and CP's Midlands DC until expelled in 1941 over differences about industrial activity during wartime. There are other refs throughout the book to the CP.

4793 Roberts, John **The Art of Interruption: Realism, Photography and the Everyday** *MUP* 1998 241pp pb A few brief, but interesting, comments on photography and the CP, esp. in the 1930s.

4794 Robson, Alec **'Spike': Alec 'Spike' Robson 1895-1979** 1987 20pp Autobiog. of NUWM activist and militant seaman; he led a strike to prevent a ship going to Franco's Spain during the Civil War.

4795 Rogers, Ted **Journeyman** *Plus 80* 2003 243pp pb YCL in the 1930s; Sunderland in the 1945 General Election; Crawley in 1950s (meets T.A. Jackson).

4796 Rolph, C. **All Those in Favour: The ETU Trial** *Deutsch* 1962 255pp pb

4797 Romero, Patricia **E. Sylvia Pankhurst: Portrait of a Radical** *Yale* 1990 334pp pb

4798 Romilly, Esmond **Boadilla** *Macdonald* 1971 196pp hb Reprint of 1937 ed. Good on his fellow I.B.ers, several of whom were in CPGB.

4799 Romilly, Giles **Gentle Revolutionary: A Portrait of Arthur Horner** in *'The Changing Nation' A.G. Weidenfeld (ed.); Contact Publications* 1948 6pp

4800 Romilly, Giles & Esmond **Out of Bounds** *H. Hamilton* 1935 310pp hb Autobiog. Amusing account of 'subversive' activities in Wellington College.

4801 Rose, Clive **Campaigns Against Western Defence: NATO's Adversaries and Critics** *Macmillan* 1985 318pp hb

4802 Rose, Jonathan **The Intellectual Life of the British Working Classes** *Yale UP* 2001 534pp A fascinating and imaginatively researched book; many refs to CP members, notably to T.A. Jackson. The chapter on the CP, with its selection of quotes from generally embittered ex-members, and where the author argues that it was the lack of moral appeal of individual members that hindered the CP's growth, is not convincing.

4803 Rosen, Harold **Are You Still Circumcised? East End Memories** *Five Leaves* 1999 163pp pb 3 generations of Jewish communists in London's East End, as described in a very well written series of 'autobiographical stories'. Contains information on Beatrice Hastings, a model and lover of the painter Modigliani, and CP member.

4804 Rosenberg, David **Battle for the East End: Jewish Responses to Fascism in the 1930s** *Five Leaves* 2011 268pp Much on the CP, Phil Piratin etc.

4805 Routledge, Paul **Mandy: The Unauthorised Biography of Peter Mandelson** *Simon & Schuster* 1999 302pp hb On his activity in Hendon YCL, plus lengthy discussion on whether he actually held a CP membership card.

4806 Routledge, Paul **Scargill: The Unauthorised Biography** *Harper Collins* 1994 296pp pb Covers Scargill's early years in the YCL, and CP involvement in NUM, especially in Yorkshire.

4807 Rowbotham, Sheila **A New World For Women: Stella Browne – Socialist Feminist** *Pluto* 1977 128pp pb In CP till 1923 – she left because she thought it didn't take feminist issues seriously enough, though she remained close; later founder of Abortion Law Reform Association. Rare socialist who campaigned openly on sexual politics.

4808 Rowbotham, Sheila **Promise of a Dream: Remembering the Sixties** *Allen Lane* 2000 262pp hb Many passing refs to the CP and individual members indicate its influence even when other far left groups were growing faster.

4809 Roy, Walter **The Teachers' Union: Aspects of Policy and Organisation in the NUT, 1950-1966** *Schoolmaster Publishing Co.* 1968 183pp Interesting section on Communist influence.

4810 Rubinstein, David **But He'll Remember: An Autobiography** *William Sessions* 1999 346pp LP member close to several leading CP educational activists, especially Sam Fisher.

4811 Rudder, Ben **Builders of the Borough: A Century of Achievement by Battersea & Wandsworth TUC** *Battersea & Wandsworth TUC* 1993 66pp pb Brief refs.

4812 Russell, Ian (ed.) **Singer, Song and Scholar** *Sheffield Academic Press* 1986 177pp Material on A.L. Lloyd, incl. important bibliography.

4813 Russell, Ralph **Findings, Keepings: Life, Communism and Everything** *Shola* 2001 346pp pb One of the better written autobiographies; joined CP when 16; describes activity at Cambridge University and in the army in India – he learned Urdu to be able to engage in local politics and became leading Urdu scholar.

4814 Ryan, Trevor **The New Road to Progress: The Use and Production of Films by the Labour Movement, 1929-39** in *'British Cinema History' J. Curran & V. Porter (eds); Weidenfeld* 1983 16pp On the Federation of Workers' Film Societies, Atlas Films, Kino, Workers' Film and Photo League, British Film Unit, Progressive Film Institute and CP involvement in these organisations.

4815 Saha, Panchanan **Rajani Palme Dutt: A Biography** *Biswabiksha; Kolkata* 2004 232pp hb

4816 Saha, Panchanan **Shapurji Saklatvala: A Short Biography** *People's Publishing House, New Delhi* 1970 104pp hb

4817 Saiyid, Dushka **Exporting Communism to India: Why Moscow Failed** *National Institute of Historical & Cultural Research, Islamabad* 1995 202pp This short but useful book, published in Pakistan, surprisingly has highest number of its Index refs to the CPGB.

4818 Saklatvala, Sehri **The Fifth Commandment: Biography of Shapurji Saklatvala** *Miranda Press* 1991 488pp pb By the daughter of the Communist MP. Mainly reproduces documents & articles.

4819 Samuel, Raphael (ed.) **Patriotism Volume 1** *RKP* 1989 330pp See chapters by Stephen Howe and Anthony Barnett.

4820 Samuel, Raphael **The Lost World of British Communism** *Verso* 2006 244pp hb The essays that originally appeared in NLR. With a bibliography of Samuel's work that includes obituaries for some CP members.

4821 Samuel, Raphael et al. **Theatres of the Left 1880-1935** *Routledge* 1985 364pp pb Chapter of autobiog. by E. MacColl plus other material.

4822 Samuel, Wayne **The Political Betrayal of Wales** *Welsh Nationalist Party* 1945 ? 16pp Incl. attack on CP's position on Wales.

4823 Samuels, Stuart **English Intellectuals in the 1930s** in *'On Intellectuals' P. Rieff (ed.); Anchor* 1970 51pp pb

4824 Saville, John **'Marxism Today': An Anatomy** in *'Socialist Register'; Merlin* 1990 25pp pb Very critical.

4825 Saville, John **Ainley, Ted** in *'DLB'* 10 2000 3pp

4826 Saville, John **Bacharach, Alfred** in *'DLB'* 9 1993 3pp

4827 Saville, John **Beauchamp, Joan** in *'DLB'* 10 2000 3pp

4828 Saville, John **Boswell, James** in *'DLB'* 3 1976 6pp

4829 Saville, John **Branson, Clive** in *'DLB'* 2 1974 9pp

4830 Saville, John **Bridgeman, Reginald** in *'DLB'* 7 1984 23pp Much on League Against Imperialism and CP.

4831 Saville, John **Chadwick, Paxton** in *'DLB'* 9 1993 8pp One of the figures behind astonishing electoral success of CP in Leiston. Saville calls him 'one of the great British natural history illustrators of the 20th century'.

4832 Saville, John **Cohen, Jack** in *'DLB'* 9 1993 7pp Full-timer for YCL and CP, 1925-68; first National Student Organiser in 1930s.

4833 Saville, John **Cohen, Max** in *'DLB'* 9 1993 2pp

4834 Saville, John **Dobb, Maurice** in *'DLB'* 9 1993 9pp

4835 Saville, John **Edward Thompson, the CP and 1956** in *'Socialist Register'*; Merlin 1994 12pp pb

4836 Saville, John **Gossip, Alex** in *'DLB'* 7 1984 6pp Incl. much on Meerut Trial & CPGB.

4837 Saville, John **Green, George** in *'DLB'* 10 2000 3pp

4838 Saville, John **Horner, Arthur** in *'DLB'* 5 1979 6pp

4839 Saville, John **Klingender, Francis** in *'DLB'* 9 1993 4pp

4840 Saville, John **Kumaramangalam, Surendra Mohan** in *'DLB'* 5 1979 2pp

4841 Saville, John **Levy, Hyman** in *'DLB'* 9 1993 7pp

4842 Saville, John **Memoirs from the Left** Merlin 2003 197pp pb Marxist historian in CP till 1956 when he became key figure in the New Left. Bibliography.

4843 Saville, John **Merson, Allan** in *'DLB'* 10 2000 3pp Historian.

4844 Saville, John **Palfreman, Bill** in *'DLB'* 9 1993 1pp

4845 Saville, John **Paxton Chadwick: Artist and Communist 1903-61** Leiston Leader 1993 32pp Reprinted from DLB Vol.9 but with some of Chadwick's flower illustrations.

4846 Saville, John **Reckitt, Eva Collet** in *'DLB'* 9 1993 5pp

4847 Saville, John **Renton, Donald** in *'DLB'* 9 1993 3pp

4848 Saville, John **Shaw, Fred** in *'DLB'* 4 1977 4pp

4849 Saville, John **The 20th Congress and the British CP** in *'Socialist Register'*; Merlin 1976 23pp pb

4850 Saville, John **The Communist Experience: A Personal Appraisal** in *'Socialist Register'*; Merlin 1991 27pp hb

4851 Saville, John **The Labour Movement in Britain** Faber 1988 166pp pb

4852 Saville, John **Valentine Cunningham and the Poetry of the Spanish Civil War** in *'Socialist Register'*; Merlin 1981 15pp pb Cunningham replied in the 1982 ed.

4853 Saxby, Jane **Jane Saxby** in *'Three Lives'*; National Federation of Community Organisations 1983 19pp pb Limited on her, and her family's, extensive activity in the CP in Liverpool, but fascinating autobiographical account of her activity in women's, co-op, and community organisations.

4854 Sayle, Alexei **Stalin Ate My Homework** Sceptre 2010 304pp hb The comedian is on form as he describes his Communist upbringing in Liverpool, his joining the YCL and then the Maoists.

4855 Scammon, Richard **The Communist Voting Pattern in British Parliamentary Elections** in *'British Election Studies,1950'*; G. Wahr Publishing Co., Ann Arbor 1951 5pp pb

4856 Schwarz, Bill **The People in History: The CP Historians' Group, 1946-56** in *'Making Histories'* Richard Johnson et al (eds); Hutchinson 1982 52pp hb

4857 Scott, George (ed.) **Remembering the Spanish Civil War, 1936-39** Aberdeen TC 1996 36pp lf See especially Bob Cooney's 'The Story of Aberdeen's Communists'; also tribute to Cooney; short biographies of Cooney and David Anderson. Also poems by and about Cooney.

4858 Seale, Patrick & McConville, Maureen **Philby: The Long Road to Moscow** Penguin 1978 349pp pb

4859 Seifert, Roger & Sibley, Tom **Revolutionary Communist at Work: A Political Biography of Bert Ramelson** L&W 2012 384pp pb CP Industrial Organiser from 1965 to 1977, and a key figure in industrial relations in this period.

4860 Seifert, Roger **Teacher Militancy: A History of Teacher Strikes, 1896-1987** Falmer Press 1987 291pp pb Esp. on anti-Communist ban on Head Teachers in Middlesex in the 1950s.

4861 Selkirk, Bob **The Life of a Worker** s.p. (?) 1967 47pp Omits details of his expulsion and re-admittance.

4862 Seltman, P.E.J. **Revisionism and Imperialism** *s.p.* 1963 16pp The whole of this Maoist pamphlet is on the CP.

4863 Seltman, Peter **What's Wrong with the British CP?** *s.p.* 1967 ?

4864 Sephton, Robert **Oxford and the General Strike** *s.p.* 1993 96pp pb Well researched; covers town and university. Useful refs to CP branch, incl. Appendix on Percy Stephensen. Concludes that CP was very weak and not influential in Oxford during the General Strike.

4865 Shadwell, Arthur **The Communist Movement: A Personal Investigation** *P. Allan* 1925 51pp

4866 Shadwell, Arthur **The Revolutionary Movement in GB** *Grant Richards* 1921 62pp pb Sketch of revolutionary forces shortly after formation of CPGB.

4867 Shallice, Andy **Remember Birkenhead** *Merseyside Socialist Research Group* 1982 18pp Unemployed riots.

4868 Shaw, Eric **Discipline and Discord in the Labour Party** *MUP* 1988 387pp hb Covers CP in 1920s.

4869 Shaw, George **On Learning to Talk with the People** *Cttee to Defeat Revisionism, For Communist Unity* 1964 4pp Maoist.

4869a Shepherd, Anna **Helen Unlimited: A Little Biggar** *The Billie Love Historical Collection* 2014 152pp Political film-maker and sculptress, Biggar worked with another Glaswegian CP member and film-maker, Norman McLaren, to produce one of the most ambitious avant-garde films of the 1930s – 'Hell Unltd.'.

4870 Sherry, Dave **John Maclean** *SWP* 1998 59pp

4871 Sherwood, Marika **Claudia Jones: A Life in Exile** *L&W* 1999 222pp pb Leading American Communist deported to UK; this book covers her political life in the UK – she played major role in establishing the Notting Hill Carnival and the West Indian Gazette. Author argues she was neglected by the CPGB. Also includes contributions from 1996 Claudia Jones Symposium.

4872 Sherwood, Marika **Kwame Nkrumah: The Years Abroad, 1935-47** *Freedom Publications, Ghana* 1996 202pp Quite a bit on his contacts with the CP. Useful for CP's approach to colonies.

4873 Shipley, Peter **Extremism and the Left** *Comservative Party* 1981 20pp Politics Today No.13.

4874 Shipley, Peter **Hostile Action: The KGB and Secret Service Operations in Britain** *Pinter* 1989 233pp

4875 Shipley, Peter **Revolutionaries in Modern Britain** *Bodley Head* 1976 256pp hb

4876 Shipway, Mark **Anti-Parliamentary Communism: The Movement for Workers' Councils in Britain, 1917-45** *Macmillan* 1988 239pp hb On organisations to the left of the CP, especially G. Aldred, but material on formation & early years of CP plus WW2.

4877 Shipway, Mark (ed.) **Sylvia Pankhurst: Communism and Its Tactics** *s.p.* 1983 25pp Brief intro. to collection of Pankhurst's articles.

4878 Shuttleworth, Antony (ed.) **And in Our Time: Vision, Revision and British Writing of the 1930s** *Bucknell UP* 2003 252pp See A. Croft 'The Ralph Fox (Writers) Group' and C. Pawling 'Revisiting the Thirties in the Twenty-First Century: The Radical Aesthetics of West, Caudwell, Eagleton'.

4879 Simon, Brian **Nahum, Ram** in *'DLB' 10* 2000 3pp Cambridge, and national, student leader; scientist.

4880 Simon, Brian (ed.) **The Search for Enlightenment: The Working Class and Adult Education in the Twentieth Century** *NIACE* 1992 334pp Much on CP, especially in 1920s and 1930s (Plebs League, Marx House) but also later.

4881 Simon, Matthew et al. **Remembering Roger: A Celebration of the Life of Roger Simon** *Privately published* 2002 26pp Much on his role at LRD.

4881a Simpson, Ann et al. (eds) **Festschrift For Jack Gaster on his 95th Birthday** *Privately published* 2002 72pp

4881b Simpson, Ludi et al. (eds) **Renate Simpson** *Privately published* 2014 38pp Celebrates the life of one of the Kuczynski sisters.

4882 Sinclair, Andrew **The Red and the Blue: Intelligence, Treason and the Universities** *Coronet* 1987 211pp

4883 Sinclair, Keith **How The Blue Union Came to Hull Docks** *s.p.* 1995 20pp

4884 Singer, Eleanor **A Memoir** *s.p.* 1998 128pp pb Interesting for links between CP and Bloomsbury; also medical and scientific circles. Author and her husband, Michael Barratt Brown, who edited this memoir were both in CP till after 1956.

4885 Sitzia, Lorraine & Thickett, Arthur **Seeking the Enemy** *Working Press* 2002

152pp pb Based on interviews with Thickett over several years. Thickett was in the CP in Australia and London – a soldier, he joined following his stint during the Korean War. An unusual and frank autobiog. of a man who drifted in and out of the CP, and employment.

4886 Skelley, Jeff (ed.) **1926: The General Strike** *L&W* 1976 412pp pb Mainly local studies & reminiscences; most contributors in CP. Personal reminiscences incl. P. Kerrigan, Bob Davies, Bill Carr, D.A. Wilson, J. Jacobs, H. Watson. Sadly, no index.

4887 Sloan, Pat (ed.) **John Cornford: A Memorial Volume** *Cape* 1938 250pp pb Cornford was Cambridge student who died in Spain. This book was reprinted in 1978 by Borderline.

4888 Smith, C.A. **Communism and Democracy** *Common Cause* 1950 12pp Speech in debate with H. Levy at Conway Hall, Jan.

4889 Smith, Chris **Technical Workers: Class, Labour and Trade Unionism** *Macmillan* 1987 322pp See Chapter 8 on TASS in the post-war period.

4890 Smith, Dai **Aneurin Bevan and the World of South Wales** *Univ. of Wales Press* 1993 359pp Esp. on N. Ablett, A. Horner, Lewis Jones.

4891 Smith, Dai **Raymond Williams: A Warrior's Tale** *Parthian* 2008 514pp pb

4892 Smith, Dai **Wales: A Question for History** *Seren* 1999 216pp pb Discusses S Wales miners and Welsh literary figures.

4893 Smith, David **Introduction to 'Cwmardy' by Lewis Jones** *L&W* 1978 5pp pb This brief biog. of the activist/novelist also appears in the introduction to 'We Live', the follow up novel to 'Cwmardy', reprinted at the same time.

4894 Smith, David **Leaders and Led** in *'Rhondda, Past and Future'* K. Hopkins (ed.); Rhondda Borough Council 1980 29pp Much on Lewis Jones, A. Horner & S Wales miners in general.

4895 Smith, David **Lewis Jones** *Univ. of Wales Press* 1982 91pp pb

4896 Smith, David **Socialist Propaganda in the Twentieth Century British Novel** *Macmillan* 1978 203pp hb With Croft's 'Red Letter Days', the most important of the books on socialist fiction for refs to the CP.

4897 Smith, Evan **Bridging the Gap: The British CP and the Limits of the State in Tackling Racism** in *'Europe's Expansions and Contractions: Proceedings of the XVIIth Biennial Conference of the Australasian Association of European Historians; Australian Humanities Press* 2010 21pp

4898 Smith, Evan **Did 1989 Matter? British Marxists and the Collapse of the Eastern Bloc** in *'Transitions Revisited: Central & Eastern Europe after the Soviet Union'* by P. Kimungyi & E. Polonska-Kimunguyi (eds); Wydawnictwo Naukowe Scholar, Warsaw 2012 27pp

4899 Smith, Geoffrey Stewart **Not To Be Trusted: Left Wing Extremism in the LP** *Foreign Affairs Publishing Co.* 1974 24pp lf

4900 Smith, Geoffrey Stewart **The Hidden Face of the Labour Party – The Unchecked Trotskyist and Communist Conspiracy Against the LP** *Foreign Affairs Publishing Co.* 1978 20pp lf Tabloid format.

4901 Smith, Harold **The British Labour Movement to 1970: A Bibliography** *Mansell* 1981 250pp hb 100 entries on the CP.

4902 Smith, James **British Writers and MI5 Surveillance, 1930-1960** *CUP* 2012 206pp Covers S. Spender, Ewan MacColl etc.

4903 Smith, Justin Davis **The Attlee and Churchill Administrations and Industrial Unrest, 1945-55** *Pinter* 1990 171pp pb

4904 Smith, Michael **The Spying Game** *Politico's Publishing* 2003 502pp pb Revised ed. of 'New Cloak, Old Dagger' published in 1996. Useful summary.

4905 Snowden, Philip **An Autobiography** *I. Nicholson & Watson* 1934 1094pp Bit on CP & ILP in 1920s.

4906 Sokoloff, Bertha **Edith And Stepney: The Life of Edith Ramsay** *Stepney Books* 1987 240pp pb Ramsay was LP councillor in Stepney and Sokoloff a CP councillor; this book refers to the work done by Stepney CP councillors and some later reflections on the CP in 1970s and 1980s.

4907 Sommerfield, John **May Day** *L&W* 1984 242pp pb This ed. has Intro. by A. Croft with material on Sommerfield.

4908 Spence, Alan **Class Struggle in Covent Garden and Other Articles** *s.p.* 1982 40pp One interesting article on CP industrial strategy 1960s-1980.

4909 Spender, Stephen **The Thirties and After** *Fontana* 1978 286pp pb Contains 'Why I Join the CP', from 'DW' Feb. 19 1937.

4910 Spender, Stephen **World Within World** *H. Hamilton* 1951 349pp hb

4911 Spiers, John et al. (eds) **The Left in Britain: A Checklist and Guide** *Harvester* 1976 168pp hb Intended as an annual guide, this one describes 'contributing organisations' – i.e. those which send publications to the associated microfilming project (CP joined in 1988). Important bibliographical tool but little on CP, apart from entries on Maoist groups.

4912 Spratt, Philip **Blowing Up India: Reminiscences and Reflections of a Former Comintern Emissary** *Prachi Prakashan, Calcutta* 1955 117pp Engaging short autobiog.; covers CP at Cambridge in early 1920s, then London (during the General Strike he was criticised at a Branch meeting for 'un class-conscious behaviour' for playing in a strikers' cricket match! In the mid 1920s he was sent to India.

4913 Spriano, Paolo **Stalin and the European Communists** *Verso* 1985 314pp hb

4914 Squires, Mike **Saklatvala: A Political Biography** *L&W* 1990 227pp hb MP for Battersea from 1922 to 1929 (from 1924 as Communist, previously as Labour). Important figure in India, too.

4915 Squires, Mike **The Aid to Spain Movement in Battersea** *Elmfield Publications* 1994 64pp pb Much on CP; incl. short biogs. of local men in the I.B.

4916 Srebrnik, Henry **London Jews and British Communism 1935-45** *Vallentine Mitchell* 1995 258pp hb Extensively researched; lengthy bibliography.

4917 Srebrnik, Henry **Sidestepping the Contradictions: the CP, Jewish Communists and Zionism, 1934-58** in *'Opening the Books'* G. Andrews et al. (eds) 1995 18pp pb

4918 Srebrnik, Henry **The British CP's National Jewish Committee and the Fight Against Anti-Semitism During the 2nd World War** in *'The Politics of Marginality'* T. Kushner & K. Lunn (eds); F. Cass 1990 15pp hb

4919 Stammers, Neil **Civil Liberties in Britain During the Second World War** *Croom Helm* 1983 240pp hb

4920 'Stammers, John' **British Workers in Action, 1800-1945** *Bombay* 1945 90pp pb 'A British Communist answers the commonly repeated charge – "every Briton is an imperialist"'.

4921 Stansky, Peter & Abrahams, W. **Journey to the Frontier: Julian Bell and John Cornford – Their Lives and the Thirties** *Constable* 1994 430pp pb

4922 Starrett, Bob **Rattling the Cage** *Ferrett Press* 1983 104pp pb Drawings and a lengthy interview with the Communist cartoonist.

4923 Steele, Tom **The Emergence of Cultural Studies, 1945-65: Cultural Politics, Adult Education and the English Question** *L&W* 1997 228pp pb Bit on E.P. Thompson, R. Williams and CP in general.

4924 Stennett, Enrico **Buckra Massa Pickney** *UPSO* 2006 430pp pb Autobiog. of Jamaican who came to Britain in 1947. Active in CP, Labour Party, trade union but especially in Black organisations – League for Coloured People, Coloured Workers' Association of GB, founder and Chairman of the African League etc.

4925 Stevens, Bertha (ed.) **Bernard Stevens and His Music** *Kahn & Averill* 1989 222pp hb Composer; left CP in 1956.

4926 Stevens, Richard **Charlesworth, John** in *'DLB' 10* 2000 6pp

4927 Stevens, Richard **Fighting on the Byways: John 'Jack' James Charlesworth 1900-93** *Nottingham TUC/KFAT/LRD* 1994 122pp pb Leading figure in Nottingham Hosiery workers' union and T.C., also Chair of LRD.

4928 Stevenson, Graham (ed.) **The Life and Times of Sid Easton 1911-91** *Friends of S. Easton/TGWU* 1992 ? 48pp Leading taxi cab militant in TGWU. Incl. Easton's reminiscences, obituary, funeral oration etc.

4929 Stevenson, R. (ed.) **Time Remembered: Alan Bush, An 80th Birthday Symposium** *Bravura* 1981 224pp hb lf

4930 Stewart, Bob **Breaking The Fetters** *L&W* 1967 200pp hb Author was founder member of CP and acted as Gen. Sec. when other leaders were imprisoned in 1926.

4931 Stewart, John **The Battle for Health: A Political History of the Socialist Medical Association, 1930-51** *Ashgate* 1999 259pp

4932 Stewart-Smith, D. **No Vision Here: Non-Military Warfare in Britain** *Foreign Affairs Publ. Co.* 1966 142pp hb

4933 Stradling, Robert **Cardiff and the Spanish Civil War** *Butetown History & Arts Centre* 1996 144pp pb

4934 Stradling, Robert **History and Legend: Writing the International Brigades** *Univ. of Wales Press* 2003 282pp hb

4935 Stradling, Robert **Wales and the Spanish Civil War** *Univ. of Wales Press* 2004 251pp pb

4936 Straight, Michael **After Long Silence** *Collins* 1983 351pp hb Cambridge in the 1930s.

4937 Stratton, Harry **In Memory of My Wife and Comrade, Lil Stratton** *s.p.* 1961 76pp hb lf Hungarian anti-fascist who married Welsh CP member and became active in Swansea CP. Includes funeral oration by Annie Powell etc. With Hungarian translation. Presumably very few printed.

4938 Stratton, Harry **To Anti-Fascism by Taxi** *Alun Books* 1984 184pp pb On Spanish Civil War.

4939 Straw, Jack **Last Man Standing** *Pan Macmillan* 2012 456pp Never a member, this autobiog. relates his brushes with the CP from his days of activism in CND and, more importantly, the student movement, plus his quizzing by security forces about his contacts with CP members on becoming a Government minister.

4940 Stretton, Hugh **George Rudé** in *'History From Below'* F. Krantz (ed.); Concordia Univ., Montreal 1985 12pp pb

4941 Sullivan, Robert **Christopher Caudwell** *Croom Helm* 1987 208pp hb Incl. info. on his activities in CP in Poplar.

4942 Suss, Henry & Chapple, Dave **Henry Suss and the Jewish Working-Class of Manchester and Salford: Interviews with Dave Chapple** *Somerset Socialist Library* 2005 216pp pb lf Suss was active in the clothing trade, serving on the Executive of the NUTGW and as Secretary of the CP's Clothing & Textile Advisory. He was the first Communist to be elected as a councillor in Lancashire.

4943 Sutherland, D.M. **Communism in the British Empire** *Niebelungen Verlag, Berlin* 1938 12pp I have been unable to trace a copy of this pamphlet, written by a leading member of the British Anti-Socialist and Anti-Communist Union, but its publishing history makes it extremely unusual and of some interest. It is listed in Alan MacKenzie's Bibliography (see Introduction).

4944 Swann, Brenda & Aprahamian, Francis (eds) **J.D. Bernal: A Life in Science and Politics** *Verso* 1999 369pp hb

4945 Swingler, Randall **Selected Poems** *Trent Editions* 2000 113pp pb See Intro. by A. Croft.

4946 Symons, Julian **The Thirties** *Cresset* 1960 186pp hb Strong on left culture (LBC, AIA, Unity Theatre) but also Spain & Unemployed Marches.

4947 Tannahill, R. Neal **The Communist Parties of Western Europe: A Comparative Study** *Greenwood* 1978 299pp

4948 Taylor, A.H. **Communism in GB: A Short History of the British CP** *Conservative Political Centre* 1951 54pp

4949 Taylor, A.J.P. **A Personal History** *H. Hamilton* 1983 278pp hb Briefly ran CP branch in Oxford with Tom Driberg. Several refs to CP but unfortunately not in index. Quite a bit on Henry Sara.

4950 Taylor, Andrew **The NUM and British Politics (2 vols)** *Ashgate* 2005; 2007 269; 357pp Most refs are in Vol.1.

4951 Taylor, Graham **The Marxist Inertia and the Labour Movement** in *'Politics and Power 1'*; RKP 1980 15pp pb

4952 Taylor, Murdoch **The YCL** in *'Youth Organisations of GB'* Douglas Cooke (ed.); Jordan 1944 4pp hb This entry on the YCL, by the Gen. Sec., emphasises 'club' activity and plays down the politics; there was a further ed. in 1946 which redresses the balance slightly. Lists branch offices and secretaries.

4953 Taylor, Richard & Young, Nigel (eds) **Campaigns for Peace: British Peace Movements in the Twentieth Century** *MUP* 1987 308pp hb

4954 Taylor, Richard & Pritchard, Colin **The Protest Makers: The British Nuclear Disarmament Movement of 1958-65** *Pergamon* 1980 190pp hb

4955 Taylor, Tom **Defend Socialism from the Communists** *ILP* 1942 12pp

4956 Temple, Richard **Horner, John** in *'DLB' 13* 2010 6pp

4957 Temple, Richard **Jones, Bill** in *'DLB' 13* 2010 5pp

4958 Temple, Richard **Nicholas, Peter** in *'DLB' 13* 2010 3pp

4959 Temple, Richard **Stokes, William** in *'DLB' 10* 2000 4pp Midlands engineers' leader.

4960 Terry, Michael & Edwards, P.K. (eds) **Shopfloor Politics and Job Controls: The Post-War Engineering Industry** *Blackwell* 1988 245pp Especially S. Jefferys on Longbridge, 1939-80 – incl. Dick Etheridge.

4961 Thayer, George **The British Political Fringe** *A. Blond* 1965 256pp hb

4962 Thomas, Frank & Stradling, Robert **Brother Against Brother: Experiences of a British Volunteer in the Spanish Civil War**

Sutton 1998 180pp hb About 2 Welshmen on opposite sides in Spain. Mostly about the Francoist Thomas, but material on Sid Hamm, a Communist who died in Spain, incl. his diary.

4963 Thomas, Hugh **John Strachey** *Eyre Methuen* 1973 316pp hb

4964 Thompson, E.P. **Beyond the Frontier** *Merlin* 1997 111pp Lectures about author's brother, Frank Thompson and his involvement in the CP prior to his fatal expedition to Bulgaria with the partisans. It was Iris Murdoch who recruited Frank into the CP. Some of Frank's poems are included.

4965 Thompson, E.P. **Caudwell** in *'Socialist Register'; Merlin* 1977 48pp

4966 Thompson, E.P. **Christopher Caudwell** in *'Persons and Polemics'; Merlin* 1994 64pp

4966a Thompson, E.P.; Winslow, Cal (ed.) **E.P. Thompson and the Making of the New Left** *L&W* 2014 288pp

4967 Thompson, E.P. **Edgell Rickword** in *'Persons and Polemics'; Merlin* 1994 8pp

4968 Thompson, E.P. **Left Review** in *'Persons and Polemics'; Merlin* 1994 7pp

4969 Thompson, E.P. **The Peculiarities of the English** in *'Socialist Register' 1965* 1965 52pp

4970 Thompson, E.P. **The Peculiarities of the English** in *'The Poverty of Theory'; Merlin* 1978 56pp Longer version of chapter from 'Socialist Register' 1965.

4971 Thompson, E.P. & Thompson, T.J. **There Is A Spirit in Europe: Memoir of Frank Thompson** *Gollancz* 1947 191pp Authors were Frank's brother and mother. Frank joined CP at Oxford; died with partisans in Bulgaria.

4972 Thomson, George **'Illusion and Reality' by C. Caudwell: Biographical Note (Introduction)** *L&W* 1966 3pp

4973 Thompson, Noel **John Strachey: An Intellectual Biography** *Macmillan* 1993 288pp Strachey was very close to the CP till 1940 – he was described by D. Caute as 'a Communist who never joined'.

4974 Thompson, Noel **Strachey, John** in *'DLB' 10* 2000 8pp Covers his relations with CP.

4975 Thompson, Willie **Scottish Communism** in *'Scottish Dimensions' – Conference Papers: History, The Nation and the Schools* 1995 9pp lf

4976 Thompson, Willie **Setting An Agenda: Thomson, Dobb, Hill and the CP Historians** *Socialist History Society* 2012 57pp pb

4977 Thompson, Willie **The End of the CPGB** *Dept of Social Sciences, Glasgow Caledonian Univ.* 1996 12pp lf

4978 Thompson, Willie **The Good Old Cause: British Communism 1920-1991** *Pluto* 1992 258pp pb The first history of the Party published after its demise; this is a critical analysis by a historian who was a long-standing member.

4979 Thornett, Alan **100 Years: Oxford & District T.C.** *Oxford TC* 1987 38pp

4980 Thornett, Alan **Inside Cowley** *Porcupine* 1998 408pp pb Trotskyist view of the car factory/car industry in the 1970s. Many, critical, refs to CP and Derek Robinson.

4981 Thornton, Carol **Reformists and Revolutionaries: Scottish Communists in the 1920s** *Dept of Social Sciences, Glasgow Caledonian Univ.* 1996 ? 12pp lf

4982 Thorpe, Andrew **Britain in the 1930s** *Blackwell* 1993 145pp Short chapter on CP.

4983 Thorpe, Andrew **Communist MP: Willie Gallacher and British Communism** in *'Agents of the Revolution' K. Morgan et al. (eds)* 2005 14pp

4984 Thorpe, Andrew **The British CP and Moscow, 1920-43** *MUP* 2000 308pp hb Looks in detail at CPGB's relations with Moscow, emphasising the complexities.

4985 Thorpe, Andrew (ed.) **The Failure of Political Extremism in Inter-War Britain** *Exeter Univ.* 1989 92pp pb Contains: '"The Only Effective Bulwark Against Reaction & Revolution": Labour & the Frustration of the Extreme Left' by A. Thorpe & ' The Failure of the Communists: The NUWM 1921-39' by H. Harmer.

4986 Thurlow, Richard **The Secret State: British Internal Security in the Twentieth Century** *Blackwell* 1994 458pp hb

4987 Thurlow, Richard **The Security Services, the CPGB and British Fascism, 1932-1951** in *'British Fascism, the Labour Movement & the State' by N. Copsey & D. Renton* 2005 20pp

4988 Tippett, Michael **Those Twentieth Century Blues: An Autobiography** *Pimlico* 1994 290pp pb The composer was in the CP for a couple of months before moving to Trotskyism and then pacifism.

4989 Todd, Nigel **In Excited Times: The People Against the Blackshirts** *Bewick Press* 1995 130pp pb Anti-fascism in the North East during the 1930s and after.

4990 Tolley, A.T. **The Poetry of the Thirties** *Gollancz* 1975 445pp Chapter on Popular Front ('Left Review', LBC, Caudwell etc. Another on Spain, Cornford etc), plus other refs.

4991 Tomlinson, John **Left, Right: The March of Political Extremism in Britain** *J. Calder* 1981 152pp pb 4pp on CP.

4992 Toole, Millie **Mrs Bessie Braddock, M.P.** *Hale* 1957 223pp hb In CP till 1924.

4993 Torr, Dona **Tom Mann** *L&W* 1936 48pp pb

4994 Tough, Alistair **Etheridge, Dick** in *'DLB'* 9 1993 5pp

4995 Toynbee, Philip **Friends Apart: A Memoir of the Thirties** *MacGibbon & Kee* 1954 189pp hb Toynbee was first Communist elected President of the Oxford Union.

4996 Toynbee, Philip (ed.) **The Distant Drum: Reflections on the Spanish Civil War** *Sidgwick & Jackson* 1976 192pp Incl. memoirs by J. Jump & T. Hyndman, and notes on Kenneth Bond. Toynbee's section covers Oxford.

4997 Tracey, Herbert (ed.) **Libels in the Daily Worker: Verbatim Report of Counsel's Speeches and Judgement** *TUC* 1940 70pp Slightly shorter version of 'Union Leaders Vindicated'. On CP's attitude to WW2.

4998 Trory, Ernie **Between the Wars** *Crabtree Press* 1974 160pp pb CP Organiser in Brighton.

4999 Trory, Ernie **Imperialist War: Further Recollections of a Communist Organiser** *Crabtree Press* 1977 242pp

5000 Trory, Ernie **Peace and the Cold War: Part 1 Labour in Government, 1940-51** *Crabtree Press* 1996 288pp pb

5001 Trory, Ernie **War of Liberation: Recollections of a Communist Activist** *People's Publications* 1987 395pp pb Third vol. of autobiog./political analysis; expelled in 1942.

5001a Trunski, Slavcho **Grateful Bulgaria** *Sofia Press* 1979 96pp Much on Frank Thompson – his student activities and mission to Bulgaria. Author interviewed various British and Bulgarian people who knew him.

5002 Tsuzuki, Chushichi **Tom Mann, 1856-1941** *OUP* 1991 289pp hb

5003 Tuckett, Angela **Ike Gradwell** *s.p.* 1980 ? 18pp

5004 Tupper, Edward **Seamen's Torch** *Hutchinson* 1938 320pp More of an anti-Communist rant than narrative or analysis.

5005 'Tyler, Wat' **Behind the Revolutionary Mask: A Critique of Neo-Maoism** *Appeal Group* 1974 58pp Critique of 'Korba' & the 'Birmingham Collective' who called for a new CP to be set up. This pamphlet calls for the Midlands DC to ban ultra-left material from the CP bookshop & ultra-lefts from the Social Club!

5006 'Tyler, Wat' **Forgotten Words** *Appeal Group* 1975 93pp Lengthy critique of CP pamphlet 'About Marxism'.

5007 'Tyler, Wat' **The Pauper Trap** *Appeal Group* 1973 46pp A miniscule Stalinist group within the CP; most of the content of their pamphlets attacks the CP for revisionism.

5008 Utley, Freda **Lost Illusion** *A&U* 1949 238pp hb

5009 Utley, Freda **Odyssey of a Liberal: Memoirs** *Washington National Press* 1970 319pp hb Friend of Shaw, the Webbs, Russell; worked for CP in Lancashire in 1930s among cotton workers. Married Russian who disappeared in the Purges; subsequently bitterly anti-Communist. This book has more about Britain than her earlier autobiog., 'Lost Illusion', which concentrates on her life in USSR.

5010 Valtin, J. **Out of the Night** *Alliance Book Corp., NY* 1941 749pp hb Pseudonym of R. Krebs; worked for C.I. – one fascinating chapter on U.K.: claims to have destroyed George Hardy's position and reduced wages at 'DW'. Accuses CP leadership of corruption.

5011 Vernon, Betty **Ellen Wilkinson** *Croom Helm* 1982 254pp pb Founder member of CP, left in 1924. Became Labour Minister of Education. Some info. on J. Walton Newbold, to whom she was briefly engaged.

5012 'Vidor, John' **Spying in Russia** *John Long* 1929 284pp Spy who infiltrated CP and NMM – calls himself 'an executive member of the Red Movement'. Mainly about his spying attempts while on a fraternal delegation, but he expounds his views of the CPGB.

5012a Virdee, Satnam **Racism, Class and the Racialized Outsider** *Palgrave* 2014 200pp hb

5013 Visram, Rozina **Asians in Britain: 400 Years of History** *Pluto* 2002 488pp Incl. Saklatvala.

5014 Wadsworth, Mark **Comrade Sak: Shapurji Saklatvala, MP – A Political Biography** *Peepal Tree Press* 1998 202pp pb Concentrates on his anti-imperialism, fight for Indian independence and race issues. Argues that Saklatvala, and Black politics, were marginalised in the CPGB. Contains texts of 2 pamphlets by Saklatvala plus letters in appendices.

5015 Waite, Mike **Sex 'n' Drugs 'n' Rock 'n' Roll (and Communism) in the 1960s** in *'Opening the Books'* G. Andrews et al. (eds) 1995 15pp pb

5016 Wakley, Tom **Communist Circus** *Clarion Socialist Youth Hostel* 1943 16pp sf Ill. by Gow.

5017 Wallace, Malcolm **Nothing To Lose ... A World to Win: A History of the Chelmsford & District Trades Union Council** s.p. 1979 144pp pb

5018 Waller, Michael **Democratic Centralism: An Historical Commentary** *MUP* 1981 155pp hb

5019 Wallis, Mick **Heirs to the Pageant: Mass Spectacle and the Popular Front** in *'A Weapon in the Struggle'* A. Croft (ed.) 1998 20pp pb

5020 Walsh, R.P. **Communists in the Unions** *Fighting Facts* 1955 ? 4pp

5021 Warburg, Frederic **An Occupation for Gentlemen** *Hutchinson* 1959 288pp hb Interesting for description of attempts by CP (followed by ILP) to woo if not recruit this respected publisher.

5022 Ward, Bert **Who'll Take the Collection? A Political Journey** s.p. 2007 90pp Autobiog. of Teesside working-class activist; a labourer who went on to Ruskin and became a lecturer. Active on the Irish issue within the CP and beyond.

5023 Ward, Michael **Red Flag Over the Workhouse: The Unemployed in SW London, 1918-23** *Wandsworth History Workshop* 1992 30pp lf Useful on early CP and local members.

5024 Ward, Paul **Red Flag and Union Jack: Englishness, Patriotism and the British Left, 1881-1924** *Boydell* 1998 232pp

5025 Warren, Des **Shrewsbury: Whose Conspiracy?** *New Park* 1980 30pp This 2nd ed. has an intro. very critical of the CP over the Shrewsbury pickets. 1st ed. was self-published in 1977.

5026 Warren, Des **The Key to My Cell** *New Park* 1982 319pp pb Autobiog. by one of the 'Shrewsbury 3' written after his break with CP. Very rare case of a prominent Communist joining a Trotskyist organisation after 1956.

5027 Watkins, K.W. **Britain Divided: The Effect of the Spanish Civil War on British Political Opinion** *Nelson* 1963 270pp hb

5028 Watkins, K.W. **Political Strikes** *Freedom Association* 1984 12pp

5029 Watson, Don & Corcoran, John **An Inspiring Example: The North East of England and the Spanish Civil War, 1936-1939** *McGuffin Press* 1966 85pp Much on Alex Robson and SS Linaria – an attempt by sailors to boycott a shipment of nitrates to Spain. Also on other CP members.

5030 Watson, Don **No Justice Without a Struggle: The NUWM in the North East of England, 1920-1940** *Merlin* 2014 276pp pb Well researched, incl. oral history records and much contemporary documentation.

5031 Watson, Elizabeth **Don't Wait For It** *Imperial War Museum* 1994 57pp pb Quentin Bell's Preface has tantalising glimpses of Watson's activities in the 1930s in the CP and AIA (of which she became Secretary). This memoir of her time as an ambulance driver in the blitz also has reproductions of some of her paintings from 1994 exhibition.

5032 Watson, George **Politics and Literature in Modern Britain** *Macmillan* 1977 190pp Has chapter 'Did Stalin Dupe the Intellectuals?' but covers all of Europe not just GB.

5033 Watt, Lewis **Communism** *Catholic Truth Society* 1932 32pp Bit on CPGB.

5034 Watters, Frank **Being Frank: The Memoirs of Frank Watters** *Monkspring* 1992 194pp pb Autobiog. of Communist organiser remembered for his role in the 'Battle of Saltley Gates'.

5035 Webster, Nesta **The Socialist Network** *Boswell* 1926 165pp hb Gloriously, eccentrically right-wing.

5036 Weiler, Peter **British Labour and the Cold War** *Stanford UP* 1988 431pp hb

5037 Weiler, Peter **British Labour and the Cold War: The London Dock Strike of 1949** in *'Social Conflict and the Political Order in Modern Britain'* J. Cronin & J. Schneer (eds); *Croom Helm* 1982 32pp hb

5038 Weinbren, Daniel **Generating Socialism: Recollections of Life in the Labour Party** *Sutton* 1997 250pp hb Lot on CP.

5039 Weintraub, Stanley **The Last Great Cause: Intellectuals and the Spanish Civil War** *W.H. Allen* 1968 340pp hb

5040 Weller, Ken **Don't be A Soldier! The Radical Anti-War Movement in North London 1914-1918** *Journeyman* 1985 96pp pb Lot of material on individuals who became active in the CP.

5041 Weller, Ken **Thring, Lillian** in *'DLB'* 8 1987 2pp

5042 Welton, Harry **The Third World War: Trade and Industry** *Pall Mall* 1959 330pp Substantial material on CP's industrial work.

5043 Werner, Ruth **Sonya's Report** *Chatto* 1991 318pp hb Key Comintern spy in China in 1930s and Switzerland in early stages of WW2. Later came to Britain, joined CP in Banbury having married a British Communist, before fleeing to GDR on being identified. Several of her sisters were active in the CPGB.

5044 Werskey, Gary **The Visible College: A Collective Biography of British Scientists and Socialists of the 1930s** *Allen Lane* 1978 376pp hb Explores in detail the relationship between the scientific and political ideas of the famous group of left-wing scientists of the 1930s and 1940s.

5045 Wesker, Arnold **As Much As I Dare: An Autobiography** *Century* 1994 578pp hb Wesker was briefly in the YCL, other members of his family (parents, aunt, uncle, sister) longer. London East End Jewish background.

5046 West, Alick **One Man in His Time** *A&U* 1969 193pp hb Autobiog. of Communist translator and literary critic.

5047 West, Nigel **A Matter of Trust: MI5, 1945-72** *Weidenfeld* 1982 196pp hb

5048 West, Nigel **Mask: MI5's Penetration of the CPGB** *Routledge* 2005 324pp Many unsubstantiated claims of CP members being Russian spies.

5049 West, Nigel **MI5: British Security Service Operations 1909-45** *Bodley Head* 1981 366pp hb Of all the spy books probably contains most, after Costello, on CP – incl. infiltration of CP by security agencies.

5050 West, Nigel & Tsarev, Oleg **The Crown Jewels: The British Secrets at the Heart of the KGB Archives** *HarperCollins* 1998 366pp

5051 West, Nigel **Venona: The Greatest Secret of the Cold War** *HarperCollins* 1999 384pp Incl. material on Ivor Montagu and J.B.S. Haldane.

5052 West, W.J. **Truth Betrayed** *Duckworth* 1987 262pp hb Some brief, but tantalising, refs to CP propaganda prior to WW2.

5053 Westacott, Fred **Shaking the Chains** *Joe Clark* 2002 402pp pb Full-time worker for CP for over 30 years, mainly in East Midlands.

5054 Westacott, Fred **The Unemployed Struggles of the Thirties and Some Personal Memories** *Self-published* 1990 ? 26pp lf

5055 Wheen, Francis **Tom Driberg: His Life and Indiscretions** *Chatto* 1990 452pp hb Debunks the commonly repeated claim that Driberg was an MI5 plant in the CP.

5056 Whitaker, Reg **Fighting the Cold War on the Home Front** in *'Socialist Register'*; *Merlin* 1984 44pp pb

5057 White, Carol & Williams, Sian Rhiannon (eds) **Struggle or Starve: Women's Lives in the South Wales Valleys Between the two World Wars** *Honno* 1998 275pp pb Incl. brief reminiscences from just one CP member, Mair E. McLellan.

5058 Baker White, John **The Red Network** s.p. 1953 38pp

5059 White, Joseph **Tom Mann** *MUP* 1991 242pp hb Chapter on his years in the CP.

5060 White, Stephen **Britain and the Bolshevik Revolution** *Holmes & Meier* 1979 317pp hb

5061 Whiting, R.C. **The View From Cowley: The Impact of Industrialization upon Oxford, 1918-39** *OUP* 1983 214pp hb Esp. Pressed Steel and Morris Motors. Much on CP, incl. interviews.

5062 Wicks, Harry; Barrow, Logie **Keeping My Head: The Memoirs of a British Bolshevik** *Socialist Platform* 1992 226pp pb One of the best books by a Trotskyist on the CP.

5063 Wicks, Harry **The General Strike** *Workers' News* 1976 16pp Intro. by J. Higgins has info. on Wicks & CP.

5064 Widgery, David **The Left in Britain 1956-68** *Penguin* 1976 549pp pb

5065 Wigham, Eric **What's Wrong With the Unions?** *Penguin* 1961 254pp pb Has a chapter 'The Red Machine' about CP and unions, plus other passing refs (but no index).

5066 Wild, R.L. **Wild Oats** *Blackwood* 1959 242pp Passing ref. to Charlie Bateman –'Winchester's only Communist'.

5067 Wilde, Arthur **The Biggest Battle is Yet to Come** *B. Lewis & D. Prudhoe/People's History of Yorkshire Vol.1* 1980 42pp pb Doncaster miner activist. This short book covers his activity to 1970s. Covers his personal life and world events, but is mostly about his CP activity (he joined in 1926) and is a particularly vivid example of the genre.

5068 Wilkinson, Ellen **Ellen Wilkinson in 'Myself When Young'** ed. Countess of Oxford *F. Muller* 1938 17pp

5069 Williams, Andrew **Labour and Russia: The Attitude of the LP to the USSR, 1924-1934** *MUP* 1989 264pp hb

5070 Williams, Chris **Capitalism, Community and Conflict: The South Wales Coalfield, 1898-1947** *Univ. of Wales Press* 1998 146pp pb

5071 Williams, Chris **Democratic Rhondda** *Univ. of Wales* 1996 304pp hb

5072 'Williams, David' **Report of the CC of the Revolutionary CP of Britain (M-L)** *Workers' Publishing House* 1983 288pp Section on CP. Maoist.

5073 Williams, Keith & Matthews, Steven **Rewriting the Thirties: Modernism and After** *Longman* 1997 221pp Esp. useful on Swingler, Montagu Slater and political theatre.

5074 Williams, Val **The Other Observers: Women Photographers in Britain, 1900 to the Present** *Virago* 1994 192pp Discusses Edith Tudor Hart and Helen Muspratt (later Helen Dunman), both leading photographers in the 1930s and CP members.

5075 Williamson, Cliff **An Antidote to Communism: Catholic Social Action in Glasgow, 1931-39** in *'Out of the Ghetto? The Catholic Community in Modern Scotland'* R. Boyle & P. Lynch (eds); *John Donald* 1998 31pp More on anti-Communism, but not without interest esp. the successful creation of an alternative to the NUWM.

5076 Williamson, Frank **Marx and the Millennium** *s.p.* 1999 238pp pb Intro. has some autobiographical material. Author involved in CP educational work in Manchester.

5077 Williamson, H. (ed.) **India and Communism** *Intelligence Bureau, Home Dept, Government of India* 1935 395pp hb Revised version of 1933 ed. (Another ed., edited by M. Saha, was published by Editions India in 1976). Covers Saklatvala, CP influence among Indian students, Meerut.

5078 Williamson, Howard (ed.) **Toolmaking and Politics: the Life of Ted Smallbone – An Oral History** *Linden Books* 1987 148pp pb Midlands' engineering activist; fought in Spain.

5079 Williamson, John **Dangerous Scot: The Life and Work of an American 'Undesirable'** *IPNY* 1969 221pp pb Last chapter covers his life in UK.

5080 Willis, Ted **Evening All** *Macmillan* 1991 244pp hb Disappointingly brief mention of YCL as Willis had edited Challenge and been Chairman of the YCL before achieving fame as a pioneer of soap opera with Mrs Dale's Diary & Dixon of Dock Green and being elevated to the Lords.

5081 Willis, Ted **Whatever Happened to Tom Mix? The Story of One of My Lives** *Cassell* 1970 198pp hb

5082 Wilson, Andrew **James Boswell: Extracting the Dream Reality** *Austin/Desmond Fine Art* 1999 40pp pb Exhibiton catalogue.

5083 Wilson, J. Havelock **The Red Hand Exploiting the T.U. Movement: The Communist Offensive Against the British Empire** *Industrial Peace Union (?)* 1926 40pp Reproduces and comments on George Hardy's 'Report to Workers' Plenum', March 1926.

5084 Wincott, Len **Invergordon Mutineer** *Weidenfeld* 1974 183pp hb Wincott, leader of the 1931 mutiny, joined the CP afterwards.

5085 Winnington, Alan **Breakfast With Mao: Memoirs of A Foreign Correspondent** *L&W* 1986 255pp pb Winnington, and brother Richard the film critic, joined the CP after Pollitt sold him a 'Communist Manifesto'. He gave up his 'career' as counterfeiter and worked for the 'DW'. Became famous for his reports from Korea during the war.

5086 Winslow, Barbara **Romancing the Revolution: The Myth of Soviet Democracy and the British Left** *AU Press* 2011 417pp hb

5087 Winslow, Barbara **Sylvia Pankhurst: Sexual Politics and Political Activism** *UCL Press* 1996 236pp pb

5088 Wintringham, Tom **The Politics of Victory** *Routledge* 1941 139pp hb Completed as Germany attacked the USSR, the book is a passionate plea for the CP to drop its anti-war line by a prominent ex-member and military expert. Interesting on the politics of the CP's A.R.P. campaign.

5089 Wood, Neil **Communism and British Intellectuals** *Gollancz* 1959 209pp hb Very critical of left-wing intellectuals for getting involved in the CPGB.

5090 Wood, Conrad **The Communist Party of India: From Leftism to United Front** in

'Britain, Fascism and the Popular Front' J. Fyrth (ed.) 1985 18pp pb

5091 Woodhams, Stephen **History in the Making: Raymond Williams, Edward Thompson and Radical Intellectuals, 1936-56** *Merlin* 2001 221pp hb Much about the CP in this collective biog. of a generation of Marxist intellectuals, historians and peace activists.

5092 Woodhouse, Michael & Pearce, Brian **Essays on the History of Communism in Britain** *New Park* 1975 248pp pb Trotskyist analysis of CP in 1920s & 1930s. Collection of articles mainly from 'Labour Review'. Reprinted as 'A History of Communism in Britain' by Bookmarks in 1995.

5093 Woods, Charlie **The Crisis in Our CP: Cause, Effect and Cure** *s.p.* 1983 34pp

5094 Worley, Matthew **Class Against Class: The CP in Britain Between the Wars** *I.B. Tauris* 2002 352pp hb Detailed and well-researched analysis of the complexities of the CP in the 'Third Period'. Much on unemployed struggles; also cultural life of the CP. Argues that despite sectarianism of the Third Period, there were many positive aspects to CP's achievements at the time.

5095 Worley, Matthew **Communism and Fascism in 1920s and 1930s Britain** in *'W.H. Auden in Context' Tony Sharpe (ed.); CUP* 2013 11pp

5096 Worley, Matthew (ed.) **In Search of Revolution: International Communist Parties in the Third Period** *I.B. Tauris* 2004 400pp Contains the ed.'s chapter on the CPGB 'To the Left and Back Again' plus J. Callaghan's chapter on India which has refs to CPGB, and there are other refs.

5097 Worley, Matthew **Labour Inside the Gate: A History of the British Labour Party Between the Wars** *I.B. Tauris* 2005 278pp

5098 Worley, Matthew **Oswald Mosley and the New Party** *Palgrave Macmillan* 2010 234pp Refs to some individuals who passed through the NP before joining the CP.

5099 Worley, Matthew **To the Left and Back Again: The CPGB in the Third Period** in *'In Search of Revolution: International Communist Parties in the Third Period'; I.B. Tauris* 2004 22pp

5100 Wright, Patrick **The Village That Died for England: The Strange Story of Tyneham** *Vintage* 1996 420pp Rural class struggle in Dorset – esp. S. Townsend Warner & V. Ackland.

5101 Wright, Peter **Spycatcher** *Viking* 1987 392pp Details of some episodes of government spying on CP.

5102 Wrigley, Chris (ed.) **A History of British Industrial Relations Vol.2, 1914-39** *Harvester* 1986 335pp Esp. R. Hyman 'Rank & File Movements and Workplace Organisation, 1914-39' and C. Wrigley 'The TUs Between the Wars'.

5103 Wrigley, Chris (ed.) **A History of British Industrial Relations, 1939-79** *E. Elgar* 1996 239pp See especially D. Lyddon's chapter on car industry.

5104 Wyatt, Woodrow **The Peril in Our Midst** *Phoenix House* 1956 70pp CP in industry.

5105 Wyncoll, Peter **The Nottingham Labour Movement, 1880-1939** *L&W* 1985 256pp

5105a Yates, Michael **Ralph Bates: Swindon's 'Unknown' Author** *ESLP* 2014 80pp Author has unearthed correspondence between Bates and Pollitt which indicate Bates was a CP member, despite Bates' later denials when he was an academic in the US.

5106 Young, George K. **Subversion and the British Riposte** *Ossian* 1984 175pp

5107 Young, James D. **The Very Bastards of Creation** *Clydeside Press* 1996 342pp Chapter on the writers James Barke and James Mitchell ('L. Grassic Gibbon') incl. their relationship to CP.

5108 Young, James D. **The World of C.L.R. James** *Clydeside Press* 1999 392pp

5109 Young, Nigel **An Infantile Disorder? The Crisis and Decline of the New Left** *RKP* 1977 490pp Analysis of CP's work in CND.

5110 Young, Thom & Kettle, Martin **Incitement to Disaffection** *Cobden Trust* 1976 120pp Covers CP in 1920s and 1930s.

5111 Zhak, Lyubov **The Fighting Scotsman (William Gallacher)** in *'Lenin's Comrades-in-Arms' Progress Publishers, Moscow* 1969 24pp

5112 Zinkin, Peter **A Man To Be Watched Carefully** *People's Publications* 1985 168pp Journalist; ed. of 'New Propellor'.

12. About the CP – Magazine Articles

I have excluded articles from newspapers and, with the very occasional exception, weekly magazines – because of the work involved but also because these articles tend to be short and topical (e.g. at the time of national Congresses, during industrial disputes). Anyone doing research into a certain event or period might want to follow this up by going through *Tribune, New Statesman* etc. Occasionally, the *Times Literary Supplement* (e.g. between April and June 1966) and the *London Review of Books* (e.g. September 1998) had articles or debates on the CP. Other papers worth looking at include: *New Times* (the paper of the CPGB's official successor organisation Democratic Left); *Red Aid Activist* (British Section ICWPA); *Jewish Forum* (Workers' Circle, Branch no. 9); *Straight Left*; papers by far left organisations too numerous to list but including *Socialist Worker* and *Red Mole* etc. Among the earlier Trotskyist papers, *Red Flag* (1933-7) and *Fight* (1936-7) are useful. Many Maoist papers, especially in the late 1960s, will also have regular articles on the CPGB.

There are also periodicals by right-wing organisations worth looking at: *IRIS News*, *Common Cause Bulletin* (which, especially in the 1960s, had many interesting snippets of industrial information), and the Economic League's *Notes and Comments*, published fortnightly, though on subscription only. Longer articles from *East-West Digest* have been included, though there was something on the CP in most issues.

Some other magazines and journals have also been omitted from this chapter: the CP reviews *World News And Views, World News, Comment, Focus, News And Views* consist largely of articles on the CP, many very short, so these are omitted. However, articles from *Inprecorr* with significant mention of the CPGB are included, though not the general 'political situation' type report and not every CC statement. *Inprecorr* articles reporting interventions by CP members at C.I. conferences and plenums are only included if there is substantial reference to CP activity or policy in Britain. Apart from articles on the CP, *Inprecorr* is full of material on industrial disputes, unemployed campaigns, colonies, the Spanish Civil War etc, which may have passing references to the CPGB but which have been omitted. From 1937 there are many fewer internal articles in *Inprecorr*, reflecting a move away from Third Period sectarianism in the international communist movement.

Articles from other CP journals have been included: *Link*, *Marxism Today*, *Communist Review* and *The Communist* – but only where they are about the CP's activity; policy statements are generally excluded. *Communist Review* [2] had an increasing number of reports in the mid 1930s on industrial disputes which include the briefest of references to the CP – these are not included. 'C.R.' is used for the earlier 'Communist Review' (1921-35), and 'CR' for its later incarnation (1946-53) – and 'Communist Review (CPB)' for that organisation's journal.

The *Communist International* is another magazine from which many articles have been listed. Initially the 'Official Organ of the ECCI', it was later published from King Street and then by Modern Books. Its numbering is chaotic; not only was this different from the Russian edition but there were special C.I. Congress issues, many were not dated and there were several series; it comes as no surprise when an editorial note in December 1931 states: 'We ask our readers not to be misled by the nominal printed date of publication'! No copies of *Communist International* appear to exist for the last quarter of 1928. I can find no explanation: perhaps there were legal problems. The *Communist International* quoted is the British edition – for a period there was a separate American edition.

The *Communist International* was not the only journal with numbering problems. Several changed from using numbers to dates and vice-versa; sometimes I have given both to avoid confusion. I have tried to be consistent, but on occasion I can only list what is on the cover. The SWP's *Socialist Review* is a major culprit – to the extent that the organisation produced a special pamphlet-cum-index to explain the numbering! The paper changed its name to *Socialist Worker Review* temporarily, but I have ignored this. If anyone ever has to work on the numbers of the *Daily Worker/Morning Star* there is a similar problem – I have come across at least 20 errors of date/numbering, some dramatic. Other journals changed name, and kept the same numbering system: the *Society for the Study of Labour History Bulletin* became the *Labour History Review* in 1990.

Some of the articles listed are obviously going to be of greater significance than others – articles in academic journals more so than polemical Maoist or Trotskyist ones for instance. I have tried to indicate some of the more important ones in the latter category but I have listed all the articles I could trace whatever the source. I have been more selective when it comes to obituaries and book reviews; included are important ones from, for example, *The Society for the Study of Labour History Bulletin*. Obituaries can be useful, even if short, as they may contain important biographical information and bibliographies (see those in *Labour Monthly* and *SSLH*). Some obituaries of members of the CP contain no reference to the Party – these have been omitted. Occasionally with short reviews and obituaries I have omitted the title of the piece and just given the title of the book plus author, and stated 'Review' or given the name of the individual and stated 'Obituary', but I have not done this with major review articles.

I have been strict about not including material prior to 1920, and this does mean some of the discussion leading up to the formation of the CP is excluded; one series of articles in Sylvia Pankhurst's *Workers' Dreadnought* from 1919-20, entitled *Towards the Communist Party*, is worthy of mention. In fact, her paper carried a lot of relevant shorter articles. For the same reason, there are no articles by John Maclean before 1920 (fortunately these are well documented elsewhere).

Also excluded are articles from *Information Bulletin: Documents of the Communist & Workers' Parties*. This was a giveaway publication printed in Czechoslovakia, mainly dealing with the USSR and Eastern Europe, but it did contain speeches and reports of all communist parties, including the CPGB.

This chapter does include entries for a few newspapers which are considered to have enough articles in most issues to justify generic inclusion rather than having to list every one; these include: *The Reasoner, Vanguard, The Leninist, RPC Bulletin*. Sometimes a sequence of articles is given only one entry – i.e. for the first in a series. Reference is usually made in the notes to any subsequent articles.

Generally, very short articles are excluded, but there are exceptions. I have listed some obituaries from *The Volunteer for Liberty*, published by the International Brigade Association; all articles in this journal are short, but these obituaries are of interest in dealing with lesser known figures (even very short ones that I have not included will be of interest to those studying the CP and the Spanish Civil War). In the case of the *Marx Memorial Library Bulletin*, I have listed over 30 of the more important articles, but there are other, shorter biographical articles that are not without interest.

On occasions, the same name will have been used by more than one organisation for journals. *Socialist Review* is assumed to be the SWP, unless stated that it is the ILP. *Communist Review* is taken as one of the three CPGB incarnations of the journal, unless stated that it is by the CPB.

A minor problem with articles is the fact that titles on the cover or in the contents page can be different from the title heading the article itself: usually I've used the latter. *New Left Review* is the main culprit here.

I have been unable to trace particular issues of some journals, so either the information given is incomplete (usually the number of pages) or I have not listed the article in question (e.g. Gertrude Godden's article 'Progress on the Communist Front in Catholic World', No. clxix, 1939), as it may not be about the CPGB. Some copies of journals are simply missing from all the national libraries in the UK and from other likely libraries (English Review, October 1950 is another). Sometimes (as in a few of the bound volumes of journals in the MML), articles have been cut out: whether this was for legal reasons and applied to all imported copies, or is simply vandalism by a user, is not always clear.

Finally, it is worth noting that it is becoming much easier to trace articles, and read them, online, as more and more publishers and newspapers upload back issues – sometimes with free access (generally political publishers), sometimes for a fee (generally academic ones). Some journals moved from printed editions to online versions, for example *What Next?* In at least one case, I have listed an online article: this is in ERAS, a fully refereed postgraduate journal in Australia, and it only exists in its online form. At the very least, most journals will have tables of contents on the web. This area is rapidly changing and in a positive way for researchers.

Articles are listed by author.

5113 **1926 Remembered and Revealed & 1926 in Aberdare** in 'Llafur' Spring 1977 35pp Reminiscences by R. Page Arnot, Len Jeffreys, Will Picton, Edwin Greening, Max Goldberg.

5114 **1956: E. Hobsbawm interviewed by G. Stedman Jones** in 'MT' Nov. 1986 5pp

5115 **20th Anniversary of the CPGB: Statement of the PB** in 'LM' July 1940 2pp

5116 **33rd Congress of CP** in 'East-West Digest' Dec. 1973 2pp

5117 **40th Congress of the CP: Commentary on the Main Political Resolution** in 'Communist' Sept. 1987 5pp Straight Left.

5118 **60 Years in the Cultural Crossfire: Jack Lindsay interviewed by Andy Croft** in 'MT' Feb. 1987 1pp

5119 **60 Years: Commemorative Issue** in 'Scottish Marxist' 21 1981 44pp Incl. 'Vale of Leven in 1920s' by Bob Saunders; 'YCL in 1930s' by M. Henery; 'Cold War Period' by B. Laughlan; 'Peace Movement in Aberdeen' by M. Rose.

5120 **6th World Congress of the C.I. – Declaration of British Delegation on the Theses on the Colonial Question** in 'Inprecorr' Dec. 27 1928 2pp Reflects wide level of arguments – the C.I. was never a monolith.

5121 **9th Enlarged Plenum of ECCI: The English Question** in 'Inprecorr' Vol.8 No.12, March 1 1928 6pp Incl. contribs by Bennett (Petrovsky), Arnot, Campbell, Larkin plus Resolution.

5122 **A Debate: J.T. Murphy (CP) v. E. Boden (SPGB)** in 'Socialist Standard' May 1930 1pp

5123 **A Preliminary Appraisal of the Recent Election in England** in 'C.I.' Nov. 15 1931 6pp

5124 **Activities of English Communists After Their Union at Leeds** in 'C.I.' 16/17 1921 3pp

5125 **Agents of Cominform Seek to Capture the Factories** in 'Labour' Sept. 1951 4pp

5126 **Allies in Action in Birmingham: Women's Advisory Cttee, Birmingham** in 'Link' Spring 1981 2pp

5127 **An Open Letter to Lancashire Communists from the CC** in 'C.R.' Feb. 1934 2pp

5128 **Annual Conference of the ILP Guild of Youth** in 'The International of Youth' Sept. 1933 2pp

5129 **Articles on CP Congress and Affiliation to LP** in 'Common Cause Bulletin' 118 1967 13pp

5130 **At the Source of the CPGB** in 'WMR' Oct. 1969 1pp

5131 **August 1, 1930** in 'C.R.' July 1930 6pp

5132 **Black Struggle and the CP: Interview with Margaret Tonge** in 'Link' Autumn 1981 1pp

5133 **Blueprint for Disaster: 'Britain's Crisis: Cause and Cure' by G. Matthews – Review** in 'East West Digest' Oct. 1975 4pp

5134 **Bob Cooney in Greenock By-Election** in 'Volunteer For Liberty' June/July 1941 2pp Commissar of British Battalion in Spain.

5135 **Bowhill and the CP** in 'The Militant Scottish Miner' March 1943 1pp Trotskyist.

5136 **British Communists and the Colonies** in 'New Commonwealth' June 24 1954 3pp Short, hostile but useful.

5137 **British Communists on the War: CC Manifesto of Oct. 7** in 'LM' Nov. 1939 2pp

5138 **British Enterprise: Communist Objectives, Tenets of the Third International** in 'The Whitehall Gazette' May 6 1926 3pp Includes an attack on Communist influence in the Socialist Sunday School movement.

5139 **British Political Parties: The Communists** in 'Fact' July/Aug. 1950 3pp Labour Party official paper.

5140 **Campaign of the YCL for the Study of 'The History of the CPSU(B)'** in 'World Youth Review' Aug. 1939 1pp

5141 **Can British Leyland Survive?** in 'Socialist Review' Oct. 1978 4pp Extracts from interview in 'Comment' with D. Robinson & 3 other CP stewards at Longbridge, with reply by 2 SWP stewards.

5142 **CND and Communist Infiltration** in 'Common Cause Bulletin' April 1962 3pp

5143 **CND and Communist Infiltration** in 'Common Cause Bulletin' 108, Jan. 1964 3pp

ABOUT THE CP - MAGAZINE ARTICLES

5144 Comintern's Message to the CPGB *in 'C.R.' June 1924* 11pp Speech by Fraternal Delegate at Manchester Congress, May.

5145 Commissar Alan Gilchrist *in 'Volunteer For Liberty' Oct. 6 1938* 1pp

5146 Communism and Youth *in 'Common Cause Bulletin' 111, 1965* 54pp

5147 Communism in Britain: Reflections on the 25th Congress *in 'Common Cause Bulletin' 59, May 1957* 3pp

5148 Communism versus Social Democracy *in 'Common Cause Bulletin' 110, 1964*, 46pp

5149 Communism: A World Menace *Anti-Socialist Union 1936* 14pp 'Information Weekly'; ed. D.M. Sutherland. Only seen one copy May 15 1936: much on CPGB.

5150 Communist Activity in the T.U.s *in 'East-West Digest' Feb. 1972* 6pp

5151 Communist Conference *in 'LRD Monthly Bulletin' No.13, Oct. 1922* 2pp

5152 Communist Election Policy *in 'LM' July 1945* 3pp

5153 Communist Teachers and NUT Elections *in 'Common Cause Bulletin' 109, 1964* 2pp

5154 Communists in Britain *in 'Times Literary Supplement' March 27 1969* 1pp Review of 'Revolutionary Movement in Britain' by W. Kendall & 'Sociology of British Communism' by K. Newton.

5155 Communists in Congress *in 'East West Digest' Jan. 1980* 3pp On 36th Congress.

5156 Communists in the Public Service *in 'Hansard' March 29 1950* 54pp

5157 Communists, Their Supporters and Spurious Peace Movements *in 'Common Cause Bulletin' 109, 1964* 50pp

5158 Comrades in Conspiracy *in 'The Economist' April 24 1954* 2pp On 23rd Congress.

5159 Conference Report *in 'SSLHB' 38, Spring 1979* 10pp On 'unofficial' T.U. movements e.g. Rego strike, Fife Miners, Seamen/Dockers; Builders.

5160 Confusionists in Conflict *in 'Socialist Standard' March 1923* 1pp On Dutt's criticism of Plebs' League.

5161 Correspondence ILP-ECCI *in 'C.I.' April 1 1934* 7pp

5162 CP Affiliation *in 'Workers' International News' June/July 1946* 3pp Editorial notes. A Trotskyist view of the CP campaign to join the LP.

5163 CP Affiliation to the LP: Transcript of the Meeting of 29 December 1921 *in 'SSLHB' 41, Autumn 1974* 17pp Intro. by Royden Harrison.

5164 CP Betrays Conscription Struggle *in 'Militant' June 1939* 1pp Paper of Militant Labour League (Trotskyist).

5165 CP Congress *in 'The Week' July 8 1943* 1pp

5166 CP Leaflet Mystery *in 'Solidarity' No.2, 1969* 3pp 'A Directive to leading members only'.

5167 CP Membership Increases *in 'East-West Digest' Sept. 1973* 2pp

5168 CPGB Lurching Into Oblivion *in 'Communist Left' (International Communist Party) Jan./June 1990* 3pp

5169 CPGB's Reply to Statement of the LP on People's Front *in 'Inprecorr' May 28 1938* 2pp

5170 Crisis in the CP: Stalinism and Trotskyism in Britain *in 'Marxist' Vol.2 No.6, 1964* 12pp Extracts from 2 internal CP docs. This Trotskyist (SLL) mag. was published by Leeds Univ. Union Marxist Society.

5171 Crisis of British Stalinism Unfolds *in 'Labour Review' Feb. 1983* 2pp

5172 Dai Francis - A Tribute *in 'Arcade: Wales Fortnightly' No.11, April 3 1981* 1pp

5173 Dare-Devil Beckett *in 'Challenge' March 14 1942* 1pp On Clem Beckett.

5174 Decision: British Communism *in 'The Marxist' (Journal of the Marxist Industrial Group) No.33, 1978* 4pp Maoist view of 35th Congress.

5175 Decisions of the National Conference of the CPGB *in 'Inprecorr' Oct. 17 1936* 2pp Sheffield Conference.

5176 Declaration of Comrade Zinoviev on the Alleged 'Red Plot' *in 'Inprecorr' Nov. 6 1924* 1pp

5177 Discussion on IPD *in 'Link' Autumn 1979* 1pp How the Draft IPD document relates to women.

5178 District Congresses *in 'Communist' (CCG) Dec. 1986* 3pp Yorkshire and N.E.

5179 District Report: Kent *in 'Communist' (CCG) March 1988* 2pp

5180 Dora Cox: Profile *in 'Rebecca' July 1982* 1pp Lifelong CP activist, mainly in Wales.

5181 Draft Programme of the CPGB *in 'C.R.' June 1924* 25pp

5182 EC YCI Resolution on the British General Strike in *'The International of Youth'* New Series No.3, 1926 6pp

5183 Eddie Dare & Mary Rosser – Obituaries in *'Praxis: Bulletin of the MML'* 152, Winter 2010/11 1pp Leading activists in the MML.

5184 Editorial View: Towards A Mass Party in *'C.R.'* Oct. 1926 7pp

5185 Edmund Frow – Obituary in *'Saothar'* 22, 1997 2pp

5186 Edward Thompson 1924-1993: Scholar and Activist in *'Socialist History'* 6, 1994 4pp Interview with R. Porter on BBC Radio 3.

5187 Edward Upward: Interview in *'Socialist Review'* Dec. 1992 2pp

5188 Election Manifesto of the CPGB in *'Inprecorr'* May 10 1929 2pp

5189 Emlyn Williams: Interview in *'Radical Wales'* Autumn 1984 4pp S. Wales miners' leader was in YCL.

5190 Eric Hobsbawm: A Historian Living Through History in *'Socialist History'* 8, 1995 7pp Interview on Radio 3.

5191 Eric Hobsbawm's Communist Party Autobiography in *'Socialist History'* 24, 2003 2pp Dated 1952. In the 1930s to 1960s, CP members were sometimes asked for an autobiographical note.

5192 Even the Best of Friends Must Part in *'Socialist Review'* Jan. 1985 1pp On split in CP.

5193 Facing Up to the Future: CP Discussion Document which led to 'New Times' in *'MT'* Sept. 1988 11pp

5194 Factions in the CP in *'Proletarian'* No.2, 1984 5pp Includes Straight Left, 'PPPS Management Cttee Faction' etc. This ed. also includes 2 pages of surprisingly interesting analysis on relations between CPGB & CPI.

5195 Fallacies of the Minority Movement in *'Socialist Standard'* March 1925 2pp

5196 Fanny Deakin in *'SSLHB'* 43 Autumn 1981 1pp Local councillor in N Staffs.

5197 Fascism, Labour and the CP in *'The Red Flag'* Aug. 1934 3pp Organ of the Communist League of GB. Review of 'Fascism and Social Revolution' by R.P. Dutt. Trotskyist.

5198 Fighters For the Cause: Interviews with Dave Goodman & Bernard McKenna in *'Red Pepper'* Nov. 1994 2pp On Spanish Civil War.

5199 Fighting Facts 1956 8pp Anti-Communist duplicated sheet ed. by R.P. Walsh, ed. of 'Catholic Worker'. 2 issues in 1956?

5200 First of May: Manifesto of CPGB in *'Inprecorr'* April 20 1935 1pp

5201 Flexibility at the Coalface: Mick McGahey interviewed by Charlie Leadbetter in *'MT'* July 1987 2pp

5202 For Communist Unity: Statement of the NCP in *'New Communist Review'* Summer 1987 10pp

5203 From Opposition to the Revolutionary Class Struggle in *'C.I.'* Oct. 15 1931 8pp

5204 From the Experience of British Communists in *'WMR'* Feb. 1967 10pp Feature incl. F. Hart on 'Communist Councillor in Scotland'; G. McLennan on 'Factory Branches'; G. Brooks on 'Public Meetings'; M. Hunter on 'Work Among Women'; B. Brooks on 'Circulation of MS'; N. Jeffery on 'Propaganda'.

5205 General Attack on the English Working Class in *'C.I.'* Oct. 1 1931 5pp

5206 General Election Manifesto in *'C.R.'* Nov. 1931 7pp

5207 General Election Manifesto in *'LM'* Nov. 1931 4pp

5208 General Plan of Recruiting Campaign in *'C.R.'* May 1931 5pp

5209 Hammer or Anvil Action Centre for Marxist-Leninist Unity 1965 Each issue of this Maoist mag. had articles on CPGB, esp. internal documents by or about Maoists in CP.

5210 Happy Birthday to Us in *'MT'* Oct. 1987 2pp 27 people were asked for their views by MT for its 30th birthday.

5211 History Group Membership Survey in *'Our History Journal'* 9, March 1985 2pp

5212 How the 'Financial Times' Boosted 'MT' in *'Labour Review'* Jan. 1983 3pp Refers to an article – not financial aid!

5213 How to Deal with Disruption in *'Socialist Vanguard'* April 1940 3pp

5214 Howard Hill – Obituary in *'SSLHB'* 41, Autumn 1980 1pp

5215 Hugo Rathbone – Obituary in *'LM'* Nov. 1969 1pp

5216 Idris Cox – Obituary in *'Llafur'* Vol.5 No.3, 1990 ? 2pp Worked for CP from 1927-69.

5217 ILP and the Comintern: Correspondence in *'C.I.'* Oct. 15 1933 8pp

5218 Immediate Tasks Before the Party and Working Class: Resolution of CC, Jan. in *'C.R.'* Feb. 1932 14pp

5219 **In Memoriam – Clive Branson** *in 'Volunteer For Liberty'* May 1944 2pp

5220 **In Memory of George Brown** *in 'C.I.' Vol XIV No.7-8,* 1937 1pp

5221 **In Memory of Harry Pollitt** *in 'WMR'* Aug. 1960 2pp

5222 1997 **In Memory: Raphael Samuel** *in 'Radical History Review'* Fall 1997 5pp Reprinted from 'The Guardian'.

5223 **Industrial Militants in Conference** *in 'East-West Digest'* July 1972 5pp On LCDTU Conference.

5224 **Interview with Hugh MacDiarmid** *in 'Scottish Marxist' 10,* 1975 12pp

5225 **Interviews** *in 'SLHS' 11* 1977 21pp Interviews with Scottish members of the I.B. Donald Renton, Tommy Bloomfield, Tom Murray; very brief but interesting refs to CP.

5226 **Ireland: Debate Between the RCG and the CPGB** *in 'Fight Racism! Fight Imperialism!' No.14,* Nov./Dec. 1981 1pp

5227 **Isabel Brown: A Life Devoted to Politics – Interview** *in 'Women's Voice'* June 1978 2pp Women's Organiser during WW2.

5228 **J.T. Murphy Expelled from the CPGB** *in 'Inprecorr'* May 12 1932 1pp Political Bureau statement. Murphy resigned, over criticism of an editorial in 'Communist Review', only to be told 'resignations are impermissible in a revolutionary organisation' and was then expelled.

5229 **J.T. Murphy in the Ranks of the Enemy** *in 'Inprecorr'* May 26 1932 1pp

5230 **Julie Burchill: Interview** *in 'Devil' Summer* 1996 34pp 'I was raised as a Communist, and basically I've considered myself one all my life'.

5231 **King Street Worried By 'Ultra-Leftism'** *in 'International'* Sept. 1969 1pp

5232 **Labour and the Communists** *in 'Socialist Commentary'* May 1946 4pp

5233 **Labour and the CP Affiliation** *in 'Socialist Commentary' (Socialist Vanguard Group)* March 1943 1pp Followed by 'The Case v. Affiliation' in April, 'The Communists & Unity' in July and 'Labour & the Communists' in May 1946.

5234 **Labour Discussion Notes 1939-43** *Socialist Clarity Group* 1975 14pp Many articles on CP, esp. on WW2.

5235 **Laurence Bradshaw (1899-1978), Sculptor** *in 'MML Bulletin' 102,* March 1983 2pp

5236 **Lessons of the Clay Cross By-Election** *in 'Inprecorr'* Sept. 22 1933 1pp Statement by CP which analyses CP election campaign.

5237 **Letter from M. Johnstone & Reply** *in 'I.S.' No.72,* Oct. 1974 1pp

5238 **Letter From the Comintern to the British ILP** *in 'C.I.'* July 15 1933 3pp

5239 **Letter from YCL** *in 'International' Vol.2 No.2,* Feb. 1969 1pp Letter from Bob Arnot (YCL National Schools Organiser) on school students & editorial reply.

5240 **Letters from the C.I. to the Party Congress** *in 'C.R.'* Feb. 1930 7pp

5241 **Lies and Propaganda Exposed** *in 'East West Digest'* April 1980 3pp On LCDTU Conference.

5242 **Manifesto of the London District Cttee on Borough Council Elections** *in 'Inprecorr'* Oct. 19 1934 1pp

5243 **Marxism and History: The British Contribution** *in 'Radical History Review' No.19,* Winter 1978 Articles on Raymond Williams, E.P. Thompson, E. Hobsbawm (incl. interview) etc.

5244 **Mass Work in the Streets** *in 'C.R.'* Dec. 1933/Jan. 1934 3pp

5245 **Maurice Ludmer – Obituary** *in 'Searchlight'* July 1981 5pp Anti-fascist campaigner in CP for many years before resigning, arguing that CP was not active enough in this area.

5246 **Militant T.U. Work & Some Proposals** *in 'C.R.'* Sept. 1933 7pp

5247 **Moments of Mass Apostasy: Interview with Ken Weller** *in 'Solidarity'* Autumn 1987 9pp Very interesting, mainly on 1956; Weller was in YCL till shortly after Hungary.

5248 **National Youth Rally** *in 'C.R.'* April 1930 3pp

5249 **North West Labour History, No.13** *NW Labour History Group* 1988 82pp This issue is a tribute to Ruth & Eddie Frow, containing interviews & reminiscences; deals with engineering industry, NUWM, the Peace Movement, WCML etc.

5250 **Notes for a Critical History of the CPGB** *in 'Workers' Broad Sheet'* Jan/Feb. 1968 14pp Published by the Maoist London Workers' Committee.

5251 **Notes on the British Party and Its Charter Campaign** *in 'C.I.'* Jan. 15 1931 4pp

5252 **NW District Congress** *in 'Communist' (CCG)* Feb. 1986 3pp

5253 **On Murphy's Expulsion from the CPGB** *in 'Inprecorr'* May 19 1932 1pp Political Bureau statement reproduced from 'DW'.

5254 **On the Discussion in the CPGB: Statement by CC CPGB** *in 'Inprecorr'* Oct. 11 1929 1pp

5255 **On the Periodical 'The Communist Review': Extract from Letter from Agitprop Central of British CP** *in 'Inprecorr'* April 9 1925 1pp

5256 **Open Letter of ECCI to Congress of CPGB & The Situation in the CPGB (Dutt & Robson)** *in 'Inprecorr'* Nov. 29 1929 4pp On forthcoming Leeds Conference.

5257 **Open Letter of the EC YCI to all Members of the YCL** *in 'Inprecorr'* Oct. 25 1929 1pp

5258 **Open Letter to the EC of the YCL** *in 'The International of Youth'* Nov. 1929 3pp

5259 **Organisation Conference on the Work Among Women** *in 'Inprecorr'* July 15 1925 1pp Incl. short but interesting report by Brown.

5260 **Organisation Section: Building Street Cells – Some Experiences in Hammersmith** *in 'C.R.'* Jan. 1933 5pp This was a regular feature till April.

5261 **Our Party and the TUC: EC CPGB** *in 'C.I.'* Oct. 30 1926 4pp

5262 **Our Party and the Workers' Charter Campaign** *in 'C.R.'* Nov. 1930 6pp By Political Bureau.

5263 **Ourselves and the LP: Thesis of the CC of the CPGB** *in 'The Communist'* Feb. 1928 17pp Replies by Dutt/Pollitt, B. Francis and J.T. Murphy in March issue.

5264 **Pages From the Life of W. Gallacher** *in 'C.I.'* Aug. 1936 3pp Review of 'Revolt on the Clyde'.

5265 **Party Educational Programme for 1953-4** *in 'CR'* Oct. 1953 8pp

5266 **Party Life** *in 'C.R.'* July 1931 5pp A regular feature till March 1932.

5267 **People's March and People's Fronts** *in 'International'* July/Aug. 1983 6pp Incl. interview with Pete Carter.

5268 **Percy Glading – Obituary** *in 'LM'* May 1970 1pp

5269 **Policy and Leadership** *in 'C.R.'* Oct. 1929 10pp Statement from the Tyneside DPC – criticises leadership for not implementing New Line vigorously enough.

5270 **Political Bureau Statement re A. Horner** *in 'C.R.'* March 1931 12pp

5271 **Pollitt-Mann Case** *in 'Free Speech and Assembly Bulletin' (NCCL)* May 1934 8pp Incl. extracts of Verbatim Report of trial for seditious speeches in S Wales.

5272 **Press Freedom a la Carte** *in 'The Communist' (BICO)* 142, Feb. 1980 6pp On arguments between BICO and L&W/CP/CPI over copyright to translation of an Engels article.

5273 **Press Freedom in Wartime: A Symposium** *in 'LM'* March 1941 11pp Incl. Wells, Shaw, Dean of Canterbury etc.

5274 **Problems of Party Building: By Sub-District Organisers** *in 'C.R.'* May 1935 3pp

5275 **Problems of Party Organisation** *in 'C.R.'* Dec. 1934 1pp

5276 **Programme for Party Education 1951-2** *in 'CR'* Oct. 1951 5pp Proposals by Central Education Dept Incl. details of Schools and publications.

5277 **Questions of Growth and Recruiting in the CPGB** *in 'Inprecorr'* May 19 1932 2pp One of Inprecorr's more important articles on the CP.

5278 **R.P.C. Bulletin** 1935 6-16pp The Revolutionary Policy Committee was the tendency in the ILP that left and joined the CP in 1935, led by Jack Gaster. Nos 21-3 (final issue) from July – Nov. 1935 relate particularly to CP.

5279 **Radek's Criticism of the CPGB** *in 'C.R.'* Dec. 1921 2pp Speech to C.I. Congress, Aug.

5280 **Ralph Fox – Obituary** *in 'Inprecorr'* Jan. 9 1937 1pp

5281 **Ralph Fox and John Cornford** *in 'Volunteer For Liberty'* Jan. 3 1938 1pp

5282 **Ralph Fox: A Tribute** *in 'Left Review'* Feb. 1937 2pp

5283 **'Reflections of a Clyde-Built Man' by J. Reid – Review** *in 'The Marxist' (Journal of the Marxist Industrial Group)* No.31, 1976 ? 6pp Maoist.

5284 **Reminiscence of Palme Dutt** *in 'Our History Journal'* 11, Jan. 1987 2pp

5285 **Reply of the CPGB to the Labour Party's Expulsion Move** *in 'Inprecorr'* Oct. 29 1924 1pp

5286 **Report of CC on Immediate Tasks** *in 'C.R.'* Jan. 1930 6pp

5287 **Resolution of CC of CPGB on the Seventh Congress of the C.I.** *in 'C.I.'* June 5 1935 2pp

5288 Resolution of the National Conference of CPGB *in 'Inprecorr'* Oct. 12 1935 1pp Welcoming Decisions of C.I.'s 7th Congress.

5289 Resolution of the Plenum of the ECCI on the Situation in GB *in 'Inprecorr'* June 23 1927 5pp

5290 Resolution of the Political Bureau on the 'DW' *in 'C.R.'* Sept. 1930 4pp

5291 Resolution of the Polit-Secretariat of the ECCI upon the Report of Comrade Bell on the Plenum of the CC of the CPGB *in 'Inprecorr'* Sept. 20 1929 1pp

5292 Resolution on the British General Strike and the YCL *in 'Inprecorr'* July 22 1926 2pp Statement by EC of YCI.

5293 Resolution on the British Labour Government: Theses & Resolution Adopted by the 5th World Congress of the CI *in 'Inprecorr'* Sept. 5 1924 2pp

5294 Resolution on the Organisational Work of the British Party *in 'C.R.'* Oct. 1926 7pp ECCI.

5295 Revolutionary Strategy in the Twenties *in 'International'* Autumn 1977 6pp Extracts from debate between J.T. Murphy & R.P. Dutt from 'C.I.' in 1925, with short intro.

5296 Rose Kerrigan 1921-1992 – An Obituary *in 'Alert Scotland'* Sept/Oct. 1995 2pp Reprinted from 'The Guardian'.

5297 Salme Dutt – Obituary *in 'LM'* Oct. 1964 1pp A shadowy figure in British Communist history; probably played significant role in links between Moscow and CP leadership in early years. Incl. a poem by Dutt.

5298 'Science and Society' *Spring 1997* 152pp The chapters in this important special issue dedicated to 'Communism in Britain and the British Empire' and edited by K. Morgan, are listed separately.

5299 Scottish Congress *in 'Scottish Marxist'* 13, 1977 7pp

5300 Scottish Congress *in 'Communist'* (CCG) Feb. 1986 1pp These reports are very partial, but useful as there is little published on local splits.

5301 Shall Communism Smash the Labour Party? *in 'The London News' (LP)* April 1943 2pp

5302 Statement of the CPGB on the ILP Conference *in 'Inprecorr'* April 13 1934 1pp

5303 Suppression of the 'DW' *in 'Socialist Commentary'* Feb. 6 1941 2pp

5304 Tasks of the CPGB: The 10th Plenum and the International Situation *in 'C.R.'* Sept. 1929 19pp

5305 The 10th Congress of the CPGB *in 'C.I.'* March 1 1929 6pp

5306 The 10th Plenum of the ECCI and the British Party *in 'C.I.'* Oct. 1 1929 6pp

5307 The 11th Plenum: Report and Discussion on the Plenum at May CC & Resolution *in 'C.R.'* July 1931 21pp Refers to 11th Plenum of the ECCI.

5308 The 12th Party Congress *in 'C.R.'* Dec. 1932 6pp

5309 The 2nd National Congress of the Young Comrades' League *in 'The Communist'* Aug. 1927 3pp

5310 The Agitational Work of the CPGB *in 'C.I.'* Oct. 15 1933 6pp

5311 The Anti-Imperialist Struggle in Britain *in 'C.R.'* July 1934 3pp

5312 The Arrest of the Twelve *in 'LM'* Oct. 1965 2pp 12 leading Communists arrested Oct. 1925 in preparation for General Strike.

5313 'The Betrayal of the Left' by V. Gollancz – Review *in 'London News'* May 1941 1pp London Labour Party publication.

5314 The Brian Pearce Dossier *in 'Revolutionary History'* Vol.9 No.3, 2006 39pp Correspondence between Brian Pearce and the CP, and some newspaper articles (1956-7).

5315 The 'British Road': An Opportunist Path to Counter-Revolution *in 'Revolution'* May 1977 10pp Maoist. Communist Federation of Britain (Marxist-Leninist).

5316 The British YCL Prepares its 7th National Congress *in 'The International of Youth'* No.2, Aug. 1933 2pp

5317 The Class Struggles in England *in 'Inprecorr'* Oct. 15 1931 1pp Leading article in Pravda Oct. 9.

5318 The Communist Party *in 'Contacts'* No.4, 1966 2pp Left-leaning sociology magazine published by Routledge – this article was probably due to the fact that Monty Johnstone was on the ed. board.

5319 The Communist Persecution in England: EC YCI *in 'Inprecorr'* Dec. 10 1925 1pp On sentencing of the 12 CP leaders.

5320 The Communists and Palestine *in 'Socialist Standard'* July 1949 1pp

5321 The Communists and Unity *in 'Socialist Commentary'* July 1943 3pp

5322 **The Comrades** in 'The Spectator' Feb. 27 1948 1pp Personal view of 20th Congress.

5323 **The Congress of the London District of the CPGB** in 'C.I.' Aug. 1936 1pp

5324 **The CP and Strike Leadership** in 'C.R.' Sept. 1934 4pp Pressed Steel strike, Oxford.

5325 **The CP and the War** in 'Workers' International News' Nov. 1941 4pp

5326 **The CP: A Feeble Last Gasp** in 'Socialist Review' 6, 1981 1pp CP's role in the 'People's March for Jobs'.

5327 **The CP: Editorial** in 'I.S.' No.31, Winter 1967 1pp

5328 **The CP: Reflection on the 32nd Congress** in 'East-West Digest' Jan. 1972 3pp

5329 **The CP: Review of 1971-2** in 'East-West Digest' Sept. 1972 5pp

5330 **The CP: Who Controls the 'Morning Star'?** in 'East-West Digest' July 1972 3pp On PPPS AGM.

5331 **The CPGB and its Application for Affiliation to the LP** in 'Inprecorr' Feb. 8 1936 1pp Letter from LP of Jan. 27 & CP's reply of Jan 30.

5332 **The CPGB and Scargill's Strike** in 'The Communist' (BICO) 180, May 1985 10pp

5333 **The CPGB and the LP: Thesis of CC of CPGB Adopted Jan. 5** in 'C.I.' March 1 1928 10pp

5334 **The CPGB and the Miners' Strike** in 'Problems of Communism (and Capitalism)' 39/40 1993 4pp Published by BICO.

5335 **The CPGB: End of the British Road?** in 'The Next Step' Oct. 1983 1pp

5336 **The CPGB's New Discourse** in 'The Communist' (BICO) 139, Nov. 1979 7pp On Thatcherism.

5337 **The Crisis in the British CP** in 'East West Digest' Sept. 1977 5pp On the NCP split.

5338 **The Crisis in the CP** in 'I.S.' No.101, Sept. 1977 3pp NCP & new 'BRS'.

5339 **The Crisis in the CP** in 'Labour Review' Nov. 1983 4pp Editorial.

5340 **The Decay of the CP** in 'Socialist Standard' Oct. 1924 3pp

5341 **The Defeats of the Twenties** in 'The Next Step' Nov./Dec. 1980 2pp

5342 **The Disunity of Theory and Practice: The Trotskyist Movement in GB Since 1945** in 'Revolutionary History' Vol.6 No.2/3, Summer 1996 40pp Like other articles from this journal, this one retains a combative 'anti-Stalinist' approach but with more research and objectivity than in most Trotskyist magazines. Probably the most important collection of Trotskyist writing on the CP.

5343 **The Election Appeal of the CPGB** in 'Inprecorr' Oct. 22 1931 2pp

5344 **The Enemy Within** in 'East-West Digest' Jan. 1972 3pp Analysis of 'Tutor's Guide & Study Material' – allegedly a confidential document!

5345 **The English Labour Government and the CP of England (sic) – Resolution of the ECCI** in 'Inprecorr' Feb. 21 1924 1pp

5346 **The First Volunteer: Felicia Browne 1904-1936** in 'Spain Today' Sept. 1949 2pp Communist artist who died in Spain – she may have been the first British volunteer in the Republican militia.

5347 **The General Secretary of the Construction Union Explains How Communists are Infiltrating His Union** in 'East West Digest' Aug. 1976 5pp

5348 **'The Good Old Cause' by W. Thompson – Review** in 'Marxist Review' Vol.7 No.10, Oct. 1992 2pp

5349 **The Great Example of the English People's Convention** in 'International Review' (U.S.) June 1941 12pp This journal was continuation of 'C.I.'.

5350 **The ILP and the C.I.** in 'C.R.' March 1934 7pp

5351 **The Immediate Tasks of the CPGB** in 'Inprecorr' May 8 1930 2pp Resolution adopted by CC and endorsed by Enlarged Plenum of ECCI.

5352 **The Kevin Halpin Story** in 'Solidarity' Vol.3 No.9, 1965 5pp About Fords' CP convenor. This issue has another very brief article on the CP at Fords and there was a longer one in Vol 2, No.11.

5353 **The Leninist** 1981 Most articles in the journal of this minute, virently leftist faction within the CP from 1981, were about the CP. Quarterly then monthly.

5354 **The Lessons of September 9 and the Next Steps: Resolution of London District Cttee** in 'Inprecorr' Sept. 28 1934 1pp

5355 **The Long and Winding Road: Britain's Communists in 1983 – Roundtable Discussion with Dave Cook, John Hoffman, Lou Lewis, Jane Woddis** in 'MT' Nov. 1983 5pp

5356 The Militants Opposing the Rent Act in *'East-West Digest'* Dec. 1972 3pp CP members in National Assoc. of Tenants & Residents

5357 The Moment of Truth: The CP Debates its Future in the Wake of 1989 in *'MT'* Dec. 1990 2pp

5358 The 'MS' and the Breakaway in *'Communist' (CCG)* March 1988 1pp

5359 The 'MT' Story; What 'MT' Meant to Me; The Last Word by M. Jacques in *'MT'* Dec. 1991/Jan. 1992 Various articles on the magazine in its very last issue.

5360 The National Council of the ILP Sabotages the United Front in *'C.I.'* Jan. 1 1934 5pp Reprinted from 'DW'.

5361 The New Policy in *'The Communist'* June 1928 2pp Debate on the new line of 'Class Against Class', continued in the following issues, esp. in Dec. 1928 when a whole issue was devoted to debate for the forthcoming Congress. Most contributions are on T.U.s, LP or CP organisation.

5362 The New Tactics of the CPGB: Editorial in *'C.I.'* April 1 1928 5pp Follows the Plenum of C.I. on the British Question.

5363 The Origins of Modern Revisionism: Report of CC of Marxist-Leninist Organisation of Britain in *'Red Vanguard'* 2, 1972 34pp Maoist view of the development of CP programmes.

5364 The Outlawry of Communism in *'Round Table'* June 1951 6pp

5365 The Parliamentary Election in GB in *'C.I.'* Nov. 1935 8pp Incl. biog. of Gallacher & some election material.

5366 The Party and the League in *'C.R.'* Oct. 1926 4pp From the Organisation Dept, on the YCL.

5367 The Police Raid on the London 'DW' in *'Inprecorr'* Oct. 1 1931 1pp

5368 The Present Situation in Britain and the Tasks of the Party in *'C.R.'* May 1930 17pp CC Resolution.

5369 The Reasoner 1956 32-40pp 3 issues: No.1, July; No.2, Sept; No.3, Nov. Ed. by E.P. Thompson & J. Saville while still in CP, though they resigned/were expelled for this publication. Important as forerunner of 'New Reasoner' and 'NLR' & as the start of the New Left.

5370 The Results of the 10th Congress in *'Inprecorr'* Feb. 15 1929 1pp

5371 The Situation in Lancashire and the Tasks of the Party in *'C.R.'* Dec. 1929 8pp Draft Resolution from Manchester DPC for District Congress in Nov.

5372 The Socialist Party v. the CP in *'Socialist Standard'* Aug. 1931 5pp Debate between P. Kerrigan & A. Shaw

5373 The Split Within British Stalinism in *'Labour Review'* Aug. 1977 7pp Trotskyist view of NCP.

5374 The Suppression of the 'DW' in *'Socialist Standard'* Feb. 1941 1pp

5376 The Tasks of the Party: Statement by the London DPC on the CC Resolution in *'C.R.'* Nov. 1929 9pp

5377 The Thirties: A Special Number in *'The Review'* 11/12 1964 94pp This issue incl. conversations with E. Rickword, C. Cockburn & E. Upward.

5378 The Trojan Horse: Communist Front Organizations in *'The British Survey'* Dec. 1959 23pp Mainly of international interest but some refs to CPGB.

5379 The Turn to Mass Work: Resolution of CC in *'C.R.'* March 1931 7pp

5380 The YCL Congress in *'C.R.'* July 1925 4pp

5381 The Youth Movement in *'CR'* Aug. 1953 3pp From Report to CP Youth Advisory Cttee

5382 Thesis on Work Among Women in *'C.R.'* Jan. 1929 5pp

5383 To the Working Men and Working Women of GB! in *'Inprecorr'* Nov. 3 1922 2pp Election manifesto signed by ECCI & EC CPGB.

5384 Towards the United Front: C.I. and ILP Correspondence in *'C.R.'* Aug. 1933 3pp

5385 Tribute to Hilda Vernon in *'Link'* Winter 1982 1pp

5386 Tributes to James Klugmann in *'MT'* Nov. 1977 5pp

5387 Trotskyist Policy and the General Election: A Reply to the 'MS' in *'Fourth International'* Winter 1970 2pp

5388 Vanguard Cttee to Defeat Revisionism For Communist Unity 1961 This Maoist paper had many articles on the CPGB.

5389 Vietnam and the Left in *'The Week'* March 13 1968 6pp Mainly a reply to Betty Reid's criticism of the Vietnam Solidarity Campaign in 'Comment' Feb. 17 1968. See also 'The Week' Feb. 28.

5390 Walter Stevens – Obituary in *'LM'* Dec. 1954 1pp

5391 **Welsh Profile ... Arthur Horner** in 'Welsh Review' Spring 1947 6pp

5392 **What the CP Has Meant to Me: Jack Davies, Helen Crawfurd, M. Dobb, J.R. Scott** in 'LM' Aug. 1940 8pp

5393 **Where the Money Comes From: Light on the Mystery of Communist Finance** in 'Labour Magazine' July 1928 4pp

5394 **Who Are Russia's Allies?** in 'Socialist Commentary' Nov. 20 1941 4pp

5395 **William Gallacher, 1881-1965** in 'LM' Sept. 1965 1pp

5396 **William Paul: A Life for Socialism** in 'MML Bulletin' 6 April/June 1958 2pp

5397 **Women in the CP: Papers by Maggie Bowden, Philippa Langton & Angela Mason** in 'Link' Winter 1982 1pp

5398 **Work of the English Young Comrades' League** in 'The Workers' Child' No.2, 1927 3pp

5399 **Worker Correspondents in GB** in 'Inprecorr' March 22 1928 1pp On their contribution to 'Workers' Weekly'.

5400 **Young Communists' New Campaign** in 'East-West Digest' July 1969 2pp

5401 A British Communist **New Battles on the Way** in 'C.I.' Jan. 30 1927 3pp

5402 A Headmaster **Communist Teachers and Their Methods** in 'Common Cause Bulletin' June 1958 6pp

5403 A Political Correspondent **The British CP** in 'Twentieth Century' May 1952 5pp Mainly on 22nd Congress and new EC.

5404 A Special Correspondent **On Leaving the CP** in 'Twentieth Century' Feb. 1954 15pp Based on interviews with 50 former CPGB members; part of larger international study (see 'The Appeals of Communism').

5405 A.G.P. **Communist Schools and Education in GB** in 'The Communist' Sept. 1927 3pp

5406 A.L.B. **Early History of the CP** in 'Socialist Standard' Jan. 1972 3pp Series of 5 articles in consecutive issues; covers up to 1935.

5407 A.W. **T.A.J. Forsakes the Cellars** in 'Plebs' Jan. 1934 1pp Criticises T.A. Jackson & CP's 'mad idea of duplicating every organisation the workers have'.

5408 Aaronovitch, Sam **The Party's Cultural Work** in 'CR' July 1952 8pp

5408a Ackers, Peter **Collective Bargaining as Industrial Democracy: Hugh Clegg and the Political Foundations of British Industrial Relations Pluralism** in 'BJOIR' Vol.45 No.1, March 2007 25pp Hugh Clegg, one of Britain's leading industrial relations academics, was in CP for a Decade until c1947. His brother Arthur (a poet and active in campaigns for China) was also in the CP.

5409 Adam, Corinna **The Comrades and Women's Lib** in 'New Statesman' Nov. 19 1971 1pp On 32nd Congress and women's involvement.

5410 Adams, S. & Cotter, Judy **Only Yesterday: Mikki Doyle Interview** in 'Link' Winter 1982 2pp Part 2 in Spring 1983.

5411 Adereth, Max **A Consistent Class Policy** in 'Communist Review' (CPB) 3, Spring 1989 6pp On CP programmes.

5412 Adi, Hakim **Forgotten Comrade? Desmond Buckle: An African Communist in Britain** in 'Science and Society' Vol.70 No.1, Jan. 2006 24pp James Desmond Buckle was a Ghanaian and lifelong member of the CP. Ed. of 'Africa Newsletter' and Secretary of the Africa Committee.

5413 Adi, Hakim **Pan-Africanism and Communism: The Comintern, The 'Negro' Question and the First International Conference of Negro Workers, Hamburg 1930** in 'African and Black Diaspora' Vol.1 No.2, July 2008 18pp

5414 Adi, Hakim **The Comintern and Black Workers in Britain and France, 1919-37** in 'Immigrants and Minorities' Vol.28 No.2/3, July/Nov. 2010 22pp Much on Cardiff and Liverpool.

5415 Adi, Hakim **The Communist Movement in West Africa** in 'Science and Society' Vol.61 No.1, Spring 1997 5pp

5416 Agit-Prop Dept of the C.I. **A Criticism of the Party Training Manual** in 'The Communist' Aug. 1928 11pp See 'CP Training'.

5417 Aldred, Guy **William Gallacher** in 'Hyde Park' No.1, Sept. 1938 1pp Lengthy critical article on Gallacher.

5418 Alexander, Bill **Britain: Tasks of Party Building** in 'WMR' Nov. 1965 5pp

5419 Alexander, Bill **The Formation and Growth of Basic Units of the Party** in 'CR' July 1951 3pp

5420 Alexander, Sally & Clarke, Richard **Jim Fyrth 1918-2010 – Obituary** in 'HWJ' 71, Spring 2011 8pp

5421 Allan, William **The Party and The Minority Movement** in 'C.R.' Oct. 1932 5pp

5422 Allaun, Frank **Culture and Politics in the Hungry Thirties** in *'NWLHSB' 17, 1992* 14pp Allaun was in the CP for 8 years, working in Collets for a while.

5423 Allaun, Frank **In Memoriam: Edmund Frow** in *'NWLHSB' 22 1997* 2pp This is followed by obituary by Kevin Morgan in same issue.

5424 Allen, Mike **Post War Dock Strikes** in *'NWLHSB' 15, 1990* 15pp

5425 Allen, V.L. **'Miners, Unions and Politics' ed. A. Campbell, N. Fishman & D. Howell – Review** in *'HSIR' No.4, Sept. 1997* 5pp

5426 Anderson, Duane C. **'The Origins of British Bolshevism' by R. Challinor – Review** in *'American Historical Review' Oct. 1978* 1pp

5427 Anderson, Paul **The CP: Is There a Fork in the British Road?** in *'Solidarity' Autumn 1985* 6pp

5428 Anderson, Perry **Myths of Edward Thompson** in *'NLR' 35, 1966* 41pp Article also entitled, inside, 'Socialism and Pseudo – Empiricism': NLR is not alone in this irritating habit of having two titles.

5429 Andrews, Geoff **'A Weapon in the Struggle' ed. A. Croft – Review** in *'Socialist History' 15, 1999* 3pp

5430 'Andrews, R.F.' **Ourselves and the LP** in *'C.R.' Jan. 1935* 3pp

5431 Arblaster, Anthony **'Proletarian Philosophers' by J. Ree – Review** in *'SSLHB' 51 Part 1, 1986* 3pp

5432 Archbold, R. **Revisionism and Culture** in *'The Communist' (BICO) 5, July 1967* 3pp Continued in no.6

5433 Archer, Mick **Open Warfare in the CPGB** in *'International Viewpoint' (United Secretariat of the Fourth International) 69, 1985* 4pp

5434 Arnot, R. Page **11th Congress of CPGB** in *'Inprecorr' Jan. 16 1930* 1pp

5435 Arnot, R. Page **11th Plenum of ECCI: Speech** in *'Inprecorr' July 6 1931* 3pp On India.

5436 Arnot, R. Page **25th Anniversary of the CP** in *'LM' Aug. 1945* 3pp

5437 Arnot, R. Page **Communism and the LP** in *'LM' July 1922* 10pp

5438 Arnot, R. Page **Dobb in the Twenties** in *'LM' Oct. 1926* 4pp

5439 Arnot, R. Page **Notes on the Communist Effort For Unity** in *'CR' April 1946* 4pp On CP affiliation to LP.

5440 Arnot, R. Page **Sixty Years Ago: CPGB** in *'LM' Feb. 1981* 4pp

5441 Arnot, R. Page **Tendencies in the British Party** in *'C.I.' Jan. 15 1929* 12pp

5442 Arnot, R. Page **The First 30 Years** in *'LM' Aug. 1950* 7pp

5443 Arnot, R. Page **Walter Milton Holmes – Obituary** in *'LM' Dec. 1973* 5pp

5444 Aronsfeld, C.C. **Communists in British Jewry: A Zionist Socialist Analysis** in *'Jewish Monthly' ed. Nov. 1947* 6pp Info. on Jack Gaster.

5445 Ashley, W. **The Menace of Communism** in *'English Review' May 1925* 7pp

5446 Ashton, Jack **Honor Arundel – Obituary** in *'Scottish Marxist' 5, 1973* 2pp

5447 Attfield, John **Conference on CP History** in *'SSLHB' 37 Autumn 1978* 1pp Report of CP conference held in May.

5448 Attfield, John **Conference on the History of the CP** in *'HWJ' 6, 1978* 2pp

5448a Aulich, Jim **Stealing the Thunder: The Soviet Union and Graphic Propaganda on the Home Front During the Second World War** in *'Visual Culture in Britain' Vol.13 No.3, 2012* 23pp CP writers, artists and designers feature in Government inspired publications as well as Communist ones, in this interesting article.

5449 Bailey, Roderick **Communist in SOE: Explaining James Klugmann's Recruitment and Retention** in *'Intelligence and National Security' Vol.20 No.1, March 2005* 25pp Appears to deal objectively with the long-standing charges of spying levelled at Klugmann while at Cambridge, though the article is more concerned with his rapid rise to the rank of major in the Cairo Bureau of the Special Operations Executive dealing with Yugoslavia during WW2.

5450 Bain, Doug **Interview with Jimmy Airlie** in *'MT' Oct. 1979* 5pp

5451 Bain, Ouaine **Culture and Enjoyment: The 'Star' Social Club** in *'Scottish Marxist' 17, 1978* 3pp

5452 Bain, Peter **From Hero to Scab: Jimmy Reid** in *'Socialist Review' March 1985* 1pp

5454 Baker White, John **Students in Revolt – The Revolutionaries** in *'Twentieth Century' Vol.177 No.3, No. 1038, 1968* 4pp Surprisingly useful article on CP and Radical Student Alliance from one of Britain's leading professional anti-Communists (and former pro-Hitlerite).

5455 Baker White, John **The Future of Communism in G.B.** in 'The National Review' July 1929 7pp

5456 Bambery, Chris **Planning the Party** in 'Socialist Review' Nov. 1993 2pp A good, concise overview of CP activity & influence in the 1930s.

5457 Bambery, Chris **The Red Years** in 'Socialist Review' June 1995 2pp Review of 4 books on CP – Fishman, Beckett, Hall, Gorman.

5458 Barker, Martin **The Merseyside Building Workers' Movement; A Case History** in 'I.S.' No.32, Spring 1968 8pp

5459 Barnsby, George **'Saklatvala' by M. Squires – Review** in 'Our History Journal' 18, 1991 5pp

5460 Barrett, Neil **A Bright Shining Star: The CPGB and Anti-Fascist Activism in the 1930s** in 'Science and Society' Vol.61 No.1, Spring 1997 20pp

5461 Barrett, Neil **The CP in Manchester and Salford, 1935-6** in 'LHR' Vol.58 No.3, Winter 1993 16pp Incl. Reports of Manchester & Salford Sub-District for 1935 & 1936 & intro.

5462 Barrow, Logie **Harry Wicks – Obituary** in 'HWJ' 31, 1991 4pp

5462a Barrow, Logie; Davis, Mary & Foster, John **Roundtable on Eric Hobsbawm's Legacy** in 'LHR' Vol.78 No.3, Dec. 2013 13pp

5463 Barry, Bernard **Angela Tuckett: Her Story** in 'WCML Bulletin' 7, 1997 3pp Activist in Bristol and Swindon. Contains bibliography and list of her Archive in the WCML.

5464 Barry, Bernard **Jane Wyatt: Unsung Activist** in 'WCML Bulletin' 6, 1996 4pp Wyatt, a headteacher, was active as a suffragette, then in the LP, CP & peace movement.

5465 Barry, Bernard **Not Just A Rambler: Benny Rothman** in 'WCML Bulletin' 9, 1999 7pp

5466 Barry, Bernard **The Courage of her Convictions: Win Langton** in 'WCML Bulletin' 14 2004 12pp Her mother was a working class suffragette & founder member of the CP; her father, a seaman and union activist, was the son of a freed slave from Guyana. Langton was a lifelong CP member, and became very active in community politics in Sheppey, then Ulverston where she was a local celebrity for her peace work; did much work for Medical Aid for Vietnam.

5467 Bateman, Don **The ILP Between the Wars** in 'NWLHSB' 5, 1978 5pp

5468 Bean, Ron **Liverpool Shipping Employers and the Anti-Communist Activities of J.M. Hughes, 1920-5** in 'SSLHB' 34, Spring 1977 5pp

5469 Bean, Ron **Militancy, Policy Formation and Membership Opposition in the ETU, 1945-61** in 'Political Quarterly' April/June 1965 10pp

5470 Behan, Brian **New 'British Road' Evades Key Questions** in 'The Newsletter' March 8 1958 1pp

5471 Behan, Brian **Rank and Filer** in 'The Spokesman' Feb./March 1972 13pp Fascinating autobiographical article.

5472 Bell, Tom & Rust, W. **10 Years of the CPGB** in 'C.R.' July 1930 11pp

5473 Bell, Tom **August 1st in England** in 'Inprecorr' Aug. 23 1929 1pp On the disappointing action of 'Anti-War Day'.

5474 Bell, Tom **Report on the CPGB** in 'C.R.' Oct. 1921 6pp Submitted to ECCI.

5475 Bell, Tom **Speech at 10th Plenum ECCI, 11th Session July 9** in 'Inprecorr' Sept. 11 1929 3pp

5476 Bell, Tom **The British Labour Party, the ILP and Communist Affiliation** in 'Inprecorr' July 21 1922 2pp

5477 Bell, Tom **The Communists and the LP in England** in 'Inprecorr' June 30 1922 1pp

5478 Bell, Tom **The CPGB Under the Banner of the Comintern** in 'C.I.' April 1929 3pp

5479 Bell, Tom **The Present Situation in England** in 'Inprecorr' Dec. 13 1921 1pp Very little on CP, but some info. on local elections: '26 candidates, 15,000 votes, 3 councillors'.

5480 Bell, Tom **The United Front** in 'C.R.' Sept. 1924 5pp

5481 Bellamy, Joan & Bellamy, Ron **Robin Page Arnot** in 'LM' Dec. 1980 5pp

5482 Bellamy, Ron **Maurice Dobb** in 'MML Bulletin' 108, Autumn/Winter 1986 8pp

5483 Bellamy, Ron **Re-establishing a Revolutionary Party** in 'Communist Campaign Review' Spring 1988 4pp

5484 Bellamy, Ron **Revisionism and the 1977 'BRS'** in 'Communist Review' (CPB) 3, Spring 1989 3pp

5485 Bellamy, Ron et al. **Pages From Our History** in 'Communist Review' (CPB) 16, Jan.

1993 4pp Reviews of various books incl. 'The Good Old Cause' plus polemic on 'DW'/'MS'.

5486 Ben Rees, D. **Centenary of a Welsh Radical: T.E. Nicholas** in *'LM'* Dec. 1979 3pp Founder member of CP, poet & Congregationalist preacher.

5487 Ben Rees, D. **T.E. Nicholas 'Niclas y Glais': Poet and Prose Writer of the Working Class** in *'MML Bulletin'* 143, Spring 2006 9pp

5488 Bennet, A.J. **The British Question at the Feb. Plenum of the C.I. & Resolution of ECCI on the English Question** in *'The Communist'* April 1928 13pp

5489 Bennet, A.J. **The ILP and a Single International** in *'C.I.'* 20 (New Series), 1926 31pp

5490 Benson, Gordon **John Maclean 1879-1923** in *'The Chartist'* Dec. 1979 5pp Incl. a lot on Maclean's relationship with CP.

5491 Benton, Sarah **Century of Destruction: Coming to Terms with Communism** in *'MT'* Oct. 1991 1pp Personal assessment of 6 years in the CP by one-time ed. of 'Comment'.

5492 Benton, Sarah **Comrades at Arms** in *'New Statesman'* May 24 1985 1pp

5493 Benton, Sarah **Star Turn** in *'New Statesman'* June 24 1983 2pp

5494 Benton, Sarah **The Left Re-aligns** in *'New Statesman'* Nov. 30 1984 2pp Includes useful chronological summary of developing split in CP.

5495 Berger, Stefan & LaPorte, Norman **Being Friendly With the 'Other Germany': Dorothy Diamond and British Support for the GDR, 1949-1961** in *'Socialist History'* 30, 2007 22pp A British Communist whose main activity was in Britain-GDR friendly societies.

5496 Berger, Stefan & Laporte, Norman **John Peet (1915-1988): An Englishman in the GDR** in *'History'* 89, 2004 20pp

5497 Berry, Joe **Daily Worker Ban** in *'Communist Campaign Review'* Autumn 1987 2pp

5498 Birch, Chris **The Aid to Spain Committee and MI5: How the Special Branch Spied On Me** in *'MML Bulletin'* 148, Autumn 2008 3pp

5499 Birchall, Ian **Left Alive or Left For Dead? The Terminal Crisis in the CP** in *'ISJ'* 30, Autumn 1985 23pp

5500 Birchall, Ian **The British CP 1945-64** in *'I.S.' No.50*, Jan./March 1972 11pp

5501 Bishop, Reg **13th Congress of CPGB** in *'Inprecorr'* Feb. 9 1935 2pp

5502 Bishop, Reg **Class War Prisoners in Britain** in *'Inprecorr'* Jan. 5 1933 1pp

5503 Bishop, Reg **Fight for the Unity of the Labour Movement** in *'Inprecorr'* Nov. 3 1934 1pp

5504 Bishop, Reg **Gains by English CP in Local Elections** in *'Inprecorr'* April 16 1931 1pp

5505 Bishop, Reg **Gallacher and the New Parliament** in *'Inprecorr'* Nov. 30 1935 1pp

5506 Bishop, Reg **Increased Terror Against Revolutionary Workers in GB** in *'Inprecorr'* Jan. 28 1932 1pp

5507 Bishop, Reg **Six Years of the London 'DW'** in *'Inprecorr'* Jan. 11 1936 1pp

5508 Bishop, Reg **The Acquittal of T. Mann and H. Pollitt** in *'Inprecorr'* July 13 1934 1pp The sedition trial in Swansea collapsed under ludicrous police evidence.

5509 Bishop, Reg **The August 1st Campaign in England** in *'Inprecorr'* July 16 1931 1pp

5510 Bishop, Reg **The Coming Borough Elections** in *'Inprecorr'* Oct. 24 1936 1pp Mainly on CP's Manifesto.

5511 Bishop, Reg **The Communist Crusade** in *'Inprecorr'* Feb. 19 1938 1pp

5512 Bishop, Reg **The Fight Against the Means Test and the Development of the CPGB** in *'Inprecorr'* Dec. 24 1931 1pp

5513 Bishop, Reg **The ILP Conference** in *'Inprecorr'* April 27 1935 1pp

5514 Bishop, Reg **The ILP in Conference** in *'Inprecorr'* April 10 1937 1pp

5515 Bishop, Reg **The LP Campaign and the Unity Campaign** in *'Inprecorr'* June 12 1937 1pp

5516 Bishop, Reg **The Municipal Elections in England and Wales** in *'Inprecorr'* Nov. 10 1934 1pp

5517 Bishop, Reg **The Struggle for Unity After the Election** in *'Inprecorr'* Dec. 14 1935 1pp

5518 Bishop, Reg **The Urban Council Elections** in *'Inprecorr'* April 13 1935 1pp Concentrates on CP gains in S Wales.

5519 Bishop, Reg **The Campaign for CP Affiliation** in *'Inprecorr'* July 4 1936 1pp

5520 Bishop, Reg **The Municipal Elections: Their Significance** in *'Inprecorr'* Nov. 9 1935 1pp 'The CP only contested about a dozen seats in order not to split the working class vote' – compare with 'Open Letter of ECCI to Congress of CPGB'.

5521 Black, Lawrence **'Labour Legends and Russian Gold: Bolshevism and the British Left, Part 1' & 'The Webbs and Soviet Communism: Bolshevism and the British Left, Part 2' by K. Morgan – Review** in *'Socialist History' 32, 2008* 4pp

5522 Black, Lawrence **Still at the Penny-Farthing Stage in a Jet-Propelled Era' – Branch Life in 1950s Socialism** in *'LHR' Vol.65 No.2, Summer 2000* 24pp

5523 Black, Robert **Communist History and the Present Crisis** in *'International Correspondence' Vol.1 No.4, March 29 1967* 3pp

5524 Blair, J. **YCL Exposed on Vietnam and Aden** in *'The Week' July 6 1967* 1pp 'Exposed' for wanting the broadest possible campaign.

5525 Bloomfield, Jon **Crossed Lines: Communists in Search of an Identity** in *'MT' April 1984* 5pp Discussion contributions followed in May, June, July.

5526 Bloomfield, Jon **Interview with Derek Robinson** in *'MT' March 1980* 6pp

5527 Bor, Michael **'Out of the Ghetto' by J. Jacobs – Review** in *'Our History Journal' 6, July 1980* 4pp

5528 Bose, Dilip **R.P. Dutt: Great Son of the Indian People** in *'LM' March 1975* 4pp

5529 Boston, Sarah **The Rego Strike** in *'SSLHB' 38, Spring 1979* 1pp Abstract of Conference paper & discussion.

5530 Bounds, Philip **Orwell and Englishness: The Dialogue with British Marxism** in *'Cultural Logic' Vol.10, 2007* 26pp

5531 Bounds, Philip **Unlikely Bedfellows: Orwell and the British Cultural Marxists** in *'Nature Society and Thought' Vol.20 No.1, 2007* 26pp Recognises Orwell's hostility to Communism but argues his cultural writings were influenced by CP writers and critics.

5532 Bowden, Maggie & Styles, Jean **Parents and Children: How Does a Communist Family Work?** in *'Link' Summer 1979* 3pp Articles on the relationship between family and Party. This article was followed by some debate.

5533 Boyle, Bill **Communist New Realism** in *'Militant International Review' No.33, Autumn 1986* 2pp Review of P. Carter's 'Trade Unions: The New Reality'.

5534 Bramley, Ted **Affiliation** in *'LM' Jan. 1946* 6pp

5535 Bramley, Ted **London's Historical Pageant** in *'Inprecorr' Sept. 26 1936* 1pp

5536 Branson, Noreen **'A Short History of Dave Morgan: An Autobiography' – Review** in *'Socialist History Journal' 20, 1992* 3pp

5537 Branson, Noreen **'Harry Pollitt' by K. Morgan & 'R.P. Dutt' by J. Callaghan – Review** in *'Socialist History' 8, 1995* 5pp

5538 Branson, Noreen **The Squatters' Movement of 1946** in *'Our History Journal' 9, March 1985* 4pp

5539 Brett, Ken **Eddie Marsden – Obituary** in *'LM' Oct. 1975* 1pp

5540 Brett-Jones, Ann **Ralph Fox: A Man in His Time** in *'MML Bulletin' 137, Spring 2003* 7pp

5541 Bright, Frank **The New Party Line and the Trade Unions** in *'C.R.' Feb. 1929* 8pp

5542 Brooks, Martin **British Youth Guild and the YCI** in *'The International of Youth' (U.S.) Oct. 1934* 4pp

5543 Broomfield, Stuart **The Apprentice Boys' Strikes of the Second World War** in *'Llafur' Vol.3 No.2, Spring 1981* 15pp

5544 Brotherstone, Terry **1956 and the Crisis in the CPGB: Four Witnesses** in *'Critique' Vol.35 No.2, Aug. 2007* 20pp Interesting introduction and then discussion at a 1999 seminar at Aberdeen Univ. between Brian Pearce, Peter Fryer, Alison Macleod & Victor Kiernan. Ranges over 1956, the Historians' Group and CP-Trotskyist relations.

5545 Brotherstone, Terry **'Communism and British Trade Unions, 1924-33' by R. Martin & 'Stalinism in Britain' by R. Black – Review** in *'SLHS' 3, 1970* 4pp

5546 Brotherstone, Terry **John Maclean 1879-1923** in *'Labour Review' Dec. 1983* 11pp

5547 Brotherstone, Terry **John Maclean and the Russian Revolution** in *'SLHS' 23, 1988* 15pp

5548 Brotherstone, Terry **Stalinism, Liberalism and British History** in *'Fourth International' Winter 1971* 3pp Review of 'Britain in the 1930s' by N. Branson.

5549 Brotherstone, Terry **'The Good Old Cause' by W. Thompson – Review** in *'SLHS' 28, 1993* 3pp

5550 Brotherstone, Terry & Pirani, Simon **Were There Alternatives? Movements from Below in the Scottish Coalfield, The CP, and Thatcherism, 1981-1985** in *'Critique' 36/37, 2005* 25pp

5551 Brown, Alan **Allen Hutt – Obituary** in *'LM' Sept. 1973* 1pp

5552 Brown, E.H. [Ernest] **Building the Party** in 'C.R.' July 1926 5pp Discussion contributions followed by T. Quelch, H. Beaken, G. Middleton, G. Gough, & R. Bond in issues to Jan. 1927.

5553 Brown, E.H. [Ernest] **Our Party and the Woollen Strike** in 'C.R.' July 1930 9pp

5554 Brown, E.H. [Ernest] **Persecution of CPGB and Offensive Against the Working Class** in 'C.I.' 18/19 (New Series), 1926 9pp

5555 Brown, E.H. [Ernest] **The Struggle in the Scottish Coalfields: The CP and the New Miners' Union** in 'C.I.' Aug. 15 1929 4pp

5556 Brown, E.H. [Ernest] **The Trial of the Communist Leaders in England** in 'Inprecorr' Dec. 17 1925 1pp

5557 Brown, Geoff **Tom Mann and Jack Tanner and International Revolutionary Syndicalism 1910-20** in 'SSLHB' 27, Autumn 1973 3pp Tanner was in the CP early on though he denied it later.

5558 Brown, J. **Smash the Sectarianism of the British League** in 'The International of Youth' (U.S.) Vol.1 No.1, 1933 ? 4pp Speech to Plenum of YCI in 1932; mainly on Lancs textile disputes & the YCL.

5559 Brown, J. **Some Questions of the United Front in England and America** in 'The International of Youth' Aug. 1933 5pp This issue published by Modern Books.

5560 Brown, J.R. **Winning the Working Youth** in 'C.R.' March 1933 8pp

5561 Brown, W.J., MP **Communism Here** in 'The Spectator' March 12 1948 1pp

5562 Brownell, J. **The Taint of Communism: The Movement for Colonial Freedom, the Labour Party and the CPGB, 1954-70** in 'Canadian Journal of History' Vol.42 No.2, 2007 23pp

5563 Bruley, Sue **Gender, Class and Party: The CP and the Crisis in the Cotton Industry in England Between the Two World Wars** in 'Women's History Review' 2, 1993 26pp

5564 Buchanan, Tom **Britain's Popular Front? Aid Spain and the British Labour Movement** in 'HWJ' 31, 1991 13pp

5565 Buchanan, Tom **'Doves of War: Four Women of Spain' by P. Preston – Review** in 'Socialist History' 24, 2003 2pp One of the subjects is Nan Green.

5566 Buchanan, Tom **Holding the Line: The Political Strategy of the International Brigade Association, 1939-1977** in 'LHR' Vol.66 No.3, Winter 2001 18pp

5567 Buchanan, Tom **Receding Triumph: British Opposition to the Franco Regime, 1945-59** in 'Twentieth Century British History' Vol.12 No.2, 2001 22pp

5568 Buchanan, Tom **The Lost Art of Felicia Browne** in 'HWJ' 54, 2002 22pp Artist killed in Spain.

5568a Buckley, Sheryl **'Revolutionary Communist at Work: A Political Biography of Bert Ramelson by R. Seifert & T. Sibley' – Review** in 'NWLHSB' 37, 2012 1pp

5569 Budden, Olive **Conference of the London District** in 'Inprecorr' Nov. 29 1929 1pp

5570 Bulkeley, Rip et al. **'If at First You Don't Succeed': Fighting Against the Bomb in the 1950s** in 'ISJ' 11, 1981 29pp

5571 Bullen, Andrew **Watching and Besetting: The Burnley Police and the 'More Looms' Disputes, 1931-2** in 'NWLHSB' 5, 1978 9pp This issue has no date or number. Quite a bit on CP (incl. ref. to the 'CP jazz band').

5571a Bullock, Ian **The Original British Ultra-Left, 1917-1924** in 'Socialist History' 44, 2014 20pp On SLP, Communist Workers' Movement etc.

5572 Burke, David **Andrew Rothstein and the Crucible of British Communism** in 'Praxis: Bulletin of the MML' 153, Autumn 2011 7pp

5573 Burke, David **Theodore Rothstein and the Genesis of British Marxism** in 'Praxis: Bulletin of the MML' 152, Winter 2010/11 10pp

5574 Burke, David & Lindop, Fred **Theodore Rothstein and the Origins of the British CP** in 'Socialist History' 15, 1999 21pp

5575 Burnham, Paul **The Squatters of 1946: A Local Study in National Context** in 'Socialist History' 25, 2004 26pp Much on relationship between CP & LP during the squatters' campaign in S Buckinghamshire.

5576 Burns, Emile **The Party's Summer Campaign** in 'CR' July 1951 5pp

5577 Burns, Emile **Take Our Policy to the People** in 'CR' Feb. 1952 3pp On public activity – with some examples.

5578 Burton, Edward **Academic Freedom and Communists** in 'Marxist Quarterly' April 1954 13pp

5579 Bush, Alan **Tasks of Cultural Workers** in 'CR' Feb. 1951 6pp Statement to meeting organised by National Cultural Cttee, Dec. 10 1950.

5580 Bush, Barbara **Forgotten Comrades: Black Colonial Labour and the Development of Anti-Colonialism in the Inter-War Years – Bibliographical Essay** in 'SSLHB' 45, Autumn 1982 6pp Some brief comments on CP's work – or lack of it – in this area.

5581 Byrne, David **Class, Race and Nation: The Politics of the 'Arab Issue' in South Shields, 1919-39** in 'Immigrants and Minorities' July/Nov. 1994 16pp Single, but interesting, ref. to how Anglo-Arab men became the backbone of a local CP.

5582 Cadogan, Peter **Stalinism and the Defeat of the 1945-51 Labour Governments** in 'Labour Review' Aug/Sept. 1958 3pp

5583 Calcutt, Andrew **1956 And All That** in 'Living Marxism' Aug. 1990 1pp On 'CP & 1956' Conference.

5584 Calcutt, Andrew **CPGB Congress** in 'Living Marxism' Jan. 1992 1pp

5585 Callaghan, John **'Class or Nation' by N. Redfern – Review** in 'English Historical Review' Vol.121 No.492, June 2006 2pp

5586 Callaghan, John **'Communist Women in Scotland' by N. Rafeek – Review** in 'SLHS' 44, 2009 3pp

5587 Callaghan, John **Colonies, Racism, the CPGB and the Comintern in the Inter-War Years** in 'Science and Society' Vol.61 No.4, Winter 1997/8 12pp Reply to M. Sherwood in Vol.60 No.2, Summer 1996.

5588 Callaghan, John **Common Wealth and the CP and the 1945 General Election** in 'Contemporary Record' Summer 1995 17pp

5589 Callaghan, John **'History of the CPGB 1927-41' by N. Branson – Review** in 'JOCS' Sept/Dec. 1985 1pp

5590 Callaghan, John **Industrial Militancy, 1945-1979: The Failure of the British Road to Socialism?** in 'Twentieth Century British History' Vol.15 No.4, 2004 21pp

5591 Callaghan, John **Jawarharlal Nehru and the CP** in 'JOCS' Sept. 1991 18pp Incl. document sent by Dutt to C.I., Feb. 1936.

5592 Callaghan, John **Looking Back in Amazement: 'Interesting Times' and the Reviewers** in 'Socialist History' 24, 2003 7pp

5593 Callaghan, John **'Mask: MI5's Penetration of the CPGB' by N. West – Review** in 'Socialist History' 30 2007 3pp

5594 Callaghan, John **Rajani Palme Dutt, British Communism and the CP of India** in 'JOCS' Vol.6 No.1, March 1990 23pp

5595 Callaghan, John & Phythian, Mark **State Surveillance of the CPGB Leadership, 1920s-1950s** in 'LHR' Vol.69 No.1, April 2004 14pp Based on freshly released government documents. Apart from pointless following of leaders, they reveal internal debate on role of USSR.

5596 Callaghan, John **The Background to 'Entrism': Leninism and the British Labour Party** in 'JOCS' Dec. 1986 24pp

5597 Callaghan, John **'The Fifth Commandment: Biography of S. Saklatvala' & 'Saklatvala: A Political Biography' – Review** in 'JOCS' March 1992 2pp

5598 Callaghan, John **'The Good Old Cause' by W. Thompson – Review** in 'Contemporary Record' Vol.7 No.2, Autumn 1993 2pp

5599 Callaghan, John **The Heart of Darkness: R.P. Dutt and the British Empire – A Profile** in 'Contemporary Record' Autumn 1991 19pp

5600 Callaghan, John **The Long Drift of the CPGB** in 'JOCS' Sept./Dec. 1985 4pp

5601 Callaghan, John & Morgan, Kevin **The Open Conspiracy of the Communist Party and the Case of W.N. Ewer, Communist and anti-Communist** in 'The Historical Journal' Vol.49 Part 2, 2006 15pp

5602 Callaghan, John **The Plan to Capture the British Labour Party and its Paradoxical Results, 1947-91** in 'JOCH' Vol.40 No.4, Oct. 2005 18pp On CP's policy of working in trade unions simultaneously at grass roots and leadership levels, and using block votes at LP Conferences.

5603 Callaghan, John **'The Political Trajectory of J.T. Murphy' by R. Darlington – Review** in 'Socialist History' 15, 1999 4pp Also reviews 'Molly Murphy – Suffragette and Socialist'.

5604 Callaghan, John **The Road to 1956** in 'Socialist History' 8, 1995 9pp

5605 Callaghan, John **'Under the Red Flag' by K. Laybourn & M. Dylan – Review** in 'IRSH' Vol.46 No.2, Aug. 2001 27pp

5606 Callinicos, Alex **A New Road for the CP?** in 'I.S.' No.97, April 1977 4pp On the 'BRS'.

5607 Callinicos, Alex **The Making of a Working Class Historian (E.P. Thompson)** in 'Socialist Review' Oct. 1993 3pp

5608 Callinicos, Alex **The Politics of 'Marxism Today'** in 'ISJ' 29, Summer 1985 41pp

5609 Callow, John **'The Death of Uncle Joe' by A. Macleod – Review** in *'Communist Review'* (CPB) 36, Spring 2002 2pp

5609a Campbell, Alan **'Bolshevism, Syndicalism and the General Strike' by K. Morgan – Review** in *'LHE'* Vol.80 No.1, April 2015 3pp

5610 Campbell, Alan & McIlroy, John et al. **British Students at the International Lenin School: The Vindication of a Critique** in *'Twentieth Century British History'* Vol.16 No.4, 2005 18pp

5611 Campbell, Alan **Communism in the Scottish Coalfields, 1920-36** in *'Tijdschrift voor Sociale Geschiedenis' (Amsterdam)* July 1992 22pp

5612 Campbell, Alan **From Independent Collier to Militant Miner: Tradition and Change in the Trade Union Consciousness of the Scottish Miners, 1874-1929** in *'SLHS'* 24, 1989 13pp

5613 Campbell, Alan & McIlroy, John **Is CPGB History Important? A Reply to Harriet Jones** in *'LHR'* Vol.68 No.3, Dec. 2003 5pp

5614 Campbell, Alan & McIlroy, John **Reflections on the CP's Third Period in Scotland: The Case of Willie Allan** in *'Scottish Labour History'* 35, 2000 22pp Allan was leader of the United Mineworkers of Scotland. Article includes discussion of other historians' work.

5615 Campbell, Alan & McIlroy, John et al. **The International Lenin School: A Response to Cohen and Morgan** in *'Twentieth Century British History'* Vol.15 No.1, 2004 26pp

5616 Campbell, Alan & McIlroy, John **The Last Word on Communism** in *'LHR'* Vol.70 No.1, April 2005 4pp Final contribution to what had been a somewhat bitter exchange on CP history.

5617 Campbell, Alan & McIlroy, John **The NUWM and the CPGB Revisited** in *'LHR'* Vol.73 No.1, April 2008 28pp

5618 Campbell, Beatrix **The Women's Movement and the Party** in *'International'* Autumn 1979 8pp Debate with C. Pugh (IMG), S. Rowbotham et al.

5619 Campbell, David **Reminiscences of 1926** in *'Scottish Marxist'* 12, 1976 4pp

5620 Campbell, J.R. **7th Congress C.I., 4th Session: Speech** in *'Inprecorr'* Aug. 28 1935 3pp

5621 Campbell, J.R. **A Congress of Confidence and Vigour** in *'Inprecorr'* June 5 1937 5pp

5622 Campbell, J.R. **After Hull – What?** in *'C.R.'* Oct. 1924 7pp On TUC Congress.

5623 Campbell, J.R. **Arguments of the Opponents of the United Front in England** in *'C.I.'* Mar/April 1936 4pp

5624 Campbell, J.R. **Growing Movement for Unity** in *'Inprecorr'* June 13 1936 1pp

5625 Campbell, J.R. **How the Workers Can Win Increased Wages** in *'C.R.'* March 1935 6pp On CP industrial work; this was Campbell's speech to Congress & was continued in April issue.

5626 Campbell, J.R. **Maurice Dobb: Communist, Economist, Historian** in *'MT'* Aug. 1967 8pp Whole issue devoted to Dobb's work.

5627 Campbell, J.R. **New Opportunist Arguments Against the C.I.** in *'Inprecorr'* July 28 1933 1pp

5628 Campbell, J.R. **Some Aspects of Our Industrial Work** in *'C.R.'* Jan. 1935 4pp

5629 Campbell, J.R. **Speech at 10th Plenum ECCI, 19th Session** in *'Inprecorr'* Oct. 9 1929 2pp

5630 Campbell, J.R. **Speech at 10th Plenum ECCI, 5th Session, July 5** in *'Inprecorr'* Aug. 21 1929 1pp

5631 Campbell, J.R. **Speech at 7th Congress of the C.I.** in *'C.I.'* Aug. 20 1935 7pp

5632 Campbell, J.R. **The 10th Congress and After** in *'C.R.'* March 1929 11pp

5633 Campbell, J.R. **The 7th World Congress and GB** in *'C.R.'* June 1935 6pp

5634 Campbell, J.R. & Messer, J.M. **The Activities of the Scottish Workers' Committees** in *'C.I.'* 11/12, June/July 1920 1pp Campbell's initials incorrectly given as 'G K'.

5635 Campbell, J.R. **The Campbell Case** in *'LM'* Nov. 1924 5pp Campbell was arrested in Aug. under the 1797 Incitement to Mutiny Act for an anti-militarist article in 'Workers' Weekly' on July 25. The charges were dropped but the 'Case' played a role in the downfall of the Labour Government.

5636 Campbell, J.R. **The Coming Congress of the CPGB** in *'Inprecorr'* May 29 1937 1pp

5637 Campbell, J.R. **The CPGB and the General Election** in *'Inprecorr'* May 3 1929 1pp 'For the first time in its history, the CPGB will enter a General Election under its own revolutionary banner, with its own revolutionary programme in opposition to the three capitalist parties, Liberal, Labour and Conservative'.

5638 Campbell, J.R. **The Workers' Counter-Offensive in the Woollen Textile Industry** in *'C.I.'* July 15 1930 6pp

5639 Canning, Audrey **William Gallacher Memorial Library** in *'Our History Journal'* 13, Dec. 1988 1pp

5640 Cant, Catherine **The British Labour Women's Conference** in *'Inprecorr'* June 30 1927 1pp On CP's influence in this conference.

5641 Cant, Catherine **Women's Day 1927 and the British Working Women** in *'Inprecorr'* Feb. 25, 1927 1pp Little on CP but notes that there were 3,000 women members compared to 600 at the same time the previous year.

5642 Carlson, O. **Six Months of Progress in GB** in *'The International of Youth'* No.1, 1924 3pp Detailed, critical view of YCL.

5643 Carruthers, Susan **A Red Under Every Bed? Anti-Communist Propaganda and Britain's Response to Colonial Insurgency** in *'Contemporary Record'* Vol.9 No.2, Autumn 1995 24pp On the IRD.

5644 Casey, Michael & Ackers, Peter **The Enigma of the Young Arthur Horner: From Churches of Christ Preacher to Communist Militant (1894-1920)** in *'LHR'* Vol.66 No.1, Spring 2001 21pp

5645 Catterall, Stephen **'Class Against Class' by M. Worley – Review** in *'Manchester Region History Review'* Vol.17 No.2, 2006 3pp

5646 Ceadel, Martin **The First Communist 'Peace Society': The British Anti-War Movement, 1932-35** in *'Twentieth Century British History'* Vol.1 No.1, 1990 29pp

5647 Chadwick, Lee **Leiston Communists and the 1939 War: A Grassroots View** in *'Socialist History Journal'* 19, 1992 8pp

5648 Chadwick, Lee **Leiston Communists and the War** in *'Our History Journal'* 19, 1992 8pp

5649 Chairman of LDCP Print Group **A Popular Workers' Newspaper** in *'C.R.'* May 1932 6pp

5650 Challinor, Ray **Harry McShane, 1891-1988 – Obituary** in *'HWJ'* 27, 1989 2pp

5651 Challinor, Ray **Memoirs of a Militant** in *'NELH'* 9, 1975 9pp Interview with Jack Parks.

5652 Challinor, Ray **Zigzag: The CP and the Bomb** in *'I.S.'* No.3, Winter 1960 5pp Curiously misnumbered as No.6.

5653 Chalmers, Doug **Interview with George Galloway** in *'Scottish Marxist'* 23, 1981 3pp Covers relationship LP/CP.

5654 Champion, Michael **Communism in Education** in *'Common Cause Bulletin'* 108, Jan. 1964 5pp

5655 Chapple, Dave **Lawrence Daly and the Fife Socialist League, 1956-62** in *'New Interventions'* Winter 1996 4pp

5656 Charteris, E. **Should the CP Be Liquidated? A Reply to M. Philips Price** in *'C.R.'* Oct. 1924 17pp

5657 Chase, Malcolm **John Saville and the 'Dictionary of Labour Biography'** in *'Socialist History'* 19, 2001 12pp Bit on CP Historians' Group.

5658 Chater, Tony **Time to Choose** in *'Communist Campaign Review'* Winter 1987 4pp

5659 Chater, Tony **British Communists Face New Tasks** in *'WMR'* March 1972 3pp On 32nd Congress.

5660 Chester, Andrew **Uneven Development: Communist Strategy From the 1940s to the 1970s** in *'MT'* Sept. 1979 7pp On CP's programmes.

5661 Childs, David **The British CP and the War, 1939-41: Old Slogans Revived** in *'JOCH'* Vol.12 No.2, April 1977 16pp

5662 Childs, David **The Cold War and the 'British Road', 1946-53** in *'JOCH'* Vol.23 No.4, Oct. 1988 22pp

5663 Cholewka, Stefan & Lahr, Sheila **'Party People, Communist Lives' ed. by J. McIlroy, K. Morgan & A. Campbell – Review** in *'Revolutionary History'* Vol.8 No.3, 2003 2pp

5664 Citrine, Walter **Democracy or Disruption: An Examination of Communist Influence in the T.U.s: Part 1** in *'Labour Magazine'* Dec. 1927 4pp Parts 2-5 appeared in the issues dated Jan, Feb, March and June 1928.

5665 Citrine, Walter **Disrupters in the Labour Movement** in *'Labour'* July 1937 1pp

5666 Clark, Alex **Memories of MacDiarmid** in *'Communist Review'* (CPB) 16, Jan. 1993 10pp Incl. discussion on his membership of CP.

5667 Clark, Alex **Personal Experiences From a Lifetime in the Communist and Labour Movements** in *'SLHR'* 10, 1996 3pp Part 2 in No.11.

5668 Clark, Andrew **'No Wonder We Were Rebels' by J. Kane – Review** in *'Communist Review'* (CPB) 21, Spring 1995 1pp

5669 Clark, David **CP Split** in *'The Leveller'* 7, July/Aug. 1977 1pp On new BRS and Sid French.

5670 Clark, Janet **Sincere and Reasonable Men? The Origins of the NCCL** in *'Twentieth Century British History'* Vol.20 No.4, 2009 25pp Discusses CP influence in the early days of the NCCL.

5671 Clarke, Willie **Communist Councillor** in *'Scottish Marxist'* 28, 1984 1pp

5672 Clifford, Brendan **Greaves and a 'Rabid Anti-National Trotskyist'** in *'The Irish Communist' (BICO)* 172, April 1980 10pp Mixes political criticism with personal attack on C.D. Greaves. About the political views of Liam Daltun.

5673 Clifford, Brendan **The Imperialist War of 1939-40** in *'The Communist' (BICO)* Dec. 1978 8pp

5674 Clifford, J. **Horner v the Political Bureau** in *'C.R.'* April 1931 31pp This defence of Horner is answered by the paper.

5675 Clinton, Alan **'Nothing to Lose ... A World to Win: A History of Chelmsford T.C.'** by M. Wallace – Review in *'SSLHB'* 42 Spring 1981 1pp

5676 Clynes, J.R. **Labour and the Communists** in *'Labour Magazine'* Dec. 1924 3pp

5677 Coates, Ken **Peter Fryer 1929-2006 – Obituary** in *'Revolutionary History'* Vol.9 No.4, 2007 4pp

5678 Cocaigne, Ellen **The Left's Bibliophilia in Interwar Britain: Assessing Booksellers' Role in the Battle of Ideas** in *'Twentieth Century Communism'* 4, 2012 12pp

5679 Cockburn, Claud **The Morning Star** in *'NLR'* 38, 1966 12pp

5680 Cohen, Gerry **Anti-Communism in Britain** in *'WMR'* March 1981 5pp

5681 Cohen, Gidon & Morgan, Kevin **British Students at the International Lenin School 1926-1937: A Reaffirmation of Methods, Results and Conclusions** in *'Twentieth Century British History'* Vol.15 No.1, 2004 31pp

5682 Cohen, Gidon **Propensity-Score Methods and the Lenin School** in *'Journal of Interdisciplinary History'* Vol.36 No.2, Autumn 2005 24pp Problems of statistical analysis in general, and relating to CPGB members at the Lenin School in particular.

5683 Cohen, Gidon & Morgan, Kevin **Stalin's Sausage Machine: British Students at the International Lenin School, 1926-37** in *'Twentieth Century British History'* Vol.13 No.4, Dec. 2003 27pp

5684 Cohen, Gidon & Morgan, Kevin **The International Lenin School: A Final Comment** in *'Twentieth Century British History'* Vol.18 No.1, 2007 5pp

5685 Cohen, J. **The Results of the January Plenum of the YCL** in *'The International of Youth'* April/May 1930 4pp

5686 Cohen, Jack **Britain: Party Education** in *'WMR'* Aug. 1962 2pp

5687 Cohen, Jack **Britain: Party Educational Work** in *'WMR'* April 1964 2pp

5688 Cohen, Jack **Critical Thoughts On Our Agitation and Propaganda** in *'C.R.'* June 1932 5pp

5689 Cohen, Jack **The CP and the YCL** in *'C.R.'* Feb. 1930 6pp

5690 Cohen, Nick **Up For Grabs: £3.5m of Stalin's Gold** in *'New Statesman'* Oct. 23 2000 2pp Arguments on the remainder of CPGB's property.

5691 Cohen, Norma **Karl Marx Was A Scouser: A Liverpool Jewish Childhood** in *'Jewish Quarterly'* 178, 2000 6pp YCL activists Eric and Eve Cohen remembered by their daughter.

5691a Cohen, Sarah **Labour Party Anti-Communism and its Limits: The Case of Sam Watson** in *'Socialist History'* 44, 2014 21pp

5692 Cohen, Sheila **Left Agency and Class Action: The Paradox of Workplace Radicalism** in *'Capital and Class'* Vol.35 No.3, 2011 19pp Compares CP with IS/SWP attitudes to workplace trade unionism, late 1970s-early 1980s.

5693 Cole, G.D.H. **Critique of British Communism** in *'This Unrest'* Ruskin College 1933 4pp Rare piece of writing by Cole on CP.

5694 Cole, Sidney **Ivor Montagu: 70th Birthday Tribute** in *'LM'* April 1974 3pp

5695 Colls, Robert **'Out of the Old Earth' by H. Heslop – Review** in *'NELH'* 28, 1994 5pp

5696 Colvin, Ray **A Communist Work In: For Re-establishing the Party** in *'Communist Campaign Review'* Summer 1987 5pp The Communist Campaign Group became the CPB.

5697 Condon, L. **British CP's 10th Congress** in *'Inprecorr'* Jan. 25 1929 1pp

5698 Condon, Richard **The CPGB: An Outsider's View** in *'Oxford Left'* Feb. 1966 5pp

5699 Conze, Edward **The Communists' Last Somersault** in *'Plebs'* Oct. 1935 4pp On 7th Congress of C.I.

5700 Cook, A.J. & Dutt, R.P. **Cook's Break with the Revolutionary Working Class: A Statement by A.J. Cook and an Editorial Reply** in *'LM'* June 1929 7pp Strong stuff from both sides! Based on Scottish Miners' problems. There were further articles on this 'debate' (eg Nov. 1929), but none specifically on CP.

5701 Cook, Dave **Interview with Vishnu Sharma** in *'MT'* Dec. 1979 5pp

5702 Cook, Dave **No Private Drama** in *'MT'* Feb. 1985 4pp On internal arguments. Discussion contributions followed in May, June, July.

5703 Cook, Dave **The Battle for Kinder Scout** in *'MT'* Aug. 1977 3pp

5704 Cook, Dave **The BRS and the CP** in *'MT'* Dec. 1978 10pp Further contributions to this debate in Feb, March, April, May 1979.

5705 Cook, Dave **The Student Movement, Left Unity and the CP** in *'MT'* Oct. 1974 11pp

5706 Cooney, Bob **Wally Tapsell** in *'Volunteer For Liberty'* May 1 1938 1pp

5707 Copsey, Nigel **Communists and the Inter-War Anti-Fascist Struggle in the United States and Britain** in *'LHR'* Vol.76 No.3, Dec. 2011 23pp

5708 Corthorn, Paul **Labour, The Left and the Stalinist Purges of the Late 1930s** in *'The Historical Journal'* Vol.48 No.1, 2005 28pp

5709 Costello, Mick **Goal: Left Unity** in *'WMR'* April 1980 5pp On 36th Congress.

5710 Coughlan, Anthony **C. Desmond Greaves 1913-88: An Obituary Essay** in *'Saothar'* 14, 1989 11pp In CP from 1934 till his death, Greaves worked full time for the Connolly Assoc. from 1951. He was a scientist, historian & poet as well as organiser. Debates about the influence of the CP will go on and on – this article shows how one member did influence events. Bibliography.

5711 Courtois, Stephane **'About Turn' ed. F. King & G. Mathews – Review** in *'JOCS'* June 1992 7pp

5712 Cowe, Bill **The Making of a Clydeside Communist** in *'MT'* April 1973 6pp Author was active in NUR during General Strike & Scottish Industrial Organiser for 16 years.

5713 Cox, Idris **50 Years Against Imperialism** in *'MT'* Oct. 1970 9pp

5714 Cox, Idris **British Congress Marks New Stage** in *'WMR'* Jan. 1974 2pp

5715 Cox, Idris **Carrying Out the CC Resolution** in *'C.R.'* Aug. 1932 4pp

5716 Cox, Idris **Communist Strongholds in Inter-War Britain** in *'MT'* June 1979 2pp

5717 Cox, Idris **Linking the Present with the Future** in *'WMR'* March 1978 7pp On 35th Congress.

5718 Cox, Idris **The 12th Party Congress and the Principles of Bolshevik Organisation** in *'C.R.'* Dec. 1932 9pp

5719 Cox, Idris **The British Party Congress and the Situation in Lancashire** in *'C.I.'* Feb. 5 1935 4pp

5720 Cox, Idris **The Need to Improve the Character and Content of Revolutionary Propaganda and Agitation** in *'C.R.'* Nov. 1932 5pp

5721 Cox, Idris **The Sign of the 'Times'** in *'Inprecorr'* June 6 1936 1pp On Horner's election as President of S. Wales Miners, in answer to article in the 'Times'.

5722 Cox, Idris **The Transformation of the Party Organisations** in *'C.R.'* Feb. 1930 5pp

5723 Cox, Idris **The World Congress and the Main Tasks of the British CP** in *'C.R.'* July 1935 4pp

5724 Cox, Idris **What to Learn from the Municipal Elections** in *'C.R.'* Jan. 1931 4pp

5725 Cox, Idris et al. **Tribute to Jack Woddis** in *'LM'* Nov. 1980 3pp

5726 Coyle, Kenny **An Unmistakable Warning: The Liquidation of the YCL** in *'Communist Campaign Review'* Winter 1987 3pp

5727 Coyle, Kenny **The CPGB and Post-Modernism** in *'Communist Review' (CPB)* 11, Autumn 1991 11pp

5728 Crawford, Ted **Professor Stuart Kirkby – Obituary** in *'Revolutionary History'* Vol.8 No.1, 2001 3pp In CP in 1929, later joined the Trotskyist movement; author suggests he may have been employed by the security services.

5729 Crawfurd, Helen **The English Working Class Today** in *'Inprecorr'* Feb. 21 1922 1pp Claims membership for CP of 10,000 and over 20,000 votes in local elections. 'During the year over 100 of our members (men and women) have been imprisoned'.

5730 Crawfurd, Helen **The Red Cross of the Working Class: Further Pages From the**

Autobiography in 'MML Bulletin' 68, Oct./Dec. 1973 4pp On W.I.R.

5731 Crawley, Aidan **A Red Under Every Bed?** in 'Encounter' Vol. XXI No.1, July 1963 5pp 'Communism in Britain is an ulcer in the body politic and not a malignant growth; it can be cured by physiotherapy rather than surgery'.

5732 Crawley, Aidan **British Communism: How the Party Draws its Strength** in 'East-West Digest' April 1972 5pp Reprinted from 'Financial Times' March 8 1972.

5733 Creaby, John **Socialism: More Than Economics, A Way of Life – Horace Green, 1907-1995** in North East History' 42, 2011 24pp Green joined the CP from the ILP; full-time CP worker in Yorkshire then Northern District. Leading figure in anti-racism from the 1960s; community activist; active in CAWU incl. on leading bodies despite ballot papers being obliged to state that he was a member of the CPGB.

5734 Croft, Andy **A Man of Communist Appearence: Randall Swingler and MI5** in 'Socialist History' 37, 2010 8pp An update on the author's biog., courtesy of newly released police files.

5735 Croft, Andy **Alick West of Marx House, 1935-7** in 'MML Bulletin' 100, April 1982 6pp

5736 Croft, Andy **'Collected Poems' by E.P. Thompson ed. F. Inglis – Review** in 'Socialist History' 20, 2001 3pp

5737 Croft, Andy **Mapless in the Wilderness: Randall Swingler and 1956** in 'Socialist History' 19 2001 26pp

5738 Croft, Andy **Proletarian Literature in the 1930s** in 'LHR' Vol.55 No.1, Spring 1990 2pp

5739 Croft, Andy **'Proletarian' Writers in Britain and America** in 'LHR' Vol.59 No.3, Winter 1994 2pp

5740 Croft, Andy **'The Crisis of Theory: E.P. Thompson, the New Left and Postwar British Politics' by Scott Hamilton – Review** in 'Socialist History' 42, 2012 2pp

5741 Croft, Andy **'Tressell: The Real Story of the Ragged Trousered Philanthropists' by D. Harker – Review** in 'Socialist History' 28, 2006 3pp

5742 Croft, Andy **Returned Volunteer: The Novels of John Sommerfield** in 'London Magazine' April/May 1983 9pp

5743 Croft, Andy **Walthamstow, Little Gidding and Middlesbrough: Edward Thompson, Adult Education and Literature** in 'Socialist History' 8, 1995 27pp

5744 Croft, Andy **Writers, the CP and the Battle of Ideas, 1945-50** in 'Socialist History' 5, 1994 24pp

5745 Crooke, Stan **Communism, Stalinism and the British General Strike** in 'Workers' Liberty' June 1996 4pp

5746 Cross, Richard **'After the Party' ed. A. Croft – Review** in 'Twentieth Century Communism' 5, 2013 4pp

5747 Cross, Richard **'Children of the Revolution' ed. P. Cohen – Review** in 'Socialist History' 19, 2001 4pp

5747a Crouch, Dave **Rising from the East: CP's role in Organising Jewish Workers in London's East End** in 'Socialist Review' June 2006 2pp

5748 Croucher, Richard **'History of the CPGB, 1927-41' by N. Branson – Review** in 'SSLHB' 52, Part 1 1987 3pp

5749 Croucher, Richard **The Coventry Branch of the MM** in 'SSLHB' 30, Spring 1975 4pp

5750 Croucher, Richard **The Coventry Toolroom Agreement, 1941-72 Part 1** in 'HSIR' 8, Autumn 1999 42pp Part 2 in following issue.

5751 Croucher, Richard **Wal Hannington (1896-1996) and the Inter-War Unemployed Movement** in 'Yearbook '98'; Magyar Lajos Alapitvany 1997 10pp Useful summary of Hannington's role, incl. relationship with CPGB leadership. English article in Hungarian journal.

5752 Crowe, Sibyl **The Zinoviev Letter: A Reappraisal** in 'JOCH' Vol.10 No.3, July 1975 26pp

5753 Crowley, Mike **Communist Engineers and the Second World War in Manchester** in 'NWLHSB' 22, 1997 10pp

5754 Crozier, Brian **Britain's Industrial Revolutionaries** in 'Interplay' Jan. 1971 3pp

5755 Cullen, C.K. **The Revolutionary Policy Committee and the ILP** in 'Inprecorr' Nov. 9 1935 1pp Author was member of the RPC who joined CP.

5756 Cullen, Stephen **Jewish Communists or Communist Jews? The CPGB and British Jews in the 1930s** in 'Socialist History' 41, 2012 20pp

5757 Curtis, Barry **James Boswell** in 'Block' No.1, 1979 4pp

5758 Curtis, Ben **A Tradition of Radicalism: The Politics of the South Wales Miners, 1964-1985** in *'LHR' Vol.76 No.1, April 2011* 18pp

5759 Curtis, Ben **Man of the People: The Place of Lewis Jones in South Wales Coalfield Society** in *'Welsh History Review' Vol.25 No.4, Dec. 2011* 20pp

5760 D.P. **The Struggle Against the General Council's 'Black Circular'** in *'Inprecorr' Feb. 2 1935* 2pp The TUC leadership tried to ban Communists from holding positions on TCs and also asked affiliated unions not to let members of 'disruptive bodies' (i.e. CP) hold office.

5761 D.R. **The Present State of Party Education** in *'C.R.' Jan. 1931* 4pp

5762 D.W. **The Party and the Working Class: Some Experiences in Bradford** in *'C.R.' Dec. 1933/Jan. 1934* 4pp

5763 Dabscheck, Braham **'Revolutionary Communist at Work: A Political Biography of Bert Ramelson' by R. Seifert & T. Sibley – Review** in *'Journal of Industrial Relations' Vol.55 No.159, 2013* 3pp

5764 Dallas, Karl **MacColl: The Man, The Myth, The Music** in *'English Dance and Song' Christmas 1989* 3pp

5765 Daniels, Gary **'The Spy Who Came in from the Co-op' by D. Burke; 'The New Civilization? Understanding Stalin's Soviet Union, 1919-1941' by P. Flewers; 'The Sixth Man: The Extraordinary Life of Paddy Costello' by J. McNeish – Review** in *'LHR' Vol.75 No.2, Aug. 2010* 8pp Books dealing with new information on spies, or alleged spies, in CPGB.

5766 Daniels, John **A Letter to a Member of the CP** in *'Labour Review' Jan. 1957* 6pp

5767 Daniels, John **The CP and Democratic Centralism** in *'Labour Review' March/April 1957* 5pp SLL.

5768 Darlington, Ralph **Shop Stewards' Leadership, Left Wing Activism and Collective Workplace Union Organisation** in *'Capital and Class' 76, Spring 2002* 33pp Argues that researchers have generally underplayed the role of socialist activists in industry and compares CP with SWP.

5769 Dash, Jack **My 'Obituary'** in *'LM' Feb. 1968* 1pp Humorous piece as performed by Dash on tv, Dec. 1967.

5770 David, Nicholas **Peter Lewis Shinnie 1915-2007 – Obituary** in *'African Archaeological Review' Vol.25 No.1/2, June 2008* 5pp Shinnie joined CP while a schoolboy at Westminster, was active at Oxford Univ., working part-time in the Ashmoelan and part-time for the CP on £3 per week. He later joined the Scottish National Party. He was a founder of African archaeology.

5771 David, Wayne **The LP and the 'Exclusion' of the Communists: The Case of the Ogmore Divisional LP in the 1920s** in *'Llafur' Vol.3 No.4, 1983* 11pp

5772 Davidson, Neil **Gramsci's Reception in Scotland** in *'Scottish Labour History' 45, 2010* 23pp

5772a Davidson, Neil **'Hamish Henderson: A Biography' by T. Neat – Review** in *'SLHS' 47, 2012* 2pp

5773 Davies, Andrew **T.A. Jackson: The Unpublished Autobiographies** in *'MML Bulletin' 102, March 1983* 4pp Incl. brief extract on the General Strike – especially the production & distribution of CP Bulletins.

5774 Davies, Brian **Heading for the Rocks?** in *'Arcade: Wales Fortnightly' No.31, Feb. 2 1982* 3pp Critical view from ex-member, but very useful & well researched analysis of CP's attitude to Nationalism.

5775 Davies, Paul **The Making of A.J. Cook: His Development Within the South Wales Labour Movement, 1900-24** in *'Llafur' Summer 1978* 21pp

5776 Davies, Rhys, MP **The 1935 Communist Manifesto** in *'New Dawn' June 1 1935* 4pp On 'For Soviet Britain'.

5777 Davies, Sam **The Membership of the NUWM, 1923-38** in *'LHR' Vol.57 No.1, Spring 1992* 8pp

5778 Davin, Anna **R.D. (Reggie) Smith 1914-85 – Obituary** in *'HWJ' 21, 1986* 2pp

5779 Davin, Delia **Jim Roche, 1909-88 – Obituary** in *'HWJ' 27, 1989* 2pp

5780 Davis, Mary & Foster, John **Eric Hobsbawm 1917-2012 – Obituary** in *'Praxis' 156, Spring 2013* 3pp

5781 Davis, Mary **'History of the CPGB 1941-1951' by N. Branson – Review** in *'Communist Review' (CPB) 26 Autumn/Winter 1997* 1pp

5782 Davis, Mary **Only Yesterday: Betty Reid Interview** in *'Link' Summer 1983* 2pp

5783 Davis, Mary **Only Yesterday: Kay Beauchamp Interview** in *'Link' Winter 1981* 1pp Part 2 in Spring 1982. Beauchamp was a CP councillor in Finsbury.

5784 Davis, Mary **Sylvia Pankhurst's Communism and the CPGB** in *'Communist Review' (CPB)* 49, Winter 2007/8 14pp

5785 Davis, Mary & Foster, John **Why Were They So Afraid of Communist Influence?** in *'American Communist History'* Vol.4 No.2, 2005 7pp

5786 Dawson, Jerry **George Garrett: Man and Writer** in *'NWLHSB'* 14, 1989 4pp

5787 Dean, Frances **'Harry Pollitt' by K. Morgan – Review** in *'Communist Review' (CPB)* 19, March 1994 3pp

5788 Deason, John **The Broad Left in the AUEW** in *'I.S.'* No.79, June 1975 9pp

5789 Deery, Philip **A Very Present Menace? Attlee, Communism and the Cold War** in *'Australian Journal of Politics and History'* Vol.44 No.1, 1998 24pp Argues the Government was justified in viewing the 1949 London dock strike as a communist threat to national security.

5790 Deery, Philip **Cold War or Class War? Comparing Communism: Britain and Australia in the 1940s** in *'Australian Studies'* 2, 1997 28pp

5791 Deery, Philip **The Secret Battalion: Communism in Britain During the Cold War** in *'Contemporary British History'* Vol.13 No.4, Winter 1999 28pp Much on the intelligence services' surveillance of CP.

5792 Deery, Phillip & Redfern, Neil **No Lasting Peace? Labor, Communism & the Cominform: Australia and GB, 1945-1950** in *'Labour History'* 88, 2005 23pp

5793 Denver, D.T. & Bochel, J.M. **The Political Socialization of Activists in the British CP** in *'British Journal of Political Science'* Jan. 1973 18pp

5794 Devine, Francis **Andy Barr – Obituary** in *'Saothar'* 29, 2004 3pp

5795 Devine, Francis **John Smethurst 1934-2010 – Obituary** in *'NWLHSB'* 35, 2010/11 5pp Historian of the NW labour movement.

5796 Devine, Francis **Ruth Frow – Obituary** in *'Saothar'* 33, 2008 5pp

5797 Devine, Pat **Annual Conference of the ILP** in *'Inprecorr'* April 20 1934 1pp

5798 Devine, Pat **Some Notes on the United Front in Britain** in *'C.I.'* Oct. 20 1934 5pp

5799 Devine, Pat **The New Unemployment Bill and the Struggle Against It** in *'C.I.'* Feb. 1 1934 5pp

5800 Devine, Pat **The United Front and the Unemployed** in *'C.R.'* Oct. 1932 5pp

5801 Devine, Pat **The National Hunger March and the National Unity Conference** in *'Inprecorr'* March 23 1934 1pp

5802 'Dexter' **Some Experiences of the United Front in GB** in *'Inprecorr'* Aug. 18 1933 1pp

5803 Dickson, Tony **Marxism, Nationalism and Scottish History** in *'JOCH'* Vol.20 No.2, April 1985 13pp Reply to James D. Young (see Jan. 1983 issue); debate centres partly on CP's analysis of Scottish nationalism. Young replied in the same issue.

5804 Dobb, Maurice **Random Biographical Notes** in *'Cambridge Journal of Economics'* June 1978 6pp This short autobiog. heads a special issue dedicated to Dobb.

5805 Doherty, Fergal **EuroCommunism in Perspective** in *'Communist Campaign Review'* Autumn 1987 4pp

5806 Dornhorst, Robert **The CPs of Western Europe: The Origins of the National Roads to Socialism** in *'Revolutionary Communist'* No.6, April 1977 17pp

5807 Dornhorst, Robert & Newman, P. **Which Way Forward for Communists? Critique of the BRS** in *'Revolutionary Communist'* No.7, Nov. 1977 18pp

5808 Douglas, Fred **Questions We Must Answer** in *'C.R.'* Feb. 1935 3pp On United Front.

5809 Douglas, H. **The Significance of the Peace Library for United Front Literature** in *'Inprecorr'* June 6 1936 2pp On the new series of CP pamphlets, but covers theory & practice of literature sales; covers 'lit. agent', bookshops, LBC. 'Even on the beaches, at cricket matches, on hikes, these pamphlets can be sold'. First two in this series reviewed in 'Inprecorr' July 4.

5810 Draper, Theodore **The Strange Case of the Comintern** in *'Survey'* Summer 1972 46pp Contains info. on Petrovsky ('Bennet').

5811 Duncan, Rob **Marjory Neilson Newbold: Tribute to a Socialist Pioneer** in *'SLHR'* 6, 1992 4pp Delegate from ILP to 2nd Congress of 3rd International in 1920; joined CP following year. Played role in election of her husband as Communist MP in 1922.

5812 Duncan, Rob **Motherwell For Moscow: Walton Newbold, Revolutionary Politics and the Labour Movement in a Lanarkshire Constituency, 1918-22** in *'SLHS'* 28, 1993 24pp

5813 Duncan, Rob 'Motherwell is Won for Moscow' by C. Fox – Review in 'SLHR' 7, 1993 1pp

5814 Duncan, Robert 'Communists and British Society 1920-1991' by K. Morgan et al. – Review in 'Scottish Labour History' 43, 2008 2pp

5815 Duncan, Robert 'Party People' by J. McIlroy et al. – Review in 'Scottish Labour History' 37, 2002 2pp

5816 Duncan, Robert The Papers of John Turner Walton Newbold, 1888-1943: An Introductory Guide in 'John Rylands Bulletin' Vol.76 No.2, Summer 1994 9pp

5817 Duncan, Robert The Revolutionary in Parliament: Walton Newbold as Communist MP (Nov. 1922-Nov. 1923) in 'Scottish Labour History' 44, 2009 18pp

5818 Durham, Martin British Revolutionaries and the Suppression of the Left in Lenin's Russia, 1918-24 in 'JOCH' Vol.20 No.2, April 1985 16pp

5819 Durham, Martin 'Little Moscows' & 'A Proletarian Science' by S. Macintyre – Review in 'Social History' Jan. 1982 3pp

5820 Durham, Martin 'The Communist Party and the War' by J. Attfield & S. Williams – Review in 'SSLHB' 50, Spring 1985 1pp

5821 Durham, Martin The Left in the Thirties in 'SSLHB' 46, Spring 1983 2pp Important review article of Gloversmith 'Class,Culture & Social Change'; Corkhill & Rawnsley 'The Road to Spain'; and Jupp 'The Radical Left in Britain'.

5822 Durham, Martin 'War of Liberation: Recollections of a Communist Activist' by E. Trory – Review in 'LHR' Vol.55 No.1, Spring 1990 1pp

5823 Dutt, R.P. Bob Stewart – Obituary in 'LM' Oct. 1973 1pp

5824 Dutt, R.P. Bourgeois Journalism and Our Press in 'C.R.' July 1932 7pp Reply to article in May issue ('A Popular Workers' Newspaper').

5825 Dutt, R.P. British Working Class After the Elections in 'C.I.' 8 (New Series), 1924 ? 23pp

5826 Dutt, R.P. Emile Burns – Obituary in 'LM' March 1972 1pp

5827 Dutt, R.P. Harry Pollitt – Obituary in 'LM' Aug. 1960 5pp

5828 Dutt, R.P. Honour to Whom Honour: Some Reflections on CP History in 'LM' May 1959 12pp Review of Pelling's 'British CP'.

5829 Dutt, R.P. 'I Believed' by D. Hyde – Review in 'LM' March 1951 4pp

5830 Dutt, R.P. India in 'C.R.' July 1930 22pp

5831 Dutt, R.P. Intellectuals and Communism in 'C.R.' Sept. 1932 9pp

5832 Dutt, R.P. Labour Unity in Britain in 'University Forward' April 1943 4pp Few articles in this CP influenced journal were directly about the CP, but this one argues strongly for CP affiliation to the LP.

5833 Dutt, R.P. Left Socialism and Communism: Notes of the Month in 'LM' April 1931 20pp Led to debate which continued to end of 1935!

5834 Dutt, R.P. Letter in 'Times Literary Supplement' May 5 1966 1pp This is most important item in series of reviews/letters between 21 April and 9 June.

5835 Dutt, R.P. New Political Course of the British CP in 'Inprecorr' Vol.8 No.11, March 1 1928 2pp

5836 Dutt, R.P. Our Election Campaign in 'C.R.' April 1929 12pp

5837 Dutt, R.P. The British Working Class Movement, The Left Wing and the CP in 'C.I.' 12 (New Series) 1925 16pp

5838 Dutt, R.P. The CP in 'Parliamentary Affairs' Winter 1951 5pp

5839 Dutt, R.P. The CP and the Advance of the Mass Movement in 'Marxist Quarterly' April 1954 16pp

5840 Dutt, R.P. The Left and Communism: Notes of the Month in 'LM' Jan. 1966 15pp

5841 Dutt, R.P. & Campbell, J.R. The New Party Line in 'C.R.' Jan. 1929 51pp Plus contrib. from: J.T. Murphy, J. Strain, W. Tapsell, E. Chase, M. Ferguson. Largely on LP.

5842 Dutt, R.P. The New Phase in Britain and the CP in 'C.I.' March 15 1928 13pp On the LP.

5843 Dutt, R.P. The Party of Victory – Notes of the Month in 'LM' April 1954 16pp

5844 Dutt, R.P. Towards the Workers' Daily in 'C.R.' Dec. 1929 16pp

5845 Dutt, R.P. The Road to Labour Unity: The Problem of Affiliation in 'LM' March 1943 10pp Continued in April & May, which also had: 'Symposium on Affiliation' 6pp; there were 3 more articles in June.

5846 E.B. Another Communist Leader Walks the Plank in 'Socialist Standard' June 1932 1pp On J.T. Murphy's expulsion.

5847 E.B. **Why the Communists Have Failed** in 'Socialist Standard' June 1930 2pp

5848 E.J.M. **Saklatvala on Socialism** in 'Socialist Standard' June 1929 2pp Critique of Saklatvala's pamphlet 'Socialism & Labourism'.

5849 E.K. **The 'DW' Makes a Beginning in Throwing Light on Party Construction** in 'Inprecorr' Jan. 12 1935 1pp Misdated as Jan. 11.

5850 E.K. **The Initiative of the 'DW' in Dealing With Questions of Party Structure** in 'C.I.' Dec. 20 1934 1pp

5851 Eaden, James & Renton, David **Comment: The Inner-Party Critics** in 'LHR' Vol.69 No.3, Dec. 2004 6pp

5852 Egan, David **Noah Ablett 1883-1935** in 'Llafur' Vol.4 No.3, 1986 12pp

5853 Eighteen, Jack **Wakey! Wakey!** in 'LM' Dec. 1969 2pp Review of 'Good Morning, Brothers' by J. Dash.

5854 Eley, Geoff **From Cultures of Militancy to the Politics of Culture: Writing the History of British Communism – 'Opening the Books' ed. G. Andrews et al. – Review** in 'Science and Society' Vol.61 No.1, Spring 1997 14pp

5855 England, Joe **How UCATT Revised Its Rules: An Anatomy of Organisational Change** in 'BJOIR' March 1979 19pp

5856 England, Joe **The General Executive Council of the TGWU: A Profile of the Members (1980)** in 'HSIR' 25/26, Spring/Autumn 2008 35pp Contains short discussion of CP members on this GEC.

5857 Enright, Tim **George Thomson, 1903-87 – Obituary** in 'HWJ' 24, 1987 3pp

5858 Ervin, Charles Wesley **Philip Gunawardena** in 'Revolutionary History' Vol.8 No.1, 2001 25pp Active in CP and among Indian exiles in late 1920s/early 1930s before joining the Trotskyist movement and becoming the founder of revolutionary socialism in Ceylon.

5859 Fair, Bill & Hughes, Alun **Pontypridd Communists in the 1930s** in 'Welsh Workers' History' No.3, 1994 12pp

5860 Fairhead, John **The Crisis in the CP & Editorial Board Reply** in 'Socialist Current' March 1957 6pp

5861 Falber, Reuben **For Left Unity: Communist Strategy in the Election Campaign** in 'WMR' Feb. 1975 3pp

5862 Falber, Reuben **The 31st Party Congress and the Fight Against the Monopolies** in 'MT' Feb. 1970 10pp

5863 Falber, Reuben **The 32nd Congress of the CPGB** in 'MT' Jan. 1972 7pp

5864 Falber, Reuben **The Party's Summer Campaign** in 'CR' June 1952 5pp

5865 Farman, Chris **King Street Crusaders** in 'Sunday Times Magazine' Aug. 30 1970 5pp Substantial article on CP history incl. interviews with leaders. Also page of interviews with ex-Communists.

5866 Farman, Chris **The King Street Crusaders** in 'History Today' Vol.62 No.2, Feb. 2012 8pp Balanced assessment of the CPGB's role in Spain. Includes short article on T. Wintringham by H. Purcell.

5867 Farrell, Alex **The Tameside Conspiracy** in 'The Next Step' April/May 1980 1pp On Tameside T.C.'s controversial meeting on Ireland (inspired by RCP) which led to its expulsion from TUC. See also the next couple of issues for more on this.

5868 Feeny, Sean **Assembly and Alliances: Interview with Jack Ashton** in 'Scottish Marxist' 28, 1984 3pp

5869 Ferguson, Maurice **Breaking Through: Mass Work in Bradford** in 'C.R.' Oct. 1933 3pp

5870 Fernbach, David **Tom Wintringham and Socialist Defense Strategy** in 'HWJ' 14, 1982 28pp

5871 Fielding, Steven **'History of the CPGB 1941-51' by N. Branson – Review** in 'Socialist History' 14, 1999 3pp

5872 Fielding, Steven **British Communism: Interesting But Irrelevant?** in 'LHR' Vol.60 No.2, Autumn 1995 3pp Review of 'Shop Floor Citizens' by J. Hinton – argues that CP is getting too much attention from historians.

5873 Finch, George **The Mass Movement of the Unemployed Workers** in 'C.R.' Nov. 1933 2pp

5874 Findlay, Gloria **A Centenary to Celebrate: Pat Devine** in 'Scottish Marxist Voice' No.7, 1998 2pp Foundation member of CPGB, served on EC of CPs of GB, Ireland and USA. Article written by his widow.

5875 Fishman, Nina **A First Revisionist Replies to Her Revisionists** in 'LHR' Vol.69 No.3, Dec. 2004 6pp Reply to McIlroy & Campbell in April 2003 issue.

5876 Fishman, Nina **'A Vital Element in British Industrial Relations': A Re-assessment of the Order 1305, 1940-51** in 'HSIR' 8, Autumn 1999 43pp

5877 Fishman, Nina & Prazmowska, Anita & Heith, Holger **Communist Coalmining Union Activists and Postwar Reconstruction, 1945-52: Germany, Poland and Britain** in *'Science and Society'* Vol.70 No.1, Jan. 2006 24pp

5878 Fishman, Nina **'The British CP and Moscow, 1920-43' by A. Thorpe – Review** in *'LHR'* Vol.66 No.2, Summer 2001 2pp

5879 Fishman, Nina & Lloyd, J. **The CPGB in 1979** in *'Problems of Communism' (BICO)* No.15, Summer 1979 18pp

5880 Fishman, Nina **The Phoney Cold War in British Trade Unions** in *'Contemporary British History'* Vol.15 No.3, Autumn 2001 21pp Anti-Communism in the TUC, 1947-9

5881 Fitzgerald, Thomas, Rev. **Communism: A Pastoral Problem** in *'Clergy Review'* Jan. 1933 10pp

5882 Fitzgerald, Thomas, Rev. **The Decline of Communism in GB** in *'Clergy Review'* Feb. 1935 10pp

5883 Fitzsimons, M.A. **'Die CPGB: Untersuchungen zur geschichtlichen Entwicklung …' by P-W Hermann – Review** in *'American Historical Review'* Oct. 1978 1pp Review in English of German article.

5884 Flewers, Paul **'Against Fascism and War' by K. Morgan – Review** in *'Revolutionary History'* Vol.3 No.3, Spring 1991 1pp

5885 Flewers, Paul **Communists for Imperialism** in *'Living Marxism'* Sept. 1989 2pp CP blamed for sending workers to their slaughter in WW2.

5886 Flewers, Paul **Cornering the Chameleons: Stalinism and Trotskyism in Britain, 1939-41** in *'Revolutionary History'* Vol.6 No.2/3, Summer 1996 30pp

5887 Flewers, Paul **From the Red Flag to the Union Jack** in *'New Interventions'* June 1995 7pp

5888 Flewers, Paul **'History of the CPGB, 1941-1951' by N. Branson – Review** in *'Revolutionary History'* Vol.7 No.2, 1999 3pp

5889 Flewers, Paul **Hitting the Pits: The CPGB and the NUM** in *'New Interventions'* Winter 1996 3pp

5890 Flinn, Andrew **Archive Notes 1: Communist Political C.V.s** in *'NWLHSB'* 22, 1997 8pp Personnel files of CP Organisation Dept

5891 Flinn, Andrew **CP Biographical Project: Communism and the British Labour Movement – A Prosopographical Analysis, Sept.** 1999 – August 2001. in *'NWLHSB'* 26, 2001 1pp Summary of the Manchester Univ. project.

5892 Flinn, Andrew **Cypriot, Indian and West Indian Branches of the CPGB, 1945-1970** in *'Socialist History'* 21, 2002 20pp Good description of the complexities of the politics of communists from the colonies in Britain, and the contradictions within the CPGB.

5893 Flinn, Andrew **Oldham: The Politics of Cotton and the 'Catholic Vote' in the 1930s** in *'NWLHSB'* 21, 1996 19pp

5894 Flinn, Andrew & Cohen, Gidon **The Abyssinia Crisis, British Labour and the Fracturing of the Anti-War Movement** in *'Socialist History'* 28, 2006 23pp Much on the relationship between CP & ILP.

5895 Flory, Harriette **The Arcos Raid and the Rupture of Anglo-Soviet Relations** in *'JOCH'* Vol.12 No.4, Oct. 1977 18pp

5896 Foot, Paul **The Lessing Legend** in *'Socialist Review'* Feb. 1998 3pp Lessing's involvement then disillusionment with CP, through her autobiog. and fiction.

5897 Ford, Glyn **'The Visible College' by G. Werskey – Review** in *'SSLHB'* 40, Spring 1980 2pp

5898 Forgacs, David **Gramsci and Marxism in Britain** in *'NLR'* 176, 1989 21pp

5899 Foster, John **Communist Renewal in Scotland, 1986-1990** in *'Scottish Labour History'* 38, 2003 20pp The final years of the CPGB and the development of the Communist Party of Scotland and Communist Party of Britain by a leading figure in the latter organisation.

5900 Foster, John **Marx, Marxism and the British Working Class Movement** in *'Praxis: Bulletin of the MML'* 155, Spring 2012 8pp

5901 Foster, John **Scotland and the Russian Revolution** in *'SLHS'* 23, 1988 12pp

5902 Foster, John **The Industrial Politics of the CP** in *'SSLHB'* 38, Spring 1979 2pp Critical review essay on 'T.U.s and Revolution' by J. Hinton & R. Hyman.

5903 Fowler, Lesley & Fowler, Alan **Ruth Frow – Obituary** in *'HWJ'* 67, 2009 3pp

5904 Foy, Noel **An Appreciation of the 21st YCL Congress** in *'Socialist Current'* Jan. 1957 2pp

5905 Francis, Dai **Dai Dan Evans – A Tribute** in *'Llafur'* Vol.1 No.3, May 1974 2pp Gen. Sec. of S Wales Miners.

5906 Francis, Hywel **Dai Dan Evans, 1898-1974 – Obituary** in *'Cyffro'* Summer 1974 2pp

5907 Francis, Hywel **The Social and Political Background of Welshmen in the I.B. During the Spanish Civil War** in *'Cyffro'* Spring 1971 4pp

5908 Francis, Hywel **The Spanish Civil War Revisited** in *'HWJ'* 32, 1991 8pp

5909 Francis, Hywel **Tribute to Will Paynter** in *'Llafur'* Vol.4 No.2, 1985 5pp Transcript of funeral oration.

5910 Francis, Hywel **Welsh Miners and the Spanish Civil War** in *'JOCH'* Vol.5 No.3, July 1970 12pp

5911 Frankau, Gilbert **Red Poison for the Bottom Dog: British Communists Exclusive Disclosures** in *'John Bull'* June 21 1930 2pp

5912 Freedland, Jonathan **My Uncle Mick, The Party and Love Betrayed** in *'The Guardian'* (G2) Feb. 14 2005 2pp On Mick Mindel, East End Jewish tailor and union activist, and Sara Wesker.

5913 French, Jean **Only Yesterday: Isabel Brown Interview** in *'Link'* Winter 1980 2pp

5914 Freund, W.M. **'Out of the Ghetto' by J. Jacobs – Review** in *'SSLHB'* 38, Spring 1979 1pp

5915 Frow, Ruth & Eddie **The General Strike in Manchester** in *'NWLHSB'* 1, 1975 5pp Esp. on Jack Forshaw, Sec. of the Salford Branch: he was arrested, denied access to medicaments for his diabetes, and kept in a cold cell where he contracted pneumonia from which he died before his trial. This article was reprinted in a later ed. of the journal (renamed 'NW Labour History') – No. 38, 2013.

5916 Frow, Ruth & Eddie **The Workers' Theatre Movement in Manchester and Salford** in *'NWLHSB'* 17, 1992 5pp

5917 Fryer, Peter **'About Turn' ed. F. King & G. Matthews – Review** in *'Revolutionary History'* Vol.3 No.4, Autumn 1991 2pp

5918 Fryer, Peter **An Unreasonable Reasoner** in *'Labour Review'* March/April 1958 3pp Open letter to E.P. Thompson.

5919 Fryer, Peter **Blimps With Little Red Flags: 'History of CPGB Vol.2' by J. Klugmann – Review** in *'Encounter'* Oct. 1969 6pp

5920 Fryer, Peter **Hammersmith and After** in *'Labour Review'* May/June 1957 3pp On CP's Special 25th Congress. Fryer confirmed this unsigned editorial was written by him in a letter to D. Cope.

5921 Fyrth, Jim **Aid Spain Movement, 1936-39** in *'Our History Journal'* 12, Jan. 1988 6pp

5922 Fyrth, Jim **Henry Collins – Obituary** in *'SSLHB'* 20, Spring 1970 1pp

5923 Fyrth, Jim **Sylvia Townsend Warner** in *'Our History Journal'* 17, May 1991 6pp Review of 2 biogs.

5924 Fyrth, Jim **The Aid Spain Movement in Britain, 1936-39** in *'HWJ'* 35, 1993 11pp

5925 Gallacher, W. **13th Congress of CPGB** in *'Inprecorr'* Feb. 16 1935 1pp

5926 Gallacher, W. **13th Plenum ECCI: Speech** in *'Inprecorr'* March 19 1934 1pp

5927 Gallacher, W. **Discussion on the 13th Congress** in *'Inprecorr'* Dec. 22 1934 1pp

5928 Gallacher, W. **John Maclean** in *'C.I.'* 30, 1924 4pp

5929 Gallacher, W. **March 6th in GB** in *'Inprecorr'* March 27 1930 1pp

5930 Gallacher, W. **Shapurji Saklatvala 1874-1936** in *'LM'* Jan. 1937 3pp

5931 Gallacher, W. **The Dumbarton By-Election** in *'C.R.'* May 1932 3pp

5932 Gallacher, W. **The Fight For the CP** in *'LM'* Aug. 1940 5pp

5933 Gallacher, W. **The Position in the Scottish Coalfield** in *'LM'* Nov. 1928 6pp

5934 Gallacher, W. **The Shettleston Bye Election** in *'Inprecorr'* July 10 1930 1pp Saklatvala was candidate.

5935 Galloway, Susan **Serving Their Time** in *'Young Communist'* (YCL/CPB) 5, 1989 ? 2pp On early YCL/CP in Fife.

5936 Gammon, Vic **'Two For the Show': David Harker, Politics and Popular Song** in *'HWJ'* 21, 1986 9pp

5937 Gardiner, Dudley **Comrades at the 'Chronicle'** in *'The Wessex Journal'* May 1997 9pp On the CP purchase of the Dorset County Chronicle in 1941, written by a printer who worked there at the time – he had no complaints as his wages were immediately doubled. The printing business was acquired for extra access to rationed newsprint, and as a backup printing press to compensate for the loss of the 'DW' – the sample monthly 'copies' were printed there.

5938 Gardner, Llew **A Comrade's Point of Departure** in *'New Statesman'* Oct. 29 1976 2pp Reminiscences by 'DW' journalist who left in 1956.

5939 Garland, R. **Jim Gardner – Obituary** in 'LM' Sept. 1976 1pp

5940 Garman, Douglas **A Revolutionary Writer** in 'Welsh Review' June 1939 4pp On Lewis Jones.

5941 Garman, Douglas **The Place, Content, and Materials of Marxist Education** in 'CR' Dec. 1948 7pp

5942 Garner, Robert **Local Labour Parties in Manchester and Salford and the Communist Question in the 1920s** in 'Manchester Region History Review' Vol.2 No.1, 1988 7pp

5943 Garnett, Jim **My Autobiography** in 'NWLHSB' 9, 1983 11pp Active in NUWM, cotton industry in Haslingden, NE Lancs. Was on EC of NMM and CP.

5944 Garriock, Jean **Erica Kathleen Hodson – Obituary** in 'Library Association Record' Vol.103 No.4, 2001 1pp Librarian who was long-term member of the CP – and a Christian Scientist.

5945 Gasquoine, Sarah **District by District** in 'Link' Winter 1982 1pp Survey of local women's work.

5946 George, Bill **Who Was Harry Pollitt?** in 'New Communist Review' 2nd Quarter 1991 2pp

5947 George, H.A. **The Communists and the Labour Movement** in 'LM' Aug. 1940 5pp

5948 Gerard, David **The Marx Memorial Library, Clerkenwell Green, London** in 'Library Review' Vol.511 No.8, 2002 3pp

5949 'Gerhard' **Plenum of the CC of the CPGB** in 'C.I.' March 15 1932 3pp

5950 Gewirtz, Sharon **Anti-Fascist Activity in Manchester's Jewish Community in the 1930s** in 'Manchester Region History Review' Vol.4 No.1, 1990 12pp Looks at rank and file Jewish activity, especially in Cheetham branch YCL (200 members, almost all Jewish working class – possibly the largest YCL branch in the country; it was also known as the 'Challenge Club').

5951 Gibbons, John **28th Congress** in 'WMR' June 1963 2pp

5952 Gibbons, John **British Communists in Congress** in 'WMR' Feb. 1966 1pp On 29th Congress.

5953 Gilby, Bill & Sime, Martin **Unofficial T.U. Militancy Among the Fife Miners in the 1920s & 1930s** in 'SSLHB' 38, Spring 1979 1pp Abstract of Conference paper & discussion.

5954 Gildart, Keith **'Persistence: The Story of a British Communist' by J. Peck & 'An Indian Landscape, 1944-46' by J. Fyrth – Review** in 'LHR' Vol.68 No.1, April 2003 2pp

5955 Glastonbury, Marion **Children of the Revolution: Matters Arising** in 'Changing English' March 1998 10pp Review essay based on 'Children of the Revolution' ed. P. Cohen.

5956 Gold, Diane **Gertie Roche, 1912-1997 – Obituary** in 'HWJ' 45, 1988 6pp Roche had leading role as steward in clothing workers' strikes of 1936 and 1970. In between she had been CP Women's Organiser in Yorkshire.

5957 Gollan, J. **50 Years of the CP** in 'MT' Oct. 1970 5pp Report to EC Sept. 12. This whole issue of 'MT' is devoted to the history of the CP.

5958 Gollan, J. **A Significant Congress** in 'LM' May 1959 8pp On 26th Congress.

5959 Gollan, J. **After the Communist Congress** in 'LM' May 1956 5pp On 24th Congress.

5960 Gollan, J. **Bob Stewart – Obituary** in 'Scottish Marxist' 6, 1974 3pp

5961 Gollan, J. **Britain: Results of the Party Building Year** in 'WMR' Sept. 1962 6pp

5962 Gollan, J. **Fiftieth Anniversary of the CP** in 'LM' Aug. 1970 3pp

5963 Gollan, J. **Great Britain: Party Building Year** in 'WMR' Aug. 1961 3pp

5964 Gollan, J. **London's Youth and Communism** in 'C.R.' April 1935 3pp

5965 Gollan, J. **The 11th National Conference of the YCL** in 'World Youth Review' May 1939 2pp Extracts from J. Gollan's Report to Conference.

5966 Gollan, J. **The CP and the Youth** in 'CR' April 1947 5pp Speech moving resolution on 'Youth' at 19th CP Congress.

5967 Gollancz, Victor **The Communists and the War** in 'The Left News' July 1941 9pp

5968 Gollancz, Victor **The Left Book Clubs, The People's Front and Communism** in 'The Left News' July 1937 2pp

5969 Goodman, Richard **The 'DW' Defeats the Foreign Office** in 'Inprecorr' April 17 1937 1pp Cockburn ('Frank Pitcairn') was forbidden from returning to Spain as 'DW' correspondent, on the pretext that he had fought on the Republican side in the early days, though this was not 'illegal' at the time. He ended up returning clandestinely.

5970 Goodwin, Pete **CP Congress** in 'Socialist Review' No.11, 1981 2pp

5971 Goodwin, Pete **Death of a Party** in *'Socialist Review'* Dec. 1983 2pp On the 38th Congress & its background.

5972 Goodwin, Pete **Fading Star** in *'Socialist Review'* 3, 1981 2pp On the 'Morning Star'.

5973 Goodwin, Pete **Is the Party Over?** in *'Socialist Review'* May 1985 3pp On forthcoming 38th Congress.

5974 Goodwin, Pete **Morning Sickness** in *'Socialist Review'* July/Aug. 1984 1pp On PPPS AGM.

5975 Goodwin, Pete **Terminal Decline** in *'Socialist Review'* July 1983 2pp On CP/'MS' split.

5976 Goretti, Leo & Worley, Matthew **Communist Youth, Communist Generations: A Reappraisal** in *'Twentieth Century Communism'* 4, 2012 9pp Brief discussion of bibliography of youth and communism in Britain.

5977 Gorman, Graham **For Communism** in *'Communist'* July 1990 3pp

5978 Gornenski, Nikifor **The Struggle of the Bulgarian People Against Fascism** in *'MT'* Sept. 1974 4pp Incl. 1 page on Frank Thompson.

5979 Grainger, G. **The Crisis in the British CP** in *'Problems of Communism'* March-April 1957 7pp

5980 Grainger, G.W. **Oligarchy in the British CP** in *'British Journal of Sociology'* June 1958 16pp On IPD debate.

5981 Gray, Robbie **E.P. Thompson, History and Communist Politics** in *'MT'* June 1979 7pp

5982 Green, Nan **The CP and the War in Spain** in *'MT'* Oct. 1970 9pp Author served in Spain in medical services and was later Sec. of I.B.A.

5983 Greig, Ian **Militant Groups in British Schools** in *'East-West Digest'* July 1969 9pp Useful summary of left-wing activity incl. YCL.

5984 Greig, Ian **The Communist Organisation in Industry** in *'East-West Digest'* Jan. 1972 11pp

5985 Grey, Eric **The Crisis in British Communism** in *'Workers' International Review'* Vol.2 No.2, 1957 7pp There are 2 other articles in the same issue also about the CP.

5986 Griffin, Ernest **Conversation with Edward Upward** in *'Modernist Studies'* Vol.2 No.2, 1977 18pp Interesting on relationship between fiction and autobiog. in 'The Spiral Ascent'.

5987 Groves, Reg **Against the Stream** in *'I.S.'* No.54, Jan. 1973 4pp Continued in following issues.

5988 Groves, Reg **Our Party and the New Period** in *'C.R.'* Nov. 1929 5pp

5988a Gurney, Peter **History and Commitment: E.P. Thompson's Legacy** in *'LHR'* Vol.78 No.3, Dec. 2013

5989 Gusev, S. **The End of Capitalist Stabilisation and the Basic Tasks of British and American Sections of the C.I.** in *'C.I.'* Oct. 15 1932 11pp To 12th Plenum ECCI.

5990 Guy, Stephen **'High Treason' (1951): Britain's Cold War Fifth Column** in *'Historical Journal of Film Radio and Television'* Vol.13 No.1, 1993 13pp Analysis of Britain's only McCarthyite film (directed by Roy Boulting), featuring a thinly disguised Communist Party engaged in sabotage. This article discusses the political climate and attitudes to the CP.

5991 H. **The Communist Wreckers** in *'Socialist Standard'* March 1924 2pp

5992 H. **The Communists and the LP** in *'Socialist Standard'* Oct. 1931 4pp

5993 H. **The CP and the General Election** in *'Socialist Standard'* May 1929 2pp

5994 H. **The Irish Elections: More Communist Trickery** in *'Socialist Standard'* Oct. 1927 2pp

5995 H. **The Rise and Fall of the CP** in *'Socialist Standard'* June 1931 1pp On CP membership figures.

5996 H. **Willie Gallacher's Political Indigestion** in *'Socialist Standard'* March 1925 2pp

5997 H.P. **The CP and the LP** in *'LM'* Feb. 1943 4pp Probably H. Pollitt.

5998 H.W. **Moscow Turns a New Somersault And Mr Pollitt Holds the Baby** in *'Socialist Standard'* Nov. 1939 2pp

5999 Hallas, Duncan **The CP and the General Strike** in *'I.S.'* No.88, May 1976 9pp

6000 Hallas, Duncan **The CP, The SWP and the Rank and File Movement** in *'I.S.'* No.95, Feb. 1977 5pp

6000a Hallas, Duncan **The United Front Tactic and the CP** in *'IS Bulletin'* May/June 1973 2pp There are other brief articles on the CP in this internal bulletin.

6001 Halstead, John **Royden John Harrison – Obituary** in *'LHR'* Vol.68 No.1, April 2003 4pp

6002 Halstead, John **The Society for the Study of Labour History and its Journal** in *'Labour and Social History in GB: Historiographical Reviews and Agendas' Special ed. of 'Mitteilungsblatt des Instituts fur soziale Bewegungen' No.27, 2002* 12pp Bit on Historians' Group.

6003 Halstead, John et al. **The Reminiscences of Sid Elias** in *'SSLHB' 38, Spring 1979* 13pp

6004 Halverson, Ron **The CP Today** in *'LM' Dec. 1980* 4pp

6005 Hanna, Vincent & Barstow, Alice **The Red Beneath Your Bed** in *'East-West Digest' Nov. 1972* 4pp On Bert Ramelson. Reprinted from 'Sunday Times', Oct. 15 1972.

6006 Hanson, A.H. **'The Sociology of British Communism' by K. Newton – Review** in *'New Society' March 13 1969* 1pp

6007 Harker, Ben **'British Communism and the Politics of Literature 1928-1939' – Review** in *'NWLHSB' 37, 2012/13* 1pp

6007a Harker, Ben **'Cold War, Crisis and Conflict' by J. Callaghan & 'Class Against Class' by M. Worley – Review** in *'NWLHSB' 29, 2004* 1pp

6008 Harker, Ben **'Communism is English': Edgell Rickword, Jack Lindsay and the Cultural Politics of the Popular Front** in *'Literature and History' Vol.20 No.2, 2011* 18pp

6009 Harker, Ben **'The Spanish Civil War and the British Left' by L. Mates – Review** in *'NWLHSB' 33, 2008/9* 1pp Points out the controversial analysis of the CP's Popular Front position.

6010 Harker, Ben **'The Trumpet of the Night': Interwar Communists on BBC Radio** in *'HWJ' 75, 2013* 21pp

6011 Harley, J.H. **Communism and the T.U.s** in *'The Contemporary Review' Dec. 1946* 5pp On TUC Congress.

6012 Harman, Chris **The General Strike** in *'I.S.' No.48, June/July 1971* 7pp

6013 Harman, Chris **The CP in Decline, 1964-70 Part 2** in *'I.S.' No.63, Oct. 1973* 10pp

6014 Harrison, Brian **Oxford and the Labour Movement** in *'Twentieth Century British History' Vol.2 No.3, 1991* 46pp

6015 Harrison, Royden & Seyd, Pat **An Interview With Len Youle** in *'SSLHB' 20, Spring 1970* 6pp Youle was in CP in 1920s, active in NUWM in Sheffield; he talks about his reasons for leaving.

6016 Harrison, Royden **Bert Wynn – Obituary** in *'SSLHB' 12, Spring 1966* 1pp Wynn was Gen. Sec. of Derbyshire Miners; left CP in 1956 and was associated with the New Left.

6017 Harrison, Royden **Communists: 'R.P. Dutt' by J. Callaghan, 'Being Frank' by F. Watters & 'Keeping My Head' by H. Wicks – Review** in *'LHR' Vol.59 No.1, Spring 1994* 2pp

6018 Harvie, Christopher **MacDiarmid the Socialist** in *'SLHS' 16, 1981* 10pp

6019 Haslam, Johnathan **The British CP, The Comintern, and the Outbreak of War, 1939: 'A Nasty Taste in the Mouth'** in *'Diplomacy and Statecraft' March 1992* 7pp

6020 Hasledon, K. **The 1st Congress of the West London Sub-District** in *'C.R.' Dec. 1933/Jan. 1934* 2pp

6021 Hawarth, F. **What We Have Learned from the Municipal Elections** in *'C.R.' Dec. 1930* 4pp

6022 Hawthorn, Jeremy **Edgell Rickword – Interview** in *'Artery' 18, 1980* 4pp

6023 Hawthorn, Jeremy **The CP and Developments in British Culture** in *'MT' Dec. 1973* 4pp Discussion contribution followed in June.

6024 Hayburn, Ralph **The NUWM, 1921-36: A Re-Appraisal** in *'IRSH' Vol.28 Part 3, 1983* 17pp

6025 Hayburn, Ralph **The Police and the Hunger Marchers** in *'IRSH' Vol.17 Part 3, 1972* 20pp On police infiltration of the NUWM & CP. There is a bit more in a follow up article in 'SSLH Bulletin' 37, 1978, by Royden Harrison.

6026 Heddon, Jon **The Left Book Club in Manchester and Salford** in *'NWLHSB' 21, 1996* 9pp

6027 Heffer, Eric **Communists and the Labour Party** in *'New Statesman' Feb. 8 1974* 2pp Criticises official LP attack on McGahey and communists in leadership of NUM.

6028 Heinemann, Margot **Poetry of the 30s: Three Left-Wing Poets – Louis MacNeice, John Cornford, Clive Branson** in *'MT' Nov. 1976* 12pp

6029 Heisler, Ron **Notes on Hugh Esson and the Glasgow Leninist League** in *'Revolutionary History' Vol.9 No.4, 2007* 2pp

6030 Heisler, Ron **Thaxted Tales: Trotskyist Versus Stalinist Pilgrims on the Anglo-Catholic Path** in *'Revolutionary History' Vol.10 Part 2, 2010* 37pp

6031 Heisler, Ron **'The Death of Uncle Joe' by A. Macleod – Review** in *'Revolutionary History' Vol.7 No.2, 1999* 2pp

6032 Helmond, Marij van **Eric Lynch: A Very Active Life** in *'NWLHSB'* 20, 1995 6pp Liverpool building worker, active in the black community.

6033 Heppell, Jason **A Rebel, Not a Rabbi: Jewish Membership of the CPGB** in *'Twentieth Century British History'* Vol.15 No.1, 2004 22pp

6034 Herbert, Michael **'The CPGB Since 1920' by D. Renton – Review** in *'NWLHSB'* 27, 2002 1pp

6035 Hevey, Muriel **Harold Smith – Obituary** in *'MML Bulletin'* 142, Autumn 2005 4pp Librarian, publisher, historian.

6036 Hevey, Muriel **The Writings of Arthur Nobes** in *'MML Bulletin'* 116, Summer/Autumn 1991 3pp Printer sacked from HMSO for CP membership.

6037 Hey, David **Kinder Scout and the Legend of the Mass Trespass** in *'Agricultural Historical Review'* Vol.59 Part 2, 2011 18pp Argues that the event was a CP 'stunt', that ignored previous long campaigns for access to the hills and that did more harm than good.

6038 Hicks, Mike **Re-Establishing the Party** in *'Communist Campaign Review'* Spring 1987 3pp

6039 Higgins, Jim **1956 and All That** in *'New Interventions'* April 1993 3pp

6040 Higgins, Jim **Origins of the CP** in *'I.S.'* No.40, Oct./Nov. 1969 3pp

6041 Higgins, Jim **R.P. Dutt: Stalin's British Mouthpiece – Obituary** in *'I.S.'* No.75, Feb. 1975 2pp

6042 Higgins, Jim **Revolutionary Trade Unionism** in *'I.S.'* No.47, April/May 1971 8pp

6043 Higgins, Jim **The Minority Movement** in *'I.S.'* No.45, Nov./Dec. 1970 7pp

6044 Hilliard, Christopher **Producers by Hand and Brain: Working-Class Writers and Left-Wing Publishers in 1930s Britain** in *'Journal of Modern History'* (Univ. of Chicago) 78, March; 2006 28pp

6045 Hinton, James **Coventry Communism: A Study of Factory Politics in the Second World War** in *'HWJ'* 10, 1980 30pp

6046 Hinton, James **Killing the People's Convention: A Letter from Palme Dutt to Pollitt** in *'SSLHB'* 39, Autumn 1979 6pp

6047 Hinton, James **Self-Help and Socialism: The Squatters' Movement of 1946** in *'HWJ'* 25, 1988 25pp

6048 Hinton, James **Sex, Violence and the Class Struggle** in *'SSLHB'* 42, Spring 1981 2pp Review article of Benson 'To Struggle is to Live' (3928); Moss 'Live and Learn' (4533); Morton & Macintyre 'T.A. Jackson' (4929).

6049 Hinton, James **'The Revolutionary Movement in Britain 1900-21' by W. Kendall – Review** in *'SSLHB'* 19, Autumn 1969 7pp Disagrees with Kendall that the C.I.'s influence in creating the CPGB destroyed a developing realistic socialist movement; also argues that Kendall overestimates John Maclean's importance.

6050 Hinton, James **The Roots of British Communism** in *'NLR'* 128, 1981 6pp Review of 'Proletarian Science' & 'Little Moscows'.

6051 Hinton, James **Warriors' Autobiography** in *'SSLHB'* 37, Autumn 1978 2pp Review of autobiogs by E. Trory & H. McShane.

6052 Hobday, Charles **'Selected Poems' by R. Swingler – Review** in *'Socialist History'* 20, 2001 3pp

6053 Hobsbawm, Eric **'The British CP and Moscow, 1920-43' by A. Thorpe – Review** in *'The Political Quarterly'* Oct./Dec. 2001 2pp

6054 Hobsbawm, Eric **A Life in History** in *'Past and Present'* Vol.177 No.1, Nov. 2002 13pp

6055 Hobsbawm, Eric **Communist History** in *'NLR'* 54, 1969 7pp

6056 Hobsbawm, Eric **Could It Have Been Different?** in *'London Review of Books'* 16, Nov. 2006 4pp Debate and reply in next 3 issues.

6057 Hobsbawm, Eric **E.P. Thompson – Obituary** in *'Radical History Review'* Winter 1994 3pp From 'The Independent'; this issue also has 2 other obits of E.P. Thompson.

6058 Hobsbawm, Eric **In Memoriam: E.P. Thompson** in *'ILWCH'* Vol.46, Sept. 1994 4pp

6059 Hobsbawm, Eric **Master of Arts: Arnold Kettle** in *'MT'* Feb. 1987 1pp Tribute at funeral.

6060 Hobsbawm, Eric **The British CP** in *'Political Quarterly'* Jan/March 1954 14pp

6061 Hobsbawm, Eric **Yvonne Kapp – Obituary** in *'WCML Bulletin'* 12, 2002 2pp

6062 Hoffman, John **An Appreciation of Maurice Cornforth** in *'MML Bulletin'* 105, Autumn 1984 7pp

6063 Hogenkamp, Bert **Film and the Workers' Movement in Britain, 1929-39** in *'Sight and Sound'* Vol.45 No.2, Spring 1976 9pp

6064 Høgsbjerg, Christian **Mariner, Renegade and Castaway: Chris Braithwaite, Seamen's

Organiser and Pan-Africanist *in 'Race and Class' Vol.53 No.2, Oct./Dec. 2011* 22pp Braithwaite, a revolutionary black seaman, who also used the pseudonym of Jones, was briefly in the CP in early 1930s, before leaving and working with George Padmore.

6065 Holbrook-Jones, Mike **Lesons of the General Strike** *in 'International' Winter 1976* 17pp Lot on history of CP prior to General Strike.

6066 Holmes, Colin **East End Anti-Semitism, 1936** *in 'SSLHB' 32, Spring 1976* 8pp Mainly consists of notes taken by Neville Laski at a private meeting he arranged between Pollitt and Herbert Morrison on Oct. 14 to discuss anti-fascist strategies.

6067 Holmes, Colin **'London Jews and British Communism, 1935-45' by H. Srebrnik – Review** *in 'Science and Society' Vol.61 No.1, Spring 1997* 4pp

6068 Holmes, Colin **The Raid on the Headquarters of the CPGB** *in 'SSLHB' 40, Spring 1980* 6pp Reproduces documents from the Home Office Closed File – incl. correspondence by Inkpin on the refusal of the prison authorities to allow him to read 'Ten Days That Shook the World'.

6069 Holmes, Walter **British Communists Prepare for Anti-War Day** *in 'Inprecorr' July 5 1929* 1pp

6070 Holmes, Walter **The 10th Party Congress of the CPGB** *in 'Inprecorr' Feb. 1 1929* 1pp Open report of strong differences, incl. refs to 'liquidatory tendencies' (sic!)

6071 Holmes, Walter **The Annual Conference of the S Wales Miners' Federation** *in 'Inprecorr' July 5 1929* 1pp More about the Communist fraction of 12 present than the Conference proper.

6072 Holmes, Walter **The ILP and the C.I.** *in 'Inprecorr' April 28 1933* 1pp

6073 Homberger, Eric **Exiles From the National Consensus: Unity Mitford and Harry Pollitt in the 1930s** *in 'Journal of European Studies' Dec. 1977* 11pp

6074 Hopkins, Stephen **The CPGB and Moscow: Report of Conference** *in 'LHR' Vol.57 No.3, Winter 1992* 12pp Organised by CP just a month before the 'transformation Conference' of Nov. 1991; all viewpoints were represented.

6075 Horne, Bob **Memories of Gallacher** *in 'Scottish Marxist' 23, 1981* 2pp

6076 Horner, Arthur **International Red Day on 1st August in GB: 10th Plenum ECCI** *in 'Inprecorr' July 24 1929* 1pp Anti-War Day.

6077 Horner, Arthur **Speech at 10th Plenum ECCI, 12th Session, July 9** *in 'Inprecorr' Sept. 17 1929* 1pp Strong criticism of Gallacher & Murphy.

6078 Horner, John **Unity, Then and Now** *in 'LM' March 1946* 4pp

6079 Howard, Stuart **Dawdon in the 'Third Period': The Dawdon Dispute of 1929 and the CP** *in 'NELH' 21, 1987* 14pp

6080 Howarth, Edmund **The Tyneside Communist Collapse** *in 'Socialist Standard' Jan. 1931* 1pp On 'the expulsion of all but three members of the Newcastle City local, simultaneously with wholesale defections from the other locals in Tyneside'.

6081 Howe, Antony **'Our Only Ornament': Tom Mann and British Communist Hagiography** *in 'Twentieth Century Communism' 1, 2009* 20pp

6082 Howell, David **Eric Hobsbawm's Interesting Times: An Interview** *in 'Socialist History' 24, 2003* 15pp

6083 Howell, David **'Opening the Books' ed. G. Andrews et al. – Review** *in 'LHR' Vol.61 No.1, Spring 1996* 3pp

6084 Howell, David **'The British CP and Moscow, 1920-43' by A. Thorpe – Review** *in 'English Historical Review' Vol.116 No.468, Sept. 2001* 2pp

6085 Howkins, Alun **George Ewart Evans, 1909-87 – Obituary** *in 'HWJ' 26, 1988* 2pp

6086 Howkins, Alun **Inventing Everyman: George Ewart Evans, Oral History and National Identity** *in 'Oral History' Autumn 1994* 7pp

6087 Hudson, Kate **Britain in 1990s: The Crisis of Socialist Theory and Prospects for the Left** *in 'New Interventions' June 1995* 2pp

6088 Hudson, Kate **Communist and Former Communist Organisations in Britain** *in 'JOCS' Dec. 1994* 7pp

6089 Hughes, Alun **Communist Parliamentary Candidates in Wales, 1921-89** *in 'Welsh Workers' History' No.1, 1994* 6pp

6090 Humber, Lee & Rees, John **The Good Old Cause: Interview with Christopher Hill** *in 'ISJ' 56, Autumn 1992* 10pp Material on how the History Group worked.

6091 Hunt, Karen & Worley, Matthew **Rethinking British CP Women in the 1920s** in 'Twentieth Century British History' Vol.15 No.1, 2004 27pp

6092 Hunt, Ken **A Topic of Conversation** in 'Folk Roots' May 1987 2pp Bit on CP's involvement in Topic Records.

6093 Hunter, Bill **A.J. Cook: Some Lessons for Miners Today** in 'Labour Review' March 1984 9pp

6094 Hunter, Bill **History of British Stalinism** in 'Labour Review' Oct. 1985 10pp

6095 Hunter, Bill **Marxists in the Second World War** in 'Labour Review' Dec. 1958 7pp See also letter by B. Farnborough in Vol 4 No.1, 1959.

6096 Hunter, Bill **Stalinism and World War Two: '1939' by F. King & G. Matthews – Review** in 'Labour Review' July 1984 8pp

6097 Hunter, Bill **The Beginning of Trotskyism in Britain** in 'Labour Review' May 1985 9pp

6098 Hunter, Bill **The Roots of the Crisis of British Stalinism** in 'Labour Review' Feb. 1985 7pp

6099 Hunter, Bill **This Was the Real Harry Pollitt** in 'Labour Review' Aug. 1983 5pp

6100 Hunter, Bill **Unmasking the Lies of British Stalinism** in 'Labour Review' Sept. 1985 10pp Continued in following issue.

6101 Hunter, Ian **'The Days of the Good Soldiers' by R. Kisch – Review** in 'NELH' 20, 1986 1pp

6102 Hunter, Margaret **26th Congress of the CPGB** in 'MT' April 1959 4pp

6103 Hunter, Margaret **Tribute to the Late Helen Crawford** in 'Scottish Marxist Voice' No.1, 1994 4pp

6104 Hutnyk, J. **The Dialectic of Here and There: Anthropology at Home and British Asian Communism** in 'Social Identities' Vol.11 No.4, 2005 17pp Refs to Saklatvala and R.P. Dutt.

6105 Hutt, Allen **Changing the Miners' Leadership** in 'The Communist' Feb. 1928 5pp

6106 Hutt, Allen **Democracy in the Scottish Miners' Union** in 'LM' June 1928 9pp See also 'LM' Nov. 1928 & June 1929 for bitter debate on the Left in the Scottish Miners & role of A.J. Cook.

6107 Hutt, Allen **Dona Torr – Obituary** in 'LM' March 1957 3pp

6108 Hutt, Allen **Organisers of Victory** in 'LM' July 1942 4pp On National Conference, May.

6109 Hutt, Allen **'The British CP: A Short History' by T. Bell – Review** in 'LM' June 1937 4pp Famous critical review; July issue carried CP Secretariat Statement: 'The Secretariat desires to advise that this book should not be considered as a history of the Party'.

6110 Hyde, Douglas **Communism in Britain** in 'The Tablet' April 10 1948 2pp

6111 Hyde, Douglas **Communism in Britain** in 'Blackfriars' Feb. 1953 3pp

6112 Hyde, Douglas **Communist Who Pulls the Strings** in 'John Bull' May 28 1949 2pp On R.P. Dutt.

6113 Hyde, Douglas **Preparations for Illegality: CPGB 1941** in 'Our History Journal' 14, Oct. 1989 10pp Important memoir by the person given responsibility for underground press work in the event of the CP being banned.

6114 Hyde, Samuel **'Please Sir, He Called Me "Jimmy!"' Political Cartooning Before the Law: Black Friday, J.H. Thomas and the 'Communist' Libel Trial of 1921** in 'Contemporary British History' Vol.25 No.4, 2011 29pp The libel case against the ed. (F. Meynell) and printer (National Labour Press) for publishing Will Hope's vitriolic cartoon bankrupted them both.

6115 Hyman, Richard **Communist Industrial Policy in the 1920s** in 'I.S.' No.53, Oct.-Dec. 1972 9pp

6116 Hyman, Richard **'The British CP and the Trade Unions, 1933-45' by N. Fishman – Review** in 'Science and Society' Vol.61 No.1, Spring 1997 3pp

6117 Hyman, Richard **Trades Unions, The Left and the CP in Britain** in 'JOCS' Dec. 1990 18pp

6118 Imrie, Malcolm **'Red Letters': The Academy in Peril?** in 'Wedge' No.1, Summer 1977 4pp This unusual article in 'a revolutionary magazine of cultural practice & theory', takes a critical but serious look at the CP's literary journal.

6119 Inkpin, Albert **British Communists in Conference** in 'C.I.' 11/12, June/July 1920 3pp On BSP's 9th Annual Congress.

6120 Inkpin, Albert **The Coming Congress of the British CP** in 'Inprecorr' May 28 1925 1pp

6121 Inkpin, Albert **The New 'Campbell' Case in England** in *'Inprecorr'* May 28 1930 1pp

6122 J.J. **The Case for the YCL** in *'C.R.'* Nov. 1923 5pp

6123 J.W. **CC Resolution: First Steps in Carrying It Out** in *'C.R.'* April 1932 9pp

6124 Jackson, Frank **Building the Opposition Inside the Unions** in *'C.R.'* Oct. 1932 2pp

6125 Jackson, T.A. **The Party Conference** in *'C.R.'* April 1924 5pp Critique of Pollitt in Feb. issue.

6126 Jacques, Martin **James Klugmann – Obituary** in *'LM'* Nov. 1977 1pp

6127 Jacques, Martin & Aaronovitch, Sam **Marxism in Britain: Past and Present** in *'WMR'* Oct. 1987 5pp

6128 Jacques, Martin **Why I Stopped Editing 'MT'** in *'The New Republic'* May 11 1992 3pp

6129 Jacques, Martin **Why Study the History of the CP?** in *'Our History Journal'* 2, July 1978 2pp

6130 James, Robert **Why Did You Join the Party?** in *'I.S.'* No.60, July 1973 1pp Very funny, if a bit insubstantial.

6131 James, T.H. **Some Mistakes in the United Front Work** in *'C.R.'* Aug. 1935 2pp About Bradford.

6132 Jay, Marie **CPGB Sides with Police** in *'Fight Racism! Fight Imperialism!'* Sept/Oct. 1980 1pp

6133 Jefferys, Steve **36th Congress of the CPGB** in *'Socialist Review'* No.1, 1980 1pp

6134 Jefferys, Steve **CPGB in 1979: Out At 60** in *'Socialist Review'* July/Aug. 1979 3pp Part 2 in next issue No.14 (5pp).

6135 Jefferys, Steve **EETPU: Decline of the Narrow Left** in *'I.S.'* No.88, May 1976 8pp On CP in the electricians' union.

6136 Jefferys, Steve **The CP and the Left** in *'I.S.'* No.58, May 1973 23pp

6137 Jefferys, Steve **The CP and the Rank and File** in *'ISJ'* 10, Winter 1980 23pp

6138 Jeffries, Jonathan **The Politics of Colonialism: Gibraltar, Trade Unionism and the Case of Albert Fava** in *'Socialist History'* 29, 2006 21pp Active in Spain during the Civil War, in Scotland during WW2, then in Gibraltar post-war where his union activites got him deported to Britain.

6139 Jenkins, Gareth **The Continuing Problems of the CP** in *'Socialist Review'* No.5, 1980 2pp

6140 Jenkins, Llew **What Can A Communist Councillor Do?** in *'C.R.'* Sept. 1934 2pp

6141 Jenkins, Mick **Cotton Struggles 1929-32** in *'MT'* Feb. 1969 7pp

6142 Jenkins, Mick **Early Days in the YCL** in *'MT'* Feb. 1972 6pp

6143 Jenkins, Peter **The Communist Predicament** in *'New Society'* May 13 1965 3pp

6144 Jenkins, D.R. **The April Local Elections in Britain** in *'Inprecorr'* May 24 1928 1pp

6145 Johanningsmeier, Edward **'Communists and British Society: 1920-1991' by K. Morgan et al. – Review** in *'Twentieth Century Communism'* 1, 2009 3pp

6146 Johnson, Alan **'Beyond the Smallness of Self': Oral History and British Trotskyism** in *'Oral History'* Spring 1996 10pp Interesting perspective on CP; incl. useful bibliog. of works on/by British Trotskyists.

6147 Johnson, Peter & Roberts, Geoff **University of the Left** in *'The Leveller'* 41, Sept. 1980 1pp On CULs.

6148 Johnstone, Charlie **Early Post-War Housing Struggles in Glasgow** in *'SLHS'* 28, 1993 23pp

6149 Johnstone, Monty **'Class Against Class' by M. Worley – Review** in *'LHR'* Vol.68 No.1, April 2003 2pp

6150 Johnstone, Monty **Combating Trotskyism in Britain Today** in *'WMR'* Jan. 1980 5pp

6151 Johnstone, Monty **Communist History: From Above and Below** in *'Socialist History'* 5, 1994 4pp Reply to K. Morgan in previous issue.

6152 Johnstone, Monty **Early Communist Strategy for Britain: An Assessment** in *'MT'* Sept. 1978 7pp Based on Paper to Conference on History of CP organised by History Group.

6153 Johnstone, Monty **Harry Pollitt** in *'SSLHB'* 35, Autumn 1977 4pp Reply to A. Rothstein's reply in previous issue. Further letter in issue 37.

6154 Johnstone, Monty **'Harry Pollitt' by J. Mahon – Review** in *'SSLHB'* 33, Autumn 1976 5pp

6155 Johnstone, Monty **James Klugmann – Obituary** in *'SSLHB'* 36, Spring 1978 1pp

6156 Johnstone, Monty **New Light on Harry Pollitt: 'Harry Pollitt' by K. Morgan – Review** in *'LHR'* Vol.58 No.3, Winter 1993 4pp See also letter in Spring 1994 by Brian Behan.

6157 Johnstone, Monty **The CP in the 1920s** in *'NLR'* 41, 1967 17pp Extended review of Macfarlane.

6158 Johnstone, Monty **The CPGB, The Comintern and the War, 1939-41: Filling in the Blank Spots** in *'Science and Society'* Vol.61 No.1, Spring 1997 20pp

6159 Johnstone, Monty **'The Good Old Cause' by W. Thompson – Review** in *'Socialist History Journal'* 20, 1992 6pp

6160 Johnstone, Monty **What Kind of CP History?** in *'Our History Journal'* 4, Feb. 1979 5pp

6161 Jones, A. **The Origins of British Reformism** in *'International'* Jan. 1973 37pp

6162 Jones, Bill **The London Busmen's Rank & File Movement of the 1930s** in *'SSLHB'* 38, Spring 1979 2pp Abstract of Conference paper & discussion.

6163 Jones, Greta **British Scientists, Lysenko and the Cold War** in *'Economy and Society'* 8, Feb. 1979 33pp

6164 Jones, Harriet **Is CPGB History Important?** in *'LHR'* Vol.67 No.3, Dec. 2002 6pp Report of Conference at Institute of Historical Research, Feb. 2002. Discusses the sometimes bitter recent differences between historians of the CP.

6165 Jones, J. Graham **Wales and the 'New Socialism', 1926-9** in *'The Welsh History Review'* Dec. 1982 28pp

6166 Jones, Jean **'Comrade Heart: A Life of Randall Swingler' by A. Croft – Review** in *'Socialist History'* 25, 2004 3pp

6167 Jones, Merfyn **Approaches to Miners' History – Review Essay** in *'SSLHB'* 43, Autumn 1981 3pp See comments on 'The Fed' by H. Francis & D. Smith.

6168 Jones, Mervyn **Why Britain Needs the Communists** in *'Twentieth Century'* Spring 1963 11pp Ex-CP member writing on the irrational perception of British Communists as 'enemy'.

6169 Jones, Michael **Theatre as a Weapon? The Emergence of Left Theatre on Merseyside** in *'Transactions of the Historic Society of Lancashire and Cheshire'* Vol.138, 1988 17pp

6170 Jones, Mike **'Glorious Summer: Class Struggle in Britain, 1972' by R. Darlington & D. Lyddon – Review** in *'Socialist History'* 23, 2003 5pp Analyses this book's assessment of CP's role in the rank and file v. union leadership debate.

6171 Jones, R.W. **Anti-Parliamentarism and Communism in Britain, 1917-21** in *'Raven'* No.11, 1990 17pp

6172 Jones, Robert **No Home But the Struggle: Interview with E. Upward** in *'The Leveller'* 11, Jan. 1978 1pp

6173 Jones, Stephen **Sport, Politics and the Labour Movement: The British Workers' Sports Federation, 1923-35** in *'The British Journal of Sports History'* Sept. 1985 25pp

6174 Jordan, Pat **Communist Party Crisis: Not the End But the Beginning** in *'International'* Dec. 1969 3pp On 31st Congress. Jordan had worked full-time for the CP before leaving in 1956 to play a leading role in the Trotskyist movement, helping to found the IMG.

6175 Jordan, Pat **The 32nd CP Congress** in *'Red Mole'* Nov. 29 1971 1pp

6176 Jordan, Pat **The British CP in Crisis** in *'Inprecorr'* (2) No.17, 1977 8pp This is the IMG's re-incarnation of 'Inprecorr'.

6177 Joss, William **The Building of Workers' Circles** in *'C.R.'* April 1934 2pp On Scotland.

6178 Joss, William **The Expulsion of J.T. Murphy and Its Lessons & Statement by PB** in *'C.R.'* June 1932 7pp

6179 Joss, William **Three Months of CP Propaganda** in *'C.R.'* Nov. 1924 7pp Author, later a member of the CEC, travelled the country assessing CP activity.

6180 Jump, Meirian **'The Spanish Civil War and the British Left' by L. Mates – Review** in *'Socialist History'* 36, 2010 3pp

6181 Just, William **With British Communists to Russia** in *'Twentieth Century'* July 1957 12pp Mixed views among a tourist group.

6182 K. **Moscow Orders More Communist Somersaults** in *'Socialist Standard'* March 1928 2pp On relations with LP.

6183 K.D. **The London C.C. Elections** in *'C.R.'* Feb. 1931 7pp

6184 Kadish, Sharman **Jewish Bolshevism and the 'Red Scare' in Britain** in *'Jewish Quarterly'* No.4, 1987 6pp

6185 Kahn, Peggy **An Interview With Frank Watters** in *'SSLHB'* 43, Autumn 1981 13pp Much on Scottish & Yorkshire Communist miners & other activists.

6186 Kahn, Peggy **Tom Mullany: Interview** in *'SSLHB'* 44, Spring 1982 9pp NUM activist in LP but interesting on CP in Yorks.

6187 Kanwar, Asha **An Interview With Arnold Kettle** in *'Social Scientist: Monthly Journal of the Indian School of Social Sciences'* 170 Vol.15 No.7, July 1987 8pp

6188 Katz, Phil **'Granite and Honey: The Story of Piratin, Communist MP' by K. Marsh & R. Griffiths – Review** in *'Praxis'* 156, Spring 2013 3pp

6189 Kay, John **Scotland's Communists** in *'Scottish Marxist'* 2, 1972 7pp

6190 Kaye, Harvey **Fanning the Spark of Hope in the Past: The British Marxist Historians** in *'Rethinking History'* Vol.4 No.3, 2000 13pp

6191 Kaye, Harvey **Towards a Biography of E.P. Thompson** in *'Socialist History'* 8, 1995 6pp

6192 Keable, Ken **'Fashioning a New World: A History of the Woodcraft Folk' by M. Davis – Review** in *'Communist Review'* (CPB) 40, Spring 2004 40pp Refs to Gladys Keable, National Organiser of Young Pioneers, and YCL (she was also the last Secretary of the International of Proletarian Esperantists).

6193 Keating, Conrad **Arthur Exell – Obituary** in *'HWJ'* 35, 1993 2pp

6194 Keirnan, Victor **Memories of the CP** in *'London Review of Books'* Sept. 17 1998 3pp

6195 Kelly, John **'Cold War, Crisis and Conflict: The History of the CPGB, 1951-1968' by J. Callaghan – Review** in *'HSIR'* 17, Spring 2004 5pp

6196 Kelly, John **Communists and the Unions** in *'Communist Campaign Review'* Spring 1988 5pp

6197 Kelly, John **'The British CP and the Trade Unions' by N. Fishman – Review** in *'HSIR'* 1, March 1996 5pp

6197a Kelly, Pat **The Contribution of Scots to Working Class Movements Abroad** in *'SLHS'* 47, 2012 24pp Several members of the early CPGB played leading roles abroad, incl. James Litterick in Canada. Also mentions John Williamson and Charlie Doyle both deported from the US to Britain.

6198 Kemp, Tom **Stalinism and the Historians** in *'Labour Review'* June 1979 10pp

6199 Kemp, Tom **The Signifcance of the 20th Congress of the Soviet CP: A Reply to John Gollan** in *'Labour Review'* June 1977 17pp 2nd part in following month's issue (29pp).

6200 Kendall, Walter **James Klugmann – Letter** in *'LHR'* Vol.57 No.2, Autumn 1992 1pp Reply by Basil Davidson in Spring, 1993; more letters in Autumn 1993 & Spring, Winter 1994.

6201 Kendall, Walter **The CPGB** in *'Survey'* Winter 1974 13pp

6202 Kenny, Michael **Recent Changes in the CPGB** in *'JOCS'* Sept. 1991 3pp

6203 Kerridge, Roy **Ranting at the Palace** in *'The Spectator'* July 9 1983 3pp On 'Marx with Sparx' Festival at Alexandra Palace.

6204 Kerrigan, Jean **Letter to Bert Ramelson** in *'Marxist'* Vol.3 No.1, 1964 5pp

6205 Kerrigan, Peter **7th Congress C.I., 7th Session: Speech** in *'Inprecorr'* Oct. 7 1935 1pp

6206 Kerrigan, Peter **Harry Pollitt** in *'CR'* Dec. 1950 6pp A birthday piece of period hero-worship.

6207 Kerrigan, Peter **Some Problems of Party Work in Scotland** in *'C.I.'* Feb. 5 1935 2pp

6208 Kerrigan, Peter **Speech at 7th Congress of the C.I.** in *'C.I.'* Aug. 20 1935 5pp

6209 Kerrigan, Peter **The CP in the Industrial Struggle** in *'MT'* Dec. 1970 7pp

6210 Kerrigan, Peter; White, R. & Jack Cohen **The CPGB and the Jubilee** in *'C.I.'* July 20 1935 6pp

6211 Kerrigan, Peter **The Struggle of the CPGB Against the Italo-Abyssinian War** in *'C.I.'* Nov. 1935 2pp

6212 Kerrigan, Peter **The Vanguard Party** in *'CR'* March 1946 5pp

6213 Keyworth, Florence **Betty Harrison – Obituary** in *'HWJ'* 8, 1979 3pp Tobacco Workers' Union.

6214 Keyworth, Florence **Women and the 'DW'/'MS'** in *'Link'* Summer 1980 2pp Part 2 in Autumn 1980.

6215 Kiernan, Victor **'About Turn' ed. F. King & G. Matthews – Review** in *'HWJ'* 32, 1991 2pp

6216 Kiernan, Victor **'Ben Bradley, Fighter for India's Freedom' by J. Jones – Review** in *'LHR'* Vol.60 No.1, Spring 1995 1pp

6217 Kiernan, Victor **Mohan Kumaramangalam in England** in *'Socialist India'* Feb. 23 & March 2 1974 4&6pp Indian Nationalist students at Cambridge in 1930s and links with CP.

6218 King, Francis **Archival Sources on the CPGB** in *'Science and Society'* Vol.61 No.1, Spring 1997 8pp

6219 King, Francis & Mathews, George **CP Library** in *'Our History Journal'* 18, Nov. 1991 2pp

6220 King, Francis **Monty Johnstone, 1928-2007 – Obituary** in *'MML Bulletin'* 146, Summer 2007 2pp

6221 King, Francis & Matthews, George **The CP Library** in *'LHR'* Vol.56 No.3, Winter 1991 1pp

6222 King, Stuart **The Comintern, the CPGB and the Minority Movement** in *'Workers' Power'* 7/8, Autumn 1978 20pp

6223 Kirk, Neville **'British Trade Unions and Industrial Politics' by A. Campbell et al. – Review** in *'ILWCH'* Vol.63, 2003 3pp

6224 Kirk, Neville **'Hobsbawm: History and Politics' by Gregory Elliott – Review** in *'LHR'* Vol.77 No.3, Dec. 2012 3pp

6225 Kirsch, Brenda **Only Yesterday: Nan Green Interview** in *'Link'* Autumn 1982 2pp

6226 Klaus, H. Gustav **Socialist Fiction in the 1930s: Some Preliminary Observations** in *'Renaissance and Modern Studies'* Vol.20, 1976 24pp About the debates in CP and Marxist circles.

6227 Klugmann, James **Communists and Socialists** in *'Marxist Quarterly'* July 1956 11pp

6228 Klugmann, James **Party Education and the BRS** in *'CR'* June 1951 3pp

6229 Klugmann, James **Party Educational Programme for 1952-3** in *'CR'* Sept. 1952 6pp Details of Schools & publications.

6230 Klugmann, James **The Christian-Marxist Dialogue in Britain** in *'WMR'* March 1968 3pp Some refs to CP's role in organising this dialogue.

6231 Klugmann, James **The Foundation of the CP** in *'MT'* Jan. 1960 10pp

6232 Klugmann, James **Twenty Years of 'MT'** in *'MT'* Sept. 1977 3pp

6233 Knotter, Ad **Little Moscows' Revisited: What We Can Learn from French and German Cases** in *'Twentieth Century Communism'* 5, 2013 18pp

6234 Knowles, Kenneth **The Post-War Dock Strikes** in *'Political Quarterly'* July/Sept. 1951 25pp

6234a Knowles, Mike **A Survey of Political Education Within the Labour and TU Movement** in *'Socialism and Education'* Vol.10 No.1, 1983 1pp Complimentary account of CP's Education Dept, under Alan Booth. Also looks at two unions and the LP itself.

6235 Knox, Bill & McKinlay, Alan **'Pests to Management': Engineering Shop Stewards on Clydeside, 1939-45** in *'SLHS'* 30, 1995 24pp

6236 Kristiansdottir, Ragnheithur **Communists and the National Question in Scotland and Iceland, c1930-c1940** in *'The Historical Journal'* Sept. 2002 17pp

6237 Kushner, Tony **Jewish Communists in Twentieth-Century Britain: The Zaidman Collection** in *'LHR'* Vol.55 No.2, Autumn 1990 9pp About the collection in Sheffield Univ. Library.

6238 Kuusinen, O. **Lessons of the English Elections** in *'C.I.'* April 1 1932 10pp Speech to the English Commission.

6239 Lane, Hilda **Why I Joined** in *'LM'* Jan. 1959 2pp St Pancras councillor.

6240 Lane, Jack **Jimmy Reid Strikes Out** in *'The Communist' (BICO)* 110, June 1977 3pp Other articles in this issue.

6241 Laporte, Norman & Worley, Matthew **Towards A Comparative History of Communism: The British and German CPs to 1933** in *'Contemporary British History'* Vol.22 No.2, 2008 28pp

6242 Laski, Harold **Great Britain and the Communists** in *'The New Republic'* Jan. 6 1926 2pp On the trial of the 12 CP leaders.

6243 Latham, Peter **Methodological Approaches to CP History** in *'Our History Journal'* 3, Oct. 1978 4pp

6244 Latham, Peter **'Unofficial' Movements in Building During the Twentieth Century** in *'SSLHB'* 38, Spring 1979 1pp Abstract of conference paper & discussion.

6245 Lauchlan, William **A Mass CP** in *'CR'* Jan. 1948 3pp

6246 Lauchlan, William **Britain: CP Factory Conference** in *'WMR'* May 1962 1pp

6247 Lauchlan, William **Closer Links Between Party and Masses** in *'WMR'* Oct. 1958 1pp

6248 Lauchlan, William **The CP and the DW** in *'MT'* June 1959 6pp

6249 Laurie, Dave **Can the CPGB Be Pushed Left?** in *'The Communist' (BICO)* 9 (10), Nov. 1967 2pp Possibly mis-numbered.

6250 Laurie, Robert (ed.) **Brighton 1926: 'The Punch'** in *'MML Bulletin'* 133, Spring 2001 8pp Reproduces text of 2 factory papers, plus introduction.

6251 Laurie, Robert **Jack Dunn – Obituary** in *'MML Bulletin'* 135, Spring 2002 1pp

6252 Laurie, Robert **The Left in the Oxford Dictionary of National Biography** in *'MML Bulletin'* 143 Spring 2006 6pp

6253 Lawrence, John **Fascist Violence and the Politics of Public Disorder in Inter-War Britain: The Olympia Debate Revisited** in *'Historical Research'* Vol.76 No.192, May 2003 30pp

6254 Lawson, Nigel **Communist Influence on Industrial Strife** in *'East-West Digest'* June 1972 5pp

6255 Laybourn, Keith **A Comment on the Historiography of Communism in Britain** in *'American Communist History'* Vol.4 No.2, 2005 8pp

6256 Laybourn, Keith **'Communism: National and International' ed. T. Saarelo & K. Rentola – Review** in *'LHR'* Vol.64 No.3, Winter 1999 2pp

6257 Laybourn, Keith **The Spanish Civil War: Political Activism and the Popular Front' – Review article on 5 books** in *'LHR'* Vol.76 No.1, April 2011 7pp

6258 Layton-Henry, Zig **Labour's Lost Youth** in *'JOCH'* Vol.11 Nos 2 & 3, July 1976 35pp Covers YCL relationship to the Labour League of Youth in 1930s.

6259 Le Brocq, Norman **The First Communist in the Jersey Parliament** in *'WMR'* July 1967 1pp

6260 Leckie, Jack **The Draft Programme of the CPGB Criticised** in *'C.R.'* Aug. 1924 6pp

6261 Lee, C.P. **Ewan MacColl: The People's Friend?** in *'NWLHSB'* 26, 2001 6pp

6262 Lee, H. **Lagging Behind** in *'C.R.'* Oct. 1932 3pp

6263 Leeson, Bob **Jack Lindsay, 1900-90 – Obituary** in *'Our History Journal'* 17, Nov. 1990 6pp

6264 Leicester, Liz **The 1970 Leeds' Clothing Workers' Strike: Representations and Refractions** in *'Scottish Labour History'* 44, 2009 16pp

6264a Leonard, Richard **Sammy Barr – Obituary** in *'SLHS'* 47, 2012 1pp

6265 Lester, Paul & Rees, Arfon **The British Leyland Road to Socialism** in *'The Communist' (BICO)* 117, Jan. 1978 6pp Attack on J. Bloomfield's analysis of BL.

6266 Levy, Martin **Revolution and Culture** in *'Communist Review' (CPB)* 62, Winter 2011/12 6pp Especially on the CP's role in the folk music revival.

6267 Levy, Sam **The 26th CP Congress** in *'Socialist Current'* May 1959 4pp

6267a Lewis, Joel A. **'Arthur Horner: A Political Biography' by N. Fishman – Review** in *'SLHS'* 47 2012 2pp

6268 Lewis, Joel A. **Clearing Out the Men of Munich: Young Communist Reactions to the Hitler-Stalin Pact** in *'Scottish Labour History'* 45, 2010 19pp International analysis with much on British YCL.

6269 Lewis, Richard **Protagonist of Labour: Mark Starr, 1894-1985** in *'Llafur'* Vol.4 No.3, 1986 14pp Leading figure in adult education; briefly in CP in early 1920s.

6270 Lindop, Fred **Interview With Harry Watson** in *'SSLHB'* 39, Autumn 1979 5pp President of Watermen's, Lightermen's, Tugmen & Bargemen's Union.

6271 Lindop, Fred **Racism and the Working Class: Strikes in Support of Enoch Powell in 1968** in *'LHR'* Vol.66 No.1, Spring 2001 23pp On the London dockers; includes analysis of CP members' responses.

6272 Lindop, Fred **The Dockers and the 1971 Industrial Relations Act, Part 1** in *'HSIR'* 5, Spring 1998 40pp Part 2 in no.6.

6273 Lindop, Fred **Unofficial Militancy in the Royal Group of Docks, 1945-67** in *'Oral History'* Autumn 1983 13pp

6274 Lindsay, Jack **Edgell Rickword – Memoriam** in *'Artery'* 24/25, 1982 ? 1pp

6275 Linehan, Thomas **Communist Activism in Interwar Britain: Motivation, Belonging and Political Religion** in *'Socialist History'* 32, 2008

6276 Little, Bob **Early Socialism in East Anglia** in *'East Anglia History Workshop Journal'* Vol.2 No.2, 1981 ? 4pp Report of conference. Info. on Leiston branch.

6276a Little, Eddie **'Revolutionary Communist at Work: A Political Biography of Bert Ramelson' by R. Seifert & T. Sibley – Review** in *'NWLHSB'* 39, 2014 1p The second time this journal reviewed this book – see Buckley, S.

6277 Little, Eddie **T.A. Jackson (1879-1955)** in *'WCML Bulletin'* 14, 2004 3pp

6277a Llacuna, Adrià **The Labour Galaxy and the Communist Solar System: An Approach to Social-Democrat Anti-Communism During the Inter-War Years** in *'Socialist History'* 44, 2014 20pp

6278 Long, Paul **Abe Moffat, The Fife Miners and the U.M.S. - Interview** in *'SLHS'* 17, 1982 13pp

6279 Long of Wroxham **The Secret Service and Communism** in *'The Nineteenth Century (And After)'* Feb. 1922 9pp

6280 Lucas, John **An Interview with Edgell Rickword** in *'Renaissance & Modern Studies'* Vol.20, 1976 9pp

6281 Lucas, John **'Red Letter Days' by A. Croft - Review** in *'Socialist History'* 5, 1994 8pp

6282 Lyddon, Dave **Trade Union Traditions, the Oxford Welsh and the 1934 Pressed Steel Strike** in *'Llafur'* Vol.6 No.2, 1993 8pp

6283 Lynch, C.F. **The Party and the YCL** in *'C.R.'* Dec. 1931 4pp

6284 M.M. **CPGB in the Struggle Against Social-Fascism** in *'C.I.'* March 15 1932 7pp

6285 M.M. **Hindrances to Factory Work in England** in *'C.I.'* May 15 1932 5pp

6286 MacDiarmid, Hugh **Towards a Communist Literature in Scotland** in *'Scottish Marxist'* 1, 1972 6pp

6287 Mace, Jane **Only Yesterday: Gladys Easton Interview** in *'Link'* Winter 1980 2pp The first in a useful series of interviews with veteran women comrades. Easton worked for the CP for 30 years.

6288 Mace, Jane **Only Yesterday: Golda Barr Interview** in *'Link'* Summer 1981 2pp

6289 Mace, Rodney **John Gorman - Obituary** in *'LHR'* Vol.61 No.3, Winter 1996 1pp

6290 MacEwen, Malcolm **Striking the Balance** in *'New Reasoner'* No.1, 1957 4pp Argues for balanced criticism of Stalin in CP (and in the New Left).

6291 MacEwen, Malcolm **The Year the Party Had to Stop** in *'The Listener'* Dec. 16 1976 2pp

6292 MacFarlane, James **Essay in Oral History: Denaby Main - A South Yorkshire Mining Village** in *'SSLHB'* 25, Autumn 1972 1pp Section on Eddie Collins, a foundation Member.

6293 MacFarlane, James **Essay in Oral History: J.T.E. (Eddie) Collins** in *'SSLHB'* 26, Spring 1973 4pp An addendum to previous item.

6294 Macfarlane, L. et al. **The CP in the Twenties** in *'SSLHB'* 14, Spring 1967 2pp Abstract of Conference paper & discussion.

6295 MacGregor, Charles **The Fight Against Cuts: Elections and the Role of the CP** in *'C.R.'* Nov. 1931 10pp

6296 Macintyre, Alasdair **'Communism and British Intellectuals' by N. Wood - Review** in *'The Listener'* Jan. 7 1960 2pp

6297 Macintyre, Donald **Close Up on Mick McGahey** in *'MT'* Sept. 1986 1pp

6298 Macintyre, Stuart **'Rajani Palme Dutt' by J. Callaghan and 'Harry Pollitt' by K. Morgan - Review** in *'Science and Society'* Vol.61 No.1, Spring 1997 5pp

6299 Macintyre, Stuart **British Labour, Marxism and the Working Class: Apathy in the 1920s** in *'Historical Journal'* June 1977 23pp

6300 Macintyre, Stuart **Red Strongholds Between the Wars** in *'MT'* March 1979 6pp On the so-called 'Little Moscows', mainly in Scotland & Wales.

6301 MacKenzie, Alan **Communism in Britain: A Bibliography** in *'SSLHB'* 44, Spring 1982 19pp R. & E. Frow wrote a brief critical letter on MacKenzie's intro. in 'SSLH Bulletin' 46.

6302 Mackenzie, Compton **Memories of Gallacher** in *'LM'* June 1966 3pp Review of 'Last Memoirs' by W. Gallacher.

6303 MacKenzie, S.P. **The Foreign Enlistment Act and the Spanish Civil War, 1936-1939** in *'Twentieth Century British History'* Vol.10 No.1, 1999 14pp On CP recruitment of volunteers for the I.B. Refs to Fred Copeman and others.

6304 MacLaine, William **The English Communists' Relief Campaign** in *'Inprecorr'* Dec. 20 1921 1pp CPGB's campaign for Famine Relief to Russia included producing 40,000 badges and appealing for donations of jewellery.

6304a Maclennan, Stewart **Andrew Clark - Obituary** in *'SLHS'* 48, 2013 1pp

6304b Maclennan, Stewart **Alex Maxwell - Obituary** in *'SLHS'* 49, 2014 1pp

6304c Maclennan, Stewart **Hugh D'Arcy - Obituary** in *'SLHS'* 49, 2014 2pp

6304d Maclennan, Stewart **Sid Paris - Obituary** in *'SLHS'* 49, 2014 1pp

6304e Maclennan, Stewart **John Kay - Obituary** in *'SLHS'* 47, 2012 1pp

6304f Maclennan, Stewart **Jack Ashton; Eric Atkinson; Irene Swan - Obituaries** in *'SLHS'* 47, 2012 1

6305 Macleod, Alison & Ambrose, Mike **'And the Scores Have Not Been Settled Yet': A Debate on the Crisis in the British CP, 1956-57** in *'Workers' International Press'* Vol.2

Nos.1/2, Winter1997/Spring 1998 5pp This was a public debate and includes contributions from Brian Pearce, R. Russell, P. Fryer et al.

6306 Macleod, Alison **'Stalin's British Victims' by F. Beckett – Review** in 'Revolutionary History' Vol.9 No.2, 2006 2pp

6307 Macleod, Alison **The Death of Uncle Joe** in 'Socialist History' 10, 1996 31pp Author was 'DW' tv critic; the article is from book of same name and is based on lengthy notes of staff meetings during the 1956 crisis.

6308 MacManus, Arthur **Working Class Education** in 'C.I.' 25, 1923 ? 6pp Interesting on relationship between CP and the Plebs League.

6309 Madeira, Victor **Moscow's Interwar Infiltration of British Intelligence, 1919-1929** in 'Historical Journal' Vol.46 No.4, Dec. 2003 18pp W.N. Ewer's 'network' that preceded the more famous Cambridge spy ring – Walter Holmes, Rose Edwardes and others. Includes info. on how CP processed Soviet funds.

6310 Mahon, John **Communist Metalworkers' Conference in London** in 'Inprecorr' Feb. 13 1937 1pp

6311 Mahon, John **Revolutionary Trade Union Work in Britain** in 'RILU' Dec. 1 1932 5pp

6312 Mahon, John **The Experience and Lessons of the Strike Struggles in Britain in 1932** in 'RILU' Vol.3 No.1, Feb. 1933 7pp

6313 Mahon, John **The Fight for Unity** in 'CR' Feb. 1951 6pp Review of activity by the London District.

6314 Mahon, John **The London District Congress** in 'Inprecorr' May 1 1937 1pp London Congresses were reported but not Scottish or Welsh!

6315 Mahon, John **The New Strike Wave and the CP** in 'C.R.' June 1934 5pp

6316 Mahon, John **The Tradition and Work of Trades Councils** in 'CR' July 1952 7pp Incl. details of ban on CP members in 1930s.

6317 Mahon, John **Word and Deed in Strike Struggles** in 'C.R.' June 1933 4pp

6318 Maisels, C. **McShane, Maclean and the CPGB** in 'The Communist' (BICO) 47, March 1972 7pp

6319 Maitles, Henry **Fascism in the 1930s: The West of Scotland in the British Context** in 'SLHS' 27, 1992 16pp

6320 Manley, John **Moscow Rules? Red Unionism and Class Against Class in Britain, Canada and the US, 1928-1935** in 'Labour/Le Travail' 56, 2005 40pp

6321 Manson, John **Communists and Workers in 'Grey Granite'** in 'Scottish Labour History' 34, 1999 5pp On the 3rd vol. of Lewis Grassic Gibbon's trilogy 'A Scot's Quair'.

6322 Manuilsky, D. **The Revolutionary Way Out of the Crisis in England: Speech at the English Commission of C.I.** in 'C.I.' April 1 1932 7pp

6323 Marlowe, T. & Whittaker, P. **The CPGB and Ireland: The British Road to Social Imperialism** in 'Revolutionary Communist' No.7, Nov. 1977 5pp

6324 Marlowe, Terry & Reed, David **The End of the British Road: The Split in the CPGB** in 'Fight Racism! Fight Imperialism!' Feb. 1985 2pp

6325 Marshall, Kate **Women and the T.U.s: Stalinists Fall Out** in 'The Next Step' Feb. 1983 1pp

6326 Martin, D. & Kirby, D. **John Saville (1916-2009): Appreciations and Memories** in 'LHR' Vol.75 No.1, April 2010 14pp

6327 Martin, David **Edmund Frow – Obituary** in 'LHR' Vol.62 No.2, Summer 1997 1pp

6328 Martin, David **'Party People, Communist Lives' ed. J. McIlroy, K. Morgan & A. Campbell – Review** in 'LHR' Vol.68 No.1, April 2003 2pp

6329 Martin, P.E. **Skipton Election and Weakness of Our Party in Lancashire** in 'C.R.' Dec. 1933/Jan. 1934 1pp

6330 Martin, Roderick **The National Minority Movement** in 'SSLHB' 17, Autumn 1968 4pp Abstract of Report & discussion.

6331 Martinov, A. **The Change in Tactics of the CPGB** in 'C.I.' April 15 1928 5pp

6332 Martynov, A. **Chartists to Communists** in 'C.I.' 22, 1926 27pp

6333 Mason, A. **The General Strike on Teesside** in 'NELH' 4, 1970 2pp

6334 Massie, A. **Some Lessons of the English Wool Strike** in 'The International of Youth' Nov./Dec. 1930 4pp This is the US ed. NB author misspelt as 'Massee'.

6335 Massie, Alex **A Bold Step Towards Youth Unity in Britain** in 'Inprecorr' June 27 1936 2pp

6336 Mates, Lewis **'A Most Fruitful Period?' The North East District CP and the Popular Front, 1935-9** in 'North East History' 35, 2004

45pp There are not many such studies of specific Districts at specific periods.

6337 Mates, Lewis **'Comrade Heart: A Life of Randall Swingler' by A. Croft – Review** in 'North East History' 36, 2005 4pp

6338 Mates, Lewis **'The Jarrow Crusade: Protest and Legend' by M. Perry – Review** in 'North East History' 37, 2006 9pp With a Reply by Perry.

6339 Mates, Lewis **The North East and the Campaigns for the Popular Front, 1938-39** in 'Northern History' Vol.43 No.2, Sept. 2006 30pp Focuses on the LP rather than CP.

6340 Matgamna, Sean **Communism and Philinistinism: Obituaries of J. Cannon & R.P. Dutt** in 'Permanent Revolution' Summer 1975 12pp

6341 Matgamna, Sean **Desmond Greaves: Obituary** in 'Workers' Liberty' No.12/13, Aug. 1989 1pp

6342 Matthews, Betty **Party Building Prospects** in 'MT' Oct. 1963 7pp

6343 Matthews, Betty **Theory Throws Light on the Road of Struggle** in 'WMR' April 1975 2pp

6344 Matthews, George **'1939: The CP and the War' by J. Attfield – Review** in 'MT' May 1984 1pp

6345 Matthews, George **A Communist Viewpoint on Britain** in 'Contemporary Review' June 1982 6pp

6346 Matthews, George **'Against Fascism and War' by K. Morgan – Review** in 'Our History Journal' 17, May 1991 6pp

6347 Matthews, George **Our Quest for a Road to Socialism** in 'WMR' April 1979 8pp On new ed. of BRS.

6348 Mauger, Sam **Communist Party Congress** in 'NLR' 35, 1966 2pp

6349 May, Daphne **The Work of the Historians' Groups** in 'CR' May 1949 2pp From a Report to the Historians' Group.

6350 McCabe, Colin **Britain's Communist University** in 'New Statesman' May 20 1977 1pp Positive assessment by non-Communist academic.

6351 McCrindle, Alex **Hugh MacDiarmid – Obituary** in 'HWJ' 6, 1978 2pp

6352 McCulloch, Gary **A People's History of Education: Brian Simon, the British CP and 'Studies in the History of Education in England'** in 'History of Education' Vol.39 No.4, 2010 20pp

6353 McCulloch, Gary **Labour, The Left and the British General Election of 1945** in 'Journal of British Studies' Oct. 1985 25pp

6354 McCulloch, Gary **Teachers and Missionaries: The Left Book Club as an Educational Agency** in 'History of Education' Vol.14 No.2, 1985 16pp

6355 McGahey, Mick **Tribute to Abe Moffat** in 'Scottish Marxist' 9, 1975 2pp

6356 McGahey, Mick **Abe Moffat** in 'LM' June 1975 2pp Funeral oration.

6357 McGee, Matthew **'Communism in Britain, 1920-1939: From the Cradle to the Grave' by T. Linehan – Review** in 'Socialist History' 35, 2009 3pp

6358 McHugh, John **'John Maclean And the CPGB' by B. Pitt – Review** in 'Revolutionary History' Vol.6 No.4, 1997 3pp

6359 McHugh, John & Ripley, B. **The Neath By-Election, 1945 :Trotskyists in West Wales** in 'Llafur' Vol.3 No.2, Spring 1981 11pp

6360 McIlhone, Bob **The CP in Congress** in 'LM' March 1935 6pp

6361 McIlhone, Bob **The Results of the British Congress of Action and National Hunger March** in 'C.I.' March 15 1934 7pp

6362 McIlhone, Bob **The Struggle of the Unemployed in Britain** in 'C.I.' April 5 1935 4pp

6363 McIlory, John **A Communist Historian in 1956: Brian Pearce and the Crisis in British Stalinism** in 'Revolutionary History' Vol.9 No.3, 2006 21pp

6364 McIlroy, John **'Adult Education and the Cold War' by R. Fieldhouse – Review** in 'SSLHB' 51 Part 1, 1986 2pp

6365 McIlroy, John & Halstead, John **A Very Different Historian: Royden Harrison, Radical Academics and Suppressed Alternatives** in 'HSIR' 15, Spring 2003 30pp Royden Harrison was in the CP and a member of the Historians' Group till 1956.

6366 McIlroy, John **Adrift in the Rapids of Racism: Syd Bidwell (Obituary)** in 'Revolutionary History' Vol.7 No.1, 1998 31pp Bidwell was initially a Trotskyist, the first member of a Trotskyist organisation to become a Labour MP, then a Left Labour MP who later in life moved closer to the CP – for which he was condemned by the author. McIlroy's articles and books are full of interesting, well researched refs to the CP and are at the same time highly polemical and combative.

6367 McIlroy, John & Campbell, Alan **Beyond Betteshanger: Order 1305 in the Scottish Coalfields During the Second World War, Part 1: Politics, Prosecutions and Protest** in *'HSIR'* 15, Spring 2003 46pp Part 2: The Cardowan Story is in No.16, Autumn 2003.

6368 McIlroy, John **Critical Reflections on Recent British CP History** in *'Historical Materialism'* Vol.12 No.1, 2004 27pp

6369 McIlroy, John **'Every Factory Our Fortress': CP Workplace Branches in a Time of Militancy, 1956-79 Part 1** in *'HSIR'* 10, Autumn 2000 41pp Second part in No.12 (52pp). Substantial and important articles.

6370 McIlroy, John & Campbell, Alan **For a Revolutionary Workers' Government: Moscow, British Communism and Revisionist Interpretations of the Third Period, 1927-1934** in *'European History Quarterly'* Vol.32 No.4, 2002 35pp

6371 McIlroy, John & Campbell, Alan **Histories of the British CP: A User's Guide** in *'LHR'* Vol.68 No.1, April 2003 27pp Looks at all periods of the literature but is largely a critique of the material produced mainly since 1980. Argues that Morgan, Fishman, Thorpe and Worley represent a revisionist tendency among historians of British Communism by downplaying Moscow's influence. Also argues that historians need to be more critical of CP members' complicity in 'Stalinism'.

6372 McIlroy, John **John Archer – Obituary** in *'Revolutionary History'* Vol.8 No.1, 2001 8pp Lifelong Trotskyist after brief membership of CPGB.

6373 McIlroy, John **John Saville, 1916-2009 – Obituary** in *'LHR'* Vol.74 No.3, Dec. 2009 9pp

6374 McIlroy, John **LHR Vol.75 Supplement – Making History: Organizations of Labour Historians in Britain Since 1960** 2010 99pp McIlroy's long article on the SSLH discusses the role of CP members in its formation and early years, quoting many sources.

6375 McIlroy, John **Look Back in Anger: Mining Communities, the Mining Novel and the Great Miners' Strike** in *'HSIR'* 18, Autumn 2004 30pp Discusses Novels by Lewis Jones, Len Doherty & Harold Heslop among others.

6376 McIlroy, John **'Memoirs from the Left' by J. Savillle & 'Interesting Times' by E. Hobsbawm – Review** in *'LHR'* Vol.70 No.2, Aug. 2005 7pp

6377 McIlroy, John **Monty Johnstone – Obituary** in *'LHR'* Vol.72 No.3, Dec. 2007 3pp

6378 McIlroy, John **New Light on Arthur Reade: Tracking Down Britain's First Trotskyist** in *'Revolutionary History'* Vol.8 No.1, 2001 47pp Joined CP at Oxford in 1921 before becoming the only known member to support the Left Opposition in 1924-5. Useful on CP organisation among students, and on the Trotsky debate. Reproduces valuable documents.

6379 McIlroy, John & Campbell, Alan **'Nina Ponomareva's Hats': The New Revisionism, the Communist International, and the CPGB, 1920-1930** in *'Labour/Le Travail'* 49, Spring 2002 40pp

6380 McIlroy, John & Campbell, Alan **Organising the Militants: The Liaison Committee for the Defence of Trade Unions, 1966-79** in *'BJOIR'* March 1999 31pp Very useful – the only academic study on the LCDTU. Concludes it was a CP front rather than independent body.

6381 McIlroy, John & Campbell, Alan **Peripheral Vision: Communist Historiography in Britain** in *'American Communist History'* Vol.4 No.2, 2005 32pp Same issue has 4 other articles on same theme, plus second article by same authors – 'Some Problems of Communist History' 15pp

6382 McIlroy, John **Reds at Work: Communist Factory Organisation in the Cold War, 1947-56** in *'LHR'* Vol.65 No.2, Summer 2000 21pp

6383 McIlroy, John **Rehabilitating Communist History: The CI, the CPGB and Some Historians** in *'Revolutionary History'* Vol.8 No.1, 2001 32pp Well researched polemic defending the view that the CI dictated all major policy of the CPGB; covers 1920-1934. The first part of the article – not by McIlroy – has a lengthy and useful bibliography marred by unnecessary personal comments as well as a more sectarian approach.

6384 McIlroy, John &, Laybourn, Keith & Campbell, Alan **Symposium: 1926 – The General Strike and Mining Lockout** in *'HSIR'* 21, Spring 2006 145pp Some interesting refs, incl. on R. Page Arnot. Useful Bibliography.

6385 McIlroy, John & Campbell, Alan **The British and French Representatives to the Communist International, 1920-1939: A Comparative Survey** in *'IRSH'* Vol.50 No.2, 2005 17pp

6386 McIlroy, John **The British CP: From World War to Cold War – Review Essay ('History of the CPGB, 1941-51' By N. Branson)** in *'LHR'* Vol.63 No.3, Winter 1998 7pp

6387 McIlroy, John **'The CPGB Since 1920' by J. Eaden & D. Renton – Review** in *'Revolutionary History'* Vol.8 No.3, 2003 4pp

6388 McIlroy, John **The Establishment of Intellectual Orthodoxy and the Stalinization of British Communism, 1928-1933** in *'Past & Present'* Vol.192 No.1, 2006 39pp

6389 McIlroy, John **The First Great Battle in the March to Socialism: Dockers, Stalinists and Trotskyists in 1945** in *'Revolutionary History'* Vol.6 No.2/3, Summer 1996 55pp

6390 McIlroy, John & Campbell, Alan **The Heresy of Arthur Horner** in *'Llafur'* Vol.8 No.2, 2001 14pp On Horner's 1931 crisis – his opposition to the Third Period & his 'trial by inquisition in Moscow'.

6391 McIlroy, John **The Jarrow Crusade, 1936: Marching Against Murder** in *'LHR'* Vol.73 No.1, April 2008 7pp

6392 McIlroy, John **'The Political Trajectory of J.T. Murphy' by R. Darlington & 'Molly Murphy' – Review** in *'Revolutionary History'* Vol.7 No.2, 1999 9pp

6393 McIlroy, John **The Revolutionary Odyssey of John Lawrence** in *'Revolutionary History'* Vol.9 No.2, 2006 88pp A version had previously appeared in 'What Next?' Nos. 26 & 27, 2003.

6394 McIlroy, John & Campbell, Alan **The Scots at the Lenin School: An Essay in Collective Biography** in *'Scottish Labour History'* 37, 2002 22pp

6395 McIlroy, John **'Under the Red Flag' by K. Laybourn & Murphy, Dylan – Review** in *'Socialist History'* 21, 2002 4pp

6396 McIlroy, John **Welsh Communists at the Lenin School Between the Wars** in *'Llafur'* Vol.8 No.4, 2003 26pp Includes info. on, among others, M. Goldberg, L. Jefferies, F. Bright, Reg Jones, Bill Williams, W. Paynter.

6397 McIlroy, John et al. **Forging the Faithful: The British at the International Lenin School** in *'LHR'* Vol.68 No.1, April 2003 30pp

6398 McIvor, Arthur **A Crusade for Capitalism: The Economic League, 1919-39** in *'JOCH'* Vol.23 No.4, Oct. 1988 24pp

6399 McIvor, Arthur **Political Blacklisting and Anti-Socialist Activity Between the Wars** in *'SSLHB'* 53 Part 1, 1988 8pp On the Economic League.

6400 McKay, Ian **Carrying the Communists' Ideas to the People** in *'WMR'* March 1982 5pp On 37th Congress.

6401 McKay, Ian **Together with the Whole Labour Movement** in *'WMR'* March 1984 6pp On 38th Congress.

6402 McKay, J. **W. Gallacher: From Infantile Disorder to Stalinist Order** in *'SLHR'* 5, 1991 3pp

6403 McKay, John **Communist Unity and Division 1920: Gallacher, Maclean and the 'Unholy Scotch Current'** in *'SLHS'* 29, 1994 14pp

6404 McKay, John **Red Clydeside After 75 Years: A Reply to Iain McLean** in *'SLHS'* 31, 1996 9pp A longstanding debate about how revolutionary the situation on Clydeside was; not all articles/books are relevant to the CP, but this one largely deals with Gallacher and the CP but the article by McLean in issue 29 hardly refers to the CP.

6405 McKeown, Neil **The CPGB on Wales** in *'The Communist'* (BICO) 46, Feb. 1972 5pp

6406 McKinlay, Alan **Jimmy Reid: Fragments from a Political Life** in *'Scottish Labour History'* 46 2011 16pp There is a response to this article by John Kay in SLHS 47, and a rely by MacKinlay in No.48.

6407 McKinnon, Alan **CP Election Tactics: A Historical Review** in *'MT'* Aug. 1980 7pp

6408 McLauchlan, John **How To Produce Factory Papers** in *'C.R.'* Feb. 1926 3pp

6409 McLennan, Gordon **50th Anniversary of the CPGB** in *'WMR'* Oct. 1970 2pp

6410 McLennan, Gordon **Communist Congress in Britain** in *'WMR'* Jan. 1968 4pp

6411 McLennan, Gordon **CP Branches in Industry** in *'CR'* Oct. 1951 6pp

6412 McLennan, Gordon **Factory Gate Meetings in Scotland** in *'WMR'* April 1964 1pp

6413 McLennan, Gordon **From Discussion to Resolution and Action** in *'WMR'* Oct. 1973 1pp On Congress procedure.

6414 McLennan, Gordon **Left Unity: Earnest of Success** in *'WMR'* Jan. 1980 6pp Interview on 36th Congress.

6415 McLennan, Gregor **'The British Marxist Historians' by H. Kaye – Review** in *'MT'* March 1985 1pp

6416 McLoughlin, Barry **Proletarian Academics or Party Functionaries? Irish Communists at the International Lenin School, Moscow, 1927-1937** in *'Saothar'* 22, 1997 18pp Quite a few refs to CPGB members, and relationship CPI/CPGB.

6417 McQuilkin, Bill **Forming a Party Branch** in *'Scottish Marxist'* 14, 1977 2pp Incl. material on history of Johnstone branch.

6418 McWhirter, Julie **Internationalism and the British Labour Movement, 1917-27** in *'SLHS'* 6, 1972 28pp

6419 Melling, Jospeh **Leadership and Factionalism in the Growth of Supervisory Trade-Unionism: The Case of ASSET, 1939-1956** in *'HSIR'* 13, Spring 2002 46pp Detailed analysis of a strong anti-Communist campaign.

6420 Melling, Joseph **'Little Moscows' by S. Macintyre – Review** in *'Our History Journal'* 7, Winter 1982 6pp

6421 Melling, Joseph **Reds Under the Collar? Clive Jenkins, White Collar Unionism and the Politics of the British Left, 1947-65** in *'Twentieth Century British History'* Vol.13 No.4, Dec. 2002 36pp Jenkins left the CP in 1954. This article has quite a bit on CP in industry.

6422 Melling, Joseph **'Shop Floor Citizens' by J. Hinton – Review** in *'HSIR'* 1, March 1996 3pp

6423 Mellini, P. **Gabriel's Message** in *'History Today'* Feb. 1990 7pp 'Gabriel' was the pseudonym of James Friell, the long-standing 'DW' cartoonist.

6424 Mepham, George **Unions and Communists** in *'Socialist Commentary'* (Socialist Vanguard Group) Jan. 1949 2pp

6425 Meredith, Christopher **McCarthyism in Britain?** in *'LM'* July 1953 4pp On the termination of Rothstein's academic appointment.

6426 Merrill, Mike **Interview With E.P. Thompson** in *'Radical History Review'* Fall 1976 22pp

6427 Miles, Andy **Workers' Education: The CP and the Plebs League in the 1920s** in *'HWJ'* 18 1984 13pp

6428 Millar, J.P.M. **The 'DW' Censorship** in *'Plebs'* Feb. 1940 2pp On 'DW' not printing NCLC adverts. Further article in March.

6429 Millar, J.P.M. **The Left Book Club's Suppressed Editorial** in *'Plebs'* July 1937 1pp

6429a Miller, Christopher W. **Forward to Obscurity? Another Dimension to the Decline of the Radical Left on 1930s Clydeside** in *'SLHS'* 47, 2012 19pp Discusses ILP and CP's policies on rearmament and pacifism.

6430 Milligan, Pat **Only Yesterday: Jenny Hyslop Interview** in *'Link'* Autumn 1981 2pp

6431 Milligan, Tony **Trotskyist Politics and Industrial Work in Scotland, 1939-45** in *'SLHS'* 30, 1995 16pp

6432 Milligan, Martin **Edinburgh People's Festival** in *'CR'* March 1952 4pp On 'People's Festival Week', 1951 – the start of the 'Fringe Festival', initiated by local labour movement with strong CP input.

6433 Mills, Sarah **Be Prepared: Communism and the Politics of Scouting in 1950s Britain** in *'Contemporary British History'* Vol.25 No.3, 2011 21pp Some Boy Scouts were expelled for sympathising with, or being members of, the YCL; Paul Garland, YCL District Secretary for the West of England, was one – he had been a scout since he was 8 and had won the highest scouting award. This article also explores the relationship between YCL and Scouts in 1920s.

6434 Mindel, Mick **Socialist Eastenders** in *'Jewish Socialist'* Summer/Autumn 1986 2pp Memories of Jewish activist, esp. in 1930s.

6435 Mitchell, Alex **British Stalinism on the Rocks** in *'Labour Review'* Nov. 1984 5pp

6436 Mitchell, Alex **Crisis of British Stalinism** in *'Labour Review'* July 1985 6pp

6437 Mitchell, Brian **Gerry Leversha: A Reflection on the CPGB** in *'Revolutionary Communist'* No.8, July 1978 2pp Reply to Leversha's article on RCG in *'MT'*, Jan. 1978.

6438 Monies, George **'The Revolutionary Movement in Britain, 1900-21' by W. Kendall – Review** in *'SLHS'* 1, 1969 2pp

6439 Monro, Stuart **Unfinished Business: The Life and Times of Ralph Fox** in *'The Ethical Record'* April 1990 4pp

6440 Montagu, Ivor **Filleted Haldane** in *'LM'* March 1969 2pp Review of BBC2 programme on Haldane ('The Last of the Polymaths' Feb. 6).

6441 Moore, Bill **'About Turn' ed. F. King & G. Matthews – Review** in *'Our History Journal'* 18, Nov. 1991 3pp

6442 Morgan, Dave **'1939: The CP and the War' ed. J. Attfield & S. Williams – Some Thoughts** in *'Our History Journal'* 9, March 1985 2pp More contributions in succeeding issues.

6443 Morgan, David **New Findings From the Moscow Archives** in *'Socialist History'* 10, 1996 4pp Brief report of Conference in Manchester.

6444 Morgan, Kevin **A.A. Purcell: An International Socialist** in *'WCML Bulletin'* 9, 1999

5pp This T.U. leader was a founder member of the CP but left shortly afterwards.

6445 Morgan, Kevin & Santana, Marco **A Limit to Everything: Union Activists and 'Bolshevik Discipline' in Britain and Brazil** in *'Scottish Labour History' 34, 1999* 22pp Compares communist industrial work in Britain and Brazil.

6446 Morgan, Kevin **Away From Party and into 'the Party': British Wartime Communism and the 1945 Election** in *'Socialist History' 37, 2010* 22pp

6447 Morgan, Kevin **Bastions, Black Spots and Other Variations: In and Beyond the Specifity of the Little Moscow** in *'Twentieth Century Communism' 5, 2013* 17pp Historiographical essay that reasseses the concept of 'Little Moscows'.

6448 Morgan, Kevin (ed.) **Cambridge Communism in the 1930s and 1940s: Reminiscences and Reflections** in *'Socialist History' 24, 2003* 39pp V. Kiernan, R. Simon, G. Barnard, R. Russell, J. Maynard Smith, C. Claydon, N. Lindop, D. Wedderburn, P. Worsley, D. Thompson, J. Bean.

6449 Morgan, Kevin **'Cold War, Crisis and Conflict: The CPGB 1951-68' by J. Callaghan - Review** in *'ILWCH' Vol.70, Autumn 2006* 3pp

6450 Morgan, Kevin **Communist Histories: 'The Enemy Within' by F. Beckett & 'The British CP and the T.U.s, 1933-45' by N. Fishman - Review** in *'LHR' Vol.60 No.3, Winter 1995* 3pp

6450a Morgan, Kevin **In and Out of the Swamp: The Unpublished Autobiography of Pete Petroff** in *'SLHS' 48, 2013* 30pp Russian-born member of SDP & BSP, returned to Russia in 1918 but the articles contains interesting refs to early CP in Scotland.

6451 Morgan, Kevin **Labour With Knobs On? The Recent Historiography of the British CP** in *'Labour and Social History in GB: Historiographical Reviews and Agendas' Special ed. of 'Mitteilungsblatt des Instituts für soziale Bewegungen' No.27, 2002* 15pp

6452 Morgan, Kevin & Duncan, Robert **Loitering on the Party Line: The Unpublished Memoirs of J.T. Walton Newbold** in *'LHR' Vol.60 No.1, Spring 1995* 17pp

6453 Morgan, Kevin **Militarism and Anti-Militarism: Socialists, Communists and Conscription in France and Britain, 1900-1940** in *'Past & Present' Vol.202 No.1, 2009* 38pp

6454 Morgan, Kevin & Saarela, Tauno **Northern Underground Revisited: Finnish Reds and the Origins of British Communism** in *'European History Quarterly' Vol.29 No.2, 1999* 37pp

6455 Morgan, Kevin **Socialists and 'Mobility' in Twentieth Century Britain: Images and Experiences in the Life Histories of British Communists** in *'Social History' Vol.36 No.2, 2011* 25pp

6456 Morgan, Kevin **The Archives of the British CP: A Historical Overview** in *'Twentieth Century British History' Vol.7 No.3, 1996* 17pp

6457 Morgan, Kevin **'The British CP and Moscow, 1920-43' by A. Thorpe - Review** in *'Socialist History' 23, 2003* 3pp

6458 Morgan, Kevin **The CPGB and the Comintern Archives** in *'Socialist History' 2, 1993* 21pp

6459 Morgan, Kevin **The Trouble with Revisionism: Or Communist History with History Left In** in *'Labour/Le Travail' 63, Spring 2009* 25pp Interesting overview of the historiography of communism in general, and CPGB in particular, while analysing one article (J. Manley 'Moscow Rules?' in 'Labour/Le Travail' 56, 2005).

6460 Morgan, Kevin et al. **Communist History Network** in *'SLHR' 10, 1996* 1pp Series of short articles on the state of current work on CP history.

6461 Morris, Aubrey **Memories and Commemorations of the Battle of Cable Street** in *'MML Bulletin' 145, Winter 2006* 8pp

6462 Morris, Margaret **The 1920s** in *'MML Bulletin' 107, Winter 1985/6* 8pp

6463 Morris, Ronald **Thomas Islwyn Nicholas, 1903-80** in *'Llafur' Spring 1981* 3pp T.I. Nicholas lived in shadow of his father, T.E. Nicholas; both were poets and were imprisoned for their pacifism.

6464 Morrison, Herbert **The ECCI's Latest** in *'Labour Magazine' May 1928* 4pp

6465 Mortimer, Jim **'Class Against Class' by M. Worley - Review** in *'MML Bulletin' 141, Spring 2005* 3pp

6466 Mortimer, Jim **'History of the CPGB, 1941-51' by N. Branson - Review** in *'MML Bulletin' 128, Winter/Spring 1997/98* 3pp

6467 Mortimer, Jim **Saklatvala: A Communist Candidate on a Labour Ticket** in *'What Next?' No.24, 2002* Reprinted from July/Aug. 2002 ed. of the Islip Unity Group Political Newsletter.

6468 Morton, A.L. **'History of the CPGB, 1927-41' by N. Branson – Review** in *'Our History Journal'* 10, Nov. 1985 2pp

6469 Moss, John **YCL Congress and Youth Problems** in *'CR'* Dec. 1952 8pp On YCL's 19th Congress.

6470 Munton, Alan (ed.) **Edgell Rickword: A Celebration** in *'PN Review'* Vol.6 No.1, 1979 32pp Despite the wide range of contributors to this supplement, there are few refs to CP, but several to 'Poetry and the People' and 'Our Times'; E.P. Thompson's is the most useful.

6471 Munton, Alan & Young, Alan **Edward Upward: A Conversation** in *'PN Review'* 19, 1980 4pp

6472 Murden, Jon **All Those in Favour Say Aye: Responses to Redundancy in the British Motor Industry, 1956** in *'HSIR'* 17, Spring 2004 37pp

6473 Murphy, Dylan **The West Yorkshire CP and the Struggle for the United Front Against Fascism During 1933** in *'NWLHSB'* 23, 1998 11pp

6474 Murphy, J.T. **After the General Election** in *'C.I.'* Aug. 1 1929 6pp

6475 Murphy, J.T. **Arthur McManus – Obituary** in *'C.I.'* March 30 1927 2pp

6476 Murphy, J.T. **Confusion on the Left** in *'The Nineteenth Century'* Nov. 1939 10pp On CP and Nazi-Soviet Pact.

6477 Murphy, J.T. **Forty Years Hard: For What?** in *'New Reasoner'* No.7, 1958 5pp Review of Pelling.

6478 Murphy, J.T. **How a Mass CP Will Come to Britain** in *'C.I.'* 9 (New Series), 1925 ? 20pp

6479 Murphy, J.T. **New Unions and Their Place in the Revolutionary Struggle** in *'C.R.'* July 1930 8pp

6480 Murphy, J.T. **Newbold's Suspension from Parliament** in *'Inprecorr'* May 24 1923 1pp On May 15 he refused to leave the Commons when ordered – he had called the President of the Board of Trade a liar over the Soviet government's supposed propaganda.

6481 Murphy, J.T. **Reflections on Our Party Congress at Manchester** in *'The Communist'* Nov. 1927 4pp

6482 Murphy, J.T. **The British Labour Party Conference** in *'Inprecorr'* July 26 1923 2pp

6483 Murphy, J.T. **The British Trade Union Congress** in *'Inprecorr'* Sept. 27 1923 2pp

6484 Murphy, J.T. **The British Working Class and the War on China** in *'C.I.'* March 30 1927 4pp

6485 Murphy, J.T. **The Coming of the Mass CP in Britain** in *'C.I.'* 13 (New Series), 1925 15pp

6486 Murphy, J.T. **The CPGB** in *'The Fortnightly'* Aug. 1943 7pp

6487 Murphy, J.T. **The Fight Against the Right Danger** in *'C.R.'* Nov. 1929 12pp

6488 Murphy, J.T. **The Lessons of the English Strike** in *'Inprecorr'* Dec. 30 1926 7pp Speech to Enlarged ECCI.

6489 Murphy, J.T. **The Party Conference** in *'C.R.'* Jan. 1924 4pp

6490 Murphy, J.T. **The Right Danger in New Clothes** in *'C.R.'* June 1930 10pp

6490a Murphy, Stewart **Fascism and Anti-Fascism on Merseyside During the 1930s** in *'NWLHSB'* 39, 2014 4pp

6491 Murray, J. Middleton **Communism and the Universities** in *'Oxford Outlook'* May 1932 9pp Theoretical – not an account of CP organisation.

6492 N.G. **The Fight Against the LP** in *'C.R.'* Dec. 1931 8pp Incl. election figures.

6493 N.H. **Main Features of British Factory Papers** in *'C.I.'* April 1 1931 4pp Author analyses 23 papers – 'as far as can be seen' only 6 are openly by Party cells – it's comforting to know that identification was difficult even then.

6494 Namboodiripad, E.M.S. **R.P. Dutt: A Tribute, An Assessment** in *'The Marxist'* CPI(M) April/June 1996 13pp Interesting comments on CPGB's influence on CPI, especially over policy on WW2.

6495 Naylor, Barry **Ramsay Macdonald and Seaham Labour Politics** in *'NELH'* 15, 1981 45pp On the Dawdon dispute.

6496 Neal, Phyllis **Women Advancing in the CPGB: Their Part in the 10th Congress** in *'Inprecorr'* March 1 1929 1pp

6497 Neal, Phyllis **Women in the British Co-operative Movement** in *'Inprecorr'* April 5 1929 1pp

6498 Neal, Phyllis **Working Women in the Coming General Election** in *'Inprecorr'* Feb. 15 1929 1pp

6499 Neavill, Gordon Barrick **Victor Gollancz and the Left Book Club** in 'Library Quarterly' Vol.41 No.3, July 1971 19pp

6500 Needham, Joseph **Desmond Bernal: A Personal Recollection** in 'MT' March 1972 3pp

6501 Neville, Dave **Barney Markson: An Old Socialist Pioneer** in 'NELH' 18, 1984 3pp

6502 Newark, F.H. **The Campbell Case and the First Labour Government** in 'Northern Ireland Legal Quarterly' March 1969 23pp

6503 Newman, Michael **Centenary of a Communist Scientist: J.B.S. Haldane** in 'New Humanist' June 1992 2pp

6504 Newman, Michael **Democracy versus Dictatorship: Labour's Role in the Struggle Against British Fascism, 1933-46** in 'HWJ' 5, 1978 22pp Compares approaches of the LP & CP.

6505 Newsinger, John **A Communist History?** in 'Socialist Review' Nov./Dec. 1979 2pp On articles in 'Our History Journal' and lack of a CP history of itself.

6506 Newsinger, John **Recent Controversies in the History of British Communism – Review Article** in 'JOCH' Vol.41 No.3, July 2006 15pp On Bruley 'Leninism, Stalinism & the Women's Movement in Britain'; Fishman 'The British CP and the TUs'; Morgan 'Against Fascism & War'; Redfern 'Class or Nation'; Thorpe 'The British CP & Moscow'; Worley 'Class Against Class'.

6507 Nicholson, Steve **Theatrical Pageants in the Second World War** in 'Theatre Research International' Vol.18 No.3, Autumn 1993 11pp Fascinating account of cabinet attempts to minimise CP influence in wartime pageants celebrating the alliance with the USSR.

6508 Nicolson, Rebecca **The Hereditary Principle: Interview with Lord Milford** in 'The Spectator' April 4 1992 2pp

6509 Norling, Bernard **American and British Communism** in 'Review of Politics' Vol.24 No.1, Jan. 1962 5pp Review of 3 books, incl. N. Wood 'Communism and British Intellectuals'.

6510 Norton, Sabena **CP Congress: A Knife in the Back of Us All** in 'The Next Step' Dec. 1979 1pp

6511 Nosaka, Sanzo **Reminiscences of R.P. Dutt** in 'LM' June 1975 3pp Author known as leading member of Japanese CP, but he had been founding member of CPGB & active till expelled from UK by British authorities in 1921.

6512 O'Connor, Emmet **Jim Larkin and the Communist International, 1923-9** in 'Irish Historical Studies' May 1999 16pp Based on latest material made available in Moscow archives; shows that the CPGB played a larger role than previously thought in early Communist politics in Ireland.

6513 O'Connor, Evelyn **Fighting for Peace, Waiting for War: Left-Wing Attitudes in Nelson to Europe and Re-armament, 1935-9** in 'NWLHSB' 22, 1997 12pp

6514 O'Neill, Redmond **Historic Compromise in the NUS** in 'International' Winter 1977 5pp Partly a response, by IMG Student Organiser, to article by K. Spours, CP Student Organiser, in 'MT' Nov. 1977.

6515 O'Riordan, Manus **Monty Johnstone and the Search for CPGB History** in 'The Communist' (BICO) 109, May 1977 6pp

6516 O'Riordan, Manus **The CPGB and the East European Trials, 1949-53** in 'The Communist' (BICO) 112, Aug. 1977 8pp

6517 O'Riordan, Manus **The CPGB and the East European Trials, 1953-6** in 'The Communist' (BICO) 119, March 1978 4pp

6518 O'Riordan, Manus **The CPGB and the Nagy Trial** in 'The Communist' (BICO) 12, May 1978 4pp

6519 Overell, Stephen **Behind the Barricades** in 'Creator' 3, 1995 6pp Unusual personal view of working on the post CPGB 'MS'.

6520 P.B. **The CP and the Miners' Fight** in 'LM' Jan. 1927 23pp

6521 P.S. **How Not to Get Socialism: The Way of the Communists** in 'Socialist Standard' Feb. 1930 2pp

6522 Page, Malcolm **The Early Years at Unity** in 'Theatre Quarterly' Vol.1 No.4, 1971 7pp

6523 Palmer, Bryan **Reasoning Rebellion: E.P. Thompson, British Marxist Historians and the Making of Dissident Political Mobilization** in 'Labour/Le Travail' 50, 2002 29pp

6524 Palmer, Bryan **Who ARE These Guys? Politics, Passions, Peculiarities and Polemics in the Historiography of British Communism** in 'American Communist History' Vol.4 No.2, 2005 11pp

6525 Papworth, Bert **'Communism and the British T.U.s' by R. Martin – Review** in 'LM' May 1970 2pp

6526 Parker, David **Rodney Hilton: A Tribute** in 'Socialist History' 23, 2003 2pp

6527 Parker, David **The Communist Party and its Historians, 1946-89** in 'Socialist History' 12, 1997 26pp

6527a Parker, David **'The Politics of New Labour: A Gramscian Analysis' by A. Pearmain – Review** in 'Socialist History' 44, 2014 4pp

6528 Parkin, Brian **The Broad Left in TASS** in 'I.S.' No.74, Jan. 1975 4pp

6529 Parsons, Steve **1956 and the CPGB** in 'SSLHB' 47, Autumn 1983 2pp See other Conference reports in same issue.

6530 Parsons, Steve **British CP School Teachers in the 1940s and 1950s** in 'Science and Society' Vol.61 No.1, Spring 1997 22pp

6531 Parsons, Steve **Nineteen Fifty-Six: What Happened in the CPGB?** in 'Revolutionary History' Vol.9 No.3, 2006 12pp

6532 Paterson, Hugh **The Glasgow University Students' Wartime CP Group: A Note** in 'Scottish Labour History' 33, 1998 3pp

6533 Pearce, Brian **'Sources for the History of the CPGB, 1920-39' by A.N. Baikova in 'Transactions of the Library of the USSR Academy of Sciences' Vol.6 (in Russian) – Review** in 'SSLHB' 11, Autumn 1965 1pp Very critical review.

6534 Pearce, Brian **For the 20th Anniversary of H. Pollitt as General Secretary** in 'International' Spring 1977 6pp Written in 1949, this article apppeared in 'Essays on the History of Communism in Britain'.

6535 Pearce, Brian **Marxists in the Second World War** in 'International' Spring 1977 2pp Originally in 'Labour Review' April/May 1959 with pseudonym of 'B. Farnborough'.

6536 Pearce, Brian **The Establishment of Marx House** in 'SSLHB' 16, Spring 1968 2pp

6537 Pearce, Brian **The Last Years of the University Socialist Federation** in 'SSLHB' 4, Spring 1962 2pp On Communist influence among students in the early 20s.

6538 Pearmain, Andrew **Twenty Years On: Whatever Happened to the CPGB?** in 'Socialist History' 38, 2011 25pp

6539 Pelling, Henry **'Harry Pollitt' by J. Mahon – Review** in 'Times Literary Supplement' Sept. 9 1976 1pp

6540 Percy, Walter **British Imperialism and Communist Anti-Militarism** in 'The International of Youth' Jan. 1928 6pp

6541 Perry, Matt **The Jarrow Crusade, the National Hunger March and the Labour Party in 1936** in 'Socialist History' 20, 2001 14pp Argues the NUWM March had more impact than the Jarrow one, despite being marginalised by the media because of its Communist leadership.

6542 Perryman, Mark **Communists and Disarmament** in 'Scottish Marxist' 25, 1982 2pp

6543 Perryman, Mark & Johnson, Alan **New Times and Class Struggle: A Debate with Marxism Today** in 'Workers' Liberty' No.12/13, Aug. 1989 7pp

6543a Petrie, Malcolm **Unity From Below? The Impact of the Spanish Civil War on Labour and the Left in Aberdeen and Dundee, 1936-1939** in 'LHR' Vol.79 No.3, Dec. 2014 25pp Much on relationship between CP, LP & ILP.

6544 Philips, Tamara & Styles, Jean **All For the Cause** in 'Link' Winter 1980 3pp 2 CP Women's Organisers reminisce.

6545 Phillips, Anne & Putnam, Tim **Education for Emancipation: The Movement for Independent Working Class Education, 1908-28** in 'Capital and Class' 10, Spring 1980 25pp

6546 Phillips, Jim **Anti-Communism and Trade-Unionism: A Brief Response to Tom Sibley** in 'HSIR' 29/30, Spring/Autumn 2010 3pp

6547 Phillips, Jim **Inter-Union Conflict in the Docks, 1954-5** in 'HSIR' 1, March 1996 25pp

6548 Phillips, Jim **Labour and the Cold War: The TGWU and the Politics of Anti-Communism, 1945-55** in 'LHR' Spring 1999 19pp

6549 Phillips, Jim **'The Scottish Miners 1874-1939' by A. Campbell – Review** in 'English Historical Review' Vol.117 No.472, June 2002 2pp

6550 Phillips, Jim **Collieries and Communities: The Miners' Strike in Scotland, 1984-1985** in 'Scottish Labour History' 45, 2010 20pp

6551 Piatnitsky, O. **11th Plenum of ECCI: Speech** in 'Inprecorr' July 6 1931 13pp Has much comparative information on CPs of GB, Czechoslovakia, USA, France & Germany on work among unemployed and factory work.

6552 Pickard, Connie **Chopwell: 'Little Moscow'** in 'NELH' 10, 1976 3pp

6553 Pimlott, Herbert **From Old Left to New Labour? Eric Hobsbawm and the Rhetoric of**

Realistic Marxism in *'Labour/Le Travail'* 56, 2005 23pp

6554 Pinel, Carl **End of the CP** in *'Socialist Standard'* May 1991 1pp Also editorial in this issue.

6555 Pirani, Simon **Scottish CP Leaders and the Miners' Strike** in *'Labour Review'* Oct. 1984 8pp

6556 Pirani, Simon **Stalinism and the Miners' Strike** in *'Labour Review'* April 1985 7pp

6557 Piratin, Phil **The CP and the Jewish People** in *'Jewish Forum'* May/June; Workers' Circle Branch No.9 1945 2pp

6558 'Pitcairn, Lee' **Crisis in British Marxism: An Insider's View** in *'NLR'* 153, 1985 20pp

6559 Pitt, Bob **Red Flag Over Saint Pancras** in *'MML Bulletin'* 132, Autumn 2000 20pp Curious episode in the late 1950s involving a group of Trotskyists in the LP in St Pancras (incl. John Lawrence and Hilda Lane) who, as Labour councillors, got the red flag flying from the Town Hall. On being expelled from the LP, they joined, temporarily, the CP. A version had previously appeared in 4 issues of 'What Next?' – Nos 7, 8, 10, 14; 1998-9.

6560 Pitt, Robert **Educator and Agitator: Charlie Gibbons, 1888-1967** in *'Llafur'* Vol.5 No.2, 1989 11pp Attended Communist Unity Convention in London but probably never joined – he was too much of a syndicalist at this stage.

6561 Plant, J.J. & MacLeod, Alison **Brian Pearce 1915-2008 – Obituary** in *'Revolutionary History'* Vol.10 No.1, 2009

6562 'Pleb' **The Popular Front: A Move to the Right** in *'Plebs'* April 1937 2pp Same issue also has T.A. Jackson arguing in favour of Popular Front.

6563 Pocock, Gerry **The Meaning of Unity Through Diversity** in *'WMR'* July 1988 8pp Dialogue on differences in international Communist movement with J. West, CPUSA.

6564 'Politicus' **British Labour and the Bolshevik Danger** in *'Fortnightly Review'* June 1921 14pp Scaremongering.

6565 Pollard, Sidney **'The Leaven of Life' by N. Connole – Review** in *'SSLHB'* 4, Spring 1962 1pp

6566 Pollins, Harold **The Rise (and Fall?) of Adult Education: 'Dons and Workers' by L. Goldman – Review** in *'LHR'* Vol.61 No.2, Summer 1996 4pp

6567 Pollitt, H. **11th Plenum of ECCI: Speech** in *'Inprecorr'* July 6 1931 4pp

6568 Pollitt, H. **12th Party Congress in Britain Marks New Turn To Bolshevik Mass Work** in *'C.I.'* Jan. 15 1933 8pp

6569 Pollitt, H. **7th Congress C.I.: Speech** in *'Inprecorr'* Oct. 30 1935 4pp

6570 Pollitt, H. & Rust, W. **Building A Bolshevik Party in Britain: Speeches to January Plenum of CC CPGB** in *'C.R.'* March 1932 13pp

6571 Pollitt, H. **Five Years of the 'DW'** in *'Inprecorr'* Jan. 5 1935 1pp From Pollitt's speech at Anniversary Celebration at Shoreditch Town Hall, Jan. 2.

6572 Pollitt, H. **In Memoriam – Shapurji Saklatvala** in *'C.I.'* Vol. XIII No.2, 1936 2pp

6573 Pollitt, H. **In Memory of the British Comrades Who Have Fallen in Spain** in *'C.I.'* Feb. 1937 3pp

6574 Pollitt, H. **On the United Front in GB** in *'Inprecorr'* Jan. 30 1934 10pp

6575 Pollitt, H. **Our Party and the Mining Areas** in *'C.R.'* May 1930 9pp

6576 Pollitt, H. **Outlines for Party Training Group Leaders** in *'C.R.'* Nov. 1925 5pp

6577 Pollitt, H. **Shapurji Saklatvala – Obituary** in *'Inprecorr'* Jan. 25 1936 1pp

6578 Pollitt, H. **Speech at 7th Congress of the C.I. Part 1** in *'C.I.'* Aug. 20 1935 9pp Part 2 – Sept. 20 (6pp).

6579 Pollitt, H. **The 13th Congress of the CPGB** in *'C.I.'* March 5 1935 11pp Part of speech to Congress.

6580 Pollitt, H. **The Communists and the ILP** in *'C.R.'* Feb. 1933 8pp

6581 Pollitt, H. **The CP and the Election** in *'LM'* July 1945 5pp

6582 Pollitt, H. **The CP and the Fight for Unity** in *'LM'* Jan. 1942 5pp

6583 Pollitt, H. **The CP and the Whitechapel By-Election** in *'LM'* Jan. 1931 6pp

6584 Pollitt, H. **The CP and Unity** in *'LM'* Feb. 1936 3pp

6585 Pollitt, H. **The CPGB and the 12th Anniversary of the October Revolution** in *'Inprecorr'* Oct. 18 1929 1pp

6586 Pollitt, H. **The CPGB in the Fight for the Masses** in *'C.I.'* Oct. 1 1932 10pp Report & Speeches to 12th Plenum ECCI.

6587 Pollitt, H. **The Derby Conference of the ILP** *in 'C.I.' May 20 1935* 8pp

6588 Pollitt, H. **The Fate of the Working Class is in Our Hands** *in 'Inprecorr' Oct. 17 1936* 1pp Speech to National Conference in Sheffield.

6589 Pollitt, H. **The Labour Party Conference: An Unreal Assembly** *in 'Inprecorr' Oct. 16 1924* 2pp

6590 Pollitt, H. **The Lesson of September 9** *in 'Inprecorr' Sept. 14 1934* 1pp Anti-fascist day of action.

6591 Pollitt, H. **The LP, ILP and the CP** *in 'C.I.' May 15 1934* 6pp

6592 Pollitt, H. **The Meeting of the CC of the CPGB** *in 'Inprecorr' Jan. 12 & Jan. 18 1936* 2;2pp Extended CC Jan. 4 & 5. Dated Jan. 11, but should be Jan. 12.

6593 Pollitt, H. **The Meeting of the CC of the CPGB** *in 'Inprecorr' June 13 1936* 1pp

6594 Pollitt, H. & Dutt, R.P. **The Parliamentary Election in England** *in 'C.I.' Dec. 1935* 15pp 2 articles.

6595 Pollitt, H. **The Party Conference** *in 'C.R.' Feb. 1924* 6pp

6596 Pollitt, H. **The Situation in Britain and the Policy of the National Government** *in 'C.I.' Jan. 15 1934* 11pp Abridged Speech at 13th Plenum ECCI.

6597 Pollitt, H. **The Tasks of the Congress of the YCL** *in 'Inprecorr' June 16 1933* 1pp

6598 Pollitt, H. **The United Front in Britain** *in 'C.R.' March 1933* 8pp

6599 Pollitt, H. **The United Front in GB: From a Speech to the Presidium of the ECCI** *in 'C.I.' Dec. 5 1934* 7pp

6600 Pollitt, H. **The United Front: Next Steps** *in 'C.I.' Jan. 5 1935* 6pp Slightly revised & abridged version of article in 'C.R.' Dec. 1934.

6601 Pollitt, H. **The United Front: Next Steps** *in 'C.R.' Dec. 1934* 8pp

6602 Pollitt, H. **The Work of the CPGB Since the 6th World Congress** *in 'C.I.' Oct. 5 1934* 9pp

6603 Pollitt, H. **The Year Which Has Passed Since the 12th Plenum of the ECCI and the Struggle of the CPGB** *in 'C.I.' Nov. 1 1933* 10pp

6604 Pollitt, H. et al. **Ram Nahum** *in 'University Forward' Vol.8 No.1, Oct. 1942* 9pp Tributes to the Cambridge scientist and student leader killed in air-raid.

6605 Pollitt, H. **CP Congress** *in 'LM' Jan. 1946* 5pp

6606 Pollitt, H. **The CP Congress** *in 'LM' July 1937* 7pp

6607 Pooke, Grant **Francis D. Klingender** *in 'Socialist History' 30, 2007* 20pp

6608 Postgate, Raymond **Communist Comedy** *in 'Socialist Review' (ILP) April 1934* 13pp Esp. on CP and LRD.

6609 Postgate, Raymond & Horrabin, J.F. **Trotsky's 'Comrades'** *in 'Plebs' July 1925* 2pp Authors reply to attacks on them in June issue of 'LM' by Dutt, Ewer & Braun. Horrabin explains why he left CP. Further letters in Aug. issue.

6610 Pottins, Charlie **How Britain's Stalinists Spied on the Left** *in 'The Original Dorril Lobster' 31, 1996* 5pp Trotskyist view.

6611 Potts, Archie **'Memoirs of the Left' by J. Saville – Review** *in 'North East History' 35, 2004* 4pp

6612 Powderly, Alan **The James Klugmann Archive** *in 'Praxis: Bulletin of the MML' 153, Autumn 2011* 3pp Includes biographical material.

6613 Powell, Glyn **Turning off the Power: The Electrical Trades Union and the Anti-Communist Crusade** *in 'Contemporary British History' Vol.18 No.2, 2004* 26pp Discusses the CP's tendancy to equate TU leadership with political leadership, as well as the anti-Communist right-wing machine.

6613a Powles, John Janey **Buchan – Obituary** *in 'SLHS' 47, 2012* 1p

6614 Power, Mike **The Party's Not Over: Interview with Nina Temple** *in 'New Statesman' Nov. 22 1991* 1pp The last interview with a CP (General) Secretary.

6615 Price, John **The Communist Wedge Again** *in 'Labour Magazine' Nov. 1932* 2pp

6616 Price, M. Phillips **Impressions of the General Election** *in 'C.I.' 24, 1923 ?* 4pp Article taken from Inprecorr Dec. 27.

6617 Price, M. Phillips **Impressions of the General Election in England** *in 'Inprecorr' Dec. 27 1922* 2pp On his campaign as official Labour candidate in Gloucester (he lost by only 51 votes).

6618 Prior, Mike **Communist Labour Relations** *in 'MT' Feb. 1978* 5pp

6619 Priscott, Dave **The CP and the LP** *in 'MT' Jan. 1974* 10pp

6620 Priscott, Dave **The Problem of Communist-Labour Relationships** in 'MT' Oct. 1977 7pp

6621 Prynn, David **The Woodcraft Folk and the Labour Movement, 1925-70** in 'JOCH' Vol.18 No.1, Jan. 1983 18pp Briefly deals with the CP's slightly ambivalent attitude to the organisation.

6622 Purdie, Bob **For a Free Debate on Stalinism and Trotskyism** in 'International' May 1969 3pp Rather arcane, but fair, contribution to the debate between YCL and Keep Left on whether to have a debate on 'Stalinism and Trotskyism'.

6623 Putnam, Tim **'Proletarian Science' by S. MacIntyre – Review** in 'Radical Science Journal' 13 1983 10pp

6624 Quelch, H. **The British LP Conference** in 'Inprecorr' July 17 1922 2pp On Pollitt's speech about affiliation.

6625 Quelch, Tom & MacLaine, W. **Report As to the Communist Movement in Britain** in 'C.I.' 11/12 June/July 1920 2pp

6626 Quelch, Tom **The Attack on the Party** in 'C.R.' Jan. 1926 5pp

6627 R.G. **The Achilles Heel of Communist Theory?** in 'This Unrest' Ruskin College 1933 15pp Reply to G.D.H. Cole.

6628 R.P. **The Fraud of 'British Bolshevism'** in 'Labour Review' Nov. 1978 8pp Review of 'Harry McShane: No Mean Fighter'.

6629 Rafeek, Neil **'Opening the Books' by G. Andrews et al. – Review** in 'SLHS' 30, 1995 2pp

6630 Rafeek, Neil **'The Enemy Within' by F. Beckett – Review** in 'SLHS' 31, 1996 2pp

6631 Rafeek, Neil **Agnes McLean, 1918-94** in 'SLHS' 30 1995 10pp McLean was an engineering worker in the CP 1942-69 who was on many of its leading bodies; she was later a Labour councillor in Glasgow.

6632 Rafeek, Neil **Mabel Skinner 1912-1996: Communist Politics Amongst a Highlands Community** in 'Scottish Labour History' 33, 1998 20pp

6633 Rafeek, Neil **Rose Kerrigan, 1903-1995** in 'SLHS' 31, 1996 12pp

6634 Ramelson, Bert **The British Communists' Strategy** in 'WMR' Nov. 1979 2pp

6635 Ramsay, Robin **'Britain's Secret Propaganda War' by P. Lashmar & J. Oliver – Review** in 'Lobster' 37, 1999 1pp

6636 Ramsay, Robin **Moscow Gold: The 'Communist Threat' in Post-War Britain** in 'Lobster' 25, 1993 4pp On CP in industry – useful for refs to Seamen's Strike of 1966. Concludes that MI5 knew details of 'Moscow Gold'.

6637 Ramsay, Robin **The Clandestine Caucus: Anti-Socialist Campaigns and Operations in the British Labour Movement Since the War** Lobster 1996 33pp Special ed. of the magazine 'Lobster'.

6638 Ratner, Harry **Remembering 1956** in 'Revolutionary History' Vol.9 No.3, 2006 4pp

6639 Ratner, Harry **Ruth Frow – Obituary** in 'Revolutionary History' 2012 2pp

6640 Rattenbury, Arnold **Total Attainders and the Helots** in 'Renaissance & Modern Studies' Vol.20, 1976 17pp Esp. on 'Our Times'

6641 Raynes, John **Communism on the Sea** in 'Empire Review' Dec. 1927 3pp

6642 Raynes, John **Communists and Rebellion** in 'The National Review' March 1929 6pp

6643 Redfern, Neil **A British Version of 'Browderism': British Communists and the Teheran Conference** in 'Science and Society' Vol.66 No.3, Fall 2002 20pp

6644 Redfern, Neil **British Communists, The British Empire and the Second World War** in 'ILWCH' Vol.65, April 2004 18pp

6645 Redfern, Neil **Winning the Peace: British Communists, The Soviet Union and the General Election of 1945** in 'Contemporary British History' Vol.16 No.1, Spring 2002 22pp

6646 'Redman, J' **British Communist History** in 'Labour Review' July/Aug. 1957 4pp Revised version of his 'The CP and the Labour Left, 1925-9'.

6647 'Redman, J.' **British Stalinists and the Moscow Trials** in 'Labour Review' March/April 1958 7pp Reprinted in 'Moscow Trials Anthology' New Park, 1967.

6648 'Redman, J.' **From Social Fascism to People's Front** in 'Labour Review' Sept/Oct. 1957 5pp

6649 'Redman, J.' **The Early Years of the CPGB** in 'Labour Review' Jan/Feb. 1958 12pp

6650 Rees, David **The Old and the New Left** in 'Interplay' Dec. 1969 4pp

6651 Rees, John & Humber, Lee **Rodney Hilton Interviewed** in 'Socialist Review' March 1992 3pp

6652 Reid, Betty **CP Archive** in *'Our History Journal'* 12, Jan. 1988 2pp

6653 Reid, Betty **The New Party Rules** in *'CR'* July 1952 6pp

6654 Reid, Betty **The Present Stage of Our Factory Organisation** in *'CR'* Sept. 1952 4pp

6655 Reid, F. **Socialist Sunday Schools in Britain, 1892-1939** in *'IRSH'* Vol.2 Part 1, 1957 30pp Bit on involvement of A Gossip; generally CP not involved after 1922 when it formally distanced itself from the movement.

6656 Reiss, Matthias **Circulars, Surveys and Support: Trades Councils and the Marches of 1936** in *'LHR'* Vol.73 No.1, April 2008 24pp

6657 Renshaw, George **How Does the Party Work? Some Problems of T.U. Work** in *'C.R.'* Dec. 1933/Jan. 1934 4pp

6658 Renton, Dave **'History in the Making' by S. Woodhams – Review** in *'NWLHSB'* 27, 2002 1pp

6659 Renton, Dave **An Unbiased Watch? The Police and Fascist/Anti-Fascist Street Conflict in Britain, 1945-51** in *'Lobster'* 35, Summer 1988 7pp See also Lobster 36 for some correspondence.

6660 Renton, Dave **Anti-Fascism in the North West: 1976-1982** in *'NWLHSB'* 27, 2002 12pp Well researched article which contrasts views and activities of left-wing and anti-racist groups.

6661 Renton, Dave **Necessary Myth or Collective Truth? Cable Street Revisited** in *'Changing English'* Oct. 1998 5pp

6662 Renton, Dave **Not Just Economics but Politics as Well: Trade Unions, Labour Movement Activists and Anti-Fascist Protests, 1945-51** in *'LHR'* Vol.65 No.2, Summer 2000 15pp

6663 Renton, Dave **Opening the Books: The Personal Papers of Dona Torr** in *'HWJ'* 52, 2001 10pp Torr was founder member of CP and its Historians' Group.

6664 Renton, Dave **Past Its Peak: 'History of the CPGB, 1941-51' by N. Branson – Review** in *'ISJ'* 77, Winter 1997 13pp

6665 Renton, Dave **The History Woman: Dona Torr** in *'Socialist Review'* 224, Nov. 1998 2pp

6666 Renton, David **Studying Their Own Nation Without Insularity? The British Marxist Historians Reconsidered** in *'Science and Society'* Vol.69 No.4, Oct. 2005 21pp Discusses the impact of popularism and nationalism on this Group's work.

6667 Reynolds, Steve **Building the Early Communist Party** in *'Bulletin of Marxist Studies'* Vol.1 No.5, Spring 1986 3pp Militant's internal theoretical journal.

6668 Richards, Frank & Turner, Phil **Stalinism, the CP and the RCG's New Turn** in *'Revolutionary Communist Papers'* No.1, March 1977 30pp Lengthy reply to discussion on changes in the CPGB with reprints of the original articles by D. Yaffe & R. Dornhorst from internal RCG documents.

6669 Richardson, Al **'Labour – Communist Relations, 1920-51' by N. Branson & B. Moore – Review** in *'LHR'* Vol.57 No.1, Spring 1992 1pp

6670 Richardson, Al **'Out of the Ghetto' by J. Jacobs – Review** in *'Revolutionary History'* Vol.5 No.1, Autumn 1993 2pp

6671 Richardson, Al **'The Good Old Cause' by W. Thompson – Review** in *'Revolutionary History'* Vol.5 No.2, Spring 1994 4pp A critical, Trotskyist, review by the journal's editor.

6672 Richardson, Al **Frank Maitland – Obituary** in *'Revolutionary History'* Vol.8 No.1, 2001 3pp Active in CP from 1930 in Edinburgh, left and joined the extremely small Revolutionary Socialist Party in 1936.

6673 Richardson, Maurice **A Worker's Notebook** in *'New Statesman'* Dec. 27 1974 Amusing memoirs of literary/political circles in 1930s; continued in next 2 issues.

6674 Richardson, Tommy **An Election Pen-Picture** in *'LM'* June 1958 2pp Councillor in Durham coalfield.

6675 Rickaby, Tony **The Artists' International** in *'Block'* No.1, 1979 4pp Many comments on CP artists. This is the original, and 'unedited', version of article that first appeared in 'HW' 6.

6676 Roberts, Edwin **From the History of Science to the Science of History: Scientists and Historians in the Shaping of British Marxist History** in *'Science and Society'* Vol.69 No.4, Oct. 2005 30pp

6677 Roberts, Geoff & Callinicos, Alex **The British Road Debate** in *'I.S.'* No.99, June 1977 6pp

6678 Roberts, Helen **Years of Struggle: The Life and Work of Robin Page Arnot** in *'LHR'* Vol.59 No.2, Autumn 1994 6pp Incl. details of deposits of his papers in Hull.

6679 Roberts, Hugh **The Student Movement and the CPGB** in 'Labour & Trade Union Review' No.26, Nov./Dec. 1991 5pp

6680 'Roberts, Owen' **Prospects for the British Labor Party ... Brightened by the Crises in Toryism and Stalinism** in 'The New International' Vol.23 No.2, Spring 1957 13pp Pseudonym of Bernard Dix.

6680a Roberts, Stephen **Memories of Dottie: Dorothy Thompson (1923-2011)** in 'LHR' Vol.76 No.2, Aug. 2011 7pp

6681 Robinson, Bruce **New Findings from the Moscow Archives** in 'Revolutionary History' Vol.6 No.2/3, Summer 1986 4pp On CP History Network conference.

6682 Robinson, Emily **New Times, New Politics: History and Memory During the Final Years of the CPGB** in 'British Politics' Vol.6 No.4, 2011 25pp 'Examines the relationship between collective memory, historical interpretation and political identity'.

6683 Robson, R.W. **A Tribute to Joe Hinks** in 'Volunteer For Liberty' Nov./Dec. 1945 1pp Hinks served as Commander of British Battalion in 1937; he worked for CP in E Anglia & died in Japanese POW camp.

6684 Robson, R.W. **Party Recruiting and Building Campaign** in 'C.R.' Feb. 1935 2pp

6685 Robson, R.W. **The 13th Plenum and the Organisation of the British Party** in 'C.R.' April 1934 3pp ECCI.

6686 Robson, R.W. **Why the Party Does Not Grow** in 'C.R.' Dec. 1934 4pp

6687 'Roebuck, C.M.' **Factory Groups** in 'C.R.' June 1924 5pp

6688 'Roebuck, C.M.' **Four Years of Struggle** in 'C.R.' Aug. 1924 9pp

6689 'Roebuck, C.M.' **The LP and the Workers' Struggle** in 'C.I.' 10 (New Series), 1925 15pp

6690 Rosen, Harold **A Necessary Myth: Cable Street Revisited** in 'Changing English' March 1998 8pp

6691 Rosenhaft, Eve **Communisms and Communities: Britain and Germany Between the Wars** in 'The Historical Journal' Vol.26 No.1, March 1983 16pp Review article of several books in German and English ('Little Moscows', 'History of CPGB').

6692 Rosser, Mary **Daily Worker/Morning Star: The Role of a Revolutionary Paper** in 'Communist Campaign Review' Winter 1987 3pp

6693 Rosser, Mary **Jack Dywien – Obituary** in 'MML Bulletin' 135, Spring 2002 1pp

6694 Rosser, Mary **Sixty Fighting Years** in 'Communist Review' (CPB) 6, Spring 1990 4pp On 'DW' & 'MS'.

6695 Rosser, Mary **The Communist Parties and Destalinisation** in 'Communist Review' (CPB) 26, Autumn/Winter 1997 3pp

6696 Rothstein, Andrew **'The British Communist Party' by L. Macfarlane – Review** in 'LM' July 1966 2pp

6697 Rothstein, Andrew **'The Revolutionary Movement in Britain 1900-21' by W. Kendall – Review** in 'LM' Dec. 1969 3pp

6698 Rothstein, Andrew **Britain: The Sixtieth TUC** in 'RILU' Oct. 1928 5pp He highlights CP involvement.

6699 Rothstein, Andrew **British Communists and the Comintern, 1919-1929** in 'Communist Review' (CPB) 10, Summer 1991 12pp N.B. says Summer on cover, Spring inside.

6700 Rothstein, Andrew **Clemens Palme Dutt – Obituary** in 'LM' May 1975 1pp

6701 Rothstein, Andrew **CP History** in 'SSLHB' 36, Spring 1978 2pp On CP policy 1939-41; a Reply to M. Johnstone (Johnstone answered in No.37).

6702 Rothstein, Andrew **From Revisionism to Liberalism** in 'Communist Review' (CPB) 6, Spring 1990 3pp On 'MFNT'.

6703 Rothstein, Andrew **Harry Pollitt** in 'SSLHB' 34, Spring 1977 6pp Reply to M. Johnstone (see previous issue).

6704 Rothstein, Andrew **Maurice Dobb – Obituary** in 'MML Bulletin' 80, Oct./Dec. 1976 2pp

6705 Rothstein, Andrew **Mr Pelling on the CP: 'The British CP' by H. Pelling – Review** in 'MT' Nov. 1958 7pp

6706 Rothstein, Andrew **R.P. Arnot – Obituary** in 'MML Bulletin' 108, Autumn/Winter 1986 2pp

6707 Rothstein, Andrew **R.P. Arnot Remembered** in 'MML Bulletin' 118, Spring 1993 3pp

6708 Rothstein, Andrew & Arnot, R. Page **The British Communist Party and Euro-Communism** in 'Political Affairs' Vol.LXIV No.10, Oct. 1985 6pp

6709 Rothstein, Andrew **The Left Wing in 1928** in 'LM' Jan. 1928 18pp

6710 Rothstein, Andrew et al. **R.P. Dutt – Tribute** in 'LM' Feb. 1975 18pp

6711 Rothstein, Theodore **The Edinburgh Conference of the LP** in 'C.I.' Special Congress Number 1922 6pp

6712 Rowan, Caroline **Dora Cox: Interview** in 'Link' Spring 1981 2pp

6713 Rowan, Caroline **Only Yesterday: Jean Massey Interview** in 'Link' Summer 1982 2pp

6714 Rowland, Anthony **'Voices' Magazine: A Cultural History** in 'NWLHSB' 34, 2009/10 4pp Ben Ainley and the CP's role in setting up this cultural magazine of working class writing.

6715 Roy, M.N. **Election Policy of the British CP** in 'Inprecorr' Oct. 23 1924 1pp

6716 Roy, M.N. **Newbold 'Explains'** in 'Inprecorr' Oct. 9 1924 1pp

6717 Russell, Ralph **On Election Policy** in 'Communist Review' (CPB) 43, Spring 2005 4pp Argues that the 1935 election was the only one the CP gave serious thought to.

6718 Russell, Thomas **Rutland Boughton – Obituary** in 'LM' March 1960 2pp

6719 Rust, W. **12th Anniversary of the 'DW'** in 'LM' Jan. 1942 1pp

6720 Rust, W. **13th Plenum ECCI: Speech** in 'Inprecorr' March 5 1934 1pp

6721 Rust, W. **Communists and the Army** in 'The Communist' June 1928 4pp

6722 Rust, W. **CP Congress at Leeds** in 'LM' Jan. 1930 5pp

6723 Rust, W. **Fenner Brockway Drops His Mask** in 'C.I.' July 15 1933 4pp

6724 Rust, W. **How the Ban Was Lifted** in 'LM' Oct. 1942 5pp

6725 Rust, W. **How the Leaders of the ILP Sabotage the United Front** in 'C.I.' Sept. 1 1933 4pp

6726 Rust, W. & Pollitt, H. **Speech at 10th Plenum ECCI, 6th Session July 5** in 'Inprecorr' Aug. 21 1929 2pp

6727 Rust, W. **The 'Daily Worker'** in 'C.R.' June 1930 6pp

6728 Rust, W. **The 'DW' and the National Front** in 'LM' Aug. 1941 3pp

6729 Rust, W. **The 12th Congress of the CPGB** in 'Inprecorr' Nov. 24 1932 1pp

6730 Rust, W. **The 12th Congress of the CPGB on the Tasks of the Revolutionary T.U. Movement** in 'RILU' Vol.3 No.1, Feb. 1933 6pp

6731 Rust, W. **The 1st Anniversary of the British 'DW'** in 'Inprecorr' Jan. 8 1931 1pp

6732 Rust, W. **The 2nd Anniversary of the London 'DW'** in 'Inprecorr' Jan. 2 1932 1pp

6733 Rust, W. **The 3rd National Conference of the YCL** in 'The International of Youth' New Series No.1, 1925 6pp This was the Organ of the EC of the YCI.

6734 Rust, W. **The British Labour Government Endeavouring to Cripple the 'DW'** in 'Inprecorr' July 17 1930 1pp

6735 Rust, W. **The Coming Congress of the CPGB** in 'C.I.' Jan. 15 1929 7pp

6736 Rust, W. **The CP Congress** in 'LM' Dec. 1932 6pp

6737 Rust, W. **The ILP Changes Its Line** in 'C.I.' June 1 1933 5pp

6738 Rust, W. **The London 'DW'** in 'C.I.' Oct. 15 1933 4pp

6739 Rust, W. **The Minority Movement** in 'C.I.' Dec. 15 1929 2pp

6740 Rust, W. **The Situation in the CPGB** in 'C.I.' Sept. 15 1930 7pp

6741 Rust, W. **The YCL Prepares** in 'C.R.' Sept. 1929 5pp

6742 Rust, W. **Towards a United Revolutionary Party** in 'LM' July 1933 9pp

6743 Rust, W. **Under the Banner of the C.I. in Britain** in 'C.I.' March 1 1934 10pp

6744 Rutherford, Malcolm **Turning Point: 'About Turn' ed. F. King & G. Mathews – Review** in 'MT' Jan. 1991 1pp

6745 Ryan, James **The Superterranean World of British Communst Historiography** in 'American Communist History' Vol.4 No.2, 2005 5pp

6746 Ryan, Paul **Apprentice Strikes in the Twentieth-Century UK Engineering and Shipbuilding Industries** in 'HSIR' 18, Autumn 2004 64pp

6747 Rycroft, Charles **Memoirs of an Old Bolshevik** in 'New Society' May 29 1969 1pp Oxbridge in 1930s.

6748 Ryder, Brian **Marxism and the LBC** in 'MML Bulletin' 123, Spring/Summer 1995 6pp

6749 Safarov, G. **The Leeds Congress of the CPGB** in 'C.I.' Jan. 15 1930 7pp

6750 Sagar, Seth **Seth Sagar's Memoirs: Part 2** in 'NWLHSB' 34, 2009/10 8pp Nelson weaver.

6751 Samuel, Raphael **The Lost World of British Communism Part 2: Staying Power** in 'NLR' 156, 1986 51pp

6752 Samuel, Raphael **British Marxist Historians Part 1** in *'NLR'* 120, 1980 77pp

6753 Samuel, Raphael (ed.) **Documents and Texts from the Workers' Theatre Movement (1928-36)** in *'HWJ'* 4, 1977 10pp

6754 Samuel, Raphael **Jews and Socialism: The End of a Beautiful Friendship?** in *'Jewish Quarterly'* No.2, 1988 2pp

6755 Samuel, Raphael **Re-opening Old Wounds** in *'MT'* Oct. 1986 2pp Reply to 'Close Up on Mick McGahey'.

6756 Samuel, Raphael **The Lost World of British Communism Part 1** in *'NLR'* 154, 1985 52pp Author uses mix of archives, memories, fiction to recreate the moral universe of the CP during its most influential period.

6757 Samuel, Raphael **The Lost World of British Communism Part 3: Class in British Communism** in *'NLR'* 165, 1987 42pp Looks at the split in the CP, then the industrial practices of the CP, workerism and the role of Communists in industry from the mid 1960s to mid 1970s.

6758 Samuel, Raphael **The Lost World of British Communism: Texts** in *'NLR'* 155, 1986 6pp One is about E. Upward.

6759 Samuels, Stuart **The Left Book Club** in *'JOCH'* Vol.1 No.2, April 1966 22pp

6760 Samuels, Stuart et al. **The English Left Intelligentsia in the 1930s** in *'SSLHB'* 14, Spring 1967 2pp Abstract of Conference paper & discussion.

6761 Sanders, William **Fighting Communism Without Gloves** in *'Labour Magazine'* June 1929 2pp On Battersea and Saklatvala.

6762 Sanderson, Heather **Eurocommunism and the new 'BRS'** in *'Communist' (CCG)* March 1988 3pp

6763 Sansom, C.J. **Anti-Communism and Apartheid: The British T.U. Movement and South Africa, 1945-54** in *'SSLHB'* 46, Spring 1983 6pp

6764 Saville, John **A Further Note on British Communist History** in *'New Reasoner'* No.8, 1959 3pp Further review of Pelling.

6765 Saville, John **E.P. Thompson – Obituary** in *'IRSH'* Vol.38 Part 3, 1993 6pp

6766 Saville, John **Robin Page Arnot – Obituary** in *'SSLHB'* 51 Part 3, 1986 3pp

6767 Saville, John **Vivien Morton, 1911-90 – Obituary** in *'Our History Journal'* 16, Nov. 1990 1pp Reprinted from 'The Guardian'.

6768 Schapiro, Rose **Inside the 'Morning Star'** in *'The Leveller'* 20, Nov. 1978 1pp

6769 Schneer, Jonathan **'The History of the CPGB, 1941-1951' by N. Branson – Review** in *'ILWCH'* Vol.56, Oct. 1999 2pp

6770 Schwarz, Bill **Claudia Jones and the West Indian Gazette: Reflections on the Emergence of Post-Colonial Britain** in *'Twentieth Century British History'* Vol.14 No.3, Sept. 2003 20pp

6771 Scott, Andrew **Britain's War Remains Imperialist** in *'Workers' International News'* June 1941 5pp

6772 Scullion, Adrienne **Glasgow Unity Theatre: The Necessary Contradictions of Scottish Political Theatre** in *'Twentieth Century British History'* Vol.13 No.3, 2002 38pp

6772a Searle, Chris **Excellence in the Ordinary: The Poetry of Peter Blackman** in *'Race & Class'* Vol.55 No.1, July/Sept 2013 14pp

6773 Seaton, Matt **Firebrands: 'The Enemy Within' by F. Beckett – Review** in *'Literary Review'* March 1995 2pp

6774 Seifert, Roger **'End Games and New Times: The Final Years of British Communism, 1964-1991' by G. Andrews – Review** in *'HSIR'* 19, Spring 2005 3pp

6775 Seifert, Roger & Sibley, Tom **Communists and the Trade Union Left Revisited: The Case of the UK 1964-1979** in *'World Review of Political Economy'* Vol.1 No.1, June 2010 14pp

6776 Seifert, Roger **English Teachers' Unions and Anti-Communism in the 1950s: The Contrasting Cases of Durham and Middlesex** in *'HSIR'* 27/28, Spring/Autumn 2009 31pp

6777 Seifert, Roger **Some Aspects of Factional Opposition: Rank and File and the National Union of Teachers, 1967-82** in *'BJOIR'* Nov. 1984 19pp Mainly on IS/SWP and Rank & File, but information also on CP in the NUT.

6778 Selkirk, Bob **Fife Miners and the CP** in *'C.R.'* March 1929 4pp

6779 Sells, David **Communist Discord** in *'The Listener'* May 30 1985 1pp On 39th Congress.

6780 Shelmerdine, Brian **Britons in an 'UnBritish' War: Domestic Newspapers and the Participation of UK Nationals in the Spanish Civil War** in *'NWLHSB'* 22, 1997 26pp

6781 Shepherd, Anna **Helen Biggar: Film Maker and Sculptor** in *'SLHR'* 10, 1996 3pp

Continued in No.11; unfortunately very little on her CP activity.

6782 Shepherd, John **Professor Philip Bagwell (1914-2006) – Obituary** in 'LHR' Vol.71 No.3, Dec. 2006 2pp

6783 Sherwood, Marika **Peter Blackman, 1909-1993 – Obituary** in 'HWJ' 37, Spring 1994 1pp Active in the Negro Welfare Association, LAI, Colonial Information Bulletin.

6784 Sherwood, Marika **The Comintern, The CPGB, Colonies and Black Britons, 1920-38** in 'Science and Society' Vol.60 No.2, Summer 1996 27pp

6785 Shields, Jim **A Survey of the London 'DW'** in 'Inprecorr' July 14 1932 2pp A 'positive criticism' for the first 4 months of 1932. Shields was CP's rep. in Moscow, later serving as ed. of the 'DW' – though this position was never acknowledged publically because of the possiblity of legal action against the paper.

6786 Shields, Jim **J.T. Murphy's Desertion to the Class Enemy** in 'C.I.' July 15 1932 3pp

6787 Shields, Jim **One Year of the January Resolution** in 'C.R.' March 1933 8pp

6788 Shields, Jim **The CPGB and Trade Union Activity** in 'C.I.' Aug. 15 1932 6pp

6789 Shields, Jim **The Issue Before the ILP Conference** in 'Inprecorr' March 23 1934 2pp

6790 Shields, Jim **The National Congress of Action and the Hunger March** in 'Inprecorr' March 2 1934 2pp

6791 Shields, Jim **United Front Developments in GB** in 'Inprecorr' April 7 1933 1pp

6792 Shipley, Peter **The British Poor Relations** in 'The Spectator' June 28 1975 1pp

6793 Short, George **The General Strike and Class Struggles in the North East, 1925-8** in 'MT' Oct. 1970 10pp

6794 Sibley, Tom **Fighting Anti-Communism, 1945-1950: The Case of the Fire Brigades Union** in 'HSIR' 27/28, Spring/Autumn 2009 38pp

6795 Sibley, Tom **'Memoirs of A Militant' by K. Halpin – Review** in 'Praxis' 156 Spring 2013 2pp

6796 Siederer, N.D. **The Campbell Case** in 'JOCH' Vol.9 No.2, April 1974 20pp

6797 Silver, Steve **70 Fighting Years: Interview with Alex McFadden** in 'RMT News' June 2010 2pp NUR activist and leader. In CP till 1950s.

6798 Silver, Steve **From Anti-Fascist War to Cold War: The Jewish Community and the Fight Against Fascism – The Defence Debate, 1946-1950** in 'Searchlight' 320, Feb. 2002 6pp On the 43 Group. Refs to Maurice Essex and Jack Perry (CP members on the Trades Advisory Council of the Board of Deputies of British Jews – and Perry was on the Board itself). Essex ran the CP Businessmen's Forum, which raised funds for Piratin's 1945 election victory. Several activists mentioned in this article also feature in the formation of the 62 Group – see 'Searchlight' 325, July 2002.

6799 Silver, Steve **They Shall Not Pass: The Jewish Community and the Fight Against Fascism – The Defence Debate, 1934-1945** in 'Searchlight' No.319, Jan. 2002 4pp Much on Cable Street.

6800 Simms, Roger **The Struggle to Found the 'DW'** in 'The Marxist: Bulletin for the '90s' No.3, May 1991 3pp Militant's internal theoretical journal.

6801 Simon, Brian **Great Britain: New Possibilities Are Opening Out in the Work Among Intellectuals & Professional Workers** in 'WMR' Oct. 1961 2pp

6802 Simons, Brian **G.C.T. Giles – Obituary** in 'LM' Dec. 1976 1pp

6803 Simons, Ralph **The Workplace and the CP** in 'MT' Jan. 1979 6pp

6804 Sinfield, George **The 'DW': Paper of the Working Class** in 'WMR' Jan. 1961 2pp

6805 Slater, H. **The Charter Campaign: A Criticism** in 'C.R.' Oct. 1932 7pp

6806 Slater, Hugh **The Tactical Line of the London DPC** in 'C.R.' June 1935 4pp

6807 Slater, Montagu **Gallacher: The Man and the Movement** in 'Inprecorr' May 30 1936 1pp Review of 'Revolt on the Cyde'.

6808 Slater, Montagu **'The British CP' by T. Bell – Review** in 'Inprecorr' April 3 1937 1pp Lengthy review, critical but not as bad as that of A. Hutt's in 'LM' in June.

6809 Slater, Montagu **The 'Daily Herald' Offensive Against Unity** in 'Inprecorr' July 25 1936 1pp

6810 Slater, Montagu **May Day in Britain** in 'Inprecorr' May 9 1936 1pp Mainly on London.

6811 Smethurst, John **Ruth Frow: A Life in Labour History** in 'NWLHSB' 33, 2008/9 1pp

6812 Smith, Cyril **Marxism and British Communist History** in 'Labour Review' June

1977 20pp Review of 4 books on CP that appeared in 1975-6.

6813 Smith, Elaine R. **East End Tailors, 1918-1939: An Aspect of the Jewish Workers' Struggle** in *'Jewish Quarterly'* Vol.34 No.2 (126), 1987 4pp Sam Elsbury and the United Clothing Workers' Union, and Sara Wesker.

6814 Smith, Evan **1968: Too Little and Too Late? The CP and Race Relations in the Late 1960s** in *'Critique'* Vol.36 No.3, Dec. 2008 21pp

6815 Smith, Evan **A Bulwark Diminished? The CP, the SWP and Anti-Fascism in the 1970s** in *'Socialist History'* 35, 2009 22pp

6816 Smith, Evan **Are the Kids United? The CPGB, Rock Against Racism and the Politics of Youth Culture** in *'Journal for the Study of Radicalism'* Vol.5 No.2, 2011 33pp

6817 Smith, Evan **'Class Before Race': British Communism and the Place of Empire in Postwar Race Relations** in *'Science and Society'* Vol.72 No.4, Oct. 2008 26pp

6818 Smith, Evan **Fighting Oppression Wherever it Exists: The CPGB and the Struggle Against Racism, 1962-1981** in *'ERAS'* 7, 2005 ERAS is an online, fully refereed post-graduate journal from Monash Univ.

6819 Smith, Evan **Industrial Militancy, Reform and the 1970s: A Review of Recent Contributions to CPGB Historiography** in *'Flinders Journal of History and Politics'* 23, 2006 13pp

6820 Smith, Evan **The Communist Party and Immigration** in *'MML Bulletin'* 145, Winter 2006 15pp 1962 to late 1970s.

6821 Smith, Evan **When the Party Comes Down: The CPGB and Youth Culture, 1976-1991** in *'Twentieth Century Communism'* 4, 2012 38pp Largely about music.

6822 Smith, Harold **John Gorman, 1930-96 – Obituary** in *'HWJ'* 47, 1999 4pp

6823 Smith, James **The Radical Literary Magazine of the 1930s and British Government Surveillance: The Case of 'Storm' Magazine** in *'Literature and History'* Vol.19 No.2, Oct. 2010 13pp Surprisingly, MI5 have a large file on this revolutionary journal – and possess one of only 2 complete collections. Its ambitious ed., Douglas Jefferies, tried to establish it as the official Comintern literary journal for Britain. It was not an official CP journal, but Jefferies was a member, and Tom Wintringham was placed on the ed. board by the CP (A.P. Roley was another board member).

6824 Smith, Lyn **Covert British Propaganda** in *'Millennium: Journal of International Studies'* Spring 1980 17pp On the anti-Communist Information Research Department.

6825 Smith, Paul **'John Maclean and the CPGB' by R. Pitt – Review** in *'New Interventions'* Winter 1996 3pp

6826 Smith, Peter **'The General Strike' by J. Skelley & 'The 1926 General Strike in Lanarkshire' by J. Maclean – Review** in *'Scottish Marxist'* 12, 1976 7pp

6827 Smith, Rose **Women and Organisation for Struggle** in *'C.R.'* July 1933 5pp

6828 Smith, Rose **Women and the Revolutionary Movement in GB** in *'Inprecorr'* Feb. 28 1931 1pp

6829 Snowman, Daniel **Eric Hobsbawm: Interview** in *'History Today'* Jan. 1999 3pp

6830 Somerville, Dennis **Celia Somerville** in *'LM'* April 1979 3pp Speech at Memorial Meeting.

6831 Spence **13th Plenum ECCI: Speech** in *'Inprecorr'* April 23 1934 1pp On YCL.

6832 Spence, W. **Experiences of the YCL of GB** in *'The International of Youth'* (U.S.) June 1934 3pp From speech at Plenum of YCI.

6833 Spender, Stephen **The Case of Edward Upward** in *'London Magazine'* March 1987 16pp

6834 Spooner, David **Stalinism and British Writing in the 1930s** in *'Marxist'* Vol.6 No.3, 1968 5pp

6835 Spooner, David **The Crisis of British Stalinism** in *'Marxist'* Vol.7 No.2, 1969 5pp

6836 Springhall, Dave **Fifty Thousand Communists** in *'LM'* May 1942 2pp

6837 Springhall, Dave **London Communists in Conference** in *'C.R.'* Aug. 1935 6pp

6838 Springhall, Dave **The Annual District Congress of the London CP** in *'Inprecorr'* June 22 1935 1pp

6839 Springhall, Dave **The Struggle for the United Front in GB** in *'Inprecorr'* July 27 1934 1pp

6840 Squires, Mike **British Communists and Elections, 1920-1935** in *'Communist Review'* (CPB) 40, Spring 2004 8pp

6841 Squires, Mike **British Communists and the Communist International** in *'Communist Review'* (CPB) 29, Spring 1999 6pp Review of 'The Political Trajectory of J.T. Murphy' by R. Darlington.

6842 Squires, Mike **'Class Against Class: The CP in Britain between the Wars' by M. Worley – Review** in 'Socialist History' 25, 2004 3pp

6843 Squires, Mike **Communists and the Fight Against Racism During the Class Against Class Period, 1928-1933** in 'Communist Review' (CPB) 32, Summer 2000 8pp

6844 Squires, Mike **CPGB Membership During the 'Class Against Class' Years** in 'Socialist History' 3, 1993 10pp

6845 Squires, Mike **'Molly Murphy: Suffragette and Socialist – An Autobiography' ed. R. Darlington – Review** in 'MML Bulletin' 129, Winter 1998/9 4pp

6846 Squires, Mike **Shapurji Saklatvala and the Fight Against Racism and Imperialism, 1921-8** in 'The Marxist' CPI(M) Oct. 1995 16pp

6847 Srebrnik, Henry **Class, Ethnicity and Gender Intertwined: Jewish Women and the East London Rent Strikes, 1935-40** in 'Women's History Review' Vol.4 No.3, 1995 17pp

6848 Srebrnik, Henry **Communism and Pro-Soviet Feeling Among the Jews of East London, 1935-45** in 'Immigrants and Minorities' Nov. 1986 20pp

6849 Srebrnik, Henry **'Salud di Heldn': Jewish Communist Activity in London on Behalf of the Spanish Republic** in 'Michigan Academician' 16, Spring 1984 11pp

6850 Stanley, Jo **'A Weapon in the Struggle' ed. A. Croft – Review** in 'NWLHSB' 24, 1999 4pp Incl. reviews of 'Children of the Revolution' & 'The Death of Uncle Joe'.

6851 Stanley, Jo **Including the Feelings: Personal Political Testimony and Self-Disclosure** in 'Oral History' Spring 1996 8pp On problems interviewing CP members. Very interesting.

6852 Stanley, Jo **Sorting the Paper Memories** in 'Socialist History' 12, 1997 9pp Describes working on the LDCP archives in LHASC.

6853 Stanley, Jo **With Panache and Probity: An Evaluation of Barry Williams' Role in the Progressive Movement** in 'NWLHSB' 31, 2006 5pp A personal and political view of a key trade union and CP figure on Merseyside.

6854 Stanton, Ernie **The Grand Old Duke of King Street** in 'Solidarity' (South London Solidarity) No.1, March 1969 4pp Syndicalist critique of the CP and the LCDTU.

6855 Stead, Nina **The British Road to Socialism** in 'The Communist' (BICO) 55, Nov. 1972 10pp Discussion continued in issues 56, 57, 59 and 60.

6856 Stevens, Bernard **Rutland Boughton** in 'New Reasoner' No. 8, 1959 8pp

6857 Stevens, Richard **Containing Radicalism: The TUC Organisation Department and Trades Councils, 1928-53** in 'LHR' Vol.62 No.1, Spring 1997 17pp

6858 Stevens, Richard **'Disruptive Elements'? The Influence of the CP in Nottingham and District T.C., 1929-51** in 'LHR' Vol.58 No.3, Winter 1993 15pp Useful local study.

6859 Stevenson, Graham **From 'The Lucas Girls' Joy' to 'We Won't Pay': Birmingham Communists in Action in the 1930s** in 'Communist Review' (CPB) 47, Summer 2006 8pp

6860 Stevenson, Graham **'Revolutionary Communist at Work: A Political Biography of Bert Ramelson' by R. Seifert & T. Sibley – Review** in 'Communist Review' (CPB) 63, Spring 2012 2pp

6861 Stevenson, Graham **'The CPGB Since 1920' by J. Eaden & D. Renton – Review** in 'Communist Review' (CPB) 38, Spring 2003 2pp

6862 Stevenson, Ronald **Alan Bush: Committed Composer** in 'The Music Review' Nov. 1964 20pp 'The only composer whose work has been officially banned by the BBC' (in 1940 – the ban was lifted when Vaughan Williams intervened).

6863 Stewart, Bob **Forty Splendid Years** in 'LM' Sept. 1960 4pp

6864 Stewart, Bob **The CP: Thirty Years** in 'CR' Aug. 1950 5pp Speech to EC.

6865 Stewart, David **A Tragic Fiasco? The 1984/85 Miners' Strike in Scotland** in 'Scottish Labour History' 41, 2006 16pp

6866 Stoecker, Walter **The Congress of the CPGB** in 'Inprecorr' Oct. 17 1922 3pp Inprecorr Supplement.

6867 Strachey, John **Communism in GB** in 'Current History' Jan. 1939 3pp

6868 Strachey, John **Notes by the Editor: The Communist Issue** in 'Socialist Review' (ILP) July 1927 5pp 'Editor's Notes' in several issues have briefer refs to the CP, especially answering Dutt's 'Notes of the Month' in LM (e.g. June 1928).

6869 Strang, Michael **From the Experience of Publishing Activity: Britain** in *'WMR'* Aug. 1961 1pp Short but interesting on range & quantity of CP material.

6870 Styles, Jean **Bessie Leigh – Obituary** in *'Link'* Summer 1978 1pp

6871 Styles, Jean **Communist Women** in *'Link'* Autumn 1973 1pp

6872 Styles, Jean **Small Steps and Giant Strides** in *'Link'* Winter 1976 2pp On women's work in S Essex & SE Midlands Districts.

6873 Surjeet, H. **Importance of Dutt-Bradley Document** in *'The Marxist' CPI(M)* Oct. 1995 6pp

6874 Surjeet, Harkishan **In Memory of Shapurji Saklatvala** in *'The Marxist' CPI(M)* Oct. 1995 3pp

6875 Surjeet, Harkishan Singh **Remembering R.P. Dutt** in *'The Marxist' CPI(M)* April/June 1996 18pp Whole issue of this journal is devoted to R.P. Dutt.

6876 Sutton, Peter **Reflections of a Cultural Worker** in *'CR'* April 1950 3pp

6877 Sweeney, Bill **Phil Filling – Memoriam** in *'Artery'* 20/21, 1981 1pp Worked for 'DW' in Scotland.

6878 Swingler, Peter **'The Rise and Fall of Revolutionary England' by A. MacLachlan – Review** in *'Revolutionary History'* Vol.6 No.4, 1997 3pp On CP Historians' Group.

6879 T.B. **'Revolutionary Political Action' Communist Brand** in *'Socialist Standard'* Oct. 1921 2pp On Poplar Board of Guardians wage reductions.

6880 T.M. **Revisionism and the British Anti-Revisionist Movement** in *'Marxist Leninist Quarterly'* No.3, Winter 1972 31pp Maoist (Communist Fed. of Britain M.L.). Useful on Maoism in CP and then outside.

6881 Taaffe, Peter **The British CP in Crisis** in *'Militant International Review'* 15, 1978 9pp

6882 Tait, William **BSISLP Documents on the Russian Revolution and the Formation of the CPGB in 1921** in *'SLHS'* 24, 1989 7pp De-Leonists & the CPGB.

6883 Tanner, Duncan **'Labour Legends and Russian Gold: Bolshevism and the British Left' by K. Morgan – Review** in *'LHR'* Vol.72 No.2, Aug. 2007 2pp

6884 Taplin, Eric **Desmond Greaves: An Appreciation** in *'NWLHSB'* 14, 1989 2pp

6885 Taplin, Eric **Edmund Frow, 1906-1997 – Obituary** in *'Manchester Region History Review'* Vol.12, 1998 1pp

6886 Taplin, Eric **'Edmond Frow: The Making of an Activist' by R. Frow – Review** in *'NWLHSB'* 25, 2000/1 1pp

6887 Tapsell, Walter **Some Critical Remarks on the 10th Party Congress** in *'C.R.'* April 1929 5pp

6888 Tapsell, Walter **The Situation of the CPGB** in *'Inprecorr'* Nov. 8 1929 1pp

6889 Tarbuck, Ken **An Appeal for Unity from Arnold Kettle** in *'The Week'* Feb. 3 1966 2pp

6889a Taylor, Elinor **Recovering Thirties Fiction** in *'Journal of Cultural Materialism'* 10, 2012 10pp

6890 Taylor, Robert **Reds Under the Bed?** in *'New Society'* Jan. 17 1974 3pp Trade unions.

6891 Taylor, Robert **The British Road from Communism** in *'New Society'* Nov. 10 1977 2pp On 35th Congress.

6892 Teanby, Keith **Leftism in the Doncaster LP, 1921-6** in *'SSLHB'* 39, Autumn 1979 1pp Pro-CP sympathies in a local LP.

6893 Temple, Richard **The Metropolitan Police and the Anti-Fascists, 1934-40** in *'Journal of the Police History Society'* No.10, 1995 11pp

6894 Terry, Mike **'British Trade Unions and Industrial Politics Vol.2: The High Tide of Trade Unionism, 1964-79' ed. J. McIlroy et al – Review** in *'HSIR'* 11, Spring 2001 8pp

6895 Tewson, Victor **People in Glass Houses** in *'Labour'* April 1948 2pp

6896 Tewson, Victor **Uphill is the Only Way** in *'Labour'* Dec. 1948 2pp

6897 Thomas, Elean **Remembering Claudia Jones** in *'WMR'* March 1987 2pp Jones was deported from US in 1955. In England she founded the West Indian Gazette and was active in the Black community.

6898 Thompson, Adam **Left Conferences** in *'The Leveller'* 34, Jan. 1980 1pp On 36th Congress, esp. congress structure & IPD.

6899 Thompson, Keith **United Behind the Bureaucrats: SWP Woos CP Trade Unionists** in *'The Next Step'* March 1980 1pp On LCDTU conference.

6900 Thompson, Keith **Wage Control and Working Class Independence: The Record of British Stalinism** in *'Revolutionary Communist Papers' (RCT)* No.4, Feb. 1979 5pp

6901 Thompson, Paul **Raphael Samuel, 1934-96 – An Appreciation** *in 'Oral History' Spring 1996* 8pp

6902 Thompson, Willie **A Good Old Cause?** *in 'Revolutionary History' Vol.5 No.3, 1994* 2pp Reply to review of his 'The Good Old Cause'.

6903 Thompson, Willie **British Communists in the Cold War, 1947-52** *in 'Contemporary British History' Vol.15 No.3, Autumn 2001* 28pp

6904 Thompson, Willie & Hobbs, Sandy **British Communists on the War, 1939-41** *in 'Oral History' Autumn 1988* 11pp Interviews with 14 Scottish Communists.

6905 Thompson, Willie **'Class or Nation: Communists, Imperialism and the Two World Wars' by N. Redfern – Review** *in 'Socialist History' 30, 2007* 2pp

6906 Thompson, Willie **End of Our History?** *in 'Socialist History Journal' 19, 1992* 3pp

6907 Thompson, Willie **'Harry Pollitt' by K. Morgan – Review** *in 'SLHS' 29, 1994* 2pp

6908 Thompson, Willie **'Opening the Books' ed. G. Andrews et al. – Review** *in 'Contemporary Record' Vol.9 No.3, Winter 1995* 2pp

6909 Thompson, Willie **'Rajani Palme Dutt' by J. Callaghan – Review** *in 'Contemporary Record' Vol.7 No.3, Winter 1993* 2pp

6910 Thompson, Willie **Scottish Communism 1962-1991: From Re-Growth to Extinction – A View from the Inside** *in 'Twentieth Century Communism' 5, 2013* 15pp

6911 Thompson, Willie **Socialist History: A Personal Note** *in 'Socialist History' 15, 1999* 3pp The final years of what had been the CP History Group, and its publications.

6912 Thompson, Willie **Stalin's Stooges? The CPGB 1920-40** *in 'Modern History Review' Feb. 1996* 3pp

6913 Thompson, Willie **The Conference on British Communists and 1956** *in 'Our History Journal' 16, Nov. 1990* 3pp

6914 Thompson, Willie **The End of the CP in Scotland** *in 'Scottish Labour History' 36, 2001* 9pp

6915 Thompson, Willie **Where Now for the CP?** *in 'Radical Scotland' 44, 1990* 2pp

6916 Thomson, George **On the Work of Party Intellectuals** *in 'CR' July 1946* 5pp

6917 Thornton, Carol & Thompson, Willie **Scottish Communists 1956-7** *in 'Science and Society' Vol.61 No.1, Spring 1997* 26pp

6918 Thorpe, Andrew **'A Weapon in the Struggle' ed. A. Croft – Review** *in 'LHR' Vol.65 No.1, Spring 2000* 1pp

6919 Thorpe, Andrew **'Class Against Class: The CP in Britain Between the Wars' by M. Worley – Review** *in 'Twentieth Century British History' Vol.14 No.2, June 2003* 2pp

6920 Thorpe, Andrew **Comintern 'Control' of the CPGB, 1920-43** *in 'English Historical Review' Vol.113 No.452, June 1998* 26pp Looks at most recently available material in Moscow, emphases CPGB's relative independence from the C.I. and considers the question of the possibility of a show trial of Pollitt.

6921 Thorpe, Andrew **CP History: A Reply to Campbell & McIlroy** *in 'LHR' Vol.69 No.3, Dec. 2004* 3pp

6922 Thorpe, Andrew **History of the CPGB, 1941-1951' N. Branson & 'Children of the Revolution' ed. P. Cohen – Review** *in 'Albion: A Quarterly Journal Concerned with British Studies' Vol.31 No.2, Summer 1999* 2pp

6922a Thorpe, Andrew **Locking Out the Communists: the LP and the CP, 1939-1946** *in 'Twentieth Century British History' Vol.25 No.2, June 2014* 15pp

6923 Thorpe, Andrew **Nina Fishman's 'Arthur Horner' and Labour and Political Biography** *in 'Socialist History' 38, 2011* 16pp

6924 Thorpe, Andrew **Stalinism and British Politics** *in 'History' 272, Oct. 1998* 20pp CP & LP attitudes to USSR.

6925 Thorpe, Andrew **'Stalin's British Victims' by F. Beckett – Review** *in 'Socialist History' 28, 2006* 4pp Rose Cohen, Freda Utley, Rosa Rust, Pearl Rimel.

6926 Thorpe, Andrew **The CP and the New Party** *in 'Contemporary British History' Vol.23 No.4, 2009* 15pp

6927 Thorpe, Andrew **'The Last English Revolutionary: Tom Wintringham, 1898-1949' by H. Purcell – Review** *in 'Socialist History' 30, 2007* 2pp

6928 Thorpe, Andrew **The Membership of the CPGB, 1920-1945** *in 'The Historical Journal' Vol.43 No.3, Sept. 2000* 24pp

6929 Thorpe, Andrew **'The Popular Front and the Progressive Tradition' by D. Blaazer – Review** *in 'LHR' Vol.58 No.2, Autumn 1993* 3pp

6930 Thorpe, Andrew **'Under the Red Flag: A History of Communism in Britain' by K.**

Laybourn & D. Murphy – Review *in 'LHR'* Vol.65 No.3, Winter 2000 1pp

6931 Thorpe, Keir **The 'Juggernaut Method': The 1966 State of Emergency and the Wilson Government's Response to the Seamen's Strike** *in 'Twentieth Century British History'* Vol.12 No.4, 2001 24pp

6932 Thurlow, Richard **A Very Clever Capitalist Class: British Communism and State Surveillance, 1939-45** *in 'Intelligence and National Security'* Vol.12 No.2, April 1997 20pp

6933 Thurlow, Richard **Soviet Spies and British Counter-Intelligence in the 1930s: Espionage in the Woolwich Arsenal and the Foreign Office Communications Dept** *in 'Intelligence and National Security'* Vol.19 No.4, Winter 2004 22pp On Olga Gray's infiltration of the CP; also on Percy Glading.

6934 Thurlow, Richard **'The Enemy Within' by F. Beckett – Review** *in 'Intelligence and National Security'* Vol.11 No.1, Jan. 1996 1pp

6935 Thurlow, Richard **The Evolution of the Mythical British Fifth Column, 1939-1946** *in 'Twentieth Century British History'* Vol.10 No.4, Dec. 1999 22pp

6936 Todd, Selina **'History in the Making' by S. Woodhams – Review** *in 'History of European Ideas'* Vol.28 No.3, 2002 3pp

6937 Todd, Selina **'Interesting Times' by E. Hobsbawm – Review** *in 'History of European Ideas'* Vol.29 No.3, 2003 10pp

6938 Toke, Dave **Treading the British Road** *in 'Clause 4 Journal'* No.2, 1977 3pp

6939 'Tom' **Experience in Work in the Enterprises in England** *in 'Inprecorr'* June 16 1932 2pp

6940 'Tom' **Party Cadres in England** *in 'Inprecorr'* Aug. 11 1932 1pp

6941 Topham, Tony **The Unofficial National Docks Strike of 1923: The TGWU's First Crisis** *in 'HSIR'* 2, Sept. 1996 38pp

6942 Tough, Alistair **The Papers of W.H. Stokes** *in 'Warwickshire History'* Winter 1989 3pp AEU official in Coventry.

6943 Tovey, Nidge **Facing Facts: Re-establishing the Party** *in 'Communist Campaign Review'* Spring 1988 3pp

6944 Townsend, Jules **The CP in Decline, 1964-70 Part 1** *in 'I.S.' No.62*, Sept. 1973 10pp

6945 Toynbee, Philip **Communism in Oxford** *in 'Isis'* May 26 1937 1pp Short but useful.

6946 'Trade Unionist' **British Communism and its Leaders** *in 'English Review'* Sept. 1927 13pp

6947 Tribe, Hubert **Clive Branson: Centenary 2007** *in 'MML Bulletin' 145*, Winter 2006 4pp

6948 Trotsky **Problems of the British Labour Movement** *in 'C.I.' 22 (New Series)*, 1926 24pp

6949 Tsirul, J. **CPGB at the Crossroads: Organisational Tasks of the Party** *in 'C.I.'* March 15 1932 7pp

6950 Tsuzuki, Chushichi **'A Proletarian Science' by A. Macintyre – Review** *in 'SSLHB'* 53, Part 1 1988 1pp

6951 Tucker, Eric **Friends and the Communist Peace Movement** *in 'The Friends' Quarterly'* Jan. 1951 5pp On the British Peace Cttee & esp. the Sheffield 2nd World Peace Congress.

6952 Turnbull, Maureen **When the CP Cheered for Churchill** *in 'Labour Review'* May 1982 7pp

6953 Turner, David **'Rajani Palme Dutt' by J. Callaghan & 'Harry Pollitt' by K. Morgan – Review** *in 'Militant International Review'* 57, May/June 1994 1pp

6954 Turner, David **'The Good Old Cause' by W. Thompson – Review** *in 'Militant International Review'* 50, March/April 1993 1pp

6955 Undy, R. **The Electoral Influence of the Opposition Party in the AEUW Enginering Section, 1960-75** *in 'BJOIR'* March 1979 15pp

6956 Upham, Martin **The Aylesbury By-Election of 1938** *in 'Revolutionary History'* Vol.1 No.3, Autumn 1988 3pp

6957 Upham, Martin **The Balham Group** *in 'SSLHB'* 30, Spring 1975 2pp

6958 Ure, J. **The BRS: A Marxist Critique** *in 'I.S.' No.50*, Jan/March 1972 6pp

6959 Ure-Smith, J. **The Establishment of a Bolshevik Newspaper in Britain** *in 'ISJ'* 18, Winter 1983 30pp

6960 'Vanguard' **And Now To Action** *in 'C.R.'* Dec. 1925 6pp

6961 Varley, Eric **The Campaign for the Party Press** *in 'The Communist'* May 1928 3pp Discusses distribution of 'Workers' Life'.

6962 Verney, Eric **The Workers' Press** *in 'C.R.'* Aug. 1924 6pp

6963 Vernon, Hilda et al. **Tributes to Pat Sloan** *in 'LM'* Feb. 1979 3pp

6964 Vevers, Simon **Scabs Charter from Euro-Stalinism** in 'Labour Review' Aug. 1985 2pp Attack on 'MT's position on the miners' strike.

6965 W.A. **International Women's Day in GB** in 'Inprecorr' March 1 1929 1pp Not 1928 as dated. Interesting refs to 1928 Conferences of Working Women's Organisations called by CP, which elected United Front Cttees of Working Women.

6966 Wadman, Howard **Left Wing Layout** in 'Typography' Summer 1937 5pp Brief analysis of typography of left publications, incl. CP and L&W; names, and praises, Alec Anderson's covers for L&W and CP Peace Library series of pamphlets among others.

6967 Wadsworth, Mark **Black Politics: A Historical Perspective** in 'Race and Class' Vol.34 No.2, Oct./Dec. 1992 12pp On S. Saklatvala.

6968 Wainwright, William **Unity the Keynote** in 'WMR' June 1959 3pp On 26th Congress.

6969 Waite, Mike **'70 Years of Struggle' by J. Berry – Review** in 'Our History Journal' 18, Nov. 1991 3pp

6970 Waite, Mike **'Children of the Revolution' by P. Cohen – Review** in 'LHR' Vol.63 No.3, Winter 1998 2pp

6971 Waite, Mike **'Enemy Within' by F. Beckett & 'The British CP and the Trade Unions, 1933-45' by N. Fishman – Review** in 'Party Politics' Vol.2 No.1, 1996 2pp

6972 Waite, Mike **Manchester's Red Army** in 'Jewish Socialist' Autumn 1994 2pp

6973 Waite, Mike **'The Education of Desire' by H. Kaye – Review** in 'Socialist History' 3, 1993 2pp

6974 Waite, Mike **The YCL and Youth Culture** in 'Socialist History' 6, 1994 13pp

6975 Walker, Pamela J. **Interview with Dorothy Thompson** in 'Radical History' 77, Spring 2000 16pp

6976 Walker, Ray **North West CPGB Publications** in 'WCML Bulletin' 7, 1997 3pp Material in the collection of the WCML, pre-computer listing. Includes some leaflets.

6977 Wallis, Dave **Backwards from Wivenhoe to Cairo: The Eighth Army and the Second World War: John Putkowski Interviews Dave Wallis** in 'Revolutionary History' Vol.8 No.2, 2002 13pp Fascinating account of a YCL member and future novelist, and soldier, in Egypt and his participation in political activities, at times verging on the mutinous (to both the army and King Street).

6978 Wallis, Mick **Pageantry and the Popular Front: Ideological Production in the 30s** in 'New Theatre Quarterly' May 1994 25pp With photos.

6979 Wallis, Mick **The Popular Front Pageant: Its Emergence and Decline** in 'New Theatre Quarterly' Feb. 1995 16pp

6980 Ward, Frank **The Battle of Marlborough Court** in 'Our History Journal' 11, Jan. 1987 4pp London squatters' battle.

6981 Ward, Paul & Hellawell, Graham et al. **Witness Seminar: Anti-Fascism in 1970s Huddersfield** in 'Contemporary British History' Vol.20 No.1, 2006 14pp One of the most detailed accounts of local CP anti-fascist activity in the 1970s, along with that of other left organisations.

6982 Ward, Stephanie **The Means Test and the Unemployed in South Wales and the North-East of England, 1931-1939** in 'LHR' Vol.73 No.1, April 2008 20pp

6983 Warren, Bill & Jones, Alan et al. **Open Letter to Members of the CPGB** in 'The Communist' (BICO) 87, June 1975 2pp 3 well known members who left over the policy of opposing the Common Market.

6984 Warren, Bill **The Programme of the CPGB: A Critique** in 'NLR' 63, 1970 16pp

6985 Waterman, Peter **Hopeful Traveller: The Itinerary of an Internationalist** in 'HWJ' 35, 1993 19pp Reminiscences of YCL/CP activist who worked for the IUS and WFTU. Interesting on internationalism.

6986 Waterson, Julie **The Party At Its Peak: 'The British CP and the Unions, 1933-45' by N. Fishman – Review** in 'ISJ' 69, Winter 1995 6pp

6987 Watkinson, Ray & Meier, Paul **A.L. Morton – Obituary/Tribute** in 'Journal of the William Morris Society' Spring 1988 2pp

6988 Watson, Don **Bobbie Qualie, 1909-1982** in 'NELH' 30, 1996 2pp Short article on an amazing character: poor, unemployed, he lived most of his life in a self-built hut and then caravan in woods by the Wear. A national weight-lifting champion, he was also an I.B.er.

6988a Watson, Don **Poles Apart: The Campaign Against Polish Settlement in Scotland After the Second World War** in 'SLHS' 49, 2014 18pp CP played significant part in this campaign.

6989 Watson, Don **Self-Help and Aid for Spain: The Hawick Workers' Mill 1936-39** in *'Scottish Labour History' 34, 1999* 5pp Brief refs to Willie Stoddart, Communist councillor in Hawick.

6990 Watson, Don **Shop Stewards of the Streets: British Communists in Local Government, 1933-39** in *'Socialist History' 40, 2012* 23pp

6991 Watson, Don **To the Head Through the Heart: The Newcastle Left Book Club Theatre Guild, 1937-39** in *'NELH' 23, 1989* 19pp

6992 Watson, David **Research Note: Black Workers in London in the 1940s** in *'HSIR' 1, March 1996* 10pp

6993 Watts, Ruth **Joan Simon: Obituary** in *'History of Education' Vol.35 No.1, 2006* 4pp

6994 Webb, Lily **Towards International Women's Day** in *'C.R.' Feb. 1931* 7pp

6995 Wedgwood Benn **The Communist Prosecution** in *'Contemporary Review' Jan. 1926* 6pp Liberal view of the trial of 12 CP leaders – criticises CP, says the words published by CP were illegal but argues the trial was unnecessary & counter-productive.

6996 Weesjes, Elke **Growing Up Communist: Theory vs. Practice** in *'Twentieth Century Communism' 4, 2012* 21pp Largely based on interviews with British and Dutch Communists who were from Communist families.

6997 Weidberg, L.E. **The Communist Party Isn't** (sic) in *'Socialist Standard' Oct. 1979* 1pp

6998 Weinberger, Barbara **Communism and the General Strike** in *'SSLHB' 48, Spring 1984* 36pp Special Branch Reports, incl. analysis of CP members arrested.

6999 Weinbren, Dan **'Red Tapes': Oral History and Left Networks** in *'LHR' Vol.60 No.1, Spring 1995* 3pp Report of Oral History Society Conference.

7000 White, H. **Winning the Middle Class** in *'C.R.' June 1935* 1pp Continued in July.

7001 White, L.C. & Houghton, Douglas **The Civil Service Purge** in *'Socialist Commentary' Sept. 1948* 4pp White, Gen Sec. of Civil Service Clerical Association, is against the purge; Douglas, Gen Sec. of Inland Revenue Staffs Fed., is in favour.

7002 White, R.M. **The Struggle of the British Unemployed and Some Lessons of the Feb. 5 Demonstration** in *'C.I.' May 1 1933* 3pp

7003 Whitehead, Andrew **Interview with Harry Young** in *'New Statesman' Nov. 6 1992* 1pp This issue also incl. article with Elizabeth Wilson's memoirs of the CP.

7004 Whitehead, E. **On Communist Unity** in *'The Spur' Sept. 1920* 1pp Letters by E. Whitehead & G. Aldred on affiliation to CP; Whitehead was elected to Provisional EC at Leeds Conference in Jan. 1921.

7005 Whitehead, E.T. **The English National Elections** in *'Inprecorr' Nov. 21 1922* 1pp On victory of Newbold in Motherwell, and other campaigns (Saklatvala, Geddes, Windsor, Gallacher, Price).

7006 Whitehead, Edgar **Five Questions** in *'Labour Magazine' Nov. 1928* 3pp

7007 Whitehead, Edgar **The Girdings of Mr Gallacher** in *'Labour Magazine' Oct. 1928* 4pp A reply to Gallacher's pamphlet 'Mondism and MacDonaldism'.

7008 Whitehead, Edgar **The Prevarications of Mr Pollitt** in *'Labour Magazine' Sept. 1928* 3pp Reply to Pollitt's response (in 'Workers' Life') to Citrine ('Democracy or Disruption').

7009 Whitehead, Edgar **The Strategy of the C.I.** in *'Labour Magazine' Dec. 1928* 4pp

7010 Whitehead, Joyce **Ruth Frow: Interview** in *'NWLHSB' 13, 1988* 10pp

7011 Whitley, J. **6th National Congress of YCL** in *'Inprecorr' Aug. 23 1929* 1pp

7012 Wicks, Harry **British Trotskyism in the 30s** in *'International' Vol.1 No.4, 1971* 7pp

7013 Wilde, Hal. **The Factory Paper** in *'C.R.' April 1931* 5pp

7014 Williams, Bert **Improving Our Agitation** in *'C.R.' Dec. 1933/Jan. 1934* 2pp

7015 Williams, Bert **The Nottingham TUC** in *'C.I.' Oct. 15 1930* 6pp

7016 Williams, Bert **The United Front** in *'C.R.' Aug. 1932* 8pp

7017 Williams, David **Communism the Greater Danger** in *'Common Cause Bulletin' 117, 1967* 32pp Also incl. biogs of EC members.

7018 Williams, David **The Challenge to Britain** in *'Common Cause Bulletin' 1975* 50pp Reviewed in 'East West Digest' Sept. 1975.

7019 Williams, David **The Communist Challenge** in *'Common Cause Bulletin' 126, Spring 1970* Continued in Nos.127-130. Incl. table of CP 'network' (organisation, publications, companies, fronts), analysis of 1969 Congress and biogs of leading members.

7020 Williams, Dick **IS, The CP and the Crawley Experience** in *'IS Internal Bulletin'* Dec. 1969 1pp How I.S. worked with and tried to influence a CP workplace branch.

7021 Williams, Evan **Memories of a Foundation Member of the CP** in *'Cyffro'* Summer 1971 5pp

7022 Williams, John Roose **T.E. Nicholas: The People's Poet** in *'Cyffro'* Vol 1 No.2, 1970 3pp In English and Welsh.

7023 Williams, Maxine **The NCP** in *'Revolutionary Communist'* No.7, Nov. 1977 7pp Mainly on CPGB not NCP!

7024 Williams, Raymond **Notes On British Marxism Since the War** in *'NLR'* 100, 1976 16pp

7025 Williams, Robert **The Liverpool Conference** in *'Labour Magazine'* Nov. 1925 3pp On Communist presence at LP Conference.

7026 Williamson, Judith **Even New Times Change** in *'New Statesman'* July 7 1989 4pp Analysis of 'MFNT'.

7027 Wilson, Alistair **50 Years of the CP in Wales** in *'Cyffro'* Summer 1971 6pp

7028 Wilson, Dan **Our Approach to Non-Party Workers** in *'C.R.'* Feb. 1935 2pp

7029 Wilson, David **Living in My Time: The General Strike & The 1931 Backlash** in *'NLR'* 97, 1976 16pp Extracts from autobiog.

7030 Wilson, Gordon **The Communist Bid for the AEU** in *'Common Cause Bulletin'* 108, Jan. 1964 7pp

7031 Wilson, Robert **Communist Party Split CPSA Broad Left** in *'Bulletin of Marxist Studies'* Vol.1 No.3, Spring 1985 4pp Militant's internal theoretical journal. About the civil service union.

7032 Wint, Guy **'Blowing Up India' by P. Spratt – Review** in *'Socialist Commentary'* Oct. 1955 2pp

7033 Winterton, E. **The Communist Congress** in *'LM'* Dec. 1944 3pp

7034 Wintringham, Tom **Growing Fighting Spirit of the British Workers** in *'Inprecorr'* Nov. 1 1929 1pp

7035 Witcop, R. **Who Are the Communists?** in *'The Spur'* Jan. 1921 1pp

7036 Wolfe, Willard **Writings on the History of Socialism in Britain, Part 2: Since 1950** in *'British Studies Monitor'* Fall 1981 28pp On Historians' Group.

7037 Wollman, Howard **'The Politics of the UCS Work-In' by J. Foster & C. Woolfson – Review** in *'SLHS'* 23, 1988 4pp

7038 Wood, Neal **The Empirical Proletarians: A Note on British Communism** in *'Political Science Quarterly'* 74, June 1959 17pp Looks at the traditionally small number of intellectuals in CPGB leadership, both absolutely and in comparison with other CPs.

7039 Woodhouse, Martin **Marxism and Stalinism in Britain** in *'Fourth International'* July 1967 7pp First in series of 4 articles (Feb. 1968, Aug. 1968, Summer 1969).

7040 Woodhouse, Michael **Syndicalism, Communism and the Trade Unions 1910-26** in *'Marxist'* Vol.4 No.3, 1966 13pp

7041 Woolley, George **Reflections on Communism in Britain** in *'New Communist Review'* Jan. 1981 6pp NCP.

7042 Worley, Matthew **'Central Books: A Brief History, 1939-99' by D. Cope – Review** in *'LHR'* Vol.65 No.3, Winter 2000 1pp

7043 Worley, Matthew **'Cold War, Crisis and Conflict: The CPGB 1951-68' by J. Callaghan – Review** in *'Socialist History'* 32, 2008 2pp

7044 Worley, Matthew **For a Proletarian Culture: CP Culture in Britain in the Third Period, 1928-35** in *'Socialist History'* 18, 2000 22pp

7045 Worley, Matthew **'History in the Making' by S. Woodhams – Review** in *'Socialist History'* 21, 2002 3pp

7046 Worley, Matthew **Left Turn: A Reassessment of the CPGB in the Third Period, 1928-33** in *'Twentieth Century British History'* Vol.11 No.4, 2000 26pp

7047 Worley, Matthew **'Party People, Communist Lives' by J. McIlroy et al. – Review** in *'Socialist History'* 24, 2003 3pp

7048 Worley, Matthew **Reflections on Recent British Communist Party History** in *'Historical Materialism'* 4, 1999 21pp Excellent introduction to recent publications; includes a balanced brief summary of relations between the CPGB and C.I.

7049 Worley, Matthew **Shot by Both Sides: Punk, Politics and the End of 'Consensus'** in *'Contemporary British History'* Vol.26 No.3, 2012 21pp CP and YCL are referred to here, along with other left groups – probably the most useful source of material, such as there is, on Communist links with the punk and post-punk music scene.

7050 Worley, Matthew **The British CP, 1920-45** in *'The Historian'* Autumn 1997 3pp Very useful bibliographical essay covering the major works.

7051 Worley, Matthew **The Communist International, The CPGB, and the 'Third Period', 1928-1932** in *'European History Quarterly'* Vol.30 No.2, 2000 23pp Concludes there was plenty of room for flexible national policies within C.I. framework.

7052 Worley, Matthew **'The Communist Party and Its Historians' by D. Parker** in *'Socialist History'* No.12 – Review in *'LHR'* Vol.64 No.3, Winter 1999 1pp

7053 Worley, Matthew **'The Political Trajectory of J.T. Murphy' by R. Darlington – Review** in *'LHR'* Vol.64 No.3, Winter 1999 2pp

7054 Wrigley, Chris **'Arthur Horner: A Political Biography' by N. Fishman – Review** in *'Socialist History'* 39, 2011 4pp

7054a Wrigley, Chris **'John Saville: Commitment and History' by D. Howell et al. – Review** in *'SLHS'* 47, 2012 2pp

7055 Wrigley, Chris **'Memoirs From the Left' by J. Saville – Review** in *'Socialist History'* 24, 2003 3pp

7056 Wynn, Arthur **Cutteslowe Wall Campaign** in *'C.R.'* Aug. 1935 3pp Campaign in Oxford to remove a wall between working class & middle class housing estates; at one stage the CP had to argue against attacking the middle class residents! CP published 'The Cutteslowe Wall-paper' & 'Children's Wall-paper' (free).

7057 Yaffe, David **Trade Unions and the State: The Struggle Against the Social Contract** in *'Revolutionary Communist'* No.7, Nov. 1977 8pp

7058 Young, Allan & Schmidt, Michael **A Conversation With Edgell Rickword** in *'Poetry Nation'* No.1, 1973 16pp

7059 Young, D.H. **CPGB: New Party of the Nation** in *'The Communist'* (BICO) 180, April 1983 6pp

7060 Young, Harry **Conference of the YCL** in *'Inprecorr'* July 9 1925 1pp Founder member of YCL.

7061 Young, Harry **The 5th Congress of the YCL** in *'The International of Youth'* No.7, Aug. 1928 13pp

7062 Young, Harry **The British YCL in Congress** in *'The International of Youth'* Jan. 1927 6pp

7063 Young, Horace (Harry) **Six Months of Nucleus Work in GB** in *'YCI Review'* May 1924 1pp

7064 Young, James D. **A Very English Socialism and the Celtic Fringe** in *'HWJ'* 35, 1993 16pp On the neglect of English socialist historians, incl. by CP Historians' Group, of the other countries in the UK.

7065 Young, James D. **Marxism and the Scottish National Question** in *'JOCH'* Vol.18 No.1, Jan. 1983 23pp

7066 Young, James D. **Neo-Marxism and the British New Left** in *'Survey'* Jan. 1967 6pp

7067 Young, James D. **Red Clydeside and Stalinist Historiography** in *'Revolutionary History'* Vol.6 No.1, 1995 3pp

7068 Zienau, Sigurd **Neglected Aspects of British Revolutionary History: 'The Revolutionary Movement in Britain, 1900-21' by W. Kendall – Review** in *'May Day Manifesto Bulletin'* May/June 1969 4pp

7069 Zilliacus, Konni **Open Letter to Gallacher and Piratin** in *'LM'* May 1946 5pp

7070 Zinoviev, G. **Declaration of Comrade Zinoviev on the Alleged 'Red Plot'** in *'Inprecorr'* Nov. 3 1924 1pp

13. Unpublished Memoirs

This chapter only includes typewritten (and occasional handwritten) memoirs in accessible libraries. There are many more bits and pieces of unfinished and unpublished memoirs, articles, funeral speeches and diaries in personal collections and in the three major collections – usually accessible by catalogue.

These entries are listed by author. All are autobiographical, unless stated, and all were members of the CP at some time of their lives. The year the memoirs were written is often not known. During the course of researching for this book, some have been published.

7071 Brewster, Frieda **A Long Journey Home** *LHASC*

7072 Collinson, Arthur **One Way Only: An Autobiography of an Old-Time Trade Unionist** *Brunel Univ. Library* 257pp Founder member who left in 1931.

7072a Cooney, Bob **Proud Years: The Story of Aberdeen's Communists** *National Library of Scotland*

7073 Cowe, William **untitled** *Gallacher Memorial Library*

7074 Cox, Idris **Personal and Political Recollections** *LHASC at the People's History Museum* 60pp There is another unpublished autobiog. at the Univ of Swansea.

7075 Cox, Idris **Story of a Welsh Rebel** *Swansea Univ.* 112pp There is another unpublished autobiog. at the LHASC at the People's History Museum.

7076 Crawfurd, Helen **untitled** *MML* 403pp The first CP Women's Organiser in 1922.

7077 Davies, Bob **The Beginning of the British CP: Personal Recollections** *MML* 100pp See also 'Our History' No. 23. Active in NW in NUWM.

7078 Dorrell, Harry **Falling Cadence: An Autobiography of Failure** *Brunel Univ. Library*

7079 Dutt, R.P. **One of the Many** *LHASC* 1st 6 chapters of his autobiog.

7080 Edward, R.H. (Bert) **untitled** *Ruskin College Library* 397pp

7081 Elias, Sid **Reminiscences** *WCML* 99pp Leader of NUWM.

7082 Etheridge, Dick **untitled** *Warwick Univ.* Leading figure at Longbridge car factory.

7083 Exell, Arthur **Abraham Lazarus alias 'Bill Firestone': Life Story** *Ruskin College Library* 40pp

7084 Exell, Arthur **My Life Story** *Ruskin College Library* 32pp

7085 Fagan, Hymie **An Autobiography** *Brunel Univ. Library* 154pp CP full time worker for 60 years.

7086 Fagg, Len **A Man of Kent** *Warwick Univ., Modern Records Centre* 154pp In CP in Ramsgate till 1925.

7087 Garman, Douglas **A Man of Quality** *Univ. of Nottingham, Dept of Manuscripts* Biog. Important literary figure who was head of CP's Education Dept between 1940 and 1950, having previously worked for Wishart and then Lawrence & Wishart.

7088 Gibson, John **untitled** *Brunel Univ. Library* 7pp Clydeside Shop Stewards.

7089 Goldfinger, David **Memoirs** *LHASC* 1954 131pp Jewish East End

7090 Heslop, Harold **From Tyne to Tone: A Journey** *Brunel Univ. Library* 293pp

7091 Horton, Ron **Richard (Dick) Pennifold** *East Sussex Record Office, Lewes* 4pp Beautifully hand-written memoir (author was artist, one of whose specialities was script) about founder member of Brighton CP. [Location: AMS6375 1/70]

7092 Horton, Ron **untitled** *East Sussex Record Office, Lewes* 1968 ? 5pp Typescript of memories of earliest days of Brighton CP by founder member.[Location: ACC 8112 14/5]

7093 Jackson, T.A. **Solo Trumpet: An Interim Report on Fifty 'Red' Years** *MML* 3 vols; much more detail than in the published ed.

7094 Jackson, T.A. **untitled** *LHASC/MML*

7095 James, T.H. **We Tread But One Path** *Rotherham Central Library, Local Studies Dept Also MML.* 85pp Yorkshire unemployed activist who fought in Spain.

7096 Jenkins, Mick **Prelude to Better Days** *WCML* 245pp Much on YCL. Full time CP official in NW.

7097 Kettle, Margot **John Gollan** *LHASC* Biog.

7098 McQuilkin, William **untitled** *Paisley Central Library, Local History Dept* 3pp

7099 Miller, Lucy **A Wasted Talent** *WCML* CP member until she started working for Harold Wilson.

7101 Murphy, Molly **Nurse Molly** *LHASC* 1958 Wife of J.T. Murphy; nurse in Spain. Ed. version by R. Darlington published in 1998 (see 'Molly Murphy').

7102 Newbold, J. Walton **Memoirs** *John Rylands Library, Manchester*

7103 Rawlings, Joe **Stormy Petrel: Struggle or Starve** *Ruskin College Library* 13pp This library also contains 2 shorter versions of his memoirs.

7104 Roche, Jim **Autobiographical Account of Events in CP, 1956-7** *Ruskin College Library* 40pp

7105 Russell, Ralph **They Think I Lost: Conclusions from a Communist Life** *LHASC* Students. India.

7106 Saklatvala, S. **untitled** *OIOC*

7107 Sutherland, Jack **untitled** *LHASC*

7108 Young, Harry **Harry's Autobiography** *Brunel Univ. Library* First National Organiser of YCL & rep. in Moscow 1922-9; YCI Secretariat; ed. by 'C.I.' 1932-5. Left CP mid 1930s for SPGB in which he remained active till his death in 1996.

14. Theses

This is the one area where I have not examined the texts. Most of titles of the theses are self-explanatory, but some may not have substantial references to the CP. And there are probably others not listed that do. Entries for 'Year' may be out by one year – occasionally there is a discrepancy between the year a thesis or doctorate is accepted and the year written.

Quite a few of the PhDs have been published – with the same, or a similar, title.

7109 Alberti, J. **The Impact of the Nazi-Soviet Pact and its Aftermath: Labour and the Left, August 1939 – June 1941** *MA; Newcastle* 1982

7110 Andrews, Geoff **Culture, Ideology and Strategy of the CPGB, 1964-1979** *PhD; Kingston* 2002

7111 Andrews, M. **Lifetimes of Commitment: A Study of Socialist Activists** *PhD; Cambridge* 1989 11 out of the 15 people studied were in CP at some time.

7112 Archer, John **Trotskyism in Britain, 1931-7** *Central London Poly* 1979

7113 Armstrong, M. **The History and Organization of the Broad Left in the AUEW (Engineering Section) until 1972, with Special Reference to Manchester** *MA; Warwick* 1978

7114 Austrin, T. **Industrial Relations in the Construction Industry** *PhD; Bristol* 1978

7115 Bainbridge, J. **'Friends of the Soviet Union': Pro-Sovietism in Britain, 1930-41** *MA; Warwick* 1982

7116 Barrett, J. **'The Busman's Punch': Rank and File Organization and Unofficial Action Among London Busmen, 1913-37** *MA; Warwick* 1974

7117 Barrett, Neil **Organized Responses to Fascist Mobilisation in South Lancashire, 1932-40** *PhD; Manchester* 1996

7118 Baxell, Richard **The British Battalion of the International Brigades in the Spanish Civil War, 1936-1939** *PhD; LSE* 2004

7118a Bayliss, Darrin **Council Cottages and Community in Inter-War Britain: A Study of Class, Culture, Politics and Place** *PhD; Queen Mary & Westfield College, Univ. of London* 1998 Material on Jack Carson and the Watling Estate ('Little Moscow') in Burnt Oak, Hendon in 1930s.

7119 Beynon, N. **Communism and Fascism and Inter-War British Art** *MA; Wales, Aberystwyth* 1987

7120 Blaazer, David **The Origins of Popular Front Leftism: A Study in the British Progressive Tradition** *PhD; La Trobe (Australia)* 1989

7121 Black, Lawrence **British Communism and 1956: Party Culture and Political Identities** *MA; Warwick* 1994

7122 Black, Lawrence **The Political Culture of the Left in 'Affuent' Britain, 1951-64** *PhD; Guildhall* 1999

7123 Boughton, J. **Working-Class Politics in Birmingham and Sheffield, 1918-31** *PhD; Warwick* 1985

7124 Bounds, Philip **British Communism and the Politics of Literature, 1928-1939** *PhD; Swansea* 2003

7125 Bowes, Nita **The People's Convention** *Warwick; MA* 1976

7126 Boys, A. **The Changing Union; A Study of the NUT, 1960-74** *MA; Warwick* 1974

7127 Broomfield, Stuart **South Wales During the Second World War: The Coal Industry and its Community** *PhD; Wales 1979*

7128 Brotherstone, Julie **The British Labour Movement, the Councils of Action and International Questions, 1917-24** *MLitt; Edinburgh 1979*

7129 Brown, G. **Tom Mann: His Life and Times, 1910-41** *PhD; Bangor 1968*

7130 Brown, J.L. **Class Consciousness Among Engineering Shops Stewards in Clydeside** *PhD; Glasgow 1981*

7131 Bruley, Sue **Socialism and Feminism in the CPGB, 1920-39** *PhD; LSE 1980*

7131a Bullivant, J. **Musical Modernism and Left-Wing Politics in 1930s Britain** *PhD; Oxford 2009*

7132 Calton, J.N. **The Party That Never Was: A Study of the Campaign for Political Integration Among Left-Wing and Radical Groups in Britain, 1929-39** *PhD; Washington 1970*

7133 Carr, F.W. **Engineering Workers and the Rise of Labour in Coventry, 1914-1939** *PhD; Warwick 1978*

7134 Carr, F.W. **The Formation of the CP in Coventry** *MA; Warwick 1969*

7135 Cleminson, Andy **The Coventry Car Industry and the Intervention of the CPGB and the I.S., 1968-76** *MA; Warwick 1987*

7136 Coupland, Philip **Voices From Nowhere: Utopianism in British Political Culture, 1925-1945** *PhD; Warwick 2000*

7137 Croft, Andy **Socialist Fiction in Britain in the 1930s** *PhD; Nottingham 1985*

7138 Cross, Richard **The Communist Party of Great Britain and the 'Collapse of Socialism': The CPGB 1977-1991** *PhD; Manchester 2003*

7139 Cross, Richard **The CPGB and the Trade Union Movement, 1979-91** *MA; Manchester 1999*

7140 Croucher, Richard **Communist Politics and Shop Stewards in Engineering, 1935-46** *PhD; Warwick 1977*

7141 Cunningham, Paul **Unemployment in Norwich During the Nineteen-Thirties** *PhD; East Anglia 1990*

7142 Defty, Andrew **British Anti-Communist Propaganda and Cooperation with the U.S., 1945-1951** *PhD; Salford 2002*

7143 Denver, D.T. **The CP in Dundee: A Study of Activists** *BPhil; Dundee 1972*

7144 Diamanti, F. **Communist and Labourist Paths to 'New Times'** *PhD; Edinburgh 1992*

7145 Donoghue, Augustine **History of the CPGB, 1939-46** *PhD; Stanford 1953*

7146 Drake, P. **Labour and Spain: British Labour's Response to the Spanish Civil War with Particular Reference to the Labour Movement in Birmingham** *MLitt; Birmingham 1978*

7147 Durham, Martin **The Origins and Early Years of British Communism, 1914-24** *PhD; Birmingham 1982*

7148 Eaden, James **'A Society of Great Friends': Rank-and-File British Communists and the Imperialist War, 1939-40** *PhD; Sheffield Hallam 1996*

7149 Eatwell, Roger **The Labour Party and the Popular Front Movement in Britain in the 1930s** *PhD; Oxford 1976*

7150 Ehrlich, Avishai **The Leninist Organizations in Britain and the Student Movement, 1966-72** *PhD; LSE 1981*

7151 Evans, A.T.B. **The Soviet Union, Comintern and the British Labour Movement, 1929-35** *MPhil; Birmingham 1983*

7152 Ewins, Kristin **Women's Writing and Political Activism in the 1930s** *PhD; Oxford 2009*

7153 Field, G. **English Left-Wing Writers and Politics in the 1930s** *PhD; London, Birkbeck 1986*

7154 Fishman, Nina **The British CP and the T.U.s, 1933-45: The Dilemma of Revolutionary Pragmatism** *PhD; London 1991*

7155 Flanagan, Richard **The Politics of the Unemployed, 1884-1939** *MLitt; Oxford 1988*

7156 Flinn, Andrew **The United Front in the Greater Manchester Area, 1933-41** *PhD; Manchester 1999*

7157 Fong, Gisela **The Times and Life of Rose Smith in Britain and China, 1891-1985** *PhD; Montreal 1998*

7158 Forde, J. **Popular Front Strategy: Betrayal or Re-Affirmation of the Socialist Cause?** *MA; Sheffield 1987*

7159 Fox, P.L. **Culture, Society and the CP, 1917-28** *MPhil; Oxford 1985*

7160 Francis, Hywel **The South Wales Miners and the Spanish Civil War** *PhD; Wales 1977*

7161 Gabbidon, C. **Party Life: An Examination of the Branch Life of the CPGB Between the Wars** *PhD; Sussex 1991*

7162 Garner, R.W. **Ideology and Electoral Politics in Labour's Rise to Major Party Status, 1918-31** *PhD; Manchester* 1988

7163 Garvie, Wayne **Mill Hill: The Making of a Mining Community** *PhD; Sheffield* 1988

7164 Goldberg, G. **The Socialist and Political Labour Movement in Manchester and Salford, 1884-1924** *MA; Manchester* 1975

7165 Goldstein, Roger **The Comintern and British Communism, 1921-26** *PhD; Columbia* 1972

7166 Goodman, G. **Who Is Anti-American? The British Left and the US, 1945-56** *PhD; London* 1996

7167 Grange, Shelley **These Bloody Reds: Ernest Bevin's Public Views of Communism and British Foreign Policy, 1945-50** *MA; Michigan State* 1983

7168 Greenwald, Norman **Communism and British Labour: A Study of British Labour Party Politics, 1933-39** *PhD; Columbia* 1958

7169 Hammond, Andy **J.B.S. Haldane and the Attempt to Construct a Marxist Biology** *PhD; Manchester* 2005

7170 Handy, T. **British CP Propaganda on Domestic Affairs, 1944-50** *PhD; Austin* 1979

7171 Harmer, H. **The NUWM in Britain, 1921-39: Failure and Success** *PhD; LSE* 1987

7172 Hayburn, Ralph **The Response to Unemployment in the 1930s with Particular Reference to South East Lancashire** *PhD; Hull* 1971

7173 Heppell, Jason **Jews in the CPGB, 1920-1948: Ethnic Susceptibility, Generational Divergence and Party Strategy** *PhD; Sheffield* 2001

7174 Holden, Len **A History of Vauxhall Motors to 1950** *MPhil; Open Univ.* 1983

7175 Howe, Antony **The Past Is Ours: The Uses of English History by the CP – Dona Torr and the Creation of the Historians' Group** *PhD; Sydney* 2003

7176 Howe, S.J. **Anti-Colonialism in British Politics: The Left and the End of Empire, 1939-64** *PhD; Oxford* 1985

7177 Howling, I.R.C. **'Our Soviet Friends': The Presentation of the Soviet Union in the British Media, 1941-5** *MA; Leeds* 1988

7178 Hubert, P.J. **Party Press and Propaganda in Parties of the Left in Britain** *PhD; Leeds* 1988

7179 Hudson, Kate **The Double Blow: 1956 and the CPGB** *PhD; London, School of Slavonic & East European Studies* 1992

7180 Humphreys, R.O. **The Left and the National Question in Wales with Particular Reference to 1979-85** *Research Project, Diploma in Labour Studies; Ruskin College* 1985 Incl. chapter on 'CP & Anti-Nuclear Movement in Wales, 1979-85'.

7181 Johnson, Iain **Women in the CP in Fife Between the Wars** *Dissertation?* 1996 Unidentified academic typescript in the Gallacher Collection in Glasgow Caledonian University. Apparently a very useful and much used document, includes original information about leading local Communist Maria Stewart.

7182 Johnstone, Charlie **The Tenants' Movement and Housing Struggles in Glasgow, 1945-90** *PhD; Glasgow* 1992

7183 Jones, D.I.L. **The United Front in the C.I.: The Debate on Affiliation of the CP to the LP, 1920-25** *MPhil; Ulster* 1976

7184 Jones, Douglas **The Communist Party of Great Britain and the National Question in Wales, 1970-91** *PhD; Aberystwyth* 2010

7185 Jones, J. Graham **The General Election of 1929 in Wales** *MA; Univ. of Wales* 1980

7186 Jones, Jean **The Anti-Colonial Politics and Policies of the CPGB, 1920-51** *PhD; Wolverhampton* 1997

7187 Jones, L. **Sylvia Pankhurst and the W.S.F.: The Red Twilight, 1918-24** *MA; Warwick* 1972

7188 Jones, Len **The British Workers' Theatre, 1917-35** *PhD; Leipzig* 1964

7189 Joyce, P. **Shop Steward Militancy: A Case Study in a London Borough During the 1970s** *PhD; LSE* 1983

7190 Jupp, James **The Left in Britain** *MSc; London* 1956

7191 Kadish, Sharman **Bolsheviks and British Jews** *PhD; Oxford* 1986

7192 Kemp, M. **The Left and the Debate over Labour Party Policy, 1943-50** *PhD; Cambridge* 1985

7193 Kendall, Walter **The Formation of the CPGB, 1918-21** *BLitt; Oxford* 1966

7194 Klotz, Daniel **Freda Utley: From Communist to Anti-Communist** *PhD; Yale* 1987

7195 Lang, Carol **The Radicalization of the British Working Class, 1910-1926, and the

Impact of the Russian Revolution PhD; City University, New York 2006

7196 Lindop, Fred **A History of Seamen's Trade Unionism to 1929** MPhil; London 1972

7197 Lopes, Antonio **The Last Fight Let Us Face: Communist Discourse in Britain and the Spanish Civil War** PhD; New University of Lisbon 2006 In English.

7198 Loughlin, S. **The British Left 'Fringe': Recruitment and Membership** MA; Manchester 1974

7199 MacDonald, G. **Aspects of Industrial Politics, 1922-31** PhD; Edinburgh 1975

7200 Macfarlane, L. **The Origins of the CPGB and its Early History, 1920-27** PhD; London 1962

7201 Macintyre, Stuart **Marxism in Britain, 1917-33** PhD; Cambridge 1976

7202 MacKenzie, Alan J. **British Marxists and the Empire: Anti-Imperialist Theory and Practice, 1920-1945** PhD; London, Birkbeck 1979 Some refs to it titled 'British Marxism ... '.

7203 Martin, Roderick **The National Minority Movement: A Study in the Organisation of Trade Union Militancy in the Inter-War Period** PhD; Oxford 1964

7204 Maslen, Joseph **Memory, Modernity and Reconstructions of Identity Amongst Veterans of Inter-War British CP Youth Politics, 1918-39/1984-5** PhD; Manchester 2008

7205 Mason, Anthony **The Miners' Union of Northumberland and Durham, 1918-1931, With Special Reference to the General Strike of 1926** PhD; Hull 1967

7206 Mates, Lewis **The United Front and the Popular Front in the North-East of England, 1936-9** PhD; Newcastle 2002

7207 McCann, S.J. **The Influence of the Formation of the CPGB and the Ideas of the Bolsheviks Upon the National Guilds League, 1919-23** Project Report; Ruskin College 1982

7208 McCrackin, B.H. **The Etiology of Radicalization Among American and British Communist Autobiographers** PhD; Emory 1980

7209 McCulloch, G. **The Politics of the Popular Front in Britain, 1935-45** PhD; Cambridge 1981

7210 Middleton, A. **The Enemy Within? A Comparative Study of the CP's Influence in Trade Unions** Project Report; Ruskin College 1992

7211 Morgan, D. **The British Labour Movement's Alternative Economic Strategy, 1966-1983** PhD; Bangor 2006

7212 Morgan, Kevin **Against Fascism and War: Ruptures and Continuities in British Communist Politics, 1935-41** PhD; Manchester 1987

7213 Mosbacher, M. **The British Communist Movement and Moscow: How the Demise of the Soviet Union Affected the CP and Its Successor Organisations** MA; Exeter 1995

7214 Mullings, M. **The Left and Fascism in the East End of London, 1932-39** PhD; Poly of N London 1985

7215 Murphy, Dylan **The CPGB and its Struggle Against Fascism, 1933-9** PhD; Huddersfield 1999

7216 Nassibian, A. **Attitudes on Clydeside to the Russian Revolution, 1917-24** MLitt; Strathclyde 1978

7217 Newton, K. **British Communism: The Sociology of a Radical Political Party** PhD; Cambridge 1965

7218 Nicholson, Steve **The Portrayal of Communism and the Soviet Union in Selected Plays Performed in GB, 1917-45** PhD; Leeds 1991

7219 Norris, G. **Communism and British Politics, 1944-48** MA; Warwick 1981

7220 Nujam, S. **A Radical Past: The Legacy of the Fife Miners** PhD; Edinburgh 1988

7221 Parsons, Steve **Communism in the Professions: The Organisation of the British CP Among Professional Workers, 1933-56** PhD; Warwick 1990

7222 Parsons, Steve **Crisis in the CPGB: The Impact of the Events of 1956 on the Membership with Particular Reference to Trade Unionists** MA; Warwick 1981

7223 Pawling, C. **Culture and Reality: A Critical Study of Christopher Caudwell** PhD; Birmingham 1981

7224 Pooke, Grant **Francis D. Klingender (1907-1955): An Intellectual Biography** PhD; Southampton 2006

7225 Powell, Glyn **The Best of All Possible Worlds? The Ideology and Practice of British Communists in the Cold War, 1953-1961** PhD; London 2001

7226 Rabinovitch, Y. **British Marxist Socialism and Trade Unionism** PhD; Sussex 1978

7227 Rafeek, Neil **Against All the Odds: Women in the CP in Scotland, 1920-1991** PhD; Strathclyde 1998

7228 Read, S.K.O. **Industrial Relations in the Road Passenger Transport Industry: A Political-Economic Analysis** PhD; Aston 1989

7229 Redfern, Neil **Historians and the Popular Front: Historiography of the CPGB, 1935-41** MA; Manchester 1994

7230 Redfern, Neil **The British CP, Imperialism and War, 1935-45** PhD; Manchester Metropolitan 1998

7231 Reid, N. **The Labour Movement in Stockport** MA; Hull 1975

7232 Renton, Dave **The Attempted Revival of British Fascism: Fascism and Anti-Fascism, 1945-51** PhD; Sheffield 1998 Useful on relationship between CP and The 43 Group.

7233 Roberts, E.A. **Marxist Intellectuals in Britain, 1933-56** PhD; London, City Univ. 1990

7234 Ross, R. **Hugh MacDiarmid and the Politics of Consciousness** PhD; Stirling 1984

7235 Savage, P.J.D. **British Communism: Which Road?** Project Report; Ruskin College 1978

7236 Saville, Ian **Ideas, Forms and Developments in the British Workers' Theatre, 1925-35** PhD; London,City 1990

7237 Sibley, Tom **Anti-Communism: Studies of its Impact on the UK Labour Movement in the Early Years (1945-50) of the Cold War** PhD; Keele 2008

7238 Side, Elke **'Children of the Red Flag': Growing Up in a Communist Family: A Comparative Research of the British and Dutch Communist Movement** PhD; Sussex 2011

7239 Simons, Guadalupe **An Analysis of the National Unemployed Workers' Movement** MPhil; Birmingham 2005

7240 Smith, David **The Re-Building of the South Wales Miners' Federation, 1927-39: A Trade Union in its Society** PhD; Wales 1976

7241 Smith, Elaine R. **East End Jews in Politics, 1918-1939: A Study in Class and Ethnicity** PhD; Leicester 1990

7242 Smith, Evan **The CPGB and Anti-Racist Politics, 1948-1981** PhD; Flinders 2007

7243 Smith, N. **Politics, Industrial Policy and Democracy: The Electricians' Union, 1945-88** PhD; Glasgow 1988

7244 Smylie, Patrick **Cold War, Partition and Convergence: Irish Communism, 1945-70** PhD; Belfast 2010

7245 Squires, Mike **The Life and Influence of Shapurji Saklatvala** PhD; Leeds 1987

7246 Srebrnik, Henry **The Jewish Communist Movement in Stepney: Ideological Mobilization and Political Victories in an East London Borough, 1935-45** PhD; Birmingham 1983

7247 Starr, W. **Christopher Caudwell** PhD; Columbia 1982

7248 Stevens, Richard **Trades Councils in the East Midlands, 1929-51: Politics and Trade Unionism in a 'Traditionally Moderate' Area** PhD; Nottingham 1995

7249 Stevenson, N. **Culture, Ideology and Politics: R. Williams and E.P. Thompson** PhD; Cambridge 1993

7250 Suart, Natalie **The Memory of the Spanish Civil War and the Families of British International Brigaders** PhD; De Montfort 2001

7251 Sullivan, R.J. **Christopher Caudwell: One Man in his Time** PhD; Brown 1985

7252 Susser, Leslie **Fascist and Anti-Fascist Attitudes in Britain Between the Wars** PhD; Oxford 1988

7253 Taylor, A. **Pitmen and Politics: The Yorkshire Area NUM and Political Activity, 1944-74** PhD; Sheffield 1982

7253a Taylor, Elinor **Popular Front Politics and the British Novel, 1934-1940** PhD; Salford 2014

7254 Taylor, R.K.S. **The Disarmament Movement and its Legacy to the Left** PhD; Leeds 1984

7255 Thayer, George **Aestheticism and Political Commitment in the Works of Edward Upward** PhD; Tulsa 1981

7256 Thomas, Nick **The British Student Movement, 1965-72** PhD; Warwick 1998

7257 Thomson, R. **Intellectuals, Labour and the Popular Front: Intellectuals and Political Commitment in the 1930s** MA; Queen's Univ. at Kingston 1993

7258 Tolland, Siobhan **'Jist a wee woman': Dundee, the CP and the Feminisation of Socialism in the Life and Works of Mary Brooksbank** PhD; Aberdeen 2005

7259 Tranmer, Jeremy **The CPGB and the Thatcher Governments: A Historical and Political Study** PhD; University of Nancy 2000

In French. A 5pp English summary appears in 'Communist History Network Newsletter' No.10, Spring 2001.

7260 Troup, A. **The Mobilization of, and Response to, 'Political' Protest Strikes, 1969-1984** *PhD; CNAA* 1987

7261 Turner, David **Reds at the Heart of Empire: Aspects of the CPGB in the Medway Towns** *PhD; Kent* 1999

7262 Upham, Martin **The History of British Trotskyism to 1949** *PhD; Hull* 1981

7263 Wailey, P. **A Storm from Liverpool: British Seamen and their Union, 1920-70** *PhD; Liverpool* 1985

7264 Waite, Mike **Young People and Formal Political Activity: A Case Study – Young People and Communist Politics in Britain, 1920-91: Aspects of the History of the YCL** *MPhil; Lancaster* 1992

7265 Walker, H.J. **The Outdoor Movement in England and Wales, 1900-39** *PhD; Sussex* 1988

7266 Watson, Don **British Socialist Theatre, 1930-39** *PhD; Hull* 1985

7267 White, Lyndon **The CP in South Wales, 1945-68** *MPhil; Cardiff* 1996

7268 Whitfield, R. **The Labour Movement in Bristol, 1914-39** *MLitt; Bristol* 1982

7269 Wilford, R.A. **The Political Involvements and Ideological Alignments of Left-Wing Literary Intellectuals in Britain, 1930-50** *PhD; Wales, Cardiff* 1975

7270 Williams, C.M. **Democratic Rhondda: Politics and Society, 1885-1951** *PhD; Cardiff* 1991

7271 Winslow, B. **Sylvia Pankhurst: Suffragette and Communist** *PhD; Washington* 1990

7272 Wood, Neal **Communism and the British Intellectual** *PhD; Berkeley* 1958

7273 Worley, Matthew **Class Against Class: The CPGB in the Third Period, 1927-32** *PhD; Nottingham* 1998

Indexes

The following indexes refer to the body of the Bibliography, not to any part of the Introduction.

a) Names

Since one of the main aims of this work is to uncover the contributions of many unknown activists of the British labour and revolutionary movements, as well as to document the better known names, this index is important. It does not cover all names mentioned in the numbered entries.

Names of authors in those chapters that are in author order, as opposed to chronological order, are not given another entry here. Some of those authors would have been in the CP, others not. The entries here are only for individuals who were in the CP. Therefore all authors of local and national publications will have an entry, if they were members.

Other entries here are for individuals who are the subject of articles or books; who are mentioned in comments on the entry (this may include the artist who designed the cover of the item); and who wrote the book that is the subject of a review. The ability to thus cross reference books and reviews will hopefully be useful. This explains why there are separate entries for Frow, E. and Frow, R. but also an entry for Frow, R. & E.: this refers to jointly written books or pamphlets.

Authors in the 'Articles' chapter and the 'About CP' chapter are not included – these are in author order, so easily accessed – but if there were two authors, and the second was in the CP, then the second name will be entered here.

Pseudonyms were used, especially in the 1920s and 1930s. These are entered in inverted commas, and appear at the end of the Index next to their real names, where known. When people wrote pseudonymously in Party journals, it is assumed that they were members. Hopefully, more of these identities will be revealed in the future.

Generally, I have left the name as printed on the original pamphlet or article, even if the customary spelling is different now (e.g. Zinovieff rather than the usual Zinoviev). When there is an error ('Inprecorr' and 'Communist International' are major culprits), I have corrected it (e.g. MacManus is spelt on one occasion as

McManus; M. Philips Price as Phillips). An interesting problem arises over A.J. Bennet. He was the Soviet Communist responsible for the work of the CPGB in the 1920s and he wrote a few pamphlets and articles under this misspelt name; occasionally he got it right and we find Bennett, but he was also commonly known as Petrovsky and Lipec – though it is believed he was born as Goldfarb. In the Index I have used Bennett.

In cases where there is more than one person with the same surname, I have tried to distinguish them by use of the first names – e.g. Devine, Pat was the father of Devine, Pat (Jnr). Bell, T. was General Secretary of the YCL – not to be confused with Bell, Tom (though his name was also Tom). I have distinguished all the Joneses.

b) Topics

I have chosen a selection of key subjects, regions, chronological periods and industries for inclusion. It is impossible to predict what aspects of the CP's activity will interest future historians – if it becomes the CP's approach to the national question, or the 1950s, then these historians will be disappointed. This is where an interactive online version is superior, but there are partial ways round such restrictions. For instance, in the case of the national question, one can search the publications of the Welsh and Scottish Districts or Wales and Scotland in the regional indexes. The Index does not include references to cities, apart from London; this is perhaps a pity, but those interested can always look in the relevant District in the Local CP chapter and the Index by Region.

Since I started work on this bibliography one controversial topic has emerged: the historiography of the CPGB. There is no Index entry for this, but the main participants in this debate will be known to many readers. The articles – for it is in journals that this debate raged – are easily traceable and there are often trails of replies in specific journals. My annotations may refer to these trails.

To avoid repetition, the entries in the chapter 'Daily Worker/Morning Star' are not included in this index under 'Daily Worker'. Similarly, entries in the National and Local CP chapters are not included in the Periods of Time index, as they are already in chronological order – so it is easy to find items dealing with 1926 or the Second World War in these chapters.

Presence in the Index does not imply importance. A short article may have several entries in the index but an important book none. For instance, *Trotskyist Politics and Industrial Work in Scotland, 1939-1945* is an article of sixteen pages and has four entries (Trotskyism; Miscellaneous Industrial; WW2; Scotland) while Willie Thompson's *The Good Old Cause*, which was the first history of the CP after its demise, has none.

Sometimes there are difficulties in deciding which subject an entry should be placed under: material on children could be in Education (usually), or Social Services or Health, depending on content.

The subjects are:

Anti-Fascist	Far Right; Jewish
Anti-Racism/Black Studies	Includes legislation; BME Communists.
Art	Includes art theory; art education; architecture; design; photography; sculpture; Communist artists; AIA.
Colonies	Excludes India.
Comintern / YCI / Other CPs	Excludes Modern Books titles.
Co-operatives	
Culture	Includes general culture; libraries (including the MML); bookshops; LBC; CP Festivals and Pageants.
Daily Worker/Morning Star	
Environment	See also Science. The word 'Environment' occurs only in one title!
Fiction	A small number of short stories and poems were published under the Party's imprints.
Film/TV	
Gay/Lesbian	
Health	
Historians' Group	
Housing	Includes Planning.
ILP	
India	Sub continent.
Ireland	
International	Excludes India, Ireland, Spain, Socialist Countries. Includes everything else: Common Market, South Africa etc.
Labour Party	Includes pamphlets/articles by the LP on the CP, by the CP on the LP and anything on LP/CP relations.
Law/Civil Liberties	Includes policing; legal cases against the CP and individual members; state surveillance of the CP but excludes spies.
Left	This refers to an analysis from a far-left viewpoint. Although a bit schematic as a category, the aim is not to be judgemental but to pinpoint those items that approach the CP from a particular viewpoint.
Literature	Includes novelists and poets (but not novels or poems – see 'Fiction'); literary criticism; literary magazines; publishing (CP & general).
Local Government	Includes Social Security etc.

Maoism	
Music	
Peace/War	Includes militarism; CP policies for, and attitudes towards, the armed forces; conscription; deserters; NATO.
Pensioners	
Religion	Includes secularism; religious members; material by or about religious organisations; Marxist-Christian dialogue. Excludes Jewish interest (see AF).
Right	Analysis from a far-right position, though generally academic studies are not included here, even if very hostile to the CP. See also 'Religion': there is a substantial body of anti-communist work from religious organisations.
Science	Includes policy statements, controversies, Communist scientists.
Socialist Countries	
Spain	Spanish Civil War.
Spies	
Sport/Leisure	Includes CP statements; CP members noted for sporting achievements; the fight for the right to roam; working-class sports organisations; DW sport annuals; Woodcraft Folk, Scouts
Structure/Organisation	Majority of these are from CP (and occasionally CI) sources. This is a selection of the most important entries.
Students	Refers to CP activity among students – not educational policy.
Theatre	
Trotskyism	
Unemployment	Includes NUWM and later activity against unemployment e.g. the People's Marches for Jobs.
Women	Excludes 'Women at Work' – see below under 'Industry'.
Youth	Excludes YCL chapter, and YCL Magazines chapter.

Pamphlets of Jewish interest are included in 'Anti-Fascism', because such a large number of pamphlets in this category cover the Battle of Cable Street and opposition to British fascists in general.

There is obviously some difficulty with figures like Jack Lindsay, who wrote on art, theatre, science, literary criticism and was a poet and novelist, and like Randall

Swingler who was a poet, novelist, critic, editor and publisher. Even Clive Branson, a lesser known figure, was an artist and poet – his name may appear in Literature, Art or Culture.

'Structure' includes Factory Groups; production of factory papers; literature distribution (but not bookshops - see 'Culture'); publicity; finance; campaigning, special conferences but not IPD/Congress material (easier to find chronologically). Excludes material on YCL, which is easy to find in YCL Indexes. It excludes issues around CP's future structure and final split (see Index '1980-1991'). It does not include every article in all the CP and Comintern journals; the quantity of these is huge.

There is an overlap between entries in 'Left' and 'Trotskyism': the latter should be about the CP and the Trotskyist movement in this country, while the former indicates a political analysis on any subject and is from a viewpoint to the left of the CP (Trotskyist, Anarchist, Maoist etc).

Perhaps a few words are necessary about the spies. My first impulse was to exclude them altogether as not shedding any light on the CPGB as such. However, many books and articles about the spies – and there is a veritable industry in this area – also discussed CP organisation among students, especially at Cambridge in the 1930s, so I have adhered to the usual criteria for inclusion. It does lead to some apparent anomalies: Philby's *My Silent War*, for example, is excluded as having insufficient references to the CPGB. I have included *Sonya's Report* by Ruth Werner, who was a key spy in the Far East for the Comintern in the 1930s and for the USSR in Europe early in the war. Werner lived in Britain between 1941 and 1950, having married a British Communist, and she actually joined the local CP branch in Banbury. However, references to the Party in *Sonya's Report* are minimal. A further problem arose with Tom Driberg. His involvement in the CP is mentioned in his posthumously published autobiography, *Ruling Passions*. However, Nigel West's *MI5* claimed Driberg was recruited by MI5 as a schoolboy to spy on the CP and was expelled when this was discovered. This version appeared in all the spy books of the 1980s, and was only rejected in Francis Wheen's *Tom Driberg: His Life and Indiscretions* in 1990. Some ambiguity is to be expected in separating fact and fiction where spies are concerned.

The 'regions' are: Scotland, Wales, London, South West, South, East Anglia, Midlands, North West, North East, Yorkshire. These areas are approximate and are not intended to correspond exactly to CP Districts. Entries in the Local CP chapter are not included here.

'Agriculture' includes fishing and food industries, plus rural issues.

'Buses' includes London Underground, as the two are often linked. 'Railways' will include some engineering, as in Acton.

'TUC' includes the STUC and Trades Councils; TUC publications; CP material about the TUC, including annual congresses.

'Miscellaneous' was potentially a huge and unwieldy category, reflecting the huge quantity of pamphlets the CP published on industrial issues, and the extensive literature on the CP in this area. For reasons of space I have excluded: book reviews (the word 'Review' appears at the end of the title of all book reviews so can be found that way); material by groups like the Economic League, IRIS, Aims of Industry – these constitute the majority of the 'Right' Index category and can be easily picked up there. I have also excluded most of the national pamphlets on general industrial questions, leaving in some key ones and those of a more specific nature e.g. on productivity, health and safety, automation, wages, young workers (usually YCL pamphlets). Also included under 'Miscellaneous' are entries on international trade unions and critiques of CP industrial policies from the Labour Party and far left. Anyone interested in CP industrial material from a particular period will be able to search 'National Publications' by year. Material on the General Strike appears under the '1926' Index.

Names

'A.F.' 530, 604
'C.B.' 154
'C.T.' 3447
'Davy' 485, 825, 3460
'Dyad' 3428
'Eccles' 908, 1372, 1411
'Espoir' 26, 40, 156, 163, 2545
'Farnborough, B.' 6535
'Gabriel' 894, 979, 2121, 2225, 3388, 3390, 3393, 3413, 3428, 3452, 3455, 3486, 6423
'Jax' 567
'Michael' 67, 128, 2988, 3321
'Pit Lad' 2995
'S.H.' 368
'Savage' 124, 150, 200
'Storm, W. 3457
'Westral' 2545
'Y.J.' 30
Aaronovitch, S. 1267, 2098, 6127
Abbott, S. 971, 2258
Ablett, N. 3911, 4890, 5852
Ackerman, M. 928
Ackland, V. 4675, 5100
Ahern, T. 965, 1189
Ainley, B. 1345, 6714
Ainley, D. 1177, 1925
Ainley, T. 997, 1183, 2602, 4825
Airlie, J. 5450
Aitken, G. 4063
Alergant, J. 1860
Alexander, B. 2249
Alexander, K. 5369
Allan, W. 3998, 5614, 4608
Allen, B. 4467
Allen, P. 2554
Allison, G. 893
Allison, J. 4551
Alsop, G. 3880
Amis, K. 3947
Anderson, A. 2557, 6966
Anderson, D. 4857, 4552, 4553
Anderson, F. 2508
Andrews, G. 5854, 6629
Annan, A. 2436

Archer, D. 2240
Archer, J. 6372
Arnot, R P. 72, 219, 304, 422, 545, 627, 703, 2921, 3409, 3750, 4155, 5113, 5121, 5481, 6384, 6678, 6706, 6707, 6766
Arnott, B. 5239
Arundel, H. 5446
Ashbee, F. 4285
Ashby, H. 3720
Ashton, J. 5868, 6304f
Ashton, M. 3738
Askins, J. 4238
Atkin, M. 2309
Atkinson, E. 6304f
Attfield, J. 2574, 5820, 6442
Attwood, A. 4151
Audit, G. 771
Aylward, B. 1743
Bacharach, A. 4826
Bagwell, P. 6782
Bain, L. 4636
Baker, B. 1170, 1243
Ball, F. 2611
Barclay, W. 2460
Barke, J. 4088, 4486, 5107
Barker, B. 2309
Barnard, G. 6448
Barnes, C. 4595
Barnsby, G. 2937, 2950, 2957, 2976
Barr, A. 5794
Barr, G. 6288
Barr, S. 6264a
Barratt Brown, M. 4884
Barrow, N. 2168
Barrow, S. 2538
Bart, L. 4286
Barton, A. 4582
Bateman, A. 1819
Bateman, C. 5066
Bates, R. 4677, 5105a
Baxter, J. 2971
Baxter, M. 2050
Beaken, H. 5552
Beardon, C. 3358

INDEX OF NAMES

Beattie, M. 4551
Beauchamp, J. 3842, 3898, 4827
Beauchamp, K. 1734, 1778, 1799, 1828, 1868, 1936, 2027, 5783
Beckett, C. 3693, 4233, 4235, 5173
Beeching, J. 2250
Behan, B. 6156
Bell, T. 3272, 4467
Bell, Tom 33, 62, 129,130, 275, 363, 565, 2208, 2542, 3500, 3909, 5291, 6109, 6808
Bellamy, J. 1284, 1347
Bellamy, R. 1330, 3717, 5481
Belsey, H. 1667
Bennett, A. 149, 154, 183, 5121, 5810
Bennett, M. 489, 3063, 3072, 3076, 3077, 3087, 3095
Benson, E. 6048
Bent, J. 1956, 1959
Benton, S. 2540
Berger, J. 3775
Bernal, J.D. 2569, 3742, 3966, 4278, 4377, 4446, 4791, 4944, 5044, 6500
Bernal, Jane 2568
Bernard, R. 2563
Berry, J. 6969
Biggar, H. 4869a, 6781
Biggs, K. 2043
Birch, C. 3920, 5498
Birch, R. 725, 4160, 4600, 4745
Bishop, R. 177, 434
Blackman, P. 3927, 6783, 2611, 6772a
Blackwell, S. 2145, 2147, 2148, 2153, 2154, 2157, 2165, 2201
Bloomfield, Jon 1425, 2181, 2183
Bloomfield, Jude 4048
Bloomfield, T. 5225
Blunt, A. 4015
Blunt, J. 2620
Bolsover, P. 757, 846, 959, 979, 1008, 3388
Bolton, Guy 4552
Bolton, George 1478
Bond, K. 4996
Bond, R. 5552
Booth, A. 1553
Booth, S. 4237
Boswell, J. 317, 325, 326, 331, 406, 417, 461, 494, 796, 3729, 4088, 4543, 4765, 4769, 4828, 5082, 5757
Boughton, R. 4416, 6718, 6856
Bourn, D. 2961
Bourne, H. 4068
Bowden, J. 3842
Bowden, M. 5397
Bowman, D. 1165, 2461
Bracegirdle, M. 4681
Braddock, B. 4992

Bradley, B. 345, 356, 529, 530, 595, 667, 2539, 3552, 4448, 4449, 6216, 6873
Bradshaw, L. 5235
Bradshaw, P. 3255
Braithwaite, C. 6064
Bramley, T. 457, 581, 1686, 1725, 1738, 1805, 1818, 1847
Branson, C. 639, 4829, 5219, 6028, 6947
Branson, N. 1638, 2975, 2977, 2978, 3717, 3722, 5548, 5748, 5871, 5888, 6386, 6466, 6468, 6669, 6922
Brennan, I. 1406
Brent, J. 4135, 4331
Bridges, G. 3126, 3263, 3375, 4467
Bright, F. 2219, 2284, 6396
Bright, G. 3725
Brooks, A. 4068
Brooks, B. 3111, 3121, 5204
Brooks, E. 580, 589, 2233, 3416, 3432, 3437, 3444, 3451, 3463
Brooks, G. 2540, 5204
Brooksbank, M. 4538
Brown, A. 1144
Brown, Eddie 4553
Brown, E.H. (Ernest) 140, 5259
Brown, G. 2278, 4438, 5220
Brown, I. 478, 506, 572, 4251, 4362, 5227, 5913
Brown, J. 5558
Brown, James 2966
Brown, John 4551
Browne, F. 5346, 5568
Browne, S. 4312, 4807
Browning, R. 2933
Buchan, J. 4088, 6613a
Buchan, N. 2550
Buckle, D. 2913, 5412, 0
Burchill, J. 5230
Burgess, G. 3854, 4147, 4764
Burke, D. 3045
Burn, G. 2572
Burns, D. 4551
Burns, E. 297, 350, 352, 360, 469, 533, 618, 654, 684, 758, 830, 883, 884, 1197, 1559, 2544, 2567, 5826
Burns, Elinor 973
Burns, R. 1982
Bush, A. 2572, 3469, 3711, 3813, 3830a, 4929, 6862
Bushell, T. 1404
Butler, E. 3450
Byrne, J. 4501
Campbell, C. 2973
Campbell, J.R. 79, 93, 117, 188, 192, 198, 222, 357, 404, 426, 486, 707, 719, 801, 966, 1025, 1124, 1202, 1209, 1234, 2414, 2434, 2516, 2600, 3443, 3472, 3475, 3672, 3684, 4567, 5121, 6121, 6502, 6796

Cannon, L. 1010, 4005
Carey, N. 2117
Carpenter, M. 3250
Carr, B. 4011, 4886
Carritt, B. 1811, 1860
Carritt, J. 1860
Carritt, M. 490
Carson, J. 7118a
Carter, P. 1563, 2953, 5267, 5533
Carver, H. 1808
Casasola, R. 4402
Caudwell, C. 3748, 3939, 4543, 4586, 4677, 4709, 4878, 4941, 4965, 4966, 4972, 4990, 7223, 7247, 7251
Chadwick, P. 4831, 4845
Challinor, R. 2944
Chapman, D. 1808
Charlesworth, J. 4926, 4927
Chase, E. 5841
Chater, T. 1335, 1341, 1353, 1373, 1485, 2050, 3270
Claiborne, B. 3718
Clair, L. 4425a
Clark, A. 2518, 6304b
Clark, E. 4329
Clark, J. 1650
Clarke, A. 1815
Clarke, I. 2568
Clarke, Mrs ? 2736
Clarke, R. 2584
Clarke, T. 4552, 4553
Claydon, C. 3082, 3098, 6448
Clegg, A. 515, 738, 766, 898, 2340, 2603, 5408a
Clegg, H. 5408a
Coates, Z. 10
Cohen, Eric 5691
Cohen, Eve 5691
Cohen, G. 1396, 2268, 3134
Cohen, H. 1167
Cohen, J. 238, 1261, 4832, 6210
Cohen, Manny 2264, 2402
Cohen, Max 4833
Cohen, Monty 3252
Cohen, P. 3933, 5955, 6850, 6922, 6970
Cohen, R. 3902, 4621, 4656, 4771, 6925
Cole, S. 1982
Coleman, P. 1743
Collins, E. 6292, 6293
Collins, H. 5922
Colyer, W. 70
Cook, D. 1378, 1449, 3267, 3954, 5355
Cooney, B. 4063, 4074, 4857, 5134
Cooper, C. 4137
Cooper, E. 4351
Cope, D. 7042, 4088a
Copeman, F. 4063, 4211, 6303
Cornford, C. 3860

Cornford, J. 4586, 4887, 4921, 4990, 5281, 6028
Cornforth, K. 1967
Cornforth, M. 429, 521, 635, 1638, 2569, 2589, 4791, 6062
Corum, A. 2572
Cose, E. 4351
Costello, M. 1307, 1451, 1480, 1518
Costello, P. 4622, 5765
Cotter, J. 3365
Cottman, S. 4311
Cotton, B. 1845
Cousins, N. 4283
Coutts, C. 3487
Coward, J. 1259, 3390
Cowe, W. 2422, 2426
Cox, D. 5180, 6712
Cox, I. 290, 368, 1152, 2355, 2363, 2376, 2384, 2386, 5216
Cox, J. 1542, 1544, 3722
Crane, G. 1095
Crawfurd, H. 5392, 6103
Croft, A. 3717, 4087, 4357, 4878, 4896, 5429, 6281, 6850, 6918
Cronje, G. 2574, 2956
Crooks, H. 1756
Crossland, V. 3107
Crossley, J. 3420
Currie, J. 2606
Daffern, E. 3860, 4106
Daltun, L. 5672
Daly, L. 5655
D'Arcy, H. 4108a, 6304b
Dare, E. 5183
Darke, M. 4668
Darton, P. 4429a
Dash, J. 3860, 3888, 4219, 5853
David, J. 2389
Davidson, J. 4074
Davidson, M. 4117
Davidson, T. 4552
Davies, B. 2922, 4886
Davies, J. 5392
Davis, A. 1823
Davis, B. 3184, 3260, 3264
Davis, L. 4121
Davis, M. 5462a
Dawson, J. 3730
Deakin, F. 211, 5196
Despard, C. 4676
Devine, Pat 2227, 2229, 2232, 2240, 5874
Devine, Pat (Jnr) 4048, 4062
Diamond, D. 5495
Dickenson, B. 2235
Dickenson, H. 2234
Dix, B. 4248

INDEX OF NAMES

Dobb, M. 2569, 2927, 3516, 4080, 4373, 4834, 4976, 5392, 5438, 5482, 5626, 5804, 6704
Doherty, L. 6375, 2550
Doll, R. 4468
Douglas, F. 2418, 2419, 2420, 2475
Douglas, J. 331, 3014, 3042
Douglass, D. 4137
Downton, A. 1688
Doyle, B. 4074
Doyle, C. 6197a
Doyle, M. 5410
Drever, G. 4553
Driberg, T. 4739, 4949, 5055
Duckworth, R. 2373
Duncan, K. 1891, 2063, 4481
Dunlop, J. 4553
Dunman, H. 5074
Dunman, J. 647, 833, 872, 1200, 1292, 2548
Dunn, B. 2028
Dunn, J. 6251
Dunstan, R. 156, 2137, 2138
Dutt, C.P. 220, 466, 6700
Dutt, R.P. 99, 152, 168, 173, 230, 231, 250, 252, 263, 289, 313, 318, 356, 378, 409, 454, 476, 510, 574, 593, 720, 735, 813, 951, 1138, 1277, 1830, 2162, 2600, 3490, 3990, 4307, 4584, 4631, 4683, 4737, 4815, 5160, 5197, 5256, 5263, 5284, 5295, 5528, 5537, 5591, 5594, 5599, 5700, 6017, 6041, 6046, 6104, 6112, 6298, 6340, 6494, 6511, 6594, 6609, 6710, 6868, 6873, 6875, 6909, 6953
Dutt, S. 4155, 5297
Dywien, J. 3497, 6693
Eaglesham, A. 3943
Easton, G. 6287
Easton, S. 4928
Eastwood, F. 3086
Ebbutt, K. 1576
Ecclestone, A. 4287
Ecclestone, D. 4287
Edwardes, Rose 6309
Edwards, R. 2195
Elias, S. 249, 6003
Elliot, A. 2962
Ellis, L. 1016
Elsbury, S. 4514, 6813
Essex, M. 6798
Etheridge, D. 1198, 4960, 4994
Evans, A. 4174
Evans, D. 5905, 5906
Evans, G.E. 6085, 6086
Evans, H. 662
Eve, M. 4473
Ewer, W.N. 5601, 6309, 6609
Exell, A. 6193
Fagan, H. 814, 1034
Fairley, J. 2552

Falber, R. 1127, 1216, 1415, 1418, 2538, 3877
Fava, A. 6138
Ferguson, A. 140, 2416, 4625
Ferguson, M. 5841
Ferns, T. 4551
Ferres, G. 2574
Field, A. 3879
Filling, P. 6877
Findlay, A. 4088a
Finley, L. 4236
Fisher, R. 2554
Fisher, S. 2554, 4669, 4810
Fitton, J. 331, 4088, 4765
Fitzgerald, J. 4501
Fletcher, G. 4056, 4574, 6565
Foles, P. 1756
Forman, S. 4137
Forshaw, J. 5915
Forster 2089
Foster, F. 1787, 1937, 1948
Foster, J. 5462a
Foulkes, F. 3699
Fox, R. 160, 3600, 3939, 4513, 4677, 5280, 5281, 5282, 5540, 6439
Francis, B. 365, 2857, 5263
Francis, D. 5172
Francis, H. 4048
Frankel, B. 4329
Fraser, H. 2435
French, S. 1656, 4229, 5669
Froom, H. 3865
Frow, E. 1162, 2782, 4232, 4355, 5185, 5423, 6327, 6885, 6886
Frow, R. 5796, 5903, 6639, 6811, 7010
Frow, R. & E. 2284, 2285, 3862, 4242, 5249
Fryer, P. 3964, 4203, 4284, 5544, 6305
Fullarton, S. 5225
Fyrth, J. 5420, 5954
Gadsby, J. 4254
Gallacher, W. 71, 118, 195, 245, 301, 310, 348, 351, 388, 434, 435, 436, 446, 451, 473, 484, 487, 491, 534, 539, 560, 561, 573, 616, 682, 691, 803, 810, 816, 831, 843, 861, 968, 1247, 2425, 2457, 2473, 2502, 2504, 2505, 3479, 3711, 3744, 3822, 3961, 4008, 4217, 4620, 4636, 4653, 4983, 5111, 5264, 5365, 5395, 5417, 5505, 5996, 6075, 6077, 6302, 6402, 6403, 6404, 6807, 7005, 7007, 7069
Ganley, C. 3912
Gardner, J. 2271, 5939
Gardner, K. 2289
Garland, P. 6433
Garman, D. 2569, 4057, 4305, 6044
Garnett, J. 2776
Garrett, G. 5786
Gascoyne, D. 4225
Gaster, J. 1811, 4046, 4608, 4881a, 5278, 5444

Gates, Mrs 2736
Geldart, D. 3205
Gibbons, C. 6560
Gibbons, J. 3426, 3435
Gibbons, T. 3725
Gilchrist, A. 5145
Giles, C. 2554
Giles, G. 812, 6802
Gillan, P. 3055, 4551, 4553
Glading, P. 293, 3887, 5268, 6933
Goldberg, M. 5113, 6396
Gollan, J. 380, 762, 836, 870, 930, 945, 1001, 1027, 1040, 1062, 1064, 1075, 1094, 1121, 1129, 1132, 1143, 1195, 1222, 1257, 1280, 1305, 1306, 1325, 1417, 1427, 1455, 2322, 2438, 2487, 2490, 2566, 3036, 3047, 3048, 3056, 3058, 3061, 3065, 6199
Goodman, D. 1616, 2337, 4311, 5198, 1957, 4074, 4284
Gorman, J. 4286, 6289, 6822
Goss, J. 3041
Gossip, A. 3755, 6655
Gough, G. 5552
Gradwell, I. 5003
Grandjean, D. 1742
Granger, W. 2753
Grant, B. 1903, 1905
Graves, B. 1685
Gray, R. 4464
Greaves, C.D. 1299, 2940, 4443a, 5672, 5710, 6341, 6884
Green, G. 4837
Green, H. 5733
Green, N. 2962, 4074, 4761, 5565, 6225, 1622
Green, R. 1625, 2969
Greenald, D. 3860
Greenhalgh, S. 2229
Greening, E. 5113
Gregory, W. 3860
Grove, D. 1645, 1646
Groves, R. 218, 4302, 4602
Gubb, F. 2553, 2554
Guest, D. 1638, 4304
Guggenheim, P. 4057
Gunawardena, P. 5858
Gunn, I. 2553
Gunter, H. 2172
Gyseghem, A. van 952
Haldane, J.B.S. 722, 3393, 3409, 3425, 4036, 4446, 4742, 4791, 5044, 5051, 6440, 6503, 7169, 3440
Hall, C. 4068
Halpin, K. 1474, 2098, 5352, 6795
Hamilton, P. 4770
Hamm, S. 4962
Hammond, J. 2242
Hannington, W. 1791, 3711, 5617, 5751

Hardy, A. 1768
Hardy, G. 4206, 4617, 5083
Harper, B. 1976
Harper, R. 1619
Harrison, B. 6213
Harrison, J. 150
Harrison, M. 1429
Harrison, R. 5163, 6001, 6365
Harrison, S. 1401
Hart, E. Tudor 4212, 4213, 4215, 5074
Hart, J. Tudor 1360, 2389
Hart, F. 961, 1092, 1136, 2467, 4551, 5204
Harvey, B. 4068
Harvey, E. 2240
Hasted, J. 3718, 4334
Hastings, B. 4803
Haston, J. 4603
Hatt, D. 4081
Haxell, F. 3699
Hayes, E. 1977
Healey, D. 4722
Healy, G. 4540, 4604, 4699
Heffer, E. 4714
Heinemann, M. 913, 2603, 4568, 4709
Henderson, H. 3711
Henderson, J. 4552
Henderson, S. 1019
Henery, M. 4538, 4551, 5119
Henrotte, E. 295
Heslop, H. 3907, 4091, 4092, 4487, 5695, 6375
Hett, K. 4268
Hewlett, B. 2342
Higgins, P. 2247
Hikins, H. 4501
Hill, C. 2569, 4976, 6090
Hill, H. 942, 4169, 4234
Hill, R. 1429
Hill, S. 4088a
Hilson, F. 944
Hilton, R. 6526, 6651
Hinks, J. 6683
Hinshelwood, H. 2410
Hitchings, G. 938
Hitchon, B. 2389, 2391
Hobsbawm, E. 40, 2926, 2961, 3348, 3359, 3369, 3717, 4077, 4166, 5114, 5190, 5191, 5243, 5462a, 5592, 5780, 6082, 6224, 6553, 6829, 6937, 4372, 6376
Hodgkin, T.L. 4192
Hodgson, G. 1534
Hodson, E.K. 5944
Hoffman, J. 5355
Hogarth, P. 1799, 1821, 1851, 2233, 3729
Hogg, R. 424
Holland, B. 1155
Holland, J. 4765
Holley, N. 1030

INDEX OF NAMES

Holmes, W. 2598, 3402, 3549, 5443, 6309
Holt, W. 3823
Hooper, B. 1626
Horner, A. 187, 371, 410, 580, 756, 1088, 4194, 4195, 4601, 4608, 4799, 4838, 4890, 4894, 5270, 5391, 5644, 5674, 5721, 6267a, 6390, 7054
Horner, J. 4956
Horrabin, F. 4006
Horrabin, J. 6609
Horrabin, W. 4006
Horton, R. 7091
Hosey, S. 4467
Howard, R. 708
Howarth, H. 2309
Howkins, A. 4273
Hudson, K. 1582, 4088a
Hunter, M. 5204
Hurst, D. 1746, 1939
Hutt, A. 292, 2410, 3474, 4550, 5551
Hyde, D. 4661, 5829, 6111
Hyett, T. 3252
Hyndman, T. 4996
Hyslop, J. 6430
Iliffe, S. 1511, 2568
Inkpin, A. 20
Jacks, D. 3339
Jackson, T.A. 4795, 51, 125, 325, 714, 2545, 2547, 2968, 4432, 4673, 4802, 5407, 5773, 6048, 6277, 6562
Jacobs, J. 4886, 5527, 6670
Jacques, M. 1289, 1324, 1416, 2566, 3338, 5359
Jacques, S. 3252
James, T. 4518
Jarrett, L. 1648
Jefferies, D. 6823
Jefferies, L. 4024, 6396, 3710
Jefferson, H.R.G. 2604
Jeffery, N. 950, 1085, 5204, 2228
Jeffreys, L. 5113
Jenkin, A. 2949, 4107
Jenkins, M. 2222, 2225, 2238, 2255, 2278, 2955
Jepps, M. 3145
Job, C. 1791
John, D. 3284
Johnson, J. 467, 4356
Johnson, V. 537, 2230
Johnston, Mary 4552
Johnstone, Monty 3252, 3259, 3275, 3276, 3350, 3375, 5237, 5318, 6220, 6377, 6515, 6701, 6703
Jones, A. 6983
Jones, B. 858, 3446, 4957
Jones, C. 4442, 4454, 4871, 6770, 6897
Jones, E. 2389
Jones, G J. 1758, 1771
Jones, George 3402

Jones, Gladys 3083, 3101
Jones, Glyn 2354
Jones, H. 1405
Jones, Lewis 2838, 3907, 4890, 4893, 4894, 4895, 5759, 5940, 6375
Jones, Reg 6396
Jones, T. Gwyn 2361
Jordan, A. 4081
Jordan, H. 2970
Jordan, P. 3821, 6174, 6176
Julius, J. 3725
Jump, J. 4996
Kane, A. 4028, 4048
Kane, J. 1137, 5668
Kapp, Y. 2915, 3840, 4460, 6061
Kartun, D. 825, 890, 1004, 3484
Katsaronas, A. 3725
Kaufman, S. 3252
Kay, Jackie 4048
Kay, John 6304e
Kaye, S. 1348, 1998, 2020, 3722
Keable, G. 6192
Keehan, J. 1754, 1851, 2089
Keith, M. 1146
Kelsey, N. 1756
Kemp, T. 3964
Kerrigan, P. 468, 567, 669, 869, 946, 1181, 2259, 2423, 4074, 4886, 5372
Kerrigan, R. 3860, 5296, 6633
Kcrshaw, H. 2227
Kettle, A. 1217, 2590, 4709, 6059, 6187, 6889
Kettle, M. 4048, 7097
Kiernan, V. 3944, 4462, 4466, 5544, 6448
King, F. 5711, 5917, 6096, 6215, 6441, 6744
Kirby, T. 1188
Kirkby, S. 5728
Kisch, R. 6101
Klingender, F. 4750, 4839, 6607
Klugmann, J. 886, 1068, 1261, 1297, 1323, 2566, 2603, 4116, 4375, 4639, 5386, 5449, 6126, 6155, 6200, 6612, 1289
Knight, E. 4502
Knight, F. 2942, 3860
Kumaramangalam, S. 4840
Landis, H. 1536
Lane, H. 6559
Langton, P. 5397
Langton, W. 5466
Lansbury, V. 4621
Latham, H. 1444
Latham, P. 2964
Lauchlan, W. 860, 927, 1012, 2496, 2509
Laughlan, B. 5119
Lawrence, J. 6393, 6559
Lazarus, A. 2563, 7083
Le Brocq, N. 741
Lee, L. 4391

Leeson, G. 4074
Leff, V. 4531
Leigh, B. 1045, 6870
Leigh, D. 4028
Lennox, J. 4552
Lesser, F. 663
Lessing, D. 5369, 5896
Levenson, S. 1163
Leversha, G. 6437
Levine, M. 4074, 4237, 4311
Levitt, V. 1815
Levy, H. 4841, 4888, 5044, 5369
Lewis, J. 2570, 3376, 4791
Lewis, L. 5355
Lewis, S. 2568
Lewis, T. 2606
Lindsay, A. 985
Lindsay, J. 2912, 3982, 4102, 4561, 4709, 5118, 6008, 6263
Litterick, J. 6197a
Llewellyn, E. 4024
Lloyd 349
Lloyd, A.L. 952, 3871, 4326, 4812
Lloyd, J. 6983
Lochore, J. 4552, 4093
Londragan, J. 4553
Lovell, B. 5214
Lovell, S. 5214
Lucas, J. 5084
Ludmer, M. 5245
Lutyens, E. 4329
Lynd, S. 747
MacColl, E. 952, 3718, 4325, 4821, 4902, 5764, 6261
MacDiarmid, H. 3711, 3982, 4763a, 5224, 5666, 6018, 6351, 7234
MacDougall, George 4553a
MacEwen, M. 1011, 2325
Macintyre, S. 2959, 2968, 3367
Mack Smith, M. 4081
MacLaine, W. 6625
Maclean, D. 3854, 4019, 4764
Macleod, A. 5544, 6031, 6850
MacManus, A. 15, 20, 100, 4495
Mahon, J. 308, 372, 592, 1017, 1064, 1067, 1238, 1821, 1865, 1870, 1877, 2641, 2684, 6154, 6539
Maitland, F. 6672
Malone, C. 31, 3750, 4575
Mandelson, P. 4805
Mann, T. 6081, 296, 503, 677, 2925, 2935, 3750, 3914, 4024, 4322, 4718, 4993, 5002, 5059, 5271, 5508, 5557, 7129
Manning, M. 1605
Margolies, D. 2582
Markson, B. 6501
Marsden, E. 5539

Marshall, L. 2167
Mason, A. 5397
Massey, G. 4025
Massey, J. 6713
Massie, A. 200, 3021
Matthews, B. 1230, 1328, 1420, 1952
Matthews, G. 589, 908, 1040, 1064, 1066, 1400, 1479, 3489, 5133, 5711, 5917, 6096, 6215, 6221, 6441, 6744
Maxwell 674
Maxwell, F. 211
McArthur, J. 4550
McBain, J. 4150
McCaig, B. 4467
McCarthy, M. 4621
McCartney, G. 4063, 4074, 4553
MacColl, E. 2550
McCourt, B. 2442, 2452
McCusker, F. 4551, 4553
McDonald, A. 2540
McFadden.A. 6797
McGahey, M. 1287, 1584, 4607, 5201, 6027, 6297
McGinn, M. 4597
McGree, L. 2773, 2777, 3866, 4239
McIlhone, B. 2491
McInnes, A. 4551
McIlven, P. 1761
McKay, Claude 4067
McKay, I. 1598, 2540
McKenna, B. 4311
McLaine, W. 32
McLaren, N. 4869a
McLean, Agnes 6631
McLean, J. 2960
McLean, J A. 4192
McLellan, Mair 5057
McLennan, G. 1367, 1411, 1442, 1499, 2517, 2519, 5204
McManus, A. 2785, 6475
McPherson, B. 2589
McShane, H. 462, 2437, 2450, 2451, 2462, 2480, 2489, 2506, 3456, 4152, 4551, 4714, 5650, 6051, 6628
McVicar, W. 4551
Meek, R. 5369
Mellor, W. 4050
Menell, W. 1356
Mercer, E. 2932
Meredith, C. 812
Merson, A. 2938, 2952, 4843
Messer, J. 5634
Meynell, F. 2545
Middleton, G. 5552
Miles, A. 2347, 2363, 2365, 2369, 2371, 2376, 2384
Miles, G. 3319

INDEX OF NAMES

Miller, John 2928
Mindel, M. 1785, 5912
Minns, F. 703
Mitchell, H. 2049
Mitchell, Johnny 4636
Moffat, Abe 535, 718, 1092, 1184, 2868, 2883, 3711, 3998, 4000, 4601, 4608, 6278, 6355, 6356
Moffat, Alex 921, 969
Montagu, I. 465, 542, 543, 544, 546, 547, 549, 675, 1275, 1298, 5051, 5694
Montefiore, D. 4412, 4608
Moore, B. 2917, 2972, 2976, 2977, 2978, 2979, 3717, 6669
Morgan, D. 5536
Morley, I. 4672
Morris, A. 4667
Morris, Margaret 2008
Morris, Max 925, 964, 1078, 2554
Morton, A.L. 828, 1507, 1588, 2121, 2931, 2946, 2974, 4077, 4466, 4709, 6987
Morton, V. 2968, 6767
Moss, B. 3481
Moss, J. 1172, 3124, 3125, 3129, 3155
Moss, L. 6048
Munby, L. 2590
Munby, S. 2289, 2292
Munro, J. 4240
Murdoch, I. 4061, 4964
Murphy, J.T. 153, 212, 247, 2296, 4111, 4112, 4114, 5122, 5229, 5253, 5295, 5603, 5841, 5846, 6077, 6178, 6392, 6786, 6841, 7053, 5228
Murphy, M. 4111, 5603, 6845
Murphy, P. 4125
Murray, A. 4553
Murray, Alex 1346
Murray, Andrew 4680
Murray, Annie 4538
Murray, E. 2592
Murray, G. 4553
Murray, J. 2667
Murray, R. 2183
Murray, S. 364, 4702
Murray, T. 4553, 5225
Muspratt, H. 5074
Myant, C. 2585, 3270
Myant, M. 2889
Mynatt, M. 4068, 4460, 4461
Nahum, R. 4879, 6604
Neal, P. 2755
Neale, R. 2939
Needham, J. 5044
Newbold, J.W. 23, 55, 63, 66, 2294, 4153, 4220, 5011, 5812, 5813, 5816, 5817, 6452, 6480, 6716, 7005, 7102
Newbold, M. 5811

Newsum, A. 4644
Nicholas, P. 4958
Nicholas, T.E. 2353, 2361, 2395, 2846, 3913, 4404, 5486, 5487, 7022
Nicholas, T.I. 6463
Nicholls, M. 2574
Nicholson, J. 1965, 2482
Niven, B. 537, 3437, 3444
Nobes, A. 6036
Norman, E. 3944
Norris, B. 4068
Norris, G. 4219
Norton, M. 591
Norwood, M. 5765, 3977
Ogden, D. 1271, 2540
O'Hara, R. 2275, 2282, 2290
Olive, P. 2540, 2558
Olorenshaw, A. 656
Osment, R. 4707
Owen, H. 377
Owen, J. 1764, 1765, 2327, 2432
Paddock, S. 3710, 4024
Page, W. 1423, 4729
Palfreman, B. 4844
Panes, A. 2179
Pankhurst, S. 3975, 4123, 4139, 4635, 4797, 4877, 5087, 5784, 7187, 7271
Papworth, B. 687, 858
Paris, S. 6304d
Parish, D. 2112, 2951, 7052
Parks, J. 5651
Pascal, R. 4080
Paul, W. 26, 39, 89, 726, 2542, 3755, 5396
Paynter, W. 1088, 2354, 4063, 5909, 6396
Peacock, A. 2945
Pearce, Bert 1576, 2171, 2391,
Pearce, Brian 3964, 4203, 4610, 4773, 5314, 5544, 6305, 6363
Pearce, D. 3338
Pearmain, A. 4088a
Peck, J. 2206, 5954
Peet, G. 4241
Peet, J. 5496
Perry, J. 6798
Perryman, M. 4088a
Philby, K. 3937, 4064, 4491, 4710, 4858
Philipps, W. 3775, 3824
Phillips, P. 3425
Pick, R. 1630
Picton, W. 5113
Pinguey, B. 4501
Pipe, R. 2119, 2124
Piratin, P. 734, 751, 800, 847, 855, 1710, 1794, 3453, 4573, 4804, 6188, 7069
Pitt, E. 4532
Pocock, G. 1458, 1552, 2573
Pollard, S. 4781

Pollitt, B. 4048
Pollitt, H. 116, 158, 279, 285, 294, 299, 300, 307, 311, 317, 322, 335, 340, 341, 343, 344, 354, 355, 359, 361, 367, 374, 375, 395, 401, 409, 415, 416, 419, 420, 421, 438, 440, 444, 449, 455, 470, 471, 474, 477, 479, 481, 495, 503, 519, 531, 548, 562, 597, 606, 619, 628, 630, 639, 641, 652, 659, 665, 689, 709, 716, 723, 727, 731, 739, 742, 749, 764, 770, 778, 782, 808, 815, 817, 826, 832, 835, 842, 854, 866, 867, 878, 881, 889, 891, 892, 894, 914, 916, 917, 919, 920, 926, 940, 949, 957, 960, 972, 981, 982, 993, 994, 1013, 1031, 1040, 1130, 1725, 1832, 1862, 2215, 2263a, 2288, 2457, 2467, 2870, 3114, 3327, 3480, 3755, 3764, 3802, 3889, 4503, 4566, 4583, 4654, 4659, 4660, 4737, 5221, 5263, 5271, 5508, 5537, 5787, 5827, 5946, 5997, 5998, 6046, 6066, 6073, 6099, 6125, 6153, 6154, 6156, 6206, 6298, 6534, 6539, 6624, 6703, 6726, 6907, 6953, 7008
Pollitt, M. 221, 389, 2595, 4749
Porte, E. 4551
Porte, I. 4551
Postgate, R. 2545, 4051, 4754
Poulsen, C. 4758
Poulton, T. 821, 1686, 3057
Pountney, E. 1670, 3665, 3691
Powell, A. 2389, 4223
Power, M. 2538, 2965, 3211, 4048
Preger, L. 4074
Price, L. 4606
Priscott, D. 1560
Proudfoot, D. 2891, 3998, 4550, 4608
Pugh, N. 1814
Purcell, A. 4337, 4655, 6444, 5609a
Purdy, D. 1431
Purkis, S. 2670
Purton, J. 1389
Qualie, B. 6988
Quelch, T. 5552
Quigley, M. 2293
Quinn, S. 4063
Ramelson, B. 1252, 1273, 1281, 1296, 1313, 1321, 1335, 1371, 1376, 1391, 1435, 4859, 2258a, 5763, 6005, 6204, 6276a, 6860
Rathbone, H. 268, 284, 5215
Rattenbury, A. 4543
Ravden, C. 2054
Rawlings, J. 4470, 4471
Reade, A. 3323, 4608, 4609, 4613, 6378
Reckitt, E. 4846
Redmond, P. 494
Rees, W. 2385
Reid, B. 629, 1311, 5782
Reid, D. 2474

Reid, J. 3157, 3164, 3346, 4440, 5283, 5452, 6240, 6406
Reith, L. 4088a
Reilly, J. 4551
Renton, D. 4553, 4847
Richards, P. 1587
Rickword, E. 376, 4095, 4102, 4369, 4543, 4677, 4967, 5377, 6008, 6022, 6044, 6274, 6280, 6470, 7058
Ridley, M. 3880
Riley, E. 2240
Rimel, P. 3902
Riordan, J. 4788, 4789
Roberts, A. 4183
Roberts, G. 6147, 6677
Roberts, H. 6679
Roberts, Jack 4184
Robinson, D. 2181, 4980, 5141, 5526
Robinson, P. 1379
Robson, A. 4794, 5029
Robson, J. 1355, 2568, 3351
Robson, P. 2240
Robson, R.W. 291, 324, 334, 342, 362, 505, 517, 541, 646, 5256
Roche, G. 5956
Roche, J. 2795, 5779
Roche, P. 975
Roley, A. 6823
Romilly, E. 4429
Rose, I. 4026, 4081
Rose, M. 5119
Rose, P. 4026, 4081
Rosen, H. 2554
Rosser, M. 5183
Rothman, B. 5465, 5703, 6037
Rothstein, A. 98, 228, 306, 309, 336, 1074, 1316, 1659, 2918, 2947, 3244, 3557, 3660, 5572, 6153, 6425
Rothstein, T. 5573, 5574
Rothwell, P. 67
Roughton, R. 4225, 4990
Rowe, C. 304, 391, 1738, 1791, 4285
Rowlandson, T. 2259
Rubens, G. 2536
Rubens, G. 2581
Rudé, G. 4231, 4371, 4466, 4940
Ruheman, B. 2948
Rushton, J. 4136
Russell, R. 6305, 6448
Russell, S. 3445
Rust, R. 3902
Rust, T. 737, 2592
Rust, W. 126, 253, 271, 276, 346, 394, 432, 504, 523, 566, 700, 2212, 2414, 2549, 2996, 3011, 3394, 3395, 3405, 3416, 3422, 3429, 3438, 3447, 3458, 3470, 3474, 3475, 3599, 3727, 4207, 4608

INDEX OF NAMES

Sagar, S. 6750
Saklatvala, S. 6467, 113, 115, 166, 201, 210, 1668, 1670, 2208, 3750, 3755, 4694, 4768, 4816, 4818, 4914, 5013, 5014, 5077, 5459, 5597, 5848, 5930, 5934, 6104, 6572, 6577, 6761, 6846, 6874, 6967, 7005, 7245
Salisbury, A. 4301
Salveson, P. 2286
Samson, P. 2103
Samuel, R. 3752, 4820, 5222, 6901
Sara, H. 4611, 4949
Saunders, B. 5119
Savage, D. 2667
Saville, J. 3956, 3964, 4403, 4629, 4773, 4842, 4920, 5369, 5657, 6326, 6373, 6376, 6611, 7054a, 7055
Saxby, J. 4193, 4853
Sayle, A. 4048, 4854
Scargill, A. 4308, 4806
Scott, J. 5392
Seal, W. 3725
Sear, H. 2572
Selkirk, B. 2886, 4140
Seltman, P. 4174
Shapiro, M. 323, 1760
Sharma, V. 1469, 1491, 5701
Shaw, F. 4848
Shaw, G. 4869
Shepherd, G. 3845
Shepherd, W. 366, 3649
Shinnie, P. 5770
Sibley, T. 5568a, 6546, 6276a
Silver, J. 3468
Silvester, F. 952
Simon, B. 1128, 1574, 2194, 6352
Simon, J. 6993
Simon, R. 1543, 2189, 4881, 6448
Simpson, T. 2854
Sims, W. 2568
Sinfield, G. 3476, 4361
Singer, J. 2159
Skelley, J. 6826
Skinner, M. 6632
Slater, M. 3729, 3953, 4102, 4543, 4692, 5073
Sloan, H. 4552; 4553
Sloan, P. 3277, 6963
Small, R. 1362, 2564, 3278
Smallbone, T. 5078
Smethurst, F. 2766
Smethurst, J. 5795
Smith, A. 2479, 2483
Smith, Harold 6035
Smith, Herbert 2550
Smith, M.J. 6448
Smith, Rose 211, 286, 298, 327, 338, 400, 2774, 3513, 4208, 4209, 4441, 4530, 4608
Smith, Rab 4551

Somerville, C. 6830
Sommerfield J. 4273, 4499, 4907, 5742
Spender, S. 4097, 4512, 4902
Spours, K. 6514
Sprague, K. 4285, 4293
Spratt, P. 4510, 4697, 7032
Springhall, D. 459, 3887, 4211
Squires, M. 2794, 3269, 5459
St John, D. 2912
Stanley, F. 1946
Starr, M. 4527, 6269
Stead, C. 3710
Stead, E. 4024
Stephensen, P. 4864, 3939
Stevens, B. 4925
Stevens, J. 3725
Stevens, P. 2150
Stevens, W. 834, 5390
Stevenson, H. 4668
Stevenson, W. 4551
Stewart, B. 5823, 5960
Stewart, J. 2984
Stewart, M. 7181
Stoddart, W. 6989
Stokes, F. 2572
Stokes, W. 4959, 6942
Stone, F. 2563
Strain, J. 5841
Stratton, L. 4937
Stubbens, V. 1756
Styles, J. 5532, 6544
Suss, H. 4942
Sussmann, J. 3081
Swan, I. 6304f
Swankie, E. 4552
Swingler, R. 4090, 4095, 4096, 4608, 4945, 5073, 5734, 5737, 6044, 6052, 6166, 6337, 4543
Tabrisky, J. 4621
Tanner, F. 27
Tanner, J. 329, 4197, 4510, 5557
Tapsell, W. 5706, 5841
Taylor, E. 3899
Taylor, G. 2274
Taylor, M. 3101
Taylor, S. 1175
Tebbs, B. 4425a
Temple, N. 4048, 6614
Thickett, A. 4885
Thomas, A. 2368, 3450
Thomas, R. 2554
Thompson, D. 6680a, 6975
Thompson, E.P. 792, 2550, 2925, 3483, 3851, 4156, 4316, 4428, 4464, 4466, 4494, 4555, 4589, 4711, 4712, 4835, 4923, 5091, 5186, 5243, 5369, 5428, 5462a, 5607, 5736, 5740, 5743, 5918, 5981, 5988a, 6057, 6058, 6191, 6426, 6470, 6523, 6765, 7045, 7249

Thompson, F. 4060, 4428, 4443, 4964, 4971, 5001a, 5978
Thompson, Willie 2574, 2889, 3266, 3336, 3338, 4367, 5549, 5598, 6159, 6671, 6902, 6917, 6954
Thompson, W.H. (Harry) 3842
Thomson, G. 3978, 4976, 5857
Thring, L. 5041
Tippett, M. 4988
Tonge, M. 5132
Torr, D. 2925, 2935, 4400, 6107, 6663, 6665
Toynbee, P. 4637
Trask, R. 3496
Tribe, K. 3367
Trory, E. 1642, 5822, 6051
Tuckett, A. 2967, 5463, 4556a
Turner, B. 204, 211, 221
Upward, E. 4677, 5187, 5377, 5986, 6172, 6471, 6758, 6833, 7255
Utley, F. 248, 3902, 4621, 7194
Veness, K. 3290
Vernon, H. 5385
Wainwright, W. 501, 516, 568, 614, 672, 1057, 1082, 1190, 3066
Walker, I. 4068
Wallace, M. 5675
Wallis, D. 6977
Wallis, P. 1610
Walshe, D. 4467
Ward, B. 2341, 5022
Ward, F. 1638
Warman, W. 2169
Warner, S.T. 4088, 4328, 4439, 4675, 4770, 5100, 5923
Warr, T. 1756
Warren, B. 6983
Waters, J. 2327
Waters, M. 3860
Watkinson, R. 2924
Watson, E. 5031
Watson, H. 2093, 4886, 6270
Watters, F. 6017, 6185
Watters, G. 4553
Weaver, H. 1837, 4529
Webb, L. 211, 221
Weller, K. 5247
Werner, R. 5043
Wesker, S. 5912, 6813
West, A. 1947, 3874, 3939, 4677, 4709, 4878, 5735
Weston, R. 3751
Westwood, J. 2163
Whalley, E. 2195, 3710, 4024
Wheeler, P. 4068
White, A. 1756
White, R. 6210
Whitehead, E. 7004

Whitfield, D. 3495
Whittaker, B. 2226, 2235, 2254
Whittenbury, J. 2243
Whyte, J. 4125
Wicks, H. 3719, 4302, 5462, 6017
Wild, S. 4063, 4074, 4237
Wiles, M. 1174
Wilkinson, E. 2208, 5011, 5068
Wilkinson, H. 3750
Willetts, R. 2930
Williams, B. 2670
Williams, Barry 6853
Williams, Bert 235
Williams, Bill 6396
Williams, Emlyn 5189
Williams, J. Roose 2350, 2374, 2395, 2845, 4267
Williams, Raymond 4156, 4427, 4709, 4891, 4923, 5091, 5243, 7045, 7249
Williams, Robert 12
Williams, S. 5820
Williamson, J. 6197a
Willis, F. 2545
Willis, T. 3252
Wilson, A. 2841
Wilson, D. 4886
Wilson, E. 7003
Winnington, A. 524, 3478
Winnington, R. 5085
Winter, E. 3161
Wintringham, T. 216, 283, 4186, 4763, 5866, 5870, 6823, 6927
Wiseman, D. 4192
Woddis, Jack 879, 1302, 1350, 1353, 1381, 1410, 1428, 1436, 3268, 5725
Woddis, Jane 5355
Woolley, G. 1958
Worswick, T. 2240
Wyatt, J. 5464
Wyatt, R. 4705a
Wynn, B. 6016
Wynn, D. 4068
Wyper, H. 1309
Yardley, C. 3184, 3260
Yates, A. 3725
Yates, S. 3725
Youle, L. 6015
Young, E. 1635
Young, H. 2983, 7003
Zaidman, L. 6237

Topics

Anti-Fascist/Jewish 289, 303, 309, 331, 425, 573, 598, 611, 624, 697, 733, 792, 940, 1008, 1171, 1172, 1237, 1284, 1347, 1348, 1390, 1412, 1414, 1426, 1449, 1454, 1469, 1483, 1491, 1516, 1517, 1576, 1668, 1783, 1795, 1817, 1889, 1945, 1947, 1984, 2005, 2027, 2044, 2062, 2172, 2178, 2184, 2318, 2329, 2444, 2563, 2612, 2965, 3031, 3182, 3183, 3211, 3266, 3423, 3433, 3722, 3751, 3829, 3830, 3836, 3849, 3894, 3904, 4007, 4016, 4021, 4047, 4071, 4072, 4073, 4117, 4201, 4231, 4294, 4306, 4319, 4353, 4354, 4356, 4378, 4434, 4442, 4454, 4457, 4458, 4469, 4480, 4497, 4498, 4502, 4521, 4536, 4542, 4573, 4667, 4707, 4741, 4768, 4769, 4777, 4778, 4779, 4780, 4803, 4804, 4871, 4897, 4914, 4916, 4917, 4918, 4924, 4942, 4987, 4989, 5013, 5045, 5095, 5132, 5245, 5354, 5412, 5413, 5414, 5444, 5459, 5460, 5527, 5581, 5587, 5701, 5707, 5747a, 5756, 5892, 5914, 5950, 6032, 6033, 6064, 6066, 6067, 6104, 6184, 6188, 6237, 6253, 6319, 6434, 6461, 6467, 6490a, 6504, 6557, 6572, 6590, 6659, 6660, 6661, 6662, 6670, 6690, 6754, 6770, 6783, 6784, 6798, 6799, 6813, 6814, 6815, 6816, 6817, 6818, 6820, 6843, 6846, 6847, 6848, 6849, 6893, 6897, 6967, 6972, 6981, 6992, 7089, 7117, 7119, 7173, 7191, 7212, 7214, 7215, 7232, 7241, 7242, 7245, 7246, 7252, 7261

Anti-Racism/Black Studies 1008, 1172, 1237, 1284, 1347, 1390, 1412, 1414, 1426, 1449, 1454, 1469, 1483, 1491, 1516, 1517, 1576, 1668, 1889, 1984, 2005, 2027, 2044, 2062, 2172, 2178, 2184, 3182, 3183, 3266, 3829, 3830, 4016, 4067, 4231, 4306, 4356, 4385, 4442, 4454, 4502, 4768, 4871, 4897, 4914, 4924, 5012a, 5013, 5132, 5412, 5413, 5414, 5459, 5581, 5587, 5701, 5892, 6032, 6064, 6104, 6467, 6572, 6770, 6772a, 6783, 6784, 6814, 6816, 6817, 6818, 6820, 6843, 6846, 6897, 6967, 6992, 7242, 7245

Art 40, 2535, 2536, 2581, 2598, 2924, 3145, 3339, 3341, 3357, 3488, 3729, 3775, 3823, 4081, 4212, 4213, 4214, 4285, 4286, 4293, 4379, 4380, 4627, 4750, 4765, 4769, 4793, 4828, 4831, 4839, 4845, 4869a, 4922, 5031, 5074, 5082, 5235, 5346, 5448a, 5568, 5757, 6114, 6675, 6966, 7119, 7224

Colonies 51, 123, 125, 220, 261, 345, 464, 585, 639, 667, 668, 734, 797, 814, 819, 879, 897, 912, 926, 951, 954, 959, 974, 1097, 1108, 1126, 1340, 1668, 1889, 1897, 2043, 2539, 2550, 2559, 2591, 2913, 3142, 3482, 3829, 3830, 3879, 3993, 4014, 4016, 4187, 4192, 4306, 4333, 4401, 4450, 4768, 4818, 4830, 4872, 4920, 4943, 5120, 5136, 5311, 5412, 5415, 5562, 5580, 5587, 5599, 5643, 5880, 5892, 6138, 6423, 6644, 6770, 6783, 6781, 6784, 6817, 7079, 7176, 7186, 7202

Communist International 1, 3, 5, 6, 7, 8, 13, 17, 20, 29, 43, 48, 64, 69, 73, 74, 82, 91, 92, 96, 141, 171, 182, 183, 184, 190, 202, 205, 237, 277, 282, 305, 340, 374, 601, 777, 805, 1157, 1206, 1231, 1424, 1444, 2195, 2561, 2987, 2989, 2994, 3001, 3010, 3013, 3015, 3022, 3029, 3035, 3039, 3040, 3123a, 3251, 3289, 3298, 3312, 3317, 3499, 3519, 3521, 3589, 3637, 3802, 3841, 3875, 3886, 3932, 3943, 3951, 3952, 4009, 4042, 4083, 4130, 4131, 4290, 4307, 4309, 4313, 4503, 4510, 4596, 4614, 4621, 4652, 4700, 4703, 4775, 4913, 4984, 5096, 5099, 5120, 5121, 5144, 5161, 5217, 5238, 5240, 5256, 5257, 5279, 5287, 5288, 5289, 5291, 5293, 5294, 5306, 5307, 5345, 5350, 5351, 5361, 5383, 5384, 5413, 5414, 5435, 5474, 5475, 5478, 5488, 5489, 5587, 5610, 5615, 5620, 5627, 5629, 5630, 5631, 5633, 5681, 5682, 5683, 5684, 5723, 5790, 5792, 5878, 5926, 5989, 6072, 6076, 6077, 6158, 6205, 6208, 6222, 6238, 6322, 6370, 6379, 6383, 6385, 6394, 6396, 6397, 6416, 6457, 6458, 6464, 6488, 6512, 6569, 6578, 6596, 6599, 6603, 6685, 6699, 6720, 6726, 6743, 6784, 6841, 6920, 7009, 7048, 7051, 7165, 7183

Co-ops 80, 104, 150, 214, 295, 348, 388, 661, 670, 822, 896, 973, 1177, 1292, 1534, 1733, 1768, 1925, 2018, 2021, 2233, 4783, 6497

Culture 114, 376, 1268, 1453, 1524, 1543, 1873, 1923, 1954, 2044, 2060, 2251, 2283, 2287, 2352, 2361, 2364, 2390, 2537, 2550, 2570, 2611, 3071, 3085, 3092, 3180, 3387, 3391, 3460, 3462, 3464, 3481, 3788, 3857, 3858, 3940, 3941, 3942, 4035, 4052, 4055, 4057, 4068, 4087, 4088, 4156, 4162, 4163, 4176, 4252, 4273, 4305, 4336, 4344, 4345, 4389, 4427, 4429, 4478, 4500, 4522, 4534, 4568, 4684, 4802, 4823, 4829, 4846, 4891, 4902, 4923, 4946, 5019, 5089, 5091, 5118, 5230, 5408, 5422, 5429, 5432, 5448a, 5451, 5530, 5531, 5579, 5678, 5948, 5968, 6023, 6026, 6187, 6203, 6263, 6296, 6354, 6429, 6432, 6499, 6507, 6748, 6759, 6760, 6850, 6876, 6916, 6918, 6978, 6979, 7044, 7087, 7110, 7159, 7233, 7249, 7272

Daily Worker/Morning Star 484, 1456, 1529, 1579, 2050, 2390, 2722, 2892, 3498, 3691, 3759, 3772, 3804, 3814, 3820, 3863, 3929, 3980, 4014, 4044, 4045, 4207, 4209, 4273, 4332, 4335, 4361, 4393, 4421, 4422, 4423, 4564, 4627, 4661, 4665, 4759, 4997, 5034, 5273, 5290, 5303, 5330, 5358, 5367, 5375, 5385, 5443, 5485, 5493, 5494, 5497, 5507, 5649, 5679, 5706, 5824, 5844, 5849, 5850, 5937, 5938, 5972, 5974, 5975, 6113, 6214, 6248, 6307, 6363, 6423, 6428, 6519, 6571, 6692, 6694, 6719, 6724, 6727, 6728, 6731, 6732, 6734, 6738, 6768, 6780, 6785, 6800, 6804, 6877, 6959

Environment 726, 1379, 1452

Fiction 144, 424, 639, 1761, 1955, 2051, 2230, 2353, 2424, 2427, 2504, 2507, 2508, 2846, 3017, 3062, 3071, 3107, 3161, 3437, 3469, 3479, 3898, 3900, 4104, 4228, 5297

Film/TV 715, 793, 862, 1170, 1243, 1536, 2963, 3144, 3834, 4137, 4381, 4382, 4383, 4452, 4565, 4814, 4869a, 5990, 6063, 6781

Gay/Lesbian 4675, 4328, 4461, 1583, 3226, 4148, 4764, 4147, 3738, 4460, 3920, 4117, 4081

Health 327, 513, 570, 603, 604, 633, 649, 699, 732, 776, 948, 1000, 1355, 1359, 1360, 1441, 1481, 1511, 1513, 1581, 1618, 1847, 1886, 1909, 1990, 2006, 2013, 2026, 2096, 2214, 2222, 2289, 2301, 2330, 2351, 2356, 2439, 2440, 2443, 2568, 2788, 2854, 3078, 3090, 3351, 4468, 4931

Historians 828, 1030, 1099, 1162, 1588, 1884, 2574, 3752, 3851, 3852, 3873, 3954, 3978, 4077, 4156, 4164, 4166, 4203, 4316, 4371, 4372, 4400, 4403, 4462, 4464, 4465, 4466, 4494, 4563, 4589, 4629, 4711, 4712, 4712a, 4713, 4730, 4835, 4842, 4843, 4856, 4940, 4976, 5091, 5186, 5190, 5191, 5211, 5222, 5243, 5420, 5462a, 5544, 5607, 5657, 5740, 5743, 5780, 5795, 5981, 6001, 6002, 6054, 6055, 6057, 6058, 6086, 6090, 6152, 6190, 6191, 6194, 6198, 6224, 6326, 6349, 6365, 6373, 6374, 6376, 6415, 6426, 6523, 6526, 6527, 6611, 6651, 6658, 6663, 6665, 6666, 6676, 6680a, 6752, 6878, 6911, 6936, 6937, 6973, 6975, 6987, 7036, 7052, 7064

Housing 323, 405, 443, 632, 654, 673, 700, 705, 710, 760, 763, 764, 838, 962, 1011, 1034, 1043, 1063, 1072, 1127, 1131, 1351, 1527, 1608, 1609, 1610, 1613, 1615, 1644, 1645, 1646, 1648, 1649, 1650, 1652, 1655, 1656, 1663, 1674, 1676, 1677, 1684, 1685, 1686, 1691, 1692, 1693, 1694, 1695, 1696, 1697, 1698, 1699, 1700, 1701, 1702, 1703, 1704, 1705, 1707, 1708, 1709, 1710, 1712, 1713, 1714, 1715, 1716, 1717, 1718, 1719, 1728, 1753, 1755, 1759, 1760, 1773, 1775, 1776, 1779, 1780, 1782, 1786, 1793, 1796, 1797, 1798, 1803, 1804, 1805, 1808, 1809, 1810, 1815, 1818, 1819, 1820, 1828, 1831, 1832, 1837, 1840, 1842, 1854, 1871, 1878, 1880, 1893, 1900, 1911, 1912, 1913, 1915, 1920, 1921, 1922, 1927, 1934, 1942, 1950, 1959, 1965, 1967, 1970, 1971, 1976, 1998, 2001, 2008, 2009, 2014, 2017, 2020, 2024, 2034, 2046, 2053, 2056, 2071, 2074, 2091, 2092, 2102, 2113, 2115, 2123, 2129, 2132, 2142, 2147, 2150, 2151, 2154, 2160, 2161, 2163, 2174, 2182, 2183, 2188, 2190, 2202, 2206, 2209, 2212, 2215, 2218, 2219, 2226, 2236, 2238, 2240, 2247, 2263, 2264, 2268, 2274, 2275, 2279, 2292, 2293, 2302, 2307, 2309, 2315, 2317, 2320, 2334, 2359, 2369, 2372, 2413, 2418, 2437, 2441, 2442, 2450, 2451, 2452, 2458, 2460, 2462, 2469, 2480, 2483, 2484, 2485, 2489, 2490, 2493, 2500, 2506, 2512, 2513, 2738, 2975, 4230, 4541, 4573, 4741, 5244, 5356, 5538, 5575, 6047, 6148, 6188, 6847, 6980, 7118a, 7182

ILP 15, 216, 264, 274, 276, 285, 296, 318, 2195, 2414, 2431, 2473, 3002, 3026, 3599, 3958, 3968, 4017, 4046, 4144, 4511, 4567, 4598, 4616, 4905, 4955, 5128, 5161, 5217, 5238, 5278, 5302, 5350, 5360, 5384, 5467, 5489, 5513, 5514, 5515, 5542, 5627, 5755, 5797, 5811, 5833, 5926, 6072, 6580, 6587, 6591, 6720, 6723, 6725, 6737, 6742, 6789, 6868, 7016

INDEX OF TOPICS

India 97, 148, 166, 168, 177, 219, 271, 293, 356, 490, 529, 530, 559, 595, 602, 639, 656, 735, 982, 1327, 1829, 1830, 2428, 3102, 3442, 3841, 3893, 3928, 3944, 4012, 4013, 4151, 4249, 4264, 4277, 4307, 4309, 4448, 4449, 4462, 4681, 4683, 4694, 4697, 4708, 4753, 4767, 4813, 4815, 4816, 4817, 4829, 4836, 4840, 4881a, 4912, 4914, 5014, 5077, 5090, 5096, 5435, 5528, 5591, 5594, 5597, 5830, 5858, 6216, 6217, 6429a, 6467, 6494, 6543a, 6846, 6873, 6874, 6875, 7032, 7105, 7106

International 34, 61, 72, 105, 151, 163, 170, 181, 268, 277, 284, 312, 369, 382, 415, 419, 420, 428, 469, 515, 601, 610, 675, 694, 698, 701, 708, 716, 738, 739, 742, 771, 840, 898, 979, 984, 1038, 1080, 1085, 1138, 1143, 1152, 1156, 1165, 1169, 1176, 1183, 1206, 1238, 1244, 1266, 1272, 1273, 1275, 1277, 1294, 1306, 1312, 1329, 1330, 1332, 1337, 1350, 1354, 1368, 1408, 1410, 1411, 1417, 1424, 1428, 1444, 1458, 1486, 1504, 1521, 1528, 1575, 1578, 1582, 1585, 1602, 1783, 1784, 1807, 1879, 1894, 1914, 1918, 1928, 1964, 2049, 2078, 2176, 2340, 2449, 2533a, 2556, 2560, 2579, 3114, 3139, 3190, 3196, 3216, 3257, 3270, 3337, 3343, 3345, 3441, 3454, 3458, 3467, 3478, 3484, 3491, 3495, 3496, 3686, 3761, 3781, 3943, 3972a, 4191, 4467, 4521, 4652, 4772, 5215, 5320, 5389, 5524, 5707, 5713, 5894, 6211, 6418, 6454, 6484, 6513, 6763, 6977, 6983, 7166

Ireland 26, 364, 491, 1299, 1334, 1352, 1367, 1406, 1437, 1537, 1754, 2040, 2072, 2080, 2562, 2940, 3194, 3727, 3728, 4599, 4632, 4676, 4701, 4702, 4703, 4705, 5022, 5194, 5226, 5272, 5672, 5710, 5867, 5994, 6240, 6323, 6341, 6416, 6512, 7244

Labour Party 22, 44, 53, 75, 86, 88, 120, 155, 158, 192, 218, 235, 247, 273, 300, 335, 336, 350, 371, 378, 394, 395, 533, 600, 618, 758, 835, 842, 889, 891, 949, 960, 1013, 1027, 1075, 1129, 1396, 1598, 1813, 1824, 2138, 2316, 2904, 2977, 2978, 2979, 3030, 3152, 3690, 3698, 3732, 3733, 3736, 3740, 3755, 3759, 3769, 3773, 3785, 3786, 3789, 3797, 3799, 3800, 3805, 3810, 3815, 3883, 3923, 3948, 3996, 4001, 4010, 4042, 4049, 4132, 4141, 4170, 4210, 4269, 4339, 4341, 4406, 4408, 4410, 4437, 4443a, 4505, 4533, 4572, 4588, 4615, 4628, 4664, 4682, 4723a, 4738, 4744, 4757, 4773, 4868, 4899, 4900, 4939, 4963, 4985, 5000, 5036, 5038, 5097, 5129, 5139, 5162, 5163, 5169, 5232, 5233, 5263, 5285, 5293, 5301, 5313, 5321, 5331, 5333, 5345, 5361, 5430, 5437, 5439, 5476, 5477, 5517, 5519, 5534, 5562, 5582, 5596, 5602, 5624, 5653, 5676, 5691a, 5708, 5771, 5832, 5840, 5841, 5842, 5845, 5893, 5942, 5992, 5997, 6027, 6078, 6161, 6182, 6239, 6258, 6277a, 6284, 6335, 6353, 6482, 6492, 6504, 6543a, 6574, 6584, 6589, 6618, 6619, 6620, 6624, 6669, 6689, 6711, 6761, 6809, 6839, 6892, 6922a, 6924, 6929, 7006, 7007, 7008, 7009, 7025, 7069, 7109, 7144, 7149, 7162, 7168, 7183, 7192, 7209

Law/Policing 116, 117, 118, 302, 460, 846, 1462, 1469, 1491, 1818, 2044, 2290, 2905, 3138, 3404, 3416, 3665, 3684, 3685, 3688, 3691, 3701, 3710, 3772, 3783, 3814, 3820, 3842, 3845, 3855, 3865, 3976, 4024, 4034, 4072, 4105, 4157, 4177, 4350, 4384, 4387, 4411, 4433, 4436, 4504, 4548, 4631, 4734, 4744, 4756, 4762, 4860, 4881a, 4902, 4919, 4986, 4987, 4997, 5012, 5048, 5055, 5101, 5110, 5271, 5273, 5303, 5312, 5319, 5367, 5374, 5375, 5497, 5498, 5508, 5556, 5571, 5593, 5595, 5635, 5670, 5728, 5791, 5895, 5915, 6025, 6068, 6132, 6242, 6253, 6279, 6367, 6399, 6659, 6796, 6823, 6893, 6932, 6995

Left 3692, 3698, 3706, 3713, 3715, 3719, 3728, 3746, 3747, 3763, 3776, 3777, 3780, 3781, 3787, 3792, 3794, 3798, 3821, 3837, 3851, 3921, 3922, 4029, 4040, 4055, 4058, 4059, 4134, 4158, 4185, 4200, 4244, 4246, 4247, 4302, 4313, 4340, 4358, 4413, 4431, 4440, 4445, 4528, 4567, 4605, 4634, 4721, 4772, 4773, 4911, 4955, 4980, 5010, 5063, 5064, 5092, 5122, 5141, 5160, 5162, 5164, 5166, 5168, 5171, 5174, 5192, 5194, 5195, 5202, 5212, 5237, 5239, , 5267, 5283, 5315, 5320, 5325, 5326, 5327, 5332, 5334, 5335, 5336, 5338, 5339, 5340, 5341, 5348, 5352, 5353, 5373, 5374, 5375, 5387, 5389, 5406, 5417, 5427, 5432, 5433, 5452, 5457, 5458, 5470, 5499, 5500, 5524, 5533, 5548, 5570, 5582, 5583, 5584, 5606, 5607, 5608, 5652, 5663, 5673, 5698, 5745, 5766, 5767, 5788, 5806, 5807, 5813, 5846, 5847, 5867, 5887, 5889, 5904, 5918, 5919, 5920, 5970, 5971, 5972, 5973, 5974, 5975, 5985, 5991, 5992, 5993, 5994, 5995, 5996, 5998, 5999, 6000, 6000a, 6012, 6013, 6031, 6039, 6040, 6041, 6042, 6043, 6065, 6080, 6093, 6094, 6096, 6098, 6099, 6100, 6118, 6130, 6132, 6133, 6134, 6135, 6136, 6137, 6139, 6161, 6171, 6174, 6175, 6176, 6182, 6204, 6222, 6240, 6249, 6265, 6267, 6318, 6323, 6324, 6340, 6366, 6370, 6387, 6392, 6405, 6435, 6436, 6437, 6505, 6510, 6514, 6515, 6516, 6517, 6518, 6521, 6528, 6534, 6535, 6554, 6555, 6556, 6610, 6622, 6628, 6646, 6647, 6648, 6649, 6664, 6667, 6668, 6671, 6677, 6681, 6771, 6812, 6834, 6835, 6854, 6855, 6878, 6879, 6881, 6889,

6899, 6900, 6902, 6905, 6944, 6952, 6953, 6954, 6958, 6959, 6964, 6986, 6997, 7020, 7023, 7031, 7039, 7040, 7057, 7059

Literature 639, 655, 1115, 2395, 2514, 2516, 2547, 2557, 2582, 2912, 2916, 2930, 3250, 3748, 3848, 3874, 3891, 3897, 3899, 3906, 3907, 3913, 3927, 3939, 3947, 3982, 4065, 4067, 4089, 4090, 4091, 4092, 4093, 4094, 4095, 4096, 4097, 4102, 4104, 4155, 4225, 4263, 4328, 4342, 4357, 4369, 4397, 4404, 4426, 4439, 4472, 4486, 4487, 4488, 4499, 4512, 4513, 4515, 4519, 4520, 4529, 4543, 4546, 4547, 4561, 4569, 4586, 4672, 4673, 4675, 4677, 4709, 4763, 4763a, 4770, 4791, 4833, 4852, 4878, 4892, 4893, 4894, 4895, 4896, 4907, 4909, 4910, 4921, 4934, 4941, 4945, 4964, 4965, 4966, 4967, 4968, 4972, 4990, 5021, 5032, 5039, 5046, 5073, 5081, 5100, 5105a, 5107, 5187, 5224, 5280, 5282, 5377, 5486, 5487, 5540, 5666, 5734, 5735, 5736, 5737, 5738, 5739, 5741, 5742, 5743, 5744, 5759, 5786, 5896, 5923, 5940, 5986, 6007, 6008, 6018, 6022, 6028, 6044, 6052, 6118, 6166, 6172, 6226, 6274, 6280, 6281, 6286, 6321, 6337, 6375, 6463, 6470, 6471, 6640, 6673, 6714, 6758, 6772a, 6823, 6833, 6834, 6889a, 7022, 7058, 7090, 7124, 7137, 7152, 7153, 7223, 7234, 7247, 7251, 7253a, 7255, 7258, 7269

Local Government/Welfare State 706, 744, 746, 824, 905, 983, 998, 1021, 1039, 1210, 1254, 1415, 1509, 1538, 1558, 1850, 1857, 1910, 1985, 2002, 2012, 2016, 2079, 2084, 2088, 2104, 2105, 2436, 2526, 2821, 4193, 4853

Maoism 2721, 3712, 3714, 3749, 3761, 3779, 3762, 3786, 3818, 3819, 4171, 4172, 4173, 4174, 4590, 4591, 4592, 4593, 4594, 4600, 4706, 4714, 4745, 4854, 4862, 4863, 4869, 5005, 5006, 5007, 5072, 5197, 5209, 5250, 5363, 5388, 5857, 6880

Music 144, 424, 952, 1079, 1757, 1955, 2353, 2572, 2928, 3017, 3062, 3071, 3224, 3469, 3711, 3718, 3813, 3830a, 3871, 3953, 3979, 4318, 4325, 4326, 4327, 4329, 4334, 4335, 4416, 4545, 4597, 4662, 4705a, 4752, 4812, 4925, 4929, 4988, 5015, 5764, 5936, 6092, 6261, 6266, 6718, 6816, 6821, 6856, 6862, 7049, 7131a

Peace 55, 91, 127, 156, 180, 183, 200, 217, 236, 283, 311, 317, 328, 341, 345, 352, 355, 357, 367, 373, 375, 377, 412, 413, 418, 438, 445, 707, 712, 759, 861, 875, 878, 880, 881, 894, 947, 981, 1057, 1082, 1110, 1122, 1132, 1141, 1145, 1190, 1258, 1298, 1353, 1485, 1496, 1523, 1542, 1544, 1640, 1641, 1666, 1724, 1727, 1729, 1730, 1734, 1735, 1736, 1737, 1739, 1867, 2077, 2111, 2121, 2125, 2127, 2143, 2192, 2197, 2200, 2300, 2322, 2414, 2422, 2519, 2587, 2983, 2985, 3121, 3146, 3225, 3440, 3471, 3700, 3721, 3764, 3787, 3971, 4028, 4106, 4287, 4295, 4531, 4585, 4617, 4626, 4652, 4689, 4782, 4801, 4953, 4954, 5040, 5088, 5109, 5110, 5119, 5142, 5143, 5157, 5164, 5249, 5464, 5466, 5473, 5570, 5646, 5652, 5894, 6069, 6076, 6453, 6513, 6540, 6542, 6721, 6951, 7180, 7212, 7254

Pensioners 1896, 1943, 1969, 1986, 1989, 2023, 3860, 4479

Religion 803, 944, 2419, 2502, 3456, 3526, 3582, 3683, 3736, 3938, 4037, 4070, 4287, 4419, 4420, 4421, 4422, 4423, 4424, 4661, 4707, 4723, 5075, 6544, 5881, 5882, 5893, 5944, 6030, 6104, 6110, 6230, 6275

Right 3682, 3683, 3684, 3686, 3695, 3696, 3697, 3700, 3704, 3705, 3721, 3724, 3726, 3734, 3735, 3739, 3741, 3753, 3754, 3770, 3771, 3774, 3778, 3782, 3783, 3784, 3788, 3791, 3795, 3796, 3799, 3806, 3807, 3810, 3812, 3820, 3876, 3884, 3885, 3886, 3938, 3959, 3961, 3962, 3967, 4005, 4039, 4043, 4086, 4167, 4265, 4274, 4288, 4299, 4300, 4308, 4346, 4347, 4348, 4352, 4384, 4388, 4418, 4419, 4420, 4425, 4455, 4539, 4570, 4581, 4626, 4873, 4888, 4899, 4900, 4932, 4943, 4948, 4961, 5020, 5028, 5033, 5035, 5058, 5104, 5106, 5116, 5129, 5133, 5142, 5143, 5146, 5147, 5148, 5149, 5150, 5153, 5155, 5157, 5167, 5199, 5223, 5241, 5328, 5329, 5330, 5337, 5344, 5347, 5356, 5378, 5400, 5402, 5454, 5455, 5561, 5654, 5731, 5732, 5754, 5983, 5984, 6005, 6011, 6254, 6564, 6792, 7017, 7018, 7019, 7030, 7132

Science 765, 1221, 1341, 2580, 2584, 2589, 2936, 3425, 3463, 3742, 3966, 4036, 4189, 4278, 4304, 4334, 4377, 4446, 4742, 4774, 4826, 4884, 4944, 5044, 5897, 6163, 6440, 6500, 6503, 6676, 7169

Socialist Countries 12, 19, 24, 28, 31, 62, 94, 111, 146, 174, 175, 179, 197, 206, 207, 211, 228, 366, 370, 379, 401, 422, 433, 489, 493, 504, 534, 541, 543, 544, 545, 546, 547, 558, 571, 730, 777, 805, 823, 867, 884, 899, 907, 908, 957, 1028, 1029, 1033, 1073, 1074, 1271, 1274, 1421, 1427, 1431, 1436, 1438, 1515, 1960, 2191, 2407, 2586, 3005, 3151, 3234, 3258, 3259, 3263, 3268, 3331, 3350, 3435, 3470, 3472, 3487, 3701, 3706, 3723, 3731, 3765, 3850, 3902, 3908, 3929,

3985, 3986, 4083, 4114, 4179, 4204, 4205, 4209, 4245, 4246, 4290, 4340, 4533, 4564, 4621, 4700, 4775, 4788, 4789, 4984, 5049, 5060, 5069, 5085, 5086, 5176, 5495, 5496, 5610, 5684, 5708, 5792, 5818, 5878, 5895, 5901, 6019, 6053, 6074, 6084, 6158, 6181, 6199, 6256, 6290, 6304, 6306, 6307, 6394, 6397, 6459, 6516, 6517, 6518, 6645, 6647, 6912, 6920, 6924, 6925, 6985, 7048, 7051, 7115, 7151, 7177, 7213, 7216

Spain 344, 359, 360, 361, 398, 399, 402, 403, 404, 432, 449, 452, 702, 767, 1559, 1822, 2221, 2278, 2337, 2488, 2962, 3055, 3390, 3629, 3661, 3693, 3725, 3808, 3838, 3840, 3861, 3881, 3895, 3896, 3973, 4052, 4063, 4066, 4069, 4070, 4074, 4082, 4103, 4104, 4111, 4129, 4135, 4183, 4186, 4211, 4222, 4223, 4233, 4235, 4237, 4251, 4253, 4292, 4296, 4297, 4298, 4304, 4310, 4311, 4331, 4362, 4391, 4392, 4394, 4397, 4429, 4438, 4513, 4516, 4518, 4553, 4579, 4580, 4644, 4725, 4746, 4761, 4763, 4779, 4798, 4837, 4847, 4852, 4857, 4887, 4915, 4921, 4933, 4934, 4935, 4938, 4946, 4962, 5027, 5029, 5039, 5078, 5105a, 5134, 5145, 5198, 5219, 5220, 5225, 5280, 5281, 5282, 5346, 5498, 5564, 5565, 5566, 5567, 5568, 5706, 5742, 5866, 5907, 5908, 5910, 5913, 5921, 5924, 5969, 5982, 6009, 6180, 6225, 6257, 6303, 6543a, 6573, 6683, 6780, 6849, 6927, 6988, 6989, 7095, 7101, 7118, 7146, 7160, 7197, 7250

Spies 3853, 3854, 3855, 3887, 3937, 3945, 3977, 3983, 4015, 4019, 4020, 4024, 4064, 4072, 4079, 4080, 4105, 4125, 4142, 4147, 4148, 4211, 4271, 4350, 4411, 4429a, 4491, 4504, 4578, 4587, 4617, 4622, 4631, 4639, 4710, 4710a, 4710b, 4732, 4739, 4740, 4751, 4756, 4764, 4788, 4858, 4874, 4882, 4902, 4904, 4936, 4986, 4987, 5012, 5043, 5047, 5048, 5049, 5050, 5051, 5055, 5101, 5449, 5498, 5593, 5595, 5728, 5765, 5791, 6279, 6309, 6635, 6823, 6932, 6933, 6935

Sport/Leisure 4451, 6037, 1163, 1404, 3049, 3133, 5703, 4356, 3693, 4235, 3450, 4516, 6433, 5465, 3466, 3468, 6988, 6621, 7265, 6659, 6173, 4453, 4233, 5173, 6192, 4122

Structure/Organisation 56, 58, 59, 60, 74, 78, 98, 129, 132, 136, 164, 240, 266, 290, 416, 508, 526, 527, 528, 680, 704, 775, 1003, 1005, 1081, 1178, 1394, 1482, 1514, 1671, 1799, 1838, 1845, 1855, 1870, 2052, 2073, 2082, 2261, 3784, 4592, 5194, 5259, 5260, 5274, 5275, 5310, 5416, 5419, 5522, 5688, 5850, 6113, 6177, 6246, 6285, 6369, 6382, 6408, 6411, 6417, 6493, 6654, 6657, 6684, 6685, 6687, 6803, 6928, 6939, 7013, 7161

Students 1283, 1302, 2177, 2471, 3364, 3803, 3854, 3872, 3944, 3947, 3966, 4015, 4061, 4064, 4080, 4147, 4187, 4473, 4491, 4609, 4637, 4671, 4722, 4813, 4832, 4834, 4840, 4858, 4879, 4882, 4939, 4949, 5077, 5454, 5770, 5804, 5832, 6217, 6350, 6378, 6448, 6491, 6514, 6604, 6679, 6747, 6945, 7105

Theatre 799, 985, 1217, 1982, 2931, 2967, 3730, 4023, 4517, 4691, 4692, 4821, 5045, 5073, 5916, 6169, 6522, 6753, 6772, 6991, 7188, 7218, 7236, 7266

Trotskyism 110, 119, 209, 301, 306, 389, 404, 409, 422, 516, 592, 1134, 1311, 1431, 1445, 1936, 2368, 3056, 3275, 3276, 3353, 3707, 3723, 3790, 3801, 3816, 3905, 3925, 3934, 3935, 3936, 3987, 3995, 4108, 4161, 4245, 4255, 4284, 4289, 4303, 4344a, 4414, 4415, 4507, 4524, 4540, 4602, 4603, 4604, 4609, 4610, 4611, 4613, 4624, 4698, 4699, 4719, 4720, 4775, 4808, 5026, 5062, 5108, 5170, 5231, 5314, 5342, 5462, 5471, 5523, 5544, 5677, 5692, 5886, 5987, 6029, 6030, 6095, 6097, 6146, 6150, 6198, 6199, 6264, 6359, 6363, 6372, 6383, 6389, 6393, 6431, 6543, 6547, 6561, 6638, 6672, 6680, 6956, 6957, 7012, 7112, 7262

Women 30, 67, 94, 128, 204, 211, 221, 249, 286, 298, 437, 443, 478, 506, 507, 569, 570, 572, 645, 685, 696, 737, 747, 798, 837, 887, 955, 1022, 1023, 1024, 1045, 1107, 1146, 1223, 1227, 1251, 1301, 1362, 1363, 1364, 1385, 1432, 1446, 1447, 1475, 1488, 1495, 1548, 1557, 1747, 1751, 1858, 1899, 1996, 2052a, 2070, 2187, 2433, 2564, 2592, 2593, 2594, 2601, 2651, 2667, 2690, 2719, 2736, 2755, 2821, 3066, 3150, 3221, 3278, 3294, 3366, 3513, 3720, 3762, 3840, 3970, 3971, 3972, 4111, 4124, 4165, 4208, 4209, 4251, 4291, 4312, 4320, 4351, 4362, 4412, 4461, 4479, 4481, 4530, 4531, 4538, 4590, 4595, 4636, 4642, 4676, 4766, 4797, 4807, 4853, 5057, 5068, 5100, 5126, 5177, 5227, 5259, 5382, 5385, 5397, 5409, 5410, 5464, 5529, 5532, 5563, 5586, 5618, 5640, 5641, 5782, 5783, 5913, 5945, 5956, 6091, 6103, 6213, 6214, 6225, 6287, 6288, 6325, 6430, 6496, 6497, 6498, 6544, 6631, 6632, 6712, 6713, 6827, 6828, 6870, 6871, 6872, 6965, 6994, 7131, 7152, 7157, 7227, 7258, 7271

Youth 121, 126, 172, 208, 238, 267, 380, 500, 638, 728, 787, 1032, 1149, 1882, 1904, 1916, 1923, 1956, 2374, 2604, 3675, 3680, 3681, 3695, 3707, 3713, 3738, 3858, 3865, 3917, 4007, 4028, 4047, 4122, 4138, 4143, 4314, 4521, 4535, 4544, 4590, 4644, 4758, 4771, 4795, 4806, 4912,

4952, 5057, 5080, 5081, 5119, 5128, 5138, 5140, 5146, 5182, 5239, 5247, 5248, 5258, 5292, 5309, 5316, 5366, 5380, 5381, 5398, 5400, 5542, 5558, 5560, 5642, 5685, 5689, 5691, 5705, 5726, 5904, 5935, 5950, 5964, 5965, 5966, 5976, 5983, 6122, 6142, 6192, 6258, 6268, 6283, 6335, 6433, 6469, 6537, 6540, 6597, 6621, 6622, 6655, 6733, 6741, 6746, 6831, 6832, 6974, 6985, 7003, 7011, 7060, 7061, 7062, 7063, 7096, 7108, 7204, 7238, 7264

Periods

Origins 3974, 3975, 4022, 4042, 4053, 4067, 4083, 4123, 4128, 4139, 4290, 4337, 4386, 4445, 4447, 4458, 4475, 4489, 4575, 4620, 4635, 4642, 4695, 4848, 4866, 4870, 4876, 4877, 5011, 5040, 5060, 5087, 5111, 5124, 5130, 5426, 5440, 5546, 5557, 5571a, 5572, 5573, 5574, 5634, 5784, 5811, 5812, 6040, 6049, 6050, 6119, 6171, 6184, 6231, 6358, 6403, 6404, 6438, 6444, 6450a, 6454, 6511, 6560, 6564, 6625, 6697, 6882, 7004, 7021, 7035, 7128, 7134, 7147, 7164, 7187, 7193, 7216

1920s 1322, 1668, 2208, 2285, 2922, 2998, 3684, 3701, 3750, 3783, 3807, 3985, 4006, 4030, 4114, 4131, 4153, 4154, 4155, 4216, 4220, 4240, 4241, 4320, 4366, 4384, 4412, 4433, 4527, 4532, 4556, 4559, 4582, 4609, 4613, 4615, 4627, 4655, 4679, 4720, 4728, 4734, 4771, 4773, 4797, 4807, 4818, 4865, 4868, 4912, 4914, 4930, 4981, 4992, 5012, 5013, 5014, 5023, 5024, 5041, 5163, 5295, 5341, 5406, 5413, 5438, 5459, 5547, 5612, 5752, 5771, 5817, 5818, 5942, 6015, 6068, 6079, 6091, 6114, 6115, 6157, 6165, 6279, 6294, 6299, 6378, 6379, 6418, 6427, 6452, 6462, 6467, 6502, 6512, 6545, 6623, 6646, 6649, 6655, 6667, 6699, 6825, 6883, 6892, 6941, 6959, 6995, 7003, 7040, 7102, 7123, 7159, 7162, 7165, 7183, 7185, 7196, 7199, 7200, 7201, 7207

1926 149, 152, 153, 157, 2066, 2595, 2597, 2669, 2790, 2816, 2921, 2953, 2960, 3003, 3136, 3137, 3220, 3319, 3832, 3932, 4040, 4148, 4302, 4313, 4441, 4455, 4490, 4495, 4549, 4606, 4612, 4646, 4864, 4886, 5063, 5113, 5182, 5292, 5312, 5619, 5745, 5773, 5915, 5999, 6012, 6065, 6242, 6250, 6333, 6384, 6488, 6501, 6520, 6793, 6826, 6998, 7029, 7195

1930s 1667, 2606, 2612, 2965, 2967, 3720, 3729, 3732, 3751, 3773, 3788, 3797, 3805, 3849, 3854, 3875, 3881, 3885, 3894, 3895, 3897, 3902, 3906, 3907, 3917, 3923, 3934, 3939, 3944, 3951, 3956, 3958, 3963, 3971, 3972, 3982, 4009, 4013, 4017, 4020, 4024, 4035, 4045, 4057, 4063, 4065, 4073, 4074, 4078, 4080, 4091, 4094, 4097, 4098, 4101, 4102, 4112, 4117, 4120, 4146, 4147, 4162, 4187, 4205, 4214, 4225, 4231, 4250, 4251, 4253, 4262, 4263, 4269, 4270, 4273, 4292, 4297, 4304, 4305, 4323, 4338, 4342, 4344, 4369, 4378, 4381, 4383, 4392, 4399, 4407, 4426, 4429, 4430, 4438, 4439, 4450, 4456, 4470, 4472, 4480, 4487, 4491, 4496, 4497, 4499, 4501, 4512, 4513, 4514, 4516, 4519, 4520, 4522, 4530, 4536, 4542, 4543, 4565, 4569, 4572, 4580, 4586, 4588, 4625, 4633, 4637, 4638, 4643, 4681, 4685, 4686, 4692, 4710, 4731, 4738, 4753, 4763, 4765, 4770, 4778, 4782, 4793, 4800, 4803, 4804, 4814, 4823, 4833, 4840, 4867, 4878, 4884, 4887, 4909, 4921, 4936, 4941, 4946, 4959, 4966, 4973, 4982, 4989, 4990, 4991, 4995, 5009, 5010, 5019, 5021, 5027, 5029, 5031, 5044, 5054, 5057, 5073, 5074, 5082, 5090, 5094, 5098, 5102, 5107, 5197, 5214, 5271, 5377, 5456, 5460, 5461, 5548, 5568, 5571, 5614, 5617, 5670, 5691, 5703, 5708, 5734, 5738, 5748, 5756, 5759, 5821, 5859, 5882, 5884, 5893, 5894, 5907, 5914, 5948, 5950, 5987, 6003, 6008, 6009, 6010, 6026, 6028, 6037, 6044, 6063, 6066, 6073, 6217, 6226, 6253, 6257, 6258, 6300, 6312, 6319, 6320, 6336, 6338, 6339, 6346, 6390, 6391, 6429a, 6434, 6468, 6473, 6490a, 6504, 6513, 6522, 6541, 6543a, 6648, 6656, 6661, 6670, 6673, 6675, 6690, 6717, 6747, 6748, 6759, 6760, 6799, 6800, 6813, 6823, 6834, 6844, 6859, 6889a, 6893, 6919, 6927, 6933, 6945, 6947, 6956, 6978, 6979, 6982, 6990, 6991, 7012, 7044, 7046, 7087, 7112, 7115, 7116, 7117, 7124, 7132, 7137, 7141, 7149, 7151, 7152, 7153, 7156, 7160, 7168, 7172, 7181, 7190, 7206, 7214, 7215, 7229, 7236, 7239, 7240, 7257, 7265, 7266, 7269

WW2 639, 740, 755, 1627, 2143, 2224, 2305, 2308, 2310, 2422, 2426, 2435, 2443, 2957, 2976, 3071, 3424, 3426, 3427, 3429, 3691, 3692, 3769, 3772, 3789, 3790, 3798, 3804, 3814, 3820, 3827, 3865, 3878, 3889, 3893, 3908, 3931, 3935, 3936, 3949, 4099, 4116, 4151, 4198, 4204, 4255, 4272, 4280, 4281, 4282, 4344a, 4349, 4363, 4364, 4408, 4428, 4443, 4482, 4485, 4524, 4567, 4619, 4652, 4792, 4918, 4919, 4955, 4964, 4971, 4997, 4999, 5001, 5001a, 5016, 5052, 5088, 5135, 5137, 5234, 5273, 5313, 5325, 5374, 5375, 5448a, 5449, 5497, 5543, 5647, 5648, 5661, 5673, 5711, 5753, 5820, 5822, 5870, 5872, 5885, 5886, 5917, 5937, 5967, 5978, 5998, 6019, 6045, 6046, 6095, 6096, 6101, 6113, 6158, 6215, 6235, 6268, 6344, 6367, 6431, 6441, 6442, 6446, 6476, 6494, 6507, 6532, 6535, 6644, 6664, 6701, 6744, 6771, 6904, 6932, 6952, 6977, 7109, 7125, 7127, 7145, 7148, 7154, 7177, 7212, 7230

1956 3487, 3723, 3745, 3821, 3851, 3869, 3964, 3969, 3981, 4108, 4203, 4245, 4246, 4340, 4343, 4358, 4478, 4554, 4555, 4564, 4610, 4835, 4849, 4850, 5114, 5247, 5314, 5369, 5544, 5583, 5604, 5609, 5655, 5737, 5860, 5896, 5918, 5938, 5979, 5985, 6031, 6039, 6291, 6305, 6307, 6363, 6529, 6531, 6638, 6680, 6680a, 6913, 6917, 6975, 7045, 7066, 7104, 7121, 7179, 7222, 831, 1093, 1794, 3703, 3829, 3844, 3891, 3924, 3996, 4005, 4252, 4356, 4382, 4410, 4436, 4477

1945-1960 4515, 4741, 4860, 4871, 4885, 4903, 5037, 5056, 5136, 5342, 5469, 5500, 5522, 5567, 5643, 5744, 5789, 5791, 5792, 5876, 5880, 5892, 5990, 6195, 6382, 6421, 6548, 6559, 6613, 6643, 6645, 6659, 6662, 6776, 6794, 6798, 6817, 6824, 6903, 7225, 7237

1980-1991 1601, 3700, 3702, 3793, 3856, 3859, 3868, 3940a, 3954, 3989, 4059, 4062, 4185, 4199, 4243, 4268, 4409, 4562, 4634, 4650, 4723, 4723a, 4724, 4898, 4977, 5093, 5117, 5168, 5171, 5178, 5179, 5192, 5193, 5194, 5202, 5252, 5300, 5335, 5339, 5353, 5357, 5427, 5433, 5483, 5485, 5491, 5492, 5493, 5494, 5499, 5550, 5584, 5600, 5658, 5690, 5696, 5702, 5726, 5774, 5805, 5856, 5868, 5899, 5970, 5971, 5973, 5974, 5975, 5977, 6038, 6087, 6088, 6139, 6196, 6202, 6203, 6324, 6325, 6435, 6436, 6538, 6550, 6554, 6555, 6614, 6682, 6702, 6708, 6762, 6774, 6779, 6906, 6911, 6914, 6915, 6943, 7026, 7031, 7138, 7139, 7144, 7180, 7213, 7259

Regions

South West 2949, 2967, 2969, 3248, 3378, 3445, 4025, 4026, 4081, 4107, 4520, 4556a, 4648, 4690, 5066, 5100, 5463, 5464, 6259, 6617, 7268

Southern 1638, 3352, 3984, 4037, 4106, 4229, 4359, 4360, 4674, 4998, 4999, 5001, 5179, 5822, 6250, 7086, 7091, 7092, 7163, 7261

London 1119, 1201, 1794, 1903, 2066, 2975, 3037, 3060, 3064, 3112, 3202, 3207, 3217, 3233, 3245, 3284, 3285, 3303, 3308, 3326, 3355, 3356, 3389, 3391, 3419, 3453, 3722, 3725, 3737, 3751, 3836, 3888, 3904, 3917, 3918, 3957, 4007, 4021, 4095, 4109, 4115, 4201, 4230, 4266, 4277, 4286, 4296, 4301, 4315, 4376, 4415, 4434, 4435, 4481, 4502, 4514, 4536, 4537, 4542, 4572, 4573, 4577, 4600, 4602, 4667, 4694, 4705, 4723, 4741, 4744, 4749, 4758, 4777, 4783, 4797, 4803, 4805, 4811, 4816, 4818, 4833, 4871, 4906, 4914, 4915, 4916, 4928, 4941, 4957, 5013, 5014, 5023, 5037, 5041, 5045, 5132, 5242, 5260, 5323, 5352, 5354, 5376, 5459, 5527, 5535, 5538, 5569, 5747a, 5783, 5789, 5912, 5914, 5964, 6020, 6047, 6067, 6188, 6237, 6271, 6273, 6287, 6313, 6314, 6434, 6559, 6583, 6659, 6713, 6761, 6798, 6806, 6810, 6813, 6822, 6837, 6838, 6847, 6849, 6852, 6879, 6893, 6947, 6957, 6980, 6992, 7116, 7118a, 7189, 7214, 7245

East Anglia 3358, 3360, 3362, 3374, 3377, 4176, 4399, 4710, 4831, 4845, 5647, 5648, 5675, 6276, 6448, 6683, 6767, 7141, 7150

Midlands 3323, 3325, 3327, 3333, 3347, 3370, 3372, 3821, 3872, 3892, 4010, 4054, 4061, 4154, 4170, 4178, 4254, 4275, 4298, 4351, 4529, 4541, 4562, 4609, 4666, 4724, 4778, 4792, 4832, 4864, 4926, 4927, 4949, 4958, 4959, 4960, 4979, 4980, 4994, 5003, 5005, 5043, 5053, 5061, 5078, 5105, 5126, 5196, 5324, 5526, 5575, 5749, 6014, 6045, 6193, 6282, 6472, 6858, 6859, 6942, 7020, 7056, 7082, 7104, 7133, 7134, 7135, 7146, 7157, 7174, 7248

North West 281, 2284, 2285, 2922, 3017, 3301, 3302, 3311, 3318, 3349, 3693, 3730, 3768, 3833, 3862, 3863, 3865, 3866, 3881, 3894, 3946, 3972, 4047, 4082, 4120, 4129, 4136, 4193, 4216, 4232, 4233, 4235, 4236, 4237, 4238, 4239, 4240, 4241, 4338, 4341, 4355, 4356, 4389, 4390, 4414, 4425a, 4438, 4470, 4471, 4501, 4516, 4530, 4590, 4821, 4825, 4853, 4854, 4867, 4942, 4992, 5008, 5009, 5076, 5127, 5185, 5220, 5249, 5252, 5371, 5422, 5423, 5424, 5458, 5461, 5465, 5466, 5467, 5468, 5558, 5571, 5703, 5719, 5753, 5786, 5795, 5890, 5893, 5915, 5916, 5942, 5943, 5944, 5950, 6026, 6032, 6037, 6142, 6169, 6329, 6389, 6444, 6490a, 6513, 6660, 6714, 6750, 6811, 6853, 6885, 6886, 6972, 6976, 7010, 7077, 7096, 7103, 7113, 7117, 7156, 7164, 7172, 7231, 7263

Yorkshire 3106, 3293, 3297, 3314, 3334, 3379, 3890, 3915, 4011, 4056, 4111, 4112, 4114, 4169, 4234, 4287, 4459, 4518, 4574, 4643, 4644, 4645, 4646, 4704, 4787, 4806, 4848, 4883, 5034, 5067, 5178, 5668, 5762, 5779, 5869, 5956, 6015, 6131, 6185, 6186, 6292, 6293, 6473, 6565, 6845, 6860, 6892, 6981, 7029, 7095, 7253

North East 2921, 3291, 3392, 3720, 3847, 3880, 3900, 4028, 4092, 4143, 4262, 4357, 4525, 4731, 4794, 4989, 5022, 5029, 5030, 5269, 5581, 5651, 5695, 5733, 6009, 6079, 6080, 6262, 6333, 6336, 6339, 6495, 6501, 6552, 6674, 6793, 6988, 6991, 7090, 7205, 7206

Wales 368, 3688, 3710, 3911, 3913, 3940a, 4024, 4069, 4115a, 4119, 4175, 4183, 4184, 4194, 4195, 4221, 4222, 4223, 4224, 4267, 4268, 4297, 4395, 4404, 4447, 4524, 4526, 4532, 4661, 4715, 4799, 4822, 4838, 4890, 4892, 4893, 4894, 4895, 4933, 4935, 4937, 4938, 4962, 5057, 5070, 5071, 5113, 5172, 5180, 5189, 5216, 5271, 5391, 5486, 5487, 5518, 5543, 5644, 5674, 5716,

5721, 5758, 5759, 5771, 5774, 5775, 5852, 5859, 5905, 5906, 5907, 5908, 5909, 5910, 6071, 6089, 6165, 6167, 6359, 6390, 6396, 6405, 6463, 6560, 6712, 6923, 6982, 7021, 7022, 7027, 7054, 7127, 7160, 7180, 7184, 7185, 7240, 7267, 7270

Scotland 462, 655, 1115, 1309, 1346, 2953, 2960, 2973, 3012, 3050, 3169, 3199, 3214, 3249, 3279, 3296, 3300, 3304, 3307, 3310, 3322, 3340, 3344, 3417, 3711, 3835, 3943, 3960, 3963, 3965, 3968, 3998, 4000, 4002, 4003, 4004, 4108a, 4138, 4140, 4141, 4150, 4152, 4217, 4220, 4245, 4256, 4257, 4270, 4292, 4337, 4345, 4352, 4386, 4440, 4476, 4480, 4486, 4493, 4511, 4538, 4546, 4547, 4549, 4550, 4551, 4552, 4553, 4553a, 4597, 4598, 4607, 4616, 4618, 4620, 4624, 4625, 4636, 4640, 4684, 4689, 4743, 4763a, 4766, 4776, 4857, 4861, 4870, 4922, 4930, 4975, 4981, 4983, 5107, 5119, 5134, 5135, 5224, 5225, 5283, 5296, 5299, 5300, 5446, 5450, 5451, 5452, 5490, 5546, 5547, 5550, 5555, 5586, 5611, 5612, 5614, 5619, 5634, 5639, 5653, 5655, 5666, 5667, 5700, 5712, 5772, 5803, 5811, 5812, 5813, 5816, 5817, 5899, 5901, 5931, 5933, 5935, 5953, 5960, 6018, 6029, 6075, 6103, 6105, 6106, 6148, 6177, 6189, 6197a, 6207, 6235, 6236, 6240, 6264, 6264a, 6278, 6286, 6302, 6305e, 6318, 6319, 6321, 6351, 6355, 6367, 6394, 6403, 6404, 6406, 6412, 6417, 6429a, 6430, 6431, 6432, 6452, 6532, 6543a, 6549, 6550, 6555, 6613a, 6631, 6632, 6633, 6772, 6778, 6781, 6825, 6826, 6865, 6877, 6904, 6910, 6914, 6917, 6988a, 6989, 7037, 7065, 7067, 7072a, 7073, 7076, 7088, 7098, 7130, 7143, 7181, 7182, 7216, 7220, 7227, 7258

Industries

Agriculture 27, 334, 396, 400, 429, 430, 450, 488, 521, 557, 575, 588, 589, 635, 636, 647, 683, 688, 748, 762, 795, 833, 872, 950, 977, 978, 1044, 1200, 1423, 1494, 1661, 2152, 2447, 2454, 2548, 3431, 3824, 4056, 4081, 4574, 4704, 4729, 6565

Buses 612, 687, 1669, 1688, 1722, 1726, 1770, 1825, 1868, 1883, 1898, 1963, 1966, 1979, 2004, 2015, 2022, 2093, 2110, 2417, 2481, 3446, 3655, 4038, 4109, 4198, 4957, 5275, 6162

Construction 347, 807, 816, 838, 970, 1448, 1682, 1769, 1836, 1837, 1907, 1944, 2007, 2048, 2964, 3218, 3741, 3866, 3905, 4108a, 4239, 4341, 4541, 5025, 5026, 5347, 5458, 5471, 5855, 6032, 6244

Docks 343, 578, 1119, 1188, 1620, 1665, 1720, 1743, 1856, 1932, 1992, 2028, 2045, 2340, 3888, 4115, 4126, 4129, 4414, 4883, 5037, 5424, 5769, 5789, 5853, 6234, 6270, 6271, 6272, 6273, 6389, 6547, 6941

Education 514, 581, 666, 774, 791, 812, 915, 919, 925, 964, 967, 1078, 1084, 1104, 1166, 1174, 1282, 1333, 1357, 1378, 1416, 1425, 1459, 1460, 1468, 1476, 1512, 1532, 1535, 1541, 1549, 1556, 1561, 1574, 1576, 1580, 1654, 1657, 1660, 1792, 1875, 1881, 1890, 1895, 1926, 1940, 1991, 2010, 2025, 2042, 2061, 2094, 2107, 2180, 2193, 2194, 2243, 2455, 2503, 2522, 2553, 2554, 2590, 2902, 3193, 3248, 3273, 3682, 3696, 4190, 4192, 4275, 4276, 4288, 4295, 4526, 4645, 4666, 4668, 4669, 4689, 4710, 4809, 4810, 4860, 4880, 5153, 5402, 5453, 5464, 5654, 6269, 6352, 6364, 6427, 6530, 6545, 6566, 6776, 6777, 6802, 6915, 6993, 7101

Electricity/Gas 1467, 1772, 1826, 1859, 1901, 1905, 2446, 3699, 3795, 4005, 4027, 4244, 4317, 4796, 5390, 5469, 6135, 6613

Engineering 695, 725, 938, 942, 971, 1083, 1181, 1233, 1493, 1763, 1764, 1841, 1846, 1863, 1892, 1917, 1937, 1946, 2112, 2310, 2973, 3050, 4099, 4114, 4150, 4160, 4197, 4198, 4232, 4236, 4241, 4355, 4358, 4364, 4394, 4402, 4413, 4440, 4600, 4674, 4745, 4785, 4792, 4958, 4959, 5078, 5112, 5214, 5539, 5750, 5753, 5788, 5872, 6045, 6235, 6528, 6631, 6746, 6795, 6942, 6955, 7020, 7030, 7080, 7083

Legislation 176, 1184, 1252, 1281, 1288, 1293, 1296, 1313, 1314, 1335, 1371, 1376, 1391, 1435, 1480, 1518, 1987, 1988, 1993, 2295, 3176, 3492, 6900, 7057

Mines 1215, 23, 35, 187, 246, 321, 338, 358, 365, 391, 397, 482, 535, 579, 580, 606, 616, 665, 709, 718, 756, 782, 826, 893, 921, 969, 972, 1016, 1088, 1137, 1175, 1226, 1358, 1540, 1555, 1584, 2085, 2196, 2199, 2242, 2284, 2299, 2306, 2308, 2312, 2383, 2408, 2599, 2600, 2953, 2995, 3122, 3246, 3291, 3321, 3738, 3744, 3807, 3843, 3847, 3880, 3900, 3907, 3911, 3998, 3999, 4000, 4002, 4003, 4011, 4024, 4032, 4091, 4092, 4115a, 4119, 4133, 4140, 4184, 4194, 4195, 4221, 4222, 4224, 4262, 4267, 4268, 4297, 4308, 4357, 4395, 4447, 4459, 4532, 4550, 4560, 4562, 4601, 4606, 4607, 4612, 4640, 4715, 4717, 4753, 4787, 4799, 4806, 4838, 4890, 4892, 4894, 4950, 5034, 5067, 5070, 5135, 5172, 5189, 5201, 5270, 5332, 5334, 5391, 5425, 5543, 5550, 5555, 5611, 5612, 5614, 5644, 5651, 5667, 5668, 5700, 5721, 5758, 5775, 5852, 5877, 5889, 5905, 5906, 5909, 5910, 5933, 5953, 6016, 6027, 6071, 6079, 6093, 6105, 6106, 6167, 6185, 6186, 6251, 6278, 6292, 6293, 6297, 6355, 6356, 6367, 6375, 6384, 6390, 6495, 6520, 6549, 6550, 6552, 6555, 6556, 6560, 6575, 6778, 6865, 6923, 6964, 7054

Miscellaneous 56, 198, 225, 383, 392, 410, 474, 492, 682, 832, 849, 855, 946, 1010, 1025, 1095, 1198, 1202, 1209, 1211, 1287, 1321, 1474, 1537, 1563, 1589, 1756, 1931, 1957, 2259, 2304,